HISTORY IN THREE KEYS

HISTORY IN THREE KEYS

The Boxers as

Event, Experience,

and Myth

Paul A. Cohen

COLUMBIA UNIVERSITY PRESS   NEW YORK

Columbia University Press
Publishers Since 1893
New York   Chichester, West Sussex
Copyright © 1997 Columbia University Press

Library of Congress Cataloging-in-Publication Data
Cohen, Paul A.
  History in three keys : the Boxers as event, experience, and myth
/ Paul A. Cohen.
    p.   cm.
  Includes bibliographical references and index.
  ISBN 978-0-231-10650-4 (cloth : alk. paper)
  ISBN 978-0-231-10651-1 (pbk. : alk. paper)
  1. China — History — Boxer Rebellion, 1899–1901. I. Title.
DS771.C67   1997
951'.035 — dc20   96–27118

Casebound editions of Columbia University Press books are printed on permanent and
durable acid-free paper.
Designed by Linda Secondari
Printed in the United States of America
c 10 9 8 7 6 5 4 3 2
p 20 19 18 17 16 15 14

The poem "The Twentieth Century," in chapter 6, is reprinted by permission of the author
and Louisiana State University Press from *Hang-Gliding from Helicon: New and Selected
Poems 1948–1988* by Daniel Hoffman. Copyright © 1988 by Daniel Hoffman.

To Benjamin Schwartz,
and to the memory of John Fairbank,
two remarkable teachers,
from both of whom I continued to learn
long after the formal instruction was over

CONTENTS

LIST OF ILLUSTRATIONS

PREFACE

Philosophers have written lengthy theoretical treatises on what historians do. What I propose in this book, as a practicing historian, is to explore the issue through an actual historical case, the Boxer uprising of 1898–1900 in China. When I first began to study history, my conception of what historians "did" was very different from what it is now. I used to think of the past as, in some sense, a fixed body of factual material which it was the historian's job to unearth and elucidate. I still think of the historian as a person whose main object is to understand and explain the past. But I now have a far less innocent view of the processes—and problems—involved. I now see the reconstructive work of the historian as in constant tension with two other ways of "knowing" the past—experience and myth—that, in terms of their bearing on ordinary human lives, are far more pervasive and influential.

Plotted at a certain level of abstraction, the Boxer uprising formed a major chapter in the narrative structure of the late Qing dynasty (1644–1912). It was the largest-scale armed conflict to occur between the rebellions of the mid-nineteenth century and the 1911 revolution. Seen as a social movement, the Boxers, many of them young farm boys made destitute by the successive natural disasters that had battered North China since the early 1890s, were a striking expression of the more general breakdown of the agrarian order in China at the turn of the century. This breakdown, characterized in many parts of the empire by high levels of popular turbulence, was also reflected in the religious beliefs of the Boxers, in particular their practice of spirit possession and frequent recourse to magic. The antiforeign dimension of the Boxer phenomenon, expressed most dramatically in the attacks on native Christians and foreign missionaries, created a profound crisis in Sino-foreign relations and eventually led to direct foreign military intervention and a Chinese declaration of war against all the powers. Finally, the lifting of the siege of the legations, the flight of the court to Xi'an in the northwest, the foreign occupation of Beijing, and the diplomatic settlement imposed on

China by the victorious powers brought on a decisive shift in Qing government policy, which in the first years of the twentieth century became increasingly (if charily) wedded to far-reaching reform. It is small wonder, taking all these different aspects of the Boxer episode together, that Mary Wright should have begun her widely read essay on the background of the 1911 revolution with the ringing pronouncement: "Rarely in history has a single year marked as dramatic a watershed as did 1900 in China."[1]

In addition to being an event, tightly woven into the larger tapestry of events comprising this period of Chinese history, the Boxers also gave rise to a potent, if somewhat contradictory, set of myths in the popular imaginations of both Chinese and Westerners. In the West, in the early decades of the twentieth century, the Boxers were widely viewed as "the Yellow Peril personified," "the very word Boxerism conjur[ing] up visions of danger, xenophobia, irrationality and barbarism."[2] Chinese intellectuals prior to the early 1920s often shared this negative perception of the Boxers, adding to the foregoing list of attributes "superstitiousness" and "backwardness." During the period of heightened nationalism and antiforeignism that marked the 1920s in China, on the other hand, while many Westerners sought to discredit Chinese nationalism by branding it a revival of "Boxerism," Chinese revolutionaries began to rework the Boxers into a more positive myth, centering on the qualities of "patriotism" and "anti-imperialism." This more affirmative vision of the Boxers as heroic battlers against foreign aggression reached a high-water mark among Chinese on the mainland (and some persons of Chinese ancestry in the United States) during the Cultural Revolution (1966–1976), at the very moment that Chinese on Taiwan (as well as many Westerners) were resurrecting the more lurid stereotype of the Boxers as fanatical, uncivilized xenophobes and pinning it on the Red Guards. During the Cultural Revolution praise was also lavished on the Boxers' female counterparts, the Red Lanterns, in particular for their alleged rebellion against the subordinate status of women in the old society.

The Boxers as *event* represent a particular reading of the past, while the Boxers as *myth* represent an impressing of the past into the service of a particular reading of the present. Either way a dynamic interaction is set up between present and past, in which the past is continually being reshaped, either consciously or unconsciously, in accordance with the diverse and shifting preoccupations of people in the present. What happens to the past — or, to be more exact, the *lived* or *experienced* past — when we perform this feat of redefinition? What happens to the experiential world of the original creators of the past when, for purposes of clarity and exposition, historians structure it in the form of "events," or mythologizers, for altogether different reasons, distill from it a particular symbolic message? If it is true, to paraphrase Paul Veyne, that events never coincide with the perceptions of their participants and witnesses and that it is the historian who carves out of the evidence and the documents the event he or she has chosen to make,[3] what are the implications of this for historical understanding? Are historians, too, ultimately fashioners of myth? Finally, if we were to unravel an event, to break it down into smaller, more discrete mini-events or units of human experience — the tedium and physical wretchedness of life in the trenches rather than the grand order of battle — what would we be left with? Just a messy and meaningless pile of data? Or, on a more optimistic note, a closer approximation of what the past was really like and what exactly happens to this "real past" when historians attempt to explain it or mythologizers to exploit it for its symbolic content?

These questions illustrate but do not exhaust the range of issues I am concerned with in this book. The first part of the book tells the "story" of the Boxer uprising, as later narrated by historians — people with foreknowledge of how things turned out, a wide-angle picture of the entire event, and the goal of *explaining* not only the Boxer phenomenon itself but how it was linked up with prior and subsequent historical developments. The second part probes the thought, feelings, and behavior of the immediate participants in different phases of the Boxer experience — Chinese peasant youths who often for reasons of survival joined Boxer units in their villages, anxious missionaries scattered across the drought-parched North China plain at the height of the uprising, Chinese and foreign inhabitants of Tianjin trapped in that city during the battle that raged there in the early summer of 1900 — individuals, in short, who didn't know whether they would emerge from their respective ordeals dead or alive, who did not have the entire "event" preencoded in their heads, and who therefore conceptualized what was happening to them in ways that differed fundamentally from the retrospective, backward-reading constructions of historians. The third part of the book explores the myths surrounding the Boxers and "Boxerism" that were fashioned in twentieth-century China — symbolic representations designed less to elucidate the Boxer past than to draw energy from it and score points, often (but not always) of a political or overtly propagandistic nature, in the post-Boxer present.[4]

My aim in scrutinizing — and juxtaposing — these different zones of consciousness is to convey something of the elusiveness of the historical enterprise, to illuminate the tension between the history that people make, which is in some sense fixed, and the histories that people write and use, which seem forever to be changing. This is really quite different from the well-known "Rashomon" effect.[5] "Rashomon," at least as it has come to be used in English, refers to the different points of view different people have of an event (different versions of the "truth"), depending on where they are situated, either literally or figuratively, in relation to that event. The different ways of knowing the past probed in this book certainly encompass differences in perspective. But they also go beyond this and address differences of a more substantive nature. Experiencers of the past are *incapable* of knowing the past that historians know, and mythologizers of the past, although sharing with historians the advantage of afterknowledge, are *uninterested* in knowing the past as its makers have experienced it. In other words, although the lines separating these three ways of knowing the past are not always clear (historians do, as we are well aware, engage in mythologization, and the makers of the past are entirely capable, after the fact, of turning their own experiences into history), as ways of knowing, they are analytically distinct. Also, as we shall have ample occasion to observe in the pages that follow, event, experience, and myth, as alternative evocations of the past, are grounded in very different bodies of historical data.

Although my principal object in this book is to explore a broad range of issues pertaining to the writing of history—the Boxers functioning as a kind of handmaiden to this larger enterprise—I hope the book will also be of interest to specialists in the China field who are centrally concerned with the Boxer episode itself and the ways in which it has been remembered by Chinese in the present century. My main contributions in this vein are in parts 2 and 3. In part 2, by far the longest section of the book, I delve into certain facets of the experiential context of North China in 1900—drought, mass spirit possession, magic and female pollution, rumor, death—in greater depth than is ordinarily the case in writing on the Boxers. While, in the process, I frequently operate as an "ethnographic historian," attempting empathetically to get at how ordinary people—Boxers, non-Boxer Chinese, missionaries—"made sense of the world,"[6] I also, with equal frequency, step back from this world to interpret what is going on in it in ways that the immediate participants about whom I am writing would doubtless find foreign.

A related but different source of tension informs part 3. In terms of the book's broader agenda, my account of Chinese mythologization of the Boxers in this part is intended to be illustrative of the mythologization process in general. But different historical events resonate with the later histories of the countries in which they occur in different ways. And in the tormented Chinese quest in this century for a modern identity that both embraces and rejects the culture of the West, the Boxers, as we shall see, have played a uniquely powerful symbolic role.

Let me say a word or two here about the choices, some of them arbitrary, others dictated by circumstance, that I have made in the writing of this book. One such choice has to do with my dual use of the term *history*. As will already have become plain to some readers, I sometimes use this term in a tight, more or less technical way to refer to the formal process of reconstruction of the past that is the historian's characteristic function. Although there is no bar, certainly, to the historian's training his or her reconstructive impulses on the experienced or the mythologized pasts (as indeed I do in parts 2 and 3), *history* in this first sense is clearly to be distinguished from *experience* and *myth*. At other times, on the other hand, as in the book's title, I use *history* in a looser, less technical fashion, to encompass the variety of ways, *including* experience and myth, in which people in general think about and relate to the past. Which of these two meanings is intended in any given instance will, I hope, be clear from the context.

Although from a strictly chronological point of view it might be argued that the *experience* part of the book ought to have come first, since the past has to be experienced before it can be historically reconstructed or mythologized, I have led with the *history-as-event* part instead. My reasons for this are two. One, quite practical, relates to my hope that this book will be of interest to people other than China specialists and that, for such individuals, it might be easier to start out with a narrative account of the Boxer episode. The second reason derives from my conviction that no one of the three approaches to the past explored in the book has logical — or epistemological — priority over the other two. Historical reconstruction, direct experience, and mythologization are, after all, all operations that every one of us performs every day of his or her life. Although professional historians spend a good bit of their time doing battle with the mythologized past or rendering the experienced past intelligible and meaningful in ways that were not available to the experiencers themselves, for most human beings experience and myth have an emotional power and importance — we may indeed call it a kind of subjective truth — that historians ignore at their peril. From this perspective, I invite readers with a modicum of familiarity with the Boxer episode not to be bound by the sequence in which the several parts of this book are printed but to read them in any order they please.

One other choice I have made pertains to the *experience* part of the book. In this part my emphasis is very strongly on the climactic phase of the Boxer movement, the spring and summer of 1900, when it had spread across much of North China and even penetrated Manchuria and Inner

Mongolia; relatively little notice is given to the pre-1900 phase of the movement, when it was still concentrated in its place of origin, Shandong
province. My reasons for this are several. First, the focal themes of the five
chapters comprising this part (drought, possession, and so on) all reached
their point of greatest intensity and impact in the spring and summer of
1900. Second, precisely because of this, the sources documenting them, on
both the Chinese and foreign sides, are far more abundant and also richer
and more diverse for this period than for the pre-1900 phase of the movement.[7] Third, and finally, we already have in English an outstanding book
on the Shandong beginnings of the Boxer phenonemon: Joseph Esherick's
The Origins of the Boxer Uprising. Although the aims of my book are quite
fundamentally different from Esherick's, it seemed to me nevertheless to
make sense, as long as it was also justified on substantive grounds, to direct
my attention to other phases of the Boxer experience and avoid needless
replication of his account.

ACKNOWLEDGMENTS

Many people have had a hand in the making of this book, and it gives me much pleasure, at last, to be able to acknowledge my indebtedness to them. I owe particular thanks to John Israel, Irwin Scheiner, Jeffrey Wasserstrom, and Madeleine Zelin, each of whom read the entire manuscript with care and, along with welcome encouragement, identified potential problems and furnished constructive suggestions for addressing them. For helpful counsel on individual parts of the book, I am grateful to Prasenjit Duara, Chang-tai Hung, Michael Hunt, Roderick MacFarquhar, Laura McDaniel, Susan Naquin, James Watson, and Ruby Watson. I also profited from audience comments following talks at Colgate, Harvard, and Wesleyan universities, and from the advice of participants in a conference on the Boxer movement held at Jinan in October 1990.

Early on in the research, Mingteh Tsou assisted in obtaining valuable Cultural Revolution-era newspaper and periodical articles from China. Mr. Tsou also put me in touch with Zhu Junzhou of the Shanghai Library, who tracked down and supplied me with rare political cartoons from the same period. At the point at which I was just beginning to familiarize myself with Boxer sources, Gail Hershatter alerted me to the existence of unpublished oral history materials from the Tianjin area, many of which, through the generosity of Chen Zhenjiang and others at Nankai University, I was able to acquire copies of on a trip to China in 1987. During the same trip I benefited greatly from talks with Lu Yao of Shandong University, one of China's premier historians of the Boxer movement.

I want to extend my thanks to a number of archivists for facilitating my use of the collections in their charge. Especially helpful in this regard were Martha Lund Smalley and Joan R. Duffy of the Divinity School Library of Yale University and Michael Miller, formerly curator of personal papers at the Marine Corps Historical Center, Washington, D.C. The custodians of Harvard's Houghton Library made my reading in the American Board of

xviii Commissioners for Foreign Missions archive an entirely pleasurable and productive experience. Dale C. Mayer of the Herbert Hoover Presidential Library responded with patience to my inquiries and sent me a large number of useful items written or collected by Herbert and Lou Hoover, who were in Tianjin during the Boxer summer.

Warm thanks are due to Lisa Cohen for her expert photo reproduction of much of the illustrative material in the book; James Hevia, Rudolf Wagner, and Catherine Yeh for advice on illustrations; Robert Forget for drawing the maps; Fan Daren for conveying to me his insights into the inner workings of the Cultural Revolution; Richard Madsen for his generous sharing of the results of oral history research he conducted among Catholic families in Hebei; and Kong Xiangji, Ma Jing-heng, and Ma Wei-yi for helping me negotiate especially troublesome Chinese terms and phrases.

I am indebted to Naoma Upham Scott for permission to quote from the diary of her father Oscar J. Upham and to Amy Cantin of the Marine Corps Historical Center for her help in procuring this permission. I am also grateful to the Association for Asian Studies for permission to use (in much expanded form) material that originally appeared in an article in the *Journal of Asian Studies* (February 1992).

Over innumerable dinners together, Sheila Levine was a warm and unfailing source of support. Over equally innumerable lunches, Daniel Little could always be counted on to help me clarify my thinking, especially on philosophical matters. Daniel Stern, an old friend, in lively conversations scattered across the years, shared with me the perspectives of one who works in a very different (although not unrelated) field. As my ideas were just beginning to take shape, Alan Lebowitz, another old friend, without any thought of hurrying me, suggested how I might eventually bring the book to a close.

Kate Wittenberg of the Columbia University Press was the first person to read the manuscript through from start to finish. I am immensely grateful to her both for her enthusiastic response and for the sure hand with which, once it was accepted, she steered the book through the publication process. At Columbia, I also owe a large debt of thanks to Roy Thomas, for the meticulous care and unsurpassed skill with which he edited the manuscript.

Finally, for showing faith in this undertaking from the outset, in the form of generous grant support, I want to acknowledge my gratitude to Wellesley College, the National Endowment for the Humanities, and the John Simon Guggenheim Memorial Foundation.

HISTORY IN THREE KEYS

PART 1

The Boxers as Event

PROLOGUE

The Historically Reconstructed Past

In March 1989 the Tony Awards administration committee ruled that the musical "Jerome Robbins's Broadway," which had received rave reviews, was not a "revival" and was therefore eligible for the award as "best musical." The decision, which ended a hard-fought battle within the committee, had important financial implications, since the show, although doing excellently at the box office, had been very expensive to produce, and the best musical award, which it was now the hands-down favorite to win, carried the potential of millions of dollars in added ticket sales. The reason for the dispute in the first place (apart from the financial stakes involved) was that, although the Robbins show as a whole had never been presented on Broadway, it consisted almost entirely of elements that had.[1] It was an open question, therefore, whether it was a new show or a revival.

The question the Tony Awards committee resolved may also be posed with respect to the past as reconstructed by historians: revival or new show? Is the consummation of the historian's labors in essence a gathering together and re-presentation of things that have already happened, or is it in important respects a new production, lacking some elements that existed in the past and incorporating others that did not? People who are not historians may well be inclined to answer that it is the former, that retrieval of the past is precisely what historians are expected to do, and if they do something other than this, the end result is not history.

The position taken in this book is the exact reverse. However counter-intuitive it may seem, I would argue (and I believe most practicing historians would join me) that the history the historian creates is in fact fundamentally different from the history people make. No matter how much of the original, experienced past historians choose or are able to build into their narratives, what they end up with will, in specific and identifiable ways, be different from that past. This is so, moreover, despite the fact that the process of narrativization in which the historian engages is not, in my

4   view, intrinsically different from the process of narrativization in which the direct experiencer of the past also engages.

Before taking a closer look at what, exactly, it is that the historian adds to the past to make it "history," let me clarify briefly the narrativization issue just raised. The problem, basically, has to do with how we go about defining the relationship between "history" (in the sense of the history that historians write) and "reality" (in the sense of the history that people make and directly experience). This has been a very controversial issue not only among historians but also among philosophers and literary theorists who concern themselves with historical matters. Some individuals (Hayden White and Paul Ricoeur are two of the best known) have taken the position that there is a fundamental discontinuity between history and reality. History, they believe, is basically narrative in form, while reality is not. Therefore, when historians write history, they impose on the past a design or structure that is alien to it. Other individuals, among whom I have found David Carr to be one of the clearest and most persuasive, argue that "narrative structure pervades our very experience of time and social existence, independently of our contemplating the past as historians." Since narrative is, for Carr, an essential component of the past reality historians seek to elucidate, the relationship between history and reality, or, as he puts it, "narrative and everyday life," is one marked not by discontinuity but by continuity.[2]

My own stance lies somewhere between these two polar alternatives, although it is closer to Carr's. I agree with Carr that narrative is a basic component of everyday existence, not only for individuals but also for communities, and that therefore the narrativization of the historian does not, in itself, create a disjuncture between the experienced past and the historically reconstructed past. However, there are other characteristics of the process of historical reconstruction, *as practiced*, that do create, if not a complete disjuncture, at least a very different set of parameters from those demarcating immediate experience.[3] At the bare minimum, all historical writing, even the best of it, entails radical simplification and compression of the past; an event, such as the Boxer episode, that took several years to unfold and spread over much of North China, is transformed into a book of a few hundred pages that can be held in the hands and read from start to finish in ten hours.

In Julian Barnes's novel, *Flaubert's Parrot*, a meditation (at least on one level) on the impossibility of ever recovering the past "as it actually was," Geoffrey Braithwaite, the narrator, makes the following observation: "Books say: She did this because. Life says: She did this. Books are where things are explained to you; life is where things aren't. I'm not surprised some people prefer books."[4] "And when you and I talk about history," Claudia Hampton, the main character in Penelope Lively's *Moon Tiger*, muses, "we don't mean what actually happened, do we? The cosmic chaos of everywhere, all time? We mean the tidying up of this into books, the concentration of the benign historical eye upon years and places and persons. History unravels; circumstances, following their natural inclination, prefer to remain ravelled."[5]

These two statements make essentially the same point: that actual experience (Braithwaite's "life," Hampton's "circumstances") is messy, complicated, opaque, while history (or "books") brings order and clarity into the chaos. One person might join the Boxer movement out of hunger; a second might join it because of hatred and fear of foreigners and foreign influence; a third might find in the movement an ideal vehicle for taking revenge against old enemies; and a fourth might support the Boxers out of fear of what would happen to him and his family if he didn't. It is the job of the historian of the Boxer movement to try to find some meaningful pattern in this jumble of motives, to transform an event of exceptional complexity and confusion into an account that is coherent and makes sense. History, in short, has an explanatory function; the historian's objective is, first and foremost, to understand what happened in the past, and, then, to explain it to his or her readership.

While I basically agree with this formulation of the historian's role, there is an oversimplification buried in the neat contrast between experience and history that needs to be addressed. The experienced past may well be messy and chaotic to the historian, but it is not to the immediate experiencer. It is not that there isn't mess and chaos in people's lives, but our lives, *to ourselves*, are not messy and chaotic. It is precisely here that the narrative function, at the level of individual, personal experience, is so important. As we live our lives, we instinctively place them in a narrative framework. We "tell stories" to ourselves that make sense of our experiences: biographical, not historical, sense. So it isn't entirely correct to say, paraphrasing Geoffrey Braithwaite, that books explain while in life things simply happen. In life, also, there is a powerful need for understanding and explanation, which all of us experience, subjectively, every moment of every day.

This need operates on a community-wide level as well. People talk with one another about their shared experiences and together construct interpretations of what is happening to them. These interpretations may take the form of well-thought-out analyses, in which case the direct experi-

6 encers of the past in effect become historians of their own experience. Or, they may be manifested in informal conversation or rumors or even gossip. Whatever the case, the interpretations advanced by the immediate participants in past events are likely to be quite at variance with those put forward by historians, who operate within a basically different field of consciousness. This was the distinction Paul Boyer and Stephen Nissenbaum had in mind when, after describing the late seventeenth-century New England social order as having been "profoundly shaken by a superhuman force which had lured all too many into active complicity with it," they observed: "We have chosen to construe this force as emergent mercantile capitalism. [Cotton] Mather, and Salem Village, called it witchcraft."[6]

Although the direct experiencer of the past has a need for order, clarity, and understanding that is, then, not all that different from that of the historian, it is driven, in general, by a quite different set of motives. Participants in the making of the past engage in a continuous process of renarrativization, reconfiguring their own past experience again and again in response to new circumstances, with a view—always—to maintaining a sense of personal integrity and coherence. A Chinese friend who had lived through the Cultural Revolution told me that, in the conversations she had with friends and relatives on her periodic visits back to China, the same individuals would remember the same experiences differently every time they discussed them. Primo Levi, shortly before his death, wrote of "the construction of convenient truth [that] grows and is perfected" the further events fade into the past.[7] As people engage in one or another form of autobiographical mythologization, in short, they—we—are concerned at least as much with the fashioning of a past that is psychologically tolerable as with uncovering the "truth" in a rigorously objective manner.

The historian, on the other hand, assigns paramount importance to constructing a picture of the past that has validity in an intellectual, rather than a psychological, sense. Although as human beings we are subject to the same spectrum of emotional needs as anyone else, in our capacity as historians our efforts to understand the past are guided by a conscious commitment (never fully realized in practice) to a socially agreed-upon and enforced standard of accuracy and truth. This commitment defines us as historians. We are all subject to other commitments as well, but if these other commitments—say, a feminist historian's desire to give voice to women who have previously been silent and, by so doing, contribute to the empowerment and liberation of women in the present and future—take precedence over the goal of understanding and explaining what happened in the past in accordance with a generally accepted set of professional guidelines, we abdicate our responsibility as historians and move in the direction of mythologization.[8] This would not be a problem, perhaps, if the truth about the past were always liberating and empowering. But if one believes, as I do, that, on both the individual and the community levels, myths are often far more empowering than truths, it has the potential to become a very real problem, indeed.

Another defining mark of the historian's craft is that it operates with known outcomes. In contrast with the participants in past events, who at the time do not know how events in which they are participating are going to turn out, the historian knows this in advance. Indeed, the process of historical reconstruction generally takes as its point of departure a known outcome and then attempts an explanation of how this outcome was brought about. Thus, although the *product* of the historian's efforts, the history he or she writes, customarily begins at some point in the past and moves forward, the historian's *consciousness* begins at a subsequent point in time and moves in reverse. The secret of the historian's success, as G. R. Elton wrote, "lies in hindsight and argument backwards."[9]

There is a problem here, which all good historians know about and do their utmost to mitigate. It is the problem of assuming, mistakenly, the necessity of the outcomes that have in fact occurred. Or, as Elton phrased it: "We know what happened next, and the risk is always considerable that the historian will fall victim to the false old proposition, *post hoc ergo propter hoc*, the succeeding event being read as a necessary consequence of the earlier event."[10]

Many practicing historians have commented on this issue. "Writing history or biography," cautions David McCullough, author of a highly regarded biography of Harry Truman, "you must remember that nothing was ever on a track. . . . Things could have gone any way at any point. As soon as you say 'was,' it seems to fix an event in the past. But nobody ever lived in the past, only in the present. . . . The challenge is to get the reader beyond thinking that things had to be the way they turned out and to see the range of possibilities of how it could have been otherwise."[11]

In a related vein, Boyer and Nissenbaum observe:

No one could have realized, back in February, or even as late as April or May, that the traditional responses of prayer and prosecution would not speedily put an end to the [witchcraft] outbreak. Something was subtly different about the situation in Salem Village in 1692, something which no one anticipated beforehand and which no one could explain at the time. . . . And yet speculation as to where events might have led . . . is one way of recapturing the import of where they did lead. And if one reconstructs those

8   events bit by bit, as they happened, without too quickly categorizing them, it is striking how long they resist settling into the neat and familiar pattern one expects.[12]

So, too, with the Boxers, it is an open question at what point they become irrevocably "the Boxers" of history. At what point does the Boxer phenomenon force itself on the consciousness of the world and cease to be an event of merely local import, even within China? As Boxer historians have repeatedly noted, it was not until December 31, 1899, that the Boxers killed their first foreigner (a missionary, S. M. Brooks, in Shandong), and, prior to May 31, 1900 (the date on which, in response to the mounting threat in the Beijing area, legation guard reinforcements began to arrive in the capital), Brooks was the only foreigner to have suffered death at the Boxers' hands.[13] If (to indulge in the sort of fruitful counterfactual speculation Boyer and Nissenbaum appear to endorse), as late as mid-May, the court had moved decisively to suppress the Boxer movement with force or the drought in North China had broken, encouraging farmer participants in the movement to return to their fields, many of the subsequent developments that transformed the Boxers into a crisis with global ramifications might never have taken place, China's own history in the first decade of the twentieth century would likely have been quite different, the Boxers as a field of academic study would very possibly never have amounted to much, and I would almost certainly not be writing this book. In probing the origins and history of the Boxer phenomenon, in other words, we have to be extremely careful, at every step along the way, not to assume with excessive haste that the outcomes we know took place were preordained.

Foreknowledge of outcomes, to summarize, empowers historians to engage in a process of explanation that is different, in important ways, from the processes of explanation engaged in by direct participants (who, among other things, do not ordinarily spend a lot of time and energy trying to figure out the origins of the events in which they are taking part). But—and this is the key point of the immediately preceding paragraphs—we must move with great caution, lest we conclude prematurely, in our reconstruction of the past, that things had to turn out the way they did.

There is another, closely related, aspect of our advance knowledge of historical outcomes that is crucially important. Such knowledge enables historians to assign meanings to prior events that literally did not exist at the time they occurred and therefore could not possibly have been known to the people who made and experienced the events (although they could, in certain circumstances, be guessed at). This process of retrospective assignment of historical meaning takes place at all levels of generality. At a fairly specific level, every major event is composed of lesser events which in other circumstances would doubtless be lost in the historical shuffle but come to be invested with substantial meaning once historians begin the process of piecing together the larger event's origins and evolution. The Marco Polo Bridge incident of July 7, 1937, instead of being a forgettable skirmish between Chinese and Japanese troops in North China, like many previous such skirmishes, is transformed into the first act in a drama known to the Chinese as the War of Resistance and to much of the rest of the world as World War II. The Chinese Communist movement's Long March of 1934–35, rather than signaling in quiet obscurity the movement's imminent expiration (as it might well have, had subsequent history taken a different turn), is heralded as an event of epic proportions that both symbolizes and makes possible the Communists' eventual triumph. Both the Marco Polo Bridge incident and the Long March become, in other words, parts of larger stories, and their historical valences change appreciably in the process.

Paralleling the part-to-whole relationship between simple and complex events, such as Marco Polo Bridge and World War II or the Long March and the ultimate victory of the Chinese Communists, we also have, at a higher level of generality, the relationship between events, simple (such as the dropping of the atomic bomb on Hiroshima) or complex (like the Second World War), and the more elaborate event structures, constituting broad substantive themes of a country's or the world's history, within which these events are nested. The part-to-whole relationship at this level may be formulated in various ways, depending on the particular event structure that is of interest to the formulator. Among the thematic contexts in which historians have placed the witchcraft outbreak in late seventeenth-century Salem, for example, are: "the history of the occult, the psychopathology of adolescence, the excesses of repressive Puritanism, the periodic recrudescence of mass hysteria and collective persecution in Western society."[14] And the atomic bombing of Hiroshima may be — and has been — seen as the beginning of the end of World War II, an especially horrible instance of white racist victimization of yellow people, or the opening act of the nuclear age.

The Boxer episode, too, formed part of a plurality of larger event structures, including (but not confined to) the pattern of recurrent domestic violence in the late imperial era, the growing problem of rural breakdown,[15] the history of conflicts between Christians and non-Christians from the mid-nineteenth century on,[16] and Sino-foreign diplomatic relations. Since these event structures extended not only backward but also forward in time, the historical meanings of the Boxer uprising were indeterminate at the time it occurred and could only be supplied retrospectively, by histori-

10 ans or others with a knowledge of post-Boxer developments.[17] Sometimes the act of supplying such meanings was performed at an even higher level of generality, the Boxer phenomenon being situated on a trajectory embracing, if not all of Chinese history, at least vast stretches of it. Harold Isaacs referred to the Boxers as "the last feeble challenge of traditionalism to the inevitability of change."[18] G. G. H. Dunstheimer situated them "at the divide between two historical eras: the Chinese Middle Age . . . and Modern Times."[19] "The patriotic, anti-imperialist Boxer movement that burst forth in 1900," according to historian Li Shiyu, "set off the second revolutionary upsurge of modern Chinese history."[20] And Zhou Enlai in 1955 hailed the heroic struggle of the Boxer movement in resisting imperialist aggression as "one of the cornerstones of the great victory of the Chinese people fifty years later."[21]

All of these statements, some of them going fairly far in the direction of mythologizing the Boxer experience, are predicated on awareness of a post-Boxer context. Implicitly or explicitly, they incorporate, like Merlin the magician or the omniscient narrator in a work of fiction, a foreknowledge of what comes next. As such, they reflect a consciousness fundamentally different from that of the direct participant in the making of the past, who, lacking such foreknowledge, still inhabits a world crowded with live possibilities, many of which—the precise ones cannot be identified at the time—will be foreclosed by the future and never come to fruition.

It would oversimplify things, on the other hand, not to point out that this distinction between the knowing historian and the unknowing participant, however important, is not absolute. Historians, also, are trapped in a present marked by indeterminacy, and this affects every phase of the process of historical reconstruction in which we are engaged, including what we choose to focus on and emphasize in our assertions about past events. Such assertions can be extremely unreliable, the more so the more general the level at which they are framed. General statements about the past (above all, I think, statements about the meaning of this or that "turning point" or "watershed") tend to have a larger mythic component than more bounded statements and, as such, reflect to a higher degree the passions and concerns of the persons making them and the times in which they live. The reason this is a problem is that the passions and concerns of the present have a way of changing abruptly and capriciously, and when this happens the general assertions about the past that embody such passions and concerns quickly lose their currency.

The point is made nicely by Vera Schwarcz in her commentary on Joseph Levenson's characterization of the meaning of the intellectual and political developments known in China as the May Fourth Movement of 1919. In his essay "The Day Confucius Died," Schwarcz writes, "Levenson had tried to endow the event of 1919 with a decisive, epoch-making significance not unlike that assigned to it by Mao Zedong in his distinction between 'new' and 'old' democracy. For Levenson, May Fourth marked a point of no return between tradition and modernity, between Western inspired solutions to China's dilemmas and the once universal truth claims of Confucianism." Ironically, not too many years after Levenson wrote his essay (1961), Confucius was dragged through the streets of Cultural Revolution Canton in effigy, a fairly clear sign that his influence in China was not moribund at all. Reflecting this and other realities, scholarship on May Fourth, according to Schwarcz, had by the 1980s moved away from the bloated language of earlier times and was less likely to embody "such extreme claims as Levenson's."[22]

The knowledge historians have of what comes next, their ability to move forward in time from any point in the past, is paralleled by their wide-angle vision, their capacity to range freely across a vast terrain, to sort out how the experiences of some individuals related to those of others and how a plurality of discrete events widely scattered over space (and time) combined to form event structures of broader scope, often — perhaps always — too broad to be encompassed in the experience of any one individual. This wide-angle vision distinguishes the historian from the participants in the making of the past.[23] But here again the advantage is a qualified one. Although, paradoxically, historians frequently have, in their reconstructive work, far more (and a more comprehensive sampling of) evidence at their disposal than was available to contemporaries, it is never enough, history being "full of missing pieces and indecipherable shards."[24]

Not only is the historian's evidence insufficient in a purely quantitative sense, it is also almost always stacked qualitatively. It does not present a representative sample of the totality of experience encompassed by the past. Nor does the evidence that survives necessarily reflect, as many might assume, the things in the past that were most important. "Survival," Daniel J. Boorstin demonstrates with depressing persuasiveness, "is chancy, whimsical and unpredictable." Because of the "happy accident" that the Babylonians wrote on clay tablets instead of on paper, "we know more about some aspects of daily life in the Babylon of 3000 B.C. than we do about daily life in parts of Europe or America 100 years ago."[25]

Boorstin generalizes from this that certain types of evidence have a greater propensity to survive than others. Besides evidence recorded on durable material (such as the cuneiform tablets of the Babylonians), these

12   "biases of survival" include evidence that is "collected and protected" by contemporaries (official documentation, for example), records pertaining to controversial issues, information relating to success as opposed to failure, and so on.[26] Any practicing historian can come up with other such evidentiary survival biases encountered in his or her own work. In the case of the Boxers, apart from a few hundred notices and other brief writings created by Boxer leaders and/or supporters and some oral history testimony collected over a half century after the uprising ended,[27] virtually all of the data that have survived—Chinese official documents (except those written by pro-Boxer officials), elite Chinese chronicles, the letters, diaries, and other writings of contemporary foreigners—are written from an anti-Boxer perspective. Rank-and-file Boxers, mostly illiterate and functioning within an oral tradition, created much in the way of history but left little to show for it. In reconstructing the perspectives of the Boxers themselves, therefore, historians must rely heavily on indirect strategies, teasing information from materials that very often are slanted against the Boxers and portray them in unflattering terms.

This sort of difficulty is one that historians encounter with great frequency, and it must be added to the other difficulties discussed earlier. It is not, however, necessary to conclude, as some have done, that because of the multitude of serious obstacles historians face, the activity in which we are engaged is without merit and our efforts at bottom little more than a sophisticated form of deception. Those who have taken such a position have tended to hold to a misguided notion (occasionally, I'm afraid, abetted by the careless assertions of historians themselves) of what exactly it is that historians are supposed to do. Because we can never meet the standard they have in mind, our efforts in their entirety are dismissed as being of questionable value.

If, on the other hand, we do not ask of historians something they cannot deliver—the past as it actually was—and recognize that the kinds of interpretive understanding and explanation historians *can* deliver are of value partly at least because of the ways in which they differ from the kinds of understanding and explanation available to the original creators of the past, all is not lost. It may well be true, as writer John Vernon has put it, that "history's ultimate unknowability" mocks those with a passionate interest in it; Vernon writes of "the powerful feeling that history is simultaneously there and not there, real and illusory—a ghost forever trailing behind, which vanishes when we turn around."[28] But it is precisely this elusive, incomplete, ephemeral quality of the past that fascinates and challenges the historian, who, with the evidence available and all the imaginative powers and skills at his or her disposal, strives to make sense of it. The end result, the kind of sense the historian makes, is not a revival of the past in its pristine wholeness. Nor is it a simple evocation of the historian's present values and wishes masquerading as a narrative about the past. (This happens, of course, all the time. But when it does, what we are confronted with is not history but mythologization.) Rather, the reconstructive effort of the historian entails a complex set of negotiations between present and past, incorporating something of vital importance from both and transforming, along the way, the consciousness that each brings to the negotiating process at the outset.

There are many other trademarks of the historically reconstructed past that I could dwell on. The characteristics discussed here—the goals of understanding and explaining, knowledge of future outcomes, privileged access to a wide-angle picture of what happened—are the ones that, over several decades of life as a practicing historian, have impressed me as the most distinctive and important. The narrative reconstruction of the Boxer episode that follows reflects, indeed is wholly dependent upon, each of these defining features of the historian's craft. It is a narrative that neither a direct participant in the episode nor one of its mythologizers would—or could—relate.

CHAPTER 1

The Boxer Uprising: A Narrative History

At the beginning of my undergraduate course in late imperial Chinese history, I ask my students to write down in two or three sentences their associations with the "Boxers" and the "Taipings." I make it clear to them that I do this less to call attention to what they don't know (although that is invariably one thing the exercise reveals) than to identify and confront them with some of the curious ways in which what they do know is patterned, the idiosyncratic, oddly misshapen cognitive map of China they have etched in their minds. The results of the quiz are remarkably consistent. Year in and year out, while a substantial majority of the students have at least a glimmer of information concerning the Boxers and are able to identify them (albeit sometimes placing them in the wrong century) as "anti-foreign" or a "rebellion" or a "revolution," well over 90 percent have never heard of the Taipings.

After announcing the results of the quiz to the class, we spend a few minutes trying to account for them. I tell my students that the Taipings launched what was very possibly the most destructive civil war in the history of the world (at least in terms of lives lost),[1] that they posed by far the most serious threat to the survival of the last imperial dynasty in China (the Qing), that for over a decade (1853–1864) they controlled some of the most valuable real estate in the country, that Westerners played a part (however marginal) in the rebellion's eventual suppression, that the Taipings' ideology was influenced in significant measure by evangelical Christianity, and—this is always the shocker—that their founder and supreme leader, Hong Xiuquan, had visions that convinced him he was the younger brother of Jesus Christ. Clearly, the Taiping uprising was an event of critical importance in the history of late imperial China; also, it had a component of Western involvement that was nothing if not intriguing. Why is it then that, in general, Americans who have not made a formal study of Chinese history have never heard of the Taipings while, in contrast, they not only have heard of the Boxers but actually know something about them?

After listening to what my students have to say in response to this question, I offer my own answer, which effectively breaks down into two parts. First, I point out, Westerners even at the time (excluding those actually resident in China) didn't pay much attention to the Taiping Rebellion or think it had much bearing on their lives. Insofar as there was any awareness of it at all, moreover, it was not generally seen as a threatening phenomenon. On the contrary, in the uprising's early phases its Christian claims excited considerable interest in Protestant missionary circles in America and Europe.[2] The Boxers, on the other hand, directly targeted Westerners and all manifestations of Western influence in China at the turn of the century and, with the siege of the legations, the assembling of a multinational relief force, and the crisis atmosphere prevailing in Western diplomatic circles, were for weeks in the summer of 1900 a familiar and frightening presence on the front pages of the world's press. People in the contemporary West knew who the Boxers were and many were horrified as lurid reports of their alleged actions gained wide circulation.[3]

Not only did the Boxers, because of the grim threat they posed to the lives and physical safety of Westerners, command far greater immediate notice than the Taipings, they also, mainly for this selfsame reason, left a lasting imprint on European and American psyches. In film, fiction, and folklore, they functioned over the years as a vivid symbol of everything we most detested and feared about China — its hostility to Christianity, its resistance to modern technology, its fiendish cruelty, its xenophobia, its superstition. Arguably, by extension, the Boxers also were emblematic of the range of negative associations Westerners in the twentieth century have had concerning the non-West in general. In stark contrast to the Taipings, who, for all their importance within the confines of Chinese history, barely scratched the surface of Western consciousness, the Boxers, willy-nilly, became a durable part of the intellectual baggage about the "Third World" Europeans and Americans still carry around in their heads.

This circumstance, the fact that the Boxers are a live — and sometimes quite emotionally charged — symbol in the West, is not necessarily a plus when it comes to reconstructing their history. Where, in the case of the Taipings, we can start with a more or less clean slate, our study of the Boxers must contend with the heavily mythologized images of them that Westerners have nurtured over the years. These images, although not without their own interest, form a kind of intellectual noise or static that historians must constantly listen for and strive to neutralize or eliminate. (This

16 is, as we shall see in part 3, even more so on the Chinese side.) As such, they pose an added challenge to those of us who would recount the Boxers' story.

The Origins of the Boxer Uprising

The Boxer phenomenon,[4] as it has been known not only to Westerners but also to many Chinese, first began to attract major attention early in 1900. For a few years prior to this it had been slowly gathering force in the area of its inception, northwestern Shandong. Then, in the winter of 1899–1900, the Boxers moved northward across the Shandong-Zhili border and spread with almost magical swiftness through a great part of the North China plain (above all, Zhili and Shanxi, to a lesser extent Henan), even spilling over into Manchuria to the northeast and Inner Mongolia to the far north.

Many of the most characteristic features of the Boxer movement in its expansionist phase — its name and principal slogans, its practice of mass spirit possession, its invulnerability beliefs and rituals, its "boxing" and deep-breathing exercises (*qigong*), as well as its nonhierarchical organization centered on boxing grounds (*quanchang* or *chang*) in rural areas and altars (*tan*) in cities (typically, in both cases, attached to temples) and composed mainly of young farmers (often mere boys), seasonal agricultural laborers, and unemployed drifters — continued patterns already established in Shandong. However, the extreme rapidity of the movement's spread in the first half of 1900 in some respects had its own dynamic and can only partly be explained in terms of the factors contributing to the much more incremental growth of the pre-1900 years.

One of the first myths about the Boxer movement that must be dispelled has to do with the term — "Boxer" (or its European-language equivalents) — that Westerners use to designate it. The Chinese term for "boxing" — *quan* or *quanshu* — refers to a range of martial arts practices, many of which have little to do with what we think of as "boxing" in the West. Since *quan* is a generic term, it is rarely if ever used alone in Chinese writing on the Boxer movement. In contemporary writing hostile to the movement the term most often encountered is *quanfei*, literally, "boxer (or boxing) bandit." Nonhostile Chinese writing on the Boxers generally modifies the term *quan* with the phrase "United in Righteousness" (Yihe), which was the name that first appeared in northwestern Shandong in the spring of 1898 and remained the name of the movement (along with the alternative and more official-sounding Yihetuan or "Militia United in Righteousness") throughout its expansionist phase.[5] Yihe Boxing referred to a particular method (or style or school) of Chinese "boxing." It was thus

distinguished from other forms — Plum Flower Boxing (Meihuaquan), Red
Boxing (Hongquan), Monkey Boxing (Houquan), Yin Yang Boxing
(Yinyangquan), Spirit Boxing (Shenquan), and the like — that were also
practiced in western Shandong in the last years of the nineteenth century.
Without in any way detracting from the uniqueness of the Boxer movement of 1898–1900, in other words, it is fair to say that this uniqueness does
not inhere in the term "Boxer."

The Boxers United in Righteousness represented a composite of two
major streams of influence: the notion of invulnerability (but not the specific rituals) associated with the Big Sword Society (Dadaohui), which
became active in Cao county, Shan county, and other parts of southwestern Shandong in early 1895, and the mass spirit possession rituals practiced
by groups calling themselves Spirit Boxers, which emerged at around the
same time in the northwestern part of the province.

The heartland of the Big Sword Society in southwestern Shandong bor-
dered on Henan and Jiangsu provinces. As with many other border regions
in China, it was not as firmly governed or politically stable as more centrally located areas. Banditry was endemic, opium growing and salt smug-
gling widespread, the gentry class not especially strong. Further contributing to the general insecurity of the area was the depletion of the normal
quota of Qing troops garrisoning it, owing to the Sino-Japanese War of
1894. In an "outlaw society, which sought as much as possible to live without interference from the state,"[6] a major concern of people with property
to safeguard was self-defense, and unofficial armed groups were frequently
called on to perform a protective function.[7] It was in this context that the
Big Sword Society emerged as an important force in the area in 1895. Oral
history materials clearly distinguish the Big Sword Society from "bandits"
and repeatedly assert that, in the initial phase of its development, the organization's sole purpose was to protect people's lives and property. Members
included landlords, rich and middle peasants, and tenants (whose mastery
of Big Sword fighting skills enabled them to protect their landlords' property). According to most accounts, the poorest people in the area rarely
joined, partly because they had nothing to protect and partly because they
couldn't afford the cash outlay required to buy swords, spears, and the
incense that members were supposed to burn daily.[8]

The founder and leader of the Big Swords until his death in 1896 was Liu
Shiduan. The group held mass meetings, partly for recruiting purposes,
generally in conjunction with opera performances.[9] The fighting technique
it practiced, known as the Armor of the Golden Bell (Jinzhongzhao), consisted of a "hard" (*ying*) form of deep-breathing exercise (*qigong*), accom-

MAP 1   Shandong and South Zhili

panied by recitation of magical formulas and the swallowing of charms. Big
Sword practitioners maintained that when this technique, which had a history going back to the mid-Qing, was carried out properly, it was as if one's
body were covered with a golden bell which bullets could not penetrate.[10]

During the spring of 1895, in response to worsening banditry in the
Shandong-Jiangsu border area, imperial orders were given to mount a
forceful campaign of annihilation. Although there was some ambivalence,
on the part of the government, toward the Big Swords, whose heterodox
religious practices were frowned upon, the court clearly distinguished
them from bandits and simply ordered that they be dispersed. In fact, they
were not dispersed and at the local level a considerable degree of cooperation emerged between the bandit-suppression activities of the authorities
and those of the Big Sword Society, as a result of which membership in the
society grew rapidly and it became a powerful player on the local scene. As
long as the Big Swords stuck to their original limited aim of protecting families and property against banditry, this cooperative arrangement persisted.
But when they became involved in conflicts with local Christian communities, it was only a matter of time before the attitude of the local authorities toward them soured.

As Esherick's analysis makes clear, the same power vacuum that enabled
banditry to flourish and facilitated the growth of the anti-bandit Big Swords
in southwestern Shandong (and northern Jiangsu) also provided an opening for an especially aggressive branch of the Catholic church—the
German Society of the Divine Word under the leadership of Johann
Baptist von Anzer—to strengthen its foothold in the area beginning in the
late 1880s. Christian communities grew, partly (as had been the case ever
since the legalization of the propagation of Christianity in China in 1860)[11]
by absorbing people in need of protection from the law. The latter were
attracted to the secure shield of the Catholic church, with its legally
immune (and convert-hungry) foreign missionary leadership. As, in these
circumstances, the line between Christians and bandits became increasingly indistinct—on one occasion in 1895 a sizable contingent of bandits,
after suffering defeat at the hands of the Big Swords, claimed membership
in the Catholic church in order to avoid being arrested by "the rich people"[12]—it was perhaps inevitable that friction would mount between the
Catholics and the Big Swords.

This friction exploded in the spring and summer of 1896 in a series of Big
Sword attacks on Christian properties in the Jiangsu-Shandong border area.
The attacks were triggered by a lineage dispute over land use in northern
Jiangsu and were not related, in any significant way, to the teachings of the

20   Catholic church.[13] Although they were, in themselves, not of great consequence (no casualties were sustained by either native or foreign Christians),
there was a significant breakdown in Big Sword discipline in the course of
the rampages, and as the Big Swords, in the ambiguous zone they occupied,
moved from (more or less welcome) guarantors of stability to (definitely
unwelcome) fomenters of disorder, the local authorities (led by future
Shandong governor Yuxian) responded by moving against their leaders. Liu
Shiduan and other Big Sword chiefs, some thirty in all, were arrested, tried,
and executed, and although the organization did not completely die out,
the heyday of its influence in southwestern Shandong was over.

Had a number of later events that were far from inevitable not taken
place and the uprising of the Boxers not occurred (or at least not on the
scale it eventually assumed), the history just summarized would very
likely never have attracted the notice of historians. Or, if it did, it would
have been as part of some other story with an altogether different import.
As it turned out, however, events following the demise of the Big Swords
imparted to the activities of the organization in 1895–96 a very considerable retrospective meaning, enabling them to occupy a place in history
both greater than and quite different from the place they would have
occupied had these events not occurred.

The first of these subsequent events was the Juye incident of November
1, 1897, in which two missionaries of the Society of the Divine Word,
Richard Henle and Francis Xavier Nies, during a visit at the residence (in
Zhangjiazhuang in Juye county) of a third member of the society, George
Stenz, were brutally murdered shortly before midnight by a small armed
band. The precise causes of the Juye incident were never established.
There is some evidence (but not conclusive) of Big Sword involvement.
There was considerable local resentment against Stenz, who although the
lone survivor (by a quirk of fate) was probably the intended target of the
attackers. By all accounts an unusually offensive individual, who regularly
engaged in the whole range of questionable practices (such as interference in lawsuits) of which the Catholic church in China had long stood
accused, Stenz undoubtedly was the object of a good deal of bad feeling
on the part of the population.[14] But there is also some evidence that the
incident was planned by a former bandit who, motivated by the desire for
personal revenge, sought to generate a career-ending crisis for the local
magistrate.

If the origins of the Juye incident were (and still are) unclear, the same
could not be said of its consequences, which were enormous. Under strong
pressure from the German government, the Chinese side agreed to the

erection of cathedrals, at its own expense, in the village where the missionaries were killed and two other places, with signs to be posted at the cathedral entrances stating: "Catholic church constructed by imperial order"; the dismissal, impeachment, or transfer of more than a half dozen local officials; and, most serious by far, the demotion and permanent removal from high office of the conservative but honest Shandong governor Li Bingheng, who, although well known for the energetic and firm stand he took against missionary abuses during his term as governor, does not appear to have been in any way responsible for the Juye outbreak. Apart from this formal diplomatic settlement, the Juye incident also provided the pretext Germany had long been looking for to seize the port of Jiaozhou and make it the centerpiece of a German sphere of influence on the Shandong peninsula.[15] This action, which was taken on November 14 and later ratified in an agreement with a harassed and (after its defeat in the Sino-Japanese War) much weakened Chinese government, in turn, supplied Britain, Japan, and other powers with the precedent they needed to negotiate long-term leaseholds of their own with China. Thus the Juye incident, which, had it occurred a decade earlier, might have been just another serious "church case," in the context of the late 1890s became the opening wedge in a process of greatly intensified imperialist activity in China, "set[ting] off a chain of events which," in Esherick's judgment, "radically altered the course of Chinese history."[16]

The direct and indirect results of the Juye incident, in combination, conveyed a clear message that, in the ongoing competition between China and the foreign powers, the latter had improved their position dramatically. The only question was how the message would be read in different parts of China, in different parts of Shandong, and among different social groups with varying degrees of translocal awareness. We know that highly educated individuals with a strong interest in national affairs and growing concern (especially after the Sino-Japanese War debacle) for China's survival as a political entity were likely to read the message with considerable alarm, regardless of whether they happened to be from Shandong or some other part of the empire. It also seems plausible that in southwestern Shandong, particularly the area in the immediate vicinity of Juye, or in the hinterland adjacent to Jiaozhou Bay on the southern coast of peninsular Shandong, people from all social strata, faced with the tangible effects of the Juye settlement, would develop a growing appreciation of the power, at least in local terms, of the Catholic church. Whether, on the other hand, ordinary people living elsewhere in China, or even elsewhere in Shandong province, would be especially concerned about or sensitive to the circum-

22 stances surrounding the downfall of a Li Bingheng (which, incidentally, proved extremely short-lived) is in my view less clear.[17]

What is fascinating about the relationship between the consequences of a historical event like the Juye incident and its origins is the degree to which the former extend beyond the latter, taking on seemingly a life of their own. It is as if we are dealing with a disjuncture between two horizons that, although historically connected, are fundamentally incongruent in range or scope. Thus the original perpetrators of the Juye incident, whatever their motives, could not possibly have imagined the far-reaching outcomes of their actions, while, conversely, the historical actors who negotiated the incident's consequences (at least the more tangible of them) neither knew nor cared what was in the minds of the original perpetrators.

This disjuncture is doubtless, in part at least, a mirage, occasioned by the mischievous habit historians have of using shorthand formulations to describe cause-and-effect relationships that are in fact a good deal more complicated. Thus, in the case at hand, if the Juye incident had taken place in a hypothetical historical vacuum, its consequences would presumably have occupied the same horizon as its causes. But because it took place in a larger context, which included causal agents unknown or of little concern to the originators of the incident — examples would be the long-standing German search for a pretext to take over Jiaozhou and the devastation of the Chinese navy in the Sino-Japanese War, which made it unthinkable for China to resist the German action with force — the eventual consequences seem out of phase with the origins. As we shall see toward the end of this chapter, the same sort of problem is encountered in the imprecise, but commonly made, assertion that the Boxer uprising constituted a watershed or turning point in the history of the late Qing, when in fact it would probably be more accurate to say that it was the Boxer Protocol of 1901 (a consequence not only of the Boxer uprising but also of a range of other causal factors, including contemporary European power rivalries) that was truly the watershed event.

Another event, or series of events, that, by contributing to the emerging history of the Boxer movement, also, retrospectively, enlarged the historical significance of the activities of the Big Sword Society in southwestern Shandong in the mid-1890s was the history of conflict between Christians and non-Christians in Guan county, Shandong, in the last decades of the nineteenth century. Although limited in scale and arguably of trivial importance in itself, this history, centering in the market town of Liyuantun, has attracted considerable attention from historians because one of the local groups opposing the Christians took the name "Boxers United in

Righteousness" (Yihequan) in early 1898 and some months later adopted 23
a slogan, "Support the Qing, destroy the foreign [or foreigner]" (Fu-Qing
mieyang), which, like the name, was identical with that used by the mature
Boxer movement as it spread across North China in 1899–1900.[18] Like Juye
(and the Big Sword Society earlier), Liyuantun thus was woven into a
much larger fabric of historical events.

Although Guan county was part of Shandong province, a piece of it
containing some two dozen towns and villages including Liyuantun had at
some point become detached and was situated (along with fragments of
two other Shandong counties) in southern Zhili. (Hence the Chinese des-
ignation of these split-off fragments as *feidi* or "flying territories.") (See map
1.) The area as a whole was one of extreme political weakness, and this was
even more true of the detached portions, which thus provided an ideal
environment for the growth of banditry, paramilitary (boxing) organizations, heterodox sects, and the Catholic church.

Friction between the Christian and non-Christian inhabitants of
Liyuantun had its inception in an 1869 agreement, a provision of which
transferred the temple property in the town to the Christians. Since the
temple was dedicated to the Jade Emperor, the top god in the Chinese pantheon, when the Christians proceeded to convert it into a church, there
was much local resistance. Over the next few decades this resistance,
which periodically took a violent turn, was led first by local gentry and later
by a group of poor peasants known as the Eighteen Chiefs (*shiba kui*). In
order to enhance their strength, the Eighteen Chiefs, whose leader, Yan
Shuqin, was a specialist of the Red Boxing (Hongquan) school, at some
point, possibly in 1892,[19] invited the support of a much larger and stronger
group called the Plum Flower Boxers (Meihuaquan), who were active in
Shaliuzhai, a village on the eastern border of Wei county (Zhili), a few
miles from Liyuantun. The Plum Flower Boxers, under the leadership of
Zhao Sanduo, were a boxing group with a long history in the area. Unlike
the Big Sword Society in southwest Shandong in 1895, their religious repertoire was extremely meager: they did not practice invulnerability rituals or
the swallowing of charms or the chanting of spells. Like the Big Swords, on
the other hand, their main purpose was generally of a protective, rather
than a predatory, nature. In fact, some of their leaders (possibly including
Zhao himself) were reluctant (at least at the outset) to take part in the anti-
Christian activities in Liyuantun, for fear that the group's good name
would be tainted and the local authorities antagonized.[20] At some point,
however, although the chronology and exact circumstances are a little
murky, Zhao Sanduo, a man known for his strong sense of justice and

24   determination to right the world's wrongs, acquiesced in Yan Shuqin's request and the Plum Flower Boxers joined the Liyuantun struggle.

Not all of them, however, and not, in the end, under the "Plum Flower" name. In April 1897 Zhao Sanduo and the Plum Flower Boxers convened a three-day public exhibition of their boxing skills in Liyuantun. Although not overtly anti-Christian, the exhibition was clearly intended as a show of strength, and in the prevailing excitement a sizable crowd attacked the temple structure, which the Christians were just then in the process of transforming into a church. In the accompanying violence, the Christians were decisively routed and the official settlement, clearly favoring the Eighteen Chiefs–Plum Flower coalition, seemed, at last, to point to a resolution of the Liyuantun difficulties. After the Juye incident in November, however, the shift in the balance of power in Shandong as a whole toward the Christian/foreign side encouraged the church to challenge the agreement, and with the downfall of Li Bingheng and the strong reassertion of the court's policy of settling church cases expeditiously to reduce friction with the foreign powers, it was only a matter of time before the original settlement came unraveled and the Liyuantun temple property was once again turned over to the Christians.

The events of 1897–98 had two important consequences. On one hand, they intensified the anger and hostility felt by many non-Christian Chinese toward the local Christian community and its foreign supporters. On the other hand, they pushed the Chinese authorities into adopting a tougher stance toward any and all organized groups that might seek to channel this resentment into overt anti-Christian acts. Thus, as Zhao Sanduo and his now expanded company of followers became increasingly engaged in direct action against Christians in the area surrounding Liyuantun in 1898, the more conservative leaders of the Plum Flower Boxers, ever fearful of antagonizing the authorities, became increasingly intent upon disengaging themselves from Zhao. It was in this context that Zhao, probably in early 1898, either voluntarily or as a result of the insistence of the less radical members of the Plum Flower leadership, changed the name of his group to Boxers United in Righteousness, an appellation conveying the sense of a coalition of Plum Flower Boxers, Red Boxers, and others, united in their righteous indignation over the inroads of the foreign-backed Christians.[21]

In response to the mounting tensions in Guan county in early 1898, not only between Christians and non-Christians but, increasingly, between the Boxers and the authorities, the latter attempted in various ways to defuse the situation. They sought to drive a wedge between the radical rustic Yan Shuqin and Zhao Sanduo, who was a definite cut above Yan in social standing and appears, even after his split from the Plum Flower Boxers, to have harbored some ambivalence about becoming overinvolved in Yan's struggle. Led by Governor Zhang Rumei, Li Bingheng's successor, the authorities also sought to transform Zhao's Boxers into officially sponsored militia.[22] Owing in part to the depletion of regular garrison forces during the Sino-Japanese War and in part to the fiscal crisis facing the government as a consequence of the indemnity ending the war, militia had assumed a growing role in keeping the turbulent Shandong-Zhili border area from getting completely out of hand. If Zhao's followers could be made into militia, it was reasoned, two birds could be killed with one stone: there would be a reduction of tension with the Christians and there would also be a general enhancement of the forces of stability in the border region.

The trouble with this strategy was that it was based on the premise that the Boxers, who by spring 1898 had spread out over much of the area, would simply, like the Big Sword Society in southwestern Shandong a few years earlier, disappear into the landscape upon being deprived of their main leadership (in this instance by co-optation rather than decapitation). This premise, unfortunately, proved invalid. The Boxers were very different from the Big Swords, much more a loose coalition of diverse constituencies than a tightly structured organization, and Zhao Sanduo's hold over them was nothing like that of Liu Shiduan and others over the Big Swords. The Boxer-to-militia conversion plan, therefore, did not work, and in late October and early November, rampaging Boxers, with the at best ambivalent involvement of Zhao Sanduo himself, attacked Christians both in the Liyuantun region and further south along the Shandong-Zhili border proper. It was during these attacks that the slogan "Fu [or Zhu]-Qing mieyang" (Support [or Help] the Qing, destroy the foreign [or foreigner]) first appeared on Boxer flags. The Qing military, not yet prepared (as it would be less than two years later) to accept the Boxers' offer of support, easily put them down. Many of the rank-and-file Boxers then accepted an official offer of amnesty, while Zhao Sanduo fled north to central Zhili.

Although this was not the end of Zhao Sanduo's career as a reluctant rebel—in 1900 he again became active in the Guan county detached area and two years later died in jail after being implicated in an antigovernment protest in nearby Guangzong county, Zhili—he ceased, after fall 1898, to be part of the main Boxer story. This story now shifted to the much larger territorial expanse of northwestern Shandong, where groups calling themselves Spirit Boxers (Shenquan), which had been in existence for several years but were not initially involved in anti-Christian activities, as they became so involved, in spring 1899, adopted the name Boxers United in

26 Righteousness, along with the key slogan "Support the Qing, destroy the foreign." The name and the slogan, however, were the extent of their connection with the Guan county Boxers. The content of the "boxing" practiced by the new Boxers United in Righteousness was far more religious in nature, including invulnerability rituals, mass spirit possession, the swallowing of charms, and the recitation of spells. Also, while the migration of a few Guan county Boxers to the new Boxer area can hardly be ruled out, the new Boxers had their own leaders and rank-and-file membership.

1.1 Boxer Flag. Inscribed on the flag is the most widely encountered Boxer slogan, "Fu-Qing mieyang." From Zhang Haipeng, ed., *Jianming Zhongguo jindaishi tuji.*

The reason the Spirit Boxers took the name Boxers United in Righteousness in the first place doubtless had to do with the notoriety the Guan
county Boxers had acquired by the end of 1898 among people in northwestern Shandong who were themselves beginning to become involved in
anti-Christian activity. If the Spirit Boxers had, for whatever reason, adopted
another name instead, it is fair to suppose in retrospect that the whole history of conflict between Christians and non-Christians in Liyuantun, not to
mention the part taken by the Plum Flower Boxers and Zhao Sanduo in
this history, would have held little interest for historians of the Boxer uprising. Historical interest in the Spirit Boxers themselves, on the other hand,
would likely have remained undiminished, owing to their substantive — not
merely nominal — importance as forerunners of the Boxer movement in its
climactic phase.

The same sort of point can be made, albeit in a somewhat different
way, in connection with a series of conflicts between Christians and non-
Christians that took place in southern Shandong between late 1898 and
late 1899.[23] These conflicts began in the southeastern coastal county of
Rizhao (just west of Qingdao) in December 1898 and spread westward to
the Jining-Jiaxiang area, not far east of Juye. Although the causes of the
incidents varied from place to place, they were in significant measure a
response to the aggressive inroads of German imperialism in the aftermath of the Juye incident — an aggressiveness reflected in the increasingly
assertive behavior of German missionaries and their Chinese Christian
followers at the local level. As in Guan county, and for some of the same
reasons (in particular the turbulent and lawless conditions prevailing in
much of southern Shandong after the war with Japan), boxing groups
again emerged. Although casting themselves in general as protectors of
local communities against the intolerable actions of the Christians in
their midst, the "boxers" engaged in activities that were not infrequently
of a distinctly predatory nature and, in the end, contributed their share to
the general lawlessness and violence of the times.

Although there were a number of different boxing groups, including (in
the far southwest) a rejuvenated Big Sword Society, the most prominent
was the Red Boxing school. Normally, like the Plum Flower Boxers, a more
or less pure fighting group with little in the way of religious ritual, the Red
Boxers in 1897 had absorbed some of the distinctive characteristics of the
Big Sword Society, including charm-swallowing and invulnerability rituals
and, most significantly, a clearly articulated, religiously sanctioned hierarchical leadership. Hence, when Yuxian, who assumed the reins of the governorship of Shandong in spring 1899, in response to the growing volatility

28 of conditions in the southern part of the province, especially in the south-west and the Jining-Jiaxiang area, applied to the Red Boxers the same policy of decapitating the leaders and dispersing the followers that, as a local official, he had applied in 1896 to the Big Sword Society in the southwest, he was once again successful.

Yuxian, the same who as governor of Shanxi less than a year later, at the height of the Boxer movement, was to take actions that would make him a lasting emblem, at least among Westerners, of the movement's worst xenophobic excesses, succeeded in restoring calm to southern Shandong in fall 1899 for a number of reasons. As just noted, his policy of decapitation and dispersion was well adapted to the structure of the groups that were its main target. It was also well suited to the social conditions of the areas in the south in which it was implemented, conditions marked by reasonably prosperous agriculture and a strong landlord-gentry presence and therefore standing to benefit tangibly from the restoration of stability and peace. Finally, the German government, as a direct corollary to its growing involvement in the building up of its sphere of influence in southern Shandong, was becoming increasingly sensitive to its own interest in the promotion of peaceful and stable conditions in the area and by the end of 1899 had made it clear to the missionaries of the Society of the Divine Word that it would no longer countenance the sort of intemperate behavior that in the course of the year had done so much to arouse popular animosity.

Esherick sees the anti-Christian incidents that began in southern Shandong in late 1898 as forming "an important background to the full-scale Boxer movement which was growing simultaneously in northwest Shandong, and would break into the open soon after the suppression of the disturbances in the south."[24] Although he is not explicit in defining what exactly this background consisted in, it is possible to argue, from his own analysis, that its most important ingredient was Yuxian himself. The success of this long-time Shandong official's decapitation-and-dispersion policy in the southwest in 1896 and again in the south in 1899 encouraged a set of expectations that were completely frustrated when, in the face of an entirely new set of conditions, he attempted to carry out essentially the same policy in northwestern Shandong in the latter half of 1899. What were these new conditions, and why did Yuxian's efforts to address them fail so disastrously?

The Spirit Boxers, whose mass possession rituals constituted the second major formative influence on the Boxers United in Righteousness (the first, it will be recalled, being the idea of invulnerability, inspired at least in part by the Big Sword Society), began to appear in northwestern Shandong in the mid-1890s. Although their center of greatest strength was Chiping county, they were distributed over ten or so other counties as well, most of them lying within the fork formed by the Grand Canal as it proceeded northward from Dong'e and the Yellow River as it flowed past Dong'e in a northeasterly direction toward the sea (see map 1). Because of its location, northwestern Shandong was especially vulnerable to natural disaster, in particular flooding. Unlike the southwestern portion of the province, it was extremely poor, with little in the way of commerce, almost no gentry or landlord presence, a sizable mobile population of destitute persons, and an

1.2 Yuxian. From Archibald E. Glover, *A Thousand Miles of Miracle in China* (London: Hodder and Stoughton, 1904).

30 unusual degree of receptivity both to sectarian religion (especially the White Lotus) and to shamanism.

It is not clear exactly how the Spirit Boxers got started. Although the oral history testimony is not completely consistent on the point, the majority of the respondents denied any link to the White Lotus sect. The importance among the Spirit Boxers of spirit possession, not typically a part of sectarian ritual, and, conversely, the complete absence in oral or written documentation on the Spirit Boxers of reference to the Eternal Venerable Mother (Wusheng laomu), the key instrument of salvation in the White Lotus belief system, seem to bear out this denial. There was general consensus, on the other hand, that the Spirit Boxers were either the same as the Big Sword Society (which had in fact become quite active in the northwest in the last years of the century) or at least had close ties to it.[25]

Different both from the Big Sword Society in the southwest and the Guan county Boxers, the great majority of those who took up Spirit Boxing, at least initially, were poor peasants. Although there were small communities of both Protestant (American Congregationalist) and Catholic (Italian Franciscan) Christians in the northwest, the Spirit Boxers were not involved at the outset in anti-Christian activities. Their original purposes appear to have been the furtherance and preservation of conventionally orthodox social and moral values: filial respect, esteem for superiors and compassion for inferiors, promotion of local harmony, resistance to greed and lust, and so on. Consonant with their generally protective stance vis-à-vis family and community, individual Spirit Boxers frequently engaged in healing. Indeed, one of the reasons for the popularity of the early Spirit Boxer leader, Zhu Hongdeng (Red Lantern Zhu), was that he treated people who were ill (his speciality was skin ulcers) and did not ask for money.

The Spirit Boxers grew steadily but undramatically during the initial period of their existence. Unthreatened — indeed, barely noticed — by the authorities, they practiced their boxing and religious rituals in the open, for all to see. Their rituals, which included bowing or performing the koutou[a] in a southeasterly direction, chanting spells, swallowing charms (after they had been burned and the ashes mixed with water), and, most important, calling upon the gods (almost all of whom were famous characters from popular fiction and opera) to possess them, were precisely the rituals soon to be practiced by the Boxers United in Righteousness during their expan-

---

[a] Also ketou, a ubiquitous Chinese ritual denoting respect for a superior and involving knocking the head on the ground while in a kneeling position; the origin of the English word kowtow.

sionist phase. Although the possession rituals of the Spirit Boxers were initially (in the time-honored tradition of Chinese spirit mediums) for the purpose of enabling them to act as healers, as they became increasingly engaged in violent encounters with Christians from the spring of 1899, healing gave way (probably under the influence of the Big Sword Society) to invulnerability as the main object of Spirit Boxer possession.

A dramatic transformation occurred among the Spirit Boxers in the last months of 1898 and the first months of 1899. Although important aspects of this change remain poorly understood, it is clear that a major factor was the catastrophic flooding of the Yellow River, which broke through its dikes, first, at Shouzhang on August 8, and twice subsequently, at Jinan and Dong'e, forcing millions of people from their homes and turning much of northwestern Shandong into a disaster zone.[26] A huge refugee population, created mainly by the flood of 1898 but also by repeated lesser floods going back to 1892, aggravated an already desperate situation and, in response, the Spirit Boxers in the winter of 1898–99 became energized and rapidly spread northward from Chiping.

A number of crucial changes accompanied this burst of new activity. Sometime late in 1898, the Spirit Boxers began to be referred to as the Big Sword Society; then, some months later, as we have seen, they took the name Boxers United in Righteousness. (This was especially true of boxers in Pingyuan, north of Chiping; in Chiping itself the name Spirit Boxers appears to have continued in use.) Around this time, Zhu Hongdeng and a monk named Benming (or Xincheng) emerged in Chiping as recognized leaders of the movement. The shift, already noted, from healing to invulnerability also took place now, possibly as a result of the influence of Benming, an accompished martial arts specialist. Finally, and in some ways most puzzling, it was shortly after the winter of 1898–99 that the Spirit Boxers began to engage in anti-Christian activities and to brandish anti-foreign slogans.

Esherick, in the absence of a clear and convincing trail of documentary evidence, hypothesizes that this last metamorphosis occurred as a result of the coming together of a number of broad factors: heightened foreign threat and concomitant Christian aggressiveness in the aftermath of the Sino-Japanese War and the establishment of the German sphere of influence in the Jiaozhou region; growing awareness in northwestern Shandong of the anti-Christian activities of the Guan county Boxers, the Big Sword Society in the southwest, and the Red Boxers and others in the southern part of the province; the disruptive effects of a major natural disaster; and the willingness of at least some of the local authorities in the northwest to look the

32   other way when it came to anti-Christian behavior.[27] This hypothesis is not unconvincing, and it may be as close an approximation to what actually happened as we will get.[28] At the same time, it fails to account for places like Zouping county (in Jinan prefecture), which, in spite of being subject to the same general forces that ostensibly resulted in anti-Christian activity in other areas of northwestern Shandong, and in spite also of having a sizable Christian community and being crowded with refugees owing to its location on the southern edge of the flood-affected area, was left "virtually untouched" by the newly anti-Christian animus of the Spirit Boxers.[29]

Whatever the specific reasons for the shift, on the part of the Spirit Boxers, toward growing involvement in violent actions against Christians, as these actions spread across the border into Zhili in the spring and summer of 1899, the foreign community reacted with predictable alarm and applied pressure on the Chinese government to respond. As a result, when Zhu Hongdeng launched attacks in two different locations in Pingyuan county in October, his Spirit Boxers experienced their first armed clashes with the forces of the Qing state.

The second of these clashes, the Battle of Senluo Temple, was especially important, in terms of its significance for the future of the Boxer movement. Those Chinese historians who are committed to a vision of the Boxer uprising as not only anti-imperialist but also antifeudal have found in the battle apparent confirmation of their own point of view. Joseph Esherick, who sees the Boxers as a loyalist movement from start to finish, maintains that the willingness of the Boxers to confront the forces of the Qing on this occasion was not motivated by antidynastic sentiment but was a direct expression of their belief that the government was "not doing enough to expel the foreign menace," that "what the Boxers were doing was undertaking, on behalf of the Chinese people, actions which the state was incapable of performing."[30] It is noteworthy, for the support it lends to Esherick's interpretation, that in the Battle of Senluo Temple the main slogan paraded by the Boxers was "Revive the Qing, destroy the foreign" (Xing-Qing mieyang).[31] Also, it was in this battle that the Boxers first began to refer to themselves as "Militia United in Righteousness" (Yihetuan), an appellation that was used increasingly from this point on and that had the effect of trading the Boxers' former identity as an organization of potentially heterodox "boxers," at best operating on the fringes of legality, for a new one as staunch defenders of the orthodox order.

Yuxian's recommendation in his memorial to the throne that the local officials in Pingyuan be punished for their complete bungling of the crisis leading up to the Battle of Senluo Temple was, in the context of the gov-

ernor's unquestioned antiforeignism and consistent policy of leniency
toward the Boxer rank and file, widely misinterpreted (by the Boxers themselves as well as by the Christians) as a censuring of these officials for having called in the troops to put down the Boxers. As such, it became the
basis for the foreign perception that Yuxian was responsible for the Boxer
movement overall and resulted in December in his removal from the
Shandong governorship.[32]

One thing is clear. In his response to the Boxers themselves, in the aftermath of the Senluo Temple affair and a rash of other violent clashes
between Christians and Boxers in November,[33] Yuxian applied the same
policy he had earlier implemented with such success in southwestern and
southern Shandong: Zhu Hongdeng, Benming, and the third major Boxer
leader in the area, Yu Qingshui, were all taken into official custody by the
end of November and in December were executed in Jinan, while ordinary
Boxers were allowed — even encouraged — to meld back into the general
population. In the different circumstances prevailing in northwestern
Shandong, however, the governor's decapitate-and-disperse policy back-
fired. In portions of the area, it is true, the Boxer movement did indeed
come to a temporary halt. But this seems to have been a consequence less
of the efficacy of Yuxian's policy than of internal quarreling within the
movement that broke out in mid-November and the heavy casualties the
Boxers incurred in the Battle of Senluo Temple (in which at least twenty-
seven Boxers were killed), causing many in Pingyuan and adjacent En
county to lose faith in the Boxers' invulnerablility rituals. In other parts of
the northwest, in an implicit rebuff of Yuxian's policy, Boxer activities gathered new energy. With the onset of winter, attacks on Christians occurred
at an accelerated pace, and by the start of 1900 the Boxers' rapid spread
northward was well under way.

The main reason for the failure of Yuxian's policy in the northwest was
the Boxer movement's capacity, like Hercules' Hydra (to borrow Esherick's
apt image), to reproduce itself (including the production of new leadership) with ease. This was owing partly to the popularity of the movement's
antiforeign agenda, partly to the increasing indications that the authorities
were themselves divided on how to respond to the Boxers, and partly, perhaps, to the relatively egalitarian social structure of the impoverished northwest, which, Esherick argues, favored the emergence of a social movement
with weakly defined lines of authority and, for this very reason, made it
more difficult to suppress such a movement by eliminating its leadership.

With respect to the last point, it is nevertheless important to note that,
in the subsequent spread of the Boxer movement across much of the North

34   China plain, the movement's seemingly effortless capacity to regenerate itself, coupled with an equally conspicuous incapacity to produce strong, movement-wide leadership, was displayed in a great variety of different social settings, some of them far more highly structured than that of northwestern Shandong. It seems, therefore, that, in accounting for the distinctive organizational character of the Boxer movement, it would be a mistake to overstate the importance of specific social context.

The Expansionist Phase of the Boxer Movement

One important factor contributing to the rapid spread of the Boxer movement, which also did much to shape the movement's special social and political character, was the dynamic of spirit possession, which as we have seen first emerged in northwestern Shandong and then remained a core feature of the movement through the remainder of its history. The streamlined, easy-to-master possession ritual the Boxers followed, although possibly characteristic of cultural and religious tendencies in North China in general,[34] was not linked to a specific social environment and thus served to uncouple the Boxer movement from the distinctive social setting in which it first emerged. The empowerment possession conferred made it enormously attractive to those at the bottom of the Chinese social scale, regardless of locale. Also, the possession ritual, by placing individuals in direct communication with their gods and enabling them, when in a possessed state, to in effect become gods, placed a major barrier in the way of the creation of a more centralized, structured, and perhaps durable, movement. "Uncontrolled spirit possession," Robert Weller has written, "more easily than other forms of religious communication, undercuts authority of all kinds."[35] The same feature of the Boxer movement that facilitated its meteoric spread across North China during the first six months of 1900 thus may well have also contributed, paradoxically, to its abrupt disintegration and almost total disappearance after the summer of that year.

    A second factor that I believe was critically important in accounting for the astonishing speed of Boxer expansion was the drought that settled in over much of North China after the winter of 1898–99. This was a sharp reversal of the problem of flooding and waterlogging that had bedeviled the farming populations of western Shandong, Zhili, and other parts of the region during the earlier part of the decade. The drought of 1899–1900 contributed to the rapid spread of the Boxer movement in a number of ways. It created a sizable population of young males who, idled by the lack of farm work, were bored and had a surplus of free time on their hands. The longer the drought lasted—and by the winter of 1899–1900, when the expansion of the Boxer movement quickened dramatically, it had continued in many areas for the better part of a year—the more the population was afflicted by hunger. Since the Boxers often had ample supplies of grain and food (acquired by force from the Christian population, by pressure and coercion from affluent Chinese households seeking protection, and by voluntary contributions from supporters in the general population), joining one's local unit was a way of filling one's belly.

Just as important as actual hunger, from a psychological point of view, was hunger anxiety. Widespread anxiety due to hunger (present or anticipated) made people more willing to risk their lives in actions of a desperate sort. It also made them more susceptible to religious constructions of reality linking the absence of precipitation to the anger of the gods over the growing inroads of Christianity and other forms of foreign influence. Such constructions were, as we shall see in chapter 2, clearly reflected in Boxer notices and handbills that were disseminated across the length and breadth of the North China plain beginning in the winter of 1899–1900, precisely the moment the Boxer movement exploded beyond the confines of its original home in northwestern Shandong.

In making the case for an animus against Christianity based on popular religious assumptions about how the cosmos functioned, I don't mean to question the concrete grievances many Chinese had against Christians living within their communities or to minimize the anger and hatred that naturally flowed from such grievances. I accept, moreover, the premise (to be amplified in chapter 2) that antiforeignism, in the pristine sense of fear of and/or hostility toward the foreign or foreign-tainted (the "other" within, in the case of Chinese Christians), was always present—and pervasive—in China in latent form. But latent antiforeignism could simmer beneath the surface for years or even decades without boiling over. It was most apt to erupt and to spread rapidly, out of control and in epidemic fashion, in an atmosphere marked by crisis. And this was, of course, above all the case if the crisis in question happened to be one that could plausibly be understood as resulting from the presence of unwanted foreign influences.

Another factor that was clearly important in accounting for the rapid expansion of the Boxer movement after the winter of 1899–1900 was the stance of the authorities. In Shandong, in December, Yuxian was replaced as governor by the vehemently anti-Boxer Yuan Shikai. Although Yuan was constrained by the court from immediately pursuing his preferred policy of extermination (in fact the first Boxer-related foreign death, that of the British missionary S. M. Brooks in Feicheng on December 31, took place

36   on Yuan's watch), in the first half of 1900 Yuan, aided by the well-trained modern force he brought with him when he assumed office, was able to keep the Boxers firmly in check.[36] Zhili, on the other hand, presented a very different picture. The governor-general, Yulu, although hardly sympathetic to the Boxers, was a notably weak official. There was not enough military force available in the province to mount an effective campaign of suppression, even had this been the clear and unambiguous intent of the authorities. And, perhaps most important, the intent of the authorities in Zhili was far from clear and unambiguous: the court was deeply divided on the question of how to respond to the Boxers (as it had been from the start), and the resulting hesitation and vacillation created an environment in which, aided by mushrooming support from within the general population, the Boxers were able to prosper.

One final factor that took a significant part in energizing the Boxer movement after the winter of 1899–1900 was the movement itself. As circular as this may sound, the fact is, once the Boxers reached a critical mass of numbers, geographical spread, and activity, it became that much easier for them to expand further and faster. Partly this was because fence-sitters who were basically sympathetic to the Boxers' aims but were wary of the dangers of getting directly involved were more apt to join the movement as it became visibly stronger. Partly it was owing to the fact that, as the Boxers became more and more influential in an area, the dangers of *not* supporting them mounted. And partly it was because, as the Boxers grew in numbers and their actions in frequency, a kind of bandwagon effect was fostered, accompanied by a good deal of noise and excitement (*renao*, to use the equivalent Chinese term), and people did not want to miss out on the action. After a certain point, it seems clear, imitation, driven by simple crowd psychology, played a crucial role in the movement's spread.

Although the above-discussed circumstances were of critical importance in accounting for the character of the Boxer movement and the timing of its rapid expansion through North China generally, note must also be taken of the special characteristics of Zhili province that made it in many ways the most logical site for the center of an antiforeign and anti-Christian explosion. Zhili's two largest cities, Beijing and Tianjin, both had sizable foreign populations, including the diplomatic corps in the case of the former. The advent of the railway and telegraph in the province,[37] in addition to serving as visible symbols of foreign penetration, had resulted in job losses in the transport and other sectors. Most significant, Zhili was among the more heavily missionized provinces in China, with a Christian population (disproportionately Catholic) of well over 100,000.[38]

MAP 2   North China and Adjacent Areas

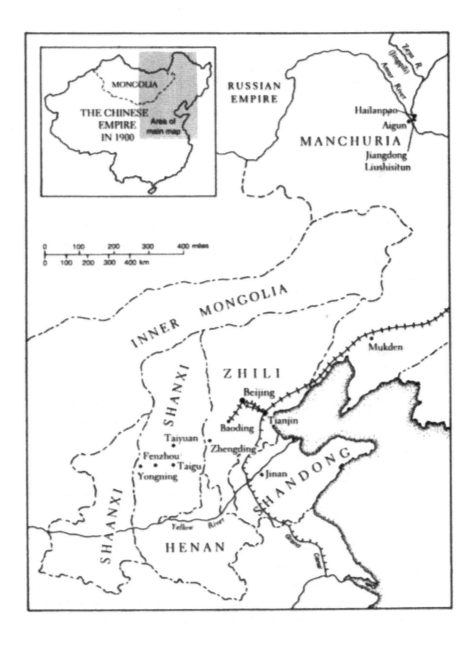

38   Although Boxers had become involved in the southernmost part of Zhili, next to the Shandong border, as early as 1898, their spectacular expansion through much of the rest of the province began only in the winter of 1899–1900. Sometimes, when people in a town or village wanted to establish an altar or boxing ground, they simply went ahead and did so, without anyone's supervision. More often, however, they would invite a boxing teacher from elsewhere (occasionally from Shandong) to assist them. Increasingly, as the Boxer presence in Zhili grew, the teachers who founded new boxing grounds or altars tended either to come from the local area or from someplace nearby. By the beginning of 1900, according to survey materials, approximately one hundred boxing grounds had been established in the southern county of Wuyi alone.[39] In the next several months the number of boxing grounds proliferated, as Boxer activities rapidly spread both into the southwestern part of the province and northward into the area of central Zhili roughly coinciding with the Tianjin-Beijing-Baoding triangle.[40]

One of the fresh developments of this expansionist phase of the Boxer movement was that, as new groups came into existence, they identified themselves with one or another Chinese trigram, the most common by far being the *kan* and *qian* trigrams.[41] Since the trigrams were associated with the Eight Trigrams sect, a branch of the White Lotus, some scholars have seen this as evidence of a Boxer–White Lotus tie. Further evidence of such a connection is found in Boxer notices, especially those circulated at the height of the movement, in which frequent reference is made to such White Lotus millenarian concepts as kalpa calamity (*jie*) and the imminent appearance of a true lord or sovereign (*zhenzhu*).[42] The question of the relationship of the Boxers to the White Lotus sect, already touched on in our discussion of the Spirit Boxer phase of the Boxer story, is an involved one; it is further complicated by the antidynastic identity periodically assumed by White Lotus followers, which makes a Boxer–White Lotus link especially attractive to Communist scholars anxious to highlight the antifeudal side of the Boxer movement.[43]

While I am inclined to agree with Joseph Esherick that, in terms of its ideas, its rituals, and its organizational patterning, the Boxers are best understood as having grown out of the popular culture of the North China plain (which contained elements of White Lotus influence), and not as centrally situated in the White Lotus sectarian tradition (as contended by Lu Yao, Cheng Xiao, Liao Yizhong, and other Chinese historians), I would also point out that, given the relative lack of hierarchical structure in the Boxer movement during its climactic phase and the corresponding freedom from external control within which individual groups operated, it was entirely possible for different Boxer units in different parts of North China to be differentially influenced by White Lotus ideas. It is even arguable, I think, that the very question, whether the Boxers were or were not connected to the White Lotus, may be too rigidly framed to account for the loose, untidy organizational reality that characterized the Boxers during this period of their development.

In matters of dress, as in their boxing and trance behavior, the Boxers imitated the martial arts performers they had so often seen in village operas. Members of *kan* trigram units generally wore red turbans, sashes, and leggings (or ankle straps), while *qian* trigram Boxers favored the color yellow.[44] Boxer units might number anywhere from 25 to 100 or more members. Typically a village would have a single Boxer unit (often called a *tuan* in the final phase of the uprising), larger villages, towns, and cities a plurality of units (which in urban areas were generally referred to as *tan* or altars).[45] According to the oral history materials, there was sometimes a further distinction made between military (*wu*) and civil (*wen*) units, the latter generally composed of Boxers with some education (mainly scholars and merchants) who might or might not take part in live combat.[46] The leader of a given Boxer unit, often chosen because of his superior boxing skills,[47] was called the *da shixiong* or Senior Brother-Disciple, the second in command was called the *er shixiong* or Second Brother-Disciple, and so on down the line, ordinary rank-and-file members simply referring to each other as *shixiong* (Brother-Disciples).

During the early months of 1900 a separate organization of female "Boxers," called Red Lanterns (Hongdengzhao),[48] also appeared on the scene in Zhili, most conspicuously (but not exclusively) in the area in and around Tianjin. Clad entirely in red and armed with red handkerchiefs and red lanterns, the members of this organization were for the most part teenaged girls and young unmarried women. The Red Lanterns had separate altars, practiced at separate boxing grounds, and had little or no day-to-day contact with the Boxers. The leadership of individual Red Lantern units paralleled exactly that of the Boxer units, the top leader being referred to as Senior Sister-Disciple (*da shijie*), the second-in-command as Second Sister-Disciple (*er shijie*), and so on.[49] Although there are occasional (and in my view not very dependable) references in the oral history materials to the direct participation of Red Lanterns in combat, they were best known at the time for the indirect assistance they provided the Boxers, owing to their extraordinary magical powers (see chapter 4). Inasmuch as Chinese historians in the twentieth century have not been especially noted for their sympathetic interest in popular religion and magic, this may be one reason why the Red Lanterns have been accorded scant notice in serious historical treatments of the Boxer uprising.[50] Another—and I believe more fun-

40 damental—reason is that, for all their importance in the religious world of the Boxers and the allure they had (on quite other grounds) for state mythologizers of the Boxer uprising during the Cultural Revolution era (see chapter 9), the Red Lanterns in fact contributed little to the history of the Boxers, when viewed (as in this chapter) as a succession of interconnected events. Indeed, they can be omitted from the Boxer story almost entirely, without significantly altering its overall thematic structure.

1.3 Red Lantern. This is a rare photograph of a Red Lantern, portraying realistically a rather plain-looking teenaged girl in a studio setting. From Li Di, *Quan huo ji*.

The members of Boxer units were for the most part local people who, in their anti-Christian and antiforeign activities, did not venture far from home. This was especially so during the first months of 1900, when Boxer actions consisted typically of the destruction (usually by fire) of churches and chapels and the looting of convert homes and other properties, usually

1.4   Boxers Setting Fire to Church. From *Quanfei jilüe*.

42   in rural areas. Important exceptions to this localist pattern began to
emerge, however, as, beginning in May, a much expanded Boxer movement became increasingly active in larger population centers, and the
repertoire of Boxer activities became less exclusively anti-Christian and
more broadly antiforeign.

Sometimes, when a major action was planned, such as the Boxer siege
in late May of Zhuozhou, a busy commercial center on the recently completed Beijing-Baoding railway line, thousands of Boxers from nearby
towns and villages came together under a unified command.[51] This was
also true, on a much grander scale, in the Battle of Tianjin in the latter half
of June and the first two weeks of July, where there was a relatively high
level of military coordination of Boxer units from the entire area under the
command of the two main local Boxer leaders Zhang Decheng and Cao
Futian. In Tianjin, although the Boxer force was made up in part of local
toughs, petty criminals, people in service trades, and boatmen thrown out
of work by the Beijing-Tianjin railway (which began operation in 1896)
and the increasing reliance on coastal steamers (instead of the Grand
Canal) for the annual rice tax shipments to the capital,[52] the vast majority
were peasant youths from the surrounding countryside, who, idled, frightened, and rendered hungry by the protracted drought, began streaming
into the city in the early months of 1900, mainly from places to the north,
west, and south.[53]

The most idiosyncratic case of Boxer activity was that of Beijing, home
both to the Qing court and to a substantial number of foreigners. Throughout the spring and on into the summer, small groups of Boxers from all over
Zhili, but chiefly from the south, filed into the city, where they became
attached to one or another of the many altars that were established there.
During the summer months, as Beijing, to all intents and purposes, came
under Boxer occupation, rank-and-file Boxers took part in the burning of
large parts of the city, the policing of the resident population, and the sieges
of the Northern Cathedral and (together with Chinese government troops
after the throne's declaration of war on June 21) the foreign legation quarter.

Internationalization of the Boxer Experience:
The Outbreak of War

As long as the Boxers confined their activities to northwestern Shandong,
they had remained an essentially local phenomenon. The dramatic expansion of the movement in Zhili during the first months of 1900, however,
elicited a growing response from an increasingly nervous foreign commu-

nity. And the escalating foreign response, in turn, forced the Chinese
court, which had vacillated for months in its policy, eventually to adopt a
clearer and more explicit (although not necessarily consistently implemented) stand with respect both to the Boxers and the foreign powers. A
triangular field of forces thus came into play, consisting of the Boxers, the
foreign governments, and the Chinese authorities, each of which affected,
through its changing behavior, the responses of the other two.

1.5   Boxer Occupation of Zhuozhou. The confidence the Boxers gained from the
siege and occupation of this important commercial center in late May was reflected
in the characters inscribed on either side of the entrance, which boasted of the
unruly character of the city's inhabitants and touted its unparalleled strategic position for the defense of the capital. From *Quanfei jilüe.*

44   For a long time there was little awareness of the Boxer phenomenon among foreigners in general. Protestant missionaries in western Shandong and southern Zhili first reported skirmishes between Boxers and local Christians in April-May 1899. But, as W. H. Rees of the London Missionary Society observed from Jizhou in southern Zhili, "such incidents are not uncommon in our mission centre." Certainly, as of spring 1899, there was still no sense — it would have been far more remarkable if there had been — of a major uprising in the offing.[54]

By the fall this situation had changed dramatically. Notice of the Boxers began to appear in foreign newspapers in early October.[55] Later in the same month, missionaries in the Beijing area reported on the spreading unrest in Shandong.[56] Rees, in mid-December, described "the rebellion" as "spreading like a prairie fire."[57] The murder of the British missionary Brooks at the end of December raised foreign alarm to a new level. Sir Claude MacDonald, the British minister, in his dispatch of January 5 to the Foreign Office, took note of the growing turmoil "secret societies" were creating in northern Shandong and made specific reference to "an organization known as the 'Boxers,'" which had attained "special notoriety" and whose "ravages [had] recently spread over a large portion of Southern Chihli [Zhili]." The growing danger to native Christians and foreign missionaries, MacDonald added, had been the subject of "repeated representations" by the foreign ministers, especially those of Germany, the United States, and Great Britain, to the Chinese government.[58]

The Chinese court, although evincing concern over the murder of Brooks and moving quickly to bring about a settlement of the case, issued a decree on January 11 which announced that people drilling for self-defense and for the protection of their villages were not to be considered bandits; the decree went on to instruct local authorities to pay attention only to whether people fomented disorder and conflict, not to whether they happened to be members of this or that society or sect. The foreign representatives in the capital reacted with apprehension to this decree, which they interpreted, not unreasonably, as an effort on the throne's part to provide the Boxers with a degree of protection and perhaps even encouragement. On January 27, Britain, the United States, France, Germany, and Italy sent identical notes to the Zongli Yamen — the Chinese government office in charge of foreign affairs — requesting publication of an imperial edict ordering the immediate suppression of the Boxers (and the Big Sword Society) in Shandong and Zhili.[59]

During the next few months the tug of war persisted. The diplomatic corps in Beijing made periodic representations to the Chinese government, protesting the inadequacy of the measures thus far taken to put down

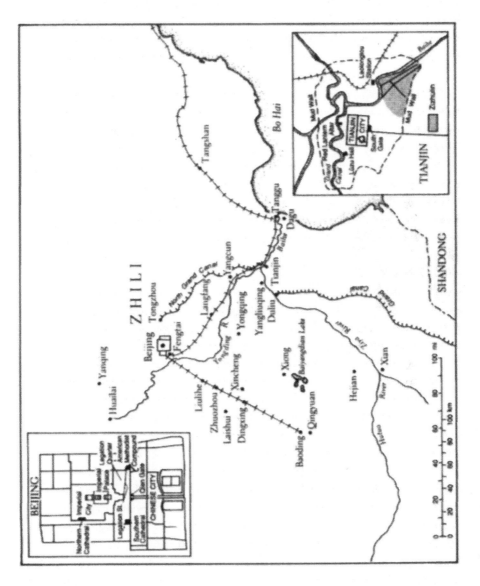

MAP 3   The Beijing-Tianjin Region

46 the rising, while the court, for its part, far from adopting a firmer policy of suppression, as late as mid-April reiterated the view that it was quite all right for good people to organize for the defense of their communities and in early May even flirted with the idea of formally organizing these local self-defense groups into "militia" (*tuan*).[60] Increasingly frustrated by the lack of Chinese official action, despite rapidly escalating Boxer-related violence in the countryside, several of the powers in April raised the level of pressure a notch by parading warships before the Dagu forts guarding the approaches to Tianjin, in a flagrant display of old-style gunboat diplomacy.[61]

If the Chinese government was being pushed, from one side, by the foreign powers, it was being pushed even harder, from the other side, by the Boxers. Inevitably, as disturbances in Zhili mounted in both frequency and severity, government forces came into direct conflict with Boxers, and the more this happened the harder it became for pro-Boxer officials to maintain the simple fiction that the Boxers were community protectors, whose main raison d'être was to guard against disruptive heterodox elements. The problem was illustrated—and also greatly aggravated—by a series of engagements between Boxers and Qing troops that took place in May in Laishui county, midway between Beijing and Baoding. The initial explosion took place in Gaoluo village in Laishui, where there had been a long history of animosity between Catholic and non-Catholic inhabitants. Boxers began to arrive in the area in the spring, and a boxing ground was established in the temple of the northern section of the village in April. Not long after this, on the evening of May 12, the Boxers, with the aid of confederates from nearby villages, burned down the church and, after killing all the Catholics (more than thirty families), disposed of their bodies in a wellpit (graphically described years later by the Gaoluo Boxer chief's grandson as a "flesh mound grave" [*rouqiu fen*]) and set fire to the victims' homes (located in the southern part of the village).[62]

Faced with this provocation, a small force of government soldiers led by Col. Yang Futong closed the boxing ground in Gaoluo on May 15 and, the following day, after being ambushed by several hundred Boxers, killed sixty of them in a one-sided government victory. A couple of days later Yang's men took twenty Boxers captive, whereupon a large force of outraged Boxers from the entire area came together to rescue the prisoners and avenge the deaths of their comrades. On May 22, in Shiting, a market town ten miles north of the Laishui county seat, the Boxers took the government soldiers by surprise and killed Yang Futong.[63]

The death of Yang, the first Qing commander to be killed by the Boxers, had a catalytic effect on the movement, which now shifted into high gear in central Zhili. During the last ten days of May a force of more than ten thousand Boxers took Zhuozhou, just northeast of Laishui on the rail line to the capital. Beginning on May 27, the Boxers also launched a succession of attacks along the Beijing-Baoding railway, ripping up tracks, destroying stations and bridges, and severing telegraph lines. On May 28 they burned down the Fengtai station on the Beijing-Tianjin railway, about ten miles from the capital. A few days later, in early June, Boxer involvement in the Baoding area also escalated.[64]

The court's initial reaction to this upsurge of activity was to seek to avoid further confrontation with the Boxers, partly because Qing military forces in Zhili were stretched perilously thin. But, by late May, as the situation worsened, the well-armed troops of Nie Shicheng (himself strongly anti-Boxer) were deployed against the Boxers along the Beijing-Tianjin railway, and in early June Governor-General Yulu for the first time urged the Zongli Yamen to request that orders be given to Nie and other Qing commanders to take decisive action to suppress the Boxer movement without further delay.[65]

If the government had moved against the Boxers with firmness a few weeks earlier, it might still have been possible to bring the rising under control and avoid serious international repercussions. As of mid-May, Boxer violence had been directed almost exclusively against native Christians and their churches and homes, only one foreign life (that of Brooks) had been lost, and no attacks had yet been launched against the railways and telegraphs. By the end of May, the situation had changed so radically that, even if the court had been strongly inclined to suppress the Boxer movement (which it was not), it is doubtful it could have succeeded.

In addition to the developments already noted, on May 28, after the destruction of the Fengtai station, the foreign ministers in the capital, fearing the loss of the rail link to the coast, called up several hundred legation guards, the first large contingent of these arriving by rail from Dagu on May 31.[66] On the same day, four French and Belgian railway engineers, attempting to escape to Tianjin from Baoding after the cutting of the Beijing-Baoding line, were killed by Boxers, and on June 1 two British missionaries met their deaths in Yongqing, directly south of Beijing. Manifestly, the Boxer movement, in the last days of May and the first days of June, had rounded an important bend, venturing into territory it had previously only threatened to enter.

Accompanying this shift in direction, antiforeign feeling among the population at large now became rampant, aroused by the calling up of the legation guards, the news that two dozen foreign ships of war had assem-

48   bled opposite the Dagu forts (in early June), the initiation of direct attacks on foreigners and on the rail and telegraph lines, the conspicuous increase in the numbers of Boxers crowding the thoroughfares to Beijing and Tianjin, and, undergirding everything, the continuation of severe drought. Significantly, when primitively armed Boxers sustained heavy casualties in a series of fierce engagements with Nie Shicheng's men along the Beijing-Tianjin railway in the first days of June (480 Boxers were killed near Langfang on June 6 alone), the Boxers, instead of being cowed into submission, became even more aggressive, emboldened by the widening support of an increasingly angry and frightened populace.[67]

Although it would be foolhardy to point to any one factor that was of greater moment than all the others in shaping the crisis that now emerged, driving China and the foreign powers inexorably toward war, a number of historians have pointed to the decisive importance of the summoning of the legation guards in late May. As Esherick has noted, on May 29, in the aftermath of the killing of Yang Futong and the assaults on the rail lines, the court, for the first time since the beginning of 1900, issued instructions to "annihilate" (*jiao*) Boxers who refused to disperse. These orders were, however, reversed almost immediately, after the foreign ministers made known their plans to summon the guards, thereby strengthening the hand of the pro-Boxer faction at court; on June 3 explicit orders were given *not* to annihilate Boxers.[68] Victor Purcell makes an even broader, if more conjectural, case for the importance of the bringing up of the legation guards in "precipitating the final crisis," arguing that "doing so made the despatch of reinforcements (under Admiral Seymour) necessary, and, to secure their retreat, the Taku [Dagu] forts had to be taken, which in its turn led to war."[69]

In early June governors-general in the Yangzi Valley provinces, fearful of imminent foreign intervention, urged the court to take forceful action immediately to suppress the Boxers. But, although the court dispatched a number of emissaries (including the pro-Boxer Gangyi) to attempt to persuade the Boxers to disperse and return to peaceful pursuits, this effort came to nought,[70] and when Nie Shicheng, also acting on imperial orders, took much stronger action against the Boxers (as we have seen), he was severely reprimanded. This pattern of inconsistency and indecisiveness continued until June 10. On the morning of this date, acting in response to an urgent telegram from the British minister, stating that the situation had become "extremely grave" and that unless arrangements were made for the immediate dispatch of a relief expedition to Beijing, it would be too late, Adm. Edward Seymour left Tianjin by train with the first contingent of an international force that by June 13 had reached almost 2,000 men.[71] Unlike the calling up of the legation guards, which had been discussed with and partially approved in advance by the Zongli Yamen, the sending of the Seymour expedition was completely without Chinese authorization. The court's response was immediate. Later on the same day (June 10), Prince Duan, a leading Boxer supporter, was appointed to the Zongli Yamen, along with three other pro-Boxer officials; Prince Duan replaced Prince Qing, a staunch opponent of the Boxers, as head of the Yamen. The hand of pro-Boxer forces at court was significantly strengthened by this move, and within days preparations were being made for war.

The Seymour expedition proceeded very slowly. Frequent repairs of the railway had to be made en route, and this made it easier for bands of Boxers to engage in harassing actions. By June 18, the expedition was still bogged down at Langfang, midway between Tianjin and the capital. On this day Qing forces, led by Nie Shicheng and Dong Fuxiang, joined a large contingent of Boxers in attacking the expedition, and the Chinese side won a major victory.[72] Unable to advance further, Seymour led the relief force back to Tianjin, which was reached on June 26, after suffering heavy casualties.[73]

While the drama of the abortive Seymour expedition was being played out, the situation in Beijing was rapidly worsening. On the evening of June 10 Boxers destroyed the British summer legation in the Western Hills outside the capital. The following day, the secretary of the Japanese legation, Sugiyama Akira, was killed near the railway station by the soldiers of Dong Fuxiang (who, unlike Nie Shicheng, was sympathetic to the Boxer cause). On the afternoon of June 13 a large force of Boxers swarmed into the city and began setting fire to churches and foreign homes; the Southern Cathedral (Nantang), in which several hundred Chinese Catholics had taken refuge, was burned to the ground, resulting in a large number of deaths. The next day, in the evening, Boxers engaged in sporadic attacks on the guards of the foreign legations.

The situation was not much different in Tianjin, where the Boxer presence had grown steadily since early March. By late May–early June, the streets of the walled Chinese city (two miles northwest of the foreign settlements) had come under effective Boxer control. Officials, on encountering Boxers, were forced to get out of their sedan chairs and demonstrate their subservience. Churches and Christian homes—and eventually any establishments with foreign associations—were plundered and burned. A prison was broken into and the inmates set free. Yulu, whose residence was in Tianjin, was coerced into opening the government's arsenals to the Boxers. Faced with a situation that was getting increasingly out of hand and that presented an immediate danger to the foreign civilian population in

50   the concession areas, foreign ships off the coast issued an ultimatum to the
occupants of the Dagu forts on June 16 and seized them the following day.

Although the court did not find out about the ultimatum until June 19
(telegraphic communication between Tianjin and Beijing having been
severed), the Empress Dowager Cixi, in the course of a series of important
conferences begun on June 16, was already moving toward a decision to go
to war. The news of the foreign ultimatum settled the matter. The diplomatic corps was informed that it had twenty-four hours in which to effect
the evacuation of foreigners from the capital. The foreign ministers, concerned about the safety of a large number of foreigners, including women
and children, making their way to the coast, were hesitant to comply with
the Chinese government's orders. Their hesitation proved justified when,
on the following day, the German minister Baron Clemens von Ketteler
was shot dead by a Chinese soldier while on his way to a meeting at the
Zongli Yamen. Within hours of the killing of von Ketteler, Protestant missionaries, many from elsewhere in North China who had taken refuge,
along with hundreds of native Christians, in the Methodist Episcopal

1.6   Boxers in Tianjin. One of the few known unstaged photographs of Boxers
other than prisoners. Courtesy of the Library of Congress.

(American) compound in the capital, were brought (with their converts) under armed escort to the legation quarter. More than 3,000 Catholics, including foreign priests and nuns (and 43 Italian and French marines), had meanwhile secured themselves in the sturdily built Northern Cathedral, two miles northwest of the legations. On the afternoon of June 20, Chinese troops, joined by Boxers, opened fire on both the legations and the cathedral, commencing sieges that were to be carried on, with varying degrees of determination, until August 14. On June 21, the court issued a "declaration of war,"[74] and the Boxers, after being officially renamed *yimin* or "righteous people," were enlisted in militia under the overall command in the capital of Prince Zhuang, Gangyi, and Prince Duan. The climactic phase of the Boxer episode had begun.

The geographical spread of the Boxer movement widened dramatically after the throne's declaration of war, extending into Shanxi and Henan in North China, and beyond North China into Inner Mongolia and Manchuria. The number of deaths resulting from the movement also escalated, well over two hundred foreigners and untold thousands of Chinese Christians being killed before the bloodbath finally ended.[75] The level of violence and disorder, on the other hand, varied greatly according to the degree to which provincial and local authorities were sympathetic to the Boxer cause. Thus high officials in the lower Yangzi provinces, determined to keep the war from spreading to the south, were able to work out an arrangement with the foreign consuls of Shanghai, according to which the Chinese authorities were to put down any antiforeign disturbances within their jurisdictions in return for which the powers would keep their armies from entering the area.[76] In Shandong also, although the Boxers (and Big Swords) experienced a revival following the clarification of the court's stance, the staunchly anti-Boxer governor, Yuan Shikai, took effective measures to prevent loss of foreign life. Although more than 300 Chinese Christians were killed in the province, by far the largest number of casualties were Boxers who ignored Yuan's orders to proceed to the Tianjin-Beijing area to assist in the fighting against the foreigners.

Forming a sharp contrast to the Yangzi provinces and Shandong was Shanxi,[77] where the uncompromisingly antiforeign Yuxian had been appointed governor in March. On July 9, forty-four foreigners (including children), after being summoned to the provincial capital (Taiyuan) for their protection, were executed under the governor's personal supervision, and by summer's end an indeterminate number of additional foreigners and some 2,000 Chinese Christians had also been put to death, many of the killings inspired directly or indirectly by the authorities.

52   Bordering on Shanxi to the north, Inner Mongolia was another area with a high death toll for both foreigners and Chinese. Boxers, mainly from Shanxi and Zhili, had streamed into the region in early summer, with support from the local officialdom. They were soon joined by Manchu-led government forces, and when one of the large churches they laid siege to was overpowered, some 3,000 Chinese Christians (mostly Catholics) were killed. Although it is impossible, because of the way in which the figures were presented at the time, to establish an internal breakdown between the number of foreign lives lost in Inner Mongolia and the number lost in Shanxi, the grand total for both areas appears to have been just shy of 180, of whom 159 were Protestant.[78]

Manchuria, northeast of Zhili, was another important arena of Boxer activity. Circumstances here were different from those in North China. There was much popular hostility in the southern part of the region to the South Manchurian Railway, which had been constructed by the Russians. Boxers began to appear in Manchuria in the spring and by late June, together with Manchu troops, had commenced destruction of the railway, in part to hinder Russian military intervention. There were also numerous attacks on Protestant and Catholic missions, resulting in the killing of more than 1,500 Chinese Christians (but few foreigners). A draconian order was reestablished in Manchuria with the Russian occupation of the entire area in the summer and early autumn.[79]

Although all told, the greatest number of foreign deaths in the summer of 1900 (over three quarters of the total) occurred in Shanxi and Inner Mongolia, a particularly serious incident took place in the Zhili provincial capital of Baoding, where on June 30 and July 1 fifteen Protestant missionaries (including children) were killed.[80] The largest number of Chinese Christian deaths also occurred in Zhili, where the Christian population was relatively numerous, the roots of the Boxer movement were deep, and the incidence of armed conflict was widespread. The greatest concentration of Christian casualties in the province was doubtless in and around the cities of Beijing and Tianjin, areas that were under effective Boxer control through most of the summer.

The only other province to experience significant Boxer-related violence was Henan, which like Zhili and Shanxi had suffered from severe drought for many months.[81] The damage resulting from Boxer activities in Henan was, however, largely confined to church burnings; no missionaries and relatively few Chinese Christians were killed.[82]

Although the most serious anti-Christian violence of 1900, as above summarized, took place after the court's declaration of war and may clearly be viewed as part of the "Boxer War" in the widest sense, in the narrower sense of armed conflict between foreign and Chinese combatants the war may be divided into several partly overlapping phases. The first two of these—the Seymour expedition of June 10–26 and the assault against the Dagu forts on June 17—have already been noted. A third phase, which because of its idiosyncratic nature is beyond the scope of this narrative to more than take note of, was the Sino-Russian conflict in the three Manchurian provinces, which began on a sporadic basis in June in the south, heated up considerably in mid-July in the Amur region (see chapter 9), and concluded with the Russian army's entry into Mukden on October 1.[83]

Overlapping in time with the third phase of the Boxer War was a fourth, the Battle of Tianjin, which began with Chinese shelling of the foreign settlements in the city (Zizhulin) on June 17. The period from June 17 to June 26, when the first of several foreign relief contingents arrived from the coast, was the time of greatest danger for the 900 foreign civilians in Tianjin (Herbert Hoover, who was there, referred to it as the period of "the black fear").[84] The siege, which resulted in heavy casualties on both sides, lasted until July 13, when the arrival of a final wave of reinforcements (bringing the combined strength of the foreign force to between 5,000 and 6,000 troops) permitted the storming of the walled Chinese city and its seizure after a day of heavy fighting.[85] The foreign victory, which was followed by several days of unrestrained killing, looting, and raping, dealt a severe blow to Boxer prospects in the Tianjin area.

The warfare in Tianjin, which pitted some of China's best-equipped troops (including the army of Nie Shicheng, who was killed on July 9) as well as Boxers against a foreign force consisting mainly of Russians and Japanese, was of a more or less conventional sort. Nothing could have been less conventional, on the other hand, than the fifth phase of the Boxer War: the assaults on the diplomatic quarter and the Northern Cathedral in the capital. Although there had been intermittent attacks earlier, both sieges began in earnest on June 20 and lasted until the arrival of the international relief force from Tianjin on August 14. The two sieges were unconventional in different ways. The assault on the Northern Cathedral was principally in the hands of some 10,000 Boxers under the overall command of Prince Duan. In almost two months of unremitting attacks, using mines, rifles, and some cannon but mainly depending on fire, the Boxers were unable to take the structure, an outcome they attributed to the superior magical powers of the foreigners within (see chapter 4).

The assault on the legations was more conventional in outward appearance. The several thousand civilians within were defended by some 400

54   foreign soldiers and over a hundred volunteers. Although there was some Boxer participation, primary responsibility on the Chinese side was borne by regular government forces, under the command of Dong Fuxiang and Ronglu. The latter, although wary of antagonizing the Empress Dowager, was not sympathetic to the Boxers, clearly understood the folly of China's having taken on all the powers at once, and made sure the siege was never pressed home. After a month of fighting that was sometimes quite heavy, a brief truce commenced in mid-July, as the court, in the wake of the news from Tianjin, tried to reach a negotiated solution to the crisis. The return of the staunchly antiforeign Li Bingheng to Beijing in late July, however, strengthened the hand of the pro-Boxer faction and stiffened Cixi's determination to continue the war. In late July and early August five officials known for their anti-Boxer views and past friendliness toward foreigners were executed by imperial order, and in early August full-scale bombardment of the legations was resumed.[86]

In both of the Beijing sieges Chinese casualties were high. Many foreigners also suffered, mainly in the assault on the legations, in which at least 66 died and well over 150 were wounded.[87] In the sixth phase of the war, the march overland from Tianjin to Beijing of the eight-power relief expedition, Chinese casualties were heavy (many of them civilians in villages and towns razed by the advancing troops), foreign casualties relatively light (if one discounts the hundreds who were unable to continue because of the paralyzing heat). Owing to interminable squabbling and to the competing commitments of several of the participants in other parts of the world, the expedition did not finally get started until August 4. The force numbered some 20,000, half of them Japanese. Once under way, it piled up one victory after another against hastily assembled and poorly led imperial troops. In the wake of the defeat of the Chinese army on August 6 at Yangcun, twenty miles out of Tianjin, Yulu shot himself. Li Bingheng, who left Beijing for the front in early August, took poison on August 11, after his own forces had twice gone down to defeat and were in flight everywhere.[88] On August 14 foreign troops entered the capital. Most Boxers had by this time abandoned their weapons and identifying red (or yellow) clothing and slipped back into the population. The Empress Dowager, Emperor, and other high court officials, disguised as ordinary people, fled westward under armed escort early on the morning of August 15.[89]

The final phase of the Boxer War consisted in mopping up and punitive expeditions by foreign soldiers, mainly in Zhili. These took place in two stages. In the first stage, military operations involving soldiers from various foreign countries were conducted in September against Duliu, an

important center of Boxer activity southwest of Tianjin, and against
Boxer strongholds south and north of the capital. The second stage, lasting from October into the following spring, was carried out under the
command of German Field Marshal Alfred von Waldersee (who did not
arrive in China until late September), and, although the soldiers of several of the powers took part, Germany took the clear lead. The city of
Baoding, the site of one of the most serious Boxer actions, was devastated
in October, its officials condemned to death by a makeshift military tri-
bunal, and its citizenry forced to pay the costs of foreign occupation.
From mid-December to the following April several dozen additional
punitive expeditions were launched under von Waldersee's direction.
Although most were aimed at objectives in Zhili, German and French
forces crossed the border into eastern Shanxi on a number of occasions
and also threatened to move into Shandong.[90]

Although the ostensible purpose of the punitive expeditions was to clear
the countryside of Boxer remnants, it was never very clear how Boxers were
to be distinguished from non-Boxers. "It is safe to say," Major General Adna
Chaffee, commander of the American relief force, said to a journalist, "that
where one real Boxer has been killed since the capture of Peking, fifteen
harmless coolies or labourers on the farms, including not a few women and
children, have been slain."[91] One motive for the key role Germany arro-
gated to itself in the expeditions was clearly the wish to avenge the killing
of von Ketteler in June and in the process expand German influence in the
Far East. Kaiser Wilhelm, in a speech at Bremerhaven on the occasion of
the departure in late July of the first contingent of German troops for the
Far East, had asserted: "Just as the Huns, a thousand years ago, under the
leadership of Attila, gained a reputation by virtue of which they still live in
historical tradition, so may the name of Germany become known in such
a manner in China that no Chinese will ever again even dare to look
askance at a German."[92] A more immediate German purpose, of course,
was to pressure the Chinese government into acceding to foreign demands
at the negotiating table. The process of negotiating a settlement of the
Boxer War had gotten under way almost immediately after the foreign
occupation of Beijing. It took a year to run its course, the final results being
incorporated in a protocol signed in the capital by eleven foreign ministers
and two Chinese plenipotentiaries on September 7, 1901.

The Boxer Protocol stipulated that Yuxian was to be executed, several
other high court officials (including Prince Zhuang) were to die by their
own hand, and that Prince Duan was to be exiled for life to Xinjiang in the
far northwest. Official missions were to be sent to Germany and Japan to

56 convey regrets for the deaths of von Ketteler and Sugiyama, and a monument erected in Beijing on the spot where the German minister had been killed. In order to ensure the future security of the powers, the forts at Dagu and other key military installations were to be destroyed; also a two-year prohibition was placed on Chinese importation of arms, an enlarged legation guard was to be permanently stationed in Beijing, and foreign troops were to be positioned at specified points between Beijing and the coast. The indemnity imposed on the Chinese was huge: 450 million taels (U.S.$333 million), to be paid in thirty-nine annual installments along with 4 percent interest on unpaid principal.[93]

Thus was written the final chapter of the Boxer episode. The detailed provisions of the diplomatic settlement were less important than the impact it had on the Chinese government and population. The severity of the indemnity greatly intensified the already considerable grip of the foreign powers over China's governmental finances and forced the Qing, in a desperate effort to generate new revenues, to begin laying the foundations for a modern state.[94] The draconian character of the settlement, together with the generally poor showing of the Chinese military in the summer of 1900 and the court's humiliating flight to Xi'an in August, placed the weakness of the Qing dynasty on full view and energized the forces of both reform and revolution in Chinese society. The court also, however reluctantly, embarked after 1900 on a program of reform that went far beyond anything previously tried and completely reshaped the environment within which Chinese politics were carried on. This environment, as it turned out, proved to be one in which the dynasty itself was unable to survive.

PART 2

The Boxers as Experience

Recovery of the experienced past in a literal sense is, as we have seen, not possible. One reason for this is that in any historical situation only a small fragment of the totality of people's experiences is ever recorded for posterity. "The trawling net fills," Geoffrey Braithwaite says of the process of writing a biography, "then the biographer hauls it in, sorts, throws back, stores, fillets and sells. Yet consider what he doesn't catch: there is always far more of that."[1] Modestly but accurately, Robert Capa called his photos of the D-Day landing "a cut into the whole event," rather than the full reality.[2] Of the tens of thousands of Chinese who took part in the Boxer movement, we have recorded traces of the behavior of only a tiny faceless (and mostly nameless) fraction. Even in the case of the hundreds of foreigners besieged in the legation quarters in Beijing in the summer of 1900, the letters, diaries, and books that many of them wrote detailing their experiences represented, at best, summaries, distillations, artful reconstructions, *not* full and exact replications.

This suggests a second reason for the impossibility of truly resurrecting the experienced past. Even if full replication of past experience were feasible, it would remain just that: replication, either in words or visual images or both, not the experience itself. In the foreign accounts of the siege of the legations, we are treated again and again to graphic descriptions of the experiential world of the besieged. But, unlike the inhabitants of this world, we cannot ourselves directly experience, minute by minute, day after day, the sweltering heat and drenching rains, the multiple sounds of gunfire in the night, the fear of being wounded or killed, the crying of "babies, tortured by heat-rash, mosquitoes and the thousands of flies," the stench of rotting pony carcasses.[3] The best that a participant account can do is provide a vivid and compelling sense of what the past was like. It cannot give us the past.

If literal retrieval of the experienced past is not a possibility, we can nonetheless form a picture of this past, or at least bits and pieces of it, in

60 our imaginations. All of us, after all, have expertise in this area. We are all experiencers ourselves, not of *the* past but of *a* past, and this personal, subjective experience affords us a basis for addressing critically and self-reflectively what it is about the experienced past that is distinctive. We cannot, in other words, recover the past as actually apprehended by the people who lived it. But we can talk about this past, describe some of its parameters, and relate at least in rough and approximate terms the ways in which it was—is—different from, on the one hand, the mythified past, and on the other, the past as a narrative of interrelated events.

One way in which it is different, suggested a moment ago in my reference to the daily trials of the foreigners besieged in the legations, is that the experienced past is deeply grounded in the senses. Indeed, although the term *experience* as used in this book refers mainly to direct participation in the making of the past, experience also has the meaning, particularly in philosophical writing, of apprehension of the world through the senses. People are sometimes acutely conscious of their sensory perceptions, sometimes blissfully inattentive to them, but on one point most would agree: without any sensory experience whatever, human existence, as we know it, would not be possible. Closely related to this sensory aspect of the lived past is the fact that experience encompasses the entire range of human emotions, and the closer our contact with real experience the more people's emotional lives—the things that make them sad or angry or nervous or bored, their worries, hatreds, hopes, fears—become foregrounded. We become aware not just of the canal that was built but also of the pain in the backs of the men who built it[4]—such awareness being immeasurably facilitated if we ourselves have experienced a comparable pain.[5]

Another distinctive property of the experienced past that historians seldom, and mythologizers never, dwell upon is the unmemorable (though not necessarily unremembered) context in which memorable experience is embedded. British soldiers in the Battle of the Somme, in addition to having to contend with more or less continous enemy shelling (7,000 men and officers were killed and wounded daily), spent a great deal of their time at the front in trenches which (in contrast with those of the Germans) were cold, often inundated with water, infested with big black rats, and filled with the smell of decaying flesh.[6] Although, for those foreigners who chanced to be in the Chinese capital in the summer of 1900, the shorthand they would use—and that would be used by others—to define their experience would generally be "the siege," a term with primarily military associations, most accounts concur that the process of surviving the siege involved much more than defense preparations. Just as in any other combat — or, for that matter, life — situation, much attention had to be devoted to such ordinary matters as the safe preparation and distribution of food, the daily testing of the water supply, the creation of a fire detail, the establishment of an effective communication system, the organization of a hospital to tend to the sick and wounded, hygienic disposition of the dead, and so forth.[7]

The past as actually lived, in short, consists of a continuum of different kinds of experience, at one end of which are experiences that, in terms of a given set of variables, are central, key, memorable, defining, and at the other end, experiences, often highly repetitive, that are of a more auxiliary or supportive sort. Another property of the lived past, one that profoundly colors all experience, is that it is outcome-blind. Citizens of Leipzig who took to the streets in the fall of 1989 to protest conditions in East Germany had no idea, at the outset, what the response of their government would be or that their protests would be woven into a fabric of events that would eventually include destruction of the Berlin Wall and German unification. "The people I worked with wanted to reform East Germany," an East German human rights activist later told an interviewer. "We never thought the country would disappear and be swallowed up by the West."[8] Individual participants in "historical events," in short, do not have the entire event inscribed in advance in their minds. They don't know where things are headed or how they are going to turn out. And this indeterminacy has an enormous impact on their consciousness, causing them to apprehend their own experience in ways that differ fundamentally from the backward-looking narrative constructions of historians.

The novelist Robertson Davies describes how different — and weirdly unsettling — the world would be if, like Merlin the magician, we could know what surprising turns the future held in store for us:

> Merlin had a strange laugh, and it was heard when nobody else was laughing. He laughed at the beggar who was bewailing his fate as he lay stretched on a dunghill; he laughed at the foppish young man who was making a great fuss about choosing a pair of shoes. He laughed because he knew that deep in the dunghill was a golden cup that would have made the beggar a rich man; he laughed because he knew that the pernickety young man would be stabbed in a quarrel before the soles of his new shoes were soiled. He laughed because he knew what was coming next.[9]

A related consequence of outcome-blindness is that the direct participants in events characteristically (although not invariably) expend a great deal of time and effort preparing for contingencies that never eventuate.

62   Such experience, of which there were numerous examples in the crisis atmosphere prevailing in the foreign community in China in 1900, becomes in a sense "wasted"—a historical throwaway. For reasons that are quite understandable, when historians get around to writing their accounts of past events they generally emphasize the things that *did* happen, rather than the things that did not.

Not only is individual experience embedded in an event structure that is unfinished and therefore indeterminate as to outcome, entire events often have meanings that are different for their immediate participants from the meanings they acquire as a consequence of future developments that at the time are unforeseen: The soldier at the front in the Battle of the Somme did not know that he was fighting in World War I. Columbus did not know that he had discovered America. The intrepid pioneers who hurried across the American continent in the early nineteenth century had no idea they were traversing "the fertile Great Plains, destined to be the granary of a great nation." ("They thought," Daniel J. Boorstin informs us, "they were crossing what on their maps was the Great American Desert. Some even sought camels to help their passage.")[10] And Boston Red Sox first baseman Bill Buckner did not know, when he allowed Mookie Wilson's ground ball to scoot through his legs in the tenth inning of the sixth game of the 1986 World Series, whether his miscue would be relegated to the status of a footnote, of little significance historically, quickly to be deleted from the consciousness of players and fans alike, or become the one thing about Buckner that, when everything else had been forgotten, would remain permanently etched in people's memories. Much, if not all, depended on the outcome of the seventh game.[11] The degree to which the meaning of the past is hostage to an as yet undefined future would appear to belie the common view among historians that, as one of us has enunciated it, "what comes after cannot influence what came before."[12]

Coupled with their lack of knowledge of—and control over—the future, either in the most immediate sense of their personal fate or in the broader sense of the outcome(s) of the event(s) in which they are participating or in the still wider sense of a future event context that is continually unfolding and in the process continually redefining the meaning of all prior events, direct participants also face limitations of a spatial nature—cultural, social, and geographical. Insofar as experience is conceived as a "text" and the experiencer as a "reader," to use the vocabulary often encountered nowadays in the academic world, different readers will read—or "construct"—the text in different ways, depending on the values, beliefs, and myths they bring with them to the reading. Thus, the same odd behavioral characteristics that in Salem, Massachusetts, in 1692 were defined by the community as proof of bewitchment would very likely, a generation later, have been treated as the beginning stages of a religious revival.[13] Similarly, while Boxer notices in the spring and summer of 1900 often constructed the Boxer movement in religious terms, as a direct manifestation of the will of Heaven, designed to extirpate foreign influence in China and in so doing appease the gods, Christian missionaries tended to turn this scenario inside out, portraying the Boxers as a satanic force and the entire Boxer episode as a full-blown battle between God and the devil. Whether in Salem in 1692 or in China in 1900, in other words, the "cultural space" a particular collection of individuals occupied had a limiting or parochializing effect on how those individuals interpreted what was taking place in their world.

In what he describes (after the hero of Stendhal's *Chartreuse de Parme*) as the "Fabrice syndrome," Eric Hobsbawm tells us that for "perfectly sound reasons . . . participants at the bottom do not usually see historic events they live through as top people . . . do."[14] People's understanding of their experience, in other words, is circumscribed by not only the cultural, but also the social, space within which they operate. Beyond Hobsbawm's top-bottom distinction, moreover, we need to differentiate among the diverse roles that people play in complex events. In the case of the Boxer uprising, we have, aside from the Boxers themselves, their foreign and native Christian targets, military personnel on both sides, representatives of the Chinese and foreign governments involved, and so on. The experience of each of these groups (assuming one can talk of a collective group experience) was partial; no two groups experienced the Boxer episode in the same way.

All experience, finally, is severely constrained by geography. Not only did Boxers in northwest Shandong and Boxers in Shanxi have different sets of experiences, it was also quite impossible for any one Boxer unit to know what was happening to all the other units at any given moment. And I'm not making a special point here of the low level of organization of the Boxer movement or the rudimentary state of long-distance communication at the time. Even under the most technologically advanced conditions—for example, the protest demonstrations in China in the spring of 1989, which were covered (at least initially) by satellite TV and whose leaders across the country were in instant touch not only with each other but also by fax and phone with Chinese student leaders abroad—the experience of individuals in any given location is framed by a limited (and limiting) set of contextual coordinates and is communicable to individuals in other locations

64 only in a partial and summary form. A leading participant in the Tiananmen demonstrations told me months after that he frequently was in the dark as to what was going on even within Beijing. That is, he knew perfectly well what he himself was experiencing but it wasn't always clear what was happening to demonstrators in other parts of the city.[15] Even within Tiananmen Square, let alone the city of Beijing, there were hotly contested "eyewitness" reports of what exactly happened on the night of the Chinese government's crackdown.[16]

Sometimes the normal constraints imposed by geography on experience are augmented by special circumstances. Luella Miner of the American Board of Commissioners for Foreign Missions (ABCFM) described in her journal the degree of spatial blindness endured by besieged foreigners in the legations as of late June:

> We are as isolated here as if we were on a desert island. Our latest news of the outside world—even of the other parts of China outside this little area guarded by foreign soldiers—is two weeks old. Did our Pao-ting-fu friends reach Tientsin in safety? Is the whole of China in turmoil? Are our Christians everywhere being slaughtered? What is happening in the Imperial Palaces not more than a mile away? Is the Emperor still alive? Has the Empress Dowager fled from the city taking as much treasure as possible with her? The bullets which sing over our heads are our only means of communication with the outside world, and their message is brief.[17]

Still another attribute of the experienced past that sets it off sharply both from the past as historically reconstructed and the past as mythologized has to do with the motivational consciousness of the experiencer. Unlike the historian, whose object is to understand and explain, or the mythologizer, who draws energy from the past to accomplish purposes of a political or rhetorical or profoundly psychological nature in the present, the direct participant's consciousness embraces the entire range of human emotions and goals. Participants, too, may seek to understand what they are experiencing, and very likely they will also mythologize it in a variety of ways. But such objectives are ancillary to the main ones, which are to enjoy, to survive, hit a homerun, kill a foreigner, pass an exam, cross a street. The motives that propel individuals and that often (although not always) take an important part in the shaping of their life experiences are infinite in their diversity.

They are also easily distorted, especially by mythologizers, but as well by historians, who, however vigorously we may guard against it, can scarcely help coercing the motivational consciousness of the past into alternative, more or less streamlined, post hoc systems of narrative meaning. The moment we perform this operation, the moment we begin to reconstruct the past, even at the most nominal level—were the Boxers an "uprising," a "rebellion," a "fiasco," or a "catastrophe"?[18]—we invest it with "associations that both illumine and deceive."[19] That is, the concepts we introduce to make the past intelligible, to "interpret," as Richard Madsen puts it, "the messy flow of concrete events,"[20] are generally (if not invariably) quite different from those in the heads of the people who created the past in the first place, and have in consequence an unavoidable distortional effect on the very reality they are designed to explicate. Madsen, in his superb book *Morality and Power in a Chinese Village*, makes extensive use of such abstract notions as "discourse," "ideal type," "paradigm," "ceremonies of innocence," "moralistic revolutionary," and "rituals of struggle" to deepen our understanding of the moral and political dynamics of a village in South China in the 1960s and 1970s. But the villagers themselves, including their key leaders during these years, would never describe their world in such language or, for that matter, seek the kind of understanding of it that Madsen offers his readers.[21]

One other characteristic of the participant's perspective on the past, as contrasted to the perspective of the historian in particular, merits notice. I refer to biographical consciousness, as opposed to historical consciousness. Individual participants in past events come together at a point not only in historical time but also in their respective biographical trajectories. Through a process of "coalescence," their individual lives merge in collective actions that we refer to as "events." These events, variably defined and labeled, acquire lives of their own, partly as symbols and metaphors, partly as organizing concepts that enable historians and other scrutinizers of the past to describe and analyze "what happened." Although on one level important components in the structure of our apprehension of the past, events, on another level, are suprahistorical, in that they represent a conflation of fragments of people's aggregate experienced lives. The people themselves, the original experiencers, the individuals who made the history in the first place, eventually fade from the picture. They walk off the set into the wings, their part in the drama finished.

This is the "dispersion" phase of the process, the phase in which individuals (assuming they survive) return to their ordinary biographical existences, retreating once more into the shadows of unnoticed, "uneventful" history: Boxers are reabsorbed into their local communities, members of the Manchu court who fled the capital in August 1900 return to take up the day-to-day business of governing, foreigners in the besieged legation quarters resume their lives in China or leave the country to take up lives else-

66   where, American marines brought from the Philippines to take part in the
       foreign relief operation are transported back to the Philippines. All who
       survive, in short, go on to do other things, to construct other parts of what
       will become "the past," to participate in other events (much as actors move
       in no preestablished pattern from play to play), leaving the "Boxer experi-
       ence" to the realm of memory, forgetting, reconstruction, distortion—a
       brief, explosive, perhaps trivial, possibly paradigmatic moment in lives that
       will encompass many other experiences before they are over.[22]

       One other facet of this coalescence-dispersion process is important.
       Although historians frequently create discrete boundaries around events,
       beginning them and ending them at specific (although not necessarily
       unchanging) points in time, individual experience tends to be basically
       continuous in nature. It operates according to its own logic, which is very
       different from the logic structuring events and the interconnections among
       events. Indeed, the kinds of connections formed at the experiential level
       will, from the standpoint of the historian, often seem downright bizarre.
       Among historians, surely, there would be a general consensus that the
       American Civil War, as an event, had nothing whatever to do with the
       Boxer uprising, as an event. Yet when a group of missionaries in Fenzhou,
       Shanxi, were trying to decide in early August 1900 whether to mount an
       armed defense against the Boxer threat, it was considered relevant that one
       of their number, Charles Price of the ABCFM, had had experience as a sol-
       dier in the War Between the States.[23]

       Other instances of this curious interplay between experience and his-
       tory abound. One frequently encountered by Americans in the early
       months of 1991 was the impact of "Vietnam consciousness" on the waging
       of the Gulf War. Again, as historical events, the Vietnam War of the 1960s
       and early 1970s and the Gulf crisis and conflict of 1990–91 were not con-
       nected. At the experiential level, on the other hand, the connections were
       manifold. Lt. Gen. Charles A. Horner, commander of the American Air
       Force in the Persian Gulf, in an interview given some months prior to the
       outbreak of the fighting, stated: "Many of us here who are in this position
       now were in Vietnam, and that war left a profound impact on our feelings
       about how our nation ought to conduct its business." A war in the Gulf, he
       said, "should not be dragged out in an effort to achieve some political
       objective." Horner's views, shared by other commanders and by millions of
       Americans, became a central feature of U.S. strategy in the short-lived Gulf
       War. They also, on the level of national psychology, spoke to broader issues
       of credibility and self-confidence, as implied by President Bush's jubilant
       declaration on March 1, 1991, that "By God, we've kicked the Vietnam syn-

drome once and for all," and the epitaph he proudly delivered a few days later, after the fighting in the Gulf had ceased: "The specter of Vietnam has been buried forever in the desert sands of the Arabian Peninsula."[24]

The aspects of the experienced past discussed above certainly do not represent a definitive inventory. They are aspects that occurred to me over several years of reading mainly about the Boxers. If I had been reading, instead, about the reform movement of 1898 in China or the founding of the Chinese Communist Party or, to move farther afield, the 1988 presidential election campaign in the United States — all events of a very different sort — my guess is I would have come up with a slightly different set of characteristics. And if my focus had been on an altogether other kind of history, history not organized around events at all but around long-term, impersonal developments — say, the growth of commerce in the last centuries of the imperial era in China or the Industrial Revolution in England — the differences would have been greater still. This variation — and more specifically the degree to which the Boxers may be viewed as illustrative of the experienced past in general — will be taken up in the conclusion.

Here I want to try to convey, however inadequately and impressionistically, something of the character of the experiential world inhabited by the Boxers and their Chinese and foreign coparticipants in the making of this segment of the past. My account will be fragmentary and incomplete, in a sense mimicking the fragmentary and incomplete quality of the actual experiences of the people involved. Even this parallelism, moreover, will at best be partial. Although, from the perspective of the Boxer episode as an entire event (the Boxers as constructed by historians), the experiences of the individual participants possessed this fragmentary, discontinuous, and ultimately incoherent quality, from the perspective of the individuals themselves, such can hardly have been the case. Cognitive science tells us that, if nothing else, individuals must have their experience coherent and meaningful.[25]

In what follows, something of this individual biographical coherence will occasionally be suggested, at least on the foreign side. On the Chinese side, because of the nature of the materials available, the best I can do is attempt to limn certain facets of a collective experiential world I believe most participants in the Boxer movement, as well as many contemporary Chinese observers of it, shared. For tens of millions of inhabitants of the North China plain, the period culminating in the spring and summer of 1900 was extraordinary in a number of ways. Protracted drought through much of the region had brought hunger and illness to many, and fear and anxiety to many more. An expanding foreign presence, manifested in dif-

68 ferent ways in different places and at different points in time, created opportunities for some but for sizable numbers of Chinese became increasingly identified as the primary source of pollution and evil in their world. The Boxer phenomenon, which emerged in this context, in some degree as a response to it, combining elements of folk religious belief centered on spirit possession, martial arts practice, and magic ritual, both reflected and contributed to the atmosphere of uncertainty and anxiety that crescendoed as the old century drew to a close. In much of the area in which the Boxers were active, rumor and suspicion became rampant among the population, occasionally reaching epidemic proportions. One other way, finally, in which the times were out of joint was that this was a period stalked by untimely death, as a result both of small-scale acts of violence and of war. Although most persons managed in the end to escape actually being killed, anxiety associated with fear of death was pervasive, among foreigners as well as Chinese, the rich as well as the poor, and in many parts of the region the sight and smell of death affronted the senses of those who survived.

These characteristics of the experiential world of North China at the turn of the century—prolonged drought, a growing foreign presence, the spread of a religio-military movement whose members practiced spirit possession and trusted in the power of magic, rumor and mass hysteria, and premature and/or violent death—converged and mushroomed in intensity in the spring and summer of 1900, feeding on each other in complicated ways. Although they impinged very differently on the lives of different groups of people—Chinese Christians, Boxers, the majority of ordinary Chinese who were neither one nor the other, elite Chinese, foreign missionaries, foreign and Chinese soldiers and officials—few were able to elude their impact entirely, and contemporary witnesses, both Chinese and foreign, repeatedly took note in their accounts of the unusual levels of excitement, anger, jitteriness, and above all fear and anxiety that prevailed. In the pages that follow I hope to capture something of this extraordinary emotional climate.

CHAPTER 2

Drought and the Foreign Presence

"I was eleven or twelve *sui*[a] at the time of the Big Sword Society disturbances. People began learning Spirit Boxing before the coming of the
flood." "The Spirit Boxers got started when I was sixteen or seventeen *sui*;
they grew rapidly after the flood." "The earliest that there was Spirit Boxing
at the Liuli Temple was during the first half of the year of the flood, when
I was seventeen or eighteen *sui*." "We had a boxing ground in this place;
the Spirit Boxers were here already before the flood. But they only practiced; it wasn't until after the flood that they became active. It was the flood
of the sixth month of the year in which I was eighteen *sui*."[1]

These statements were made by elderly inhabitants of northwestern
Shandong in response to questions put them by members of the Shandong
University History Department in surveys conducted in early 1960 and the
winter of 1965–66. The flood referred to by the respondents, and used by
them (significantly) as a memory marker to locate the point in time at
which the Spirit Boxers became active in their localities, was that of the
Yellow River, which burst its dikes at several locations beginning on August
8, 1898. Described by contemporary foreigners as "MORE APPALLING AND
DISASTROUS than any within living memory," the Yellow River flood of 1898
wreaked devastation on large portions of western Shandong. Thirty-four
counties in all were affected, thousands of villages inundated.[2] Millions of
people who were lucky enough not to drown or die from disease or starve
were reduced to a diet of willow leaves, wheat gleanings, and cottonseed
mixed with chaff and pits;[3] many others abandoned everything and, like
disaster-afflicted farmers since time immemorial in North China, migrated
elsewhere and begged (or even stole) to survive. By the winter of 1898–99

[a] Chinese are considered to be one *sui* (year) old at birth; they then add another *sui* at
the start of every new lunar year. The age count in *sui* is therefore always at least one
year greater than the Western age count.

70   the northwestern section of Shandong was saturated with refugees made homeless not only by the great flood of August 1898 but by a succession of lesser inundations that had taken place annually since 1892.[4]

Neighboring Zhili was also beset by persistent flooding during the 1890s, to the point where large stretches of the province had become heavily waterlogged by 1898. In the summer of that year the same drenching rains that had resulted further south in the flooding of the Yellow River caused the waters of the Hutuo River southwest of Tianjin to overflow their banks, submerging portions of Shenzhou, Raoyang, Anping, Xian, and Dacheng. Serious floods also occurred between Beijing and the city of Tangshan (to the east) and just north of Tianjin at the junction of the lower reaches of the Yongding River and the North Grand Canal. In the latter area, according to an official report, several dozen villages were completely submerged, "nine out of ten homes were deserted," and the suffering was extreme. In Zhili as a whole, fifty-two departments (*zhou*) and counties were affected by the floods.[5]

Agriculture in North and Northwest China had always depended on "timely" precipitation: the right amount of rain falling at the right time.[6] During much of the 1890s in western Shandong and Zhili there had been too much rain, and severe flooding and waterlogging had resulted. After the winter of 1898–99, however, this pattern abruptly reversed, too little or no rain falling in a vast region embracing Shandong, Zhili, Shanxi, and Henan in North China, Shaanxi and Gansu in the northwest, and Inner Mongolia.[7] Insufficient precipitation was certainly no stranger to this area. The great famine of 1876–1879, brought on mainly by drought, is said to have taken as many as nine and a half million lives, Shandong and Shanxi being especially hard hit.[8] The drought at the turn of the century, although less severe than the one a quarter century earlier, was, like it, distinguished by its geographical extension and duration. Drought was the common fate of millions of farmers and their families over a long period of time. And for the vast majority of these people, many of whom were old enough to have vivid recollections of the famine of the 1870s, it was a frightening experience.[9]

Flood and Drought

Although both flood and drought are calamities that take huge tolls in human suffering, they differ from one another in important ways.[10] For one thing, floods originate in specific geographical locations: particular rivers whose waters become so swollen by the spring thaw or by heavy summer rains that they overflow their banks or burst their dikes (at specific locations) and temporarily form alluvial lakes covering limited (though not necessarily small) stretches of low-lying land. Droughts, by contrast, although certainly influenced by the climatic characteristics of a given geographical region, are not tied (like floods) to the particular physical features of a region. There is the potential, therefore, for a major drought, like the one that struck North and Northwest China in 1899–1900, to embrace a much vaster territorial area than a major flood and, correspondingly, to inflict harm on a far greater number of people.[11]

If one basic difference between flood and drought has to do with spatial placement, another derives from the very different ways in which they are situated in time. Floods occur at specific moments in time, and if they are of sufficient gravity can (as we have seen) become permanent memory markers in the minds of their victims. This time-specific character of floods is

2.1 AND 2.2   Images of Starvation from North China Famine of Late 1870s. These images originally appeared in a Chinese pamphlet. In figure 2.1 the starving stand in pools of blood; in figure 2.2 a corpse is being carved up to provide food for the living. From Committee of the China Famine Relief Fund, *The Famine in China* (London: C. Kegan Paul, 1878).

72   strengthened by the fact that they are generally of limited duration. The suffering floods cause may be terrible, but when the rains stop and the flooding subsides survivors are often able to return to their villages, repair and rebuild their homes, and resume their work routines, sometimes even benefiting from a new layer of rich alluvial soil deposited by the retreating flood waters.

If severe enough to result in famine, droughts, too, may become memory aids, especially in oral traditions. "The occurrence of other events of personal or public significance," David Arnold reports, are often recalled "by locating them in relation to the date of a particular famine, which acts as the pole around which all other experiences and impressions are organized and collected." The capacity of famine to form "a link between the world of personal memory and the broader domain of collective consciousness" is exemplified by the Indian and African peasant habit of using such traumatic incidents as "personal reference points" for telling their ages or recalling other dates and events.[12]

Still, as compared to floods, droughts behave very differently and have a very different kind of impact on people's lives. "The major difficulty in preparing a quantitative definition of drought," William Dando writes, "stems from drought being a 'non-event' as opposed to such a distinct event as a flood."[13] Drought is in fact such a paradigmatic nonevent that it is frequently used as a metaphor, in sports and other spheres, for all manner of things that are expected or counted on to happen but don't. When in the spring of 1991 New York Yankee rookie Hensley Meulens, widely touted as the team's "next great home-run hitter," went fifteen games before hitting one out of the park, it was almost predictable that the next day's headline would read "After 15 Long Games, Meulens Ends Drought."[14] (Conversely, in business, politics, and other areas, "rainmaker" has come into the language as a metaphor for someone who makes good things happen.)[15] While it is not generally difficult to pinpoint the termination of a drought, drought does not, like flood, have a sharply defined onset. Indeed, a drought doesn't become a drought until a certain amount of time has gone by—exactly how much depending on a wide range of physical, biological, and subjective factors.[16] This is one reason why the incidence of drought, both spatially and temporally, is so unpredictable and governments and peoples are so often unprepared for it, witness the "near panic" of the British government when confronted with the drought that afflicted the United Kingdom in 1976.[17]

Similarly, the suffering occasioned by drought is not sudden and dramatic, like that generally resulting from flood, but slow-moving, incremental, and of indeterminate duration. Drought, in fact, is a superb example of the indeterminacy—uncertainty with respect to the future—that characterizes experience in general.[18] The longer a drought lasts, the more urgent and pressing become such questions as: When will it rain? When will the drought end? Will it end in time? Put succinctly, the focus of disasters created by flood (*shuizai*) is on something that has happened, while the focus of disasters resulting from drought (*hanzai*) is on something that has not happened. The latter, arguably, is harder to deal with psychologically.

The *Times of India* in the summer of 1899 captured the combination of anxiety, hope, and a misplaced trust sometimes resulting in paralysis that often characterizes the human response to drought. "While hope has not yet been relinquished," the paper editorialized in late July, "great anxiety is felt on all hands lest the rains . . . in western India and the Deccan should be a failure." A month further into the drought, the Kathiawar correspondent summed up the desperate situation occasioned by the failure of the monsoon rains: "From week to week the hope of rain continued. Now it was bound to come, they said, because such and such a festival fell on such and such a day. Then it was another date on which the rain could not possibly fail. Finally, the festival of Shri Krishna, they held, was bound to bring it. And while the people were procrastinating, the cattle were dying, the land was unirrigated where it might have been artificially moistened, and there was no preparation."[19]

Yet another difference between flood and drought with emotional ramifications is that the former, unlike the latter, is often, in part at least, a consequence of human failing; when flood prevention measures—forestation, dredging, dike construction and repair—are possible but are not taken, either because of insufficient experience and skill or because of negligence or outright corruption on the part of those responsible for flood control administration, preventable flooding sometimes occurs. When this happens, the victims, once their immediate fears for their safety and survival have subsided, are apt to become angry and to direct their anger at the local authorities. Drought, on the other hand, is not as easy to account for in terms of strict human agency (although human beings can under certain circumstances do a great deal to mitigate its effects) and historically has more often been understood as resulting from the action of supernatural forces that need to be propitiated or cosmic imbalances that require correction.

The Religious Construction of Drought

In China, where it had been widely believed for centuries that there was a link between human behavior and the actions of Heaven, as expressed

74   through nature, it was not at all uncommon to blame droughts and other
       natural calamities on official misconduct and to seek to alleviate the crisis
       by changing either the conduct or the official.[20] "I have heard," one censor
       commented in response to the drought of 1876–1879, "that if one woman
       suffers an injustice, for three years there will be no rain." Another censor,
       citing the precedent of a three-year drought during the Han dynasty fol-
       lowing the unjust execution of a filial wife, connected the 1870s drought to
       the disruption of heavenly harmony caused by excessive judicial torture.[21]
       In the spring of 1901, in the changed political climate that emerged after
       the suppression of the Boxer movement, a teacher in Taiyuan, which was
       still experiencing severe drought conditions, complained that local offi-
       cials (presumably under foreign pressure) were providing famine relief to
       the Christian population but not to non-Christian farmers, who were left
       to starve to death in the fields. "With human affairs thus," he intoned, "can
       one hope that Heaven will let fall a timely rain?"[22] A similar pattern of
       explanation was encountered in the aftermath of severe flooding. In the
       wake of a flood in Fuzhou in July 1900, a lengthy poem was circulated
       attacking the crimes of Governor-General Xu Yingkui and expressly link-
       ing the flood to Xu's support of the policy of containment of the Boxer War,
       which in turn was seen as occasioning Heaven's anger.[23]

       Correction of human misconduct in order to reestablish cosmic har-
       mony has been one means of responding to drought. Another, which
       seems almost universal in societies regularly afflicted by drought, has been
       direct propitiation of the gods through prayer and other rain-inducing cer-
       emonial practices. In precolonial Botswana in southern Africa, where rain-
       making was considered to be "the most important" of all the magico-reli-
       gious functions of the chiefs,[24] such ceremonies ranged from the sacrifice
       of a black ox on a former chief's grave to the ritual murder of a child (or
       exhuming of an already dead one) and use of its body parts in rainmaking
       medicines.[25] Millions prayed for rain during the drought that extended
       over western India in the summer of 1899.[26] In Massachusetts a day of pub-
       lic fasting was proclaimed on June 15, 1749, "on occasion of extream
       drought," and on August 24, 1749, a day of "general thanksgiving" was
       announced "for the extraordinary reviving rains, after the most distressing
       drought . . . in the memory of any living."[27] Even in modern secular
       America, with its general trust in scientific explanation of the physical
       world and its extraordinary technological capability, when a serious
       drought hit the Midwest in the summer of 1988, Jesse Jackson, then cam-
       paigning for the Democratic nomination for president, prayed for rain in
       the middle of an Iowa cornfield, and an Ohio florist flew in a Sioux medi-

cine man from one of the Dakotas to perform a rainmaking ceremony, which thousands came to watch.[28]

Similarly, in China, prayer and other rituals, both official and popular, were routinely offered to counter the effects of drought. Kenneth Pomeranz has written about the Handan rain shrine in southern Zhili, where in the late Qing the popular custom of combating drought by taking water from the Shengjinggang well (in Handan) and then putting it back after it rained was increasingly overtaken by official rituals, centering on the removal of a tablet from the well and its return with an additional tablet following the fall of rain.[29] In response to the famine of the late 1870s, the young Guangxu Emperor offered public prayers at five state temples, including the Dagaodian near the rear entrance to the imperial palace, where he prostrated himself before an image of the Jade Emperor. Prayers were also offered by the governors-general and governors of the stricken provinces.[30] And there are reports of comparable efforts (including bans on the slaughter of animals)[31] made by the court and by provincial and local officials in various parts of Zhili, Shandong, and Shanxi in the spring and summer of 1900.[32]

Drought, Anxiety, and the Spread of the Boxer Movement

Prayer, however, even when offered up by the most powerful people in the realm, does not always work. And, as a drought continues and people become more and more desperate, restlessness, anxiety, and ultimately panic easily set in. To imagine how profound the panic can be among impoverished farmers and poor city folk living in a society with little in the way of a "safety net," it is illuminating to look at the reactions of the newly unemployed in California in the early stages of the recession that began in the latter half of 1990. "The hardest thing," observed the part owner of a small marketing company in Huntington Beach that had recently gone out of business, "is to see how panicked people are. . . . Right now, I don't have a dime. I'm worried about buying things like sugar. I'm that close to losing my home. Now is when the nerve systems are really going." A young film editor from Hollywood, noting the "prevailing air of uncertainty," expressed a lack of confidence "about the future."[33]

Uncertainty about the future governs virtually all phases of human experience. But it does not always produce anxiety. For anxiety to result, the uncertainty must bear on an aspect of life that is of vital importance: a child's safety, one's performance in a play or a sporting event, the fate of a loved one engaged in combat, the time frame of one's own mortality, the security and dependability of one's livelihood. It was the last-named area of

76   uncertainty that was shared by Californians in 1990 and Chinese farmers in North China almost a century earlier. Different societies, however, are differentially susceptible to the effects of natural or social disasters,[34] and in the case of the drought of 1899–1900 in China (or that of 1899 in western India), because of the absence of a well-functioning crisis support system, it was much more a matter of life and death.[35]

2.3   Rain God. The Chinese prayed and offered sacrifices to a variety of gods in time of drought. The one whose rainmaking responsibilities were most specific is shown here, standing amid the clouds with a watering can in his hands. From C. A. S. Williams, *Outlines of Chinese Symbolism and Art Motives*, 2d rev. ed. (Shanghai, 1932).

A wide range of sources, including gazetteers, diaries, official memorials, oral history accounts, and the reports of foreigners, indicate a direct link between the spread and intensification of the Boxer movement, beginning in late 1899, and growing popular nervousness, anxiety, unemployment, and hunger occasioned by drought. As early as October 1899, Luella Miner (ABCFM) identified drought as one cause of growing Boxer-related unrest in northwestern Shandong.[36] In the Beijing area, where for many months very little rain had fallen and the wheat seedlings had completely withered, popular feeling was described as unsettled and volatile, owing to drought-induced hunger, and from late April 1900 contagious diseases began to break out with increasing frequency and seriousness.[37] In other parts of Zhili it was much the same. American legation secretary W. E. Bainbridge, noting that during the preceding year "there had been insufficient rain" and that "the entire province was on the verge of famine," concluded that conditions were "peculiarly favorable to its [the Boxer uprising's] friendly reception. . . . As Spring advanced and early Summer approached with no rains to aid the crops, the excitement . . . reached a fever heat."[38] From Zhuozhou, just southwest of Beijing, apprehensions were expressed in early June that, if it did not rain soon, it would become increasingly difficult to control the thousands of Boxers who had gathered in the area.[39] A gentry manager of a *baojia*[b] bureau just west of Tianjin reported that in the spring of 1900 young farmers idled by the drought often took up boxing because they had nothing else to do with their time.[40] The relationship among drought, idleness, and augmented Boxer activity found blunt corroboration in the testimony of a former Boxer from the Tianjin area: "*Gengzi* [1900] was a drought year and there was nothing to do, so we began to practice Yihe Boxing."[41]

Liu Mengyang, a reform-minded (and anti-Boxer) member of the local Tianjin elite, in one of the most detailed eyewitness accounts of the progress of the movement in Tianjin, used the persistent drought, almost as a drum roll, to periodize the escalation of Boxer activity and support in the city:

> During the second month [of the 26th year of Guangxu, March 1–30, 1900] there was no rainfall. Rumors proliferated. . . . A comparatively large number of people began to practice boxing, and since the authorities didn't look very closely into what was going on, the bandits became increasingly intrepid. . . .
>
> During the third month [March 31–April 28] there was still no rain. Epidemic disease spread and the calamity began. The Boxer bandits, taking ad-

---

[b] The *baojia* was a local-level mutual security system.

vantage of the situation, fabricated a formula which went: "Drive out the foreigner and, in due course, the rains will fall and dispel our misfortune." . . .

During the fourth month [April 29–May 27] there was still no rain.
Officials from the governor-general down to the county magistrates repeatedly . . . offered up prayers. But the severe drought persisted and was even
made worse by fierce winds. The Boxer bandits everywhere started to set up
altars. . . . They lorded it over everyone in the streets, making the population
nervous. Yet all looked up to them as gods, and even the authorities dared
not mess with them . . . .

During the first ten days of the fifth month [May 28–June 6] the severe
drought continued. The railway between Beijing and Tianjin was destroyed. . . . The Boxer bandits in Tianjin now became still more violent and
unreasonable.[42]

Drought conditions in large areas of Shanxi had by summer 1900
become, if anything, even worse than in Zhili. In many places there had
been no rain at all since winter. Farmers were without work. The prices of
wheat and rice had shot up. Hunger was widespread and popular anxiety
at a high pitch. A missionary report stated that the "organization of the
Boxer societies spread rapidly throughout the province when so many were
idle because of the drouth."[43] The gazetteers of Qinyuan, Quwo, Lin, Jie,
Linjin, Xiangning, and Yuci counties all connected the first emergence of
the Boxers in mid- or late June to the protracted drought in their areas.
Moreover, it was alleged that famine victims regularly joined in when the
Boxers stirred up trouble.[44]

I do not at all want to suggest that the expansion of the Boxer movement in the spring and summer of 1900 was due to drought alone. Within
a given area, the official stance toward the Boxers, pro (as in Shanxi) or
con (as in Shandong), played a role of perhaps equivalent weight.
Nevertheless, drought—and the range of emotions associated with it—
was a factor of crucial importance. It is significant, in this connection, that
in a number of instances when rain fell to interrupt the drought and possibly bring it to an end, Boxers (as well as Big Sword Society members)
dropped everything and returned to their fields. Esherick observes that
when "a substantial penetrating rain" fell in early April along the Zhili-
Shandong border, peasants went home to plant their spring crops, "quiet-
ing things down considerably."[45] After being defeated by the foreign forces
in Tianjin during a torrential downpour on July 4, fleeing Boxers are
reported to have said to one another: "It's raining. We can return home
and till the soil. What use is it for us to suffer like this?" The following day,
accordingly, most of them dispersed.[46]

Oral history accounts from Shandong tell a similar story. In late June 1900, during the drought in the western part of the province, a Big Sword Society leader from Zhili named Han Guniang (Miss Han) was invited to a Big Sword gathering at the hemp market at Longgu, just west of the Juye county seat. Rumored to be a Red Lantern with extraordinary magical powers — it was said that, in addition to being able to withstand swords and spears, "when she mounted a bench it turned into a horse, when she straddled a piece of rope it turned into a dragon, and when she sat on a mat it turned into a cloud on which she could fly" — Han Guniang took charge of food distribution. Within a short time, upwards of a thousand people joined her Big Swords. The grain she handed out had been seized from the supplies of rich families. "After two or three days," one account continues, "there was a big downpour. The next day there were no Big Swords anywhere in sight. They were all gone. The reason these people had come in the first place was to get something to eat. As soon as it rained, they all went back to tend their crops."[47]

Lin Dunkui, who has made a special study of the role of natural disasters in the history of the Boxers, concludes that "from the time of the first outbreak of the Big Sword Society right up to the high tide of the Boxer movement, a sizable number of peasants were prompted to take part in these movements mainly by the weather."[48]

The Missionary Response to the Drought

Although the experience of missionaries in North China in the summer of 1900, especially ones stranded in isolated areas of the countryside, was very different from that of Chinese farmers, the missionaries, too, faced a situation defined by life-and-death uncertainty. And they too hoped desperately — and prayed — for rain. The immediate fear of the missionaries, of course, was death not from hunger but at the hands of hungry Chinese. This fear and the corresponding one on the Chinese side were amply expressed by Rowena Bird of the ABCFM in letters and journal entries written from Taigu, Shanxi, only weeks before her death (on July 31). On June 25 Bird wrote: "These are most trying times — famine threatens the people with starvation — the dry, hot weather makes all ill, and the Boxers are threatening the destruction of the country by robbing and killing missionaries and Christians. . . . The country is full of the wildest rumors and threats. The people have nothing to do but talk and they talk of killing the foreigners and Christians and we feel that the end may not be far off for any of us . . . things grow worse and worse and if the rains hold off it is hard to

80 say what violence may not ensue. We know God could send relief thru rain if He thot best, and we know all our interests are in His hands."[49]

If the absence of rain aroused feelings of fear and anxiety on all sides, the opposite was also true. When, a few days after the above lines were written, a light rain began to fall, the relief among the Taigu missionaries was palpable. "We are hoping much from this blessed rain," Bird wrote, "that possibly has come just in time to save us all . . . there is still a chance to plant late millet if enough rain comes."[50] In a similar vein, (Mary) Louise Partridge wrote from Liman, a village near Taigu, on June 19: "It clouded up last night & began to rain. This morning I was so thankful because a good rain would mean safety. It's because its [sic] so dry that they make any disturbance here, not *Boxers*. . . . You must know that this is ordinarily a quiet people but now they are rendered desperate by hunger and fear of starvation."[51]

In a journal entry of June 30, Eva Price, an ABCFM missionary stationed in Fenzhou, Shanxi, contributed her ruminations on the meaning of the drought for Chinese and foreigners: "If copious rains would fall and now! Crops could be sown, the idle starving people would have field work, and the prospect of good fall crops would relieve the situation for us here as nothing else could do. Oh, that our merciful Heavenly Father would bless us by adding to what He has so mercifully done for us, this other great blessing."[52]

Other Shanxi missionaries also focused on the connection between drought, Chinese hunger, and foreign fear. As early as June 1899, shortly after she and her husband opened a mission station in Yongning, Olivia Ogren of the China Inland Mission (CIM) reported: "This region was suffering from famine, caused by long-continued drought. This kept increasing in severity after our arrival, and people began gradually to blame us for keeping away the rain."[53] In the jittery mood then prevailing, mobile unemployed people were particularly subject to suspicion. "In consequence of the drought," observed E. H. Edwards of the Baptist Mission Society, ". . . many people were wandering about picking up a precarious living, and not a few of them were accused of being in the pay of foreigners for bad purposes, and killed at sight."[54]

Missionaries elsewhere in North China experienced the drought in much the same terms as their Shanxi coworkers. "The joint powers," Sarah Boardman Goodrich wrote on May 25 from Tongzhou, a dozen or so miles east of the capital, "have discovered they have no power. Not a seed planted and starvation staring thousands in the face helps to increase the dislike to foreigners. We simply feel it our duty to stand in our places, not knowing what a day may bring forth."[55] Luella Miner, also in Tongzhou, reported

that after the burning on May 28 of the Fengtai station (on the Beijing-
Tianjin rail line)—"the first overt act of the Boxers in this region"—missionaries and Chinese Christians prayed "earnestly for rain, which might
improve the situation by sending some of the Boxers into the field to
work."[56] Three weeks later, after relocating to the capital, Miner observed
that on the afternoon and evening of June 18 the first substantial rain in
nearly a year fell in the Beijing area, and expressed the hope that it would
avert famine and furnish employment to some of "the idle hordes for
whom Satan has been finding mischievous work. Perhaps there would be
fewer Boxers in the land," she added, "but for the long-continued drought
and the desolate brown fields."[57]

In Baoding it was much the same story. Mrs. F. E. Simcox (American
Presbyterian) wrote in mid-April: "There is great need of rain. The ignorant attribute this drought to the foreigners who have 'offended heaven.' "
In a letter of June 2, Horace Pitkin (ABCFM), after describing the growing
threat in the area to Protestants and Catholics alike, commented with
terse urgency: "Dry as powder—oppressive duststorm—God give us rain.
That would quiet things a moment. . . . We can't be sure of a single day's
life. Pray for us. Pray for rain." After the killing of all fifteen foreign
Protestants in Baoding on June 30 and July 1, according to Luella Miner,
it rained, confirming, from the Boxer point of view, the rightness of their
cause and conduct.[58]

Missionary fear of drought-related unrest extended to Henan as well.
"Prolonged droughts had destroyed the prospects of a good harvest," a CIM
medical missionary observed on the eve of his hurried departure for
Hankou, "and the people were in a restless condition, ready for anything in
the way of uprising and excitement. They were incensed at the failure of
all their prayers and rain processions; no rain had fallen. 'It must be the foreigners' fault,' they said; 'let us get rid of them.' "[59]

The consensus missionary assessment of the critical importance of
drought in 1900 was cast in more general terms by Arthur H. Smith
(ABCFM) in his retrospective effort to account for the timing of the Boxer
outbreak: "There were special causes for a popular rising during the spring.
The drought was great and practically universal. For the first time since the
great famine in 1878 no winter wheat to speak of had been planted in any
part of northern China. . . . The ground was baked so hard that no crops
could be put in, and at such times the idle and restless population are ready
for any mischief."[60]

Fundamentally the same analysis was also made in the reports of the foreign ministers in Beijing to their governments. The American minister,

82   Edwin H. Conger, in a dispatch of May 8, 1900, described the situation in
Zhili in the following terms: "The people are very poor; until yesterday
practically no rain has fallen for nearly a year, plowing has not been and
can not be done, crops have not been planted, the ground is too dry and
hard to work in any way, and consequently the whole country is swarming

2.4   Report on Drought. In a missionary's postcard to his parents, dated June 23,
1900, note is taken of the continuation of the drought in south and central Zhili.
From Archibald E. Glover, A *Thousand Miles of Miracle in China* (London:
Hodder and Stoughton, 1904).

> June 23rd 1900
>
> Dearest Parents, thank God all is well with us. The mail service is at present interrupted, as the Boxers have cut the communication between Tientsin & the interior, & have partially destroyed the railway at Pao-ting Fu. So we cannot tell when you may receive letters. Just now, the post offices are not forwarding. I write this in the hope that it may possibly reach you, and allay any anxiety you may be feeling about us. It will not be long before the mail service is running regularly, as word from Mr Wm Cooper, who is at Pao-ting Fu, says that things are quieting down, & the railway is being quickly repaired: & you will then have all our news. In God's mercy we have had heavy rain at Lu-an, enabling the people to sow their seed. In most other parts, the drought continues. Don't be anxious about us. "Ye believe in God: believe also in Me." And join us in believing prayer that the things that are happening may turn out to the furtherance of the gospel & the glory of God's Christ. Fondest love. Your own son, Archie. (Let Stanley Smith know.)

with hungry, discontented, hopeless idlers, and they . . . are ready to join any organization offered. . . . If the rain, now commenced, continues copiously, I apprehend we will hear little more of the 'Boxers.' "[61]

Even after the Chinese government in mid-May began to take more serious suppressive measures against the Boxers, Claude M. MacDonald, the British minister, stated his conviction that "a few days' heavy rainfall, to terminate the long-continued drought which has helped largely to excite unrest in the country districts, would do more to restore tranquillity than any measures which either the Chinese Government or foreign Governments could take."[62]

In one important respect the understanding of the diplomats differed from that of the missionaries: it was cast in completely secular terms. For Christians at the close of the nineteenth century God's hand was literally everywhere. If He wanted His flock to survive, He would deliver them from danger. If He wanted the missionaries to continue in their work, He would see to it that their material needs were satisfied. And if, as Rowena Bird had written, "He thot best," He "could send relief thru rain."[63] Conversely, if the Christians faced a deadly threat like that of the Boxers — "so plainly the work of the devil, saturated with superstition and witchcraft, reeking with cruelty, diabolical to the last degree, an open revolt against Jehovah and his Anointed"[64] — it was not because God was asleep on the job. God did not sleep. The Boxer uprising took place because He had permitted it to take place. His dealings were sometimes "mysterious," and it was not always easy for mere mortals to understand why He allowed certain things to happen. But good Christians knew that, although it was necessary in such circumstances to walk "by faith, not by sight,"[65] in the final analysis everything that transpired "must be," as Luella Miner put it, "among the 'all things' which are working together for the good of God's kingdom, and of China," or, in Dwight Clapp's phrasing, "for the glory of God in the end, tho we can't see how now."[66]

The Boxer Construction of the Drought

What is fascinating is the degree to which contemporary Chinese—non-Boxers as well as Boxers—also viewed everything that happened in the world, including whether it rained or not, as being in the control of Heaven or "the gods." Indeed, although the Chinese construction of reality differed greatly in specifics from that of the missionaries, in a number of broad respects it formed almost a mirror image of the missionaries' construction. Where the missionaries saw themselves as representatives of the Lord,

84   sometimes describing themselves as "God's soldiers"[67] and often believing
quite literally that they had been called by Jesus Christ to go to China to
labor for that country's salvation, in jingles repeated and notices circulated
throughout North China in 1900 the Boxers were often portrayed, in comparably salvific (as well as martial) terms, as "spirit soldiers" (shenbing) sent
down from Heaven to carry out a divine mission or, which amounted to the
same thing, as mortals whose bodies had been possessed by spirits (thereby
rendering them divine) for the identical purpose.

Again, where the missionaries constructed the Boxer movement as a
satanic force, whose capacity for evil knew no bounds, the Boxers (and, one
presumes, millions of Chinese who were not active participants in the
movement) saw the missionaries, and by extension all other foreigners (as
well, of course, as Chinese Christians and other Chinese who in one way
or another had been tainted by foreign contact), as the root source of evil
in their world, the immediate reason for the anger of the gods. The explanation of the drought found in Boxer notices was embedded in a full-blown
religious structuring of reality; the notices also provided participants in the
movement with a clear program of action designed to mollify the gods and
restore the cosmic balance. Such notices began to be widely circulated at
least as early as the beginning of 1900. (It is doubtful that one would
encounter drought-related notices much before this date, as it was probably not until the late months of 1899 that people in North China began to
experience the protracted dry weather as a "drought.")[68] In February of this
year the Tianjin agent of the American Bible Society reported the following text to have been "posted everywhere" in North China: "On account
of the Protestant and Catholic religions the Buddhist gods are oppressed,
and our sages thrust into the background. The Law of Buddha is no longer
respected, and the Five Relationships are disregarded. The anger of
Heaven and Earth has been aroused and the timely rain has consequently
been withheld from us. But Heaven is now sending down eight millions of
spiritual soldiers to extirpate these foreign religions, and when this has
been done there will be a timely rain."[69]

Boxer notices were often written in doggerel, which made them easier
to circulate orally. A portion of one of the most widely disseminated examples (in Esherick's translation) went as follows:

They proselytize their sect,
And believe in only one God,
The spirits and their own ancestors
Are not even given a nod.

Their men are all immoral;
Their women truly vile.
For the Devils it's mother-son sex
That serves as the breeding style.

...

No rain comes from Heaven.
The earth is parched and dry.
And all because the churches
Have bottled up the sky.

The god[s] are very angry.
The spirits seek revenge.
En masse they come from Heaven
To teach the Way to men.[70]

Sometimes the essence of the notices was distilled in jingles that even a small child could recite from memory. Chen Zhenjiang and Cheng Xiao supply two of these: "*Shale yangguitou, Mengyu wang xia liu*" (When the foreign devils have been killed, A heavy rain will fall); and "*Yangren shajin, Yu yu huan yu, Yu qing jiao qing*" (When the foreigners have all been killed off, Rain will come when we call for rain, And it will be clear when we want it to be clear).[71]

Frequently Boxer notices took the form of a personal reprimand from the Jade Emperor, widely regarded by the Boxers as their guardian deity.[72] In the following broadside, which appeared in late spring 1900 in Beijing, Tianjin, and other locations in Zhili and Manchuria, the target of the Jade Emperor's admonishment is Prince Qing, who was head of the Zongli Yamen at the time and strongly opposed to the Boxers:

> Prince Qing during the *zi* hour [11 P.M.–1 A.M.] of the night of the 9th day of the 4th month [May 7] had three dreams in succession.
>
> The Great Jade Emperor instructed him to switch from Catholicism[c] and return to the orthodox Way of the Great Qing: You have a Chinese official's salary, and yet you lend assistance to the foreigners. If you don't change your ways, it will be too late to repent. Since the Catholics and Protestants do not abide by the teachings of Buddhism, violate the Way of the Sages, and everywhere treat the common people of the Qing just as they please, now the Lord on High is very angry and prevents the rain and snow from falling. He

---

[c] Prince Qing was not in fact a Christian. The notice refers to him as such to discredit him because of his involvement in the management of foreign affairs.

86   has sent down 80,000 spirit soldiers to instruct the sacred society of the
       Boxers, with a view to using human strength to protect China, drive out the
       foreigners, and sweep away the bunch [who follow] the devil images of other
       countries [i.e., Chinese Christians]. Before long hostilities will commence.
       . . . The Jade Emperor has a merciful heart. Wishing to save the world and
       bring relief to the people, he issues an advance notice: Starting from the 18th
       day of the 4th month [May 16], don't take trains in the interest of speed, lest
       you meet with death on the rails. On the 18th day of the 5th month [June 14],
       all railways throughout the area will be destroyed. When this date arrives you
       are enjoined absolutely not to ride the trains. Pass on one copy [of this
       notice] and avert calamity to one family; pass on ten copies and avert disas-
       ter to a whole area. If you read [the notice] and don't disseminate its con-
       tents, calamity will surely strike you. After waking up from your dream, write
       down [these words] in order to save the world.[73]

Occasionally Boxer notices were pitched directly at Chinese Christians.
The following placard was posted in Taigu, Shanxi, at the height of the
movement in the summer:

       The gods of happiness and wealth issue these instructions for the informa-
       tion of the members of the Catholic and Protestant religions: You have aban-
       doned the gods and done away with your ancestors, causing the gods to be
       angry so that the rains do not fall from the sky. Before long heavenly soldiers
       and heavenly generals will descend to earth and wage a great battle with the
       adherents of your two religions. It is a matter of great urgency that you
       quickly join the Boxers and sincerely mend your ways, so that when the time
       comes [for the great battle], your entire families do not suffer harm.[74]

The writings of the Boxers were numerous and diverse, and not all of
them attempted to link foreign religious incursions, heavenly anger, and
drought. A great many of them, however, did.[75] Chen Zhenjiang and
Cheng Xiao suggest that this linkage was a propaganda device used by the
Boxers to encourage the masses to burn down churches and drive out the
missionaries,[76] the implication being that the Boxers themselves did not
fully accept the premises of the narrative structure embedded in their writings. While it is entirely possible that some of the authors of these placards,
as well as some rank-and-file Boxers, did not in fact subscribe to the
analysis contained in them, the likelihood is that the great majority did.
Esherick maintains that "without a doubt" the placards "reflected the
beliefs and hopes of most Boxers in the Beijing-Tianjin area."[77] There is
every reason to believe, moreover, that this judgment held true for the population at large as well. "There come the foreign devils," a missionary
reported hearing a street boy call out on a visit to the Chinese city of

Tianjin in May 1900, "that[']s why we don't have any rain."[78] Chen and Cheng themselves acknowledge implicitly that the "propaganda" of the Boxers could only be effective if it appeared credible to large numbers of people. And contemporary observers, both Chinese and Western, were quite explicit in their confirmation of this supposition.[79]

I would take it a step further and argue that in an ecological setting in which people periodically suffered from severe hunger, owing to actions of nature that were unpredictable and beyond human control, the most natural thing in the world for many of society's members was to predicate a supernatural connection between the immediate cause of the hunger—lack of precipitation—and some form of inappropriate human action—the intrusion, in this case, of a foreign religious rival—that was perceived as upsetting the normal balance of the cosmos. Such a pattern of thinking had been deeply etched in Chinese cultural behavior for centuries. It is also a pattern that has been widely displayed in other cultures (especially agrarian ones) in many different historical eras.

It would be a mistake, I believe, to characterize this mode of thinking as supracultural or intrinsically human. In late twentieth-century societies, in which modern science exerts a profound shaping influence, there are vast numbers of people who would not seriously entertain any explanation of drought cast in other than strictly natural terms. Supernatural agency is, nevertheless, a very widely encountered cultural construction. A classic statement of the logic informing this construction is found in the Old Testament, where God announces to His chosen people:

> If you will earnestly heed the commandments I give you this day, to love the Lord your God and to serve Him with all your heart and all your soul, then I will favor your land with rain at the proper season—rain in autumn and rain in spring—and you will have ample harvest of grain and wine and oil. I will assure abundance in the fields for your cattle. You will eat to contentment. Take care lest you be tempted to forsake God and turn to false gods in worship. For then the wrath of the Lord will be directed against you. He will close the heavens and hold back the rain; the earth will not yield its produce. You will soon disappear from the good land which the Lord gives you.[80]

Other examples abound. Muslims in Nigeria in 1973 interpreted the drought of that year as a sign of "the wrath of Allah against mankind." For Christians in late Elizabethan England, the famine of the 1590s "showed that God was angry with the people."[81] Among the Beng of Ivory Coast, where the gravest of all possible offenses to the Earth is the act of sexual intercourse in the forest or in the fields—an act certain to result in a drought threatening to the entire Beng people—a minor drought in 1980 was brought to an end

88   only after the meting out of appropriate punishment to a guilty couple.[82] In Botswana in the nineteenth century it was widely believed that a prolonged drought was caused by the incursions of Christianity, especially after a renowned rainmaker, upon being baptized, abandoned his rainmaking practices. When, after a series of disastrous years, the local missionary (David Livingstone) left and the tribe of the converted rainmaker also moved elsewhere, sure enough, the drought broke.[83]

"Whatever the precise cause," generalizes David Arnold, "there was no doubting the divine provenance of famine. . . . The involvement of the elements—the failure of the rains, the unseasonal frosts and floods—seemed to place causation beyond human reach and to provide sober confirmation of man's subordination to god and nature."[84] Still, while the basic premise that natural disasters are to be accounted for by some supernatural agency acting in response to human wrongdoing appears with great frequency, the particularities of a society's response to such disasters, the "structures of meaning" (to use Geertzian language) within which it interprets them,[85] will be shaped by the special cultural forms and historical experience of that society. Thus, in China in 1900 the fact that the gods were angry was not distinctive; what was distinctive was that this anger was occasioned by the disrespect foreigners were perceived to have shown such specifically Chinese teachings as Confucianism and Buddhism, in which native gods had a strong proprietary interest, and the alleged defections from these teachings of growing numbers of Chinese. Similarly, while in more ordinary times the human agency responsible for the disruption of cosmic harmony might typically have been identified as the misconduct of Chinese officials, in 1900, at a time of increasing foreign pressure and mounting crisis in China's foreign relations, it was not surprising to find the blame for drought shifted from the domestic to the foreign arena.

The same sort of analysis may be applied to the instructions for crisis remedy that we find in many of the Boxer notices. The first recourse for people faced with drought is, as we have seen, to offer up prayers and perform a range of rain-inducing rituals. But when such conventional means fail to produce relief, and the anxiety occasioned by the drought deepens, people often resort to more heroic measures. The generic element here is scapegoatism, the identification of a human agency deemed responsible for the crisis and the punishment of that agency. But the forms of scapegoatism vary enormously in different cultural and historical settings. In some places, Arnold tells us, old women have been accused of being witches who malevolently drive away the rain clouds with their sorcery. The drought in the southeastern African country Malawi in 1949 was blamed on old men with gray hair or bald heads and on brickmakers, both of which categories were seen as gaining from the absence of rain. "When the monsoons failed in Gujarat in western India," Arnold continues, "the Bhil *adivasis* or tribals suspected Bania traders of stopping the rain deliberately so as to profit from the resultant dearth and high prices. To break this spell the Bhils forced a Bania to hold a water pot on his head at which they fired arrows until the pot broke and released the rains."[86]

Far more extreme measures were taken in late medieval European millenarian movements, as analyzed by Norman Cohn. In 1420 in Bohemia, Cohn writes, "people saw themselves as entering on the final struggle against Antichrist and his hosts. . . . No longer content to await the destruction of the godless by a miracle, . . . preachers called upon the faithful to carry out the necessary purification of the earth themselves. . . . 'Accursed be the man [stated one widely circulated tract] who withholds his sword from shedding the blood of the enemies of Christ. Every believer must wash his hands in that blood.' "[87]

Boxer Motives: Anti-Imperialism, Antiforeignism, or Anxiety Over Drought?

The crisis remedy proposed by the Boxers in 1900 reveals a close kinship to that described by Cohn for the millenarian movement of 1420.[88] In one placard after another, the Chinese people are enjoined to kill off all foreigners and native Chinese contaminated by foreigners or foreign influence. Only after this process of physical elimination of every trace of the foreign from China has been completed will the gods be appeased and permit the rains once again to fall.

What is peculiar here and needs somehow to be accounted for is why at this particular moment in Chinese history there was such an extreme response to the foreign presence. Chinese had often shown a tendency, during times of military or cultural threat, to lapse into a form of racial thinking that categorized outsiders as fundamentally different and called for their expulsion, and this tendency had been greatly magnified in the nineteenth century with the appearance of "physically discontinuous" Westerners, who also happened to be carriers of a symbolic universe that diverged radically from the Chinese and, directly and indirectly, challenged the validity of the Chinese cultural world.[89] From the early 1800s, people who had had contacts of any sort with Westerners were regularly referred to as "Chinese traitors" (*Hanjian*).[90] More specifically, there had been efforts prior to the Boxer era to link natural disasters (as well as the fail-

90   ure of Chinese prayers to relieve them) with the presence of Christians.[91] And of course there had been no end of anti-Christian and antiforeign incidents in China in the decades leading up to 1900. Never before, however, had there been a movement like the Boxers, uncompromisingly dedicated to the stamping out of foreign influence and backed, all the evidence indicates, by the broadest popular support. How do we explain this?

The reasons are without doubt very complex. Chinese historians, insisting upon the "anti-imperialist and patriotic" (*fandi aiguo*) character of the Boxer movement, tend to assign primary responsibility to the intensification of foreign imperialism in the last years of the nineteenth century.[92] My own view is that the vocabulary of anti-imperialism is so deeply colored by twentieth-century Chinese political concerns and agendas that it gets in the way of the search for a more accurate, credible reading of the Boxer experience. This is not to deny that imperialism was a fact of life in China at the turn of the century or that it formed an important part of the setting within which the Boxer movement unfolded. It was only one causal agency among several, however, and its gravity relative to other causal forces varied considerably from place to place and over time. Furthermore, action taken against the more tangible reflections of imperialism—missionaries and Chinese Christians, railways, telegraphs, foreign armies, and the rest—could, when it occurred, derive from a range of possible motives; it need not have been inspired by either "patriotism" or "anti-imperialism." To superimpose this vocabulary on the Boxer movement, therefore, is to risk radical oversimplification of the complicated and diverse motives impelling the Boxers to behave as they did.

There are really two problems here, although they are easily conflated. One, just alluded to, is the problem of oversimplification, the assignment (sometimes explicitly, sometimes implicitly) of a dominant or even uniform set of motives to the participants in events, even when the evidence is fairly strong that their motives were not in fact unitary at all. It is reasonable to suppose that some Boxer behavior may, indeed, have been actuated by patriotic or anti-imperialist impulses. But it also makes sense, as we have seen in the preceding pages, to interpret Boxer actions as having, possibly to a quite considerable degree, been the product of a religious construction of the world in which foreigners—outsiders—were seen as holding the key to the cosmic disturbances that were troubling and frightening Chinese in 1899–1900. And finally, no different from the participants in other major historical events, the Boxers and their immediate antecedents sometimes acted—and there is ample evidence to support this—from motives that were notably idiosyncratic, self-serving, highly personal, even trivial in character, flinging mud in the faces of historians intent upon finding important and compelling meaning in the events of the past.[93]

Figuring out which kind of motive was uppermost in the minds of Boxers in any given instance is no mean task. The task is made vastly more difficult by a second problem, which I will call the impenetrability of experience. Experience is sometimes thought of as the basic empirical data of the past, which it is the historian's job to interpret and explain. What is left out of this formulation is the degree to which experience itself incorporates interpretation, before the historian ever gets to it. People are not the passive recipients of the experience they undergo. They engage, rather, in an active process of structuring and ordering, assigning to their experience meaning that, in turn, is conditioned by relevant prior experience, the cultural framework within which they function, their emotional state and individual psychic (as well as physical) needs at the moment, and so on. As if this subjective, often highly ambiguous, quality of experience were not enough of a problem for historians, we are also faced, very often, with a situation in which the immediate experiencer of the past remains mute or articulates what a particular experience was like, what it meant, only after a considerable period of time has elapsed, at which point the articulation is likely to be subject to new environmental forces (not to mention memory loss) that significantly alter the experience's original meaning.

Thus, to cite again the example of the Salem witchcraft outbreak of 1692, although the adult inhabitants of Salem Village eventually decided that the bizarre actions of their children were a consequence of witchcraft, "nobody knew then, or knows now," in the judgment of Boyer and Nissenbaum, "precisely what it was the girls were experiencing. They never told; perhaps they did not know themselves."[94] Another example may be drawn from the behavior of millions of Chinese farmers who, during the Sino-Japanese War of 1937–1945, became supporters of the Communist Party. In an influential book published in 1962, Chalmers Johnson argued that the main reason for this was Communist identification with (and exploitation of) the political force of nationalism, which the Japanese invasion—and in particular the brutality of Japanese "mopping up" campaigns in the countryside—had aroused among the Chinese peasantry. Other scholars, however, have been sharply critical of the "Johnson thesis," insisting that, at least in certain parts of China, factors such as social and economic reforms or the organizational strength of the CCP were more important in generating peasant backing. There have been attempts to resolve this controversy by pointing out that different factors were more critical in different places and at different times. A major problem with the whole debate, however,

92   has been that the subjects whose behavior is under scrutiny, the Chinese
peasantry, have from the outset been largely voiceless.[95]

The Boxers present a closely analogous problem. We have hundreds of
samples of Boxer writing—handbills, wall notices, charms, slogans, jingles,
and the like. And even though most if not all of these may be assumed to
have been composed by Boxer leaders or elite Chinese sympathetic to the
Boxer cause rather than by rank-and-file participants in the movement,
there is, as argued earlier, little doubt that they incorporate values and
beliefs widely shared among the Boxers in general, not to mention millions
of Chinese who witnessed and often supported, but were not directly
engaged in, the activities of the Boxer movement. Still, as crucially important as these materials are in establishing the mindset of the Boxers, they
fall well short of supplying the kind of intimate tracking of experience that
we get, say, from the memoir literature of participants in the Cultural
Revolution or the heresy trial testimony of the sixteenth-century Italian
miller Menocchio or the letters, journals, and even poems composed by
British soldiers in the trenches in World War I.[96] In fact, it was not until
after 1949 that elderly survivors of the Boxer uprising, mainly in western
Shandong and Tianjin and other parts of Hebei (Zhili) province, were
finally given a chance to describe more or less in their own words their
experiences at the turn of the century. As useful as these oral history materials can sometimes be, however, their value is circumscribed by the
advanced age of the respondents, the remoteness in time of the events
under discussion, the political and ideological constraints built into the
environment within which the interviewing was conducted, the specific
questions the interviewers posed, and the editorial process by which the
resulting responses were structured.[97]

Consequently, in attempting to get at the range of motives that impelled
the Boxers to attack foreigners, foreign-made objects, and foreign-influenced Chinese, we are regularly faced with the necessity of inferring these
motives from Boxer actions, of reading back, as it were, from behavior to
intent. This is one of the more dangerous kinds of business in which historians must unfortunately all too often engage, as it presents us with an
open invitation to discern in the experience of the past the values, thought
patterns, and psychological orientations that make the greatest sense to us
in our own day.

Although on a macrohistorical level we hear much of the intensification of foreign imperialism that took place in China in the years following
the Sino-Japanese War of 1894, it is arguable that, unlike drought, a conspicuously growing foreign presence was not, in 1899–1900, the common

experience of the vast majority of Chinese inhabiting the North China plain. Whether we train our sights on expanded communities of native Christians or the growth in strength of the Catholic and Protestant missionary bodies or the construction of railways and telegraphs or the intrusion of foreign armies, the experience of direct confrontation with the foreign or foreign-influenced remained, for those living away from large urban centers, a sporadic and highly localized one in these years. Despite a substantial increase in the numbers of Protestant and Catholic converts in China as a whole in the 1890s — from approximately 37,000 Protestants in 1889 to 85,000 in 1900,[98] and from about 500,000 to over 700,000 Catholics between 1890 and 1900[99] — there were still, in 1899–1900, large stretches of North China that had Christian communities of negligible size or none at all. Similarly, in the case of both the Catholic and Protestant missionary efforts in the empire, although impressive growth occurred in the last decade of the century,[100] this growth was far more in evidence in certain areas — the greatly expanded Catholic presence in southern Shandong, for example[101] — than in others. Again, as of 1899–1900, the only railway lines that had been completed in North China were the Beijing-Baoding line, the Beijing-Tianjin line, and the line extending northeastward from Tianjin, through Tangshan, into Manchuria.[102] And, leaving out the military activities of the Russians in Manchuria, foreign troop movements in the Boxer summer were largely confined to Tianjin and Beijing, their immediately surrounding areas, and the corridor connecting these two cities (although in the months following the lifting of the siege of the legations, as we have seen, punitive expeditions were carried out in other parts of Zhili and in eastern Shanxi).

In other words, despite an overall expansion in the opportunities for direct contact with foreigners, foreign-influenced Chinese, and foreign technology in the last years of the century, these opportunities were not evenly distributed throughout North China. Furthermore, there is the curious circumstance — curious, at least, if one interprets the behavior of the Boxers as having been guided in significant measure by anti-imperialist impulses — that the areas where the impact of imperialism was greatest often did not coincide with those areas in which the Boxers were most active. This was especially true in Shandong, where the arenas of greatest foreign economic activity — the eastern and southern coasts — were conspicuously free of Boxer involvement and where approximately half of the missionized areas also were left untouched by the Boxers.[103] Mark Elvin, who includes southern Zhili as well as Shandong within his purview, is so struck by the weakness of the link between "Boxerism and the religious and

94 foreign irritant usually supposed to have caused it" that he questions whether it can serve as "a convincing sufficient explanation" of the movement's origins.[104]

I am not particularly concerned here with the origins of the Boxer movement. I do, however, believe that there is room for a fresh understanding of the range of motives that lay behind what was perhaps the Boxers' most distinctive and defining characteristic: their antiforeignism. The reality of Boxer antiforeignism — and the antiforeignism of many millions of Boxer supporters and sympathizers — is not at issue. What is at issue is the underlying meaning of this antiforeignism. Was it a reflection of simple hatred of foreigners owing to their foreignness? Or did it result from anger over specific foreign actions? Or did it spring from fear and anxiety and the need for a credible explanation for the problems — above all, drought — occasioning this fear and anxiety?

My own view is that antiforeignism, in the sense of fear and hatred of outsiders, was there all along in China in latent form, but that it needed some disturbance in the external environment, a rearrangement of the overall balance of forces within a community or a geographical area, to become activated. Chinese antiforeignism thus functioned in much the same way as fear of witchcraft in late seventeenth-century Salem or anti-Semitism in 1930s Germany. In each of these instances outsiders — Westerners in China, people accused of being witches in Salem,[105] Jews in Germany — lived more or less uneventfully within their respective communities when times were "normal." But when something happened to create an "abnormal" situation — economic insecurity in Germany, apprehension concerning the enormous economic and social forces transforming New England in the late 1600s, anxiety over drought in turn-of-the-century North China — and people sought in desperation to address their grievances and allay their insecurities, outsiders became especially vulnerable.

The specific circumstances favoring outbreaks of antiforeignism in North China in 1899–1900 varied from place to place. In Shandong, escalating Boxer anti-Christian activity in late 1899 resulted (under foreign pressure) in the replacement as governor of Yuxian, who had followed a policy of leniency toward the Boxers, with Yuan Shikai, who, after the killing of the British missionary S. M. Brooks on December 31, pursued an increasingly strong policy of suppression. In Zhili province, especially in the Beijing and Tianjin areas and the corridor connecting the two, there was a relatively high level of exposure to the full range of foreign influences and, from the winter of 1899–1900, to rapidly growing numbers of Boxers.

In Shanxi, where there were no significant manifestations of foreign influence apart from the missionaries and native Christians, there was a governor (Yuxian having been transferred there in March) who was deeply antiforeign and pro-Boxer.

Although the precise mix of factors was thus variable, the drought was shared in common throughout the North China plain. It was this factor, more than any other, in my judgment, that accounted for the explosive growth both of the Boxer movement and of popular support for it in the spring and summer months of 1900. Missionary reports and oral history accounts occasionally used the term "famine" to describe conditions in North China at the time.[106] This was, for the most part, a loose usage; severe famine did not appear until the early months of 1901, mainly in Shanxi and Shaanxi.[107] The evidence is overwhelming, on the other hand, that *fear* of famine, with all its attendant bewilderment and terror, was extremely widespread. As has often been the case in other agricultural societies, moreover, the uncertainty, anxiety, and increasingly serious food deprivation accompanying the Chinese drought—the *delírio de fome* or "madness of hunger," in the arresting formulation of Nancy Scheper-Hughes[108]—seem to have inclined people to be receptive to extreme explanations and to act in extreme ways.[109] The year 1900 was not a normal one in China. The menace of inopportune death was everywhere. And, as can be seen in the periodic eruptions of mass hysteria and the apparent readiness of many members of society to give credence to the most spectacular religious and magical claims of the Boxers, there was a strong disposition on the part of the population to depart from normal patterns of behavior.

CHAPTER 3

Mass Spirit Possession

When we took up Spirit Boxing [Shenquan], we were first told . . . to write down on a piece of red paper our names, home villages, and how many we were. The six of us then kneeled down and burned incense; we didn't burn white paper. We requested teachers. I requested Sun Bin.[a] They requested Liu Bei, Zhang Fei,[b] and such people. We requested the gods to attach themselves to our bodies [qiushen futi]. When they had done so, we became Spirit Boxers, after which we were invulnerable to swords and spears, our courage was enhanced, and in fighting we were unafraid to die and dared to charge straight ahead. This is how it was when the six of us became Spirit Boxers.

Xie Jiagui, former Boxer, Chiping county, Shandong

It is reported that when they practice boxing they assemble several untutored boys who stand facing the southeast. The teacher pulls the right ear of each youngster with his hand and has him recite a charm three times. The charm goes as follows: "I beseech the Holy Mother of the West Emituofo [Amitabha]." When they've completed the charm the boys fall to the ground on their backs and almost stop breathing. After a brief interval [the teacher] makes them get up and dance or he gives them sticks to serve as swords and they pair off and fight, as if engaging an adversary. They really behave as if they are drunk or in a dream state. After a long while the teacher strikes each boy's upper garment with his hand and calls out his real name. Thereupon the lads suddenly return to their senses and stand erect like wooden chickens. They have no recollection of the boxing techniques [they've just used]. It's as if they are completely different people from the ones fighting a few moments earlier.

Sawara Tokusuke, Japanese resident, North China

On that day [May 27, 1900], after arriving in Xiong county [in Baoding prefecture, Zhili], the members of my family went to have a look at the boxing

---

[a] A one-legged warrior of the Warring States period (403–221 B.C.).
[b] Liu Bei was a political leader, Zhang Fei, a general, during the Three Kingdoms period (third century A.D.). Both were also characters in the *Romance of the Three Kingdoms*.

ground at the temple. They were told that boys ten or so years of age, after practicing there for seven or eight days, became invulnerable to swords. I certainly didn't believe this. But on the first day of the fifth month [May 28], as we passed through the village of Gaoqiao, the driver said that there was a boxing ground at the temple there. So I got down from the cart to go see. I saw that the people there were all young lads of thirteen or fourteen, the youngest of them no older than eight. On an altar there were three tablets arranged, one in honor of Guansheng,[c] another in honor of Huanhou [the posthumous title of Zhang Fei], and a third in honor of Zhao Zilong.[d] After paying their respects to these gods, the boys positioned themselves solemnly on either side of the altar. Suddenly . . . their faces turned red and they stared straight ahead. Frothing at the mouths, they began to shout and laugh and strike blows with their fists and feet. Even those who were only seven or eight years of age leaped several feet into the air. They moved forward and retreated, got up and lay down, turned to the front or to the rear in unison, as if directed by a single person. Some of the local elders, seeing that I had come to look, asked whether we had anything like this in the south. I asked them: "Who teaches the boxing?" In reply they said: "There is no boxing instructor at all. Only gods who attach themselves to the boys' bodies, after which the latter are able to do the [boxing] exercises. It is called Spirit Boxing [Shenquan]. After eighteen days of practice, they achieve mastery."

Local official, Zhili

The method of the Boxers is as follows: They write an incantation on a piece of paper. After rinsing their mouths [for ritual purification] and chanting the incantation they suddenly fall to the ground. After a short while they get up and begin to dance in a frenzied manner and talk as if in their sleep. Then they either state that Guandi has descended [xiajiang] or that Kongming[e] has attached himself to their bodies [fushen].

Anze county (Shanxi) gazetteer

From the time of the arrival of the Senior Brother-Disciple [da shixiong] in Taiyuan, the numbers of Boxers in the streets of the city grew. They practiced their boxing in small groups on the streets. One time as I was going from Willow Lane to Xixiao Wall I saw a youngster of fifteen or sixteen going

---

[c] Also known as Guandi or Guangong, the God of War. By late Qing times, Guansheng had become possibly the most popular god in the northern Chinese pantheon. He was the deified version of the historical figure, Guan Yu, a famous general of the Three Kingdoms period. Guan Yu also was a character in the *Romance of the Three Kingdoms*.
[d] The courtesy name of Zhao Yun, a famous general of the Three Kingdoms period, also a character in the *Romance of the Three Kingdoms*.
[e] The courtesy name of the Three Kingdoms prime minister Zhuge Liang, who also was a character in the *Romance of the Three Kingdoms*.

98   through his boxing drills. Facing toward the southeast he performed the
          koutou and chanted Tangseng, Shaseng, [Zhu] Bajie, [Sun] Wukong,[f] and
          the like. After this he fell to the ground, scrambled to his feet, and then with
          greatly increased energy practiced the martial arts.

                                              Jia Xianju, resident of Taiyuan

The foregoing accounts,[1] the first from Shandong, the next two from Zhili,
the last two from Shanxi, describe in different ways and with different
details the core religious experience of the Boxers as they spread across the
North China plain in the spring and summer of 1900. Whether one
chooses to construe the Boxers as "a religious uprising" with antiforeign
aims (the position taken many years ago by Jerome Ch'en)[2] or as an antiforeign (or anti-imperialist) movement that expressed itself in religious terms
(the stand of many Chinese historians),[3] there is no disputing the fact that
the world the Boxers inhabited was one saturated through and through
with religious and magical beliefs and practices. The Boxers counted on
these beliefs and practices for protection in an environment fraught with
danger; they also used them as their main cognitive apparatus for understanding and explaining—to themselves and to others—what transpired in
this environment (see chapter 4).

The Spirit Possession of the Boxers

Central among the religious practices of the Boxers was spirit possession,
which by the summer of 1900 appears to have become virtually ubiquitous within the movement. The phrase most often used in the sources to
denote "spirit possession"—*jiangshen futi*—refers to a process whereby a
god descends and enters (literally, "attaches itself to") the body of a Boxer.
The possession ritual varied widely. The individual seeking to be possessed by a god might face southeast[4] or recite a charm or perform the
koutou or burn incense or engage in some combination of these and
other actions. Generally the god would be "requested" (*qiu*) or "invited"
(*qing*) by name to attach itself to the person's body. Once it had done this,
the Boxer entered an altered state of consciousness, accompanied by
behavioral changes (similar to those attending spirit possession in other
cultures where it occurs)[5] and often greatly enhanced physical prowess.

---

[f] Tangseng was the Tang-dynasty monk Xuanzang; Zhu Bajie and Sun Wukong were two
of his disciples. Along with Shaseng, they figured centrally in the novel *Journey to the
West*, Tangseng as the "Tang monk" (or "Tripitaka"), Shaseng as "Sha Monk," Zhu Bajie
as "Bajie," and Sun Wukong as the "Monkey King" (or "Monkey").

This change in state was sometimes referred to as *shangfa* or "entering into the magic."

Boxer possession rituals were generally conducted in the open for all to see. Guan He, an astute (albeit unfriendly) eyewitness chronicler of the movement in Tianjin, described the range of different behaviors possessed Boxers in that city manifested:

> There are those who move slowly with their eyes closed and those who stare straight ahead and walk forward with erect bearing. There are cases in which a few people hold one person up and cases in which a person supported by two other persons staggers like one who has had too much to drink. In some instances, holding a sword, they dance about wildly, and pedestrians don't have time to get out of the way. In other instances several of them, clutching weapons, walk in single file. Sometimes, mounted on horses, they provide people with protection and guidance. Sometimes they place those who have been wounded or are already dead on their shoulders and take them home. There are even cases in which a bandit [i.e., a Boxer] will hold a stick embellished on the top with a bloody object which he claims is the heart and liver of a foreigner. Coming or going, they are unaware of what they are doing. Confused, disoriented, they don't seem like normal people.[6]

Guan He, in addition to supplying interesting detail on the external appearance and behavior of possessed Boxers, also exemplifies a problem we face in attempting to probe the Boxers' religious world. We have a fair amount of data relating to this world. But, apart from the occasional oral testimony of former Boxers recorded a half century or more after the original experience, almost all of our information has been filtered through the minds of hostile (or at best unempathetic) outsiders: contemporary native and foreign observers, in the first instance, and more recently Chinese and foreign scholarly analysts. How confident can we be that such information is reasonably free of distortion?

Quite confident, I believe. For one thing, the oral history testimony, mainly from northwestern Shandong and the Tianjin area, while of perhaps questionable utility when it presents information that is fully consistent with the ideological mindset of the Communist historians soliciting it (graphic depictions, for example, of the outrageous behavior of foreign missionaries and Chinese Christians), may be assumed to be somewhat more reliable when it describes Boxer practices (such as spirit possession) that fly in the face of Communist values and beliefs. One example, from Shandong, appears at the head of this chapter. Another comes from a former Boxer from the Tianjin area, who was captain of a rifle unit under the command of Liu Shijiu (Nineteen Liu). This man described the

100   harangues Liu would deliver to his Boxer troops before they entered combat: "When you've reached the field of battle," he shouted, "as soon as the gods have entered your bodies you'll go up to heaven, and the devils [foreigners] will have no way to attack you."[7]

For another thing, there is a remarkable degree of consistency in the contemporary Chinese and foreign accounts of Boxer religio-magical beliefs and practices, despite the fact that these accounts were produced independently in different geographical locations. It seems reasonable to suppose, therefore, that the Boxers' behavior as well as verbal claims are reflected in these accounts more or less faithfully, especially when (as is not infrequently the case) confirmation is found in the oral history testimony of the Boxers themselves. Again, in the half century since World War II, there has been a great deal of scholarly interest in Chinese popular religion, especially among Western anthropologists and historians, and although much of this interest, at least initially, focused on the southern rim of the Chinese culture area, there appears to be a substantial correspondence between certain popular religious beliefs in the South and those attributed to the Boxers in North China. Finally, there is a considerable scholarly literature pertaining to spirit possession in other parts of the world, and the parallels in this literature to aspects of Boxer religious experience are often quite illuminating.

Boxer Religion and Chinese Popular Culture

The last two factors, by diminishing the otherness of Boxer religious behavior with respect, in the first instance, to China and, in the second, to broader human norms, take us a long way toward the demystification of this behavior. Certainly, in the context of prior Chinese experience, the Boxers were not nearly so unique as Westerners—and perhaps, in more recent times, many Chinese as well—have imagined. Whether one focuses on the Boxers' martial arts activities—their "boxing"—or their invulnerability claims or their attraction to the heroes of Chinese popular literature and theater (opera) or their spirit possession rituals—all prime contributors to Boxer exceptionalism in the minds of Westerners—an examination of Chinese popular culture discloses an abundance of comparable phenomena, not only in the Boxer homeland in the North but also in South China, and not only prior to the Boxer uprising but right up to the present day.

A few examples relating to invulnerability rituals may be cited to illustrate the point. In the Wang Lun rebellion of 1774 in Shandong, the insurgents used a variety of magical techniques, including spells, a group of women warriors waving white fans, and the chant "guns will not fire," to avoid injury.[8] The members of the Qinglianjiao (Azure Lotus Sect), which was active in South China during the Daoguang reign (1821–1850), had a tradition of Spirit Boxing, used charm water (*fushui*) to spread their teachings, and, once possessed by the gods, acquired a range of martial arts skills that (they claimed) made them unafraid of firearms (*bu wei qiangpao*).[9] Among the participants in an armed tax revolt in the southern Hunan county of Leiyang in 1843 was a monk who was able "to stop up the muzzles of guns" with incantations.[10] The Armor of the Golden Bell (Jinzhongzhao), which began to be used in the mid-Qing and was based on a mix of "hard" (*ying*) *qigong*, secret formulas, and charms, was (as pointed out in chapter 1) the basis for the fighting methods and invulnerability rituals of the Big Sword precursors of the Boxers in southwestern Shandong in the 1890s.

A similar mix of *qigong*, training in self-defense, religious rituals and magical techniques, and invulnerability claims has also frequently been encountered in the twentieth century. In southern Zhejiang in the mid-1930s the main adversaries of Communist guerrilla bands were Big Swords, who fought with double-edged swords and red-tasseled spears and before battle swallowed magic pills made of herbs, cinnabar, and the ashes of paper slips on which incantations had been written. The pills were believed to confer invulnerability to bullets, but their efficacy could be countered either by bamboo pitchforks or dirty cloth.[11] During the same years, in eastern Fujian, Big Swords fought in a state of trance induced by magic potions, charms, and incantations; their sense of invulnerability wore off if they either tripped or came into contact with water.[12] The Red Spears, active in North China during much of the first half of the twentieth century, made extensive use of a variety of invulnerability rituals, including spirit possession.[13] The members of the Tieguanzhao (Armor of the Iron Gate), an offshoot of the Red Spears composed of unmarried women, believed that if, on the field of battle, they recited a magic formula, enemy bullets would fall harmlessly into the baskets they held in their hands.[14] Another group of women affiliated with the Red Spears, variously known as the Lanzihui (Basket Society) or Hualanhui (Flower Basket Society), dressed in white and, carrying a basket in one hand and fan in the other, were able by waving the fans to cause bullets to drop into their baskets.[15] Invulnerability to bullets was claimed for the virtuous among members of the Xiantiandao, a sect organized for community self-defense against banditry in Shunyi county (north of Beijing) in the late 1930s.[16] Similar claims were made by some *qigong* masters in the 1980s and early 1990s.[17]

102   Some of the conclusions derived from the serious study of Chinese popular culture in the postwar decades are relevant to our understanding of the
embeddedness of Boxer religious experience in this culture. One such
conclusion is that, at the village level, the sharp boundaries between the
"secular" and the "sacred," to which modern Westerners are accustomed,
simply did not exist. The gods of popular religion were everywhere and
"ordinary people were in constant contact" with them.[18] These gods were
powerful (some, to be sure, more than others), but they were also very close
and accessible. People depended on them for protection and assistance in
time of need. But when they failed to perform their responsibilities ade-
quately, ordinary human beings could request that they be punished by
their superiors.[19] Or they could punish them themselves. "If the god does
not show signs of appreciation of the need of rain," Arthur Smith wrote
toward the end of the nineteenth century, "he may be taken out into the
hot sun and left there to broil, as a hint to wake up and do his duty."[20] This
"everydayness" of the gods of Chinese popular religion and the casual,
matter-of-fact attitude Chinese typically displayed toward their deities
doubtless contributed to the widespread view among Westerners both in
the late imperial period and after that the Chinese were not an especially
religious people. It would be more accurate, I believe, to describe the fabric of Chinese social and cultural life as being permeated through and
through with religious beliefs and practices.[21]

But not always with the same degree of intensity and certainly not with
equal discernibleness in all settings. This is another facet of Chinese popular religion that, because it does not entirely square with the expectations
of Western observers, has occasioned a certain amount of confusion and
perplexity. Sometimes religion appears to recede into the shadows and to
be largely, if not altogether, absent from individual Chinese consciousness.
But at other times it exercises dominion over virtually everything in sight.
Thus, the martial arts, healing practices, and the heroes of popular literature and opera often inhabit a space in Chinese culture that seems unambiguously "secular." But it is not at all unusual, as clearly suggested in the
accounts of Boxer spirit possession transcribed at the beginning of this
chapter, for these selfsame phenomena to be incorporated into a fully religious framework of meaning.

Although this may, at first glance, seem puzzling, it ought not to be. In
China, as elsewhere, when life is more or less problem-free, either on an
individual or a collective level, religious belief tends to find less overt
expression. But when personal problems (such as infertility or family illness or a failing business) arise or a communal or societal crisis (such as

natural disaster or foreign invasion or, on a more abstract level, a growing sense of national cynicism and alienation) materializes, people are more apt to have recourse to a range of options of a religious nature. These options are always there in a dormant state, and belief in their efficacy, although by no means universal, appears to be widespread.

Spirit Possession and Spirit Mediumship

The two different types of crisis just referred to, individual and collective, have elicited different forms of spirit possession in response. When faced with personal crises, individual Chinese in all parts of the country have for centuries sought out the services of spirit mediums (often referred to in Taiwan, Singapore, and Hong Kong by the Hokkien term *tâng-ki*).[22] These people, when in the possessed state, serve as intermediaries between ordinary human beings and the supernatural. They heal the sick, exorcise evil spirits, predict the future, mediate interpersonal conflicts, enable barren women to become pregnant. Mediums in the Canton area, as described by Jack Potter, also have the power in certain circumstances to command the services of "spirit soldiers," who are able to perform such tasks as recovering the souls of children that a hungry ghost has kidnaped for ransom.[23] Although mediums perform a range of different services and spirit mediumship has assumed different forms in different parts of the Chinese culture area,[24] in general the accent is on *communication* between the supernatural and human worlds.[25] Spirit mediumship is a "helping profession," and the individual spirit medium, by virtue of his or her training and aptitude, is not infrequently seen as performing a protective function on behalf of the local community, safeguarding the community against the whole array of dangerous and malevolent forces to which ordinary people are subject.[26]

Although the physical symptoms accompanying trance, as experienced by the Boxers, seem very much like those presented by Chinese spirit mediums,[27] suggesting a common neurophysiological basis, the sociocultural meaning of Boxer spirit possession was fundamentally different. Prior to the winter of 1898–99, it is true, the Spirit Boxers were much concerned with healing the sick, especially after the disastrous flooding of the Yellow River that took place in August and September 1898. Also, even after this date, as the purpose of Boxer possession shifted increasingly to invulnerability (as a consequence of the rising levels of violence between Boxers and Christians), possession trance continued to be seen as serving a protective function with regard to the community. In other respects, however, Boxer

104   possession functioned in very different ways from the possession accompanying Chinese spirit mediumship. For one thing, even before the winter of 1898–99, possession among the Spirit Boxers was a *mass*, not an individual, phenomenon. And, for another, although the Boxers in their placards and public notices and on their flags frequently referred to their role as protectors of the Qing dynasty or of China,[28] one senses very strongly that, on a personal level, the overwhelming object of Boxer invulnerability rituals was less community protection than *self*-protection.

    Erika Bourguignon, looking at possession trance globally, distinguishes between societies, such as Palau (in the western Pacific), in which possession trance plays a predominantly *public* role, serving the needs of the community, and societies—the Shakers of St. Vincent in the West Indies or the Maya Apostolics of Yucatán—in which the function of trance is a mainly *private* one, focusing on its importance for the individual, "who believes himself 'saved' as a result of the experience and . . . derives euphoria and personal strength from it."[29] Bourguignon sees these ideal-typical functions of trance, the public and the private, as endpoints of a continuum and she recognizes that, in some societies, possession appears to serve both roles simultaneously. Certainly this was the case with the Boxers. In fact it would not be wide of the mark to argue that the broad range of individual (private) needs spirit possession satisfied within the context of the Boxer movement (the precise mix varying from one Boxer to another) constituted a major reason for the ease with which Boxer possession developed into a mass (public) phenomenon in the last years of the nineteenth century. Self-preservation, in an immediate sense, and national preservation, on a more abstract level, were mutually reinforcing.

Spirit Possession, Theater, and Personal Empowerment

The appeal of spirit possession and its rapid spread, first among the Spirit Boxers in northwestern Shandong and increasingly, after the winter of 1899–1900, among Boxer groups in Zhili, Manchuria, Shanxi, and elsewhere, was clearly related to the intensified sense of crisis that swept over the North China plain at this time, the result in part of worsening relations in certain locales between Christians and non-Christians, in part of the growing visibility of Boxers (and boxing) in villages, cities, and on major thoroughfares across the region, and in part of mounting anxiety and suffering throughout the North China countryside owing to drought.

    A major attraction of spirit possession to prospective Boxers was that it dramatically enhanced the power of individuals who, socially, were at or near the bottom of the scale, biologically, were often in a weakened condition as a result of prolonged drought, and, militarily, stood at a generally primitive stage in terms of training and weaponry. On the most obvious level, the empowerment resulting from possession took the form of improved fighting skills and invulnerability to sword and bullet. Less obvious, but no less crucial, the exercise of divinely assisted Boxer military power against foreigners and the manifestations of foreign influence was, as we saw in chapter 2, widely believed to be the most effective means of addressing the problem of drought. Least obvious, but perhaps most crucial, spirit possession was immensely empowering psychologically. Robert Weller, who has studied the mass possession movement that took place in Guangxi on the eve of the Taiping uprising and personally witnessed the collective possession experience of members of the Religion of Compassion (Cihuitang) on Taiwan, argues persuasively for "the emotional and aesthetic power of trance performances." Other forms of communication with the gods, Weller writes, pale before the "thrill of the arrival of extraordinary beings" that takes place when the spirit speaks through the mouth of a possessed person.[30]

Again we see here the intimate relationship between the individual and the collective sides of spirit possession. Weller's main emphasis is on the role that trance plays in attracting followers to possession-centered religious movements—the powerful appeal of "the visible ability of the gods to transform human personality."[31] But it is clear that the underlying basis of the appeal is the witness's recognition that he or she, too, can experience this form of empowerment.

Crucial to Weller's argument is the premise that spirit possession makes good theater. "No one," he assures us, "sleeps through the service when possessed Holy Ghost people in the West Virginia mountains begin to pass rattlesnakes around."[32] Examples from other cultures confirm this. Robin Horton witnessed a complex "war-game" enacted by Kalabari (West Africa) in the context of possession, which featured changing drum rhythms, convulsive shaking, wild (and potentially dangerous) swordplay, and dancing. "After the final bout of swordplay, the drummers work up to a climax and the spirit rushes headlong into the cult-house. In a few minutes the priest emerges, dressed once more in his everyday clothes, no longer possessed, and looking exhausted." "Every move of the game," according to Horton, "is followed with delight by the spectators."[33] John Beattie and John Middleton, on the basis of a wide range of other data, emphasize the "dramatic quality" of much African possession ritual, which they feel provides "lively entertainment," "a means of catharsis," and a therapeutic "relief of anxiety."[34]

106   The situation in China is not dissimilar. In a discussion of "the *tâng-ki* as spectacle," David Jordan reports that, in the late Qing, Taiwanese *tâng-ki*, called from one village to another to perform, were said to have been carried in sedan chairs in stately procession along country roads, accompanied by banners and large drums; he also describes the physical abuse possessed *tâng-ki* in late twentieth-century Taiwan inflict on themselves in the context of religious processions and the overall atmosphere of fun and excitement that characterizes the mood of those watching such performances.[35] Jordan makes the additional point, not unrelated to Boxer possession experience, that the rapid healing of wounds resulting from *tâng-ki* self-mortification is interpreted by onlookers as an indication of "the miraculous nature of the performance."[36] Along similar lines, Margery Wolf observes that the purpose of lying on a bed of nails or lacerating the body with swords or a prickball "is not to subjugate the flesh as in early Christian ritual, but to prove that the gods do not allow their vehicles to feel pain from these injuries and will protect their *tang-ki* from permanent damage."[37]

The relationship between Boxer spirit possession and theatrical performance was, if anything, even more complex than the above-noted examples, providing a splendid illustration of David Johnson's observation that "the distinction between entertainment and religion" so natural to Westerners "did not seem that obvious to most Chinese."[38] Certainly, possessed Boxers, with their strange physical behavior and often high levels of martial arts accomplishment, put on a good show for the crowds of people who gathered to watch them. But, beyond this, the cultural language in which Boxer possession was expressed, its cultural patterning,[39] showed the deep imprint of Chinese popular theater. The locations of altars and boxing grounds at which possession rituals were commonly enacted were, as often as not, the very same places—the open spaces in front of temples— at which village theatrical performances were staged, in conjunction (usually) with religious festivals and fairs.[40] The gods by whom Boxers were most frequently possessed—Guandi, Monkey (Sun Wukong), Zhang Fei, Zhao Yun, Zhu Bajie, and the like—were the heroes of such works of popular fiction as the *Romance of the Three Kingdoms* (*Sanguo yanyi*), *Journey to the West* (*Xiyouji*), and *Enfeoffment of the Gods* (*Fengshen yanyi*), which in turn were the main sources of material for the itinerant storytellers, puppet shows, and village operas familiar to all inhabitants of the northern Chinese countryside. The stylized swordplay of popular theatrical performances was virtually indistinguishable from the swordplay of possessed Boxers. Even the latter's speech, a contemporary tells us, was "like the declamatory delivery of opera actors on stage."[41] Small wonder that, in the

early years of the twentieth century, Chinese intellectuals hostile to the
Boxers identified popular opera as a crucial factor in both the origins and
eventual defeat of the movement.[42]

The Martial Patterning of Boxer Possession Ritual

The fighting techniques the Boxers learned (at least in part) from the combat scenes in village opera performances may well have served them poorly in real combat.[43] But the powerful gods into whom possessed Boxers were transformed were an enormous source of psychic strength. As in other parts of China, and, indeed, other cultures in which possession takes a prominent part, the possessed Boxer underwent a true change in personality and status, becoming emancipated from an existence that was in all respects miserable and identified, however temporarily, with the "rich and powerful figures of legend and history."[44]

3.1   Boxer/Performer. This stylized rendering of Liu Shijiu, a Boxer leader in the Tianjin area, conveys nicely the theatrical dimension many observers saw in the physical movements of Boxers. From *Jing-Jin quanfei jilüe*.

108   What is interesting is the degree to which, in this as in other respects, the possession experience of the Boxers was less distinctive, in the context of Chinese popular culture overall, than one might think. C. K. Yang observed long ago that the mythology and lore found in fictional literature were "an outstanding source of religious knowledge for the Chinese people."[45] A specific instance of this has been supplied by Wen-hui Tsai, whose researches reveal that, as of the 1970s, a sizable percentage of gods with historical backgrounds worshiped at temples in Taiwan were also heroes in the three popular novels, *Enfeoffment of the Gods*, *Romance of the Three Kingdoms*, and *Romance of the Sui-Tang* (*Sui-Tang yanyi*).[46] The first two of these, it will be recalled, were also important sources for the Boxer pantheon. Even more telling for our purposes, of the four gods most often invoked by spirit mediums in Singapore, two, Monkey and Guandi,[47] were equally favorites of possessed Boxers.

Aside from the apparent popularity of certain gods throughout China, partly as suggested above because of their links to works of historical fiction of universal appeal, like *Journey to the West* and the *Romance of the Three Kingdoms*, and partly as a result of the role of the state in late imperial times in promoting countrywide the worship of such gods as Guandi,[48] another characteristic of Boxer religious ritual that was less specific to the Boxer experience than one would suspect was its martial flavor. Although Guandi was possibly the most popular god in the Boxer pantheon,[49] it is not clear that this was because he was the God of War; Guandi may indeed have been worshiped with particular intensity in periods of armed conflict, but he happened also, in Duara's words, to be "probably the most popular god in the villages of North China" in general.[50] Conversely, it appears to be common in possession ritual in widely scattered parts of the Chinese culture area to appeal for the aid of "heavenly armies," "celestial generals," and "spirit soldiers" in countering problems that have no military bearing whatever. We have already seen one example of this in the case of a medium in the Canton region who called on spirit soldiers to recover the kidnaped souls of a client's children. The daggers that mediums in southern Fujian in the late nineteenth century thrust through their cheeks, upper arms, or shoulders were called "general's heads" (*junjiang tou*) and had hilts consisting of the head of a commander of the heavenly army; since the "celestial generals" these daggers represented were, according to de Groot, the most "powerful and dangerous enemies" of the whole range of evil and harmful influences, when implanted in the body of the medium they endowed him with all the terrors the celestial armies themselves inspired.[51]

Elliott cites other examples from his research in Singapore. A mid-twentieth-century Singapore medium's invocation to Sun Wukong (Monkey) stated in part: "We, your human followers, respectfully invite you. You can change into seventy-two different forms. We . . . beseech you to descend speedily, for we know that when the order is given the Heavenly Army will come to our aid as quickly as we hope." Another invocation, acquired from the same temple in Singapore and addressed to the Third Prince (San taizi),[g] stated: "All your generals are exercising their powers above the altar. They make sand fly, stones roll and caves open. Come quickly to cure our sickness and save us from misery. May 80,000 soldiers come riding down from Heaven. We, your followers, respectfully invite you."[52] In an unambiguously military context, Boxer notices, as we saw in chapter 2, also made frequent reference to 80,000 or 8 million spirit soldiers descending from Heaven to help the Boxers extirpate the foreign religion and drive all foreigners from China.[h] But it seems likely that such allusions to divine military assistance in the case of the Boxers represented less a completely new creation than an adaptation of an already militarized religious ritual to a historical setting in which *real* military help happened to be needed.

Popular Attitudes Toward Spirit Possession

An important question that is often raised in discussions of spirit possession is: Does possession *really* occur? Or is it only simulated? There are really two questions here, one having to do with what the person alleging to have been possessed believes, the other having to do with what is believed by the people watching possession behavior. There is no simple answer to these questions. Nor should it be assumed that the answer is the same for all cultures or for any one culture at all times. For example, genuine dissociation is reported among a number of West African peoples and the Alur of East Africa. But among other East African peoples the situation seems more ambiguous. A former Nyoro medium, acknowledging a measure of deception, stated: "I thought that all the same it would be good for the patient if I did what I was required to do." John Beattie, commenting on this admission, conjectured that the "religious ritual or drama" the woman per-

---

[g] The third son of a general who fought for the Zhou dynasty in the twelfth century B.C., the Third Prince was widely known in Daoist and Buddhist legend for his great strength and miraculous powers and was a celebrated hero in stories and on the stage.

[h] The number *eight*, viewed as auspicious in Chinese popular culture, is often found in Boxer writings.

110   formed might be "pleasing to the spirits and an effective means of influ-
encing them, even when it is recognized . . . to be a dramatic performance,
and not taken to be literally 'true.' "[53]

John Middleton, on the basis of his study of the Lugbara (also of East
Africa), went a step further, judging the distinction between "real" or "simulated" possession to be "a somewhat meaningless one": "Lugbara diviners
are putting on a dramatic performance of some skill, and this would seem
to be as important, if not more so, than [sic] being 'really' possessed. . . . in
Lugbara perhaps no possession is 'real' in any medical sense, yet is [sic] perfectly 'real' in the context of divination."[54]

In China we find a comparable spectrum of possibilities. Margery Wolf
has recounted an event that took place in 1960 in a northern Taiwanese village in which she was carrying on research. A woman in the village suddenly began to display symptoms of "mental illness, spirit loss, possession
by a god, and shamanism." The woman's fellow villagers, who witnessed
her aberrant behavior, were divided as to whether she had become men-
tally ill, her claims to being possessed only a pathological fantasy, or had
been truly possessed by a god. What is of interest about Wolf's account is
that the central issue faced by the villagers (at least most of them) was not
whether it was *possible* to be possessed by a spirit or a god, but whether possession was actually occurring *in this instance*.[55] Belief in the possibility of
possession appears to have been a given not only in Wolf's village in northern Taiwan but in many other parts of the Chinese culture area as well.[56]

Certainly this was the case in North China at the turn of the century.
Virtually all accounts of the lightning-quick spread of the Boxer movement, first, in the winter of 1899–1900, from Shandong into Zhili, and,
thereafter, from Zhili into Manchuria, Shanxi, and other areas, refer to the
broad acceptance among the common people of the entire range of Boxer
supernatural claims. A careful observer from Tianjin estimated that eight
out of ten people, including officials, believed that the Boxers were emissaries of the gods.[57] Another Chinese chronicler of the movement, from
just west of Tianjin, remarked on the astonishment of observers at the
"whirlwind" speed with which the Boxers spread through the cities and
towns of the entire region from late January 1900: "Youngsters only a few
years old performed the *koutou* and invited the gods [to possess them].
They had no proper teachers, but their boxing techniques and swordsmanship were as if the result of long training. Their activities spread instantaneously and in a completely spontaneous fashion over hundreds of
miles. It seemed a phenomenon incapable of being brought about by
human agency, only by the agency of Heaven."[58]

Among foreign witnesses, it was much the same. "Though professing to know nothing beyond the domain of sense," Robert Hart proclaimed in 1900, "the Chinaman is really an extravagant believer in the supernatural, and so he readily credits the Boxer with all the powers he claims."[59] One of the more astute missionary observers, Rowena Bird (ABCFM), wrote in July 1900 from Taigu, Shanxi: "One of the strongholds the Boxers have got here is through superstition — they teach their tactics first to young boys, and these boys take the lead in every desperate deed, and elder people stand in awe of them and believe that they have supernatural powers. Then the rapid spread of the movement springing up as it has in village after village, hundreds in a day, makes even intelligent people believe it is the revenge of the gods against the religion that disregards their power."[60]

Boxer Attitudes Toward Possession

And what of the Boxers themselves? Did they believe that they were truly possessed by the gods? Or were they only play-acting? Or, as in the case of the Lugbara diviners discussed by Middleton, was the distinction essentially a "meaningless" one? Although former Boxers, in their references to the possession ritual in the oral history materials, don't offer an explicit answer to this question,[61] there is little doubt in my mind that all of these alternatives embody some measure of truth. The Boxers, it is important to remember, were a very heterogeneous movement, including not only ordinary peasants but also Daoist priests, Buddhist monks and nuns, demobilized soldiers, members of martial arts organizations, seasonal farm laborers, transport workers hurt by the advent of the railway and steamship, urban gang members, and vast numbers of unemployed drifters (*youmin*) made destitute by the successive natural disasters that impinged on North China in the last years of the nineteenth century.[62]

Not only did participants in the Boxer movement come from a wide range of social strata and occupational backgrounds, they also, as one might expect, brought to their involvement a great diversity of motives. Poor people sometimes joined the movement to put food into their stomachs. Rich people, afraid of being victimized by the Boxers, established (or made contributions of grain and money to) altars and boxing grounds as protection for themselves and their families.[63] Sometimes, as the following statement by a former Boxer from an affluent Tianjin merchant family makes clear, they even went further: "My family, in order to obtain protection, sent me to join up with the Boxers. A few other sons of wealthy merchants went along with me, also for the purpose of gaining protec-

112   tion."[64] There were undoubtedly individuals who, as reported with tire-
some regularity by Chinese and foreigners hostile to the Boxers and occasionally acknowledged by the Boxers themselves, used their participation
in the movement as a cover for the avenging of old grievances that had
nothing to do with the Boxers' stated aims.[65] And it is no less certain that
many of the adolescent males who constituted such a large proportion of
the movement's following were attracted by the sheer noise and excitement
(*renao*) of becoming a Boxer, the opportunity to practice and attain expertise in the martial arts (especially welcome to farmers rendered idle by the
drought),[66] the exhilaration of performing in front of crowds of credulous
onlookers, and the satisfaction that came from lording it over a population
that, by the summer of 1900, had either become supporters of the Boxers
or thoroughly cowed by them.[67] These personal motives, however, did not
necessarily displace or compromise motives of a more public and widely
shared nature, such as loyalty to the dynasty or antiforeignism or the related
conviction (discussed in chapter 2) that the Boxers had it in their power, by
stamping out foreign influence, to bring an end to the drought plaguing
much of North China at the turn of the century.

By the same token, there is no reason in my judgment to assume that only
Boxers who joined the movement out of the "purest" of motives were capable of being possessed. My strong suspicion, admittedly unprovable, is that
there was a continuum in this respect that stretched from those Boxers, on
one end, who consistently entered a full trance state, to those, on the other
end, who deliberately faked possession in order to win over their audiences
or achieve some other advantage. As an example of the latter, Liu Mengyang
says that, from the time in June 1900 when the rumor became widespread in
Tianjin that Guandi was assisting the Boxers in the fighting then in progress,
there was a veritable epidemic of Boxers claiming to have been possessed by
this god: "One Boxer bandit attached to the Great Awakening Temple got
into an argument over this with a Boxer bandit from some other place, and
neither would give ground. Boxer A said to Boxer B: 'You're just pretending
to be Guangong,' to which Boxer B rejoined: 'You're the one who's doing the
pretending.' Unable to resolve their dispute, they asked a bandit chieftain to
decide for them. The bandit chieftain said: 'I am the one who has been truly
possessed by the spirit of Guangong. You two are charlatans. You have the
audacity to assume the name of another in order to trick people. You should
be killed!' He then brandished his sword and made as if to chop off their
heads, whereupon A and B refrained from further wrangling."[68]

In between the endpoles of those who became truly possessed and those
who engaged in out-and-out deception were probably the vast majority of

Boxers who sometimes achieved a trance state and sometimes did not, and who, in a culture in which "life" and "art," "reality" and "performance," were so deeply intermeshed, were very possibly incapable of clearly distinguishing the one from the other. David Johnson's analysis is extremely pertinent here. Johnson's researches into the relationship between "opera" and "ritual" have led him to conclude that these two institutions, which he regards as the "most important institutions of non-elite community life" in the imperial era, "were profoundly akin because for both, *performance* was fundamental." "Opera," Johnson continues, "had a great advantage over ritual as a master metaphor: it portrayed all facets of life, it was intentionally 'life-like.' As opera became more dominant, religion, and the rest of Chinese life, began to be 'operaticized.' "[69]

The Rapid Spread of Boxer Possession in 1900: Contributing Factors

There is one other issue, closely related to the above, that needs to be touched on briefly before we leave the subject of Boxer possession. "Even the dogs in the street in West Kerry know that the 'otherworld' exists," Irish poet Nuala Ní Dhomhnaill writes, "and that to be in and out of it constantly is the most natural thing." In much the same spirit, Katherine Gould-Martin has observed that Taiwanese "consider it quite easy to go into trance."[70] Gould-Martin's assertion — as also Dhomhnaill's — is about a specific society or culture. Others have made similar statements about the *circumstantial factors* facilitative of possession, irrespective of culture. Can we point to anything either in the cultural traditions of North China or the circumstances present in that area in 1899–1900 that may have made it comparably "easy" for Boxers to become possessed?

Cheng Xiao has contended that in North China, as compared to the south, it was relatively easy for the possession ritual to spread. In South China, according to Cheng, shamanism was a more specialized and structured phenomenon. The ability to act as a shaman was passed on by teachers to their followers, and, because of the procedures that had to be mastered, it was difficult for the general run of people to "become gods." In the north, by contrast, it was much simpler to achieve this end. There were, in general, no strict rituals or standards to be followed. All that was necessary to become possessed by a god was to write out charms or recite incantations, and these were so simple and easy to memorize that even illiterate people had no trouble mastering them. Thus, when the Spirit Boxers moved out of Shandong in the winter of 1899–1900, the possession ritual

114   they took with them caught on rapidly among the inhabitants of Zhili and
other parts of North China.

Cheng Xiao cites, as an earlier precedent for the rapid and easy spread
of spirit possession in North China during the Boxer period, a possession
case involving a Patriarch's Assembly (Zushihui) in Xincheng county (in
Baoding prefecture) in 1826. The originator of the group was one Hu Jijiao
(Oxhorn Hu). Hu had heard that calling down the gods was an efficacious
way of healing people, so he made off with a few spirit tablets from a patriarch's hall in another village and set up his own assembly, gathering followers and using possession to cure people of their assorted ills. According
to Zhili Governor-General Nayancheng, who investigated the case, the
Patriarch's Assembly migrated from Henan to the Baiyangdian Lake region
in Zhili (just east of Baoding), and from there continued to spread northward through one county after another. It used the same methods as originally used by Hu Jijiao; as a result, Nayancheng complained, it was next to
impossible to delve into its activities. The model of dissemination followed
by Hu Jijiao's movement, Cheng Xiao concludes, had distinct similarities
to that used by the Boxers later on. Both were forms of propagation by "radi-
ation," without strong organization or articulated leadership; people simply patterned their own behavior after the behavior observed in others.

Part of Cheng Xiao's argument is that the phenomenon of mass possession, as it emerged in the first years of the twentieth century, not only in the
north but in other parts of China as well, was generally linked to an antiforeign agenda. The national crisis of these years was widely perceived as a
consequence of "foreign aggression," and calling down the gods for help
and protection against such aggression was the most accessible and powerful weapon available to ordinary Chinese caught up in the crisis.[71]

I would, as earlier indicated, strongly support this view. However, I
would add to it two other factors that may possibly have had a significant
bearing on the ease with which the possession ritual spread at the turn of
the century. One was the extreme youth of many of the Boxers, as noted in
numerous accounts, both Chinese and foreign. (According to an oral history informant from the Tianjin area, contemporaries called the Boxers the
tongzijun or tongzituan, "youth army" or "youth militia.")[72] The motives
that attracted adolescent males to the Boxer movement in general also
applied to their participation in the possession ritual. It was exciting. It alleviated the anxiety that was the constant companion of many in North
China in 1900. And it afforded an opportunity for a relatively powerless element in society to alter dramatically its moral, political, and social position.
Something very similar to this was to happen in the early stages of the

Cultural Revolution, as adolescent Red Guards, for a brief time, achieved a heady and quite unaccustomed dominance in local Chinese society. It was very likely also a factor in the part adolescents took in the Salem witch-craft outbreak of 1692 and the religious revival known as the "Little Awakening" which began in Northampton, Massachusetts, in 1734. In both the Salem and Northampton cases, according to one highly regarded analysis, young people experienced a "breathtaking" "reversal of status," as they "at least momentarily broke out of their 'normal' subservient and def-erential social role to become the *de facto* leaders of the town and (for many, at least) the unchallenged source of moral authority."[73]

It may be worth noting that in all of these historical episodes young peo-ple behaved in ways that were viewed by at least some members of their surrounding communities as odd or "abnormal." Given the very different constructions different societies have placed on "adolescence" (in some

3.2 Child Boxer. Since many Boxers were little more than boys, contempo-raries often used such terms as "youth army" (*tongzijun*) and "children's brigade" (*wawadui*) to characterize them. From *Yihetuan*, vol. 1.

116   instances raising the question whether such a developmental stage even existed),[74] I am more than happy to leave it to the child psychologists to speculate about any general propensity teenagers may have to be experimental in their behavior, to "try on different identities," and so forth. I am less hesitant, on the other hand, to entertain the view that young people, in a wide range of cultural settings, may be more inclined than adults to succumb to group pressure, get caught up in mass movements, even "lose themselves" in one craze or another. A psychological link between the youthfulness of many members of the Boxer movement and the ease with which the possession ritual became a mass phenomenon in 1900 does not seem at all far-fetched.

One other aspect of this link that is of interest is the belief apparently still found in some parts of China that young males have a special facility for becoming possessed. It is possible that this belief is related to the ancient Chinese notion that children who were still virgins possessed an undisturbed quality that made it easier for them to serve as mouthpieces of the gods and assist the latter in the combating of evil.[75] It is worth noting, in any case, that a number of widely used terms for spirit medium in the southern Chinese culture area include the term *tong* or "youth" (despite the fact that many mediums today are not male or particularly young). One such term, introduced earlier in this chapter, *tongji* (Mandarin for *tâng-ki*), literally means "youth diviner" or (with the two characters reversed) "divining youth" and is used in Fujian, Taiwan, Singapore, and elsewhere in the south. Another, *jiangtong*, or "the youth into whom [the spirit] descends," is encountered in southern Guangdong. Elliott, writing about Singapore, states that, although anyone may become a spirit medium, "youths of under twenty are the most suitable candidates," especially those with unfortunate horoscope readings. "Such people are expected to lead blameless but unhappy lives, and to die young. They are chosen by the *shen* [gods] because they can at least be of value to society by lending their bodies for this purpose."[76]

In North China at the turn of the century a similar connection may have existed in people's minds. Sawara and Ouyin claimed that when the Boxers established an altar in Zhili, their primary method of recruiting new members was, in a possessed state, to scour the immediate area for young males. Upon finding such persons, they entered their homes and seized them. If family members protested, the possessing god, speaking through the mouth of the Boxer, announced that the boy in question had a predestined affinity with the god, whereupon the family dared not resist further.[77] In Shanxi a CIM missionary reported that in early July a Boxer placard posted in Daning called on "schoolboys" to form a "Children's Witchcraft Band."[78] Another Shanxi missionary supplied an interpretation of this concentration on young lads that was current at the time: "A large proportion of the Boxers were boys, as they were *more susceptible to the spirits* than mature men. Many children were won from among the poorer people, by the promise of perpetual safety from all calamity if they would give their sons to this righteous crusade."[79] Although a number of historians of the Boxer movement also have alluded, at least in passing, to the greater susceptibility of young people to the possession ritual,[80] we still await a systematic investigation of the importance of this factor in accounting for the ritual's rapid spread across North China in 1900.

A second factor that in all likelihood contributed to this spread has received even less attention from scholars. I refer to the severe hunger experienced by large numbers of people in North China at the time. In the literature on possession, it is interesting to note, a connection is often drawn, in the most widely disparate cultural settings, between food deprivation and dissociation. "Most Africans who hope to be possessed," M. J. Field tells us, "are careful to fast."[81] Informants in North Palau claim that a person can induce trance by "fasting and then chewing a large quantity of betel rapidly."[82] Umbandists in Brazil, although they don't abstain completely, prepare themselves for trance by avoiding heavy meals and alcohol on days when they hold public sessions.[83] Fasting is sometimes part of the preparation followed by shamans in Siberia prior to calling on their spirits.[84] And a *tâng-ki* in Singapore, according to Elliott, is supposed to vomit all of his food and experience a significant drop in body temperature before entering trance.[85]

In fiction as well we find occasional evocations of a relationship between food deprivation and dissociation, a classic instance being *Wuthering Heights*, in which the demise of the central character Heathcliff is related to, if not directly brought on by, his refusal in the last four days of his life to consume any food. During this period, in which he becomes paralyzed— we might indeed say "possessed"—by memories of his "immortal love" Catherine, Heathcliff's manner and expression combine the extremes of anguish and euphoria. He is described as having an "unnatural . . . appearance of joy under his black brows; the same bloodless hue, and his teeth visible, now and then, in a kind of smile; his frame shivering, not as one shivers with chill or weakness, but as a tight-stretched cord vibrates—a strong trilling, rather than trembling." "I'm animated with hunger," he observes, "and, seemingly, I must not eat."[86]

There is, in short, persuasive evidence of a direct physiological connection between food deprivation and altered consciousness, the onset of dis-

118   sociation conceivably being facilitated by the lowered blood-sugar level resulting from abstention from food.[87] Although food deprivation in the above cases was, with the possible exception of Heathcliff's, self-induced,[88] there is no reason why the same physiological relationship should not pertain in the context of involuntary hunger, as experienced by the inhabitants of North China at the turn of the century.[89] There is, moreover, the further possibility, clearly relevant to the latter group, that possession, through release of the body's natural painkillers, the beta endorphins,[90] may reduce the pain of hunger, thus serving as a kind of self-therapy.

The biophysical linkages between hunger and trance remain poorly understood. Much better documented are the psychological connections between the two. Sometimes these are culturally patterned in distinctive ways. For example, among the Ojibwa Indians of North America, who are hunters and gatherers, failure in the quest for food provokes a double anxiety, resulting in part from the threat of starvation and in part from the lowered self-esteem of the unsuccessful food-provider; this anxiety is alleviated by a form of therapeutic possession (by the *wiitiko* spirit), which is accompanied by the ravenous consumption of food. An analogous therapeutic possession occurs among the Gurage of Ethiopia in response to the intense anxiety experienced by Gurage men (again for social as well as physiological reasons) in connection with prolonged food deprivation.[91] But, as William A. Shack who has studied the Gurage observes, although there may be good "social anthropological explanations of spirit possession among socially deprived persons . . . , the bread and butter issue is that an empty belly and gnawing hunger pains will stimulate anxiety behaviour among most normal men in any society."[92]

This, certainly, appears to have been the case in North China in 1900. The epidemic of spirit possession that took place in connection with the spread of the Boxer movement across the region was unquestionably a religious phenomenon. But it was also anxiety behavior of the first magnitude.[93] The vast majority of individuals who participated in the "possession craze" (*jiangshen re*)[94] of the time were not accustomed in their previous existences to being possessed by the gods; they got caught up in such behavior now owing to a number of factors, among which hunger anxiety—along with the desire to use supernatural sanctions against those deemed responsible for the hunger[95]—may well have been paramount.

CHAPTER 4

Magic and Female Pollution

At midnight on the eighteenth day [June 14, 1900] three churches [in Tianjin's Chinese city], the one inside the West Gate, the one in front of the garrison headquarters, and the one at the entrance to the granary, were burned down by the Boxer bandits. . . . While the church at the granary entrance was burning, the flames spread to a dozen or so private residences next door and across the street. The bandits passed the word around that, just as they were setting fire to the church in question, some woman from across the way had come out of her home and spilled dirty water. Their magic was therefore destroyed, and the misfortune extended [beyond the church]. On the basis of this [explanation], the families whose homes had been burned down didn't resent the Boxer bandits; they all cursed the woman. People who have complete faith in the Boxer bandits' claims say that, as [the Boxers] were on the point of setting fire to the churches, several dozen Red Lanterns ascended high into the air and circled around each church once. After this the Boxer teacher recited an incantation and pointed toward the doorway of the church with a stick of incense, at which point the fire started. . . .

After burning down these churches, the Boxer bandits issued orders to all families not to eat meat for three days. They also instructed women not to go out of their homes at night and not to throw dirty water into their courtyards, lest they give offense to the gods and incur blame. . . .

On the twenty-second day [June 18], from early morning until noon, the sound of gunfire was constant. Supporters of the Boxer bandits said: "When the fighting began between the Boxers and the foreigners, the foreigners were unable to hold their own. Then, suddenly, in the midst of the foreign army there stood a naked woman. The Boxers' magical powers were thwarted, and they dared not advance."

Liu Mengyang, resident of Tianjin[1]

Boxer Magic and the Question of Efficacy

Chinese, as well as foreigners, who have written on the Boxer movement, either as contemporary witnesses or latter-day scholars, have consistently—

120   it sometimes seems almost instinctively—ridiculed the movement's vaunted magical powers. Ai Sheng, a native of Dingxing county, southwest of Beijing, for example, recounted an incident in which several hundred Boxers set fire to a few dozen Christian homes in a village (Cangju) in the county in May 1900. While the fire burned, a strong wind rose up and fanned the flames. Everyone in the village said that this was because of the magic wrought by a group of Red Lanterns who had erected a mat shed near the site of the fire. "While the Red Lanterns slept in the shed," they reported, "their souls mounted to the clouds and called on the strange wind to help [the Boxers] in battle." Ai Sheng later interrogated the regiment commander who investigated the incident: "When you went to Cangju and pulled the Red Lantern women out [of their shed] and stripped them of their clothes and flogged them with a large whip until their flesh was raw, did you see any evidence of their being able to ride the clouds?" The regiment commander smiled and did not respond.[2]

This mocking stance has, for reasons that are plain enough, been displayed with greatest frequency in connection with the Boxers' invulnerability claims. "If the bandits' magic can protect against gunfire," the staunchly anti-Boxer official Yuan Chang intoned, "how is it that on the seventeenth and eighteenth days [of the fifth month of gengzi, i.e., June 13–14, 1900], when the bandits launched repeated assaults against the legation quarters on East Jiaomin Lane [Legation Street], the foreign soldiers' firing instantly killed several bandits?"[3] The American missionary, Luella Miner, after reporting that a band of thirty to forty Boxers had scattered when fired on by marines in Beijing on June 14, quipped: "These bullet-proof Boxers don't seem to like the smell of foreign powder!"[4] And, along similar lines, F. W. S. O'Neill of the Irish Presbyterian Mission in Manchuria wrote in early July 1900: "Young girls also enter the [Boxer] Society, and they especially are said to be bullet-proof. On the occasion of [the] first attack at Tiehling [Tieling] the Chinese troops were led by a maiden on horseback. She was shot in the head, and died, of course. But the story was that she became alive again."[5]

Chinese scholars in the late twentieth century, while honoring the Boxers for their patriotic resistance to foreign aggression, have been equally dismissive of Boxer magical claims. "The 'magical powers' of the Boxers weren't magic at all," writes one historian, "they were simply a combination of traditional qigong, sorcery, and martial arts. Although that acclaimed mystery of mysteries, the Boxer technique of rendering oneself impenetrable to swords and spears [daoqiang buru], had a credible component, it was mostly a matter of deliberate exaggeration and artful deception."[6]

The assault on Boxer magical claims is remarkable for two reasons. First, there is its astonishing consistency, all the more striking because of the diverse quarters from which it has emanated. Skeptical Confucian elites in the late Qing perceived Boxer magic as evidence of the credulousness of the "ignorant populace." Christian missionaries, operating on the comfortable assumption that people outside the West "know no true spiritual religion,"[7] dismissed Boxer magic as rank superstition. Scholars in the People's Republic of China, friends neither of Confucian elites nor of Christian missionaries, have taken from the former the view of Boxer magic as an expression of the generally "low cultural level" of the Chinese people at the time,[8] and from the latter the characterization of it as "superstition" (though more, to be sure, in the sense of its being unscientific than of its being the handiwork of Satan). And yet, despite their differences, for all of these critics, the bottom-line standard to which Boxer magic has been held—and against which it has invariably been found wanting—has been empirical efficacy. As Ai Sheng expressed it, the Boxers' invulnerability rituals "frequently worked in inconsequential trials but not in real fighting."[9]

The trouble with the empirical-efficacy test—and this is the second remarkable aspect of the attacks on Boxer magic—is that it largely misses the point. When the rites of medieval Catholics failed to result in miracles, people didn't stop performing them. When Protestant prayers for deliverance in the summer of 1900 went unanswered, the Christian faith of those who survived often became even stronger. Prayers and other ceremonies designed to induce rain sometimes "work" and sometimes don't, yet it seems an invariable rule the world over that when drought conditions prevail, the stock of rainmakers goes up. And, on a more mundane level, it often takes but a single victory to convince sports fans and players that "wearing a certain article of clothing, or doing or *not* doing a particular act can influence the results of a game,"[10] despite repeated empirical proof that it does not. Empirical efficacy, as a test of magico-religious validity, is the ultimate cheap shot and as such has been universally used to discredit other people's beliefs. And yet people, even of "high cultural level," continue to believe. They continue to make, as hardheaded psychologists who study superstition are wont to put it, "false correlations between a particular act and a particular result."[11] Why?

This is a difficult question, and it is answered differently in different religious settings. One answer questions the very premise on which the challenge to magico-religious ritual is often founded, to wit, that such ritual must be immediately and discernibly efficacious. Thus, Mary Douglas writes of the Dinka herdspeople of the southern Sudan: "Of course Dinka

122   hope that their rites will suspend the natural course of events. Of course they hope that rain rituals will cause rain, healing rituals avert death, harvest rituals produce crops. But instrumental efficacy is not the only kind of efficacy to be derived from their symbolic action. The other kind is achieved in the action itself, in the assertions it makes and the experience which bears its imprinting." "So far from being meaningless," Douglas adds, "it is primitive magic which gives meaning to existence."[12]

In responding to the same question, Christian missionaries at the turn of the century, although they would not have disagreed entirely with Douglas's formulation (assuming replacement of the phrase "primitive magic" by the term "prayer"), would certainly have put the emphasis elsewhere. Prayer, for Christians, might indeed inform existence with subjective meaning. But the inner logic of events, in objective terms, was knowable only to God. God could be counted on to "bring forth the good to the *greatest number*,"[13] and one could be certain that, whatever transpired, in the end it would be for the furtherance of His Kingdom.[14] But, in the daily workings of human life, His plan was often beyond comprehension, and all Christians could do in the face of this was trust in it absolutely, even when their prayers were of no avail.

The Boxers had yet other ways of accounting for the inefficacy of their rituals without imperiling the belief system on which they were based. Sometimes, when Boxer rituals failed to work properly, it was explained in terms of the insufficient training or insincerity or spiritual inadequacy (or impurity) of the person enacting them. But much more often, as we shall see presently, the Boxers pointed to sources of pollution in the external environment, countervailing magical forces that had the power to destroy the efficacy of the Boxers' own magic.

For all that separated the Dinka, the Christians, and the Boxers, in the ways in which they dealt with the issue of ritual efficacy, there was one thing that drew them—and perhaps all other religious practitioners—tightly together. Their religious and magical practices had as a paramount goal the affording of protection and emotional security in the face of a future that was indeterminate and fraught with danger and risk. Through their rituals, each sought to exercise some degree of control over the uncertainty—or, as I called it earlier, the outcome-blindness—that is one of the defining marks of human experience.[15]

Magic as a Means of Environmental Control: Fighting and Burning

The resourcefulness of the Boxers in this regard—the array of magico-religious means they used to control their immediate environment, to make it less dangerous, more predictable—was impressive. The two areas of activity in which Boxer magic was deployed most extensively were, not surprisingly, also the ones in which the danger, either to individual Boxers or to the Boxer cause, happened to be greatest. I refer to fighting, mainly against Chinese Christians and foreign expeditionary forces, and to the destruction by burning of churches and the homes and shops of native Christians. The need for magical protection in the case of the former activity was self-evident.[16] In the case of the latter, it was more indirect, having to do with the Boxers' relationship to the population of a given locale. If the Boxers were able to burn down Christian buildings through magical means, this would redound to the credit of the movement and garner local support. If, on the other hand, the fires they set, by whatever means, spread to the homes and shops of non-Christians, the Boxers ran a substantial risk of incurring popular enmity.

The Boxers were reported to have command of a wide range of magical skills in combat situations, apart from their possession-conferred invulnerability powers. Frequently, as they were about to go into battle, they chanted rhymed incantations, such as the following (which was widely used in Yanqing, Huailai, and other counties northwest of Beijing in the summer of 1900): "Disciples in the world of men, stop up the barrels of guns; guns in unison sound, bullets scatter all 'round."[17] Many Tianjin residents apparently accepted the claim that when a rank-and-file Boxer received a bullet or shell wound the teacher had only to rub it and it healed instantly, and the additional claim that when a Boxer was killed in action it was only necessary to recite an incantation to restore him to life. The magical skills of some Boxer teachers and brother-disciples were more highly developed still: approaching bullets and shells simply followed the contours of their clothing and dropped harmlessly to the ground,[18] or, alternatively, the foreigners' guns were stopped up so that they were unable to fire.[19] In Beijing it was said that when the Boxers went into battle, men and horses were more than ten feet tall and the swords of the former were so numerous that it was impossible to resist them. Like their brothers in Tianjin, moreover, when bullets struck their clothing, they rolled off like rain drops, not injuring them in the slightest.[20]

Cao Futian and Zhang Decheng, the top Boxer commanders in the Tianjin region, were alleged to have exceptional magical powers. They were able to make themselves invisible and to disappear into the earth. They had the power to be in two places at once. While they slept their souls roamed about and reconnoitered foreign troop deployments. When Cao Futian went into battle, he carried in his hand a millet stalk two feet long which, he said, was really a precious sword given him by the Jade Emperor;

124 all he had to do was point the stalk in the enemy's direction and one after another their heads fell to the ground.[21] In a similar vein, according to one former Boxer, Cao is said to have announced to his men, as they were advancing toward the Laolongtou Railway Station to attack the Russians: "All of you who are empty-handed, with no weapon, take a stalk of *gaoliang*

4.1 AND 4.2   Boxer Leaders in Tianjin Area. Zhang Decheng and Cao Futian (on horseback). The banner next to Zhang's sedan chair is inscribed "Number One Unit Under Heaven," the name of the famous Boxer altar Zhang founded in Duliu in spring 1900. From *Jing-Jin quanfei jilüe*.

and continue your forward advance. When you get to the front lines, it will turn into a real gun [or spear]."[22]

No less powerful than the magic of Cao and Zhang was that of the female auxiliaries of the Boxers, the Red Lanterns. These young women and girls, it was maintained, were able to protect the Boxers during combat. "Each time we went into battle," a former Boxer recalled, "a brother-disciple would hold a piece of rope in his hand and . . . direct the fighting. The Boxers would fight down below, while the Red Lanterns would watch from above, appearing, suspended in the sky, no larger than a chicken's egg."[23] They could send swords flying through the air without looking and from a distance lop off enemy heads. They were also able to hurl bolts of fire and, using their magic, make off with the screws holding together the foreigners' artillery. When the Red Lanterns stood erect and did not move, their souls left them and engaged in battle. Foreign guns were paralyzed in

126   their presence.[24] They also had extraordinary healing and restorative powers. Zhao Qing, a former Red Lantern from Ziya in Jinghai county,
recalled that, once the senior sister-disciple of the Ziya Red Lantern altar
had gone into trance, all she had to do was clap her hands in the direction
of a sick person and the person became well. The leading Red Lantern in
Tianjin, Huanglian shengmu (Holy Mother of the Yellow Lotus), was said
to be able to heal wounds by sprinkling clear water on them; she also had
the power, by rubbing the bodies of the dead, to restore them to life.[25]

    Arson in China at the turn of the century, especially in cities like
Tianjin and Beijing, where homes and shops were often flimsily constructed and crowded together in close proximity, was exceptionally hard
to control. The Boxers, therefore, had to take special magical measures to
contain the fires they set in these cities. Liu Yitong, who was more receptive to Boxer claims than most Chinese elites, insisted that the Boxers had
a remarkable capacity to know which homes belonged to Christians and
which did not and that, by burning slips of paper and invoking the help
of their gods, they were able to ensure that only the former were burned
down. As an example, Liu recounted an incident in which the Boxers on
June 9–10 set fire to two churches in Tongzhou (some miles east of the
capital). One of the churches was located very close to a granary. The
local magistrate performed a *koutou* in the direction of the fire and
prayed to the gods to protect the granary. Suddenly, as it was related to
Liu, there appeared in the air a god in golden armor who stood atop the
flames and then disappeared. Neither the granary nor the homes on
either side of the church were damaged. Everyone said it was Guandi
making his power manifest.[26]

    Tang Yan, a skeptical visitor to Beijing from Jiangnan, reported that on
June 13 the Boxers set fire to a church in the eastern section of the capital.
Tang was not present at the scene. But everyone, according to his account,
said that all they saw was the senior brother-disciple of the Boxers reciting
incantations over and over again in front of the church, whereupon all of a
sudden the fire broke out. They also said that the fire didn't spread to the
homes of neighbors on either side of the church and that only church members were killed in the conflagration.[27] Thinking this most bizarre, on the
next day Tang Yan himself watched as the Boxers set fire to two churches.
There was a sizable crowd of onlookers, he reported, all shouting their
encouragement. Yet the owners of the homes nearby were content to burn
incense outside their doors, seemingly secure in the faith that they would
not be harmed.[28] As of mid-June, it would appear, there was still a high level
of acceptance of Boxer claims on the part of the Beijing populace.

One of the more detailed general accounts of the Boxers' fire-setting methods was supplied by Zhongfang Shi. First, according to him, the Boxers called down their gods to possess them. Immediately thereafter their countenances changed. They looked very angry and appeared strong enough to lift a weight of one thousand *jin*. They made huffing and puffing sounds. Then they grasped double-edged swords and pointed them in the direction of the homes of non-Christians for the purpose of safeguarding these homes from the flames. After doing this, they each held a long stick of burning incense and knelt in a row in front of the home to be burned down. Bystanders were also ordered to kneel. The Boxers, with their burning incense sticks in their hands, then performed the *koutou*, mumbled incantations, and threw the incense sticks into the home designated for destruction. The home immediately burst into flames. If anyone tried to extinguish the fire, the Boxers, assuming this person to be a Christian, seized him and had him put to death.[29]

There were also accounts of more powerful incendiary techniques available to the Boxers. It was reported, for example, that when they destroyed the section of the Beijing-Baoding railway running from Liulihe to the capital on May 28, they simply went along the tracks pointing sticks of *gaoliang* and shouting "burn, burn" (*shao, shao*), whereupon the tracks burst into flame.[30] A Boxer teacher in a certain county was said to be able to set fire to churches by reciting an incantation, stamping his foot on the ground, and shouting "burn."[31] A former Boxer from Tianjin recalled that when the Boxers burned churches in that city, all they had to do was point at their target and it would catch fire.[32] An eyewitness to the burning on June 14 of the large church at the base of the wall inside Xuanwu Gate in the capital reported that the Boxer leader stuck a charm written on yellow paper on the church door, then waved a red banner and shouted "burn," at which point the fire broke out.[33] Other Boxers were able to set fire to people's homes by simply bowing three times with hands clasped, while facing southeast, and shouting "burn, burn, burn."[34]

The most powerful magic of all, in incendiary as in combat activities, was that possessed by the Red Lanterns, whose specialties — possibly reflecting a response to the "world-shrinking" magic implicit in the telegraph, powerful weaponry, and steamships of the foreigners — were flying and controlling the strength and direction of the wind. One observer reported on June 8 from the capital that there had been much talk of late about these young women, who every night between the hours of nine and one were said to cruise through the heavens and serve as intermediaries in the setting of fires; it was for this reason, people said, that there had been such

128   an increase in the number of churches and Christian homes burned down in the Beijing area.[35]

On June 18 during the fighting in Tianjin a dust storm made the blaze in the foreign section of the city (caused by Chinese gunfire) burn with great intensity. Boxer supporters, according to Liu Mengyang, circulated word that the fires had been set by the magic of the Boxer teacher and that Red Lanterns perched on the southeastern corner of the city wall, by waving their red fans, had made the fires burn all the more fiercely. Upon hearing this, people repeatedly offered up prayers to the Buddha.[36]

The most impressive claims with respect to the incendiary magic of the Red Lanterns related to their ability, by waving their fans, to fly. After becoming accomplished at this, they soared through the sky to other lands where they set fire to foreign buildings and homes.[37] By mid-June, according to one tally, sixteen of eighteen foreign countries had already been destroyed by this means.[38] In a variation on the same theme, young women clad entirely in red and with red kerchiefs in their hands were said to have descended from the heavens in Baoding. When they threw them, their red kerchiefs turned into red lanterns, and with red lanterns everywhere a great fire instantly ignited.[39]

The Frustration of Boxer Magic: Female Pollution

Boxer magical rituals, of course, frequently did not have their desired effect, and in such instances the Boxers were regularly called upon to explain why. Sometimes, as already noted, they did this by pointing to some moral failing in the person performing (or otherwise involved in) the ritual. When a Boxer was killed in the fighting in Tianjin, for example, and people asked the Boxer teacher how it was that, if the Boxers were invulnerable to bullets, there were still casualties among them, the teacher replied that the person in question must have been a corrupt man and therefore the gods would not possess him.[40] A specific instance of this was recalled by a former Boxer from the Tianjin area, who said that one day he had seen a senior brother-disciple take part in the beating of a fat man, without making any effort to verify that the man was a Christian (*ermaozi zhiyan*).[a] Later, in the fighting at Zhangjiawo, the senior brother-disciple's invulnerability techniques didn't work and he was wounded by a foreign

---

[a] *Maozi*, or "hairy person," in late Qing times was a derogatory colloquialism for Westerners; *ermaozi* ("secondary hairy person") generally referred to Chinese Christians or to other Chinese who were in the employ of or had dealings with Westerners. *Zhiyan* ("straight eye") was an epithet for Chinese Christians which appears to have been used mainly in the Tianjin area.

bullet.[41] Along similar lines, when the Holy Mother of the Yellow Lotus's healing methods were of no avail, she is said to have asserted: "This person has committed transgressions in his life. The gods will not help and therefore he cannot be made better."[42] Occasionally, the Boxers attributed the failure of their magic to a malfunction in cosmic timing. In late June someone asked Cao Futian to explain why, although the fighting had gone on for a long time already, the Boxers still hadn't been able to destroy Zizhulin (the foreign concession area in Tianjin). Cao replied that the Boxers had confronted the foreigners prematurely, that the proper time had not yet arrived, and that it was therefore impossible to destroy Zizhulin. The proper time, he added, would be the eighth month.[43]

Far more often, the Boxers accounted for the inefficacy of their magic by reference to something in the environment that, because of its dirtiness or impurity, was inimical to it. After being defeated on July 4 in a battle in Tianjin that took place during a downpour, the Boxers said that, because of the heavy rains, the gods had refused to possess them (*shen bu fushen*).[44] On the morning of June 16 the Boxers set fire to a foreign-affiliated building in the southern section of the capital. The manager of a neighboring establishment, apparently fearful that the fire would spread, tried to douse the flames with urine from a chamberpot that happened to be sitting nearby. This provoked the anger of the gods, according to the Boxers, and the fire quickly spread to many other buildings. When the Boxers found out who had splashed the urine, they are said to have seized him and thrown him into the flames. But it was already too late.[45]

A more detailed account of this conflagration, which resulted in the destruction, according to official estimates, of over 1,800 shops and 7,000 homes in one of Beijing's most affluent districts,[46] was supplied by Nigel Oliphant, a British employee in the Chinese postal service:

> It appeared that the Boxers first intended only to burn the patent medicine stores, where the fire started. Their leader explained to the crowd that by standing round the burning buildings and holding their hands in a certain way with the fingers close together, and also by muttering certain charms, they would prevent the fire from spreading to the adjoining buildings. Later on, when a theatre next door caught, the people accused them of being frauds; but they explained by saying that one of the crowd had thrown a bucket of dirty water on one of the burning houses, and that their leader, noticing this act of insolence, had opened his fingers, and that now the fire must be allowed to do its worst.[47]

Dirty water, as a destroyer of magic, was unquestionably related in Boxer minds to the most powerful magic-inhibitor of all: women,[48] and more par-

130 ticularly uncleanness in women, a category that, for the Boxers, included everything from menstrual or fetal blood to nakedness to pubic hair. Water was of course a symbol of *yin*, the primeval female principle in China, and there was a long-held belief that the symbolic representations of *yin* could be used to overcome the effects of such phenomena as fire (including gunfire), which was symbolic of the male principle, *yang*.[49] Several groups of rebels in the late Ming had used women to suppress the firepower of government troops.[50] During the insurgency of 1774 in Shandong, Wang Lun's forces used an array of magical techniques, including strange incantations and women soldiers waving white fans, in their assault on Linqing. The imperial defenders of the city were at first frustrated by the effectiveness of the rebels' fighting tactics. An old soldier, however, came to the rescue with this advice: "Let a prostitute go up on the wall and take off her underclothing . . . we will use *yin* power to counter their spells." When this proposal was carried out and proved effective, the government side adopted additional measures of a like sort, including, as later recounted by Wang Lun himself, "women wearing red clothing but naked from the waist down, bleeding and urinating in order to destroy our power."[51]

Such magic-destroying strategies were clearly well established in Chinese minds. The nurse who took care of the famous writer Lu Xun when he was a little boy once told him the following story about her experience with the Taiping rebels: "When government troops came to attack the city, the Long Hairs [the Taipings] would make us take off our trousers and stand in a line on the city wall, for then the army's cannon could not be fired. If they fired then, the cannon would burst!"[52] More generally, the Taiping practice of strictly segregating males and females, until the insurgency was over, was almost certainly related to fear of the subversive properties of the *yin* principle in a combat environment.[53]

The power of women, above all menstruating women, to counter ritual efficacy—a power commonly encountered in other cultures as well[54]—continued to be widely recognized in the twentieth century. When invulnerability rituals were in progress among the Red Spears, females were forbidden to look, as it was held that "if a female (the *yin* element) watched, the spirit would never descend into the male's body."[55] In Singapore it was said that if a *tâng-ki* cut himself as part of his trance performance and there happened to be a menstruating woman nearby, he might have great difficulty stopping the bleeding.[56] A similar danger was reported by Emily Ahern for the northern Taiwanese village in which she carried on her research. From time to time, according to Ahern, the villagers believed it necessary to purify the image of one or another of their gods by carrying it over a bed of hot coals. Ordinarily, the men who performed this firewalk were not burned, despite being barefooted, because the god's spirit possessed them. The presence of a menstruating woman, however, could prevent the god's spirit from entering them and their feet might be severely burned.[57]

At issue in all of these cases was, to borrow Ahern's phrasing, "the gods' extreme sensitivity to pollution."[58] For the Boxers, completely dependent as they were on the gods but unable in the last analysis to ensure a pollution-free environment for them to operate in, this turned out to be a major stumbling block.[59] When the flames from burning churches in Tianjin on June 14 spread to non-Christian homes in the vicinity, the Boxers' explanation, as presented in Liu Mengyang's chronicle (excerpted at the beginning of this chapter), was that a woman had come out of her home and splashed dirty water on the ground. Other local accounts of the same event omitted the reference to dirty water and gave as the Boxers' explanation of the disaster either simply that a woman had come out of her home or that there were women in the neighborhood who were "unclean" (*wuhui*) and that this had "destroyed the magic" (*baifa*).[60]

On June 16, the date of the great fire in the capital, Liu Yitong reported, there were two water vats located at one end of the bridge at Zhengyang Gate (popularly known as Qian Gate). As the Boxers together with the fire brigade were about to try to put out the blaze, an old woman led four young girls over to the water vats. They knelt around them and by some mysterious means counteracted the power of the gods. The water vats broke, the buildings in the Zhengyang Gate area burned down, and several thousand homes outside the gate also were reduced to rubble.[61]

Although in the second of these two lapses in Boxer incendiary magic, women apparently operated as intentional polluters, it was much more common, as in the first, for them to be portrayed as unintentional ones (or, as Mary Douglas says at one point, "involuntary source[s] of danger").[62] In contrast with this, in most of the examples that we have of female pollution in combat or combat-related situations, the pollution was clearly intentional, women—or, what amounted to the same thing, some object associated with women—being used by the Boxers' enemies to overcome them.

The Boxers regularly attributed the casualties they suffered in fighting with the foreigners in Tianjin to the latter's placement of a naked woman in the midst or in front of their forces, which broke the power of the Boxers' magic.[63] The story was also circulated and widely believed by the populace that a naked woman straddled each of the many cannon mounted in the foreign buildings in Zizhulin, making it impossible for the "gunfire-repelling magic" (*bipao zhi fa*) of the Boxers to work properly.[64]

132   According to another story that made the rounds in Tianjin in early
June, when Nie Shicheng (who, it will be recalled, was firmly anti-Boxer)
was preparing to engage the Boxers in battle, he was fearful of their magic
and therefore had the proprietor of a rice shop in the city go to the red-light
district to obtain a supply of menstrual cloths (*jingbu*). The Boxers maintained that when they fought Nie's army the officers and soldiers all had the
cloths wrapped around their necks, as a result of which the power of the
Boxers' magic was broken (*po qi fa*) and they sustained heavy casualties.[65]

The most frequent references to the polluting power of women in
Beijing were in connection with the Boxers' siege of the Northern
Cathedral, in which approximately 3,400 people, mostly Chinese Catholics, more than half of them women and girls, had taken refuge in June.[66]
Among the various explanations the Boxers are said to have offered for their
repeated failures to take the cathedral and the heavy losses they suffered in
these attempts were the following: Naked women had come out of the
building. The defenders had hung the skins of women (*furen pi*) and other
"dirty things" (*huiwu*) from the spires (tactics also employed, it was alleged,
in the defense of the foreign legations). Naked women were nailed to the
church facade. Countless naked women with "dirty things" in their hands
stood on top of the walls. The foreigners had cut open the bellies of pregnant women and nailed them to the building. The foreign defenders had
a "ten-thousand woman flag" (*wan nü mao*), woven from women's pubic
hair, which, when they used it to direct the fighting from the church
steeple, prevented the Boxers' gods from possessing them.[67]

From the perspective of the Boxers, the fighting they were engaged in
in the summer of 1900 was not to be understood as a military conflict in
the conventional sense (conventional, that is to say, in our sense). Much
more fundamentally, it was to be seen as a contest to determine whose
magical skills—and by extension, in the case of foreign and Chinese
Christian adversaries, whose gods—were more powerful and would prevail. There is some evidence, it is interesting to note, that the Christian
antagonists of the Boxers operated from a broadly similar perspective:
Chinese Catholic survivors in southeastern Zhili apparently believed that
the appearance of the Virgin Mary above their church was instrumental in
protecting them from a number of Boxer attacks between December 1899
and July 1900,[68] and foreign missionaries, threatened by fire, regularly
attributed life-saving shifts in the direction or strength of the wind to the
hand of God.[69] For their part, the Boxers, when they experienced setbacks,
at the hands of Chinese government troops (prior to the throne's "declaration of war" against the foreign powers) or foreign forces or armed Chris-

tians, attributed them not to their adversaries' superior firepower but, almost invariably, to their more effective magic. Repeatedly, we are told, Boxer efforts to overpower churches in southeastern Zhili were thwarted by the image of a white-clad woman, whose presence stopped them in their tracks and deprived them of their powers.[70] And the white-bearded leader of the Catholic defenders of the Northern Cathedral, Bishop Favier, was transformed into a "devil prince" (*guiwang*), two hundred years of age, who, in addition to being highly skilled as a strategist, practiced sorcery, was expert at divination, had the power to render himself invulnerable by daubing his forehead with menstrual blood, and had gained complete ascendancy over the minds of the other "devils."[71]

4.3   Bishop Favier. From J. Freri, ed., *The Heart of Pekin: Bishop A. Favier's Diary of the Siege, May-August 1900.*

134   A similar sort of analysis can, I believe, be made with respect to the
Boxers' incendiary activities. These activities were, from the Boxer point of
view, not something separate from the larger conflict in which they were
engaged; indeed, given the primitive state of their weaponry, arson was,
quite literally, the most potent form of firepower generally available to the
Boxers.[72] There was, however, one crucial difference between the magical
dimension of fighting and the magical dimension of burning. In the case
of the latter, the polluting forces that thwarted the Boxers' magic were for
the most part not, as in the case of the former, deliberately brought into
play; rather, they appear to have been inadvertent, introduced as often as
not by people who were supporters of the Boxers (or at least wished it to
appear as such).

Measures to Ensure the Efficacy of Boxer Magic

Despite this difference, the measures adopted by the Boxers to counter the
agents of pollution that threatened their magical powers did not clearly differentiate between intentional and inadvertent pollution. The *effects* of the
pollution, after all, were the same either way. All the Boxers could do,
therefore, was to take any and all available precautionary steps to negate
these effects and fashion as favorable an environment as possible for the
operation of their magic.

To accomplish this purpose, the Boxers in the summer of 1900, in the
repeated instructions they issued to the populations under their control
(most conspicuously, though by no means exclusively, in Beijing and
Tianjin), had recourse alternately to intimidation, appeals to the calamity-
aversion psychology of people and their instinct for self-preservation, and to
claims on the populace's overall support of the Boxer cause. On the last day
of the fifth month, for example, the Boxers sent people through the streets
of Tianjin shouting out orders that all households were to burn incense and
change the following day from the first day of the sixth to the first day of the
eighth month, the number eight being viewed as auspicious and the eighth
month as the most propitious time for the Boxers to vanquish their enemies. Cao Futian and Zhang Decheng announced that with this calendri-
cal change, before three days had passed, they would destroy Zizhulin and
drive the foreigners to the sea. All Tianjin residents, according to one
account, accommodated themselves to the change. Even pawnshops wrote
"eighth month" instead of "sixth month" on the tickets they issued their
customers. No one dared any longer to refer to the sixth month.[73]

To maximize the number of people reached by their instructions, the
Boxers frequently concluded their placards with one or another version of

a standard formula designed to induce people to disseminate the placard's contents. A typical example went: "After you have seen this notice, pass it on quickly. Pass on one copy and avert calamity to one family. Pass on ten copies and avert calamity to a whole village. If you fail to take the notice down and circulate it, you can count on losing your head."[74]

4.4　Boxer Notice. This fairly representative Boxer notice, issued from Shandong, contains a variety of instructions to the populace. Those who disobey the instructions, the notice asserts, will be defenseless against foreign gunfire. By circulating the notice people will safeguard themselves and their families against calamity. From *Yihetuan dang'an shiliao*, vol. 1.

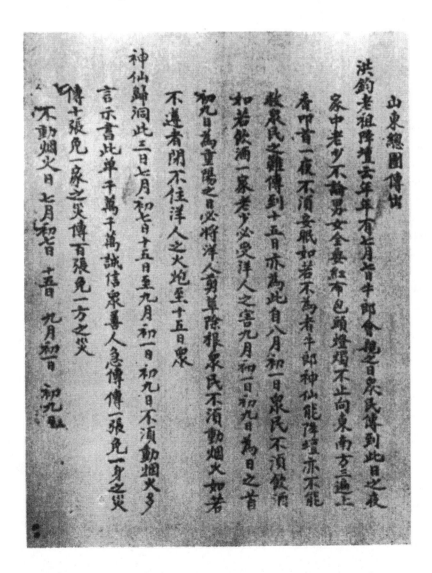

136   In the period from June 16 to June 19, the Boxers in Tianjin suffered a number of military reverses and popular confidence was shaken. The Boxers therefore ordered all households to place on their doors a "doorway incantation to keep out gunfire" (*bihuo men zhou*):

> The cave entrance in the north is open,
> The iron buddha is requested to come out,
> The iron buddha is seated on the iron lotus throne,
> Iron helmet, iron armor, iron-walled fortress,
> Stop the gunfire so it cannot come in.[75]

In both Tianjin and Beijing the Boxers frequently instructed residents to burn incense (sometimes for the entire night),[76] abstain from meat on specified days or for a specified number of days,[77] *koutou* facing the southeast,[78] not set off firecrackers,[79] and not use dirty water or throw it in the streets or courtyards, for fear of offending the gods.[80] People were also ordered to affix various objects colored red (auspicious and life-giving) to the outsides of their homes and to other places, as a protection against danger.[81] On July 7, for example, all households in Beijing were notified that they were to light red lanterns each evening in front of their entranceways, to assist in the Boxers' magical efforts to exterminate the foreigners. Henceforth, after nightfall, the roads and streets of the capital became like so many fiery dragons.[82] A Boxer notice first posted in Zhengding prefecture and then copied and circulated in Shanxi instructed people to put realgar, lime, black soybeans, green pepper, and prickly ash in red cloth bags and suspend the bags, along with five willow twigs, behind their front doors, to counter the blood-smearing black magic of the "devils."[83] Zhongfang Shi reported that on June 15 the Boxers ordered all households in the capital to make little bags of red cloth, fill them with cinnabar, mung beans, tea leaves, and such things, and either nail them to their doors or carry them on their persons; on June 29 they issued instructions for all houses and shops to nail a piece of tapered red cloth to their door fronts; on July 11, in celebration of apparent damage to the Northern Cathedral as the result of a mine explosion, they ordered all shops and homes to affix over their doorways red cloths inscribed with the words "Precious Sword of the Red Heaven" (*hongtian baojian*).[84]

Sometimes, in the prevailing excitement and confusion, conflicting orders were issued. In Tianjin it was said that the Boxers went around one evening spreading the word that everyone should cover their chimneys with red paper in order to safeguard against foreign artillery. But some individuals insisted that if people covered their chimneys the eyes of the female immortals would be closed, making it impossible for them to move through the sky. Therefore, everyone climbed up on their roofs and tore off the red paper they had just put in place.[85] Yang Diangao, reporting from the capital, suggested another reason for conflicting orders to the populace. On July 11, according to Yang, groups of one corps of Boxers distributed magic charms consisting of yellow paper with vermillion writing to all homes with instructions, if they wished to avert misfortune, to paste them on the crossbeams above their doors. On the following day another corps of Boxers, while patrolling the streets, saw the charms. They said that the orders to put them up had not come from the "true corps" and issued instructions for them to be removed at once.[86]

Because of the danger women posed to the effective operation of the Boxers' magic, restrictions were repeatedly placed on their activities. After the burning down of the three churches in Tianjin on June 14, women were instructed not to go outside their homes after dark and not to splash dirty water into their courtyards, "lest they give offense to the gods and incur blame." If a woman left her home in a sedan chair, she was to cover the opening in front with a square of red cloth, so as not "to break the power of the Spirit Boxers' magic."[87] At a later point, Guan He reported that, to safeguard against defilement, women in Tianjin were forbidden to go outside their homes at any hour, and that those who violated this injunction (sometimes unknowingly) were killed. As a result of this order, Guan complained, he was unable (initially) to move his family to a safer location.[88]

According to the anonymous author of *An Account of One Month in Tianjin*, during the Battle of Tianjin, the wind blew constantly from the southeast; since the foreign forces were situated to the southeast, the Chinese side was always going against the wind and it was hard for the soldiers to keep their eyes open. The Boxers therefore walked through the streets, calling on all residents and shopkeepers to burn incense and pray for a northwesterly wind. The incense was to be burned every night, continuously without interruption. When people lit the incense, they were to *koutou* 360 times and in the middle of a table place five bowls of clear water and five steamed breads. These weren't to be moved. Nor was it permitted for women to take charge of the incense-burning ritual, "for fear of destroying the magic" (*kong po qi shu*).[89]

A particularly comprehensive set of restrictions on the behavior of women was supplied by the same chronicler: "The Boxers suddenly issued orders that women inhabitants of all shops and homes were not to enter the market for seven days, that they were not to stand outside their doorways for seven days, that for seven days they were to sit cross-legged on their beds

138   with their feet not touching the ground, that for seven days they were not to comb their hair or wash their faces, and that for seven days they were not to bind their feet. For seven days men and women were to wear red clothing and eat vegetarian meals."[90]

It is perhaps significant that in Chinese numerology the number seven is associated with women as a *yin* element: "At 2 x 7 years = 14 'the *yin* path opens' (i.e., onset of menstruation). . . . At 7 x 7 years = 49 the menopause ensues."[91] This may account for instructions designed to weaken the *yin* force during the prescribed seven-day period. By the same token, depending on context, the same number (seven) was capable of being linked to a quite different set of injunctions and prohibitions. In July in various places in Zhili (including the cities of Zhuozhou and Beijing and Huolu county in Zhengding), the Boxers issued orders that on the seventh day of the seventh month (August 1), which was the festival of the Cowherd and the Weaving Girl, everyone, young and old, male and female, was to wrap red cloth around his/her head, keep candles burning continuously, and face southeast and *koutou* three times. No one was to sleep the entire night. If people failed to do any of these things, the Cowherd and the other gods and immortals would be unable to descend to their altars and protect them from calamity. Also, on this day, no one was to light fire for cooking; if people lit their fires it would not be possible to stop the bullets of the foreigner.[92]

The causal relationship between constraints on women's behavior and Boxer success was neatly summed up in a jingle the Boxers of Tianjin led the populace in singing as they walked through that city's streets: "When women don't dress their locks, we can chop off the foreigners' blocks; when women don't bind their kickers, we can kill all the foreigners with snickers: ha, ha."[93]

The Magical Power of Virginal Women: The Red Lanterns

If, in China in general in the latter years of the imperial era, the foreigner came to be seen as the quintessential "other," frightening and dangerous but also powerful and admired, much the same could be said of women and girls as they appeared in the more delimited magico-religious world of the Boxers at the turn of the century.[94] As in Chinese popular religion generally, the power of females in the Boxers' world was complex and many-sided. In the examples just cited, adult women were consistently portrayed as potent hindrances to the efficacy of the Boxers' magical repertoire and therefore in need of severe restriction in their daily activities. Younger females, often no more than girls, on the other hand, in their guise as Red

Lanterns,[95] were viewed as the possessors of magic that was even more powerful than that of the Boxers themselves. As one account put it: "Although
the magic of the Boxers is great, they still fear dirty things. The Red
Lanterns are in fear of nothing."[96] As a concrete expression of the high
regard the Boxers placed in the power of the Red Lanterns, a notice was
posted in the capital toward the end of July, announcing that since the
Boxers had been unable to overpower the Northern Cathedral themselves,
they had issued a special request to two of the leading Red Lanterns in the
Beijing area, the Holy Mother of the Golden Sword (Jindao shengmu) and
the Venerable Mother of the Pear Mountain (Lishan laomu), to assist them
in this undertaking. The Holy Mother of the Golden Sword is said to have
entered the capital on July 29 with a large retinue of Red Lanterns and
Boxers and to have taken part in the siege from that date.[97]

Although there is evidence of a modest Red Lantern presence in Shandong and Shanxi,[98] by all accounts the main center of Red Lantern activity was Zhili, in particular the area in and around Tianjin. Liu Mengyang,
who although hardly a friend of the Boxers wrote one of the fullest and
most reliable chronicles of their activities in the Tianjin area, maintained
that there were numerous Red Lanterns in the villages and towns north and
west of the city in the spring of 1900.[99] Liu's description of the interaction
of these mostly adolescent females with the population of Tianjin, including the Boxers, speaks volumes for the awe in which they were held at the
time: "When they walk through the streets, they avoid women, who are not
allowed to gaze upon them. The people all burn incense and kneel in their
presence; they call them female immortals and dare not look up at them.
Even the Boxer bandits, when they encounter them, fall prostrate on their
knees by the side of the road."[100]

How do we account for the remarkable power attributed to the Red
Lanterns at the time, at least in the popular imagination? The term
Hongdengzhao, which I have generally translated as "Red Lantern," has a
number of meanings in the context of the Boxer movement. In the earlier
phases of the movement, in Shandong, it was the name of a martial arts
organization. But it also referred to a technique used to confer invulnerability to bullets, and as such had some of the same protective qualities as
the Iron-Cloth Shirt (Tiebu shan), the Armor of the Golden Bell, and
other forms of "hard *qigong*." Indeed, it was sometimes known (as late as
the summer of 1900) as the Armor of the Red Lantern (also "Hongdengzhao" in Chinese, but with a different character for "zhao").[101]

It was not until the spring of 1900, apparently, that "Hongdengzhao"
first took on the new meaning of a separate organization of female teen-

4.5　Red Lanterns Assist in Siege of Northern Cathedral. The Red Lantern to the left rear (holding a lantern in her hand) has flung a magical rope between the opposing sides, protecting the Red Lanterns in the middle from the crossfire. From V. M. Alekseev, *Kitaiskaia narodnaia kartina: Dukhovnaia zhizn' starogo Kitaia v narodnykh izobrazheniiakh* (The Chinese folk picture: The spiritual life of old China in folk graphic art) (Moscow, 1966).

agers allied with the Boxers. In writings that circulated in Zhili in the course of this year it also referred to a religious belief, clearly influenced by White Lotus millenarian ideas, that light would triumph over darkness and that, on the arrival of the kalpa on the fifteenth day of the eighth month, the Red Lanterns would rise in rebellion and light up the world. The suffering that would be experienced at that time would make the suffering of the present look like child's play. "This suffering," a typical announcement that appeared in Beijing began, "is not to be reckoned suffering. On twice four add fifteen [that is, the fifteenth day of the eighth month], the streets will be lit up by red lanterns. Then there will be real suffering."[102] All people, it was understood, if they wished to escape the horror of kalpa calamity, should place their full faith and trust in the Red Lanterns.

It is not implausible to suppose that the awe in which the Red Lanterns were held in Tianjin and elsewhere in the summer of 1900 was, in some measure, owing to the beliefs just described. For some reason, however, these beliefs are barely referred to in the major contemporary chronicles of the Boxer movement, in spite of the fact that the authors of these accounts were generally hostile to the Boxers and would happily have seized the opportunity to blacken the "bandits'" reputations even further by identifying their female counterparts with the illegal White Lotus sect.[103] My guess is that the reason the religious meanings attached to "Hongdengzhao" occupy such a small place in contemporary accounts is quite simply that they did not have very wide currency at the time. If we seek a source for the unusual popular deference paid to the Red Lanterns, therefore, we are probably best advised to look elsewhere.

A good place to begin, in my view, is with the special status the Red Lanterns had as young females who, being presexual and in many cases very probably also prepubescent, were largely if not entirely free of the ritual uncleanness characteristic of adult women in China.[104] The Red Lanterns were said to range in age generally from 12–13 to 17–18 *sui* (roughly 11–12 to 16–17 by Western counting).[105] This age spread, together with the probability of a relatively late onset of menstruation owing to contemporary dietary standards (not to mention the added effects in 1900 of the protracted drought in North China), meant that some portion of these teenage (and preteenage) females, possibly a quite sizable one, had still not experienced (and, even more important, would not generally have been perceived by society as having experienced) menarche.[106]

Menstruation, in any case, was viewed as far less polluting than sex and childbirth in China, partly (it appears) because of the vastly greater quantities of blood involved in the latter.[107] It was possible, therefore, in certain

4.6   Red Lantern. This mannered representation, unlike the Red Lantern earlier shown (figure 1.3), projects an impression of elegance and glamour (epitomized by the figure's tiny bound feet), possibly in an effort on the artist's part to discredit the Red Lanterns' allegedly presexual status. Neither of these contemporary images conveys even a hint of the heroic and fiercely courageous character assigned to the Red Lanterns during the Cultural Revolution years (see figure 9.3). From *Jing-Jin quanfei jilüe*.

circumstances even for menstruous women, by rejecting marriage, to purify themselves. This was the path followed by such heroines of popular Chinese religious literature as Miaoshan and He Xiangu.[108] It was also the road taken by the silk-reeling marriage resisters of southern Guangdong, although their motives appear to have been more economic than spiritual in nature.[109] While I certainly do not wish to argue that the girls and young women who joined the Red Lanterns in 1900 did so expressly in order to avoid the pollution attendant upon marriage—many of them were too young to be concerned about such matters and, in any case, we have scarcely any Red Lantern voices directly talking to us about their inner feelings[110]—whatever their motives, the end result was the same. In an environment in which the paramount danger was thought to derive from female pollution, the Red Lanterns, unexposed to the sexual and childbirth defilement resulting from marriage and, in the nutritional conditions prevailing at the time, very likely in many instances even premenstrual, were, relatively speaking, pollution-free.

Indirect support for this analysis is furnished by the fact that when unfriendly observers of the Boxer movement wanted to discredit the Red Lanterns, they did so not by pointing to the apocalyptic—and dangerously antidynastic—religious ideas with which they were occasionally identified but rather by emphasizing their illicit sexual behavior. One contemporary told the story of a Red Lantern aged seventeen or eighteen *sui* who disappeared one night and only returned a few days later. When her parents, who were suspicious, questioned her closely, she said that she had flown to Russia and had burned down the capital of that country. This was official business, she added, and her parents had best not try to place obstacles in her path or she would have to kill them. The mother and father believed their daughter and henceforth did not interfere in her activities. Afterward, however, it was alleged by some people that the young woman was really having an affair and only pretended to be a Red Lantern so that she could go to meet her lover.[111]

Other contemporaries alluded to the Holy Mother of the Yellow Lotus' long history of promiscuous conduct.[112] Still another, Guan He, who repeatedly disparaged the Holy Mother as a "local Tianjin prostitute," described the respectful treatment she had received in encounters with Zhili Governor-General Yulu and with the son of Li Hongzhang (for decades China's leading official), and took note of the report that the foreigners, after capturing her, had decided to send her on tour through the countries of the West. He then recounted a humorous exchange with a

144   friend. The friend said that for a prostitute to flout ceremony in an audience with a governor-general and be treated with deference by a nobleman (Li's son) was enviable. Guan replied that, in his judgment, even more enviable was the chance to travel to Europe and America, to visit famous places like London, Paris, Berlin, and Washington. That he, Guan He, had never had the good fortune to be appointed to the retinue of a diplomatic envoy and had also neglected to seek a position as one of the Holy Mother's incense-serving boys, so that he might travel the globe, was truly to be regretted. Guan's friend responded that, if it were in fact as he described it, then Guan was evidently not on the level even of a local prostitute. The two men clapped their hands and laughed heartily.[113]

The issue, of course, is not whether the contents of stories such as these were "true." What is important is the cultural belief system the stories incorporate. For the Boxers and doubtless many non-Boxers as well, the source of the Red Lanterns' special power was their purity. For Chinese hostile to the Boxers, therefore, there was no better way to challenge the foundation of Red Lantern power—and by extension the legitimacy of the Boxer movement overall—than by calling into question this very purity. (The same tactic was used incidentally against the Boxers themselves in contemporary woodcuts depicting them visiting prostitutes and stealing grain.)[114] The key point, however, is that, although the two sides, pro-Boxers and anti-Boxers, disagreed on whether the Red Lanterns were pure, they appear to have shared a common cultural belief that purity (moral/sexual) was good and, in some sense, empowering.

An analogous point may be made with respect to the material on Boxer magical beliefs and practices in general, as introduced and elaborated in the pages of this chapter. Certainly, there were skeptics among the population, and there was unquestionably a great deal of intimidation and coercion.[115] Moreover, there is ample evidence of people suspecting individual Boxers of fraud when the latter were unable to demonstrate convincingly the efficacy of their magic. But not having faith in this or that Boxer's magic was a very different thing from not believing in Boxer magic at all. The overwhelming testimony of contemporary observers, Chinese and foreign, is that, as we saw in chapter 3, the great majority of Chinese at the time were quite prepared to accept the premises underlying the Boxers' magico-religious claims. Many of these premises were deeply rooted in beliefs that had long been a central feature of Chinese popular culture and constituted, in the language of Lévi-Strauss, a shared "gravitational field" of belief.[116] Even among people who, in calmer circumstances, might be resistant to such beliefs, moreover, there was a greater inclination than usual to pay them heed in the tense, jittery atmosphere that enveloped North China in the spring and summer of 1900—an atmosphere marked by extreme fear and anxiety, credulousness, rumor, and even, at certain moments and in certain places, something approaching mass hysteria.

CHAPTER 5

Rumor and Rumor Panic

The month before last Yizhong told me that when a certain photographic studio [in the capital] had been set on fire some fresh litchis from Guangdong were found inside. When they were passed around and examined, the consensus was that they were gouged-out human eyeballs.[a] Everyone bristled with anger. People didn't realize that what they had found was a food product that was sweet and refreshing. It was like mistaking a camel for a horse with a swollen back. In the unsettled conditions of the present, eight or nine out of ten things one hears are rumors of this "tiger-in-the-market-place"[1] sort.

Ye Changchi, Beijing official

On a certain day red-colored marks that looked like bloodstains suddenly appeared on people's doorways. On account of this rumors sprang up all over alleging that the blood had been smeared by Christians. One rumor had it that, if there was a bloodstain on a doorway, the Boxers' magic would not work. Another claimed that in only a hundred days time [the people within the house] would kill each other off. Still another alleged that in only seven days the house would catch fire. No one knew who had said "in only a hundred days" or "in only seven days." Those who repeated these statements didn't realize how absurd they were; those who heard them believed them to be true. How detestable is the ignorance of these foolish people.

Liu Mengyang, resident of Tianjin

Various stories were set afloat as to the power of the missionaries to prevent rain, ascribing almost superhuman strength in the way of controlling the elements. Clouds were constantly being driven away by fierce winds, which led to the story—thoroughly believed by all the people—that we went into our upper rooms and drove the clouds back by fanning with all our might. The

---

[a] For years one of the most widely circulated charges against Catholic missionaries had been that they removed dying converts' eyes (usually under cover of administering extreme unction), which they then used for medicinal and other purposes.

story was changed as regards the T"ai Yüan Fu [Taiyuan] missionaries, that
they were naked when doing the fanning.

C. W. Price, American missionary, Shanxi

One day a rumor spread from Tianjin to certain places in the Beijing area to
the effect that, when the foreign soldiers and Boxers fought, the Boxers only
had to bow and, without taking a step, could advance forward. If they bowed
once, they advanced several hundred steps. If they bowed three times, they
engaged the foreign soldiers directly, and before the latter had a chance to
fire their guns they were killed. . . . Therefore the foreign armies all went
down to defeat.

Guan He, resident of Tianjin

On that night [the seventh day of the seventh month (August 1, 1900)], . . .
inhabitants [of Taiyuan, Shanxi] became alarmed for no reason. The men
howled and the women cried. All night long they remained agitated. The next
morning when they were questioned they said a black wind [*heifengkou*][b] had
come, but in fact no one had seen it. Also, they didn't know what evil spirit the
black wind represented. Nevertheless, from this time on, the mood of the people in the city remained unsettled. They said the black wind emerged at night
to bring harm to people. Everyone, male and female, old and young, carried
leather whips to protect themselves and drive off the black wind. (Word having gotten around that the black wind feared leather whips, whips for a time
became very expensive.) This strange situation lasted for half a month.

Liu Dapeng, teacher, Taigu, Taiyuan[2]

Ralph L. Rosnow, summarizing recent research in the field of rumor generation and transmission, characterizes rumors as "public communications
that are infused with private hypotheses about how the world works."
Rumors, he elaborates, "give vent or expression to anxieties and uncertainties as people attempt to make sense of the world in which they live."
The creation and passing of rumors, he hypothesizes, occurs when there is
an optimal combination of four variables: personal anxiety, general uncertainty, credulity, and "outcome-relevant involvement" (by which he means
an individual's personal stake in whether a rumor's content turns out to be
true or false).[3]

Rosnow, in another context, distinguishes "rumor" from "gossip," suggesting that while rumors tend to be about a topic of emotional importance

[b] The "black wind" or, as here, "mouth [*kou*] of the black wind" was a terrible wind that
was believed to accompany or signal the arrival of a kalpa calamity. It was associated with
White Lotus teachings that frequently became intermingled with Boxer beliefs at the
height of the uprising; it was also related to popular wind-divination beliefs.

148 to the teller, gossip need not be. "Gossip," he observes, "is small talk, a kind of intellectual chewing gum, while rumors have the feel of something of great substance."[4] More pertinent for our purposes—and also more difficult to characterize with confidence—is the distinction between rumor and belief. Ordinarily (although not invariably) we think of rumors as being *spread*, beliefs as being *held*. Rumors, by definition, contain unverified information, while for beliefs that are held with conviction the question of verification generally does not arise. Of course, it is often the case that beliefs are not held with conviction. Or they may be so held under conditions that are temporary in nature—a period, for example, of high anxiety, when people are more apt than otherwise to suspend disbelief, especially when other members of their communities are engaged in a similar suspension of disbelief—and then relinquished when these conditions have subsided.

Beliefs, in the form of stereotypes, also may influence the degree to which a rumor finds acceptance and what sort of spin the person who hears and transmits the rumor chooses (often quite unconsciously) to put on it. Rosnow tells of an especially grisly rumor that erupted in Detroit in the winter of 1967–68: A mother and her young son were in a department store. The boy at one point went to the lavatory. When he did not return, the floor supervisor, at the mother's request, entered the lavatory, where he found the boy lying unconscious on the floor, castrated. Salespeople recalled some teenage boys having gone into the lavatory shortly before the boy entered and then leaving prior to the boy's discovery. What is interesting is that, almost predictably, when this rumor was told in the white community, the teenagers were black, the boy and his mother, white, while the exact reverse occurred when it was told in the black community. "Given that such rumors are intrinsically disturbing," Rosnow observes, "passing them may be a way of validating one's prejudices as much as sharing one's fears . . . in an attempt (not always successful) to dissipate discomfort."[5]

The Number and Variety of Rumors in 1900

Li Wenhai and Liu Yangdong, in their very interesting analysis of the social psychology of the Boxer period, point out that at no other juncture of modern Chinese history did rumors flourish as they did at the turn of the century.[6] This unusual proliferation of rumors was widely noted at the time. In Dengzhou, on the northern coast of the Shandong peninsula, "rumors fell like snow in winter."[7] In Beijing, in the early summer of 1900, Ye Changchi observed (as we have already seen) that "in the unsettled conditions of the present, eight or nine out of ten things one hears are rumors." As the influence of the Boxers spread in May, according to Guan He, "rumors and falsehoods filled the ears on a daily basis." Guan speculated on the reasons the population of his city, Tianjin, now became such easy prey to rumor-mongering: "The root evil is still that the people are uneducated and know of nothing but ghosts and spirits, while the educated do not understand the times and lack fixed views about anything. Deceiving them is therefore easy and frightening them not hard."[8] Liu Dapeng, a local teacher who supplied over a dozen examples of rumors that circulated in the villages of Taiyuan county in July and August, described a population in that area that was in a state of near total panic, inclined to sudden outbursts of violence and prepared to believe almost anything. "For the rampant spread of rumors," Liu declared, "no time was worse than the juncture of summer and autumn of the 26th year of Guangxu [July-August 1900]."[9]

Foreign observers also attested to the widespread rumors. The *North-China Herald*'s Tianjin correspondent reported in early June: "The public mind (native) here is almost inconceivably excited. No rubbish is too preposterous for belief—the Boxers can fly, they can spit fire; even the most sober-minded, sensible Chinese are persuaded that they (the Boxers) are immune to steel and lead. The infection is running to craziness." Grace Newton (American Presbyterian) wrote from Beijing on May 30 that the city was "so full of wild and exaggerated rumors that it is next to impossible to tell the truth" and again on June 2: "I could fill a mail bag with the rumors we have heard."[10] Luella Miner wrote (in May) of the "absurd rumors" with which the town of Tongzhou and surrounding villages had become filled. Foreigners were accused of hiring people to poison wells. Foreigners were "responsible for the terrible drought." If people burned kerosene, which was all imported from abroad, their eyes would drop out after two days, and if they inhaled the odor from foreign matches, some other dreadful thing would happen to them. Miner, who was exceptional among the missionaries of the day for being possessed of a highly developed sense of humor, recounted a fantasy that struck her during the hymn-singing at a Sunday afternoon women's meeting: "I could hardly keep from shaking during the singing of the first hymn because I had a vision of a roomful of people with their eyeballs all rolling down into their laps and around on the floor like marbles."[11]

The great variety of rumors that circulated in North China in the spring and summer of 1900 may usefully be seen as a symbolic roadmap to the wide-ranging emotions buffeting people at the time. As always, in a setting characterized by a scarcity of reliable information and an abundance of

150 credulity, there was, for certain individuals, an irresistible temptation to fabricate rumors for the sake of material gain or some other form of personal advantage. During the Battle of Tianjin, it was reported that the face of the Guandi statue in one of the temples in the Tianjin area had suddenly broken out in a profuse sweat, it being claimed that this was because of Guandi's efforts in behalf of the Chinese side in the fighting. As word of the miracle spread, worshipers converged on Guandi temples in droves to express their gratitude. According to the recorder of this rumor, what actually had happened was that the Buddhist monks in the original temple were having difficulty making ends meet, as a result of the sharp fall-off in temple incense-burning (occasioned presumably by the extreme scarcity and resulting price inflation of incense owing to the heavy emphasis the Boxers placed on family incense burning for protective purposes).[12] The monks, therefore, secretly placed ice inside Guandi's hat, and when the ice melted in the summer heat it ran down the statue's face, looking just like sweat. The monks spread the word all over, to publicize the miracle and encourage people to come to the temple with their alms.[13]

Another example of what we may call the charlatan syndrome was reported by Luella Miner during the siege of the legations. Because of the complete cutoff in communication between the besieged and the outside world during the initial weeks of the crisis, the legation quarters were aswirl with rumors and Chinese "soldier-spies" were regularly despatched to find out what they could about the anticipated relief expedition from Tianjin. Miner's sense of the absurd again rose to the occasion in a journal entry (of August 1) describing the report of one such individual: "The soldier-spy came as usual to give his information and collect his dollars, but having marched our foreign troops too rapidly, so that we ought to be able to hear their cannonading from the city wall, he was obliged to have them retreat. He landed them back at Ma-t'ou [Matou, less than halfway from Tianjin to the capital] this morning, and if we had given him time, he would doubtless have marched them in good order all the way to Tientsin." The soldier-spy, confirming foreign suspicions, was revealed to be "a yellow-journalist of the worst type" when a letter arrived from the Japanese general in Tianjin dated July 26 and announcing a delay in the departure of the relief force because of transport difficulties.[14]

People also generated rumors to explain phenomena that seemed to them otherwise inexplicable.[15] Sometimes, as in the Detroit example cited earlier, such rumors gave expression to people's stereotypical beliefs and prejudices; at other times, they were deeply conspiratorial in nature. Thus, in June 1900, when Nie Shicheng, in response to telegraphed orders from

Zhili Governor-General Yulu, took his well-armed modern forces to Tianjin to deal with the mounting crisis in that city, the Tianjin population, keenly aware that Nie, a steadfast opponent of the Boxers, had recently fought a series of bloody battles against them along the Beijing-Tianjin railway, reviled him as "Devil Nie" (Nie guizi). The Boxers, against this backdrop, fabricated the rumor that Nie was in league with the foreigners and had been bribed by them to suppress the movement in Tianjin.[16] Ironically, Nie Shicheng fought against the foreigners in the Battle of Tianjin and was killed in action on July 9. A former Boxer's recollections managed to preserve the conspiracy rumor intact, while at the same time accounting for Nie's death at the hands of his alleged coconspirators: Nie had made a secret peace with the French, so the foreigners would not attack him. Nie's army was outside the south gate of the city. As the French forces approached, Nie, to disguise the conspiracy, waved his flag and ordered his men to fire in the air. The French, not realizing that this was a ruse, thought Nie's men were firing on them. They attacked and Nie was killed![17]

Wish Rumors

Many rumors, as we might expect, were energized by wishful thinking. Among foreigners trapped in the legation compound in the hot summer months, such thinking quickly became a staple of life. "Rumors of troops coming to our relief," reported Sarah Goodrich in late June, "are the order of the day." On July 8, weeks before the foreign relief force even left Tianjin, she wrote in her journal: "Yesterday the French Minister was sure he could hear artillery not farther than six miles away. Last night some said Russian troops were at the Western Hills, and would come in this morning by seven o'clock." After hearing "good rumors," according to Emma Martin (Methodist Episcopal), people often sang "Tramp, Tramp, Tramp the Boys are Marching," to try to make themselves believe it was so.[18]

In a particularly elaborate example of wish rumor on the Chinese side, the Tianjin Boxers on July 4 told people that their teacher, after rendering himself invisible, had entered the foreign concession (Zizhulin), where he came upon a tall building that was vacant. Making himself visible again, he went inside. The building had four stories. There was nothing on the first two floors. But the third floor was filled with gold, silver, pearls, and precious gems, and on the fourth floor he encountered an elderly foreign couple seated facing each other. The couple performed the *koutou* before the teacher. They said that they were husband and wife and were over one hundred years of age. Suddenly bursting into tears, they said they knew that

152 the teacher's magic was very powerful and also knew that he was to come on that day. Therefore, they were waiting for him. They said that the foreign countries had only firearms to rely on. Today the foreigners were to be destroyed. Heavenly soldiers had come into the world. The firearms would not fire. The foreign countries had therefore resigned themselves to being extinguished. They invited the teacher to go to the middle floor and help himself to the gold, silver, pearls, and jewels. They then announced that they were going to die. When they had finished talking, they both seized pistols and shot themselves in the chests.

"The Boxers," we are told, "took much pleasure in telling this story and the people of Tianjin were convinced it was true. Suddenly, they spread the word that the government forces and Boxers had repulsed the foreign armies and that the Chinese had taken Zizhulin. . . . The news circulated noisily through the streets of Tianjin. Only after a long time had passed did people discover that it had no basis in fact."

A related rumor that circulated at the same time asserted that the foreigners had fled Zizhulin, that the government forces and Boxers had entered the area and quartered themselves there, and that within the concession they had found forty crates, each containing 280,000 *liang* of gold (1 *liang* = 50 grams). Neither the government troops nor the Boxers took the gold; instead they presented it to the governor-general's yamen (office) to be used for relief purposes.[19]

There were a number of wishes symbolized in these rumors, and they had to do with people's deepest and most pressing concerns. On the most obvious level, of course, there was the wish, shared by both the Boxers and the population at large, that the Chinese side would be victorious in the Battle of Tianjin and the foreigners go down to defeat. (This wish was also given expression in the woodcut art of the day, which frequently showed the foreigners being overwhelmed by the Chinese in military encounters or humiliated by them in some other way.)[20] In an area suffering from the effects of protracted drought, there was also the wish, expressed in the second rumor (and implying a possible divergence of interest between the Boxers and the general population), that ordinary people (not the Boxers or the government soldiers) would be the beneficiaries of the precious-metal windfall discovered in the foreign concession. Finally, and perhaps least obvious, the first rumor incorporated the fantasy that the foreigners (as represented by the truth-telling elderly couple) accepted the efficacy of Boxer magical claims and had bought into the master narrative of the heavenly nature of the Boxer movement and its mission, thereby confirming in the most powerful way the validity of the Boxer cause.

Another wish rumor, from the same source, disputed the report that   153
after the foreigners' victory in the Battle of Tianjin in mid-July the Boxer
leader Zhang Decheng had been captured and put to death. On the contrary, according to the rumor, after his capture Teacher Zhang had made
himself invisible and gone to the market town of Duliu, where under his
leadership the Boxers experienced a revival. (Duliu was the base for

5.1   Battle of Tianjin. This is a detail from a larger patriotic print depicting the use
of a variety of weapons (including explosives) by glowering Chinese troops in a victory over the foreigners. From C. P. Fitzgerald, *The Horizon History of China*. By
permission of The British Library.

5.2   Execution of Russian and Japanese Soldiers. This print shows Russian and Japanese prisoners being hauled before Prince Duan and Dong Fuxiang for judgment (upper right), and their subsequent execution (upper left). From H. C. Thomson, *China and the Powers: A Narrative of the Outbreak of 1900.*

Zhang's famous "Number One [Boxer] Unit under Heaven," which he had
established there in the late spring.)[21] Several tens of thousands of new
recruits joined up. Boats coming from Tianjin were detained and their car-
goes of clothing and other articles seized.

In this rumor, we find encoded not only the fantasy of the indestruc-
tibility of the Boxer movement[22] but, again, the notion that participation in
the movement would be materially rewarding. The author of the account
in which the rumor is reported states that on July 21 he journeyed to Duliu
himself and found it completely quiet, with no trace of Boxers.[23]

At the time of the circulation in the Tianjin-Beijing corridor of the
rumor alleging bowing to be part of the Boxers' magical repertoire when
engaged in combat against foreigners, a story was told of a Tianjin rickshaw
puller who inadvertently offended a foreigner and was about to be
rewarded with a thrashing. The frightened rickshaw puller instinctively
bowed, whereupon the foreigner threw away his stick and fled in panic.
Although comical from our perspective and doubtless also from that of the
skeptical Chinese writer who recounted this rumor, from the standpoint of
Chinese who believed in Boxer magic, the story's deeper symbolic meaning was that, like the fable about the ancient couple in the building in
Zizhulin, it confirmed foreign acquiescence in the Chinese worldview.[24]

Some of the "wish rumors" spread in the summer of 1900 had a decid-
edly political cast and appear, from their contents, to have been generated
by elite supporters of the Boxer movement. One such, playing on widespread hostility to Li Hongzhang for allegedly having betrayed China's
interests at the Shimonoseki peace conference of 1895, claimed that Li's
nephew was the son-in-law of the Japanese emperor. Another was the
"Twenty-Five Article Treaty," printed and circulated in Hengzhou, Hunan,
on July 3–4, 1900, in conjunction with the burning down of Italian,
French, and British church buildings in that city. This was a completely
fabricated document, assuming the form of an edict issued by the Empress
Dowager. Patriotic and intensely antiforeign in tone, it called for an almost
complete rollback of the imperialist incursions of the preceding decades,
including cancellation of all of China's indemnity obligations, Japan's
return of Taiwan to China, Germany's return of Jiaozhou, Russia's return
of Dalny (Dalianwan), foreign payment to China of 400 million taels to
compensate it for its military expenses in the Boxer War, payment of an
additional 400 million taels to the Boxer forces to compensate them for
their expenses, confiscation of all churches in China and expulsion of all
missionaries, restoration of Chinese supervisory power over Korea and
Annam, Japanese payment of tribute to China as in Qianlong times, the

156 performance of the *koutou* by Japanese and Westerners when received by Chinese officials, a doubling of the duties collected on foreign imports into China and also of those collected on goods exported from China to foreign countries, a prohibition of foreign travel in China for pleasure, and so forth. That the "Twenty-Five Article Treaty" went beyond the simple antiforeignism of most Boxers is indicated by its clear acceptance of trade and other forms of intercourse with foreign countries, provided Chinese sovereignty was fully respected.[25] That it represented wishful thinking is clearly shown in the Boxer Protocol of 1901, which reflected far more faithfully the harsh realities of the Sino-foreign relationship at the time.

Dread Rumors

It is no surprise to learn that, in an environment stalked by drought and the threat of untimely death, another major category of rumors that were epidemic in North China in the spring and summer of 1900 were those driven by fear and anxiety. The connection between drought and the explosive growth of rumors was made by many observers, Chinese and foreign. In Tianjin Liu Mengyang reported that, when the rains still did not fall in March, "rumors proliferated," generally targeting the foreigners and Christians.[26] C. W. Price of the ABCFM in Shanxi wrote in his diary in the second half of June: "It was about 1st June that we began to hear vague rumours of unusual unrest and talk against the foreigners and Church. This was caused by the continued drought, which was already being felt in the scarcity of food, and also by the lack of any useful employment for the people, so that they could congregate in the streets and talk over grievances, seeking to find a reason why this suffering should come upon them."[27] Olivia Ogren of the CIM in Yongning, Shanxi, after noting the growing restlessness of the local population owing to the "long-continued drought and threatened famine," described some of the specific rumors that began to circulate shortly after the first arrival of Boxers in the area in mid-June: "Whispers soon were repeated . . . to the effect that the Boxers wore buttons which kindled fires (celluloid), and that they were stealing girls to recruit [into] the 'Red Lantern Society.' Absurd stories stating [sic] the arrival of foreign soldiers in packing-cases, and that 'the Heavenly Soldiers,' as the Boxers were called, had flown away into heaven at their approach."[28]

Fear rumors, as the observations of Ogren suggest, were greatly encouraged by violence and the threat of harm. Roland Allen recounted a story initially related by the friend of a Christian in the capital in early June: The friend was returning home one evening when he saw a boy of about sixteen walking down a street marking certain doors (but not others) with a piece of white chalk and then bowing before each marked door. Presently, as the boy's behavior was noticed, people came to their doorways in a state of great agitation and began to discuss what it portended—whether the marked houses signified friends or foes of the Boxers, the saved or the doomed. The Christian's friend went up to the boy, seized him by his queue, and asked him what he meant by such foolishness. The onlookers seemed astonished at the boldness of this man who dared to interfere with the secret emissaries of the Boxers, and the boy himself at first tried to brazen it out, but when the man threatened to take him to the police station, he fell to his knees and protested that he was only doing it as a practical joke to frighten people. "So men lived in those days," commented Allen, "ignorant what might be the meaning of the simplest acts, a prey to wild terrors roused by any unusual sight or sound."[29]

Sometimes being "prey to wild terrors" had dire consequences. As a small detachment of American marines was about to set out from Tanggu to relieve the foreign community in Tianjin in June, all sorts of rumors were spread about the fate (including ambush by fanatical Boxers) that awaited them. One frightened young marine, with little if any combat experience, rushed about from one Chinese to another at the marine camp, desperately seeking details on what might be expected if the marines were indeed ambushed and he were captured. The natives accommodated him with a generous supply of bloodcurdling tales of all the tortures to which captured enemies were subjected, and the poor fellow was soon on the verge of a breakdown. No sooner did the marines get under way than a shot rang out. The agitated young man, "after hysterically shouting something about ambushes," had put a bullet through his heart and died instantly.[30]

Recent research on rumor control indicates that, while anxiety is often a source of rumors, it can also be aggravated by them.[31] Indeed, it has been suggested that rumors may be viewed as "a kind of opportunistic information virus, thriving because of their ability to create the very anxieties that make them spread."[32] This reciprocal action between rumor and anxiety was a familiar experience in North China in 1900. In the Tianjin area in late May–early June, at a time when people's nerves were already frayed owing to the drought and the rising incidence of Boxer-related violence, rumors calculated to further aggravate popular anxiety rose on all sides: "There was a rumor that the [Boxer] bandits cut off men's queues[c] when

---

[c] It was widely believed among the populace that sorcerers used queue-clipping to steal men's souls.

158 they weren't looking.[33] There was a rumor that red circles drawn by the Boxers at night had suddenly begun to appear on people's doors. And there were also countless other rumors designed to terrorize their hearers, with the result that the Christian inhabitants of Sanyi village in the vicinity of Tianjin, in great fright, fled their homes under cover of dark. Popular anxiety intensified owing to this."[34] In the area around Taiyuan in July and August there were frequent alarms sounded that the foreigners were about to enter the city or that the Christians in such and such a village had risen in rebellion. Each time a rumor started, according to Liu Dapeng, the people became frenzied with fear. Two incidents recounted by him follow:

> On the ninth day of the sixth month (July 5), after the sounding of the second watch, a rumor suddenly spread among the residents of Wangguo village that the Christians from Dongji Gully were coming to kill them. The people were panic-stricken and everyone fled. Before long the inhabitants of Three Family village, Long Lane village, North-South Great Monastery, Little Station Camp, and Little Station village were in a state of utter turmoil. People screamed and cried out for help. Men, carrying their wives on their backs, sons their mothers, fled by the light of the stars in all directions. Some hid in nightsoil pits, others in pigpens, still others in reed fields, rice paddies, and lotus ponds. The bedlam lasted the entire night. Only when dawn broke did people discover that it was a false alarm.

> On the fifteenth day of the seventh month [August 9, 1900], in the dead of night, someone reported that several hundred armed Christians from Willow Grove village [in the vicinity of Taiyuan] had taken advantage of the night to cross the Fen River in a westward direction and, to avenge their group's grievances, were acting in a wantonly brutal manner. The villagers upon hearing this became agitated and a thousand of them assembled and went to the southeast corner of the village, where they arranged themselves in several rows and waited with their weapons. When they peered toward the distant banks of the Fen in the bright moonlight, it seemed as though there were people there, a row of whom were swarming toward them. When they wiped their eyes and looked again, it seemed that the people had stopped and were no longer advancing. They were by turns afraid and suspicious, but no one dared to go and investigate. When dawn broke, they realized that what they thought had been people were actually young millet stalks in the fields swaying in the breeze. They had been so nervous that "every bush and every tree looked like an enemy." This really happened.[35]

Tang Yan, a teacher enroute from Beijing to Huaian county (in western Zhili) in mid-June, noted a similar condition of jitteriness in the localities through which he passed. Twice in two nights rumors circulated that armed Christians were about to launch an attack on the town in which his inn was located. The first night this proved to be a false alarm. On the second occasion, just as Tang was about to go to bed, he suddenly heard the jingle of horse bells, followed by someone knocking with urgency on the inn door and shouting: "Several hundred secondary hairy ones [Christians] have already gone up the mountain. They're not far away. Hurry and make yourselves ready." The innkeeper awoke in a state of fright and became agitated. Tang and his traveling companions told him of the rumor of the previous night (which, as it turned out, had been ignited by the sound of gunfire from a neighboring county) and eventually persuaded him to calm down and go back to sleep.[36]

Rumors that were linked to a sudden change in circumstance had unusual potency and were widely believed. On August 15, the day after the arrival of the foreign expeditionary force in Beijing, word spread far and wide that the foreign soldiers were trigger-happy and were going to blow up the entire population. Those who valued their lives, therefore, abandoned their homes and possessions and fled the city.[37] In Tianjin, after the foreigners took the city in mid-July, it was much the same, except that the target of the rumors shifted. Chinese Christians, according to Governor-General Yulu, were reported to have disguised themselves as Boxers by putting on red or yellow turbans ("It was impossible to identify them") and to have concealed mines both inside the city and in the area immediately surrounding it.[38] In another, more elaborate, rumor, word spread that on such and such a day Chinese government troops were going to attack Tianjin with heavy artillery. Gen. Song Qing had carried nine cannon into the city. Land mines had been hidden in certain places. A huge force of Boxers was coming from somewhere to seize the city by force. The residents of Tianjin, according to Liu Mengyang, were terrified and the numbers of those seeking to escape from the city soared.[39]

Rumors similar to the "total destruction" ones just described were also rampant in early June among foreigners in Beijing, as tensions mounted in that city. Mary Porter Gamewell (Methodist Episcopal) described the prevailing mood: "Rumors fill the air. A new edict only seems to give permission for further violence. At the Post Office they say we are safe. At the legations they say we are safer in Peking than in Tientsin. Yet the Chinese say tomorrow is set as the day for the destruction of all foreigners in Peking!"[40]

In situations where there was no change of circumstance and the same rumors were spread day in and day out, on the other hand, there was sometimes a tendency to discount the rumors. "Were it not that the day has been set for our extermination at least fifty times since I came to China,"

160   Courtenay H. Fenn (American Presbyterian) wrote from Beijing on May 3, "it would be difficult to keep a restful mind."[41] When Fei Qihao (Fei Ch'i-hao), a Christian associated with ABCFM missionaries in Fenzhou, Shanxi, was urged on August 14 to flee for his life, as his foreign patrons in Fenzhou were all to be killed, Fei said that this made little impression on him, as he "had been hardened to hearing such rumors. For two or three months there had not been a day when men had not been saying on the street: 'Today the foreigners will be killed,' or 'Tomorrow the houses will be burned.' "[42] In somewhat different circumstances, it was of course possible to dismiss the specific timing incorporated in a rumor but still give credence to its underlying message. In the journal of Rowena Bird, although rumor after rumor proved unfounded, the death that the rumors predicted closed in on the author with fearsome inevitability.[43]

Danger, Uncertainty, and the Proliferation of Rumors

All the rumors so far discussed, whether circulated among foreigners or Boxers or ordinary Chinese or Chinese Christians, and whether centering on wishes or on fears, flourished because of the crisis situation virtually everyone in North China faced in the spring and summer of 1900. Like many crises, this one was made up of two essential ingredients: a sense of immediate danger and an agonizing shortage of information either about what was happening (or had already happened) elsewhere in space or about an indeterminate future that held tightly within its grip the answers to people's most pressing questions.

The agony of uncertainty in such situations and the role that rumor plays as a palliative appear universal and have been attested to again and again. Rosnow asserts that "rumors flourish in an atmosphere of uncertainty because they attempt to relieve the tension of cognitive unclarity."[44] "In circumstances where numbers of people are together without adequate information, such as concentration or prisoner-of-war camps," Gustav Jahoda writes, "a series of rumours almost invariably arises. Although most of these tend to be largely untrue, they do at least serve to still for a while the suffering caused by uncertainty."[45]

"War rumors" present a special case, but one that is highly pertinent to the situation in North China in 1900. Paul Fussell confirms the judgment of Rosnow and Jahoda in the following insightful commentary: "In the prevailing atmosphere of uncertainty for all and mortal danger for some, rumor sustains hopes and suggests magical outcomes. Like any kind of narrative, it compensates for the insignificance of actuality. It is easy to understand why soldiers require constant good news. It is harder to understand why they require false bad news as well. The answer is that even that is better than the absence of narrative. Even a pessimistic, terrifying story is preferable to unmediated actuality."[46]

The most dramatic instance of the "false bad news" phenomenon on the foreign side in 1900 was the announcement in mid-July that all foreigners in the capital (save two) had been killed on July 6–7. Headlines such as the following appeared in much of the world's press: "ALL MASSACRED IN PEKING," "PEKING MASSACRE IS CONFIRMED," "MASSACRE STORY ACCEPTED AS TRUE," "ALL BELIEVED TO HAVE PERISHED." Accounts of the massacre were filled with details: The attack had been launched by the Boxers' main supporter at court, Prince Duan. The streets around the legations were strewn with dead bodies of Chinese as well as Europeans. Prince Qing, a leading anti-Boxer figure, upon hearing of the assault, had brought in his own troops, but these were outnumbered and defeated and the prince himself slain. In celebration of his victory, Prince Duan had distributed 100,000 taels and huge quantities of rice to the Boxers. The *New York Tribune*, in an article datelined London, July 17, after denouncing the "utter worthlessness of all the detailed accounts which have been, or may be, published," stated authoritatively that, despite confusion over the date, "the fact that the massacre was complete and ruthless cannot be questioned." There was "profound gloom" at the highest official levels in Washington, London, and other world capitals. As the rumor panic continued, the accounts of what happened became ever more detailed. Then, magically, news was received that nothing at all of what had been reported contained even a grain of truth.[47]

One of the things that happens in situations marked by great danger and an almost complete absence of reliable information is that "standards of plausibility" change. Just at the moment when the hunger for information is greatest, as a result of the danger, access to information is cut off. In such circumstances, people become far more suggestible than they would otherwise be, prepared to accept as fact assertions that in a calmer state they would instinctively challenge.[48] They hope for the best, but imagine the worst. And if the predisposition to think badly of a particular category of people is already in place, certain kinds of rumors, which attribute terrible acts to such people, are much easier to accept as factual. In the United States in the 1980s charges of cannibalism, the eating of human feces, and the drinking of urine and human blood, leveled against satanic cults, were believable to many people because of widespread prior acceptance of the symbol of Satan as evil incarnate coupled with a long-standing fantasy that

162   there actually existed groups of human beings in America pledged to Satan's service.[49] In much the same fashion, in the Western world in July 1900 it was relatively easy to be persuaded that a massacre of all foreigners in Beijing had been carried out because Westerners at the time assumed that the Chinese were entirely capable of just such behavior.

Generic Rumors: Antiforeign and Anti-Christian Lore

Predictably, a similar pattern may be discerned on the Chinese side in 1900: the "false bad news" about foreigners and Christians that was widely disseminated in this year was readily believed by masses of Chinese in part because they had long been conditioned to think ill of precisely these categories of people. In contrast with many of the rumors dealt with so far in this chapter, which have tended to be situation-specific and nonrecurrent, these rumors were more generic both in nature and in content. Also, because they threatened not just the Boxers but the entire Chinese population, the former, by spreading them and not infrequently portraying themselves as protectors against their injurious effects, were able to use such rumors to broaden support for their cause. One variety of "false bad news" rumor drew on the venerable Chinese tradition of scabrous, harrowing, often racist lore about foreigners in general and Christians in particular. The other, although also in this instance targeting foreigners and Christians, may best be represented as a form of mass panic or hysteria of a sort commonly encountered in previous periods of Chinese history (not to mention crisis situations elsewhere in the world) and focused unequivocally on death.

The Chinese store of anti-Christian and antiforeign lore embodied a number of themes. Although some of these themes were traceable as far back as the late Ming, they became especially pronounced after 1860 when foreign missionaries for the first time in over a century were given permission to operate throughout the Chinese empire. Sometimes this lore focused on the weird social and sexual practices of foreigners—and by extension Chinese Christians, who had in one way or another been contaminated by foreign contact. These practices included improper mixing of the sexes, copulation during religious services, mother-son incest, the smearing of menstrual fluid on the face, serial copulation with young girls who had been purchased and placed under a spell, and so forth. People who engaged in such behavior were defined explicitly or implicitly as enemies of the moral and civilized orders; lest there be any doubt as to their lack of qualification for being considered human, they were often represented pictorially as sheep, pigs, and other animals.[50]

Another theme of anti-Christian and antiforeign lore was more sinister, directly threatening the Chinese populace at large in the most gruesome ways and presenting Westerners (the external enemy) and Chinese Christians (the enemy within) as the very essence of evil. A Christian in Hunan was said to have cut off the queues of men, the nipples of women, and the testicles of little boys. The practices of Catholic priests were particularly suspect. The administration of last rites was, as we have seen, easily misconstrued as masking the priests' real purpose, which was to gouge out the dying person's eyeballs. The establishment of orphanages for abandoned children was another Catholic practice that was readily misunderstood. In the aftermath of an antimissionary incident that took place in Nanchang, Jiangxi, in 1862, some of the inhabitants of that city, when asked by representatives of the governor whether the missionaries' practice of rearing abandoned children was not a good thing, replied: "Locally, our rearing of abandoned children is limited to taking in and nursing the newly born. But in their orphanage the boys and girls bought are all over ten *sui*. Do you think that their purpose is to rear children or to avail themselves of this as a pretext for cutting out their vital organs and severing their limbs?"[51]

During the major incident that took place at Tianjin in 1870, suspicions surrounding the Catholic orphanage in that city were again a factor, aggravated in this instance by an epidemic in the orphanage in June that raised significantly its already high death rate and a rash of kidnappings that had broken out in Tianjin in the spring and that many residents (including non-Catholic foreigners) believed had been encouraged by the imprudence of the Catholic sisters in offering monetary "inducements to have children brought to them in the last stages of illness, for the purpose of being baptized *in articulo mortis*."[52]

Mutilation of the human body and traffic in its parts, often associated in China with kidnapping scares, and done for a variety of medicinal purposes (such as the concoction of immortality pills and potions), struck at the deepest fears of the Chinese people and had been capital offenses since the Ming period. Barend J. ter Haar has shown that these fears were part of an oral tradition stretching back at least to the Song dynasty and has argued persuasively that dismemberment, disfiguration, drugging for nefarious purposes, and other horrific charges were consistently used by ingroups (social or ethnic) to attack and demonize the members of outgroups. Rumors alluding to such behavior thus fit not only into a tradition of lore about Christians and Westerners but also into a wider tradition that had been evolving for centuries and of which the nineteenth-century anti-Christian and anti-Western tradition was but an adaptation.[53]

164   Such rumors proliferated in the summer of 1900. Two Catholic nuns living north of Tianjin were killed by a crowd of angry Chinese after (according to a former Boxer from the area) charges circulated that, among their other crimes, the nuns specialized in the kidnapping of children, whom they then turned over to church members to gouge out their hearts.[54]

Liu Yitong, one of the contemporary observers most sympathetic to the Boxers, wrote that on June 10, as tensions mounted in Beijing and the surrounding region, a large group of Christians streamed into the capital. The women's noses had been pierced and a cord passed through them. The reason for this was that, when their husbands had been hacked to death by the Boxers, the women became terrified and wanted to apostatize. The foreigners, furious at them for betraying the faith, gave them a drug, where-

5.3   Catholics Gouging Out Eyes of Chinese Christians. According to the righthand text of this late nineteenth-century poster, the gods cannot be fooled: people who gouge out the eyes of others will have their own eyes gouged out in return. The text on the left goes on to warn "dead devils" (Chinese Christians, who have become dead to all virtue) that while those with sight may seek to become blind, the blind can never recover their sight. To drive the point home, in the foreground are two converts whose eyes have already been removed by the foreigners, after whom they now crawl submissively. From *Jinzun shengyu bixie quantu*.

upon they pierced their own noses and passed the cord through them, enabling the foreigners to lead them like camels. After reaching the capital, the foreigners concealed the women in the Northern Cathedral. They covered the women's bodies with a medicinal plaster. When the plaster was pulled off, the women died. The plasters were then sold to people for two foreign dollars. Many of the people who bought them also perished.[55]

On July 1, Liu reported, three bricklayers presented themselves at the camp of one of the Chinese commanders in Beijing. They said they had worked for the foreigners for twenty-one years, but now they were so hungry they couldn't stand it any longer. The food and water supplies of the foreigners in the legation quarters were already exhausted. Therefore, the foreigners hid in the tunnels underneath the city and butchered people and horses to eat.[56]

One of the names the Boxers had for Christians, as we have seen, was "straight eyes" (*zhiyan*). They explained this, according to Guan He, by alleging that, after joining the Christian religion, Chinese often took foreign medicine, whereupon they could only stare straight ahead and no longer had the eye movements of normal people. This was one of the ways in which the Boxers were able to distinguish Christians from the rest of the Chinese population.[57]

Ye Changchi, one of whose friends in the capital related to him the story of the litchis in the photographic studio that had been mistaken for human eyeballs, was told by another friend that, after the Boxers burned down a dispensary, they found a stiff object which they thought was a cure-dried human being. There was much noise and excitement, but later it was discovered to be only a wax figure. Still another acquaintance told Ye of the formation of a "dead spirit column" (*yinhun zhen*) to defend against the Boxers. The people who formed the column, presumably Christians, ripped open the bellies of pregnant women (perhaps to generate dead spirits) and chased each other around naked to prevent the gods from possessing the Boxers.[58]

Since the Boxers believed that human eyeballs were needed for photographic work, they were said to have tied up the manager of a photo shop and forced him by means of torture to show them where he hid his supply of eyes.[59] It was also reported that, in an effort to make reality conform to fantasy, some of the girls in a missionary-run school for the blind in the capital were detained and "urged to confess that the foreigners took out their eyes."[60] In Tianjin in the summer of 1900 people said that the top leader of the entire Boxer movement, a 108-year-old man with unrivaled magical powers, on a secret inspection trip to Zizhulin had gone into a foreign building in which he came upon three earthen jars, one containing

166   human blood, another, human hearts, and a third, human eyes.[61] A particularly grisly body-parts story that circulated in Beijing alleged that Westerners confined the female members of church congregations and, after cutting out their vaginas, sold the women for three taels apiece.[62]

The anonymous author who recorded the last rumor commented cynically that the rumor had deliberately been spread by the Boxers "in order to enrage the people and cause them to hate the Westerners."[63] Such skepticism was not uncommon among elite contemporaries. But it was by no means universal. There were many other individuals, including highly educated ones, who although strongly disinclined to give credence to the more miraculous claims of the Boxers, accepted without hesitation the accusations they circulated about Christians and Westerners. Thus, Yun

5.4   Catholics Removing Fetus. Foreign missionaries were often accused of extracting the fetus and placenta from pregnant women for medicinal and alchemical purposes and for sorcery. In this poster, circulated in the late nineteenth century, the foreigners are depicted wearing green hats, symbolic of a person who has been cuckolded. The text on the right articulates the importance in the Confucian tradition of bearing sons; that on the left urges the speedy elimination of heterodoxy (Christianity) and the destruction of the foreign devils. From *Jinzun shengyu bixie quantu.*

Yuding, who frequently disparaged Boxer magic in his diary, describing it at one point as "black arts to stir up and delude the foolish people," in an entry dated June 14 (5/18) observed without a hint of skepticism that the Boxers, in ransacking churches, had found "numerous vile objects, including several dozen jars containing such things as human eyeballs, hearts and livers, and penises. There were even instances," he wrote, "of flayed human skins and hollowed out pregnant wombs, thought to be objects used by sorcerers to bring harm to their victims. These things were too ghastly to look at. Passersby were all overcome with grief and rage."[64]

Rumors such as the ones just described operated in complex and often contradictory ways. On one hand, they intensified popular fears and anxiety that were already present at the turn of the century as a result of other factors. On the other hand, they became a means of alleviating tension and stress, partly by enabling individuals to share their fears collectively and partly by transforming popular fear into popular anger concentrated on the actions of hated outsiders.

The rumors thus operated in a way somewhat analogous to "contemporary legends," as discussed by folklorists and sociologists.[65] Although some contemporary legends (also called urban legends or modern legends or exemplary stories) are quite benign, more frequently they contain horrific subject matter of one sort or another: Babies, kidnapped in Latin America, are used to provide spare parts for organ transplants in the United States. Children (or sometimes more specifically blonde, blue-eyed, virginal female children) are abducted and sacrificed by satanic cults in America. Young female clients of Jewish clothing shops in France are kidnapped and sold by the proprietors of the shops into forced prostitution.[66] And in China, at the turn of the century, the body parts of human beings are cruelly extracted by China's enemies for a range of fiendish purposes. Legends such as these often draw on centuries-old archetypal myths and vary in detail as they are told and retold over space and time. They serve, to a degree at least, to contain the chaos characteristic of situations pervaded by fear and uncertainty by naming the stress (even if only metaphorically) and locating its source. Thus they offer a clarifying narrative in a murky and threatening setting in which "even a pessimistic, terrifying story," to repeat the apt phrasing of Fussell, "is preferable to unmediated actuality."

Generic Rumors: The Well-Poisoning Scare

The second form of generic rumor that was very widely circulated in North China in 1900 also focused on actions allegedly taken by foreigners

168   and Christians for the purpose of bringing dire harm to the Chinese population. Sometimes, as we have seen, foreigners and Christians (and occasionally, in an ironic reversal, Boxers) were accused of smearing blood or
some other red substance on the doors of people's homes. The rumors
triggered by such acts, although various, always focused on the harm
promised to the homes' occupants: either they would fall sick and possibly
die or they would go mad and kill each other or they would burn to death
or their children would be kidnapped.[67] A Boxer notice announced that in
the prefectural city of Zhengding (in western Zhili near the Shanxi border), on the night of June 22, everyone went insane after touching the circles and crosses smeared in blood on their doors.[68] The Boxers, in addition
to spreading such charges, in their other role as society's protectors also
counseled people that, if they found blood markings on their doors, they
could prevent further harm by removing them with a mixture of lime and
human urine.[69]

Similar rumors accused the foreigners and Christians of cutting human
figures out of paper and placing them in the streets, where after coming to
life they would bring death to large numbers of people,[70] of depositing on
the roads cakes laced with poison for unsuspecting people to pick up and
eat,[71] and of stealing children.[72] But by far the most widely circulated rumor
of this genre was one that charged foreigners and Christians with contaminating the water supply by placing poison in village wells. This rumor
appeared in Caozhou, Shandong, as early as 1899, where it was readily
believed owing to the prevalence of typhus and "a certain sort of plague."[73]
During the spring and summer of 1900 the well-poisoning charge became
"practically universal" in North China "and accounted for much of the
insensate fury" directed by ordinary Chinese against Christians.[74]

Well-poisoning was regularly alluded to in Boxer notices, which not
infrequently incorporated recipes for herbal remedies to counter the effects
of the poison. Thus, a placard posted in Beijing concluded with the following warning and guidance: "At present there are foreigners who secretly
have placed poison in the wells. To neutralize the poison simmer seven
smoked plums, five *qian* [1 *qian* = 5 grams] of eucommia bark, and five
qian of *maocao* [coarse grass?] in water and swallow."[75] Such information,
of course, while again putting the Boxers forward as society's guardians and
saviors, also served, inevitably, to confirm and exacerbate the populace's
worst fears.

In addition, the well-poisoning charge supplied a ready-made vehicle
for people to avenge private grievances that had nothing to do with the
Boxer movement and its publicly professed goals. Liu Dapeng reports that,

in the latter half of July, every day brought reports of villages in Shanxi putting to death poisoners.[76] Liu's assertion, however, needs to be placed alongside Rowena Bird's observation, frequently reiterated in her letters and journal, that the people killed were often "outside" people, who had nothing whatever to do with the local foreign community. Conditions, Bird wrote from Taigu on July 6, "are growing more and more desperate, new outrages are committed each day, till not only Christians but people generally are fearful for their lives. . . . Last night two men, not Christians, were killed in a village near[by], on the charge that, hired by the foreigners, they were poisoning wells and scattering medicines. These men had no connection with us, and respectable men in the village went security for the[m], but it was no use, they were at once burned to death."[77]

The well-poisoning scare in North China in 1900 came as close as anything at the time to a mass panic. Elvin has suggested that the population of the area in which the Boxers were most active in the latter part of 1899 and early 1900, stretching from Qingzhou and Weixian in northwestern Shandong to Tianjin and Tongzhou (outside the capital) in Zhili, was particularly prone to mass hysteria.[78] In support of this hypothesis, he draws attention to two other panics that erupted in the region in the latter years of the nineteenth century. One was a flood scare fomented in 1872 by the Shengxian sect, which was active in the area south of Baoding. The leaders of this sect, according to the *North-China Herald*'s Baoding correspondent, proclaimed that "on a certain date a flood of waters would devastate the country, and only the faithful few who prepared themselves for its coming by building boats, [*sic*] could escape—like another Noah—from the ruin that would overtake the land. Boats were built in immense numbers, and far and wide provision was made for the fated day." This day came and passed, however, "to the confusion of those whose arks, ready provisioned for a voyage, stood unconcealed before their doors. Many broke up their boats at once, but every here and there in that district you still [twenty years later] come across them half-decayed and used for all sorts of purposes."[79]

The second instance of mass hysteria cited by Elvin was a kidnapping panic that began in Tianjin in 1897 and spread rapidly to other parts of Zhili and Shandong. This panic targeted foreigners as the main culprits and was, in many ways, a dress rehearsal for the rumor scares of the Boxer period. "From Tientsin," the *North-China Herald* reported in late June, "we hear . . . that a state of absolute panic reigns in the city. The natives cannot sleep at night for fear of kidnappers, and they are being urged on by anti-foreign intriguers, and rascals who have baser ends to serve, to vent their spite on foreigners." Such kidnapping rumors apparently were circulated annually

170   in Tianjin, "about the time of the advent of the grain junks from the south," when there was in fact a greater or lesser amount of buying and kidnapping of children mainly by Cantonese junkmen. This year, however, the rumors were "unusually virulent," owing to the imminent reopening of the Roman Catholic cathedral that had been destroyed in 1870, unemployment fears attending the completion in June of the Beijing-Tianjin railway, and a number of other factors. The completion of the railway had given rise to tales in the capital "about children buried under the ties and slain to solidify the bridges." The old stories of hearts and eyes being dug out for foreign use were revived "and found ready credence." In one part of Shandong a captured kidnapper was said to have confessed to having sold a heart and two eyes to the foreigners for 100 taels, and in another part a notice was posted stating that 500 hypnotists had been dispatched from Tianjin to victimize children. Many unfortunate Chinese wrongfully accused of being kidnappers were subjected to horrible judicial deaths.[80] Then, by late summer or early fall, like the flood scare of 1872 and comparable outbreaks of mass hysteria in other places and times, the kidnapping rumors died out, as suddenly and enigmatically as they had begun.[81]

    That there were prior instances of mass hysteria in the same region in which the Boxers were active from late 1899 into the summer of 1900 is undeniable. The question is: How unusual was this? Did the bouts of mass panic that can be documented for the Zhili-Shandong region result, as Elvin suggests, from the special characteristics of the inhabitants of this area or was such hysteria encountered more generally in China in situations in which, for whatever reason, collective anxieties were at a high pitch? This is not the place to attempt a comprehensive answer to these questions. It is enough to note that the researches of a number of scholars suggest that such mass panics occurred in many parts of China and with considerable frequency. The queue-clipping scare of 1768 studied by Kuhn had its origins in Zhejiang province and was mainly concentrated in east-central China. Ter Haar has documented a wide range of mass panics from the late sixteenth century onward, some centered on queue-clipping, many on kidnapping fears, and erupting not only in North China but also in Fujian, northern Hubei, Guangxi, Guangdong, and especially the lower Yangzi region.[82]

    Ter Haar also makes several other points that are pertinent here. One of his key arguments—a thesis which, incidentally, the main thrust of Elvin's analysis supports—is that violent action taken against Christian missionaries and converts was, more often than not, an adaptation of preexisting cultural and social patterns that were of long standing and, in their origins, had nothing to do with foreigners or Christians. Even more pertinent for our purposes is ter Haar's insistence upon the importance of situational factors—as opposed to the behavioral proclivities of the populace of a given region—in generating conditions conducive to mass hysteria. Thus, the antiforeign disturbances that took place in the Yangzi River valley in 1891 occurred against a background of heightened tension owing to drought (which hit city-dwellers, the main perpetrators of the riots, especially hard) and were part of a pattern of intensified criminal violence in the area that was unconnected with missionaries or foreigners. More generally, ter Haar points out that rumors spread more rapidly—and rumor panics tended to break out with greater frequency—in densely populated areas with well-frequented channels of trade and travel, which would apply, of course, not only to North China but also to the other regions in which the panics he discusses took place.[83] Another situational factor bearing on the extent and rapidity of rumor circulation, which my own reading of Boxer-era materials strongly suggests, is the response of the authorities, both central and local, to the initial appearance of rumors. One reason why North China experienced such an epidemic of rumors in the spring and summer of 1900 was the uncertainty of the court at the outset as to how to respond to the Boxer movement and its eventual decision to support it, which, from the populace's point of view, seemed to throw a cloak of legitimacy over even the wildest of Boxer claims. The spread of rumors, in such circumstances, instead of being contained (which was usually the Chinese government's interest with respect to rumors), was encouraged, and nowhere was it encouraged more than in Shanxi province, which had a governor (Yuxian) well known for his strong pro-Boxer and antiforeign feelings. This may help to account for the exceptional jitteriness of the Shanxi population, as documented by Liu Dapeng, on the Chinese side, and Rowena Bird and other missionaries, on the foreign.

Leaving aside the question of whether the population of North China, or at least large portions of it, showed an unusual susceptibility to mass hysteria, I would suggest that a question that is of at least equal interest has to do with the content of the hysteria in this case. Why mass poisoning? And why, in particular, the poisoning of public water sources? If one accepts the view that rumors convey messages and that rumor epidemics, in particular, supply important symbolic information concerning the collective worries of societies in crisis, one approach to answering such questions is to try to identify the match or fit between a rumor panic and its immediate context. In the case of kidnapping panics, which have a long history not only in China but in many other societies as well, the focus of collective concern is the safety of children, who (as the term *kidnap* seems to imply) are almost always seen as the primary victims.[84] Rumors of mass poisoning, on the other hand, are far more appropriate as a symbolic response to a crisis, such as war or natural disaster or epidemic, in which *all* the members of society are potentially at risk.

Such is, in fact, exactly what we find to be the case. Charges of well-poisoning and similar crimes were brought against the first Christians in Rome and the Jews in the Middle Ages at the time of the Black Plague (1348). During the cholera epidemic in Paris in 1832 a rumor circulated that poison powder had been scattered in the bread, vegetables, milk, and water of that city. In the early stages of the Great War, rumors were spread in all belligerent countries that enemy agents were busy poisoning the water supplies. Newspaper accounts in 1937, at the onset of the Sino-Japanese War, accused Chinese traitors of poisoning the drinking water of Shanghai.[85] Within hours of the great Tokyo earthquake of September 1, 1923, which was accompanied by raging fires, rumors began to circulate charging ethnic Koreans and socialists not only with having set the fires but also with plotting rebellion and poisoning the wells.[86] And rumors of mass poisoning proliferated in Biafra during the Nigerian civil conflict of the late 1960s.[87]

In many of these instances, the rumors targeted outsiders (or their internal agents), who were accused, symbolically if not literally, of seeking the annihilation of the society in which the rumors circulated. This, of course, closely approximates the situation prevailing in China at the time of the Boxer uprising. Like the charge that the foreigners were the ones ultimately responsible for the lack of rain in the spring and summer of 1900, rumors accusing foreigners and their native surrogates of poisoning North China's water supplies portrayed outsiders symbolically as depriving Chinese of what was most essential for the sustaining of life. The well-poisoning rumor epidemic thus spoke directly to the collective fear that was uppermost in the minds of ordinary people at the time: the fear of death.

CHAPTER 6

Death

Several thousand Boxers had assembled in Zhangdeng [township in Qingyuan county, Zhili]. It was the eighth day of the fifth month [June 4, 1900]. At sundown there was a huge commotion along with sounds of shrieking and wailing. It was discovered that the Boxers had burned several dozen Christian families to death. A workman who went to have a look reported that the men of the families had fled, leaving only the women, who were incinerated in their homes. When one young woman escaped from the flames, her belly was cut open with a sword by the Boxers. One could hear the sound of skin separating from bones. Several Boxers grabbed the woman by the thighs and arms and threw her back into the flames. The savagery was unspeakable. The stench traveled for several *li*.

Ai Sheng, resident of Dingxing county, Zhili[1]

The Boxers didn't kill people indiscriminately. We killed people with a purpose in mind. . . . When we wanted to kill people we made sure they were secondary hairy ones [Christians].

Li Yuanshan, former Boxer, Tianjin[2]

On the way [from the capital to Tianjin in late August 1900] we passed villages and scattered farms, all absolutely deserted. The crops were ripening in the fields, but there was no one to look after them or to reap them. They were left to rot. At a season when in ordinary years the country is alive with busy folk, when every field has its watcher's booth, when every threshing-floor is rolled afresh, and men, women, and children, all turn out to bring in the harvest, now not a soul was to be seen. We went into house after house, broken cups and plates lay upon the floor, an evil stench warned the intruder from corners, the water from the wells had a strange taste savouring of disease and death.

Roland Allen, British chaplain, Beijing[3]

174   On this day [GX 26/5/29 or June 25, 1900] someone saw a corpse on the slope
by the Lüzu Hall.[a] It was a man who had been killed by the [Boxer] bandit
chief Cao Futian. His testicles had been cut off and his head severed and
placed between his thighs, facing upward stiff and motionless. It was
unspeakably horrible. These people regard life as a trifling matter. When
they kill a person, they rarely dispatch him with a clean blow of the sword;
more often they slash indiscriminately with their swords and chop the body
into pieces. The horror of the slaughter they perpetrate is even worse than
that of the punishment of death by dismemberment.

Liu Mengyang, resident of Tianjin[4]

Within the capital and in an area outside it extending over a hundred *li* in
all directions, the dead numbered in the tens of thousands. Corpses were
piled up everywhere with no one to bury them . . . and the stench of the rotting flesh and bones strewn across the roadways was unbearable. The
extreme suffering of the common people was everywhere in evidence.
Thousands of homes were burned down by the raging flames, which day and
night lit up the sky. In my judgment, the capital has not suffered such cruel
devastation since the beginning of the Qing.

Hong Shoushan, resident of Beijing[5]

The Boxers cut our Christian babies in pieces and now the Japanese and
Russians have returned double, quadruple, for all they gave. The stories the
soldiers tell us are too horrible to put on paper.

Sarah Goodrich, American missionary, Beijing[6]

When the story of the Boxer uprising is told, the high points, depending on
one's point of view, are generally the characteristics of the Boxers as a
movement (their superstition, backwardness, xenophobia, patriotism) or
the martyrdom endured by the Christian community or the righteousness
and heroism of the foreign military response or the consequences of the
uprising (or more precisely its diplomatic settlement) for China's subsequent history. We of course hear of the deaths that occurred. But, more
often than not, this part of the story is told in the flat, impersonal language
of statistics, even when, as in the following statement by Harold Isaacs, a
certain amount of feeling informs the telling: "Before the bloodletting of
1900 was over, more than 200 *foreign devils* and a reported total of some
30,000 *secondary devils* (Chinese Christians) had been killed, and an
Allied punitive expedition that marched from Tientsin to Peking, and later

---

[a] A shrine in honor of Lü Dongbin (Tang or Song), one of the Eight Immortals of Daoist
tradition. Located just west of the Tianjin city wall, the Lüzu Hall was the site of a major
Boxer headquarters, established by Cao Futian in the first half of June.

fanned out over northeastern China, took many times more that number in gross retribution. There was Christian martyrdom; then there was looting, rapine, and slaughter by the avenging Christian armies."[7]

Death, in such accounts, becomes a collective marker. It stands as a metaphor for the cruelty of the Boxers or the brutality of the foreign relief forces or the suffering of the Christians or the slaying of innocents. But its meaning as an expression of individual experience is largely lost. It is this experiential side of death that I want to try to reclaim in the pages that follow, focusing on the death and destruction that resulted from combat and other acts of violence.

Apart from such actualized death, there was of course the much broader phenomenon of death anxiety, which, as we have seen in the immediately preceding chapters, was on a lot of people's minds in North China in 1900. Farmers idled by the continued failure of the rains in the spring became progressively more hungry and also progressively more nervous, especially (one imagines) those of them over thirty who retained vivid memories of the death and horror wrought by the famine of the late 1870s. Young Boxers spent many hours learning and practicing invulnerability rituals designed to confer immunity to death, and much of the Boxers' magic was specifically directed either at ensuring the death of their foes or protecting against the death of their supporters among the general population. The anxiety rumors that were rampant throughout the region in the spring and summer typically had as their central content images of death or grave bodily harm; even the wish rumors that also had wide circulation may plausibly be seen as providing emotional release from the fear of death. Finally, as if other sources of death anxiety were not already abundant enough, notices posted all over North China repeatedly concluded with dire warnings of the catastrophic end sure to befall those who chose to ignore the Boxers' message.

The actual experience of death was not as pervasive as the death consciousness just described. But it was pervasive enough. Decreed public executions either of anti-Boxer officials or of foreign missionaries were, it is true, carried out in only a few places (Beijing in the case of the former, Taiyuan and other localities in Shanxi in the case of the latter). And in many parts of North China, where the Christian population was of negligible size or nonexistent or the Boxer movement had not taken firm root, there was relatively little major violence. But in many other parts of the region, there were Boxer pogroms against Chinese Christians — and sometimes reverse "pogroms" led by Christians against non-Christians. Moreover, although the parts of North China that had direct experience of full-scale warfare — principally the Tianjin and Beijing areas and the corridor

176 connecting them—were fairly limited in geographical scale, much vaster areas, including parts of Manchuria and Shanxi and much of Zhili, experienced the terror of foreign campaigns of retribution from late summer 1900 until the spring of 1901—a subject that, although often alluded to, still awaits comprehensive study by Western scholars.[8]

What is noteworthy about the experience of violent death in 1900 is not that it was not widespread but that it was not uniform. Different individuals experienced death in different ways. Some were victims, others perpetrators, still others witnesses. Some wrote of the sights and sounds of death—and of death's distinctive smells. Others described the terrors that they personally or people they knew or had observed had gone through in the face of death. And many recounted the fearful choices that had to be made. The experience of death, in short, like the experience of anything, was a highly individual matter. It was also, more perhaps than any other form of experience, supremely biographical. History, after all, does not die, nor does society. It is the individual who dies. Because of death's unique properties as the terminator and terminus of life, the fear and apprehension surrounding it are key to the formation of biographical consciousness; they tend to pull people away from history and society, toward an intense concern with their own personal destinies.

Much of the literature on death, I discovered when I first looked, has to do with the formal and informal rituals people in different cultures have devised to ease the transition across this greatest, and most final, of life's divides. A disproportionate share of the death that people in China experienced in the summer of 1900, however, was raw death, unadorned by ritual of any kind. And, so, death, the ultimate object of the anxiety that was so pervasive at the time, also, because of the way in which it was encountered, became an added source of this very anxiety.

Witnesses

Images of horror—of brutality, physical destruction, and immense human suffering—presented themselves to millions of inhabitants of North China in 1900. Ai Sheng, in his chronicle of Boxer activities in Dingxing and neighboring Laishui county, described several incidents that occurred in his area. On May 12 an armed group of several hundred people led by Boxers killed over thirty Catholic families in Gaoluo village in Laishui, then stuffed the bodies into a wellpit and burned down the victims' homes. On July 13 a friend returning from Yizhou, just west of Laishui city, reported that the Boxers there had beheaded four female members of a

Christian family and hung the males from a tree. Then they made a banner, killed the men, and offered them as a sacrifice to the banner. "The whole town turned out to watch, thinking they could now look forward to peace and well-being. How," the friend intoned, "can popular sentiment be moved by such evil acts?"

On August 17, three days after the entrance of the foreign relief force into the capital, fleeing Chinese troops arrived in the Dingxing area in large numbers, creating a good deal of havoc. A local Boxer leader, Wang Luoyao, stole into the county seat and, together with bandits, smashed the lock on the south gate, permitting the routed soldiers to pour in. The soldiers looted the markets and there was much firing of guns. Ai Sheng had managed to evacuate his immediate family from Dingxing two days earlier. Four members of a cousin's family, less fortunate, threw themselves into the ancestral well and died.[9]

Guan He recounted an incident in the Tianjin area in which Boxers, after robbing several dozen Christians, dug a huge pit, drove their victims into it, and filled it with earth and stones. "The sounds of the screams and the sight of the suffering," he wrote, "were unbearable."[10]

Also in the Tianjin area, a man named Zhang reported that, when passing through Yang Family village on July 1, he came upon two corpses by the roadside, one male, one female, with fresh sword wounds all over their bodies. Two small children, a boy and a girl, lay crying next to the bodies. Horrified at the sight and afraid the children would starve to death, Zhang took them home with him.[11]

Foreign missionaries, not surprisingly, had especially fearsome stories to relate about Boxer cruelty to Christians. Olivia Ogren (CIM), in Yongning, Shanxi, reported that the man who had worked as postman for the local missionaries "had been caught by the Boxers, dragged from prison, where the official had sought to protect him, and beheaded. His head was, along with many others, nailed to the city wall, until his widow was released from prison, when she took it down." Some Christians, Ogren continued, "had been maimed for life. One grey-headed old man had been hanged by his thumbs for half a day. Others had had a cross cut on the forehead by a sword."[12]

In Beijing, Courtenay Fenn described the consequences of the terror unleashed by the Boxers on the night of June 13: "In the following days . . . there came into our compound the straggling remnants of our native Church, wives without husbands, husbands without wives, parents without children and children without parents! The Boxers, with prepared blacklists, had gone throughout the city, hunting down all who had been con-

178   nected with the foreigners, cutting them down, hacking them to pieces, or carrying them off for more terrible torture in a Boxer camp."[13]

During the early days of the Battle of Tianjin, according to Liu Mengyang, many inhabitants of the city tried to flee. It was hard to take the river route out of the city, however, as the Boxers had blocked it with boats. At Yangliuqing, a market town not far to the west, the Boxers insisted on searching all boats passing through. The pretext was that they were looking for spies, the real reason (according to Liu) was plunder. Sometimes the Boxers falsely accused people of being Christians, killed them, and threw their bodies into the river; if enough people were dispatched in this way in succession the waters of the river changed color. Liu also reported (on June 26) that, ever since the onset of the Boxer rising, almost every day corpses could be seen floating in the Grand Canal in Tianjin. Most of them were missing limbs. All had been killed and disfigured by the Boxers. "On one day a female corpse without its head, still clutching the dead body of a child, came downstream. It was a dreadful sight to behold."[14]

According to James Ricalton, a photographer sent by his publisher to China to obtain a visual record of the Boxer uprising, several times a day coolies with poles were sent to a particular spot on the Baihe (White River) in Tianjin "to set free the accumulation of bodies and allow them to float down stream." Ricalton claimed to have seen "heads and headless trunks in this flotsam of war." Although in the stereograph he took, there were only a few bodies in view, at other times he reported having seen much larger numbers, "especially in the morning, after a night's accumulation." Many of the dead, according to him, had been killed by the foreign relief forces, many others by the Boxers, and "doubtless a considerable number" were suicides.[15]

Earlier, on July 5, Ricalton had taken a military barge from Tanggu to Tianjin. Here is his graphic account of what he observed along the way: "Many mud villages were passed . . . , from most of which the inhabitants had fled back into the country. We were constantly passing dead bodies floating down, and, on either bank of the river, at every turn, hungry dogs from the deserted villages could be seen tearing at the swollen corpses left on the banks by the ebb tide. It was forty miles of country laid waste, deserted homes, burned villages, along a river polluted and malodorous with human putrefaction."[16]

Prior to the conclusion of the Battle of Tianjin in mid-July, Guan He and his wife fled the city and made their way south by boat. Guan described what they saw: "There were many corpses floating in the river. Some were without heads, others were missing limbs. The bodies of women often had their nipples cut off and their genitalia mutilated. . . . There were also bodies in the shallow areas by the banks, with flocks of crows pecking away at them. The smell was so bad we had to cover our noses the whole day. Still, no one came out to collect the bodies for burial. People said that they were all Christians who had been killed by the Boxers and the populace dared not get involved."[17]

On her way by boat from Beijing to Tianjin on the North Grand Canal in late August, Emma Martin, who had nursed wounded foreigners in the makeshift legation hospital during the siege, described the results of the

6.1 Bodies Floating in Baihe in Tianjin. This photograph, taken by James Ricalton, also shows shell-damaged buildings along the French bund. Courtesy of the Library of Congress.

180   relief force's northward trek earlier in the month: "Scores of dead Chinese had been shot along the way and their bodies left to rot in the sun or be eaten by dogs and worms. Many of the bodies were in the water and sometimes the stench was dreadful. We had to use this river water for cooking and I had to drink it once."[18]

Not all deaths were the direct result of combat. On July 11, during the siege in Beijing, Nigel Oliphant reports that the French captured twenty Chinese on Customs Road and, as they would not give any information, "slaughtered the lot in cold blood," one corporal "polishing off fourteen with his bayonet in record time."[19] Only a little less summary was the justice meted out in Tianjin after a Chinese assassinated a French officer on a foreign settlement street. A dozen or so coolies were promptly rounded up and rushed to military headquarters, where they were executed "on evidence," according to the assessment of Herbert Hoover, an engineer in China at the time, "that merits rank with the Salem witchcraft, and again demonstrates that the foreigner himself can be a barbarian."[20]

For the residents of Beijing and Tianjin, the horror of the summer of 1900 was divisible into two phases: an initial period during which effective control was in the hands of the Boxers and a later one, beginning in mid-

6.2   French Interrogation of Chinese Prisoners. After questioning, according to the source of this photograph, prisoners were routinely shot. From J.-J. Matignon, *La Défense de la Légation de France (Pékin, du 13 Juin au 15 Août 1900)* (Paris: Libraires Associés, 1902).

July in Tianjin and mid-August in Beijing, during which both cities came under foreign occupation. The point of transition between the two phases was particularly gruesome. With the foreign conquest of Tongzhou (a dozen or so miles east of the capital) on August 12, routed Chinese soldiers began to flood into Beijing, and the inhabitants of the city became panicky. The gates were closed. There were few people on the streets. Boxer altars were demolished and all other signs of the Boxers' existence destroyed. Shops were closed for trade, families barred their doors. Many thought of fleeing. But with the city gates barred, it was hard to leave, and with soldiers all about looting and killing, one wouldn't have wanted to step out of doors anyway. Boxers not native to Beijing vanished, Boxers native to the city changed their dress. In a day and a night, according to one account, all traces of the Boxer presence had disappeared.[21] An old soldier accompanying the imperial entourage on its flight west described the circumstances attending the foreign assault when it came. People in the Imperial City lit fires and burned themselves to death. Many women, unable to flee, threw themselves into the moat, which became so clogged with bodies that the water stopped flowing. Corpses from the fighting were piled high along the roadways.[22] Luella Miner, after climbing up the tower of the Qian Gate, shared her reactions to what she saw on the afternoon of August 16: "It was a sad afternoon, and I know now that war is hell. . . . There were bodies of Chinese soldiers and Boxers lying below the wall, the buildings on the side nearest the legations were a mass of ruins, and we saw party after party of poor refugees, men, women, and children, fleeing from the doomed city. We watched some of the towers over the city gates burning, and many other fires."[23]

In Tianjin, a month earlier, it was much the same. A Chinese eyewitness described in some detail the pandemonium that ensued with the final burst of foreign troops into the city on July 14:

> People rushed about in all directions, in dread of what was to come next. When someone shouted that the North Gate was open and that it was possible to leave by it, the whole city converged on the North Gate. In an instant the press of the crowd was such that one couldn't move. . . . The foreigners and Christians climbed the drum tower [in the center of the city]. From this vantage point they saw the crowd at the North Gate unable to get out and fired repeatedly on it, each volley resulting in the deaths of several tens of people. . . . The greater the numbers of people killed, the greater became the numbers of those fighting to escape. Some were killed by the shells. Some lost their footing and were trampled to death. Some people were hacked to death by the swords people were using to slash their way through the throng.

182   Some were thrown to the ground. . . . When those in front fell, those behind also fell. The more people were trampled upon, the more people died. The pile of trampled bodies grew higher and higher. . . . A woman led a child by the hand. Just as they were pushing and squeezing their way forward, a shell struck and the child fell to the ground. Wailing and weeping, the woman said: "I fled for the sake of this piece of flesh. Now it's gone." She then turned around and went back home. Another woman held an infant in her arms. The woman was hit by a shell and dropped to the ground. The infant at her breast continued to make baby sounds and cry. The pedestrians trampled on them and the infant died, too. Dead from bullets, dead from artillery shells, dead from swords, dead from trampling. It was horrible. . . . The corpses were piled several feet high. After three days of cleaning up, following the foreigners' entry into the city, the streets still were not clean.[24]

Liu Mengyang's recounting of a walk he took through the city on the morning of July 16 supplied additional detail. Strolling eastward along Needle Market Street, he saw white flags hanging from all the shopfronts. The atmosphere was gloomy. There were few pedestrians. Continuing east he reached the beginning of Needle Market Street and turned south. He saw dead bodies lying helter-skelter by the roadside. Going further south, he came to the bridge outside the North Gate. The city moat was filled with corpses, a head sticking out here, a foot there. There were foreign soldiers everywhere, also some Chinese mercenaries in foreign uniform. Liu felt afraid as he walked and dared not look into the soldiers' eyes. When he got to Wooden Bridge Lane, he thought he would cut through and return home via Needle Market Street, the way he had come. However, halfway down the lane, he came upon three bodies blocking his path. Unable to proceed, he retraced his steps and took a more roundabout route home. "Although I didn't see many sights on this stroll," Liu wrote in the concluding lines of the main part of his chronicle, "the atmosphere of gloom and desolation was unbearable. After I got home, I chanced to think back over everything. It was as though a great many dead bodies were ranged before my eyes. Recalling the painful experience [of the preceding few months], I felt heartbroken and depressed."[25]

As both Chinese and foreign observers noted, there was little to choose between Chinese and foreign brutality in the summer of 1900. During the occupation of Tianjin, foreign soldiers constantly humiliated and harassed the local population, frequently raping the women, especially in the Hedong section (east of the river), which was occupied by Russian and German troops.[26] In August a foreign force went to Duliu, Zhang Decheng's base, and burned down more than half the town. Many inhabitants, includ-

ing law-abiding subjects, were killed or injured and many women raped.[27]
In the terror visited upon Tianjin after the foreign victory, some residents
apparently hid their valuables in coffins along with the remains of dead family members. The foreign soldiers, on getting wind of this, broke open virtually every newly buried coffin in the suburban and guild cemeteries, flinging the bodies by the roadside to be eaten by wild dogs and pigs. When the
relatives of the deceased came to identify the corpses, the skeletal remains
were already incomplete. The coffin of a former Tianjin prefect, Li Shao-
yun, was reported to have been broken into on three separate occasions. "If

6.3   Dead Defenders at South Gate of Tianjin's Chinese City. Ricalton, who claimed
that the bodies belonged to Boxers, took this photograph immediately after the foreign
entry into the city. Courtesy of the Library of Congress.

184   we look at this in light of the doctrine of karma," a Japanese chronicler intoned, "what did this man do while alive that was so bad as to merit such cruel treatment?"[28]

The day after the arrival of the foreign relief force in Beijing, Luella Miner wrote in her journal:

> The conduct of the Russian soldiers is *atrocious*, the French are not much better, and the Japanese are looting and burning without mercy. . . . The Russians all the way up from Tientsin butchered women and children without mercy, and women and girls by hundreds have committed suicide to escape a worse fate at the hands of Russian and Japanese brutes. Our American soldiers saw them jumping into the river and into wells, in T'ungchow [Tongzhou] twelve girls in one well, and one mother was drowning two of her little children in a large water jar. . . . It is easy to say that China has brought this calamity on herself—that this is not war but punishment—but when we *can* distinguish the innocent from the guilty why stain the last pages of the century's history by records which would disgrace the annals of the dark ages? Sweet lessons in "western civilization" we are giving to the Chinese.[29]

Lest it be thought that Americans were invariably above reproach in their conduct during and after the Boxer War (as contemporary American accounts generally seemed to imply), one British officer in Beijing entered the following comment in his diary for August 15: "The Americans I watched some time, lying in wait at the end of each street and shooting every Chinese that showed his head."[30] Americans, moreover, including even some missionaries, were among the most vigorous defenders of the reprisals and looting that took place in the war's aftermath.[31] It is only fair to note, on the other hand, that Washington prohibited its forces from participating in punitive expeditions against the Chinese population in the winter of 1900–1901, and the record of the American occupation force in the capital received high grades from the Chinese officials of the day.[32]

There was broad agreement among contemporary Chinese and foreign observers that German conduct in the months after the war was far less exemplary.[33] Gao Shaochen, who served as magistrate of Yongqing county (directly south of Beijing) from mid-June 1900 until late the following year and wrote a detailed account of his efforts to contain the violence in his jurisdiction, described a serious incident that took place on February 13, 1901. On this day more than a thousand German troops arrived at the west entrance of Yongqing city and, without warning, opened fire, killing some two hundred Chinese soldiers and civilians. The population, stunned, scurried frantically in all directions. Gao ran into an officer of the Chinese garrison leaving the city on foot. Suddenly, German soldiers started to beat the two men with their rifle butts and then tied their queues together and kicked and punched them, to the point where they sustained serious injuries. After this, the German officers made them kneel for a long time in the snow. They then ordered their troops to surround the city, in which four hundred people were still trapped, and to fire continuously. Gao, after payment of a generous sum of money, obtained his release from his foreign captors. On reaching the west entrance of the city, he heard cries and came upon the four hundred trapped residents, kneeling in rows, about to be shot. After some melodramatic moments, including (as Gao tells it) an offer on his part to sacrifice his own life to save the lives of his people, the German officer was moved and, praising Gao for his courage and compassion, pardoned them all and counseled them thereafter to be good people. The Germans then beat their drums, blew their horns, waved their flags, and left. "When I went back into the city," Gao concluded, "dead bodies were strewn everywhere, creating a heartrending scene." He quickly issued burial instructions for those corpses that could be identified and gave further orders for the thirty or so dead soldiers to be interred together and a joint stele erected at the gravesite.[34]

The cruelty, extreme violence, and generally unpredictable behavior of German soldiers was also encountered in the area directly west of Tianjin. Liu Xizi, a gentry manager of the Yangliuqing *baojia* bureau, wrote that, when the Germans passed through a place, "it was like the sudden arrival of a hurricane." Everywhere, officials, gentry, and commoners had been killed or injured by them. Although, in the end, Liu's own village was spared, partly because of good luck and partly because it had taken the precaution of stockpiling supplies that the Germans would be likely to requisition, the villagers lived in a state of constant fear and wariness.[35]

Perpetrators

Up to this point, I have mainly focused on death as experienced by witnesses. What about the emotional reactions of those more immediately involved in the business of killing and being killed, the combatants themselves? It seems abundantly evident that, among the latter, a combined process of depersonalization and demonization often took hold, making it possible to kill, mutilate, and otherwise violate fellow human beings with little or no sense of remorse. Years later a former Boxer gave symbolic expression to this process when, in recalling an angry mob's killing of two Catholic nuns near Tianjin, he used the term *zai*, normally reserved for the slaughtering of animals, to describe the crowd's action.[36]

186   Dehumanization operated, it is clear, on all sides of the conflict. Although "Boxerism" in the twentieth-century West became, in the minds of many, emblematic of the savagery and barbarism specifically of the non-Western world, to more than a few Westerners actually on the scene in China in 1900 the human race resisted such tidy bifurcation.[37] Indeed, it seems fairly plain that all human beings, without regard to race, educational level, class, ethnicity, or cultural background, have the capacity in certain situations—war perhaps being the most common—to define their adversaries as less than human and then treat them accordingly.[38]

Even more remarkable, perhaps, than the ability of human beings to behave as savages toward other human beings is their capacity, in the face of death, to experience simultaneously the more familiar emotions of fear, sadness, compassion, courage, even shame. Laurie Lee, who fought in the Spanish Civil War, described the climactic moment of his experience in that conflict: "I headed for the old barn where I'd spent my first night. I lay in a state of sick paralysis. I had killed a man, and remembered his shocked, angry eyes. . . . I began to have hallucinations and breaks in the brain. . . . Was this then what I'd come for, and all my journey had meant—to smudge out the life of an unknown young man in a blur of panic which in no way could affect victory or defeat?"[39]

One possible starting point for unraveling the paradox of the contradictory behavior of men in war is the recognition that death has two faces, which are experienced in fundamentally different ways. Death is ordinary, in the sense that it happens to all human beings without exception. This is the face of death that people who grow beyond childhood encounter on a virtually daily basis. It may occur as a result of natural causes or unnatural ones. It may happen singly or plurally. It may be impersonal in the sense that one does not know the individual who has died and only reads about it in the newspapers or sees it on television, or it may be intensely personal, as in the death of a family member or friend. It may inspire horror or anguish or, since it is someone else's death and not one's own, profound relief. Or, especially in the case of mass death that repeats itself to the point of becoming routine, it may elicit a response of pervasive numbness. But, however it manifests itself, ordinary death has one characteristic that is defining: it is the death that happens to others.

The other face of death, far from ordinary, is the death that each of us, individually, experiences. This death occurs only once. Because it entails not only the end of physical existence but also a complete rupture of consciousness, its prospect is profoundly disturbing and people respond to it with powerful emotions.

Ordinary death and extraordinary death are, of course, two sides of the same thing, in the sense that each individual's death, although unique and therefore extraordinary for that individual, is an "ordinary" death for everyone else. Moreover, to the extent that, at some level of our consciousness, when we encounter the death of others we are reminded of our own mortality, there is also a deep subjective connection between these two faces of death. This subjective link is, I would guess, especially strong in situations, such as warfare, where death is not a by-product of other activities but the paramount objective of the central activity everyone is engaged in. Killing and getting killed, after all, are what war is ultimately about.

Viewed in this way, it is not at all remarkable to find, alongside the heartlessness and cruelty so conspicuous among combatants both Chinese and foreign in 1900, a range of other behavioral characteristics of a more "human" nature. Although it was common, as we have seen, for elite Chinese and foreigners to deride the performance of the Boxers in combat, there were those, within both groups, who took at least partial exception to this judgment. Yang Mushi, a Qing army officer who fought against the Boxers in the Xincheng area in late May and early June, reported to Nie Shicheng that the Boxers' main strength lay in their numbers and the fact that they were "not afraid to die." Ai Sheng, a persistent Boxer critic, also conceded that, when in a possessed state, the Boxers "invariably faced death unflinchingly."[40] Herbert Hoover made much the same point, at least implicitly, in his account of the behavior of Boxer fighters on the first day of the Chinese assault on the railway station in Tianjin (June 18): "The Boxers came in front, and their charges, almost up to the muzzles of the Russian guns, were the charges which only fanatics can perpetrate. In charging, when one was shot his companions would raise him from the ground, shake him, and try to set him on his feet, apparently believing that it could not be death."[41] A German officer who had participated in the Seymour expedition confirmed that the Boxers simply did not believe they could be killed: "I . . . saw some of the Boxers running up to our men armed only with knives. They would be hit by a bullet, but would get up again and recommence running; sometimes even after three or four shots they would rise. In one body I counted no less than four wounds."[42]

Roland Allen supplied a similar appraisal of Boxer fighting valor in his recounting of a battle that took place on August 20 between Bengal Lancers and a small band of Boxers armed only with swords and spears in the imperial hunting park south of the capital: "The Boxer, inflamed with fanatic zeal, is almost as mad as a Dervish. One of them, it was said, though pierced right through the body, yet struggled free and renewed the attack."

188   "Such conduct," he added, "was unknown in the Japanese war, and probably had not been seen since the rising of the T'ai P'ings. It was only another proof that the Chinese can fight and will fight, in his own cause, whilst he will not fight when led by officers in whom he reposes no trust, in a cause which he does not understand."[43]

Along with frequent demonstrations of personal courage, the Boxers, as their casualties mounted in fighting against adversaries who were almost invariably better armed, also became progressively more frightened. During one of the climactic battles in the conflict in Tianjin, we are told, some two thousand Boxers were killed. Chinese government troops, having previously sustained very high casualties themselves, were scornful of the Boxers' invulnerability claims and ordered the Boxers to the front lines, on pain of death. The Boxers advanced with their swords and, when the foreigners fired on them, got down on their knees and prayed to Heaven for protection. This, however, was of no avail, and after the Boxers up front were killed, the ones behind were terrified and tried to flee. When the government soldiers saw this, they were furious and fired their guns at the retreating Boxers. The huge number of Boxer deaths in the battle, therefore, was only partly owing to the firepower of the foreigners.[44]

On another occasion, according to Liu Mengyang, when Qing commander Song Qing ordered them to defend a certain location, the Boxers all fled to escape foreign artillery. Greatly angered, Song instructed his troops to kill the Boxers, whereupon the latter threw their turbans, sashes, and weapons into the streets and scattered. Some Boxers hid in lanes and tossed their identifying clothing over the walls into people's courtyards. In the upshot, several hundred Boxers were killed, prompting the following caustic pun from Liu: "The Boxer bandits can't *hamper* [*bi*] guns, but they can *scamper* [*bi*] from guns."[45]

On August 19, a group of Boxers under the leadership of Liu Shijiu (Nineteen Liu) ran into a foreign force of over a thousand soldiers west of Tianjin. The Boxers were armed with antiquated rifles (commandeered from the gentry of Yangliuqing), which did not have much range and sounded like firecrackers when discharged. The foreigners waited until the Boxers' ammunition was spent, then surrounded them and fired volley after volley into their midst. "Unfortunately," wrote Liu Xizi, "the spirit soldiers of yore were suddenly turned into spirits [*gui*]." But "the most unbearable thing of all to see and hear," he added, in a grim reminder of Melville's assertion that "All wars are boyish, and are fought by boys," was the "children in their early teens lying by the roadside, with wounds to their arms and legs, crying out for their fathers and mothers."[46]

Like Liu Xizi—and Laurie Lee—the Boxers also were capable of hollowing out a quiet space in the noise of war for the demonstration of personal compassion. Luella Miner recounted an incident involving the thirteen-year-old son of a Chinese pastor from Baoding, whose entire immediate family had been killed by Boxers. The boy was later caught by a group of Boxers sixteen miles south of Baoding and was about to be put to death when one of his captors, after discovering that he was all alone in the world, stepped forward and announced that he would adopt the boy as his own son. The boy's deliverer, whom Miner identifies as one of three bachelor brothers, "all notorious bullies," kept the boy in his home for three months, "tenderly providing for every want," and, when it was subsequently found out that he had an uncle, also a pastor, who was still living, personally escorted him to Baoding to reunite them. The interesting thing about Miner's account is its demythologization of the Boxers. Even as Boxer behavior in general is represented by such characteristically lurid adjectives as "cut-throat" and "blood-thirsty," a lone Boxer, described in the account as "the terror of the region," is shown to have feelings of tenderness and compassion.[47]

On the foreign side, too, there was a wide range of reactions in situations shadowed by death. The young American marine who was so frightened at what he had heard about Chinese treatment of captives that he killed himself before ever experiencing combat was surely not the only foreigner terrified of meeting a horrible end.[48] There were others, on the other hand, who clearly had greater stores of fortitude. At the climactic point in the Battle of Tianjin, Ricalton described a scene of flatboats filled with wounded Japanese being evacuated from the front: "The spectacle they present is pitiful in the extreme; the bottoms of the boats are crowded with wounded men, some sitting, some lying, all in the hot sun; they are just brought from the muddy field where they have lain and moaned away a dreary night. The silence is funereal; they are not dead men; they are the wounded, many of them mortally; yet no word is spoken, even by the men poling the boats slowly along."[49] Lt. Richard A. Steel, a British subaltern who was part of the foreign relief expedition that left Tianjin for Beijing on August 4, confirmed the stoic courage of the Japanese: "Their wounded never uttered a sound, and I saw lots carried past me with horrible wounds, some actually joking with the stretcher bearers."[50]

Emotions of a quite different sort, reflecting the process of demonization earlier noted, were expressed by U.S. Marine Pvt. Oscar Upham when, during the pause in the fighting in Beijing on July 17, the Chinese began removing their dead from the Qian Gate wall: "its about time as they

190   have been lying there under our noses for near three weeks as they lower them off the wall in straw matting we can see heads and limbs fall out and flatten when they hit the ground, we are very thankful to them for removing their dead as the stench has been something awful for a dead chinaman has a peculiar oder [*sic*] all his own some of the bodies were lying within 3 or 4 feet of our barricade and were quite an inducement to the flies and I think all of the flies in Peking were here."[51]

Upham, as he described his own behavior in his log, was almost a caricature of the hardbitten marine for whom killing was part of a day's work. He related an incident that took place on August 14: "One of the Chinees [*sic*] had taken shelter behind the fence that faced Legation St. and was pumping away at us as fast as he could load, one of the 14th Inf. men spot-

6.4   Japanese Doctors Attending Their Wounded after Battle of Tianjin. Courtesy of the Library of Congress.

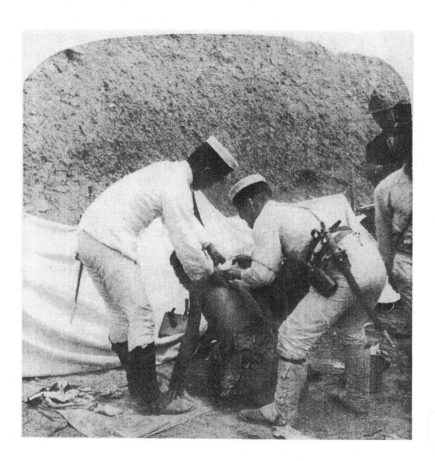

ted him and pointed him out to me, and said 'there he is! shoot him! shoot him!' I asked him why he didn't do a little shooting himself, he did[n't] answer but kept jumping up and down and yelling 'shoot him!' I tried two shots without affect [*sic*] but the third did the business, he was afterward found with a bullet hole through his head."[52]

Other foreign soldiers showed themselves to be more vulnerable. Richard Steel, who in January had been appointed aide-de-camp to Lord Curzon, the British viceroy of India, and was then assigned in June to China to serve as orderly to General Gaselee, the commander of the British contingent of the foreign relief force, related his personal responses to the action he saw enroute from Tianjin to the capital: In the fighting on August 5 a Chinese shell "burst just a few yards from me, killing and wounding several followers and mules and made me feel devilish uncomfortable for a bit. I'd never seen a man killed before!" And several days later: "The heat was *awful*, the whole road being littered with men fallen out, Americans, Japs, and ours. The country is so dense with crops we couldn't see anywhere, and the flies and bad water made life pretty sickening. Everywhere one came across dead bodies of Chinese and mules and horses in various degrees of foul decomposition. I nearly catted dozens of times. We couldn't go on, as men and beasts were absolutely cooked."[53]

In a letter to his sister, Pvt. Harold Kinman of the First Marine Battalion, who initially saw combat in the Philippines, then in China, and, after recovering from a wound in the U.S. Naval Hospital in Yokohama, again in the Philippines, provided an American perspective on the march from Tianjin to Beijing: "That march is imprinted on my memory that nothing can efface. It was full of terrible experiences, short of water, and forced to march after you were almost unable to walk. Fighting for your life every day, surrounded by Chinese Imperial troops numbering from 30,000 to 40,000 strong. Cutting your way out at the point of the bayonet while the shot and shell were flying all around you." On one occasion, after "putting the Chinese to utter rout," the marines watched as the crack British cavalry, composed of Sikhs, turned and fled in the face of a Chinese charge. Appalled at the "cowardice" of the Sikhs, the Americans, according to Kinman, sprang to their feet and charged the Chinese cavalry with fixed bayonets: "There were hundreds killed and wounded we gave no quarter nor asked for any so you see we took no prisoners we killed them all that fell into our hands. I will now close my letter by wishing you all a Merry Christmas and a Happy New Year."[54]

The last line of Kinman's letter calls attention to one of the more bizarre characteristics of death when, as in war, it is encountered in wholesale

192   form: death, even the most appalling death, becomes in such circumstances routine and is readily incorporated into the dailiness of life. Fussell tells of the American sailor on dangerous duty in the Pacific in World War II who, just after annihilating a Japanese with his 20-mm installation, records in his diary news from his hometown paper: "Waltham [Massachusetts] High is still undefeated [in football]. It looks like they will be state champs this year." He then, a page later, sets down dispassionately the details of the carnage suffered aboard the nearby USS *Denver:* "Men with broken backs, eyes blown out, bodies crushed, etc."[55]

Similar juxtapositions, equally discordant, were not uncommon in 1900, at least in the more personal accounts that we have from foreign pens. Sarah Goodrich reported a "comparatively quiet" day in the June 26 entry of her siege diary: "Desultory fighting. Sand-bags the order of the day. Cleaned up the yard. Also cleaned up a men's and a ladies' toilet room. Visited the north part of the compound, and looked through the loop-hole. Saw seven dead horses, and as many dead Boxers, dogs, and deserted streets. Treachery expected tonight."[56] Oscar Upham described the killing of a Russian soldier at the next loophole over from his in late June: "he was smoking a cigarette and blowing the smoke out through the loophole we told him to knock it off, one of the Chinees [*sic*] sharp shooters spotted him and put a slug through his head he straightened up and turned towards me, I saw the blood spurting from his head he fell back into Pvt. Moody's arms, dead, we buried him in the Russian Legation."[57]

Richard Steel on August 15 (the day following the arrival of the allied troops in the capital) "went out into the Board of War with Dering and shot some pigeons for dinner and saw some ghastly sights, dead Chinese." And four days later: "Heard a looting party of marines was going to Prince Kung's [Gong's] house and went with them along a road *horrible* with Chinese corpses in all stages of decomposition and was nearly sick. Kung's palace is a perfect wonder of wealth, and we carried away any amount of treasure for the common fund." On September 17 Steel joined a combined force of Germans, Americans, and British on a "Boxer-hunting" expedition in the Western Hills. The Boxers were taken by surprise and fifty of them killed: "I counted thirteen dead Boxers myself. We explored the temples and pagoda and returned with the German force to Peking. . . . I have not seen any place in China yet to compare with the beauty of this valley."[58]

Herbert Hoover, amid a sea of Chinese death in Tianjin, accounted for the negligible number of foreign civilian casualties during the siege of Zizhulin (two killed and five or six wounded) with an engineer's humor: "Of the 900 civilians in the settlement not more than 100 ever went out during firing so that we may say that only 100 were exposed and these scattered over one square mile—so that supposing the hittable area of a person is 7 sq. feet then a person had one chance in about 1,800,000 of being hit by any given missile, or the 100 persons exposed would need 18,000 missiles before one was hit."[59]

The routinization of death was tied partly to the frequency with which death was encountered, its commonplaceness. "We hear of the slaughter of the Christians daily," wrote Emma Martin in mid-June, "till we are so accustomed to hearing horrible things that we are not shocked any more."[60] But the almost lighthearted spirit characterizing the diary entries of Richard Steel, not to mention the playful tenor of Hoover's foreign survival calculus, suggests another factor, aside from repetition, that may have been at work in some circumstances. I refer to the sense of buoyancy, almost exhilaration, experienced by those who, after close encounters with death, felt comparatively safe. There was nothing lighthearted, certainly, about Steel's earlier reactions to the fighting he experienced on the march from Tianjin to the capital or Hoover's account of the "black fear" that prevailed among foreign civilians in Tianjin during the first period of the siege, before the arrival of foreign reinforcements.[61]

As for Emma Martin, although she grew accustomed to the incessant reports of horrors occurring elsewhere, she never became jaded in her reactions to her own experiences in the legation hospital, where she worked the night shift. One evening, after sitting beside a young German bleeding to death from a wound in the liver ("a large overgrown boy with light hair and blue eyes—somebodys darling"), she was called on to assist in removing the bullet from a Russian shot through the chest. No sooner had the Russian been "fixed up" than six American marines came in "carrying one of our boys shot in the head." Martin described what she observed next and her reactions: "He was vomiting and a little stream of blood trickeled [sic] along the path and on the veranda. They put him on the table but he died that very minute and we could not help it. Oh, the horrors of war. I felt like crying but there was no time or place for we found the Russian was having a hemorrhage."[62]

Most of the tears shed in the summer of 1900 were doubtless of this sort, tears of sadness and grief. But there were also tears of anguish, even rage. On June 16, the date of the huge blaze set by the Boxers in the southern quarter of Beijing, Tang Yan, while at the rice market inside the Fucheng Gate, came upon a weeping woman who complained with bitterness: "At first they said they were going to kill the foreigners, but up to now not a single foreigner has been hurt. The ones killed have all been Chinese who

194   were worshipers of things foreign. What's more, not a single man has been hurt. The only ones killed have been women and children. Things being this way, how can the turmoil truly be brought under control? I am very frightened." When Tang heard this, he claims to have been left speechless, as none of the comments of his educated friends in the preceding several days had been so clear-sighted and resolute.[63]

Victims

The woman with whom Tang Yan spoke made a sociological observation about the deaths that had occurred (presumably in the capital area) through mid-June and expressed her fear concerning the pattern that seemingly lay behind them. Others in North China in the summer of 1900 articulated fears of a far more immediate and personal nature, as they faced the prospect of possible — or, in the case of missionaries away from Beijing and Tianjin, often almost certain — death. The level of fear for these individuals varied from group to group. It varied over time, in response partly to the progression of events and partly to a process of familiarization that could moderate fear even in situations in which the actual threat remained more or less unchanged. And it varied in accordance with class, gender, and race — poor Chinese, especially in cities like Tianjin and Beijing, being more endangered than their more affluent compatriots, women being more at risk than men owing to Boxer pollution beliefs, and Chinese in general, whether Boxers or Christians or neither, being far more vulnerable than foreigners (with the important exception of missionaries stranded in the interior).

The evidence, for all of these variables, is most abundant with reference to Tianjin and Beijing, where roughly parallel situations prevailed. In both cities the first distinction to be drawn, in respect to exposure to death, was between the foreign-protected areas (the legation quarter and Northern Cathedral in Beijing, Zizhulin in Tianjin) and the Chinese residential and commercial areas. Within each of these areas, however, there were further distinctions to be made, based partly on timing but mainly on race or class or both.

In Tianjin, Herbert Hoover's observations are again extremely useful. The foreign settlement lay along the Baihe, which flowed from Tianjin to the sea. The original site of the settlement had been about two miles southeast of the walled Chinese city. But over time the area in between the two had become filled "with a jungle of one-storied Chinese houses and a maze of narrow alleys," so that by 1900 the foreign settlement could be said to form one end of greater Tianjin and the original walled city the other end (see map 3).[64]

At the beginning of the siege all foreigners not involved in the defense of the settlement were moved to a small area in the center. This was surrounded by a ring, approximately three miles in circumference, which was garrisoned by foreign soldiers. "It was in the centre," Hoover wrote, "that the melodrama and comedy were played—the rim was nearly all tragedy." For the majority of foreigners in the center, the most severe "mental shock" of the Chinese bombardment was at the very outset. The foreigners knew they were greatly outnumbered, that they were situated "on a perfectly open plain with no natural defence," and that if the Chinese continued the level of "frenzy" of their initial assault for two days more, "it would have been the end." On the second day of the siege, "with the smoke of many burning buildings pouring over the settlement, with the civilians erecting barricades across the streets for the final rush, the terrific bombardment, the constant sound of rifle-fire in the distance, and the knowledge, if not the sight, of the scores of wounded brought in from the lines, it all seemed bad—very bad. It was really the climax of terror, of the black fear, as it was of the fighting." After this, the majority of foreign civilians moved into a sturdy stone municipal building (Gordon Hall), which had bombproof catacombs underneath. "Here," Hoover reported, "pandemonium reigned. . . . Midst the shriek and bang of shells and the distant crack of rifles, the nearer howls of the babies and sobs of the hysterical, and with the drawn tenseness of hundreds of faces around, even the nerves of those who might have been strong if isolated in their own homes, soon gave way."

Although the worst was now over, this was not known at the time, and it wasn't, as earlier noted, until the arrival of foreign reinforcements from the coast that the "black fear" finally lifted. Foreign civilians were, nevertheless, relatively safe, as long as the foreign defense perimeter held and as long as they stayed indoors. All foreign residences were constructed of brick and stone, and virtually every house had some nook that was bombproof. If, on the other hand, one ventured out into the streets, which Hoover described as "canals of moving lead," one clearly took one's chances. Everyone who did so, according to him, had narrow escapes, and "anything less than the puncture of one's hat or bicycle tyre by a bullet was considered of no especial moment."[65]

The situation was far worse for the three or four thousand Chinese—employees of foreign firms, people who worked in Chinese government offices, and refugee Christians—who were also sequestered in the foreign settlement. For these individuals, living in fragile Chinese houses, the "ter-

196   rors of the bombardment" were greater and many were killed. None had
laid in provisions for a siege. There was little water available, as the coolies'
carts which in more ordinary times delivered it from the river were not
allowed on the streets after the beginning of the siege. And, as if this were
not enough, the two main Chinese quarters within the settlement, the one
in the French concession and the one on Dagu Road in the English concession, were set on fire by the foreigners, who were afraid that they harbored assassins and offered cover for the approach of the Chinese enemy.
No official measures, according to Hoover, were adopted to relieve the
unfortunate inhabitants of these quarters, who were forced into the streets,
absolutely destitute, "where they were oft times brutally treated by the soldiers." What succor they received came from Catholic fathers, whose com-
pounds gave shelter to a thousand converts as well as to nonconverts who
sought them out, and individual foreigners "who went from place to place
securing refuge for terrorised Chinese, who took them rice and accompanied them for water, buried their dead, and doctored their wounded."[66]

In Beijing similar distinctions prevailed, although the disparity in circumstances between Chinese and foreigners appears to have been less
great in the siege of the Northern Cathedral than in that of the legation
compound. The occupants of the Northern Cathedral—3,420 in all (once
the siege began), of whom 71 were Europeans (43 of them French and
Italian marines) and well over half women and children—faced almost
constant shelling from Boxers and Chinese troops. But the structural
strength of the church, combined with the ineffectualness of the Chinese
bombardment, lessened the final death toll from this source.[67] There were,
of course, close calls. Bishop Favier wrote of a twenty-five-pound cannon
ball falling on his bed just after he had left it and of a Mauser bullet passing through the hat of the other bishop, almost depriving him of his coad-
jutor.[68] On one occasion, moreover, the explosion of a mine killed half a
dozen Italian marines and over eighty Chinese, including many infants.[69]
On the whole, however, the over 400 deaths that occurred during the siege
of the Northern Cathedral were attributable far more to disease and starvation than to Chinese bullets. The principal victims, not surprisingly,
were the Chinese. There were outbreaks of smallpox, which took the lives
of many children ("seven to eight are dying every day"), and on August 5
Favier wrote that "the question of food is the only one that now engages our
attention: we can resist balls, bullets, and bombs, but we can make no resistance against famine." Dogs that had just finished feeding on the bodies of
dead Boxers were by this point being hunted, killed, and eaten by the
Chinese, supplementing a diet that as of early August had been reduced to

little more than leaves and roots. On the date of the arrival of the foreign expeditionary force, after already suffering weeks of starvation rations, the besieged, now numbering some 3,000 persons, were down to their last 400 pounds of food.[70]

As compared to the situation in the Northern Cathedral, the foreign community in the legations—473 civilians (mostly missionaries and diplomats and their families) and a little over 400 military personnel[71]—represented a much greater proportion of the total number of besieged persons (3,800–4,500, depending on who was counting and who got counted);[72] it was also a far more heterogeneous group of individuals.

There were other differences as well between the two sieges. The puzzling truce that began on July 17 and resulted in a considerable respite in the Chinese assault on the legations—the lull in the fighting lasted until the beginning of August—had no counterpart in the siege of the Northern Cathedral, which was unremitting. Also, while there was a small medical staff available in the legation quarter, there was no doctor or surgeon in the Northern Cathedral to tend to the sick and wounded.

From a psychological point of view, a major difference between the two sieges was that the people sequestered in the Northern Cathedral remained, from first to last, totally cut off from the rest of the world, whereas the besieged in the legations began to receive reliable messages from outside shortly after mid-July. When, on July 18, a Chinese Methodist courier returned to the legation quarter with a message from the Japanese consul in Tianjin announcing that a foreign force of over 33,000 troops would be leaving that city shortly, Luella Miner expressed relief that "the strain and stress of this terrible siege is over."[73] Such relief eluded the Catholics in the Northern Cathedral until the very end. (In one of a number of attempts to establish contact with the outside world, a messenger was dispatched to the legations on August 10 to inform the French minister of the dire situation of the besieged; he was captured by the Boxers, flayed, and his skin and head put on display within a few yards of the cathedral walls.)[74]

The build-up of tension in the Northern Cathedral was made all the more acute, moreover, because of the rapidly deteriorating food situation there. This points to one other major difference between the two sieges. Foreigners in the legation compound complained about the monotony of a diet which, regardless of a person's station in life, consisted "mainly of rice, millet, cracked wheat, brown bread, horse-flesh, and some more rice!"[75] But they never really had to worry about starving to death.

The same was not, unfortunately, true of the Chinese besieged in the legations, whose living conditions were, in almost every respect, far worse

198   than those of the foreigners. Chinese in the Northern Cathedral fared poorly, but so did the Europeans, and when Bishop Favier talked about "our" situation, he clearly meant to include everyone. In the numerous accounts left by foreign participants in the legation siege, the several thousand Chinese refugees who shared the experience seldom got mentioned at all, and when they were referred to it was almost always as "them" or "they." As early as July 1, Nigel Oliphant reported that the Christians (Chinese) were "dying like sheep from smallpox &c." Roland Allen, in one of the few references to the refugees in his diary, described their circumstances as of early August: "The Christians . . . were beginning to feel the pangs of famine; they were fed on a mixture of a little grain, chopped straw, and other fodder, which made a coarse and revolting kind of bread. Besides that, they had the entrails and heads of the ponies killed for the foreigners and a few dogs. The child mortality amongst them was said to be high."[76] Other missionaries depicted the living conditions of the Chinese Christians in similar, if less graphic, language.[77]

The food situation was somewhat better for the several hundred male converts who volunteered for heavy labor under conditions of extreme danger. These were given coupons, which enabled them to supplement their diets with a little horsemeat and a bowl of rice. Their family members, who had to cook for themselves, were also entitled, on presentation of a coupon at the commissariat, to roughly a pound of rice per person per day (but no horsemeat). People without male laborers in their families or without families at all were apparently not entitled to anything and had to fend for themselves, unless they were sick, in which case, on presentation of a coupon from a doctor, they could obtain a little over a pound of wheat flour.[78]

Oliphant, while conceding that "we do not reckon Chinese converts &c. in our casualty lists," reported that "quite a number of these poor creatures, who really do work hard for us, have lost their lives [to] . . . the enemies' bullets."[79] Miner also heaped praise on the "courage and faithfulness of our Chinese Christians, in working on barricades and trenches, where bullets sometimes fell in showers, where they were scorched by the summer sun, or drenched by the pouring rain."[80] The Christians themselves, as reported by Lu Wantian, a Chinese Methodist who served as a labor recruiter and supervisor, complained bitterly of the treatment they received, especially at the hands of the British during the early days of the siege. "The work at the British legation is crushing," they explained to Lu, "and they don't feed you enough. And if you do not carry out their orders to the letter, they flog you to get you to do so. Therefore, we don't want to go there." On another occasion, they told Lu: "We're exhausted. At this point we prefer death to life. The British legation mistreats people, and even if it means dying we don't want to go there." The Chinese Christian workers, it is interesting to note, gave the non-Christian Japanese much higher grades for compassion: "For them we are ready to risk our lives."[81]

For those inhabitants of Tianjin and Beijing who lived outside the foreign enclaves, death was a more or less constant companion from late spring through early fall 1900, and the fear of it shaped the lives of all individuals. The racial distinction between foreign and Chinese, of course, did not obtain here, since everyone was Chinese. But other distinctions, especially ones derived from class and gender, did. Different people, depending on their life circumstances, were differentially vulnerable to the threat of death and were therefore affected by it in different ways and to different degrees.

A partial exception to this rule was susceptibility to fire, which appears to have been at least as great for the rich as for the poor. The huge conflagration that ravaged much of the southern section of Beijing on June 16 destroyed one of the most affluent sections of the city. And the frequent fires accompanying the fighting in the Chinese city of Tianjin from mid-June to mid-July attacked the homes and shops of the better-off classes along with those of the destitute. In fact, Ricalton reports that lower-class homes in Tianjin, because they were constructed mainly of clay and unfired brick, often escaped destruction from fire (although not from shelling).[82] In general, although reliable figures on deaths sustained as a result of the fires in either Beijing or Tianjin are unavailable, it is not unreasonable to assume that the total value of property lost was greater among the wealthy than among the poor. Zhongfang Shi, who witnessed the large fire of June 16 in the capital, said that although there were only a few casualties, owing to its having been a daytime fire, the value of the property destroyed was unfathomable.[83]

In the days immediately following the June 16 blaze, the Boxers set fire to many other sites in the capital. Zhongfang Shi described in graphic terms the hysteria and fear that gripped the population:

> For days on end, during the daylight hours, thick smoke could be seen, billowing up into the sky one moment, dispersing the next. Everywhere people circulated stories that such and such a place had caught fire or that so-and-so's whole family had been killed; or there would be shouts that the foreign buildings on East Jiaomin Lane had caught fire, and everywhere people would cry out "Burn incense, destroy the devils." One person would start the shouting, then everyone else would chime in. People were in a constant state of agitation. At night, the fires glowed brightly in all directions and everything was red for a long time. Many families stood on the ridges of their

200   roofs to see into the distance. From far off you could hear the sounds of men and women yelling. All night long, until daybreak, the households on every street were in a state of terror, and everyone was petrified. People acted irrationally and forgot to eat and sleep. They were all afraid that near them there might be Christians residing or property belonging to Christians, that the Boxers would be provoked to set these places on fire, that the calamity would spread in every direction, making no distinction between good people and bad, and that they would die without a proper burial.[84]

Sometimes, according to Zhongfang Shi, bands of twenty to thirty Boxers would go about identifying homes or shops as Christian, whether or not they really were, and promptly burn them down. The people who lived or worked in such places and their neighbors were naturally terrified. They would get down on their hands and knees and plead with the Boxers, who sometimes let them off if they contributed a certain amount of silver or grain to the Boxers' altar, the amount varying in accordance with the family's circumstances. The more prosperous families lived in constant dread that the Boxers would come to their homes and strip them bare.[85]

In Beijing, at least prior to the arrival of the foreign expeditionary force in mid-August, the dangers from shooting and bombardment, as opposed to fire, were mainly confined to the spaces around the legation quarter and the Northern Cathedral. During and right after the fighting in Tianjin, by contrast, the entire Chinese section of that city was exposed more or less constantly to shelling. Although it stands to reason that the families of poor shopkeepers and manual laborers were more vulnerable than elite families (if for no other reason than that they did not have servants to go out and fetch food, water, and other necessities for them), the exposure of the latter was not inconsequential. Guan He, an educated, reform-minded man who fled south with his household prior to the conclusion of the fighting, describes the state of fear and paralysis that governed elite lives in the initial phase of the conflict:

> Day after day my family members all lie on the floor on mats, the window lattices sealed off by wooden furniture to keep shells from entering. We are very weary but are unable to close our eyes; although we are famished it is hard for us to swallow food. The women and children face each other but don't speak, as if dull of wit. Sometimes I open the door and go out to have a look around. The people going back and forth are all Boxers, there are red turbans everywhere, the glitter of swords is blinding, and in every direction there is the sound of gunfire, like firecrackers going off in rapid succession. To myself, I figure that, of all the things I have seen and heard in my whole life, this is the most singular.[86]

As with the inhabitants of Zizhulin, people in the Chinese city of Tianjin who for any reason ventured outside their homes courted serious danger. On one occasion, around midnight, hearing that the fires burning to the southeast were especially fierce, Guan He went up to the roof of his dwelling to have a look. When a bullet suddenly whizzed past his ear, his body shook and he slipped and almost fell. Guan quickly went back down, bullets flying all about him. On another occasion, a bullet narrowly missed hitting one of Guan's friends, who had fled with Chinese government forces after their defeat in a battle against the Russians.[87]

Another Tianjin resident described a harrowing experience he had on July 18, after the foreign occupation of the Chinese city. On this date, after moving his family for safety's sake to the foreign firm at which he was employed, he returned home to get some things they had left behind. The shelling was intense. After reaching his home he heard a huge noise and loud cries outside. On going out to find out what had happened, he saw his neighbors fleeing through the streets, screaming as they ran, some with no clothes on their bodies, others without shoes on their feet. A shell had hit and destroyed the roof of the home to the left of his own. As bullets were flying all over and another shell had struck the ground, causing his house to shake, he fled with the crowd and made his way back to the foreign firm. When halfway there, he encountered foreign soldiers who asked to see his pass (passes having been issued to all Chinese living or working in the foreign settlement). In his confusion and panic, he of course had left it at home. The foreign soldiers thought he was a spy and were about to shoot him when an old friend who was a Catholic happened along and persuaded them to release him into his custody.[88]

During the summer of 1900, residents of Tianjin and Beijing lived in dire fear not only of fire and of bullets and shells but of many other things as well. The foreigners were not the only ones concerned about spies. The Boxers were positively paranoid on the subject. During their occupation of Tianjin, they patrolled the streets by day, summarily executing Christians if they encountered them, while at night, as they made their rounds, if they saw people behaving suspiciously, they accused them of being enemy agents and killed them on the spot.[89] At Dongfu Bridge, a Boxer checkpoint, there were Boxers lined up on both sides, armed with swords, looking for spies. When a rickshaw crossed, according to Guan He, they raised the curtain and looked inside: "If they identified you as a spy, you were not permitted to defend yourself."[90]

Since the Boxers frequently misidentified people as Christians, this was another source of anxiety at the time, one to which no one really was

202   immune. Ye Changchi, an official in the capital, tells of a close call he had on June 23, as he was escorting his wife and children to a safer location outside the city. On pulling up at an inn for the night, they encountered ten Boxers armed with swords who questioned Ye closely. When one of Ye's family members pulled down the rickshaw curtain, the Boxers became suspicious and shouted "secondary hairy ones." Ye raised the curtain, stepped down from the vehicle, and explained to the Boxers that he was a conscientious official from Beijing who planned to return to his job in the city as soon as he had made arrangements for the safety of his family. Persuaded by what they had heard, the Boxers, one after another, called out "Good man, good man," and left.[91]

Guan He and his family had a similar experience. When, during the Battle of Tianjin, the Boxers relaxed their prohibition against women venturing into the streets, Guan and his wife decided to take their son and leave the city. To offset the negative effects of his wife's impurity, Guan, in accordance with Boxer instructions, had the rickshaw carrying her and his son covered with a red quilt. Still, the Boxers struck and pierced the curtain over the rickshaw opening several times, and on one occasion one of them asked: "Who is inside the rickshaw? Is it a straight eye?" Guan bowed with hands clasped and said, "This young lady belongs to the family of Master Zhou of the first section *baojia* bureau," whereupon the Boxer nodded and left. Guan's maternal uncle, it turned out, had indeed held this position, and since he had tried cases at the prefectural and county levels, most Tianjin people were familiar with his name.[92]

Not everyone accused of being a Christian was so fortunate. A friend told Guan He that, after the start of the Battle of Tianjin, some Boxers saw a woman running in the distance and called out to her: "Where is the straight eye fleeing to?" The woman heard them and, kneeling, said: "I am not a straight eye. I am the wife of so-and-so of such-and-such a place." To this the Boxers replied: "Your forehead is marked. How can you deny it?" They thereupon seized her, took her to the area outside their altar entrance, and killed her forthwith.[93]

The forehead marking was explained when, after the killing of a husband and wife named Cui in the vicinity of the Wenchang Temple in Tianjin, someone asked a Boxer: "In looking for Christians to kill, how do you know a person is a Christian before killing him [her]?" The Boxer replied: "Christians all have a cross on their forehead. You people with ordinary eyes can't see it, but we [Boxers], once we get into our magic [*shangfa*], are able to make it out clearly."[94]

Since it was not in fact possible to differentiate between Christians and non-Christians, a common practice during the Boxer summer, attested to in numerous accounts, Chinese and foreign, was that of settling old scores by falsely accusing people of being followers of Jesus.[95] The fear of being so charged was greatly aggravated by one of the more common Boxer methods of ascertaining the validity of such indictments. The accused party was hauled off to a Boxer altar, where he or she was made to burn slips of paper. If the ashes flew upward, the charge was determined to be false and the accused was given a reprieve; if, however, the ashes failed to rise (after, according to some accounts, three burnings), the person was judged to be a Christian and was beheaded. Many innocent (that is, non-Christian) persons were wrongly killed in these circumstances, prompting Zhongfang Shi to remark: "How cruel to treat human life as a child's sport and rely on whether ash rises or not as the basis for deciding whether a person should live or die."[96]

A form of vulnerability generally more applicable to upper- than to lower-class Chinese was the Boxer injunction against owning or trading in anything foreign or even, in the case of shopkeepers, using the term "foreign" (*yang*) in their shop signs. People violating this order were liable to be killed. Shops that violated it were sometimes burned down, sometimes looted by the poor. Since kerosene-burning lamps were included in the prohibition (kerosene being a foreign import), people in the capital spilled their kerosene into the streets. When word was circulated that, after the Christians had all been killed, students who read foreign books would be next, many families owning such books consigned them to the flames. After the Beijing Boxers put his Sino-Western primary school to the torch, the future philosopher and rural reconstructionist, Liang Shuming, only seven at the time, furtively burned all his English textbooks.[97]

Although it was the exception, sometimes even the poorest elements of society ran afoul of the Boxer abhorrence of things foreign. Since rickshaws were frequently referred to as *Dongyangche* ("Eastern vehicles"), a name containing the character for "foreign," rickshaw pullers in Tianjin changed the name of the vehicles they pulled to *taipingche* ("great peace vehicles") and affixed to them a piece of red paper with the new name written on it.[98]

Sometimes the Boxers were able to capitalize on the terror they sowed among foreign-contaminated elements of the populace. On one occasion, the Tianjin Boxers, led by Zhang Decheng, looted two businesses that dealt in foreign goods and burned some of the items. They then seized the manager of one of the businesses, along with his entire family, and planned to put them all to death. After mediation by a number of bystanders, however, they agreed to spare their lives in exchange for payment of a 10,000-tael fine.[99]

Apart from being a spy, a Christian, or a person who possessed or traded in things foreign, one other source of death fear at the height of the Boxer

204   movement was being female. This was the complaint of the woman at the Beijing rice market whose perspicacity so impressed Tang Yan. Especially vulnerable were women with unbound feet. "If any were killed," a contemporary from Dengzhou, Shandong, later recalled, "it would be the women with natural feet. For a woman to have natural feet was then a sure sign of being connected with the foreigners."[100] Being female appears to have been a special problem in Tianjin, where, as we saw in chapter 4, the Boxers, to safeguard against defilement, placed repeated restrictions on the movements of women. A number of women who were either unaware of or chose to violate the proscription against venturing out of doors were actually killed, according to Guan He.[101] As an ironic reflection of the unrelenting vulnerability of Tianjin women in the summer of 1900, women fleeing the city on July 14, as the Battle of Tianjin reached its climax, wore red to avoid being killed by Boxers and, as a result, were frequently shot by foreign soldiers, who suspected them of being Red Lanterns.[102]

The personal jeopardy in which many individuals in Beijing and Tianjin found themselves during the summer of 1900 forced them to confront difficult, often painful choices, choices that were far more biographical than historical in meaning. As a person with a strong interest in foreign learning, Guan He claims that he had in his home some three thousand volumes (*juan*) of English-language books and books printed lithographically or from movable type, all objects, according to him, sufficient at the time to place one's life in jeopardy. Nevertheless, even though everybody in the neighborhood knew about his interests, he chose to risk not destroying his library and in the end managed to elude discovery (although, he claimed, members of his extended family in South China were sure that, as a result of his exposed position, he had met up with some terrible fate).[103]

As the military situation in Tianjin deteriorated in the early summer, a neighbor confided to Guan He that if they didn't find a way of escaping, they were sure to meet with disaster. Guan He, agreeing, returned home to talk matters over with his wife. But their servants, still feeling themselves in danger from the Boxers, were unwilling to leave. Guan's wife, moreover, said: "I would prefer to sit tight and die in this room than be disgraced and victimized by the bandits [Boxers] in the streets." "Her words," Guan commented, "were fitting but full of sadness."[104]

Zhongfang Shi faced a similar situation some weeks later, after news of the fall of Tongzhou and the imminent arrival of foreign troops reached the capital. "Although ordinarily a calm individual," he wrote, "when faced with this chaotic, life-and-death situation, with ten family members, including an elderly mother and a wife and children, all depending on me to take

care of them, I was in a state of some emotional turmoil, anxious and confused, not knowing what was the best course of action. All I could do was
make a clumsy effort to console them, relieve my mother's anxiety, quiet
the turbulent feelings afflicting everyone, and commit our lives to fate."[105]

Foreigners, above all foreign missionaries, also faced hard choices in
1900. Sometimes these choices, as with Guan He's books, had to do with
things. Emma Martin tells of the visit she and a physician colleague made
in the second week of June to the Methodist Episcopal hospital in the capital to collect drugs, dressings, and instruments that might be of use in case
of hasty flight or siege: "It is hard to tell just what one ought to take and
what leave. . . . It is strange how things, beautiful and costly things, lose
their market value when one stands face to face with death. So we . . . try
to select what we think will be most useful to us or will keep life in us the
longest if we should be besieged."[106]

The choices were more excruciating when they had to do with human
beings, often, in the case of missionaries, converts, who in the event of
flight would have to be left behind. On the eve of the murder on June 20 of
Clemens von Ketteler, the German minister, the Chinese government had
circularized the diplomatic corps, giving the foreign community twenty-
four hours in which to vacate the capital. A number of missionaries penned
urgent letters to the American minister, pleading with him not to leave.
"Oh! how we prayed," wrote Sarah Goodrich, "knowing that to remain
meant death—massacre—while going meant forsaking our Chinese,
wronging their souls, for they could die happily if we died with them. It
made it a hard question, the hardest I ever met." With the killing of von
Ketteler, the dilemma was eased, as it was quickly decided that for the foreigners to travel from Beijing to Tianjin was too dangerous and that the
wiser course was to congregate in the legation quarter. "God again delivered us," commented Goodrich with evident relief, "for they said the
Chinese could go [to the legations] with us."[107]

Missionaries in the interior, away from the large and to some degree
protected cities of Beijing and Tianjin, also confronted agonizing choices
in the summer of 1900, focused mainly on whether staying where they
were or leaving for the hills or the coast offered the greater chance for survival.[108] The ones who chose to stay in place described with poignancy the
emotional strain of waiting for almost certain death. "Nights are continual
hours of anxious suspense," wrote Eva Jane Price in Fenzhou, Shanxi, on
June 30, "starting at every sound, and imagining an unruly mob surrounding us and taking our lives. . . . Our friends at home will have suspense but
not such as ours when the heart refuses to act properly and knees and legs

206 shake in spite of all effort to be brave and quiet, trusting in God."[109] "If you want to know how folks feel facing death," ruminated (Mary) Louise Partridge in a letter of June 19 from Liman (a village near Taigu, Shanxi), "don't read Robert Hardy's Seven Days' [sic] or that story in one of the late Independents. Ask some one whose [sic] been there. . . . It has impressed me strongly that I ought to write some messages to my family and special friends, but I just can't, my courage isn't equal to it. I can only keep up by following my accustomed regular routine. . . . I am ready & not afraid. That's all I can say."[110] Horace Pitkin (ABCFM), in Baoding, wrote simply: "We can't go out to fight—we have no soldiers. We must sit still, do our work—and then take whatever is sent us quietly."[111]

Not knowing whether one would live or die was, of course, also the daily experience of soldiers in the summer of 1900. While waiting in Tianjin in early August for the allied relief force to begin its march to the capital, Harold Kinman, with more than a whiff of youthful melodrama, wrote his sister: "We move for pekin not later than day after tommorow. I hope the good lord spares me to come back to you. But we are going to fight the greatest battle at Pekin that has been fought for one hundred years. . . . Good Bye maybe for a few days maybe Forever. Love to Father sister uncle and Tom and Elwin. do not worry iff any thing happens Itt is all for the best some body has to give their lives for their country."[112]

Waiting in suspense was also the lot of Chinese Christians, especially in locations with high concentrations of Boxers, such as the area in and around the town of Zhuozhou, on the main artery connecting Beijing and Baoding. Two American missionaries who visited the area in May described the state of mind of Christians living there as one of "appalling horror, beside which the anxieties which beset us were light. There, in the country, they knew nothing certain. They heard of places all round them being pillaged, and their fellow-Christians ruined, maltreated, mutilated, murdered. They knew not at what hour the scourge might fall upon them. Every rumour of Boxer approach filled them with terror."[113]

The situation for native Christians was, if anything, worse two months later in Shanxi, after confirmation of the officially supervised executions of missionaries and converts in Taiyuan on July 9 reached Christian communities scattered about the province. Rowena Bird, in Taigu, reported on July 13 that with this news many of the Chinese in the employ of the missionaries prepared to leave, the feeling being that "although death is probable at home, it is certain here." The night before, according to Bird, the Taigu missionaries themselves had been "almost ready to start for the hills, thinking it one chance for life, but the danger from the Boxers and robbers and perils of all kinds are *so* great. What could we do?" "If you never see me again," she concluded what was to be her last letter, "remember I am not sorry I came to China. Whether I have saved anyone or not, He knows, but it has been for Him and we go to Him."[114]

Bird, like other foreign victims of the events of the Boxer summer, at least got to put into words for posterity the thoughts in her head and the feelings in her heart on the eve of her death, which, along with the deaths of five other American missionaries and several Chinese Christians, occurred in Taigu on July 31, at the hands of a combined force of some three hundred Boxers and soldiers.[115] The final thoughts and feelings of the great preponderance of people whose blood was shed in 1900—the Boxers themselves, native Christians, government soldiers, and many ordinary Chinese who fell into none of these categories—remained unrecorded. This muteness, so characteristic of the experienced past in general, has been evoked, with special reference to the Boxer era, by the poet Daniel Hoffman:

A squad of soldiers lies beside a river.
They're in China—see the brimmed gables piled
On the pagoda. The rows of trees are lopped
And the Chinese soldiers have been stopped
In their tracks. Their bodies lie
In bodily postures of the dead.

Arms bound, legs akimbo and askew,
But look how independently their heads
Lie thereabouts, some upright, some of the heads
Tipped on their sides, or standing on their heads.
Mostly, the eyes are open
And their mouths twisted in a sort of smile.

Some seem to be saying or just to have said
Some message in Chinese just as the blade
Nicked the sunlight and the head dropped
Like a sliced cantaloupe to the ground, the cropped
Body twisting from the execution block.
And see, there kneels the executioner

Wiping his scimitar upon a torso's ripped
Sash. At ease, the victors smoke. A gash
Of throats darkens the riverbed. 1900. The Boxer

208   Rebellion. Everyone there is dead now.
         What was it those unbodied mouths were saying?
         A million arteries stain the Yellow River.[116]

One answer to the question concluding Hoffman's poem has, of course, been supplied by historians, in their efforts to understand and explain the Boxer episode. Another, as we shall see in the next part of this book, has been provided by mythologizers, operating from a quite different set of premises and guided by motives of a more plainly presentist character. Unfortunately, the answer of the unbodied mouths themselves, giving voice to the thoughts and feelings of the immediate Chinese experiencers of this moment out of the Chinese past, must forever remain locked in silence.

6.5   Beheaded Boxers. A stereograph by B. W. Kilburn. From Barbara P. Norfleet, *Looking at Death* (Boston: David R. Godine, 1993). Courtesy of Harvard University.

PART 3

The Boxers as Myth

PROLOGUE

The Mythologized Past

Historians, much like art restorers removing the grime from old masters, not infrequently set for themselves the express task of stripping away the layers of myth that conceal from view the true face of the past. This is what John Keegan and Paul Fussell attempt in their classic studies of the boredom, cruelty, and fear of ordinary soldiers at the front.[1] It is what Vera Schwarcz had in mind when she wrote, referring to the demythologization of May Fourth, that it "might yet become what it really was: the halting, confused movement of a small group of intellectuals trying to awaken themselves."[2]

But there is a potential downside to this process of historical restoration, which Schwarcz herself, in the same piece, alluded to. "To bring May Fourth back down to human scale," she wrote, ". . . is to risk reducing it to a truly marginal event . . . an event of *merely* historical significance, with no claim upon the values, loyalties, ideals of the present."[3] Other examples of this negative aspect of demythologization abound, from all areas of life. Gabriel García Márquez's fictional portrayal of Simón Bolívar as a foul-mouthed, flatulent hypochondriac "capable of crossing the Andes bare-foot, naked, and unprotected, just to go to bed with a woman" threatened to deprive Latin Americans of one of their few genuine heroes.[4] The Library of Congress's release of Thurgood Marshall's papers shortly after his death, by unveiling in the most intimate detail the processes by which the Supreme Court operates, risked stripping the Court of an aura thought by some to be essential to its authority and legitimacy.[5] And the cleaning of the frescoes on the ceiling of the Sistine Chapel dispossessed art lovers permanently of a Michelangelo they had known and cherished.[6] The dismantling of the mythologized past, in short, is seldom pain-free: It entails a loss, often irreversible, not unlike that resulting from death, that can be severely disturbing and may, because of this, be stubbornly resisted.[7]

"Myth," in everyday parlance, often implies something "fabricated" or "not true." My use of the term here, although not excluding this connota-

212   tion, is broader, more ambiguous, and focused on a somewhat different set of concerns. Not the least of these concerns is the very issue of what, indeed, "truth" is in a historical sense. Once assertions about the past enter deeply into people's minds (and hearts), it is arguable that they acquire a truth of their own, even if this truth does not at all coincide with what actually happened at some point in past time. At the very least such assertions are true statements about what people *believe* and therefore must occupy a central place in any history of human consciousness.

Beyond this, insofar as what people believe (regardless of whether it is "true" or "false" in the ordinary sense) exerts a powerful influence not only on how they feel and think but also on their behavior, such beliefs become agents that generate and condition historical action of the most undeniably "real" sort. "The past is a malleable substance," observes one writer, "which we work into expressive shapes that in turn shape us."[8] During the twentieth century the myth of the American frontier has more than once influenced Washington's foreign policy and also through books and films shaped popular beliefs concerning violence, masculinity, race, material progress, and a host of other matters.[9] The legends created and circulated in China's treaty ports in the early decades of the century helped the British inhabitants of cities like Shanghai to define themselves as a community and also provided rationales for periodic treaty-port attacks on British government policy.[10] Myths gain their potency from their ability to persuade. It doesn't matter whether the Opium War (1839–1842) in fact ushered in the beginning of the "modern" era in Chinese history. If most Chinese believe it did, as appears to be the case, and if the belief is deeply enough held, it becomes, on some level, "true" regardless—an efficacious working myth.[11]

Although any aspect of the past has the potential to live on as myth in the present,[12] certain events and persons, because they resonate with themes of broader historical scope and importance, have this potential to a pronounced degree. Thus, in American history, where racism has been such a pervasive historical force, figures like Abraham Lincoln and Martin Luther King who helped to ameliorate the condition of African-Americans are often treated in larger-than-life terms. In France—and indeed the world—the French Revolution, although long viewed by historians as a troublesomely contradictory event, remains (among other things) serenely emblematic of the unending quest of human beings for freedom and democracy.[13] And, to take a perhaps more complex case, in China in the twentieth century, where the West has been by turns hated as an imperialist aggressor and admired for its mastery of the secrets of wealth and power, the Boxers, because they attacked both the West and its modern secrets, have been alternately praised and reviled.

On the level of intentionality, the past treated as myth is fundamentally different from the past treated as history. When good historians write history, their primary objective is to construct, on the basis of the evidence available, as accurate and truthful an understanding of the past as possible. Mythologizers, in a sense, do the reverse. Certainly, mythologizers start out with *an* understanding of the past, which in many (though not all) cases they may sincerely believe to be "correct." Their purpose, however, is not to enlarge upon or deepen this understanding. Rather, it is to draw on it to serve the political, ideological, rhetorical, and/or emotional needs of the present.

On the level of actual operation, the distinction between history and myth, as alternate ways of relating to the past, is much less clear-cut. Truth-seeking, as a *goal*, may be an absolute for historians. But insofar as the questions historians ask and the concepts they use to organize the data of the past are profoundly shaped by such variables as gender, class, country, ethnicity, and time, the *act* of seeking the truth tends to be highly relative.[14] "All historians," as Eric Hobsbawm has put it, whatever else their objectives, are engaged in "the invention of tradition," "inasmuch as they contribute, consciously or not, to the creation, dismantling and restructuring of images of the past."[15] Even the most accomplished of historians, in other words, in the process of challenging one mythologized past, inevitably fashion others.[16]

This point is made with great succinctness by Stanley B. Alpern in a discussion of African historiography: "The emotional element in modern African studies," Alpern writes, "has too often led to the replacement of derogatory old myths by patronizing new ones. In an effort to show that blacks are as good as anyone else, a point that had to be emphasized given the legacy of pseudoscientific claptrap to the contrary, many serious Africanists (as distinct from the latest mythmakers) have been tempted to claim too much. What we have seen, in effect, is historiography as ego massage."[17]

If the quest of historians for past truth is unavoidably imperiled, to a greater or lesser degree, by their rootedness in the here and now, mythologizers, however unembarrassed they may be about their present-mindedness, are seldom wholly indifferent to the credibility of the myths they frame about the past. To begin with, they may not view their reading of the past as mythologized at all — or themselves as mythologizers. But even when mythologization is at its least innocent (and most premeditated), it

214   achieves its effect typically not through out-and-out falsification but through distortion, oversimplification, and omission of material that doesn't serve its purpose or runs counter to it. The mythologized past need not be historically accurate. But if it is to be effective in persuading or mobilizing people in the present, it must be bound by at least a loose conception of "truthfulness." The people marching in the streets of Beijing in the spring of 1989 may be described as "prodemocracy demonstrators." Or they may be described as "counterrevolutionary rebels." But they may not plausibly be described as "abortion-rights activists."

Another difference between historians and mythologizers is that, where historians deal in (or at least are supposed to deal in) complexity, nuance, and ambiguity, mythologizers generally operate with a one-dimensional view of the past, wrenching from the past single characteristics or traits or patterns that are then portrayed as the essence of past reality. This process of essentialization is nicely illustrated in the plethora of myths that have grown up around Columbus over the years, each catering to the needs of a particular group of people. For many Europeans, ever since the sixteenth century, Columbus has epitomized "the explorer and discoverer, the man of vision and audacity, the hero who overcame opposition and adversity to change history." For erstwhile American colonists who had suffered under the rule of George III, Columbus became a symbol of "escape from Old World tyranny." Italian-Americans in the late twentieth century celebrate Columbus's Genoese origins, while African-Americans and Native Americans of the same era, focusing on Columbus's involvement in the slave trade and his brutal treatment of the Indian populations of the Caribbean, have refashioned him into a powerful symbol of imperialism and racist exploitation.[18] Each of these mythic representations of Columbus is, of course, in some sense "true" and has genuine links to a genuine historical past. But, like photographs, which always leave out far more than they include, the kind of truth they convey is fundamentally ahistorical—subjective, one-sided, egregiously incomplete. It is not until contending mythologizations are drawn together, juxtaposed in such a way that they begin to temper and qualify one another, raising questions instead of dismissing them, that we move in the direction of a more historical understanding of the past.

The example of Columbus also calls to mind one of the most durable myths about the mythologization of the past: that it is more likely to take place and achieves its most grotesque shapes when the aspect of the past being mythified is one characterized by a dearth of reliable evidence.[19] This mistaken notion is based on the assumption, not at all unreasonable, that when a great deal is known about something, there is a built-in safeguard against the sort of subjective imposition characteristic of myth. Accurate understanding, the argument runs, rests on a foundation of information; the more information, the more accurate the understanding. As self-evident as this reasoning may appear, it is, sadly, not at all borne out by reality. While in the Black Athena controversy over the ethnic/racial origins of Western civilization mythologization has, perhaps, been facilitated by the comparative sparsity of the evidentiary record,[20] mythologizers have never been timid about taking on phases of the past, such as the French Revolution or the life of Martin Luther King or the Boxer uprising, on which the documentary record is seemingly inexhaustible in its variety and scope.

Mythologization of the past comes in many shapes and forms. One variety, which we may call "everyday" mythologization, is embedded in the storehouse of images of the past that ordinary people in all societies carry around in their heads. It crops up unpredictably, at odd moments, and is often articulated in wonderfully inventive, occasionally ironic ways. Geremie Barmé reports reading a modernized version of the famous Boxer invulnerability chant—"Knives and halberds won't penetrate us, nor electric batons shock us" (*daoqiang bu ru, diangun bu chu*)—on the banner of a citizens' support group parading around Tiananmen Square in the spring of 1989.[21] In a similar vein, a young protester, expressing the mood of self-confidence, elation, and invulnerability that had become so infectious during the early stages of the demonstrations, told Orville Schell only half-jokingly: "We are like the Boxers of 1900. We believe that not even bullets can pierce us!"[22] The essentializing of Boxer "invulnerability" was also encountered, less ironically, during the crackdown when activist workers, on hearing that the Chinese army was killing civilians on its way into the center of Beijing, threw wet blankets over their shoulders (presumably for protection against teargas) and jogged down Chang'an Avenue in the direction of the soldiers chanting "*daoqiang bu ru*."[23]

On the foreign side, Ruth Altman Greene, a daughter of China missionaries, whose childhood was spent in a world in which "China" and "Boxers" and "terror" were inextricably linked (she was born in 1896), summons up the chilling memory of a family meal in which suddenly her "brother—ever of liveliest imagination and flair for the dramatic—rose from the table, caught up an apple off his plate, speared it on his knife and, brandishing it, ran wildly round the table shouting, 'I'm a Boxer! I'm a Boxer!' " "That apple was a head," Greene comments, "and it was mine. For years I winced at the word *China*."[24]

216   In a less morbid vein, the writer Liu Xinwu, in a talk at Harvard in 1987, mentioned that on a visit to Japan in the early 1980s he had been taken by his hosts to a department store in Tokyo, where he was flabbergasted by the rich array of goods on display. By the time he got to the third floor, Liu said that he was so filled with rage that he felt just like a "Boxer" and wanted to burn the whole store, with all its wonderful contents, to the ground. The irony here, of course, was that Liu didn't really feel like a Boxer at all. He didn't hate the "modern" commodities in the department store; nor did he hate his foreign hosts. What he hated (it was clear from the talk)—and what caused him such pain—was China's inability, in embarrassing contrast to Japan, to produce these things herself.[25] (The irony of Liu's remarks will be less apparent to observers of Chinese manufacturing prowess in the last years of the twentieth century.)

Another commonplace form of mythologization is autobiographical, that is, the mythologization we all engage in as we continually rework our prior lives so as to make them coherent and congruent with the changes in self-conception that we pass through as we navigate along our biographical trajectories. In her moving ethnography of an elderly Jewish community in Venice, California, Barbara Myerhoff writes that in her subjects' quest for "the integrity of the person over time," the creation of "personal myths" often took precedence over "truth and completeness."[26] This form of mythologization, although a vital aspect of everybody's personal experience, is unfortunately not easily gotten at in the case of the Boxers because of the nature of the materials available.

Still another kind of mythologization, often far more powerful than history in fixing images of the past in people's minds, is that found in poetry, drama, fiction, art, and film dealing with historical subject matter. The Salem witch trials, it has been argued, are better known in the late twentieth century through the work of a playwright, Arthur Miller, than through the writing of historians.[27] And yet, ironically, The Crucible, which appeared in 1953, was an effort on Miller's part to say something not about Salem but about a far more immediate threat to the well-being of the American body politic: McCarthyism.

Mythologization of the Boxers in the arts in China, like their mythologization in general, has tended to gravitate between the extremes of vilification and praise. Of more than 5,000 poems composed by elite Chinese either during or in the immediate aftermath of the uprising, some 90 percent, according to one study, viewed the Boxers with contempt, describing them by such pejorative terms as "bandits" (daozei), "rebellious people" (*luanmin*), and "thugs" (*baotu*).[28] This was also true of the novels of the late Qing that took the Boxers as their central subject matter. On the other hand, as noted in chapter 5, contemporary popular woodcuts often depicted the Boxers as patriotic heroes who vanquished their foreign adversaries on the field of battle.[29]

Positive portrayal of the Boxers in Chinese literature had its heyday, as one might expect, after the Communists came to power in 1949. The editors of a collection of Boxer stories for young people, published in 1961, took note of the "heroism, tenacity, simplicity, and resourcefulness" of the Boxers and evinced the hope that young readers, "inspired and strengthened by the stories," would "throw themselves into the cause of constructing and defending socialism in the motherland!"[30] The celebrated writer Lao She, a Manchu whose father, a member of the Imperial Guards, had been a casualty of the fighting in Beijing in the summer of 1900 and whose mother, when he was a boy, had filled his head with grisly stories of the crimes committed by the foreign forces in the capital, decided in 1960 to write a play commemorating the sixtieth anniversary of the Boxer rising. Titled *Shenquan*, or "The Spirit Boxers," the play revolves about a poor farmer from the area west of the capital, Gao Yongyi, who, after experiencing cruel exploitation at the hands of the local Catholic church (and its foreign priest) and the tragic suicide of a niece as a result of the coercive behavior of a family of local bullies, forms a Boxer unit to take revenge against his—and his fellow villagers'—oppressors.[31]

Lao She's romanticization of the Boxers as courageous heroes, anti-imperialist patriots, and Robin Hoodesque redistributors of wealth—after burning down the Catholic church Gao's Boxers distribute grain and cloth to the needy—followed the standard Communist script in fairly straightforward fashion.[32] In the more freewheeling literary world of the 1980s, Chinese writers began to depart from this script and, in the process, with growing temerity to disidentify with the Boxers. In Liu Xinwu's semifictional account of the rioting that took place in Beijing on May 19, 1985, following the Chinese soccer team's loss to Hong Kong, the central character Hua Zhiming emphatically distances himself and the other rioters from the Boxers of 1900 ("Now *they* were xenophobes"). The mob's targeting of foreigners and Hong Kong people during the 1985 incident had more to do, the narrator explains, with "jealousy of those who had been making a lot of money than . . . concerted antiforeign sentiment." No xenophobes, Hua and his comrades were "the most ardent consumers of popular Hong Kong culture and Japanese products."[33]

218   Farcical treatment of the Boxers also became an option in the 1980s. In
Wang Shuo's *Qianwan bie ba wo dang ren* (No man's land), first published
in late 1989,[34] a main theme, again, is China's effort to regain face vis-à-vis
the outside world—this time owing to her defeat in an international sports
competition at Sapporo. The person chosen to represent the country in
this effort, described by Geremie Barmé as "a Chinese Everyman who can
redeem national pride and who is also, in an important sense, a sacrificial
victim to that pride," is Tang Yuanbao. Tang, "a crooked pedicab driver," is
skilled in the most powerful form of Chinese *gongfu*—Damengquan (literally, "Great Dream Boxing")—which he has learned from his father,
who has the honor (dubious as it turns out) of being "the last living Boxer."
In the Sapporo martial arts rematch, in preparation for which he is put
through the most excruciating training by his backers (including castration
when it is learned that only women are eligible to participate), Tang com-
petes against athletes from all over the world to see who can endure the
most humiliating treatment. After performing "the ultimate feat of self-
humiliation"—with a sharp knife he cuts the skin around his neck and
peels off his face—Tang is acclaimed "uncontested world champion" in a
ceremony that is televised in China and sparks a national celebration. Prior
to this, Tang's father has been arrested on charges of betraying the Boxer
movement and causing the fall of the Qing dynasty—no statute of limitations here—and is convicted not only of the former charge but also of
responsibility for the spectrum of "social disorders, evils and general corruption" in the China of his own day. The elder Tang, already over a hundred years old, is sentenced to life imprisonment!

Wang Shuo's satire is important for our purposes because it evokes some
of the most powerfully contradictory ways in which the Boxers survive in
Chinese consciousness in the late twentieth century. On the most pro-
saically ideological level, the Boxers are treated in the work as a "positive"
force: the central figure's father is, after all, arrested by the authorities for
having betrayed the Boxer movement. But when one pokes a little deeper,
the images in the work relating explicitly or implicitly to the Boxers—fighting techniques that are unreal (dream boxing), patriotism via national self-
humiliation, victimization by the state (the arrest of "the last living
Boxer"), the scapegoating of the powerless as a means of addressing serious
social problems (the pillorying of Tang's centenarian father as "public
enemy Number One")—are also images of self-loathing that have been
deeply etched in the minds of Chinese intellectuals and have surfaced
again and again in this century in national discussions of cultural self-def-

inition such as (to take the most recent example) the "culture fever (or craze)" (*wenhua re*) of the 1980s. The farcical Boxer imagery in *No Man's Land* is used only on a superficial level to attack the Communists; the more important target of Wang Shuo's novel, it appears, is the Chinese condition in general.

While mythologization in literature — and also the other arts — encompasses the entire range of tonalities, from the most positive to the most negative, another form of mythologization inclines generally toward the positive. I refer to "local boosterism," as embodied typically in monuments, shrines, stela, and memorials, erected partly to keep alive the memory of the local boy (or girl) who made (or did) good and partly to enhance the image and promote the fortunes of the local place itself. The memorial created in the mid-1980s in honor of Boxer leader Zhao Sanduo in his home village (Shaliuzhai) in Wei county in southern Hebei (formerly Zhili) includes a large white plaster bust of Zhao rendered in the Mao-era heroic mode, a full-length traditional-style Chinese painting of him (also larger than life), which makes him look for all the world like a mandarin, and, to complete the symbolic reworking of Zhao from illegitimate rebel into respectable exemplar of orthodoxy, a formal biography (white characters against black background) that immediately calls to mind the biographies in the official dynastic histories. The irony evoked by the Zhao Sanduo memorial lies in the diverse and contradictory sources of symbolic validation (Maoist and traditional Chinese) the memorial incorporates. For a dozen or so foreign visitors in October 1990 (of whom I happened to be one), there was much irony as well in the warm and spirited welcome extended by the villagers, many of them direct descendants of the Boxers, to people who at least culturally were descendants of the Boxers' archenemies of yesteryear — a welcome carried even to the point of urging us to sign a guestbook marking our participation in this oddly celebratory pilgrimage.[35]

Local boosterism is, at bottom, an exercise in public remembering. Not all commemoration is celebratory, however, as evidenced by the range of activities, both annual and ongoing, designed to keep alive memory of the Holocaust.[36] As the example of the Holocaust also suggests, commemoration need not be focused on individuals. Indeed, anything that has happened in the past that someone thinks is worth commemorating can be commemorated. No sooner did reliable news reach the foreigners in the legation quarters in August 1900 that the allied relief force had left Tianjin and would soon arrive in the capital than a notice was posted offering a prize for the best design for a medal to be struck "as a

220   memorial of this strange experience." One of the designs entered in the competition had three figures representing Europe, America, and Japan standing hand in hand on the head of a dragon[37]—a neat example of instant mythologization, in light of the "miserable international jealousies" that, in the view of one careful observer, "disgraced" the "relief of Peking from its very inception."[38]

In Salem, Massachusetts, to take a somewhat more complicated case, an event which when it happened embodied the very essence of fear, intolerance, and blind hatred—the witchcraft outbreak of 1692—has in an odd twist of fate become the primary reason for which the town is today known and also over the years a substantial source of commercial profit for its inhabitants. Every day is Halloween in Salem. The witch-on-a-broomstick logo appears on everything from the badges of the town's police force to the uniforms of its high school football team. As of 1990 a thousand people who claimed to be witches lived in the town, some making their livings from the practice of witchcraft. And, as plans were being laid in 1992 for the 300th anniversary of the witch trials, it was hard for some of the planners to decide whether what they were planning was a commemoration of an event filled with horror or a celebration of everything that event had done to make Salem what it was.[39]

Anniversaries are among the most common—and potentially powerful—forms of commemoration of the past. If the event being commemorated is generally viewed by later generations in negative terms, as in the case of the Salem witch trials, a major purpose of the anniversary commemoration is likely to be educational in nature.[40] Thus, one member of the tercentenary committee appointed by the mayor of Salem suggested "Lest We Forget" as a working theme for the year-long commemoration process, and a variety of symposia, lectures, theater performances, and public school programs took place.[41] Often, however, people use anniversaries to reexperience a past with which they feel a strong positive sense of connection. One of the most heralded sporting events of the twentieth century was the rematch between Joe Louis and Max Schmeling at Yankee Stadium on June 22, 1938. Even before it took place, the Louis-Schmeling fight, because it pitted a black American against a white man from Nazi Germany, was connected in people's minds with larger contemporary issues having little to do with boxing. Fifty years later, in 1988, these issues were directly alluded to when Jesse Louis Jackson, who like so many African-Americans of his generation was named after Louis and as a presidential aspirant clearly saw himself as a beneficiary of Louis's knocking down of racial barriers, recalled his hero's first-round knockout of Schmeling in soaring mythical language: "Up from the ghetto of Detroit rose a young David who slew Hitler's Goliath."[42]

In other instances people seize on the opportunity afforded by anniversaries to argue for a completely revised understanding of the past and to challenge the appropriateness of the way (or ways) in which a person or event has previously been commemorated. This is what happened on the occasion of the 500th anniversary of Columbus's voyage to the "New World," as we have seen. It also happened in 1989, at the time of the bicentennial of the French Revolution, when a profusion of books conveying a revisionist, far less upbeat view of that event appeared in print.[43]

In all cases, it seems, anniversaries form an emotional bridge between present and past that is ever subject to reconstruction in response to the shifting preoccupations of people — and governments — in the present. After more than a year of listening to foreign charges of brutality and savagery in its handling of the protest demonstrations that rocked China in the spring of 1989, the Chinese government decided to use the 90th anniversary of the foreign relief force's invasion and occupation of Beijing at the time of the Boxer episode to launch a counteroffensive. In mid-August 1990 a flurry of articles appeared in the Chinese press which, in addition to emphasizing the standard post-Tiananmen themes of renewed vigilance against imperialist aggression (now taking the more subtle form of "peaceful evolution") and the crucial leading role of the Communist Party in China's modernization, made a special point of reminding readers — sometimes in excruciating detail and with careful attention to documentary support — of the brutal and savage acts committed by foreigners against the Chinese people in the summer of 1900. These atrocities sufficed, one article concluded, to lay bare the sham nature of "the so-called 'Western civilization' continually trumpeted by the allied forces and their home governments."[44]

One last variety of mythologization — perhaps it is best described as a genre — is that encountered in newspapers, periodicals, and books. Sometimes generated in the minds of private individuals, sometimes orchestrated with varying degrees of cynicism by the state, this category of mythologization (really two categories insofar as it may emanate from either society or the state) has the potential to reach a very large number of people and is also in some ways the most readily accessible. For these reasons, I shall concentrate on it in the chapters that follow, describing and analyzing the ways in which the Boxers were mythologized during three different periods of the twentieth century in China: the New Culture movement (pre-May Fourth), the anti-imperialist struggles of the 1920s,

222 and the Cultural Revolution. My purpose in these pages, reflecting the dual aims of the book as a whole, will be twofold: first, to scrutinize the working procedures of mythologizers and identify what is distinctive about their perspective on the past (especially in comparison to that of historians), and, second, to explore the part taken by mythologization of the Boxers in particular in the history of Chinese consciousness in the twentieth century.

CHAPTER 7

The New Culture Movement and the Boxers

Joseph Levenson once observed that although Christianity had been rejected in China in both the seventeenth and the twentieth centuries, the grounds of the rejection in the two eras were radically different. "In the seventeenth century," he wrote, "Chinese opposed Christianity as un-traditional. In twentieth-century China, especially after the first World War, it was the principal anti-Christian cry that Christianity was un-modern. In the early instance, . . . Christianity was criticized for not being Confucian; this was a criticism proper to Chinese civilization. In the later instance, Christianity was criticized for not being scientific; and this was a criticism from western civilization."[1]

Certainly, one might quibble with the neatness of Levenson's formulation. In addition to the contrasting bases for Chinese anti-Christian sentiment in the two centuries, there were also important elements of continuity, such as the widely held belief (in both periods) that Christianity was irrational and superstitious, unworthy of the attention of serious folk.[2] Levenson's basic point, nevertheless, stands: Although there was opposition to Christianity in both periods, the cultural, intellectual, and psychological context for the opposition changed in crucial ways.

Paradoxically, an analogous pattern may be discerned in the case of Chinese denigration of the Boxer movement, itself ferociously anti-Christian. In the contemporary Chinese press and in the diaries and other accounts kept by elite chroniclers of the movement, the Boxers tended almost invariably to be perceived (like Christianity from the seventeenth through the nineteenth centuries) in the context of the age-old distinction between orthodoxy and heterodoxy. The whole range of pejorative terminology associated with *xiejiao* or "heterodox sects" was thrown at them. They were identified as "Boxer bandits" (*quanfei* or *tuanfei*),[3] who stirred up "turmoil" and "disorder" (*luan, bianluan*)[4] and "misled" (*huo*) or "incited" (*shanhuo*)[5] the masses with their "deceitful" (*gui*) claims.[6] Contemporary

224   authors, as we have seen, also ridiculed and expressed skepticism toward the magical prowess of the Boxers, although they were quick to acknowledge its effectiveness in attracting followers among the benighted masses. The masses—the "ignorant people" (yumin)—were widely portrayed as credulous folk, who could be made to believe almost any form of nonsense.[7] Boxer leaders were accused of deliberately duping their followers with claims of invulnerability in order to bolster the latter's courage.[8] In the view of one writer, only 20 percent of the general population—consisting of Muslims, people with a thorough grasp of reason, and people who had a deep understanding of the overall situation—were sufficiently clearheaded to withstand the propaganda onslaught of the Boxers.[9]

This critical perspective on the Boxers—as well as on Chinese society more generally—was also found in the writings of reform-minded Chinese at the turn of the century,[10] although with the reformers one begins to detect a shift in the intellectual context informing the criticism. For the philosopher Liang Shuming's father, Liang Ji, who was an official in Beijing in the summer of 1900, the Boxer movement brought home the ignorance and superstition of the masses of his countrymen and underscored the need for national regeneration to go beyond the elite and embrace the populace at large.[11] The reform leader Kang Youwei, in an unpublished essay of late 1900 or early 1901, conjectured that the net result of the "turmoil" (luan) created by the "Boxer bandits" (quanfei) and of the ensuing devastation of the capital by the foreign relief forces might actually be a plus for China: "Heaven's way of laying the foundation of China's modernization and of preparing the ground for the sage emperor's [Guangxu's] restoration."[12] Kang's disciple, Liang Qichao, in an influential essay of 1902, faulted the widespread popularity of fiction for the rampant superstitions that had, on the one hand, hindered the building of railways and the opening of mines in China and, on the other, contributed to the calamitous rising of the Boxers.[13] Another of Kang's followers, Mai Menghua, condemned the Boxers' "indiscriminate xenophobia" as a barbaric stance that could only be harmful to China's interests.[14]

The reformers' criticism of the Boxers was intellectually transitional: they saw the Boxers as imperiling the emergence of a reformed, "progressive" China, but they also betrayed a lingering concern for the movement's threat to Confucian rationalism and the Confucian social order. When Chinese revolutionaries, who were also beginning to appear on the scene at the turn of the century, condemned the Boxers, the condemnation tended to come more unambiguously from Western culture.[15] Zou Rong, an admirer of the martyred reformer Tan Sitong and one of the most culturally iconoclastic of the early revolutionaries, set the tone in his famous 1903 pamphlet, *The Revolutionary Army* (*Gemingjun*). In this tract Zou distinguished between barbaric revolutions (*yeman zhi geming*), which were pointlessly destructive and intensified people's suffering, and civilized revolutions (*wenming zhi geming*), which engaged in destruction in order to pave the way for construction and, by establishing the rights of freedom, equality, independence, and autonomy, enlarged people's basic store of happiness. Held up by Zou as models of the second kind of upheaval were the English, American, and French revolutions. (Zou, in his preface, specifically acknowledged his indebtedness to such "great thinkers" as Rousseau and Washington.) A prime example of the barbaric form of revolution, as befitted a nation of ignorant slaves, was the Boxer uprising.[16]

Although dealt with only in passing, the Boxers, in Zou Rong's hands, took a giant step in the evolution from history to myth. Chroniclers of the uprising such as Liu Mengyang, Guan He, and Zhongfang Shi, although defining it in terms of a preestablished vocabulary ("bandits," "turmoil," "heterodoxy") that was highly pejorative, nonetheless sought, at least on some level, to elucidate the Boxer movement—to provide a contemporary record of its origins, course, principal characteristics, and dénouement. Zou Rong was different. He could not have cared less about explaining or understanding the Boxers. The aim of his tract was to encourage the Chinese people to engage in a revolutionary act that would replace Manchu rulers with Han, monarchy with republic, and a country of slaves with a country of free people. The Boxers, for Zou, were a symbol of everything in Chinese society he wanted destroyed.

The "civilized" revolution Zou Rong wanted actually took place in 1911. Although it resulted in the overthrow of the Manchus and the installation of a republican form of government in place of the ancient imperial system, however, the consensus among Chinese intellectuals was that it worked hardly any change at all upon Chinese society, that China as a human organization had, if anything, gone from bad to worse. Certainly this was the outlook of Lu Xun, who in his famous short story, *The True Story of Ah Q* (*A Q zhengzhuan*, 1921), ridiculed the superficiality of the revolution's impact: "The people of Weizhuang . . . knew that, although the revolutionaries had entered the town, their coming had not made a great deal of difference. The magistrate was still the highest official, it was only his title that had changed; . . . the head of the military was still the same old captain. The only cause for alarm was that there were also some bad revolutionaries making trouble, . . . cutting off people's pigtails the day after their arrival."[17]

226   The New Culture movement, in which Lu Xun was a major participant, is conventionally said to have begun around 1915, although many of
the specific positions with which it is identified can be traced to the turn of
the century. One of the movement's cardinal objectives was to refashion
Chinese society, the living embodiment of all the assorted ailments inher-
ited from China's traditional culture. The traditional culture, which many
in the movement rejected as barbaric (Lu Xun, in another well-known
story, A Madman's Diary [Kuangren riji, 1918], described it as "man-eat-
ing"),[18] was to be replaced by a new culture, washed of the noxious influences contaminating the old and patterned largely if not entirely on the
culture of the modern West. The same objective was also pursued by the
Chinese state during this period. The state's motives included the traditional one of wishing to prevent social unrest (frequently associated with
"superstitious" beliefs and practices), but they also embraced the newer
goal, shared with New Culture figures, of removing all hindrances to
China's becoming a modern society.[19]

    The Boxers, in this context, were a convenient peg on which to hang all
that the participants in the New Culture movement found most objectionable and threatening about the old culture. Paramount here, especially
for people wedded to the values of science and reason, were the superstitions and irrationalism they perceived as endemic in Chinese society.
Under the playful title "The Boxers' Conquest of the Westerners," the following squib appeared in the first issue of the short-lived Weekly Critic
(Meizhou pinglun) in December 1918:

> Some folks say that at the French embassy at present they indulge in
> planchette writing and invocation of the gods. Doesn't this imply that the
> Westerners believe in ghosts and spirits too? I say, not so at all. Decadence in
> official circles, whether in China or abroad, is nothing new. Moreover,
> although there is a tiny minority of scholars in foreign countries who are
> fond of things strange and are given to discoursing on ghosts and demons, it
> isn't as in China, where ghosts and demons and things miraculous pervade
> the thoughts of the entire society.[20]

    Two things are noteworthy about this brief item. First, the fact that the
term "Boxers" (Yihequan) occurs conspicuously in the title but not at all
in the text suggests unmistakably that "Boxers" (or "Boxerism") is intended
to represent the main subject matter of the text: belief in ghosts and spirits.
Second, belief in ghosts and spirits is asserted to be ubiquitous in China;
hence, Boxerism is understood to symbolize a prime trait of Chinese culture in general.

Denigration of Boxer superstition from the vantage point of a newfound commitment to the science and rationalism of the West was commonplace in the writings of New Culture figures. Jiang Menglin (Chiang Monlin), a recent convert to Western science in turn-of-the-century Shanghai, referred to the Boxers as "a fanatical cult claiming magical powers." Wang Xing-gong, who studied science in England and became a chemistry professor at Beijing University, took a strong stand against the supernatural and saw such events as the Boxer rising as the tragic consequence of misplaced reliance on faith. And Hu Shi, in a speech at Yanjing University in 1925, pointedly contrasted Boxer superstitiousness to the rationalism of his own day.[21]

Such disparagement, however, while significant, is of less interest to me than the further—and more crucial—step involving identification of the Boxers with the superstitious, irrational, blindly ignorant, barbaric tendencies of Chinese society as a whole. This was not an identification that was made with great frequency by New Culture intellectuals. The truth is, for most of these persons, the Boxers were such an embarrassment they preferred not to think about them any more than was absolutely necessary. It was, however, made by a few influential figures, explicitly and with force. In the process the existential issue of what a modern Chinese cultural identity might look like was joined.

Chen Duxiu, Lu Xun, and the Boxers

The most striking example was an essay by Chen Duxiu that appeared in the fall of 1918 in *New Youth* (*Xin qingnian*), the leading journal of the day. Chen, who had been a cofounder of *New Youth* several years earlier and would go on in 1921 to become the first head of the Chinese Communist Party, wrote his essay amid the din created by crowds in the streets of Beijing celebrating the victory over Germany in World War I. He was disinclined to go out and join the revelers, he says, mainly because he did not feel that China had had enough of a part in the Allied victory to warrant such public jubilation. When he heard people outside elatedly exclaiming about the destruction of the von Ketteler Monument, erected at German insistence on the spot in the capital where the German minister had been killed in June 1900, he was even less inclined to leave the quiet of his study. Instead, Chen informs us, he pulled out some old materials on the Boxers, so that he could have another look at that "laughable, frightening, infuriating, tragic" set of events.

After reproducing lengthy excerpts from these materials to jog the memories of his forgetful compatriots, Chen issued the warning that, if some-

228   thing were not done to prevent it, China could expect a recurrence of the
Boxer unrest, the foreigners would again invade the country, and instead of
a single von Ketteler Monument there would be stone memorials everywhere. He then embarked on an extended discussion of the factors contributing to the Boxer rising:

> Of the causes leading to the Boxers in the past, the first was Daoism. . . . The
> entire array of superstitions and heterodox teachings . . . are rampant
> throughout society as a result of the efforts of the *yin-yang* school, the
> alchemists, and the Daoist priests down through the ages. The Boxers were
> the crystallization of every superstition and heterodox teaching in the entire
> society; that is why when they opened their mouths [after being possessed by
> spirits] they claimed to have received orders from the Jade Emperor to
> destroy the Westerners.
>
> The second cause was Buddhism. Buddhism made two contributions to
> the Boxers. The first was Buddhist philosophical theory, which entailed the
> acceptance of a spiritual world transcending the material. . . . Another facet
> of Buddhism that was an important constituent element of the Boxers was
> the whole range of superstitions involving the exercise of magical power. . . .
>
> The third cause was Confucianism. Although Confucius did not speak of
> gods and spirits, he also never rejected supernatural beings categorically.
> Furthermore, the general idea of the *Spring and Autumn* [*Chunqiu*, a
> Confucian classic] can be completely summed up in the four words "Revere
> the king, expel the barbarian" [*zun wang rang yi*]. Doesn't [the slogan]
> "Support the Qing, destroy the foreigner" [Fu-Qing mieyang] paraded by the
> Boxers have the same meaning as "Revere the king, expel the barbarian"?
>
> Chinese opera . . . was the fourth cause of the Boxers. . . . The gods
> invoked by the Boxers were mostly opera heroes with their "theatrical make-
> up" and "martial posturing": Guan Yu, Zhang Fei, Zhao Yun, Sun Wukong,
> Huang Santai, Huang Tianba, and the like.[22] Opera is particularly popular
> in Tianjin, Beijing, and Fengtian, so it was exceptionally easy for the Boxers
> to spread. When the Boxer gods presented themselves, their speech was
> modeled on the spoken parts in the operas and their gestures were modeled
> on the prescribed movements of the opera actors. These were things that
> people from Beijing, Tianjin, and Fengtian saw with their own eyes; it's not
> something I'm making up.
>
> The fifth . . . cause consisted of the conservatives with their hostility to
> new learning and their magnified sense of their own importance. . . . Since
> the barbarians weren't conversant with the ethical teachings of China's sages
> and wise men, that made them savage beasts; as for those Chinese who fell
> in with and advocated emulation of these savage beasts, weren't they even
> more worthy of being killed? Therefore, in 1898 they killed or drove into
> exile the members of the reform party who had fallen in with the savage

beasts, but they still weren't content; only in 1900, with the appearance of the Boxers, intent upon preserving the national essence and the three teachings and determined to kill off all the savage beasts, did these celebrated Confucian officials become completely content, feeling that [the problem] had been solved in a fundamental way.

The heart of Chen's argument was that these five causes of the Boxer uprising were all present in 1918 unchanged: "Although the name 'Boxers' hasn't yet reappeared, the ideas of the Boxers and the reality of the Boxers are everywhere throughout China and are in the ascendant. Can we be sure that the Boxers will not reemerge in the future? And if they do reemerge in the future, can we be sure that we won't again have to erect a monument to our national shame?" After detailing an array of superstitious and magical practices that he said were still followed across the land, Chen concluded:

> Looking at it from the point of view of the above facts, it may be concluded that the causal agencies capable of bringing the Boxers into existence in present-day China are not a whit less prevalent than they were on the eve of 1900. The future may therefore be foretold. If the people of China wish to be rid of present and future monuments to national shame, they must see to it that the Boxers do not reemerge. And if they want to see to it that the Boxers do not reemerge, they have no choice but to eradicate the whole range of causes that brought the Boxers into being.
>
> There are at present two paths open to us: one is the path of light that leads toward republicanism, science, and atheism; the other is the path of darkness leading toward autocracy, superstition, and theism. If our people do not wish for a revival of the Boxers, if they are loath again to contemplate the erection of humiliating memorials like the von Ketteler Monument, which of these paths, in the last analysis, shall we take?[23]

Chen Duxiu's essay is a classic instance of the mythologization of the past. What he essentially argues is that A — a broad array of superstitious, unscientific, conservative ideas — was the direct cause of B — the Boxer rising — and that since in his own day A is still widespread in China, if something is not done quickly to root it out, B is bound to reappear. From the standpoint of historical logic, Chen's argument is gravely flawed. However important certain ideas may have been in the shaping of the Boxer movement, few historians would claim that ideas alone were accountable for the movement's origin and development. Furthermore, if the ideas in question were as deeply and permanently etched in Chinese societal and thought patterns as Chen suggests, one wonders why "the Boxers" were not a permanent feature of Chinese life. The fact that they were not, that they had

230   not appeared on the scene prior to 1898–1900 and that they disappeared after that time, casts a heavy shadow of doubt upon the simplistic and, paradoxically, not very "scientific" correlative reasoning with which Chen seeks to persuade his readership.

None of this, however, would faze Chen in the slightest. Chen's objective in this piece is not to advance understanding of the Boxers as a historical phenomenon. What he really wants to do is bring about a decisive transformation in the beliefs and attitudes of his contemporaries. Other Chinese—the throngs in the streets of the capital in November 1918 announcing the demolition of the von Ketteler Monument, Chen Duxiu himself in 1924 (as we shall see), a long line of Chinese Marxist-Leninists stretching at least into the 1980s—might argue that the main weight that needed to be lifted from China's back before its development could proceed in a "normal" fashion was foreign imperialism. In 1918, Chen Duxiu contested this logic sharply, maintaining that imperialism, as symbolized by the von Ketteler Monument, was not the cause of China's difficulties but the consequence. The cause of China's difficulties, which made such monuments possible, indeed probable, was the intellectual condition of Chinese society as symbolized by the Boxers. China's energies therefore should be directed not toward the elimination of superficial emblems of national shame but toward the creation of a new kind of society—republican, scientific, atheistic—that would, by its very nature, preclude similar occasions for national humiliation in the future.

The notion that China's real problem lay deep within its own culture—and the use of the Boxers to dramatize this notion in symbolic terms—is also encountered in a brief satirical note by Lu Xun that appeared in the same issue of New Youth:

> Recently, there have been a fair number of people scattered about who have been energetically promoting boxing. I seem to recall this having happened once before. But at that time the promoters were the Manchu court and high officials, whereas now they are Republican educators—people occupying a quite different place in society. I have no way of telling, as an outsider, whether their goals are the same or different.
>
> These educators have now renamed the old methods "that the Goddess of the Ninth Heaven transmitted to the Yellow Emperor" . . . "the new martial arts" or "Chinese-style gymnastics" and they make young people practice them.[a] I've heard there are a lot of benefits to be had from them. Two of the more important may be listed here:

[a] The Goddess of the Ninth Heaven (Jiu tian xuannü), according to tradition, instructed the Yellow Emperor (China's mythical first emperor) in the martial arts.

(1) They have a physical education function. It's said that when Chinese take instruction in foreign gymnastics it isn't effective; the only thing that works for them is native-style gymnastics (that is, boxing). I would have thought that if one spread one's arms and legs apart and picked up a foreign bronze hammer or wooden club in one's hands, it ought probably to have some "efficacy" as far as one's muscular development was concerned. But it turns out this isn't so! Naturally, therefore, the only course left to them is to switch to learning such tricks as "Wu Song disengaging himself from his manacles."[b] No doubt this is because Chinese are different from foreigners physiologically.

(2) They have a military function. The Chinese know how to box; the foreigners don't know how to box. So if one day the two meet and start fighting, it goes without saying the Chinese will win. . . . The only thing is that nowadays people always use firearms when they fight. Although China "had firearms too in ancient times" it doesn't have them any more. So if the Chinese don't learn the military art of using rattan shields, how can they protect themselves against firearms? I think — since they don't elaborate on this, this reflects "my own very limited and shallow understanding" — I think that if they keep at it with their boxing they are bound to reach the point where they become "invulnerable to firearms." (I presume by doing exercises to benefit their internal organs?)[c] Boxing was tried once before — in 1900. Unfortunately on that occasion its reputation may be considered to have suffered a decisive setback. We'll see how it fares this time around.[24]

In a subsequent number of *New Youth* a man named Chen Tiesheng, older than Lu Xun and apparently with some military background, wrote an irate response to Lu, charging him with having totally confused two things that were as different as night and day: "I don't know what sort of person Mr. Lu Xun is; probably he's a young man. In any case the mind of this gentleman seems a bit muddled. How could he mix up the Boxer bandits and the art of attack and defense? I don't know if Mr. Lu ever saw the Boxer bandits. If he had he would never make such foolish insinuations." Chen went on to argue that the Boxers had been savage beasts who seduced people with lies and were in the thrall of the supernatural, whereas the practitioners of the art of attack and defense operated according to the most exact rules and followed the way of humanity. Chen found Lu Xun's claim that the foreigners didn't know how to box "preposterous," and challenged him, if he really believed that to be so, to account for the fact that the word "box-

[b] Wu Song, one of the heroes of the novel *Shuihu zhuan* (Water margin), was famous for his mastery of the martial arts.
[c] Lu Xun refers here to *neigong*, a regimen of breathing exercises (*qigong*) closely associated with Chinese boxing.

232 ing" existed in foreign countries. Finally, Chen used satire himself to ridicule Lu, especially for his naïveté: "Firearms must indeed be used. But when in battle one becomes involved in close fighting—this doubtless is not something Mr. Lu knows about—one must also use the magical arts of the Boxer bandits. In army middle school, I recall, they still taught the art of the sword and spear, and the methods that were used and the diagrams that were drawn fell well within the sphere of the art of attack and defense. Here again Mr. Lu shows himself to be a true foreign Boxer bandit" (in the sense that Lu had no comprehension of Chinese boxing at all).[25]

In his response to Chen Tiesheng, Lu Xun pointed out that the main intent of his original note had been to address a "social phenomenon" (she-hui xianxiang), whereas Chen's attack was a reflection of his private attitude. Lu explained the distinction by reference to a book on the new martial arts that Chen Duxiu had cited in his von Ketteler Monument article. The author of the preface to that book had expressed an attitude of strong sympathy not only for the Boxers but also for their supernatural claims. This would be of little consequence, Lu tells us, if it were just the opinion of an isolated individual. But the fact that the book had received the government's imprimatur, had been warmly received in educational circles, and was being used as a text all over the country made it into a real social phenomenon—a social phenomenon, moreover, advancing the mentality of "supernaturalism" (guidaozhuyi). Lu went on to say that he realized that there must be some experts in Chinese boxing who did not believe in the supernatural. But since these individuals did not step forward and state their position publicly, their views remained hidden by the prevailing trend in society.

Lu's defense against the specific charges raised in Chen's attack was fairly straightforward. With respect to the item concerning the foreign word "boxing," for example, he countered: " 'Boxing' is indeed a term that is found in foreign countries. But it is not the same as China's daquan [boxing]; so with respect to China's it may be said that they 'don't know how.' It's very much like their using 'Boxer'—one of their own words—for quan-fei [Boxer bandits]; would one say, because they have such a word, that the foreigners also have Boxer bandits?"

Lu concluded with a concise summation of his position: "If Chinese boxing is regarded as a special skill and there are a few individuals whose pleasure it is to seek out an instructor and practice it, I have no objections whatever; that is a small matter. What I am at present opposed to are two things: (1) educators treating boxing as a fashionable thing which all Chinese without exception must take up; and (2) the promoters of boxing

for the most part embracing the psychology of the 'supernatural' [*guidao*] —
which is an extremely dangerous sign."[26]

The fascinating thing about the exchange between Lu Xun and Chen Tiesheng is that a fair amount of heat was generated, especially on the side of Chen, between two individuals who, at least with respect to the essentials, were not really that far apart. Chen Tiesheng, after all, was in full agreement with Lu Xun that the Boxers were to be condemned as purveyors of rank superstition, and Lu Xun, for his part, was prepared to accept, if warily, a degree of social legitimacy for Chinese boxing. What, then, was the problem?

The crux of the problem, I would argue, is that Chen viewed the Boxers as history and therefore dead, whereas Lu viewed them as myth and therefore very much alive. For Chen Tiesheng, the Boxer rising was an episode out of the past that, however horrible and repugnant, was over and done with. Precisely because the Boxers were a thing of the past, it was possible to deal with Chinese boxing—the martial arts—as a completely separate realm of human activity, insulated from, even immune to, the negative associations evoked by the historical Boxers. What infuriated Chen was that Lu Xun, a young upstart who clearly knew nothing about either the historical Boxers or Chinese boxing, had gratuitously collapsed the distinction between the two, sullying in the process the good name of the martial arts in China.

Lu Xun, of course, saw things very differently. Born in 1881, he was not at the time he wrote his piece quite as inexperienced as Chen made him out to be, although by his own admission he was indeed an outsider as far as Chinese boxing was concerned. But none of this, in any case, had much bearing on the matter at hand. What was of consequence was that the two men had completely disparate areas of concern. Where the paramount issue for Chen was the reputation of Chinese boxing, for Lu Xun it was the far broader question of the present and future orientation of Chinese culture. Lu, like Chen Duxiu, saw Chinese culture as mired in superstition and irrationality and firmly believed that China's survival depended on its capacity to root out these deadly qualities. In such circumstances, a phenomenon like the Boxer movement, so widely understood by New Culture intellectuals as the quintessential embodiment of these qualities, was hard to view as mere history. From Lu Xun's perspective, it was not he that was guilty of confusing "Chinese boxing" and the "Boxers," but Chinese society itself. As long as superstition and irrationality remained ubiquitous in this society, it would be extremely hard for Lu and others like him to share the perception of Chen Tiesheng that the Boxers were dead.

234   Although my emphasis in the foregoing analysis has been on mythologization of the Boxers as part of the effort of New Culture figures to bring about China's cultural renovation, it would be a mistake to view the war Chen Duxiu, Lu Xun, and others were waging as simply an intellectual engagement between the forces of light and the forces of darkness. "We educated ones," wrote the historian Gu Jiegang in 1925, "are too far from the people; we consider ourselves cultured gentlemen and them as vulgar; we consider ourselves as aristocrats . . . and revile them as mean people."[27] The elitism Gu alluded to had been made explicit a dozen years earlier by Jiang Menglin when he wrote (not without concern): "our motto is government of the people, for the people, and by the educated class."[28] What the comments of Gu and Jiang clearly suggest is that the negative stance of New Culture intellectuals toward China's traditional culture also had a social underside. It was not just a matter of modernists attacking tradition, of the new culture versus the old; it also reflected an elitist antipathy toward the popular culture participated in by several hundred million ordinary Chinese.

This pronounced antipopular strain on the part of Chinese elites, Communist as well as non-Communist, continued long after the New Culture era was over.[29] As earlier suggested, moreover, it was not a strain that was confined exclusively to the private sphere. Assuming a variety of disguises—the "Superstition Destruction movement" of the Guomindang in 1928–29, the campaign against the "Four Olds" during the Cultural Revolution, the persistent drive to eliminate "feudal superstition" (fengjian mixin) in Deng Xiaoping's China—it was also embodied in the policies of a succession of Chinese governments in the course of the twentieth century.[30] It seems safe to conclude, therefore, that when the Boxers (in absentia) came under attack during this period for their superstition, backwardness, ignorance, and xenophobia, they were being treated as a proxy for a more generalized popular culture that, not only for intellectual reasons but also (at least to a degree) for social ones, was heartily despised by China's intellectual and political elites alike.

The Western Analogue and the Issue of Chinese Cultural Identity

It may be helpful at this point to compare New Culture mythologization of the Boxers with their (on the surface at least) not dissimilar mythologization in the West. Although there have been exceptions (generally emanating from people on the political left), the overriding tendency among Westerners in the twentieth century has been to portray the Boxers in stridently negative terms.[31] In the years immediately following the uprising, the Boxers were a prime focus of Yellow Peril demonology. Throughout the century they have been understood single-dimensionally as an emblem of barbarism, cruelty, irrational hatred of foreigners, and superstition.

This pattern made its first appearance while the uprising was still in progress. Typical were the following stanzas from a poem written by a woman from Dubuque, Iowa, and published in *The Independent* in August 1900 during the siege of the legations:

> Day after day, while screaming shells are flying,
> And throb barbaric drums,
> Our own folk wait, amid the dead and dying,
> For help that never comes.
>
> Millions of yellow, pitiless, alien faces,
> Circle them round with hate;
> While desperate valor guards the broken places,
> Outside the torturers wait.[32]

Similar themes were struck in a cartoon printed in the *Brooklyn Eagle* during the siege, which depicted the powers wielding the broom of civilization and sweeping China clean not only of Boxers but of the whole range of repellent characteristics generally associated with them in Western minds (see figure 7.1).[33] Early European film treatments of the Boxer episode, with titles like "Boxer Attack on a Missionary Outpost," capitalized on the contrast between foreign heroism and Chinese villainy.[34] Ralph D. Paine's *The Cross and the Dragon*, a short adventure novel serialized in the popular young people's magazine *The Youth's Companion* in 1911–12, pitted American Protestant missionaries in North China against the "Big Knives," who although not explicitly identified with the Boxers had all of the more distinctive Boxer traits and were dedicated to driving every foreigner from China.[35] One of the men interviewed by Harold Isaacs for his classic work *Images of Asia* recalled "the sensation of terror" aroused by accounts of the Boxers he had read as a boy and was so traumatized by *The Cross and the Dragon* in particular that, when some years later he unexpectedly received word that he was to be sent to China, Paine's story — and the lurid illustrations accompanying it — rose to haunt his dreams.[36]

Although the first popular American novelist to write about China, Frances Aymar Mathews (1865?–1925), did not treat the Boxers in detail, the "legacy of the Boxers" was, in one scholar's judgment, clearly seen in her portrayal of the Chinese as "cruel and revengeful."[37] This generally unflat-

236 tering characterization continued in other works of fiction published in the 1920s.[38] It was also encountered in the foreign journalism of the period, which emphasized the Boxers' primeval xenophobia (see chapter 8), and it reemerged several decades later during the Cultural Revolution, when the irrational violence and antiforeignism associated with the Boxers were commonly evoked in critical Western commentary on the Red Guards.[39]

Although the specific traits linked with the Boxers in the minds of Westerners were almost identical with those singled out by Chinese intellectuals in the first decades of the century, the settings within which the two mythologization processes evolved were fundamentally different and this ensured that the meanings of the processes would also be very differ-

7.1 Anti-Boxer Cartoon: "The Open Door That China Needs." The unappealing traits commonly associated with the Boxers in the West are clearly depicted in this cartoon, which appeared in the *Brooklyn Eagle* during the siege of the legations. From *The Literary Digest*, July 14, 1900.

ent. For Westerners, armed with a generally untroubled sense of self-confidence and superiority in the moral and cultural spheres, fueled (and even sometimes justified) by the West's position of unquestioned military and economic preeminence, the threat posed by the Boxers—symbolically— was to a world already in place. For New Culture Chinese, on the other hand, it was the very opposite. Intent not on preserving the existing China but on fashioning a completely new one, along with a new and modern Chinese cultural identity, from the perspective of Chen Duxiu, Lu Xun, and others, the threat represented by the Boxers—again symbolically—was to a world waiting to be born.

In another respect as well the seeming parallelism between the two mythologizations masked a crucial difference. From the vantage point of people in the West, the antiforeignism, superstition, savage brutality, and backwardness of the Boxers constituted a coherent whole, all the parts of which were equally menacing to a world Westerners held dear. But for those Chinese in the first decades of the twentieth century who were completely comfortable rejecting Boxer superstition and backwardness, Boxer antiforeignism, which targeted not only modern Western culture (which they were attracted to) but also foreign imperialist encroachment (which the vast majority of them found abhorrent), presented a more complicated problem. This problem—the problem of Boxer antiforeignism and its assessment—was central to the new mythologization of the Boxers that took shape in the 1920s.

CHAPTER 8

Anti-Imperialism and the Recasting of the Boxer Myth

When the past is treated as myth, its meaning is governed to an overwhelming extent by the concerns of the present. As the center of gravity of present concerns shifts, therefore, the meaning of the past necessarily shifts along with it, sometimes to a quite extraordinary degree. Something very much along these lines took place in China in the 1920s, as the preoccupations of the New Culture movement, which were fundamentally oriented toward cultural renovation, gave way to a new set of concerns that were far more political, both in their underlying premises as to how the world operated and in their understanding of the action program that flowed from these premises.[1]

To be sure, the New Culture movement, in the sense of a collection of individuals who held that the task of remaking China was first and foremost a cultural one, did not just disappear. Many Chinese intellectuals, including people as diverse as Hu Shi and Lu Xun, continued to attach overriding importance to China's cultural transformation. Nevertheless, more and more Chinese, frustrated by the glacial pace of cultural change and profoundly influenced by a succession of jolts in the political sphere that underscored the continuing grip of imperialism on China's fortunes, gravitated to the view that the political problem had to be dealt with first. Such political shocks as the betrayal of China's interests at the Versailles Peace Conference (the immediate occasion for the protest demonstrations that broke out in Beijing on May 4, 1919) and the killing of unarmed student demonstrators by British police in Shanghai in the May Thirtieth Incident of 1925, in combination with the emergence of a revolutionary politics centered on the fledgling Chinese Communist Party (CCP) and reorganized Guomindang and strongly influenced by Lenin's theory of imperialism, channeled the anger of politically engaged Chinese increasingly in the direction of a bitterly anti-imperialist nationalism. As animosity toward the foreign powers, and in many instances toward foreigners personally, reached new levels of intensity, some of these individuals discovered new and far more positive meanings in the Boxer experience.

Positive mythologization of the Boxers was of course not entirely new in China. At the turn of the century Prince Duan and other archconservative figures at the Qing court, identifying with the antiforeign animus of the Boxer movement, consistently portrayed the Boxers as loyal, righteous, and patriotic. Their viewpoint was immortalized for the contemporary English-reading public by the Edinburgh-educated anti-imperialist Gu Hongming: "The Empress-Dowager, Prince Tuan [Duan] and his Boxer lads are not the enemies, but the real true friends of Europeans, and the true European civilization that has been trying to realise itself since the last Great Boxer rising in Paris in '89 [!]." The "real enemies of Europe, of the world and of true civilization," against whom (according to Gu) the "Boxer lads" had risen, were the "modern European usurers, called financiers and capitalists" — "the sneak and the cad who have just entered into partnership to cheat, swindle, bully, murder and rob the world and finally to destroy all civilization in the world."[2]

Gu's quirky cosmopolitanism reached its apogee in a Scottish-style ballad celebrating the exploits of Prince Duan and the Boxers, which he composed in 1900 in honor of the sixty-sixth birthday of the Empress Dowager. The first verse and refrain read as follows:

> To the Lords of convention 'twas Prince Tuan who spoke:
> E're the King's crown go down there are crowns to be broke;
> Then each Boxer lad who loves fighting and fun,
> Let him follow the bonnets of bonnie Prince Tuan.
>> Come fill up my cup, come fill up my can;
>> Come saddle my horses, and call out my men;
>> Unfurl the banner and let fire the gun,
>> For it's up with the bonnets of bonnie Prince Tuan.[3]

Not only among conservatives but among reformers and revolutionaries as well there were, from the outset, those who discerned in the Boxer experience at least some redeeming qualities. The famous translator Yan Fu, although viewing the Boxers (not untypically) as an "uprising of the superstitious mob and of ignorant and worthless armed bandits," also was impressed by the spirit of the Boxer armies: "One cannot say that there were not patriots among them."[4] And an article of March 1901 in *Kaizhilu* (A record of new knowledge), a short-lived journal started by radical Cantonese students in Yokohama in December 1900 (and the recipient of a 200-yen donation from Sun Yat-sen),[5] gave a glowing account of the

240 Boxers' contributions to Chinese independence: "The Boxers knew very well that they were hopelessly outnumbered and outpowered. But actuated by patriotic feeling and driven beyond the limits of forebearance, against overwhelming odds they braved every danger, in the hope that the Chinese people might enjoy a day in which they would resist the foreigner and stand up on their own. . . . Although the Boxers suffered a crushing defeat and are held in contempt by people, do we Chinese realize that they also planted countless sturdy roots and sowed the seeds of national independence on China's behalf?"[6]

Sun Yat-sen himself, addressing (in 1903) the question of the preservation or dismemberment of China, not only praised the Boxers (albeit with qualification) but also made the all-important shift (at least implicitly) from treating the Boxers as "them" or "other" to treating them as "us," as representative of the spirit of the Chinese people. Such a shift was essential if the Boxers were to be tapped for their mythic power:

> Though the Chinese are meek and not martial, they will resist to the death. . . . Even though the Chinese submit to a slave dynasty [the Manchus], they will still defend their villages. . . . Look at the Boxers. Suspecting dismemberment, they rose in violent resistance to the foreigners and fought like madmen. . . . Only they were stupid . . . and did not know the value of firearms and merely depended upon naked blades. . . . If they had cast aside these crude weapons and changed to modern ones, it is doubtful whether the allied expeditionary force would have achieved such quick results. But the Boxers consisted only of Chihli [Zhili] people. If the entire country were aroused, there would be no comparison.[7]

While some patriotic Chinese (like Sun) were able to identify at least to a degree with the Boxers themselves, others found it easier to draw inspiration from the memory of the humiliations suffered during and in the immediate aftermath of the Boxer rising. One of the purposes behind a meeting of merchants and gentry held in Jiaxing, Zhejiang, in 1910 was precisely the keeping alive of such memories.[8] The short-lived *Anhui suhuabao* (Anhui common speech journal), established by Chen Duxiu in February 1904 and edited by him until its demise in August 1905, ran a series of pictures marking the humiliation of the nation (*guochi*) during the Boxer period (see figures 8.1 and 8.2).[9] By focusing on China's victimization at the hands of foreign imperialism, rather than on the Boxer movement per se, the sometimes distasteful particularities of the movement were de-emphasized and the Boxer experience was assimilated to the broader—and more broadly acceptable—theme of China's "century of imperialism."

This was the safe harbor to which positive mythologization of the Boxer episode could always retreat. During the politicized 1920s, however, some Chinese patriots showed themselves willing to chart a more adventurous course, portraying the Boxers, even with their shortcomings, as consummate anti-imperialists.

The Spiritual Legacy of Boxer Resistance

The shift from the New Culture perception of the Boxers as backward, superstitious, and irrational to the post-May Fourth view of them as patriotic anti-imperialists was nowhere more dramatically demonstrated than in an article of September 1924 by Chen Duxiu, at the time secretary-general of the Chinese Communist Party.[10] The occasion was the anniversary of the signing of the Boxer Protocol on September 7, 1901. On the recommendation of the Anti-Imperialist Federation, the newly constituted Guomindang, now closely allied with the CCP and in its militantly anti-imperialist phase, designated September 7 a "National Humiliation Day" and the week following as an "Anti-Imperialism Week."[11] In this context, the earlier scattered praise of the Boxers as patriots swelled into a chorus in the radical press, with the CCP-sponsored *Xiangdao zhoubao* (The guide weekly) pointing the way.

Chen Duxiu's article appeared in a special number of *Xiangdao zhoubao* marking the September 7 anniversary. He began by asserting that the Boxer rising was no less important an event in modern Chinese history than the 1911 revolution. Most people, however, not only failed to appreciate this but also harbored two mistaken views about the Boxers. The first such misconception was the tendency to loathe the Boxers for their "barbarous antiforeignism" (*yeman de paiwai*):

> They only see the antiforeignism of the Boxers; they don't see the reasons for the emergence of Boxer antiforeignism: the bloody oppression suffered by the whole of China from the Opium War on at the hands of foreign armies, diplomatic officials, and missionaries! They only see that the Boxers killed a German minister and a Japanese secretary; they don't see that the British [in 1858] took Guangdong Governor-General Ye Mingchen in custody to India where he died, and also paraded him about in public in a glass enclosure! They only see that the Boxers brought harm to the lives and property of a few foreigners; they don't see that the military and commercial aggression of imperialism has brought harm to the lives and property of countless Chinese! They only see the brutality and ferocity of the killing and arson committed by the Boxers; they don't see the still greater brutality and ferocity shown by

242 the imperialists in their forced sale of opium, the burning of the Summer
Palace, their seizure of Jiaozhou Bay, and all the rest! . . . They criticize as
reactionary and superstitious the Boxers' call to support the Qing and destroy
the foreigners and their reliance upon the authority of the gods; they forget
that today's China is still dominated by an Eastern spiritual culture consisting of patriarchal morality, feudal politics, and the authority of the gods!

It is true that the Boxers were unavoidably reactionary, superstitious, and
barbarous; but the entire world (China, of course, included) still exists in a
state of reaction, superstition, and barbarism. Why censure only the Boxers?
Why, especially, given the importance of the Boxers in the movement of

8.1 AND 8.2 "National Humiliation Pictures." *Figure 8.1:* After the foreign forces took
Tianjin in July 1900, "shameless" Chinese "who cared for nothing except saving their own
skins" carried flags proclaiming that they were "people who submitted" (*shunmin*) to the
foreign occupiers. The foreigners detested such persons and killed them anyway. From
Anhui suhuabao, October 1905, no. 15. *Figure 8.2:* Following their occupation of
Manchuria, the Russians seized Chinese and forced them to repair the railways for them.
They did not pay them regular wages and flogged them when their work was unsatisfac-
tory, "treating them no differently from horses and oxen." From *Anhui suhuabao*,
September 1905, no. 14.

national resistance? Instead of loathing the barbarism of the antiforeign Boxers of those years, we should loathe the civilization of the warlords, bureaucrats, unscrupulous merchants, university professors, and newspapermen who at present curry favor with the foreigners!

In 1918, writing from a perspective that stressed the preeminent importance of culture and was uncritically admiring of the West, Chen Duxiu had castigated the Boxers for their barbarism, conservatism, rampant antiforeignism, and above all their superstition. In 1924, having shifted to a perspective dominated by nationalism, Chen did not deny these Boxer qualities that he had formerly found so repugnant; instead, he now found new ways to legitimize them: Boxer antiforeignism had to be understood in terms of the foreign oppression and exploitation that had given rise to it. Boxer barbarism was nothing in comparison to the savage brutality of foreign imperialism. If all societies were permeated by conservatism and superstition, what was so exceptional about the conservatism and superstition of the Boxers? And, finally, what did "barbaric" and "civilized" mean anyway? In a world in which the main source of evil was foreign imperialism, was uncompromising opposition to imperialism therefore "barbarism"? And was currying favor with imperialism the mark of "civilization"?

244   The second widespread misconception, Chen continued, was the view that, since the Boxer affair was the crime of a minority, the powers should not, on this account, have punished the entire Chinese people with a huge indemnity. In challenging this misconception, Chen was explicit—where Sun Yat-sen had earlier been only implicit—in his identification of the Boxers with the Chinese people as a whole. All Chinese, he insisted, not just the Boxers, had suffered from imperialist oppression. The idea that the Boxers, because they had rebelled against this oppression, should be treated as culpable and singled out for punishment, while the majority of Chinese, because they had been subservient to the foreigners, should be rewarded for their subservience by not being punished reflected, in Chen's judgment, a complete failure of logic. "Thank God," he concluded, "for the barbarous minority of Boxers, who have preserved a measure of honor for the history of the Chinese nation!"[12]

Chen Duxiu reiterated his revised view of the Boxers several months later in *New Youth*. The Boxers, he wrote, were one of four great national movements in China's petty bourgeois phase of development (the other three being the 1898 reform movement, the 1911 revolution, and the May Fourth movement): "The Boxers, in their contempt for the treaties, their repelling of foreign force, foreign goods, and Christianity, and their attacks on Christians and others who had dealings with Westerners—the running dogs of imperialism—were beyond reproach. The Boxers' trust in the power of spirits and their rejection of all science and Western culture were of course their deficiencies, but these are the deficiencies of all backward agrarian societies, so we can't single out the Boxers for special blame." The real deficiencies of the Boxers, Chen went on to argue, were their lack of organization, which caused the movement to disintegrate after suffering defeat, and their cooperation with, and co-optation by, reactionary elements, which lost them the good will of the progressive forces of society.

Although his substantive point of view had changed completely from 1918, Chen Duxiu's object in his 1924 essays on the Boxers was in an operational sense no different from the object of his earlier piece on the von Ketteler Monument. Now, as then, his aim was not to probe the events of the past for greater historical understanding but to use a particular reading of the past (to which he may well have subscribed with complete earnestness) to change the outlook of educated compatriots in the present. The most pernicious effect of the defeat of the Boxer movement—an effect that still in his view shaped the psychological climate in China in the 1920s—was the pervasive belief among Chinese intellectuals that "antiforeignism was barbaric and disgraceful." This psychology had done untold harm to the spirit of resistance to foreign imperialism. And it was Chen Duxiu's intention, using his very considerable powers of persuasion, to change it.[13]

Chen was not alone. Other contributors to the special September 7 anniversary number of *Xiangdao zhoubao* were equally intent upon legit-imizing anti-imperialist attitudes among the Chinese public and sought desperately to chip away at the psychological barriers that stood in the way of such legitimation. Since the most intractable of these barriers, as Chen Duxiu clearly saw, was the deep-rooted assumption, largely derived from the Boxer experience, that there was something somehow unsavory or shameful or uncivilized about being antiforeign—and by extension anti-imperialist—a major item on every contributor's agenda was the reshaping of public memory of the Boxers.

No one made the point more explicitly than Peng Shuzhi, a protégé and close ally of Chen Duxiu in the early years of the Communist movement:

> If we want to buoy up the national revolutionary spirit of China and destroy the slavish mentality of fawning upon foreign countries, . . . we must first reintroduce the significance of this date [September 7, 1901] in the history of China's oppression at the hands of international imperialism, and in partic-ular we must reassess the true value of the Boxer movement in the history of China's national revolutionary movement. We should proclaim on behalf of the Boxers the wiping out of the bad name given them over twenty-three years by the imperialists and their running dogs, and clear up the basic mis-conceptions concerning the Boxer movement harbored in the minds of the general run of Chinese.[14]

While Peng Shuzhi addressed the attitudinal set of the Chinese popu-lation as a whole, Cai Hesen focused his efforts more directly on the Guomindang and its alleged revolutionary character. Cai, a major figure in the early history of the Chinese Communist movement and a close friend of Mao Zedong, began his essay with the observation that the foreign bourgeoisie and imperialists—the enemies of the Boxer movement—were not the only ones to proclaim the movement a "barbarous Chinese antifor-eign action"; Chinese compatriots, even revolutionaries, were given to publicly condemning the Boxers in much the same terms. In contrast to the Boxer movement, which they announced to the imperialists was "an evil perpetrated by a minority of the ignorant, uneducated populace," their own revolution was "civilized behavior, which went even further than the Manchus and warlords in respecting the foreign treaties and safeguarding foreign lives and property."

Cai, like Chen Duxiu and Peng Shuzhi, acknowledged the defects of the Boxer movement. Nevertheless, he saw it as having "sacred historical value,"

246   especially when compared to the Revolution of 1911: "The Revolution of 1911 seems on the surface to represent an advance over the Boxer movement, in that in form and in spirit it appeared to have undergone a process of modern bourgeoisification; yet, in actuality, this revolution was a complete failure, and its significance was not as great as that of the Boxers. The Boxers failed because they were not modern; the 1911 revolution failed because of its ludicrously blind imitation of modern bourgeoisification."

After elaborating on this comparison, Cai explicitly identified the legacy of the Boxers, focusing in particular on what the Boxers had to offer to the reconstituted Guomindang of his own day: "Since the Guomindang's reorganization at its first congress this year, it has been possessed of a first-rate and clear-cut political program; if in their day the Boxers had had a comparable anti-imperialist political program, the Boxers could have led the Chinese national revolution to a successful conclusion. Conversely, if the present-day Guomindang, possessing such a fine political program, were to be supplemented by the authentic anti-imperialist spirit of the Boxers, the Guomindang would be even better fitted to lead the Chinese national revolution to success." The great legacy of the Boxers to the history of the Chinese national revolution, Cai concluded, was "the spirit of antiforeignism"—a legacy he earnestly hoped the Guomindang would inherit.[15]

A key event in the development of anti-imperialist nationalism in the 1920s was the May Thirtieth Incident of 1925. The incident had its origins in a Chinese workers' strike protesting low wages at a Japanese textile mill in Shanghai in February. When a preliminary settlement was rejected by the mill's owner, the workers struck again and on May 15 sent an eight-man delegation to negotiate with the owner's representatives. Violence ensued and a Japanese guard fired on the Chinese workers, killing one of them and wounding the seven others. The Shanghai Municipal Council (mostly British) responded to this clash not by apprehending the Japanese guard but by arresting a number of the Chinese workers for disturbing the peace. Then on May 22, college students and workers held a public memorial service in honor of the worker who had been killed and used the occasion to make speeches attacking the Japanese mill-owner. The arrest of many of the participants in the memorial service led to a 3,000-student protest demonstration in Shanghai on May 30. British police fired into the crowd, killing eleven and wounding many more. Also, some fifty of the demonstrators were arrested. The events of May 30 sparked anti-imperialist protests, strikes, and boycotts throughout China, which did not finally subside until December, when the responsible British police officials were dismissed and the dead and wounded were indemnified by the Municipal Council.[16]

Insofar as the May Thirtieth movement was not only fiercely anti-imperialist but also had the significant involvement, at every stage, of China's
fledgling industrial proletariat and was partly shaped in its propaganda and
strategy by the CCP, it was a quite different event from the May Fourth
movement six years earlier. These differences had a noticeable impact on
post-May Thirtieth Communist discourse on the Boxers. This discourse
tended to be a good deal more ambivalent than before, much depending
on the immediate context within which a writer wrote. Tang Xingqi, for
example, after noting (in the summer of 1925) that foreign observers of the
May Thirtieth movement were predicting a revival of "Boxer bandit turmoil" (*quanfei zhi luan*), went to some pains to distinguish between the
Boxer and May Thirtieth movements. The former, he contended, was "a
pure antiforeign movement," opposed not only to foreign oppression but to
all foreign intercourse, while the latter was specifically *anti-imperialist* in
nature, opposed to all those (domestic or foreign) who exploited and
oppressed China, but not to those nations (like the Soviet Union) that
treated China in a spirit of equality.[17]

The problem of the relationship between antiforeignism, which was
sometimes good, sometimes bad, and anti-imperialism, which was always
good, was a difficult one, the resolution of which seemed to hinge on whom
one was addressing at any given moment. Prior to the May Thirtieth movement, when the emphasis of Communist publicists was on the legitimation
of anti-imperialist sentiment among educated Chinese in general (Chen
Duxiu) or among non-Communist revolutionaries in particular (Cai
Hesen), the tendency was to portray antiforeignism in a favorable light,
even to collapse the distinction between antiforeignism and anti-imperialism altogether. During and after the summer of 1925, however, in the face
of persistent efforts in the foreign press to delegitimize the new form of
nationalism that the May Thirtieth movement represented by identifying it
with Boxer-style antiforeignism,[18] Communist writers, although not aban-
doning their positive sense of historical connection to the Boxers, felt constrained to draw a clear line of demarcation between Boxer antiforeignism
and May Thirtieth anti-imperialism, as well as between the nature and
characteristics of the two movements.

Tang Xingqi represented one effort in this direction. A far more comprehensive analysis was developed by Qu Qiubai in a "special September
7th issue" of *Xiangdao zhoubao* (1925) marking the twenty-fourth anniversary of the signing of the Boxer Protocol. Qu, who was to take over from
Chen Duxiu as general secretary of the CCP in August 1927 and at the time
of writing was himself a leading participant in the May Thirtieth move-

248   ment, began his article with a series of questions clearly identifying the immediate nature of his concern: How could the May Thirtieth massacre have happened? How can we overturn the Boxer Protocol and the entire unequal treaty system? Why does the May Thirtieth movement offer greater hope of success in the struggle to liberate the masses than the Boxer movement of twenty-six years ago?

The last of these questions is the one that is most pertinent for us. Qu, like Chen Duxiu, defended the Boxers against the label of "uncivilized antiforeignism" and lashed out at those educated Chinese who thought that, by viewing the Boxer movement as the creation of a minority of ignorant people, they could distance themselves from the Boxers and in so doing provide a basis for accommodation of the very historical force, imperialism, that had brought the Boxers into being. Since, Qu retaliated, the behavior of the imperialists was a necessary consequence of the development of capitalism in the West, if there had been no Boxer movement, the foreigners would have found some other pretext for attacking China and obtaining the privileges reaped in the Boxer Protocol. It was wrong, therefore, to regard the Boxers as a fringe phenomenon, to marginalize them. The Boxers were a movement of national liberation directed against imperialism, and for their spirit of resistance they deserved to be accorded the highest honor.

These were the strengths of the Boxer movement. But the Boxers also had numerous defects in Qu's judgment. They had a superstitious and reactionary ideology. They rejected all foreign goods and opposed every manifestation of scientific culture. They espoused a rarified national essence. They had a quasi-religious organization that required blind obedience to their leaders. And, above all, they lacked a progressive, organized, and powerful class to serve as the mainstay of the movement, with the result that their ideology reflected a narrow form of nationalism that enabled them to be antiforeign but failed to propel them in the direction of domestic class struggle and opposition to the Manchus and made them vulnerable to manipulation by the ruling classes.

While the May Thirtieth movement represented a continuation of the Boxers' movement of resistance to aggression, in its methods, organization, and tactics it differed from the Boxers in basic ways. The times in which the two movements occurred also were marked by important differences, not the least of which was that in 1900 the general run of "scholar-officials" and "civilized people" abetted the imperialists in vilifying the "Boxer bandits" and crushing the spirit of resistance of the masses, whereas, after the events of the summer of 1925, opposition to imperialism, calls for the abolition of the unequal treaties, and the general spirit of resistance had become increasingly widespread among the population. What was to be feared in the May Thirtieth context, according to Qu, was the restoration of a narrow form of nationalism. Views such as "the nation transcends all" and "workers are not permitted to engage in class struggle" were frequently to be found in the bourgeois press and were even articulated by Guomindang leaders. This was, he continued, "the new Boxer danger," the danger consisting in the possibility that such elements would cause the laboring masses to compromise with the bourgeoisie, lose their class consciousness, and abandon the class struggle, resulting in a complete destruction of the movement for emancipation.[19]

It was characteristic of the complexity of the Boxer symbol in Qu's hands that in one and the same article the Boxers were honored for their bold spirit of resistance to imperialism and reproached for their willingness, born of inadequate class consciousness and a too narrowly conceived nationalism, to compromise with the enemy (the Qing dynasty). This accorded with what appears to have been the general tendency in Communist writings of this period to treat the Boxers favorably when the issue was imperialism and less favorably when the issue (or issues) under discussion had to do with what later Communists would call "feudalism." Qu Qiubai's article dealt with both sets of issues, but since his paramount concern was with the class consciousness of the May Thirtieth movement, he spent more time pointing out the deficiencies of the Boxers than extolling their strengths.

Communist writing in which the principal focus was on the threat to China's patrimony as a nation (imperialism) rather than on its evolution as a society (feudalism) was more likely to distill from the Boxer experience an affirmative message. Thus, Li Dazhao, one of the cofounders of the CCP, in an article of March 1926 marking the first anniversary of the death of Sun Yat-sen—a nationalist, not a communist—referred to the Boxer movement as part of "the Chinese people's national revolutionary history of resistance to imperialism."[20] And even more pointedly, Long Chi, in an article of September 1926 commemorating the twenty-fifth anniversary of the signing of the Boxer Protocol and written in the context of the movement for treaty revision—a movement the appeal of which was first and foremost to nationalistic impulses—wrote:

> The anniversary of September 7 is once again upon us. No matter how much the imperialists vilify the Boxers, no matter how imperfect the Boxers themselves were, their spirit of resistance to imperialism can never be obliterated and will always be worthy of our veneration. . . . As a consequence of the

250   defeat of the Boxers, we suffered the imposition by the imperialists of a still
heavier set of chains—the 1901 treaty. But if we want to cut through these
chains, and all the other chains as well, our only recourse is to revive among
the people the spirit of the Boxers, adding to it the element of organized,
uncompromising struggle—only then will we be able to make imperialism
yield. . . . It is incumbent upon us at last to change September 7 from an
anniversary of national humiliation into an anniversary marking the freedom
and independence of the Chinese nation.[21]

Although Communists took the lead in the 1920s in recasting the Boxers
as anti-imperialist patriots, they were by no means alone. Throughout the
decade a succession of overlapping political movements was spawned—
anti-Christian, educational rights, student, treaty abolition—all of which
angrily attacked foreign imperialism and called for the elimination of its
influence in Chinese affairs. It was hard, in the circumstances, not to identify, at least in spirit, with the Boxers. There was frequent praise of Boxer
anti-imperialism in the pages of *Fei Jidujiao tekan* (Special anti-Christian
issue), a magazine put out by the Anti-Christian Federation in September
1924.[22] Radical participants in the educational rights campaign of 1924–25
transformed the Boxers, in Jessie Lutz's phrasing, from "traditional peasants" into "warriors against imperialism."[23] In the aftermath of the May
Thirtieth Incident, antiforeign students in Hunan openly proclaimed
themselves successors of the Boxers.[24] In a circular telegram of December
1925 the Anti-Christian Federation pointed to "the patriotic movement of
the Boxers" as the lone exception to the long-standing tendency of the
Chinese people to allow themselves "to be hypnotized and asphyxiated by
the Christian apostolate."[25]

One of the most intriguing non-Communist treatments of the Boxers as
patriots was an article published some months after the May Thirtieth
Incident by a Chinese student in America, I. Hu. Hu's piece—which bore
the provocative title "Did the Boxer Uprising Recur in 1925?"—began by
resurrecting the image of the Boxers as cruel and heartless, but then, in a
curious twist, turned this image on the British themselves:[26]

The differences between this [Boxer rising] and the other one a quarter of a
century ago are: that the Boxer [i.e., the British] is no longer depending on
spears and swords and defying foreign armed soldiers, but depending on
rifles and machine guns and defying native unarmed students; that he is not
any more ignorant or superstitious but trained and educated under a nation
that carries the epithet "Gentleman." . . . [The Boxers] were the ones who
gave the order "Shoot to kill"; they were the ones who rejoiced in the killing
and tried to justify the actions. Did the Boxer uprising recur in 1925? Yes, it

did, and with the same if not higher degree of ferocity and cool-bloodedness, but in an entirely different situation and with a totally diverse motive.

As Hu proceeded to identify the key elements of situation and motive that distinguished 1900 and 1925, he quickly shifted in his manipulation of symbols from a sadistic Boxerism of indiscriminate killing to a romanticized one of courageous resistance to unjust foreign oppression. In the process, he detached the Boxer image from the foreign perpetrators of the killings of 1925 and affixed it securely to the Chinese victims. By the end of his article, Boxerism had come to stand for the spirit of patriotic resistance to foreign imperialism, wherever and whenever it occurred:

> The foreign imperialists fooled themselves when they thought that in 1900 the Boxer was defeated once for all; and they will fool themselves again if they take the temporary tranquillity in China to mean the abatement and disappearance of this nationalistic spirit. With or without obstacle, the spirit will go on among the people. . . . Just as the world has witnessed, twenty-five years ago, our first but unsuccessful battle to check imperialism, so will the world witness, twenty-five years from now, the greatest spectacle in human history, our last battle that demolishes imperialism forever.[27]

Although Hu's feelings about the British in 1925 and about their Chinese victims were unambiguous, his feelings about the Boxers—and Boxerism—were plainly marked by the most profound conflict. In this he was not atypical. The Boxer experience was so complex and fed into such diverse and contradictory themes in the history of China in the twentieth century that it was often hard for Chinese who were both patriotic and progressive to get a firm handle on it. In the nationalism-charged decade of the 1920s, many, like Hu and most of the Communist writers dealt with earlier, found ways to dispose of their uncertainties and fashioned a vision of the Boxer experience that was, on balance, affirming. Many others, perhaps no less patriotic but not generally as radical, held fast to a perception of the Boxers that was unambiguously hostile.

The Persistence of the Negative Myth

Characterizations of the Boxers that were of a basically deprecatory nature were put to widely divergent uses in the 1920s. While foreigners repeatedly evoked fears of a resurgent "Boxerism" to delegitimize Chinese nationalism, Chinese used the same symbolic associations to dramatize the ongoing barbarism and brutality of foreign imperialism. Local Chinese authorities were not averse, on occasion, to raising the specter of Boxerism, in the

252   sense of unruly mob behavior ("turmoil"), to justify their suppression of
anti-imperialist political activity. Finally, on both the Chinese and foreign
sides, there were those whose support of, or sympathy with, the force of
nationalism impelled them to draw as clear a line as possible between this
force, which they perceived as modern and progressive, and Boxerism,
which they defined as the very essence of reaction.

Foreign disparagement of Chinese nationalism in the 1920s was apt to
be most conspicuous among foreigners actually resident in China, not only
because of their direct exposure to anti-imperialist and antiforeign activity,
but because the local British press, on which they mostly depended for
news and analysis, tended to take a harshly dismissive view of the "new
nationalism."[28] Even before the May Thirtieth Incident, the *North-China
Daily News* (January 7, 1925) referred to the appearance of "symptoms
closely resembling those that were noted before the Boxer outbreak . . . formation of secret societies, distribution of violently anti-foreign leaflets and
the like,"[29] and the *Birmingham Post* (March 2, 1925) published an article
expressing its China correspondent's fears that the "anti-Christian and antiforeign propaganda" then being carried on among the educated classes by
Bolshevik agents might precipitate a Boxer-type outbreak.[30] As the May
Thirtieth movement got under way, explicit Boxer comparisons in the foreign press became more and more frequent. But, as Wasserstrom points
out, it was not necessary to be explicit. When the *North-China Herald* and
North-China Daily News described the anti-imperialist activities of
1925–1927 as "antiforeign," "xenophobic," "savage," and "irrational," they
used these terms as code words that clearly invoked the phantom of the
Boxers without having to refer to the Boxers directly.[31]

Not only was it unnecessary to name the Boxers in order to draw on their
mythic energy, once the mindset of Chinese antiforeignism became
deeply enough implanted in foreign minds, the mindset itself sometimes
became father to the evidence used to substantiate it. Thus, an American
cameraman, after being expelled from Canton by the local authorities for
his attempts to "frame" pictures showing outrages against foreigners by
Cantonese strikers and pickets after the May Thirtieth Incident, went to
Shanghai, rented one of the local Chinese movie studios, and staged a
whole set of pictures showing the activities of strikers and pickets and the
forcible seizure and confiscation of foreign goods. The pictures, duly identified as depicting antiforeign activities in Canton, were published in a
double-page spread in a London illustrated paper.[32]

Foreign use of the Boxer image — as well as that of Bolshevism — to den-
igrate Chinese nationalism reached a high-water mark in the early months

of 1927 at the time of the Northern Expedition[a] and the accompanying   253
upsurge of Sino-foreign tension. A cartoon in the January 27, 1927, issue of
the *North-China Daily News* combined both images in the form of a
"Russo-Boxer," portrayed as an inciter of mob violence (see figure 8.3).
Even more explicit was a special supplement of the same paper entitled
China in Chaos, published in April for the purpose of persuading the West
that military force, not conciliation, was the only medicine that would cure
the Chinese sickness. The supplement editors, realizing that the two most
powerful rhetorical devices at their disposal were the linking of nationalism
with Boxerism and the stirring up of Western fears of Russia and
Bolshevism in general,[33] proposed in the introduction "to demonstrate that
'Nationalism' is not a spontaneous Chinese patriotic movement but is a
new form of Boxerism with much Russian inspiration behind it."[34]

The use of Boxer symbolism to discredit Chinese nationalism in *China
in Chaos* is sometimes implicit, as when "nationalism" (always in quotation marks to highlight its alleged bogus quality in China) is referred to as
"mob action" and described by such terms as "barbarous," "antiforeign,"
"hideous," and "disgusting savagery." Just as often, it is explicit. "The spirit
of the [nationalist] movement, as manifested in propaganda, diplomacy
and mob action, is," we are told, "destructive and malevolent, never hope-
ful nor constructive. It is intellectual Boxerism, for which it is much harder
to find an apology than for the excesses of illiterate coolies and farmers in
1900." A news item recounting a Chinese attack on a Wesleyan mission
compound is headlined "The New Boxerism in Red Hupeh." Another
item, reporting anti-Christian attacks in Fujian in response to rumors of
suspicious activities at a Spanish Catholic orphanage, bears the headline
"Boxer Charges Revived." An editorial comment on the Communist inspiration behind Chinese "nationalism" states: "Communism and atheism
among the student intelligentsia, and Boxerism among the semi-criminal
riff-raff (euphoniously known in Red literature as the peasants and workers)
are the obvious ends of all agitation in China as in other fields of Soviet
work." As a final example, a correspondent in Changde (Hunan), after noting that numerous placards of an antiforeign, anti-Christian, and in some
cases pro-Communist tenor had been displayed of late in the streets, commented: "Thus are the people being inflamed for a second Boxer uprising
and the authorities do nothing to check all this orgy of hatred and wilful
misrepresentation."[35]

---

[a] A military campaign, under the command of Chiang Kai-shek (Jiang Jieshi), the goal
of which was the political reunification of China.

254   The tactic of devaluing the behavior of political adversaries by identifying it with Boxerism was most widely prevalent among foreigners.[36] But it was occasionally encountered on the Chinese side as well, especially in the aftermath of the May Thirtieth Incident. We have already seen one instance of this in the article by I. Hu, in which the author charged the British with

8.3   Sapajou, "MAKING THINGS MOVE. The Boxer with the match: 'Ah ha! Something's going to happen now!' " From *North-China Daily News*, January 27, 1927.

having staged a rerun in 1925 of the Boxer rising of a quarter century before.   255
On June 1, 1925, the Shanghai Executive Branch of the Guomindang,
clearly responding to foreign criticisms of Chinese behavior, issued a manifesto stating that the conduct of the British in May had been "worse than
that of the Boxers."[37]

In a similar vein, in the June 14, 1925, issue of *Guowen zhoubao* (National
news weekly), an editorial writer, after noting that ever since the uprising of
the Boxers in 1900, "Boxer" (Yihetuan) had been viewed as "a general term
for irrational, uncivilized, cruel behavior" and that in recent years foreigners had taken to applying this label to all organized movements of the
Chinese people, observed: "On the occasion of the May Thirtieth Incident,
Western police from the International Settlement killed students indiscriminately for several days running and arrested many thousands of
Chinese on their own authority. The only name I can think of for them is
foreign Boxers [*yang Yihetuan*]."[38] In the next issue of *Guowen zhoubao*, the
same point was made in cartoon form: A huge foreign soldier was shown
bayonetting a tiny, unarmed Chinese, identified by the soldier as a "Boxer."
The caption underneath read "Who is the Boxer?" (see figure 8.4).

8.4   "Who is the Boxer?" From *Guowen zhoubao*, June 21, 1925.

256   While the overriding tendency in the 1920s was to apply Boxer symbolism in the context of Sino-Western interaction, since the Boxers stood not
just for antiforeignism but also for turmoil, instability, and the general
threat of "mob rule," it was not unheard-of for Chinese authorities to use
the Boxer symbol against their fellow citizens. In Wuhu in 1922, the governor and chief of police criticized anti-Christian student activists for stirring
up disorder and issued dire warnings of a second Boxer rebellion if peace
were not restored. The same grim specter was invoked by the Defense
Commissioner of Changsha in December 1924 to justify the banning of a
Christmas Day rally that was to have climaxed the educational rights campaign in Hunan.[39] Intramural use of the Boxer symbol appears, however, to
have been a relatively minor theme in the 1920s, and even where it
occurred, if the few instances I have encountered are an accurate indication, the Sino-foreign dimension (taking the form in the above two examples of student anti-imperialist activism) was never completely absent.

In all the instances recounted in this section, either of two forms of
political behavior—one involving the mobilization of native antiforeign,
anti-Christian, nationalist, or anti-imperialist sentiment, the other, foreign
suppression of the actions resulting from such mobilization—was deval-
ued by *identifying* it with Boxerism. In other instances the very opposite
occurred, as Chinese nationalists and their foreign supporters sought to
legitimize the force of nationalism by *distancing* it from the Boxers. In both
categories of cases, it is well to emphasize, it was the negative rather than
the positive Boxer symbol that was appealed to.

After explaining why it was necessary to oppose Christianity, the
author of a pamphlet circulated in Shaanxi in August 1925 wrote: "But pay
close heed! I am not counseling you to rise up in bands like the Boxers or
to massacre the missionaries and set fire to the churches. Those are barbarous actions, which are no longer in vogue. Let us be content to rip off
the mask that covers their true countenance."[40] In much the same way,
student activists from Canton reported in 1926 in *Wusa jinian* (Commemorating May Thirtieth) that by strict adherence in their propagandistic activities to the Guomindang program to overthrow imperialism
and warlordism and unite with the world's oppressed, their movement
had avoided the fundamental mistake of becoming xenophobic and turning into a Boxer-like phenomenon.[41] Even the "Christian general" Feng
Yuxiang, in a speech of June 26, 1925, to his officers, advocating a Chinese
military response to the May Thirtieth killings, is said to have remarked:
"Can we sit by peacefully in the face of these things? I think not. It is not
a matter of repeating the mistakes of the Boxers. But it cannot be demand-

ed of us that we permit them to make mincemeat of us without saying or doing a thing."[42]

Moderate Chinese intellectuals of the 1920s also went to some length to distinguish the nationalism of their own day, which they viewed as a wholesome development, from Boxerism. Hu Shi, in a 1925 speech at Yanjing University aimed at getting mission schools to secularize and "forego [sic] their purpose of religious propaganda," asked his audience to understand that, although "the Boxers were easily put down because theirs was a superstitious and undirected movement . . . it would be impossible for any military force to check the present nationalistic movement because it is deeply rooted in the minds of the members of a great nation." Hu further noted that, while he was not one of those "extreme" types "who praise the Boxer movement as one of the heroic tragedies in the history of Chinese national development" or "who advocate the use of the term 'anti-foreign' as a watchword for mass propaganda among the people," the actual program of Chinese nationalists—abolition of existing customs regulations, abolition of extraterritoriality, Chinese control of all education, prohibition of religious propaganda by foreigners, and the canceling of all special privileges granted to foreigners in China—was "not so radical as is its watchword."[43]

An equally forceful statement—like Hu Shi's, staunchly patriotic, moderate in its own political stance, yet not wholly unreceptive to the more radical positions of others—was made by Cai Yuanpei. Cai, president of China's leading institution of higher learning, Beijing University, was traveling in Europe in 1925 and issued a "manifesto to all nations" in July to counter European misconceptions about the May Thirtieth movement. The greatest of these misconceptions, according to him, was the view that May Thirtieth was a simple replay of the Boxer rising of 1900. Cai challenged this view by pointing out certain basic differences between the two events: First, the initiators of the Boxer movement were uneducated northern Chinese who did not understand the difference between Catholics and non-Catholics, were ignorant about firearms, believing they could use magic to protect themselves against such weapons, and were spurred on by unenlightened people at court who thought that if all the foreigners in China could be killed, China's problems with foreign countries would be over. In sharp contrast to this global ignorance, the participants in the May Thirtieth movement were people who understood the world situation and had a clear grasp of the actual strength of the various nations. Second, unlike the Boxers, who wanted to kill off all foreigners, those taking part in the current unrest in China confined themselves to tactics of noncooperation. Third, whereas the Boxers opposed all foreign countries, the present

258   Chinese demonstrators opposed only Great Britain and Japan. A fourth difference, Cai concluded, was that the Boxer movement was restricted geo-
graphically to Beijing and such provinces as Zhili and Shanxi, while the
political unrest generated by the May Thirtieth Incident was China-wide
in scope.[44]

Lu Xun, impressed by the fact that some Englishmen had acknowledged that England was at fault in the May Thirtieth Incident (thereby
evincing a capacity for moral self-criticism he judged "sadly lacking"
among his own countrymen), observed with characteristic acerbity that
"despite everything, I still think that the foreign devils are more civilized
than the Chinese."[45] Lu's specific judgment here is of less interest than his
raising of the issue in the first place. This issue—the question of who was
the more civilized and, by extension, what constituted civilized behavior—
was of paramount importance for Chinese intellectuals in the twentieth
century; it was precisely because of its importance that the Boxer symbol
carried such a high charge.

There was, in fact, throughout the 1920s, a considerable segment of foreign opinion that not only was highly critical of foreign behavior in China
but also took an affirmative stance toward the development of nationalism. Like Hu Shi and Cai Yuanpei, the articulators of this opinion, when
they alluded to the Boxer symbol, generally did so in order to establish difference, not identity,[46] to legitimize Chinese nationalism rather than to
discredit it.

Typical of this "liberal" perspective on events in China within the
Western press was *The Nation*, whose editors consistently refused to yield
to the sort of simplistic, anti-Chinese analysis found in such outlets as the
North-China Daily News and *North-China Herald*.[47] In an article that
appeared in June 1925, for example, Stanley High, a member of the
Methodist Board of Foreign Missions, drew a sharp distinction between
the Boxer uprising of 1900 and the anti-Christian movement of his own
day, which he felt (clearly echoing Hu Shi)[48] constituted "a more serious
challenge to the program of the Christian Church in China." "The massacres of 1900 were brought about at the instigation of the governing
Manchus and directed against Christians in a final, futile effort to halt
China's advance from her old aloofness and isolation toward a place in the
modern world. . . . The present anti-Christian movement is not sponsored
by the advocates of reaction. It is led, in fact, by those who claim to be the
most aggressive and the most modern proponents of progress. . . . Instead
of mob violence the method of the present attack on Christianity is that of
propaganda." High, acknowledging the sincerity and depth of Chinese

nationalistic sentiment, judged it "wholly superficial" to conclude that the anti-Christian movement of the 1920s was "fundamentally a result of Bolshevik propaganda."[49]

Again, during the climactic phase of the Northern Expedition in the early months of 1927, *The Nation* not only reacted sympathetically to Chinese nationalism, it also took it seriously. "The 'old China hands' have refused to believe that the new Nationalism in China was more than a passing effervescence," wrote the author (unidentified) of a January article entitled "China's War of Independence," "and they and the Powers which trusted their judgment are reaping the harvest of their blindness."[50] Another piece, entitled "China—Vaccinated," identified the West as the source both of China's troubles and of the means by which it was seeking to overcome them: "Chinese Nationalism today is not the blind anti-alienism of Boxer days. . . . Those who charge the missionaries with responsibility for it have a measure of justice on their side; those who blame the penetration of foreign business are equally right; those who say the tens of thousands of returned students have brought back the revolutionary spark are also justified. Western influence in China has acted like a vaccination; it has first made the patient ill, while at the same time inoculating him with the germs of resistance to the disease."[51]

Even in the emotion-charged days and weeks following the Nanjing incident of March 24, 1927, in which soldiers of the National Revolutionary Army terrorized the foreign population of Nanjing and took the lives of seven foreigners, *The Nation* resisted the widespread foreign tendency to interpret what had happened as a recurrence of Boxerism.[52] Cautioning against foreign military intervention (which would be "a plain warning to China that for her there is a White Peril"),[53] it characterized the recent antiforeign and anti-Christian outbreaks as "mere excrescences," which "would disappear quickly if the foreigners did not defend with such an insane show of force privileges which they must know they will soon lose."[54]

Moderate Chinese, like Hu Shi and Cai Yuanpei, and liberal foreigners, like the editors of *The Nation*, by frontally challenging the pervasive foreign tendency in the 1920s to draw on negative Boxer symbols to stigmatize Chinese nationalism, seemed at first glance to demythologize the Boxer movement, to restore it to its historical self. The fact is, in their efforts to validate nationalism by distancing it from any and all association with the Boxers, they, too, no less than nationalism's detractors, were engaged, however inadvertently, in a process of mythmaking. Like the people whose views they contested, their principal interest was not in gaining deeper

260 insight into the Boxer experience (a task for historians) but in using this experience as a repository of negative symbolic information for the clarification of present political stands. In countering one use of the Boxer image (the discrediting of Chinese nationalism), they therefore ended only in the creation of another (its legitimation).

In fact, the multiple, even conflicting, uses to which the Boxer symbol was put in the 1920s stand as perhaps the most intriguing aspect of the mythologization process as it was manifested during these years. Just as, in American frontier history, the figure of Daniel Boone (1734–1820) could be seen by some as the archetypal hero in the winning of the West, and by others (in particular, representatives of the more developed white society of Boone's day) as one who, in forsaking the industry of agriculture for the idleness of hunting, had "reverted to the savage stage" and become a "white Indian,"[55] or, in World War II, Joan of Arc could be portrayed by French resistance fighters as a symbol of national independence, a "selfless fighter against foreign occupiers," and by the puppets of those self-same occupiers, the Vichy authorities, as a heroine in the German struggle against the English (who had, indeed, been the historical Joan's archenemies),[56] the Boxers, too, spoke in different voices to different people.

A basic reason why some phases of the past possess this multivocal quality is that they are inherently complex, often embodying ambiguous, implicitly contradictory strains. For the multiple voices to find optimal expression, however, an additional condition must be met: the contradictions in question must tap into major contested issues in a people's history. In nineteenth- and twentieth-century China, the influence of the West — and how it was to be viewed — constituted just such an issue, and the Boxers, with their promiscuous, indiscriminate antiforeignism, excited this issue in the most flagrant way. How people mythologized the Boxers in specific situations, however, depended very much on what was going on in China at the time. In the 1920s, when the overriding concern was the continued humiliation of the imperialist presence, Boxer mythologization tended to center, in one way or another, on the theme of anti-imperialist nationalism. During the Cultural Revolution and again in the post-Mao 1980s, on the other hand, as the issues changed, the meaning of the Boxer experience and the ways in which the Boxers were remembered also underwent significant changes.

CHAPTER 9

The Cultural Revolution and the Boxers

The mythologization of the Boxers during the Cultural Revolution (1966–1976), as compared to that of the early decades of the twentieth century, was distinctive in a number of respects. First, it was different in content, answering to the specific thematic needs of the period. Second, as the requirements of historical understanding yielded to those of political correctness, the Boxers as myth completely displaced the historical Boxers, to the point where even historians, when they wrote on the Boxers, wrote as mythologizers. Third, Cultural Revolution mythologization of the Boxers was orchestrated to an unprecedented degree in the officially controlled press as part of the state's overall effort to establish "ideological hegemony" over society.[1] No longer was it possible, as in the 1920s, for private individuals to mythologize the Boxers in divergent ways. A single standard was imposed on all.

The last point requires further comment. During the first half of the twentieth century, Chinese mythologization of the Boxers had taken place within a generally pluralistic environment. In such an environment the standard for judging "good" mythmaking was how persuasive it was, how effectively it made its point in comparison with competing evocations of the Boxer experience. In an authoritarian setting, such as existed in China in the 1960s and 1970s, it was a quite different matter. The standard for judging good mythologization now was how correct it was politically, how closely it adhered to the government's line. The fact that the state, in these circumstances, became the sole arbiter of how the Boxer movement was to be interpreted and that this interpretation became compulsory fare for everyone in society did not, however, mean that the substantive content of Boxer mythologization during the Cultural Revolution was uniformly objectionable to all Chinese. On the contrary, although some unquestionably did find it repugnant, many others, especially perhaps among the young, found it both credible and highly compelling.

262   Although the treatment of the Boxers in heavily mythic terms spanned the entire decade of the Cultural Revolution, it reached unusual levels of intensity at two junctures: during the spring of 1967, when the Red Guards were still running strong and the attack on head of state Liu Shaoqi was coming increasingly into the open, and in 1974–1976, in connection partly with the anti-Confucian movement and, on a far larger scale, with the ongoing campaign against the Soviet Union.[2] In all these instances the Boxers—and their female counterparts, the Red Lanterns—were used both as positive models to be emulated and as symbolic ammunition in attacks against domestic and foreign enemies.

The Attack on Liu Shaoqi

In March 1967 the radical intellectual Qi Benyu published a major article in the Chinese theoretical journal *Red Flag* (*Hongqi*) that signaled the beginning of a new stage in the Cultural Revolution assault on Liu Shaoqi, generally known in the esoteric coding of the time as "China's Khrushchev" or "the top party person in authority taking the capitalist road." The article, which Mao himself went over and embellished, was entitled "Patriotism or National Betrayal?—On the Reactionary Film *Inside Story of the Qing Court.*"[3] Although framed as an authoritative critique of the historical film *Qinggong mishi* (The inside story of the Qing court) and prescribing what the correct attitude ought to be toward three of the film's themes (imperialist aggression, the Boxer movement, and the reform movement of 1898), the underlying purpose of the article was to condemn Liu Shaoqi and the "revisionist" line with which he was identified.

As was so often the case in Cultural Revolution polemics, there were also subtexts embedded in this main text, not the least of them being the desire of Jiang Qing—wife of Mao and a major force within the cultural realm during the Cultural Revolution years, as well as the political patron of Qi Benyu (described by one writer as "a page in the presence of his queen")[4]— to avenge herself for humiliations experienced in the early 1950s at the hands of enemies in the cultural establishment.[5] It is in this context that an otherwise unexceptionable film took on magnified political importance.

Although *The Inside Story of the Qing Court*, which was based on the popular play *Qinggong yuan* (The malice of empire),[6] dealt mainly with fin de siècle court politics and had less than five minutes of footage directly relating to the Boxers,[7] Qi Benyu (speaking for Mao and Jiang Qing) was less concerned with the film's actual contents than with the negative political messages that could be distilled from it. Since Liu Shaoqi was alleged to have praised *The Inside Story of the Qing Court* as "patriotic" and to have repeatedly ignored Mao's and Jiang Qing's efforts to have it banned,[8] once the film's character as a negative political text had been authoritatively explicated, it could be used as prima facie evidence in the case being built up against Liu.

Among the political messages encoded in *The Inside Story of the Qing Court*, according to Qi, the most important for our purposes was its "deep-rooted class hatred" for the Boxer movement. The film and its praisers, turning everything upside down, portrayed the imperialist aggressors "as envoys of civilization while slandering as 'barbarous rioters' the heroic and indomitable Yi Ho Tuan [Yihetuan] who resolutely resisted imperialist aggression." In addition to seeking to discredit the patriotic role taken by the Boxers in the struggle against imperialism, the film also distorted their relationship to the feudal ruling class, slanderously making them out to be "partisans" of the Empress Dowager Cixi.[9]

Within weeks of the appearance of Qi Benyu's critique, Red Guard groups began to print cartoons venomously attacking Liu Shaoqi for, among other things, his alleged contempt for the Boxers.[10] There was also a dramatic upsurge of articles on the Boxers in the press. These materials all build on Qi's piece. They repeat the same themes, highlight the same Boxer slogans, and reproduce many of the same quotations from Mao and Lenin and such foreign participants in the Boxer-era fighting as von Waldersee and Seymour. Most important, at no point do any of the materials I have seen diverge in the slightest from the ideological stance embodied in Qi's article. The articles do, on the other hand, explore new themes not explicitly dealt with by Qi Benyu (such as the analogy between the Boxers and the Red Guards) and establish new emphases (such as the role of the Red Lanterns). Moreover, they introduce a substantial amount of material pertaining to the Boxers that is not found in the original critique.

One of the most intriguing aspects of these articles is the attention lavished on the Red Lanterns. The Red Lanterns come in for only passing mention in serious historical accounts of the Boxer uprising, and it seems clear that their actual historical role was of limited importance.[11] Even during the Cultural Revolution, in general discussions of the Boxer movement, the Red Lanterns tended to be treated as a distinctly minor theme. A popular booklength account of 1972 made two brief references to them.[12] A history (1973) of Boxer involvement in Tianjin devoted only three of seventy-five pages to the Red Lanterns, in spite of the fact that Tianjin in the summer of 1900 was by general consensus the high-water mark of Red

264   Lantern activity.[13] Even in Qi Benyu's article there were only three brief paragraphs dealing specifically with the Red Lanterns.

How, then, are we to explain the sudden burst of Chinese media interest in the Red Lanterns in the spring of 1967? The most obvious answer is that the Red Lanterns shared a number of characteristics with the Red Guards, who at this time were a dominant force in Chinese political life. Both organizations had three-syllable names—Hongdengzhao and Hongweibing—starting with the word *red* (*hong*),[a] in addition to which the Red Lanterns, we are told again and again, were clad from head to foot in red, armed with red-tasseled spears, and carried red scarves and red lanterns in their hands.[14] Also, like the Red Guards, the Red Lanterns were young, consisting mostly of teenagers, and they were rebellious, with a decided preference (as mythologized) for behaving outrageously toward civilized idols. It was small wonder, given this array of common attributes, that one group of Red Guards chose to call itself the "Red Lantern Fighting Force" (Hongdengzhao zhandoudui).[15]

Another possible reason for the press's emphasis upon the Red Lanterns at this juncture was the symbolic association with Jiang Qing's model revolutionary opera *Hongdeng ji* (The red lantern). This opera, first staged in 1964, had by late 1966 become one of only a handful of operas still being performed in China.[16] The story is set in the Northwest in the 1940s and tells of the heroic resistance to Japanese aggression of a Communist guerrilla fighter, Li Yuhe, his mother, and his daughter, Li Tiemei. Li, who is a railway switchman, shortly before he is killed by the Japanese, gives his red signal lantern to his daughter for safekeeping. The lantern, described by the daughter as a "priceless treasure . . . our heirloom" and by the father as an object to "be passed from hand to hand,"[17] clearly symbolizes the transfer of revolutionary commitment from one generation to the next. The concluding lines of the narrative version of the opera read: "Advancing on the road of people's war under Chairman Mao's guidance, a powerful revolutionary armed unit was taking up a new fight. Shoulder to shoulder with the people, and with the red lantern to light the way forward, this revolutionary force was to win one major victory after another and wipe out the aggressors."[18]

The red lantern symbolism is amplified in a euphoric notice of the opera that appeared in *People's Daily* in May 1967: "*Hongdeng ji* has demonstrated the lofty aspirations and sentiments of the proletarian revo-

---

[a] A color that, in addition to symbolizing good fortune for Chinese in general, also had strongly favorable connotations for the Communists.

lutionaries of our era. Having seen the 'red lantern' and learned from the   265
'red lantern,' we have hung the red lantern of Mao Zedong's thought in our
hearts. This red lantern points the way for us to storm and breach the
citadel of the old world, to rebel vigorously against imperialism, revisionism, and the handful of top powerholders in the party taking the capitalist
road, and to carry the revolution through to the finish!"[19]

Jiang Qing's active promotion of opera reform, with her husband's backing, had been a prime means by which she had built up her own power
base and simultaneously undermined that of old foes in the cultural arena
whose treatment of her in Shanghai in the 1930s, when she was trying to
establish herself in the theater, had aroused deep feelings of bitterness and
rancor.[20] During the 1960s, and especially after the onset of the Cultural
Revolution, as Jiang's personal authority in the cultural realm soared, she
was able increasingly to push her own agenda. The Qi Benyu article,
which first disclosed the conflict she had had with culture officials in 1950

9.1   Red Guard Cartoon Attacking Liu Shaoqi. In front of a flag emblazoned with the
words "rise in rebellion," a heroic, larger-than-life Boxer stands over the head of a foreigner he has apparently just decapitated. Liu Shaoqi points contemptuously at the Boxer
and mutters to himself: "Disorderly rabble, barbaric, barbaric!" From *Dadao Liu Shaoqi
yilianhuan manhua ce.*

9.2   Li Tiemei. The heroine of Jiang Qing's revolutionary opera *Hongdeng ji* holds high the red lantern received from her father and symbolizing the generational transfer of revolutionary commitment. From *Renmin ribao*, May 13, 1967.

over *The Inside Story of the Qing Court*, was one step in this direction. Another may have been the spate of articles on the Red Lanterns that began to appear in the press in mid-April, shortly after the publication of Qi's piece. Whether or not Jiang Qing had anything directly to do with the articles, their implied evocation of *Hongdeng ji*, a major expression of her new revolutionary culture, and their exploitation of the symbolism of heroic young women, dressed in red, lighting the revolutionary path with their red lanterns, was the perfect embodiment of her particular brand of feminism.

Whatever feminist subthemes might be embodied in the articles, it was clear that their overriding objective was to defend the Cultural Revolution and its most concrete incarnation the Red Guards against the counterattacks of the number one enemy Liu Shaoqi. After briefly introducing the Red Lanterns, an editorial of April 14 in *Wenhuibao* went on to make the familiar point that one's attitude toward the Boxers and the Red Lanterns was a sure indication of whether one was a real revolutionary or a fake one. There was nothing accidental, therefore, about the fact that "China's Khrushchev" (Liu) detested the Boxer movement and the revolutionary young generals of the turn of the century. For the Red Lantern revolutionary young generals had been resolute in their anti-imperialism, while "China's Khrushchev" was terrified of imperialism, worshiped imperialism, and was on good terms with imperialism (*kongdi, chongdi, qindi*); the Red Lantern revolutionary young generals had been uncompromising in their spirit of rebellion, while "China's Khrushchev" preached bourgeois reform, prettified bourgeois democracy, and vainly sought a capitalist restoration in China. Finally, the editorial pointed out that, given his bitter hatred of the revolutionary movements of the past, Liu's hatred of the revolutionary movement of the present day and his desire to suppress its most concrete embodiment, the Red Guards, were hardly surprising. The Red Guards, however, not to be intimidated, were determined to carry on and develop the revolutionary spirit of the Red Lanterns and, under the leadership of Chairman Mao and his thought, repulse the enemy's every attack.[21]

The same issue of *Wenhuibao* devoted an entire page to laudatory Red Guard statements about the Red Lanterns. A number of these statements drew explicit parallels between the Red Lanterns and Red Guards, focusing on the behavior of the two groups, what they stood for, and the slanderous charges both were subjected to by hostile contemporaries. Two Red Guards from the Fudan University History Department, for example, after invoking the same theme of revolutionary succession found in the opera *Hongdeng ji* ("The soldiers of the Red Guard will always carry on and develop the spirit of revolutionary rebellion of the daughters of the 'Red

268 Lantern'!"), observe that the Red Lanterns and Red Guards are "blood brothers and sisters," that both are "heroes who dare to rebel," but that where the Red Lanterns fought the imperialists with swords and spears, "we Red Guards, with our pens as weapons, make rebellion against the powerholders in the party taking the capitalist road." The Red Lanterns and Red Guards, the authors continue, both are "revolutionary new things," with such enormous vitality that no force, however great, can stifle their growth and maturation. Yet just as a handful of counterrevolutionary revisionists and capitalist-roaders openly praise as "patriotic" a film that slanders the Boxers and the Red Lanterns as "disorderly rabble" (wuhe zhi zhong) "who appear as if under a magic spell," imperialists and revisionists slander the Red Guards as "fanatical youth" (kuangre shaonian) intent upon "destroying world civilization."[22]

Some of the writings of this period supplied concrete information on the Red Lanterns.[23] Others drew specific parallels between the Red Guards and either the Red Lanterns or the Boxers. Still others, such as the colored posters with which Tianjin was blanketed in the early years of the Cultural Revolution, adopted a hortatory tone, urging the Red Guards to view the Boxers as their spiritual ancestors.[24] Regardless of their precise focus, however, the basic intent of all these materials was the same: to put the symbolic resources of the past to work in support of current preoccupations.[25] Sometimes this intent was explicitly stated. An article in *People's Daily* in late April 1967, for example, noting the parallel between the place-name changes wrought in the capital by the Boxers and by the Red Guards (in August 1966), observed: "From 'Cut Off the Foreigners Street' and 'Stop the Foreigners Bridge' to 'Anti-Imperialism Road' and 'Anti-revisionism Road'—the birth of these street signs possessing distinctively revolutionary character was far more than a simple change of names; it was a symbol of the victory of the revolutionary mass movements of the Boxers and the Red Guards."[26]

Sometimes, on the other hand, the symbolic connection between the actual Boxer experience and the mythologization of this experience during the Cultural Revolution was not made explicit and was very likely unconscious or even completely inadvertent. I have in mind, in particular, the soaring, apocalyptic quality of Cultural Revolution prose, with its Manichaean worldview, its emphasis on "new things" or "newly emerging things" (xinsheng shiwu), its harping on the replacement of the decrepit old world by a pristine new one, and so on. The concluding lines of a *Guangming ribao* article of late April 1967 offer a typical example: "Let us continue to hold high the banner of revolutionary rebellion, to carry the Great Proletarian Cultural Revolution through to the end, to carry world

revolution through to the end, to thoroughly destroy the old world and 269
erect a new world of bright red Mao Zedong Thought! Long live the revolutionary rebel spirit of the 'Red Lanterns'! Long live the Red Guards!
Long live invincible Mao Zedong Thought!"[27] Such rhetoric was pervasive during the Cultural Revolution, especially in the early, Red Guard

9.3 Cultural Revolution Depiction of Red Lantern. The only thing this Red
Lantern has in common with contemporary representations is the quality of youth.
The clothing and hairstyle have been modernized and the feet unbound. Most
important, the Cultural Revolution Red Lantern has exchanged the reserve and
elegance of her forebears for the persona of a fiercely rebellious warrior, who, sword
in hand, takes her place side by side with male Boxers in the fight against the foreigner. From *Hongdengzhao* (Shanghai, 1967).

270   phase; by no means was it reserved for references to the Boxers.[28] But it resonated with the millenarian strain found in many of the handbills and notices that circulated in North China in 1900 during the climactic phase of the Boxer movement,[29] suggesting a deep, inner connection between the Boxers and the Red Guards that, unlike such obvious and oft-noted shared attributes as youth, redness, and rebelliousness, tended to go entirely unacknowledged.

The Attack on Confucianism

After their brief flurry of notoriety in the spring of 1967, the Red Lanterns receded from the front lines of Cultural Revolution pen warfare.[30] When they reemerged in the mid-1970s, the political context had changed dramatically. The Red Guards had long since been either banished to the countryside or killed in fighting with government troops. Liu Shaoqi had been toppled from power and died in prison. Such were the vagaries of the Cultural Revolution that even Qi Benyu, less than a year after the publication of his *Red Flag* article attacking Liu, had himself come under attack as a "counterrevolutionary double-dealer" who, among his assorted "crimes," had collected "black information" on none other than his erstwhile political patron Jiang Qing.[31]

In the mid-1970s the overriding political issue, as far as the Red Lanterns were concerned, was the anti-Confucian campaign, which had been initiated in the late summer of 1973. Although on one level this campaign, like others of the 1973–1976 period, was a vehicle through which radical ideologues in Shanghai under Jiang Qing's patronage and veteran party bureaucratic leaders in Beijing waged their continuing struggle for personal and ideological power, on another level it was exactly what it claimed to be: a renewed effort to root out such old habits and tendencies associated with Confucianism as bureaucratism, abhorrence of physical labor, and the subordination of women.[32] It was in connection with the last issue, in particular, that the Red Lanterns experienced a brief revival.

References to the Red Lanterns as a symbol of rebellion against the "feudal Confucian ethical code" had also abounded in 1967.[33] But the main emphasis at that time had been on the parallel between the Red Lanterns and the Red Guards. When the Red Lantern symbol was resurrected in 1974–1976 its main focus was not on youth and redness, as in the earlier period, but on the issue of female emancipation in a patriarchal society. For hundreds of years, we are told, the feudal reactionary ruling class of China, in order to safeguard its position, had based itself on the falsehood perpetrated by Confucius that "only girls and mean people are hard to raise." Following the precepts of Confucian morality, China's rulers had insisted that women neither look nor listen nor speak nor move unless it was in accordance with the proper rules of etiquette. Confucian scholars attempted to subjugate women with the spiritual shackles of "the three obediences and the four virtues" (*sancong side*);[b] the more malicious of them even incorporated this ideology of gender oppression into didactic tracts with such titles as *The Classic for Girls* (*Nü'er jing*), *The Classic for the Moral Improvement of Girls* (*Gailiang nü'er jing*), and *Valuable Advice for the Boudoir* (*Xiuge jinzhen*). The heroines of the Red Lantern, no longer willing to tolerate this terrible situation, fearlessly attacked "the traitorous teachings of Confucius and Mencius," broke through the constraints of the Confucian ethical code, and "inscribed a glorious page in the history of the revolutionary struggle of the women of our nation."[34]

During the anti-Confucian campaign, Lin Hei'er, the most famous of the Red Lanterns and their leader in the Tianjin area, was fashioned into a potent legend, symbolizing both patriotism and women's emancipation.[35] According to the legend, Lin was the daughter-in-law of a boatman who transported goods along the Southern Grand Canal. During the spring of 1900, her father-in-law got into a scrape with a foreigner, and the local authorities, fearful of giving offense, arrested him and threw him into jail. Lin Hei'er, when she heard this, exploded with anger and henceforth bore a deep hatred for the foreigners and their Chinese minions. The Boxers by this point had spilled over from Shandong into Zhili, and Lin, after meeting with the Boxer leader Zhang Decheng, was made head of the Red Lanterns of Tianjin. In June, as fighting broke out between the Boxers and foreigners in the Tianjin area, Lin, now renamed Huanglian shengmu (Holy Mother of the Yellow Lotus), paid a call on Zhili Governor-General Yulu, who even after the court's declaration of war against the foreigners was continuing to harass the Boxers. Lin berated Yulu in harsh language, warned him against making further trouble for the Boxers and Red Lanterns, and insisted on his support in the future. As she talked, Yulu kept nodding his head, like a hammer pounding away at garlic. He acceded to every one of her demands. In high spirits, with Lin Hei'er at their head, the Boxers and Red Lanterns returned. The Holy Mother of the Yellow Lotus

[b] The three obediences: to one's father before marriage, one's husband after marriage, and one's son after one's husband's death; the four virtues: morality, proper speech, modesty, diligence.

272   had stormed the governor-general's yamen, lectured Yulu, and gained a dazzling victory.

Under Lin Hei'er's leadership, the Red Lanterns of Tianjin developed apace. Each day at dusk they assembled to practice their swordsmanship, and every few days they paraded around the city, brandishing their swords as they marched through the streets. Once, when the Red Lanterns were patrolling in the vicinity of the Southern Grand Canal, they encountered a boat coming from Tianjin. When they stopped it to interrogate and search the passengers, they were handed a calling card on which was inscribed the name of none other than Li Zhongpeng (Jingshu), the son of the Chinese traitor Li Hongzhang. The Red Lanterns flung the card into the canal and reprimanded Li: "Do you think that just because you are the son of Grand Secretary Li you can disobey Boxer regulations?" Li's son was petrified and begged for mercy.

Apart from maintaining public order and apprehending spies, the legend continues, the Red Lanterns also performed such tasks as gathering military intelligence, transmitting news, giving first aid to the wounded, hauling provisions, and boiling water and preparing meals. When there were major battles, they even buckled on their armor and got into the thick of the fighting. They took part in the burning of a number of Christian churches in the Tianjin area in mid-June. They also participated in the famous battle at the Tianjin railway station (Laolongtou) on June 18. The station had been occupied by Russian troops, who had behaved with particular brutality toward the civilian population in the vicinity. In the June 18 encounter a joint Boxer–Red Lantern force defeated the Russians, inflicting over five hundred casualties. The Tianjin population celebrated by presenting them with mung bean soup and victory cakes inscribed with the words "The sacred Boxers [Yihe shen tuan] have won a complete victory."

"In this fierce battle, the daughters of the Red Lantern displayed enormous courage! Clad entirely in red, like a mass of flame, they confronted the most vicious bandits and, filled with righteous anger, shouted the resounding slogan: 'The hell-raising Red Lanterns, Fear neither gun nor cannon. With our short-hilt swords, We lop off the foreigners' heads.' When the Czarist Russian invading forces heard this deafening battle cry they were so terrified that they got cramps in their calves!"

In July, unfortunately, the Boxers suffered a severe setback in Tianjin and were forced to retreat, overwhelmed by the foreigners' superior fire power and brutal tactics. In this conclusive engagement, Zhang Decheng sustained serious wounds and Lin Hei'er was captured and later executed. The legacy of these heroic leaders, however, did not die. The mere mention of the Boxers struck terror in the hearts of the enemy, as did the sight of the Red Lanterns: "The red lantern of the Red Lanterns is a symbol of the militancy of Chinese women; the daughters of the Red Lantern are the vanguard of the opposition of Chinese women to imperialism! Mountains may be leveled and the seas may be emptied, but the red lantern of revolution will never be extinguished!"[36]

The Lin Hei'er legend[37] follows closely the conventional Communist reading of modern Chinese history as a two-front struggle waged by the Chinese people against imperialism and feudalism. Lin's humiliation of Yulu and Li Hongzhang's son, on the home front, and her bravery and heroism in battle, on the foreign front, were themes found in a thousand other stories of the Cultural Revolution era. What distinguishes the story of Lin Hei'er — and this may be all that distinguishes it — is that Lin was a woman.

It is easy to dismiss the kind of feminism embodied in the Lin Hei'er legend as "patriarchal feminism," in that its sole claim is that women are capable of experiencing the same emotions, holding the same attitudes, and engaging in the same kinds of behavior as men. What such disparagement fails to take into account is the emotional impact of the multiple empowerment Lin Hei'er represents. When Lin launches into her tirade against Yulu, it isn't just a working-class person talking up to a member of the ruling class, it is also a female in a patriarchal society talking down to a male. Similarly, when her Red Lanterns engage the imperialist forces in battle, it is not simply a case of primitively armed Chinese fighting against a powerfully armed foreign foe — a theme played over and over again in Boxer mythologization — but also of women fighting side by side with men.

This last form of empowerment was closely related to another, also symbolized by the Lin Hei'er story, which we may call "victim power." I refer to the kind of power that accrues when the good guys are defeated by the bad guys in a contest in which the odds are heavily stacked in favor of the latter, who are portrayed as behaving with particular viciousness and brutality. In experiential terms, victims in the summer of 1900 were, almost by definition, powerless (see chapter 6). Once mythologized, however, they could become very powerful indeed. Such empowerment was, as noted above, built into the mythologization of the Boxer story in general; it was by no means confined to female Boxers.[c] Nevertheless, when the victims were females — or anyone conceived as relatively vulnerable and defense-

---

[c] Or, for that matter, to the Boxer movement. Victim power was the central theme of the "national humiliation days" that were an important expression of Chinese nationalism in the first half of the twentieth century. Recall the annual commemorations of the signing of the Boxer Protocol discussed in chapter 8.

274 less (unarmed student protesters, for example)[38] — the emotional impact was greatly magnified. In the revived campaign against Soviet revisionism that straddled the last years of the Cultural Revolution and the first years of the post-Mao era, Chinese mythologizers played this empowerment of the vulnerable for everything it was worth.

9.4 Cheng Shifa, "Boxers heroically resisting the invading army." The theme of primitively armed Boxers fighting against powerfully armed foreign aggressors was not confined to the Cultural Revolution years. This illustration is from a book published in 1956: Bao Cun, *Yihetuan* (Shanghai).

The Attack on Soviet Revisionism

The Soviet Union had been a target of Chinese propaganda warfare since the early 1960s, well before the start of the Cultural Revolution, and it continued to be attacked in the Chinese media long after the Cultural Revolution was over. Anti-Soviet propaganda went through different stages, however, in response to changes in the Sino-Soviet relationship and the international situation in Asia. Thus, as the Chinese felt themselves increasingly threatened by the Soviet Union militarily in the mid-1970s, the usual charges of Soviet revisionism were supplemented by shrill denunciations of Soviet social imperialism, hegemonism, and big power chauvinism.

Although the most dramatic confrontation between the USSR and China had come in 1969, when the two countries fought a succession of pitched battles along their common frontier, the Soviet military buildup in Asia, which had begun in 1965 under Brezhnev, actually intensified during the 1970s (partly in response to the 1969 clashes) and continued into the 1980s.[39] Against this general backdrop the fall of the Saigon government in the spring of 1975 presented China with a worrisome situation. A *People's Daily* editorial of May 9, 1975, warned that "the Soviet social imperialists . . . are leaving no stone unturned in their efforts to replace the U.S. imperialists at a time when the latter are becoming increasingly vulnerable and strategically passive." Deng Xiaoping, using pithier language, expressed essentially the same sentiment when he cautioned the leaders of the Philippines and Thailand "to beware of the tiger coming from the back door while pushing out the wolf from the front door."[40]

Even before the collapse of Saigon, as the war in Vietnam wound down, Chinese fears of Soviet military encirclement inevitably grew. This was, I suspect, the major factor behind a new anti-Soviet campaign that was launched in 1975. Like the earlier attack on Liu Shaoqi, this campaign also took as its point of departure the alleged negative treatment of the Boxers in a work from the cultural sphere. In this case, however, the object of attack was not a historical film but a historical book, *Novaia istoriia Kitaia* (The history of modern China), edited by the well-known Soviet Sinologist S. L. Tikhvinsky and published in Moscow in 1972.[41] It was significant, in light of the fact that this was a campaign against Soviet revisionism, that the Tikhvinsky book embodied a revised Soviet understanding of modern Chinese history.[42] Also significant, given the historical nature of the campaign's immediate target, those who took part in it appear to have been mainly historians, and the campaign was waged largely in academic jour-

276 nals, many (although not all) of them from institutions in the Northeast (Manchuria), where Czarist Russia had played a dominant political and military role during the Boxer era and the Soviet threat in the mid-1970s was most palpable.

Characteristically, the starting point for the Chinese campaign against the Tikhvinsky volume was less the actual analysis of the Boxer movement contained in it than the language it used to describe and evaluate the Boxers. Emphasis on correct language had been a central component of the Confucian tradition in China, it being widely held from the time of Confucius himself that language, by shaping attitudes, had a direct bearing on behavior. In the discourse of the international communist movement as well, although the understanding of the philosophical relationship between language and behavior was very different, proper labeling or categorization of people and events had been an important feature from the outset. Under simultaneous pressure from two disparate but (on this point at least) mutually reinforcing intellectual traditions, it thus became a matter of course for Chinese historians during the Communist period to pay the very closest attention to the proper use of evaluative language. Correct labeling literally defined reality—an emphasis that, when carried to extremes, as in the Cultural Revolution, resulted in a complete collapse of the customary distinction between historians and mythologizers.

This was painfully evident in the Tikhvinsky case. In their book Tikhvinsky and his associates, while affirming the Boxers in the abstract, are alleged to have described them in concrete terms as ignorant, superstitious, blindly antiforeign, conservative and backward, wanton murderers and arsonists, complete rejecters of European culture and the latest achievements of science, and impotent before the heavily armed forces of the imperialist powers, while conversely heaping praise on Czarist Russia for its efforts to establish peace and order in the Northeast and to introduce the benefits of Western civilization into the area.[43] In response to this effort simultaneously to delegitimize the Boxers and whitewash turn-of-the-century Russian imperialism, Chinese historians mounted a varied and spirited defense. They repeatedly quoted from the scathing denunciation of Russian motives and conduct found in Lenin's 1900 essay "The War in China."[44] Students and teachers from the history department of Beijing Normal University procured statements from Chinese of various backgrounds (including a few surviving former Boxers) defending the Boxers under such rhetorical headings as "Who were the real murderers and arsonists?" and " 'Ignorant' and 'backward' or the main force of the revolution against imperialism?"[45] One of these statements (by a member of the

People's Liberation Army) pointed out that the pejorative language used by Tikhvinsky and his coauthors to defame the Boxers was little more than a replay of contemporary foreign characterizations of the uprising as "a savage antiforeign disturbance" marked by "wanton burning and killing" by "Boxer bandits" (*quanfei*).[46] And Wu Wenxian, a staff member of the Heilongjiang Provincial Museum, to show that the Soviet revisionists' positive appraisal of Czarist actions in China was also nothing new, introduced a 1905 Moscow publication on the construction of the Chinese Eastern Railway, which loudly proclaimed the "glorious achievement" of Czarist Russia in bringing "Western civilization" to the people of the Northeast and "suppressing banditry and disorder" there.[47]

Some historians, applying conventional Marxist-Leninist analysis, argued that the behavior of the Boxers was a natural by-product of the action of imperialism on Chinese society. Thus, the superstitious aspects of the movement were a direct reflection of the backward conditions fostered by imperialist aggression. Boxer destruction of foreign railways, telegraphs, and commodities was partly, like the smashing of machinery by British workers at the beginning of the Industrial Revolution, a product of insufficient understanding of the nature of the enemy and partly an outgrowth of legitimate hatred spurred by the economic inroads of imperialism.[48] More generally, since it was an ironclad law of history that oppression and exploitation begot resistance, the uprising of the Boxers was a natural outcome of the forces that had been operating in China since the Opium War.[49]

By far the most effective defense at the disposal of Chinese historians, in combating the negative portrayal of the Boxers in the Tikhvinsky book, was to turn this portrayal on its head by showing that in fact it was Russia, not China, that had behaved in savage, barbarous, uncivilized fashion at the turn of the century.[50] We have already noted the charges of brutality against civilians brought against the Russian occupiers of the Laolongtou railway station in Tianjin. Russian forces were also accused of butchering the greater part of the citizenry of Beitang, a large market town due east of Tianjin;[51] looting and smashing priceless treasures from the imperial palace in the capital, even using the paper from Chinese books and artwork to wipe themselves after defecating;[52] and committing every kind of atrocity against the population of Heilongjiang (in northern Manchuria).

It was the last-named example of Russian savagery, focusing on the massacres of unarmed Chinese civilians in two locations on the Russian side of the Amur in the summer of 1900, that Chinese historians found particularly compelling.[53] The Sino-Russian Treaty of Aigun (1858) had established the Amur River in the area of Aigun (a town on the Chinese side) as

278   the boundary between the Chinese and Russian empires. However, many Chinese continued to live in towns and villages on the Russian side of the river. As Boxer activities in the Northeast intensified in late June and early July, 1900, the Russian government decided to move troops into the area on the pretext of suppressing the "rioters" and reestablishing order. On July 13 five Russian naval vessels steamed down the Amur, and on the 14th Russian troops forced their way ashore. When the Qing garrison at Aigun resisted, hostilities broke out. It was in this context that Russian atrocities took place at Hailanpao (Blagoveshchensk), just north of the junction of the Zeya (or Jingqili) and Amur rivers (and a focal point, it is worth noting, of Cultural Revolution-related violence and serious Soviet-Chinese tension in 1969), and at Jiangdong Liushisitun (literally, "the sixty-four villages on the east bank"), an area immediately south of Hailanpao (see map 2).[54]

On the eve of the first massacre the Russian authorities at Hailanpao announced that they were going to transfer all Chinese inhabitants of the town to the other (Chinese) side of the Amur and that the doors of their homes should be left unlatched. On July 16 the Russians herded several thousand Chinese, including women and children, into the police station, whereupon their residences and shops were looted clean. Then they rounded up Chinese villagers from the surrounding area, killing all those who offered resistance. As the numbers detained mounted, the police station could no longer hold them all. So in the evening they were taken to the courtyard of a lumber mill by the bank of the Zeya River. The next day, July 17, the first batch of Chinese residents, numbering 3,000–3,500, were escorted by Cossack soldiers to a point on the shore of the Amur six miles north of Hailanpao. Those who fell behind on the way were hacked to death by the Cossacks. At that time the narrowest stretch of the river was still seven hundred feet wide and the current was very swift. According to a contemporary Western account, the Cossacks ordered the Chinese to swim across. The ones who entered the water drowned immediately, while those who were afraid to go in were shot or bludgeoned to death by the soldiers. Within half an hour the river bank was piled high with the corpses of Chinese. Another account, this one by a Chinese, reported that, after the Chinese had been forced to the river's edge, Russian cavalry suddenly arrived and began to attack the prisoners with their weapons. The prisoners, caught by surprise, tried to flee and were drowned in the Amur.

The other massacre took place at Jiangdong Liushisitun, which had been occupied by Russian troops since April. On July 17 the Russians began to burn down the homes of the villagers in the area. In one instance they herded people into a large house and set fire to it, incinerating numerous Chinese alive. Other inhabitants of Jiangdong Liushisitun were divided into groups and driven toward the bank of the Amur, where those who didn't drown attempting to cross were murdered in cold blood on the shore.

Chinese who witnessed the massacres from Aigun on the opposite shore said that they saw Russian troops surround a large number of Chinese prisoners by the river's edge. They then heard an enormous noise and could make out Russian soldiers with swords and axes hacking and chopping at random, cutting up corpses and smashing bones. Sounds of wailing and weeping filled the air. The mortally wounded died on the bank of the river. The lightly wounded died in the river. Those who weren't wounded at all and tried to escape by swimming across the river drowned. "It was ascertained that more than five thousand people were either massacred or died from drowning."

An elderly person who was present at one of the massacres recalled it in the following language: "The Russian troops forced the Chinese toward the river as if tossing dumplings into a pot. The ones who refused to enter the water they stabbed with their bayonets or hacked with axes. Some of those whom they pushed into the river could swim. When the Russian soldiers saw this they shot them dead. As if this weren't enough, the Russian troops also tied the queues of two or three men together and then pushed them into the waters. They thought up every conceivable means to prevent people from crossing the river alive."

An official Russian account stated that "the testimony of all eyewitnesses forces one to believe that [the Russians] were not in fact ferrying the Chinese across the river but were intent upon killing them all off or drowning them." Another Russian account, by an officer who surveyed the scene three weeks after the massacres, stated: "It is hard to estimate how many corpses we saw on this day, but . . . on a single small spit of sand we counted over 150 bodies. It may be inferred that the total number of Chinese corpses was great."

After the massacres on the Russian side of the Amur, which Chinese allege resulted in the violent deaths of over 15,000 of their compatriots and left another 10,000 homeless, the Russians turned their attention to Aigun and nearby villages on the Chinese bank, which they razed in August. "The inhabitants of Aihun [Aigun]," according to one Chinese work, "numbered 50,000 prior to the ravages and burning committed by the soldiers; during the calamity of *gengzi* [1900] two out of ten died in the fighting, while three out of ten died from epidemic diseases."[55] On a wider scale, during the Boxer period the Russians are said to have killed over 200,000

280   Chinese inhabitants of the areas north of the Amur and east of the Ussuri (areas, that is, under the jurisdiction of the Russian empire).[56]

In the propaganda war against Tikhvinsky and Soviet revisionism, it was the two massacres described above that Chinese writers returned to again and again. War is war, and for most people it will always evoke horror. But one has only to think of the mass killing of incarcerated Polish officers in the Katyn Forest in World War II or the slaughter of the village population at Mylai during the Vietnam War or the butchering of over two hundred Palestinian men, women, and children in the refugee camps of Sabra and Shatila in 1982 to appreciate that massacres—the indiscriminate killing, often by exceptionally cruel means, of defenseless (or relatively defenseless) humans—occupy a unique place in people's emotions. War, for all its attendant suffering and pain, appears still to be viewed by the vast majority of human beings as a legitimate last resort in the resolution of conflict, and people who engage in war are not generally regarded as uncivilized for that reason. Massacres are different: unacceptable, illegitimate, beyond the pale.

The best Chinese defense against the Soviet charge that the Boxers were uncivilized "bandits" who "killed and burned" was, therefore, to present evidence, in the form of Russian massacres against Chinese civilians, that the real killers and burners were none other than the self-proclaimed emissaries of Western civilization in the Northeast, the Russians themselves. "In the last analysis," one writer asked rhetorically, "was Czarist Russian imperialism carrying out a 'mission civilisatrice' in China or was it pursuing a policy of naked criminal aggression? History is the best proof."[57]

History may, indeed, be the best proof. But only in certain circumstances, and only when it is appealed to for answers to questions that are genuinely open-ended. When the questions are closed and the appeal to history is not for answers but for confirmation of positions that have already been arrived at, history may offer comfort but it "proves" nothing. To put it somewhat differently, the object of Chinese historians in the present instance was not to understand the past but to control it, and the reason that they, as well as their Soviet counterparts, were so intent upon controlling the past is that they were both caught up in a process that was fundamentally political, not historical, in its basic nature and aims.

That such was the case was acknowledged with almost embarrassing transparency by the Chinese participants in the campaign. Tikhvinsky and his collaborators, they charged, by not even alluding to the Russian atrocities and by characterizing Russian conduct in the Northeast as a "civilizing mission," gave proof positive that they were writing history for political purposes.[58] This charge, moreover, was reinforced by the Soviet allegation that the real reason Chinese historians were so enamored of the Boxers as a topic of research was that the Boxers, apart from being useful for fanning nationalistic rage against the Soviet Union, accorded perfectly with the Chinese propaganda requirements that "to rebel is right" and "there is great disorder in the world." Such charges and allegations, the Chinese parried, completely unmasked the sinister political motives behind the Soviet revisionists' attacks on the Boxers, making it crystal clear that the real Soviet aim was none other than to oppose the revolutionary upsurge of the peoples of China and of the Third World against the social imperialist hegemonism of the USSR.[59] "An important combat mission of the present-day historical profession" in China was, therefore, to expose these motives and criticize the "shameless slanders" to which they gave rise.[60]

One of the more impressive of such exposures, from the point of view of historical documentation, concluded with the following words of warning:

> After the Soviet revisionist renegade clique ascended the stage, it pursued a policy of restoration of capitalism at home and of expansionism abroad, thereby becoming social imperialism. In order to realize the pipe dream of "world empire" that the old czars were unable to realize, they have falsified history in a hundred and one ways, covering up the old czars' criminal aggression against China. They hope by prettifying the policy of aggression of the old czars to prepare the way for the colonialist aggression of their new czars. But this is only wishful thinking! We warn the Soviet revisionist renegade clique: When your ancestors, the old czars, were around, they committed aggression everywhere. But their quest for world domination came to no good end and they were overthrown by the people. Now you have inherited the mantle of the old czars and are trying in vain to realize the pipe dream of "world empire" that the old czars were unable to realize. In the end there is no way that you will be able to improve upon the old czars. Your efforts, too, are doomed to fail![61]

Chinese vindication of the Boxers against the charges of Tikhvinsky and his associates is interesting in a number of respects. First, the symbolic repertoire associated with the Boxers has been internationalized. We have already encountered the Boxers during the Cultural Revolution as symbols of patriotism, revolutionary youth, and female emancipation. Now there is an extension of the concept of emancipation to embrace movements of national liberation in Asia, Africa, and Latin America, and the criticisms leveled by Soviet historians against the Boxers are understood as a reflection of Soviet opposition to the aspirations for freedom of the peoples of the entire Third World.

282 Second, the language employed in the assault on the Tikhvinsky volume is, like Chinese Communist campaign rhetoric in general, marked not only by a complete absence of discipline and restraint but also by lavish reference to battles, fighting, struggles, enemies, fronts, and combat missions.[62] The vocabulary of historical discourse has become effectively militarized; the writing of history has turned into a form of warfare.

Finally, there is the all-important matter, already touched on, of the relationship between history and politics. One must not, of course, read this material with a sense of the absurd, or the entire edifice will crumble. There is nothing wrong, after all, with Chinese historians accusing Soviet historians of accusing Chinese historians of using history for political purposes. History and politics, all the combatants knew, were inseparable. The point was not to write history that was free of politics; it was to write history that embodied the correct politics.

But one could only write history with the correct politics if one had the correct politics to begin with. History, as one Chinese historian put it, taking his cue straight from Marx and Engels, was an ideological thing, and the changes it went through had their sources in changes in people's social relations and in class struggles of an intense and complicated nature. Thus, the revisionist retrogression in Soviet historiography was a direct reflection of the retrogression taking place in the history of contemporary Soviet society. The Soviets' so-called reanalysis of history was nothing other than the restoration of bourgeois historiography—"the reflection in the ideological sphere of the restoration of capitalism in the Soviet Union." And the defiance by Tikhvinsky and his coauthors of the teachings of Lenin, their poisonous slandering of the anti-imperialist and patriotic Boxer movement, was "a reflection of the degeneration of Soviet socialism into social imperialism" and answered to "the political needs . . . of the Soviet revisionists' new colonialism."[63] Soviet historians, in short, lived and worked in a society that was moving in the wrong direction. There was no way, therefore, that they were going to get their history right.

Mythologization and Credibility

If even the best historians inadvertently fashion myths, it is also true that good mythmakers rarely display complete imperviousness to history. Thus, even during the Cultural Revolution, when the mythologization of the Boxer experience, not to mention other phases of the Chinese past, reached new heights, and no Chinese historian was so foolhardy as to challenge the process publicly (although some were apparently fortunate enough not to have to participate in it), the picture of the Boxers that was presented to the Chinese public was by no means unconnected to the past. In fact, the state-directed mythologization of this era went to some lengths to establish the appearance of historical credibility.[64] Accounts of the Amur massacres were, as we have seen, substantiated by official and nonofficial Russian sources as well as the oral testimony of surviving witnesses. The introduction of the Red Lanterns in the spring of 1967, in conjunction with the attack on Liu Shaoqi and the upsurge of Red Guard activity, was accompanied by extensive reference to specific source materials: participant accounts,[65] slogans, songs,[66] and the like. *Guangming ribao* even published an entire page of such materials, drawn from documentary collections, with full citations.[67]

From a historian's vantage point, to be sure, much is missing from such an effort. Sources may be cited accurately, but there is no attempt to deal with them critically. One would never guess, for example, that the actual evidence for direct Red Lantern involvement in combat is extremely thin.[68] Even more mischievous, sources are wrenched from their context in order to provide support for the mythologizer's thematic agenda. In the above-cited *Guangming ribao* issue, one of the items quoted to document the heroism and courage of the Boxers and Red Lanterns states: "Regardless of whether the Boxers died at the hands of the Christians or the soldiers or the law, they invariably faced death unflinchingly." There is no hint of the immediately following phrase in the original, which suggests that Boxer indifference to death was at least partly owing to their ability, when possessed by spirits, to fall into a semiconscious, trancelike state.[69] (If this were even partially the source of their courage, of course, it would detract substantially from the image of the Boxers as patriotic heroes.)

Finally, Cultural Revolution writers were shamelessly selective in their exploitation of the documentation available to them. Nowhere in any of the materials that I have seen, to cite just one instance, is there any mention of the famed magical prowess of the Red Lanterns, in particular their abilities to control the wind and to fly.[70] Spirit possession, invulnerability rituals, and magic, despite their importance in the religious-cultural repertoire of the Boxers and Red Lanterns, did not fit the sanitized picture Chinese mythologizers were intent upon constructing during the Cultural Revolution. Therefore they were deliberately omitted.[71]

Beyond these specific distortions, there were the more general patterns of misrepresentation inherent in the patently political motives that informed discussions of the Amur massacres, the exaggerated importance attached to the Red Lanterns within the Boxer movement as a whole, the consistent conflation of Boxer "antiforeignism" with "patriotic anti-imperi-

284 alism," and the insistence upon treating the Boxer phenomenon as something to be praised or castigated rather than understood and explained.

And yet, for all the problems this picture creates for the historian, accustomed to reconstructing the past according to well-defined rules, for the general public, untutored in such rules and unaware or only dimly aware of their
importance, the Cultural Revolution portrayal of the Boxers was, I would
argue, far from complete nonsense. Whether it conformed to what actually
"happened" was beside the point. What mattered was that it was cognitively
plausible—it *could* have happened—and was, for many Chinese, emotionally satisfying.

The 1980s and the Renewal of Tension Between History and Myth

As the Cultural Revolution drew to a close and it became possible once
again for historians to be historians, the distinction between history and
myth gradually and somewhat tentatively reemerged. This was evidenced in the evolution of the handling of the Amur massacres of 1900.
An article that appeared in June 1977 (almost a year after the "official"
end of the Cultural Revolution) indicated that the campaign against the
Tikhvinsky book was still in progress but at the same time hinted that it
was running out of steam. The article begins with the obligatory quote
from Lenin's "The War in China," the treatment of the massacres themselves is typically brief and hackneyed, and the piece on the whole is
quite polemical in tone. There is, moreover, a complete absence of any
sense of historical problem. On the other hand, the Tikhvinsky volume,
although referred to sarcastically toward the end of the article as a "brilliant masterpiece" and scolded for its apologetic stance toward the crimes
of the "old czars," is identified only by title and not by the name of its
chief editor.[72]

In 1980–81, Xue Xiantian, a historian attached to the Institute of
Modern History of the Chinese Academy of Social Sciences, published
two articles on the massacres that went a long way toward reestablishing
them as a proper object of historical research. The first of the articles,
which appeared in China's leading historical journal, *Lishi yanjiu*
(Historical studies), focused on perhaps the most explosive aspect of the
massacres: the question of how many people had actually been killed.
Significantly, Xue's treatment of this question is almost clinical in its detachment. He sifts through a wide range of conflicting evidence and in
unpolemical language subjects it to careful and thorough analysis. Most
important, there is no overt political agenda in the piece. Tikhvinsky is not

mentioned anywhere. There is no homage to Lenin. The analysis appears to be guided by a genuine sense of historical problem.[73]

In the second article, which appeared in *Jindaishi yanjiu* (Modern Chinese historical studies) in 1981, Xue takes a clear pro-Chinese political stance. But his approach, once again, is fundamentally problem-oriented, and his treatment of the problem he sets for himself—an inquiry into Russia's real motives for perpetrating the Amur massacres—is seriously historical. There are no attacks on the "lies" and "fabrications" of Soviet historiography. And although the conclusion Xue arrives at—that Russia's main objective was territorial expansion at China's expense—was the politically safe conclusion, it may also have been historically accurate. In any case it is supported in the author's hands by reasoned argumentation and an impressive array of sources, including some in Russian and Japanese.[74]

Xue Xiantian's articles signal a clear retreat from the sort of mythologization that accompanied the campaign against the Tikhvinsky history. It is not that politically influenced handling of the Amur massacres disappeared in China in the 1980s. The emotive force of Chinese patriotic feeling, in combination with the constraints of operating within a political system the authoritarian character of which had moderated only to a degree, placed definite limits on the capacity of Chinese historians to address dispassionately and without bias a topic that, because of its nature, was bound in any case to carry a high political voltage. It seems, nevertheless, undeniable that there was a genuine reassertion of a historical agenda.

A comparable development could be discerned in post-Cultural Revolution handling of the Red Lanterns. The turning point in this case was an article by a Gansu historian Wang Zhizhong that appeared in 1980. Insofar as a major purpose of Wang's piece was to debunk the "revolutionized" (*geminghua*) and "modernized" (*xiandaihua*)—and hence in his view unhistorical—picture of the Red Lanterns fashioned by Qi Benyu and other Cultural Revolution writers, Wang could not be said to be entirely lacking in political purpose. In the course of the article, nevertheless, he went a long way toward not only stripping the Red Lanterns of the highly politicized and mythologized veneer they had acquired during the Cultural Revolution but also redefining them—much as Xue Xiantian had done in the case of the Amur massacres—as a historical problem.[75]

Clearly, the departures represented by the writings of Xue Xiantian and Wang Zhizhong did not signal complete reversals of previous historiographical patterns. Rather, if we think of the historical past and the mythologized past not as diametric opposites but as two poles of a continuum, we may say that the center of gravity of Chinese treatment of the massacres

286 and the Red Lanterns shifted from the extreme mythologization end of the continuum part way back toward the historical end. Where, during the Cultural Revolution, the text was political correctness and historical understanding was at best a weak subtext, in the 1980s political and historical texts became locked in real competition, with one or the other predominating in response to a broad range of factors.[76]

If this was true with respect to the massacres and the Red Lanterns, it was even more true of the treatment of the Boxer experience in general. Here, however, in addition to the competition between historical and political texts, there was the added complicating factor of two fiercely competing political texts: the one tied to the long-standing Communist commitment to revolution, especially peasant revolution, the other reflective of the renewed emphasis in the post-Mao era on modernization. The fact that modernization, accompanied by spirited Chinese interaction with the rest of the world, became the guiding policy of the Deng leadership beginning in the late 1970s prompted some historians to take a more critical stance toward the various manifestations of Boxer antiforeignism.[77] Few Chinese, on the other hand, were prepared to go quite as far as Joseph Esherick in repudiating the revolutionary ("antifeudal") interpretation entirely and seeing the Boxers as a loyalist movement from start to finish.[78]

Boxer historians in the 1980s engaged in a great deal of controversy over specific issues, sometimes pointing to real divergences in historical interpretation,[79] sometimes reflecting differences in political or ideological orientation.[80] The 1980s also witnessed the compilation and publication — always the safest course in a politically charged field — of numerous compendia of original source materials, often drawn from archival collections.[81] Excellent work was done on the social psychology of the Boxers and the impact on the movement of folk religious and sectarian ideas,[82] the latter a domain that had been declared nonexistent during the Cultural Revolution. Also Chinese historians produced an impressive number of in-depth empirical studies of specific phases of the Boxer experience.[83]

The impression is nevertheless unmistakable, at least from the vantage point of a Western historian, that the goal of extricating the historical Boxers from the mythologized Boxers has not been an easy one to achieve. It has been a relatively simple matter for Chinese historians to reject the cruder forms of mythologization that prevailed during the Cultural Revolution era. But the New Culture movement mythologization of the Boxers as superstitious (*mixin*) and the 1920s mythologization of them as anti-imperialist and patriotic (*fandi aiguo*) have been much harder to overcome.[84] These mythologizations spring from two of the most powerful discourses defining twentieth-century Chinese intellectual commitment: the one centering on unqualified faith in science and rationality (scientism), the other emphasizing national sovereignty and the conquest of any and all forces (above all, imperialism) subversive of it. Constrained—perhaps even blinded—by these overpowering currents, many Chinese historians do not see the portrayal of the Boxer movement as "superstitious" or "anti-imperialist and patriotic" as mythologization at all but as historically accurate descriptions, the one pointing to a key deficiency of the movement, the other identifying one of its towering strengths.[85]

My own sense is that both of these vocabularies, because they are so heavily freighted with twentieth-century political and cultural commitments, undermine the historian's quest for a more truthful understanding of the Boxer experience. To define the popular religious beliefs and practices of the Boxers as "superstition" is to adopt an essentially hostile stance toward them, making it more difficult to acquire a deeper appreciation of how these beliefs and practices appeared to the Boxers themselves and the functions they served in the Boxers' intellectual and emotional world. Similarly, to superimpose upon the Boxer movement the label "anti-imperialist and patriotic" is to radically oversimplify—and hence seriously hinder inquiry into—the diverse and complex motives impelling the Boxers to behave as they did in a context in which imperialism, however important, was only one among several powerful causal agencies and action taken against the effects of imperialism was not necessarily powered by either "patriotism" or "anti-imperialism."

A closely related reason Chinese historians have found it so difficult to free themselves more fully from mythologized constructions of the Boxer experience is that the Boxers raised, in the most striking way, what has very possibly been the central issue of cultural identity in the last century or so of Chinese history: the ambivalence with respect to the West.[86] Often this ambivalence has been expressed in coded language, as in the periodic references in this and the two previous chapters to the distinction between "civilized" and "uncivilized" behavior, the West sometimes exemplifying the former, sometimes the latter. Equally often, it has been articulated very directly, as in the following reflections of the educator, Jiang Menglin, upon his boyhood feelings about Westerners in turn-of-the-century Shanghai: "The foreigner appeared to my mind half divine and half devilish, double-faced and many-handed like Vishnu, holding an electric light, a steamboat, and a pretty doll in one set of hands, and a policeman's club, revolver, and handful of opium in the other. When one looked at his bright side he was an angel; on the dark side he was a demon."[87]

288   Cast in more general language, the West during the nineteenth and twentieth centuries has represented both imperialism, which is bad, and modernity (the secrets of "wealth and power"), which is good. Both of these, moreover, served equally as *cause* and *target* of the Boxer movement. Thus the Boxers—as history—have had a kind of built-in potency, rendering them exceptionally usable in later Chinese consciousness. When the West is defined as aggressor and exploiter (the demonic West), Boxer resistance to it has been deeply satisfying to patriotic Chinese (as we saw in our examination of the mythologization of the Boxers in the 1920s) and readily treated in laudatory terms. But when the West is seen as the wellspring of modern life (the angelic West), Boxer machine-bashing—the Luddite-like attacks on Western telegraphs, railways, and steamships[88]—has often been a source of acute embarrassment and roundly condemned. Indeed, to those Chinese intellectuals, like Lu Xun and the early Chen Duxiu, who saw China's troubles in the nineteenth and twentieth centuries as primarily rooted not in Western imperialism but in structural defects at the very heart of Chinese culture, Boxer antiforeignism, savagery, and above all superstition easily became metaphors for the Chinese condition in general.

If the Boxer episode as history encompassed substantive themes that resonated with unresolved issues pertaining to Chinese cultural identity in the twentieth century, the reverse has also been true. That is, the continued difficulty Chinese intellectuals since the late Qing have experienced in establishing what it means to be Chinese (a problem most recently vented in the fevered cultural debates of the mid- and late 1980s)[89] has made it uniquely difficult for historians to come to terms with the Boxers and to define their place in Chinese history. What is more, this is not a problem that is likely to go away any time soon. It is not, after all, unnatural or surprising that Chinese should experience love-hate feelings toward the West—or, for that matter, their own past. And as long as this ambivalence remains, the Boxers, because of the particular themes they evoke, are likely to continue their extraordinary life as a storehouse of symbol and myth.

CONCLUSION

One meaning of the word *key*, as used in the title of this book, is borrowed from music and refers to the tonal system of a composition. Another refers to a device or instrumentality that provides entrée to something. Both meanings are vital to the approach I have adopted in these pages. *Event*, *experience*, and *myth* point to different ways of getting at the meaning of the past, of accessing it, and—ultimately—knowing it. But they also suggest different ways in which the past may be configured or shaped, each operating according to different principles and imparting a very different inflection or "tone." These tonal differences, as some readers may have detected, are even echoed to a degree in the prose of the book's several parts, the main contrast being between the chapters comprising part 2, where I try as far as possible to enter into the emotional worlds of the people I am writing about, and parts 1 and 3, where I am more disposed to maintain a certain distance from the subject matter, resulting in a less personal, somewhat more "scholarly" style of exposition.

There are a few questions that still need to be raised. One has to do with the matter of representativeness. In this book, in an effort to gain a clearer picture of what historians do, I have examined the distinctive characteristics of event, experience, and myth in reference to a single—and in many ways highly singular—episode out of the past, the Boxer movement and uprising at the turn of the century in China. I have assumed, of course, that buried in the particularity of the Boxers are universals that are applicable to other historical events. It is now time to scrutinize this assumption more closely.

Let me begin by disposing of an issue that may be troubling some readers. I am not interested here in all aspects of the past, only in those aspects directly engaging the *consciousness* not only of the historian but also of the experiencer and mythmaker. This leaves out a whole category of historical writing, which is focused on long-term, impersonal developments (fre-

290 quently but not necessarily social or economic) that, however important, are generally too incremental to be noticed and therefore rarely, if ever, engage people's passions. The writing that encompasses such developments assumes, like all historical writing, a narrative form,[1] expressing the consciousness of the historian-narrator (historians never lose *their* consciousness). But it leaves little or no room for the consciousness of the agents of history, the individuals who make and experience the past, and it is doubtful anyone would ever set out to mythologize price inflation in eighteenth-century China or agricultural change in northern Europe during the late feudal era.

If we omit those facets of the past that, whatever their cumulative effect on people's lives, are so slow-changing as to go undetected — French historians often refer to such developments as the *longue durée* — and train our attention instead exclusively on the facets that individual human beings experience on a conscious level, there is a lot still left. In fact virtually everything is left that people ordinarily think of when they contemplate the past as an arena in which "things happened." The real question for us, then, is whether the Boxers, for all their distinctiveness, may still be taken as illustrative of the consciously apprehended past in general. My answer to this question, it will surprise no one, is strongly in the affirmative.

When viewed as an event, reconstructed after the fact by historians, with the goal of understanding and elucidating what happened and why (as in part 1), the Boxers, I would argue, are as appropriate for illustrative purposes as any other phase of the past. Indeed, since the focus, in all such reconstructive effort, is on the consciousness of the historian, rather than that of the direct participant or mythologizer, there is no reason why historical reconstructions even of the more impersonal parts of the past (as opposed to "events" and "individuals") cannot be used to exemplify what historians do. The contents of every historical event are, of course, unique. Moreover, some events, like the Boxer movement, are complex, occurring over vast stretches of time and space, while others, such as the first performance of a new Broadway play or the death of a national political leader, are relatively simple (although their ramifications may not be). But the historian's structuring of these events — the narratives we tell about them — operates according to a fairly distinctive set of principles regardless. One of these principles, which is absolutely fundamental, is that, unlike the mythologizer, the historian seeks to understand and explain the past. Another, no less important, is that, in contrast to the participant experiencer, historians know in advance the outcomes of the events they seek to reconstruct. A third principle, again distinguishing the historian from the immediate participant, is the former's freedom from the constraint of spatial location. Unlike the original agents of history, the historian is endowed with what I earlier referred to as wide-angle vision—the capacity to discern how the experiences of different individuals in the past related to one another and how a profusion of discrete events widely distributed in space (as well as over time) interconnected to form event structures of broader compass.

The suitability of the Boxers as an illustrative case, when the past is viewed as experience (part 2), is somewhat less straightforward. Here, after all, the spotlight is trained not on the consciousness of the historian-reconstructor but on that of the historical agent, and while we may argue with confidence that historians, regardless of their subject matter, always do more or less the same thing, surely the same cannot be said of the people who made the past in the first place and directly experienced it. Wars, election campaigns, baseball games, first loves, and final exams all refer to intrinsically different kinds of experience. The number of different kinds is infinite, and the individual experience is always unique. How, then, can an event like the Boxer episode, in which the key areas of experience included such things as drought, spirit possession, magic, rumor, and death, be taken as illustrative of the experienced past in general? Indeed, isn't the very notion of experience "in general" a contradiction in terms?

The answer—and, although more complex, it is no different really from that given to the question of the representativeness of the Boxers *qua* event—has several levels. At its most concrete and particular, the experience of those involved in the Boxer summer was, like the experience of participants in any phase of the past, unique and nonduplicable. On a somewhat more general level, on the other hand, this was less the case: world history, after all, is full of popular movements in which religion and magical rituals played a key part, antiforeign feeling was a driving force, rumor and incredulity were pervasive, and war, bloodshed, and dying predominated. On the most general (or formal) level, finally, such phenomena as indeterminacy (outcome blindness), emotional engagement, multiple motivation, cultural construction, and biographical consciousness appear to characterize all human experience, regardless of the specific, concrete forms in which it is expressed.

The kinds of historical data available for the reconstruction of different experiential worlds will, of course, vary according to the idiosyncrasies of historical circumstance. Except at the most superficial level, for example, it is impossible to explore the biographical consciousness of the Boxers because very few Boxers were literate and none appear to have left detailed

292 contemporary accounts of their experience.[2] There is a profusion of documentation, on the other hand, relating to such facets of the Boxer experience as the high levels of anxiety occasioned by the uncertainties attending prolonged drought and premature death and the pervasive tendency of Chinese and foreigners alike to interpret their experiences in terms of prior cultural patterning. We cannot reconstruct the Boxer experience in its entirety, in other words; but we can certainly gain access to significant portions of it, and at a certain level of generality, in so doing, we can gain insight into the experienced past more broadly considered.

The problem of the Boxers' representativeness as myth is different, but not fundamentally so. The main difference is that many parts of the past—and I refer here expressly to the consciously experienced past—do not survive, in any significant way, as myth. To live on as myth, as noted in the prologue to part 3, an event or person must embody characteristics or themes that seem especially pertinent to the concerns of people and/or governments in later times. Columbus is important to Italian-Americans because, when viewed as the discoverer of America, he is emblematic of the contribution people of Italian ancestry have made to American life. In a quite different way, Columbus is also important to Native Americans because the harshness of his actions toward the Indian peoples living in America at the time of his arrival symbolizes the oppression Native Americans have suffered throughout their history at the hands of people of European ancestry.

On the Chinese side, to take an example very different from the Boxers, the Taiping movement and uprising have been mythologized in a wide variety of ways. In the last years of the Qing, the radical journal *Minbao* hailed the Taiping founder, Hong Xiuquan, as one of China's great nationalist revolutionaries (along with the first emperor of the Ming dynasty and Sun Yat-sen).[3] The Guomindang in the early 1920s and the Chinese Communists, throughout the period of Maoist dominance, also identified with and saw themselves as carrying on the Taiping revolutionary tradition.[4] Individual Taiping leaders, in heavily mythologized form, have figured centrally in Chinese Communist political wars. After being sumptuously praised in the historiography of the 1950s, for example, the able commander Li Xiucheng, because of the confession he made (following torture) to Zeng Guofan after the Taipings' defeat, was reviled during the 1960s as a traitor to his class and regularly deployed as a negative symbol in Cultural Revolution attacks on revisionists.[5] And Chinese historians, in the late 1970s and early 1980s, in their attacks on "feudal despotism" in general and (more guardedly) the "patriarchal despotism" of Mao Zedong in particular, regularly drew parallels between Mao's slide into increasingly autocratic leadership after 1958 and that of such past political leaders as Hong Xiuquan.[6]

The Taipings, as one might expect, have also been a favorite source of local-level mythmaking, especially in the area of their origin near Canton. Sun Yat-sen, who came from the same part of southern Guangdong as Hong Xiuquan, is said to have admired and identified with the Taiping leader ever since his childhood days.[7] Refugees in Hong Kong reported that in the mid-1950s Guangdong peasants, viewing Hong as an all-purpose spokesman for popular resistance to the coercive power of the state, looked for him to return from the dead to lead them in opposing the cooperativization of their land.[8] Recent work on the Hakka minority of southern China shows how Christian members of this ethnic group have integrated a positive vision of the Taiping movement (whose founders were Christian-influenced Hakkas) into the invented traditions that form part of their definition of themselves as a community.[9]

Although the particularities of Taiping and Boxer mythologization differ greatly (the Taiping experience does not, for example, like that of the Boxers, resonate in a special way with the issue of modern Chinese cultural identity), the underlying processes involved do not. In both cases—as indeed in all instances of mythologization of the past—the emphasis is less on what actually happened than on how what happened is transformed and recast by later people for their own purposes. Invariably, particular themes from the past are identified, simplified, magnified, and highlighted, to the point where they become sources of energy in the present, making it possible for present and past to affirm and validate one another, sometimes in powerful ways. The themes so used may or may not be part of the actual historical past—it isn't clear, for example, that real Red Lanterns ever saw themselves as rebelling against the Confucian social conventions that hobbled Chinese women at the end of the nineteenth century—but they must, if they are to work effectively as myths, possess at least a degree of plausibility. They must be believable, even if not true.

On the matter of the Boxers' representativeness, to summarize, I would draw essentially the same conclusion with respect to each of the alternative avenues of access to the past explored in this book. At the most concrete and specific level, the Boxers, whether viewed as event, experience, or myth, are undeniably unique. This uniqueness, however, has embedded within it broad recurrent patterns encountered in all phases of the consciously experienced past, making it perfectly feasible, at a more general level, to appropriate the Boxers—or, for that matter, any other historical episode—for illustrative purposes. We don't study lions in order to learn

294   about giraffes, but we can study either lions or giraffes to enrich our understanding of the animal kingdom.

Another issue that invites further comment has to do with the comparative validity of event, experience, and myth, as ways of knowing the past. Are we to understand the experienced past as being privileged over the historically reconstructed one because it is more real? Or the historically reconstructed past as preferable to the mythologized one because it is truer? Although at one point in my development as a historian I would not have hesitated to answer "yes" to both of these questions, my growing conviction is that each of the three approaches, despite manifest tensions among them, possesses a solid kind of legitimacy within its sphere.

This is fairly well accepted with respect to the polarity between the experienced and the historically reconstructed pasts. Although we see the ways in which they differ, we have no trouble valuing each in its own right. We may delight in confronting, for the first time, the historical reconstruction of a part of the past—a war, say, or a social movement—in which we ourselves have directly participated, marveling in the new information and perspectives it supplies. But we retain a special emotional attachment to the original experience, our own past, that no amount of historical redoing can touch—unless, of course, as memory fades, the experienced past and the historically reconstructed one become hopelessly confused in our minds.

The situation with respect to the value of myth is more complicated and potentially problematic, although perhaps less so in regard to the relationship between myth and experience than that between myth and history. Experience, as we have seen (for example in chapter 4), does not take place within a cultural void. As people encounter "life," they instantly "process" it in terms of the myths that have formed a vital part of their socialization. Boxers do not hesitate to identify the gods who possess them as the historical and literary figures they have learned about from early childhood or to understand the failure of their magic in terms of deep-seated cultural beliefs about female pollution. Christian missionaries almost instinctively interpret the Boxer movement as the work of Satan. Such mythic constructions are ubiquitous in the world of experience and form an inseparable part of it. But, as merged as they seem—and perhaps are—at the moment an experience is first registered (the immediate past), they remain analytically distinct. This distinctness becomes especially clear when, in reviewing the personally experienced past from a more remote point in time, we inadvertently mythologize it. The process of constantly reworking one's own experienced past, which I have called autobiographical mythologization, obviously does violence to the original expe-

rience. "However honest we try to be in our recollections," a character in
Davies' *World of Wonders* cautions, "we cannot help falsifying them in
terms of later knowledge."[10] But, at the same time, as Barbara Myerhoff has
argued so compellingly,[11] autobiographical mythmaking has a clear value,
in that it helps to preserve a sense of psychological coherence and personal
integrity over time.

The value of myth in the context of the relationship between myth and
history is vastly more complicated. Professional historians see it as part of
their responsibility to distance their reconstructions of the past from the
"vulgar," mythologized understandings of the general population. We
shrink from accepting a simple, idealized vision of Abraham Lincoln as
"the great emancipator" and feel in duty bound to point out that, despite
his personal concerns about slavery, Lincoln's priority, from start to finish,
was not to free the slaves but to save the Union.[12] Similarly, we challenge
the simple view of World War II as "the good war" and insist on calling
attention to the fact that, although many Americans believed the war was
waged, at least in part, to vanquish an ideology based on racial difference,
the United States government, in addition to fielding a military force seg-
regated along racial lines, also in the name of wartime exigency systematically incarcerated over 100,000 persons residing on the West Coast for no
other reason than their Japanese ancestry.[13] Nevertheless, despite our best
efforts, the mythic power of a Lincoln or of a World War II — the emotional
investment in an essentialized understanding of certain individuals and
events that isolates out one strand from a complex picture and emphasizes
it to the exclusion of all else — remains serenely intact. And this is true even
for historians when we're not behaving as historians. The most disciplined
purists among us will doubtless always be prepared to substitute empirically demonstrated truths for long-cherished myths. But the majority of historians are happiest when laying siege to other people's mythologized
understandings, not their own. Indeed, the very notion that the truth about
the past — what historians seek to attain — is necessarily and always of
greater value than what people want to *believe* is true about the past may
itself be little more than a myth. There are, it is well to remember, several
different kinds of value — moral, intellectual, emotional, aesthetic — and an
assertion about the past that ranks high in respect to one of them may not
rank very high at all in respect to the others.

One last issue, related to but distinct from the one just discussed, bears
scrutiny. This concerns my own role, as author, in the several parts of this
book. Each part, after all, explores a different realm of consciousness: the
consciousness of the historian in the first part, that of the participant expe-

296   riencer (or historical agent) in the second part, and that of the mythologizer in the third. And yet, in all three parts, my own consciousness, as historian-narrator, is also at work. This presents no problem in the first part of
the book, since the consciousness of the author and that of the historian-
reconstructor of the Boxer episode are one and the same. But what about
the second and third parts, where this is not so?

In the experience portion of the book, I, as historian-author, select the
specific themes to be presented: drought, spirit possession, magic, and so
forth. I also explore analytical issues — the role of youth and hunger (and
hunger anxiety) in the rapid spread of the Boxers' possession ritual or of
prepubescence in the collective fantasies that existed concerning the Red
Lanterns — that it would never have occurred to the Boxers themselves to
raise. Similarly, in the myth section, in addition to identifying how the
Boxers were mythologized in different time periods, I analyze the *process*
of mythologization in ways that the mythologizers themselves would likely
resist. In both parts, in other words, in the course of playing the conventional historian's role of reconstructor of the past — in this instance the
experienced and mythologized pasts — I also introduce a consciousness,
my own, that is certainly different from and may even run counter to that
of the people whose consciousness I am probing.

It would be foolish to maintain that this is not a problem. The question
is: how serious a problem is it? The answer hinges partly on what as a historian one is capable of doing and partly on what one aspires to do.
Although it is clearly not within the bounds of the historian's capability to
resurrect the experienced past in its pristine form, it is certainly possible, in
the case of both the experienced and the mythologized pasts, to reproduce
live voices from those pasts (although not necessarily the voices one might
ideally wish to reproduce), and this is as good a way as we have of evoking
what the people we are studying (whether experiencers or mythmakers)
themselves thought and felt.

I have done this repeatedly in the second and third parts of the book.
But to have done only this would have been to do only a portion of what I
initially set out to accomplish. Since, from the outset, it was my hope not
merely to present examples of event, experience, and myth but to scrutinize analytically their distinctiveness as ways of knowing the past, it was
essential to introduce my own intelligence as a historian into the scrutinizing process. It may well be that, in so doing, I have created a situation
in which different consciousnesses, the scrutinizer's as well as the scruti-
nized's, are in a state of tension with one another. But, apart from being

unavoidable, it occurs to me that there is a palpable benefit, in terms of greater historical understanding, to be derived from this very tension.

Essentially, the problem I am addressing here is that of the historian's "outsideness." This outsideness can take a variety of specific forms: American historians writing about the Chinese past, male historians reconstructing the experience of women, white historians probing black history. It can also—indeed must always—take the more general form of people in the present attempting to elucidate the experience of people in the (sometimes remote) past. In all of these cases, the historian's outsideness, precisely because it is outside, has the potential to misconstrue and distort, to introduce meanings alien to the material under examination. And it is in this respect, clearly, that outsideness can be a problem.

But the historian's outsideness can also be an asset. It is an essential part of what makes us different both from the immediate experiencers of the past and from the past's mythologizers, enabling us, in our capacity as historians, to render the past intelligible and meaningful in ways unavailable to either. In addition to attempting, with all the attendant risks, to re-create the consciousness of the experiencer and/or the mythologizer of the past, in other words, we also seek to form a bridge between those worlds and the world of the people of our own day, making possible some degree of useful communication between the two. Akin to the translator, whose job is to render a text not only faithfully but also meaningfully from one language into another, historians act as mediators between present and past. In the complex process of negotiation that ensues, we must curb our outsideness as we try to understand the consciousness of the people we are studying (in the past). But we cannot curb it—on the contrary we must capitalize on it—in the effort to explain this consciousness meaningfully to the people for whom we are writing (in the present). Historians, in short, not unlike translators, must be acquainted with two languages, in our case those of the present and of the past, and it is the need to navigate back and forth between these two very different realms, incessantly, sensitively, and with as much honesty as possible, that is the ultimate source of the tension in our work.

ABBREVIATIONS

ABCFM	American Board of Commissioners for Foreign Missions
CCP	Chinese Communist Party
CIM	China Inland Mission
FRUS	United States. *Papers relating to the Foreign Relations of the United States, 1900*. Washington, D.C.: 1902.
GX	Guangxu reign (1875–1908)
HDYYDJ	"Hebei diqu Yihetuan yundong diaocha jilu." Unpublished oral history transcripts, Nankai University, Tianjin.
HJZH	"Hebei Jingzhou, Zaoqiang, Hengshui diqu Yihetuan diaocha ziliao xuanbian." Compiled by Shandong daxue lishixi Zhongguo jindaishi jiaoyanshi. In *Shandong daxue wenke lunwen jikan* 1 (1980): 157–94.
LMP	Luella Miner Papers (North China Mission). American Board of Commissioners for Foreign Missions, Papers. Houghton Library, Harvard University.
NCH	*North-China Herald and Supreme Court and Consular Gazette*
NYT	*New York Times*
PP:1900	Great Britain. Parliamentary Papers. *China No. 3 (1900)*. London: 1900.
SYDZX	*Shandong Yihetuan diaocha ziliao xuanbian*. Compiled by Lu Yao et al. Jinan: 1980.
TDYYDB	"Tianjin diqu Yihetuan yundong diaocha baogao." Compiled by Nankai daxue lishixi 1956 ji. Mimeographed. Reissue of original 1960 mimeographed edition. Tianjin: n.d.
TYJ	*Tianjin yiyue ji*. Anonymous. In *Yihetuan* 2:141–58.
YHT	*Yihetuan*. 4 vols. Shanghai: 1951.

NOTES

Preface

1. Wright, "Introduction," 1.

2. Wasserstrom, "The Boxers as Symbol," 10–11.

3. Veyne, *Writing History*, 40.

4. Although the mythologization of the Boxers in the twentieth-century West is also touched on occasionally, this mythologization has had its own inner dynamic. To treat it properly would take us deeply into Western fears and fantasies, resulting both in a blurring of the book's focus and an unnecessary addition to its already considerable girth.

5. The reference is to the famous Kurosawa film dealing with a rape-murder in eleventh-century Japan and the different versions the four people who witnessed it had of what happened.

6. Darnton, *The Great Cat Massacre*, 3.

7. A partial exception to this is in the area of oral history testimony. Although there are unpublished oral history materials relating to 1900, focused mainly on Hebei (Zhili) province and more specifically on the Tianjin region, and I have found them (especially the earlier ones gathered in the 1950s) to be exceptionally useful, the interview materials covering the pre-1900 period in Shandong (partly published) are both more extensive and more systematically arranged.

PART 1 / *Prologue: The Historically Reconstructed Past*

1. *NYT*, Mar. 10, 1989, C4.

2. Carr, *Time*, 9, 16; see also ibid., 65, 73, 168–69, 177. For White's views, see his "The Question of Narrative in Contemporary Historical Theory," 1–33; for Ricoeur's (which are discussed admiringly in White's article), see his *Time and Narrative*, vol. 1.

3. Carr, in the final part of his book, explicitly acknowledges some of the characteristics of historical narration that seem to set it apart from participant narration. The differences, however, are of a practical rather than a formal sort, and form, rather than practice, is what counts for the author. Thus, in practical terms, the historian has hindsight, while the subjects about whom he or she writes do not. But in formal terms people in the present also have a kind of hindsight—Carr calls it "quasi-hindsight"—inasmuch as they are able to anticipate future outcomes and

302   act *as if* the future they anticipate will in fact be realized. See Carr, *Time*, 168–77; also ibid., 60–62.

4. Barnes, *Flaubert's Parrot*, 168.

5. Lively, *Moon Tiger*, 6.

6. Boyer and Nissenbaum, *Salem Possessed*, 209.

7. Levi, *The Drowned and the Saved*, 27.

8. This problem is encountered in all historical scholarship. It is posed most conspicuously by scholars who are candid about their extraprofessional social and political commitments. See, for example, Gail Hershatter, "Subaltern." Hershatter, a first-rate social historian, raises the problem implicitly but does not actually address it in her article.

9. Elton, *Return to Essentials*, 7.

10. Ibid., 65.

11. David McCullough, interviewed in *NYT*, Aug. 12, 1992, C10.

12. Boyer and Nissenbaum, *Salem Possessed*, 20–23.

13. Esherick, *Origins*, 269–70, 287, 304; Purcell, *Boxer Uprising*, 247 (G. Nye Steiger is quoted in ibid., to the same effect); and Kobayashi Kazumi, "Minshū shisō," 256–57.

14. Boyer and Nissenbaum, *Salem Possessed*, xi.

15. Particularly good on this is Bastid-Bruguière, "Currents," 535–602, esp. 576–602.

16. The Boxer uprising, according to Ding Mingnan ("Jiaoan de kaocha," 27), "might be said to have been China's biggest *jiaoan*" ("church case"). Ding's periodization of *jiaoan* for the years from the Opium War to the eve of the 1911 revolution is in ibid., 39–40.

17. This did not, of course, keep contemporaries from trying (with Carr's "quasi-hindsight") to divine the deeper meaning, in terms of the future, of the events they were living, or had just lived, through. "This episode of to-day," Robert Hart wrote in reference to the siege of the legations, "is not meaningless—it is the prelude to a century of change and the keynote of the future history of the Far East: the China of the year 2000 will be very different from the China of 1900!" (*Essays*, 49). Thomas F. Millard, commenting on the ease with which "the psychological moment . . . when the decisive change takes place" may be overlooked, ventured "to suggest that, aided by the perspective of time, the future historian will fix this turning point for China somewhere among the years from 1900 to 1906" (see his *The New Far East*, 217–18).

18. Isaacs, *Images of Asia*, 143.

19. Dunstheimer, "Le mouvement des Boxeurs," 415.

20. Li Shiyu, "Yihetuan yuanliu," 18.

21. Zhou made his oft-quoted statement in a speech in Beijing welcoming a visiting delegation from the German Democratic Republic. The speech is in *Renmin ribao* (People's daily), Dec. 12, 1955.

22. Schwarcz, "Remapping May Fourth," 25. Levenson's essay was a review of Chow Tse-tsung's *The May Fourth Movement: Intellectual Revolution in Modern China*.

23. The apparent exceptions that come to mind are presidents, generals, and other people in leadership positions, who, especially in an era of high-tech elec-

tronic communication, are able to make instant and virtually simultaneous contact with a multitude of different points in space. Even in such exceptional circumstances, however, I would guess that there is much that does not get communicated at the time—the details in a field commander's personal journal, for example, or, even better, an infantryman's letters to his mother—that does, with luck, end up in the historian's portfolio of evidence.

24. The words are novelist John Vernon's, in his "Exhuming a Dirty Joke," 35.

25. Boorstin, "The Historian," 28–29.

26. Ibid.

27. For an excellent, annotated collection of over 150 Boxer writings, see Chen Zhenjiang and Cheng Xiao, *Yihetuan wenxian*. Boxer oral history testimony and some of its limitations are discussed in ch. 2, n. 97 of the present volume.

28. Vernon, "Exhuming a Dirty Joke," 35.

1. *The Boxer Uprising: A Narrative History*

1. It is not uncommon to place the number of deaths attributable directly or indirectly to the Taiping uprising at more than 20 million.

2. In 1853, for example, the enthusiasm in English missionary circles over Taiping Christianity encouraged Hudson Taylor (later to become one of the most influential missionaries in the nineteenth century) to break off his medical studies and depart posthaste for China (Dr. and Mrs. Howard Taylor, *Hudson Taylor*, 180–84). On the evolving Western Protestant response to Taiping Christianity, see Cohen, "Christian Missions," 551.

3. It is worth noting also that, in contrast with the Taiping era, by 1900 the West was in telegraphic contact with China (although not with Beijing during the summer), and this heightened the sense of immediacy surrounding events there.

4. In my reconstruction of the history of the Boxers in this chapter, I have relied to a greater extent than elsewhere on secondary sources. My indebtedness, especially with respect to the Shandong phase of the story, to Joseph Esherick's path-breaking study will be obvious to everyone who has read it. In recapitulating this phase, I have also been much influenced (as was Esherick) by the basic plotting of the story found in the oral history materials gathered (and partly published in 1980) by Lu Yao and other historians at Shandong University. Apart from my main purpose, already indicated, of providing an example of how a historian approaches the past, the ancillary purposes of this chapter are to supply a brief but reliable account of the Boxer episode—something not now available in English—and to advance a few interpretations that differ somewhat both from Esherick's and from those found in a good deal of the scholarship that has come out of China. See Esherick, *Origins*; SYDZX.

5. I follow Esherick's translation of "Yihe." It has traditionally been rendered "Righteous and Harmonious" or "Righteous Harmony" in English-language writing on the Boxers (see, for example, Tan, *Boxer Catastrophe*, 36–37; Purcell, *Boxer Uprising*, 163). Esherick (*Origins*, 154–55) argues persuasively that the real meaning of "Yihe" is to join together to uphold the cause of righteousness. The same point was (as Esherick notes) made at the time by the British minister to China, Sir Claude MacDonald. "The idea underlying the name," MacDonald observed, "is that the members of the Society will unite to uphold the cause of righteousness,

304   if necessary by force." See his dispatch to Salisbury, Jan. 31, 1900, in PP:1900, 13. Lu Yao and Cheng Xiao advance a similar interpretation in their *Yihetuan yundong*, 53.

    6. Esherick, *Origins*, 19.

    7. For the distinction between protective and predatory collective violence as alternative responses to environments marked by scarcity, see Perry, *Rebels*.

    8. See, in particular, Wu Mengzhou (80), Cao county, Mar. 1960, SYDZX, 19–20; Li Zhaoxiang (79), Cao county, Mar. 1960, ibid., 20; Cai Jingxun (82), Shan county, Mar. 1960, ibid., 20–21; Su Yuzhang (76), Shan county, Mar. 1960, ibid., 22. In this and other references to oral history materials, the figure in parentheses indicates the age of the respondent.

    9. For one of the more extended accounts of such gatherings, see Chen Laohan (80), Shan county, Mar. 1960, SYDZX, 11.

    10. See Chen Zhenjiang and Cheng Xiao, *Yihetuan wenxian*, 6, 138–40; Naquin, *Millenarian Rebellion*, 30–31; Esherick, *Origins*, 55, 104–109.

    11. See Cohen, *China and Christianity*.

    12. Su Yuzhang (76), Shan county, Mar. 1960, SYDZX, 22. Su gives GX 20 or 1894 as the date of the incident; Esherick (*Origins*, 113) says it should be 1895.

    13. See Su Guifang (83), Dangshan county (Jiangsu), Mar. 1960, SYDZX, 25–27, for an especially long account of the factors contributing to the dispute.

    14. Popular recollections (probably exaggerated in some respects) of the outrageous behavior of the Christian community in Juye at the time (all gathered from interviews with Juye residents in 1960) are in Li Ruitang (78), SYDZX, 34; Yao Liangtong and Yao Laicheng, ibid.; Zhao Xianming, ibid., 34–35; Zhang Peijing, ibid., 35; Yuan Fengyun (73), ibid.; Liu Mide (70), ibid.; Xu Titang, ibid., 35–36; Li Wenkui (78), ibid., 36; Li Xinling (68), ibid.

    15. The classic treatment of the German sphere is John E. Schrecker, *Imperialism*. According to Schrecker (33), when Kaiser Wilhelm first heard about the Juye murders, a few days after their occurrence, he reacted euphorically, seeing the incident as a "splendid opportunity" to realize Germany's ambitions in Shandong.

    16. Esherick, *Origins*, 123.

    17. I differ slightly from Esherick on this point. I would certainly agree with him (*Origins*, 134–35) that the meaning of the punishment of Li Bingheng was not lost on the local authorities of Shandong and was apt to have an immediate effect on their treatment of Christian communities in their jurisdictions. I would also agree (ibid., 152) that the impact of Li's punishment was likely to be felt, even by ordinary Chinese, in an isolated town like Liyuantun (in northwestern Shandong), in which conflict between Christians and non-Christians had festered for decades (to be discussed below). I am less sanguine than he appears to be about the response of "the average villager" of the western part of the province overall (133). It is also worth pointing out that, despite the terms of the Juye settlement, Li Bingheng, not long after his removal from the Shandong governorship, was appointed to other high posts (Tan, *Boxer Catastrophe*, 104).

    18. The Guan county events are dealt with in Esherick, ch. 6. See also Lu Yao, "Guanxian Liyuantun jiaoan," 77–90, and Lu Yao's earlier article, "Lun Yihetuan de zuzhi yuanliu," 65–97. Both of Lu Yao's articles are reprinted with minor revisions in Lu Yao and Cheng Xiao, *Yihetuan yundong*. The second piece, which is

somewhat broader in scope, has also appeared in a translation by K. C. Chen and David D. Buck, entitled "The Origins of the Boxers."

19. This is the date given in Lu Yao, "Guanxian Liyuantun jiaoan," 82; Esherick (*Origins*, 151) is less precise.

20. Esherick (*Origins*, 151), relying mainly on the oral history account of Guo Dongchen (80), who had been Zhao Sanduo's secretary, asserts that Zhao initially was reluctant to go to the aid of the Eighteen Chiefs but was eventually persuaded by his disciples. (See especially Guo's testimony in SYDZX, 269. Elsewhere, it is worth noting, Esherick strongly contests the reliability of Guo's assertions; see Esherick, *Origins*, 376n57.) Lu Jingqi, relying mainly on Wang Yuntai's unpublished account of Zhao Sanduo's activities, maintains that, after some initial hesitation, Zhao, responding to repeated requests from Yan Shuqin, decided in favor of going to the aid of the Eighteen Chiefs. Other Plum Flower leaders, however, demurred, and it was in these circumstances that Zhao, to preserve the reputation of the Plum Flower Boxers, created a splinter group with a new name, into which he absorbed those Plum Flower Boxers who wanted to take part in the anti-Christian activities in Liyuantun. The name of the new group was Yihequan or "Boxers United in Righteousness." See Lu Jingqi, "Zhao Sanduo Yan Shuqin," 211.

21. The various dates given by different scholars for the adoption of the new name are discussed in Lu Yao and Cheng Xiao, *Yihetuan yundong*, 49–53; they themselves argue persuasively for the early 1898 date as the correct one (see also Esherick, *Origins*, 136). Esherick (153–54, 162) maintains that Zhao was *forced* to adopt the new name; Lu Jingqi, 211, suggests that the change was more voluntary in nature (see n. 20 above).

22. As part of his argument in favor of this strategy, Zhang claimed in a memorial of June 30 that the Boxers United in Righteousness were derived from a militia of the same name that had existed in the middle of the century. Esherick argues (*Origins*, 160), with cogency, that this was a fabrication on Zhang's part. It became, nevertheless, the basis for the thesis, first advanced by George Steiger and then by Dai Xuanzhi, that the Boxers of 1899–1900 had originated in government-sponsored militia. This thesis has been convincingly demolished, in a number of his writings, by Lu Yao. Steiger, *China and the Occident*, 128–46; Dai Xuanzhi, *Yihetuan yanjiu*, 5–19, esp. 10–11; Lu Yao, "Zuzhi yuanliu," 82–87; Lu Yao and Cheng Xiao, *Yihetuan yundong*, 54–63; Lu Yao, ed., *Qiyuan*, 118–36.

23. For a convenient province-by-province chart of "church cases" in all of North China between 1896 and 1899, see Lu Yao and Cheng Xiao, *Yihetuan yundong*, 82–84.

24. Esherick, *Origins*, 187.

25. See SYDZX, 120–31; Esherick, *Origins*, 219–22. Esherick acknowledges the contribution of a debased version of the White Lotus religion to the popular culture of northwestern Shandong, out of which (in his view) the Spirit Boxers emerged. But he forcefully rejects any organizational link between the Spirit Boxers and the White Lotus sect. Lu Yao and Cheng Xiao (*Yihetuan yundong*, 101–18), although clearly distancing themselves from the Lao Naixuan view that the Yihe Boxers of the late nineteenth century were identical with the Yihe Boxers of the late eighteenth century, differ from Esherick in seeing the Spirit Boxers/Yihe Boxers as emerging centrally out of the White Lotus tradition.

26. For additional details, see Esherick, *Origins*, 177–81.

27. Sometimes local officials went a good bit farther than this. In the fourth or fifth month of GX 25 (May 10–July 7, 1899), a large meeting was held at Zhangguantun in Chiping to mark the victory of the Boxers in a dispute with local Christians. The meeting, accompanied by an opera performance (which the Christians were required to put on to mark the settlement), lasted for four days and was attended by several thousand persons. The magistrate of Chiping, Yu Xian (not the same as the Yuxian who was governor), who was sympathetic to the Spirit Boxers, attended the gathering personally. With this kind of encouragement, boxing grounds sprang up all over the county, and every village was reported to have students of Spirit Boxing. SYDZX, 81, 143–46; Esherick, *Origins*, 229.

28. See, especially, Esherick, *Origins*, 226–29.

29. Elvin, "Mandarins," 118. Elvin, noting that in addition to the refugees from the great flood of late summer 1898 there were institutionalized seasonal migrations from the flooded river plain, concludes (ibid.) that "the contribution made by refugees to anti-Christian violence should not be overestimated."

30. Esherick, *Origins*, 254; also 253.

31. This slogan, although first used (in slightly different form) in the context of the Boxer movement in Guan county in fall 1898, was not an original creation of the Boxers. In one or another variation—for example, *bao-Qing* ("protect the Qing") or *shun-Qing* ("follow [or submit to] the Qing"), preceding *mieyang*—it appeared at about the same time in connection with anti-Christian activities in Hubei and in Dazu county, Sichuan. Liao Yizhong, Li Dezheng, and Zhang Xuanru, *Yihetuan*, 88; Kobayashi Kazumi, "Minshū shisō," 251, 253. Kobayashi (ibid., 250–56) has a detailed discussion of the evolution of this most famous of Boxer slogans, arguing that the word "Qing" referred not to the reigning dynasty but to China in general; for a somewhat different interpretation, which links successive changes in the first part of the slogan—from *shun-Qing* to *bao-Qing*, *zhu-Qing* ("help the Qing"), or *xing-Qing*, to *fu-Qing*, and finally to *sao-Qing* ("sweep away the Qing")—to the developing attitude of the Boxers toward the state power, see Satō Kimihiko [Zuoteng Gongyan], "Quanliguan," 895–900.

32. Esherick, *Origins*, 256.

33. A detailed table of Boxer attacks on Christians in Shandong, covering the period from May 1899 to Jan. 1900, is in ibid., 259–63.

34. This argument is advanced in Cheng Xiao, "Minsu xinyang," 296–301. Cheng Xiao's analysis is presented more fully in ch. 3.

35. Weller, *Resistance*, 84. On the political ramifications of spirit possession in the context of mass movements, I have found much stimulation in Weller's work, in particular his analysis of the Guangxi phase of the Taiping movement. In addition to ibid., 69–85, see his "Popular Tradition, State Control, and Taiping Christianity," 183–206. An interpretation similar to Weller's, but applied specifically to the Boxers, is in Kobayashi Kazumi ("Minshū shisō," 244–45). Kobayashi makes a special point of the fact that the Boxers, unlike the Taipings, had (and were possessed by) a plurality of gods, each with independent authority, with the result that they were unable to generate either charismatic leadership or a strong military/administrative organization.

36. Liao Yizhong, Li Dezheng, and Zhang Xuanru, *Yihetuan*, 91–101. The harsh policies Yuan pursued against the Boxers in the early months of 1900 are detailed on pp. 95–96. Popular hatred toward him was reflected in the following jingle: "After we've killed the bastard Yuan, it'll be easier for us to get on" ("Shale Yuan yuandan, women hao chifan") (ibid., 101). The murder of Brooks was not premeditated and may not even have directly involved Boxers. Some sources give the date of his death as December 30. For a possible basis for the confusion and an attempt to dispel it, see Purcell, *Boxer Uprising*, 290–91, 325.

37. Zhili was in 1900 the only part of China (except for Manchuria) with completed railway lines: the Beijing-Tianjin line, the Beijing-Baoding line, and a line extending from Tianjin northeastward through Tangshan.

38. It is impossible to get precise figures organized by province and year. In 1896, according to Latourette, the Jesuits in southeastern Zhili (Xian county) had a native following of 43,736, and the Lazarists (who had jurisdiction over the rest of the province), six years earlier, a Christian community under them numbering about 62,000. MacGillivray gives an aggregate count for the entire province for 1905 of over 197,000, but given the dramatic increase in the Catholic population in Zhili in the years immediately following the suppression of the Boxers, we may suppose the totals for 1900 to have been well below this figure. Protestant numbers at any point in time were far lower than Catholic and did not substantially alter the overall picture. (As of 1918–1921, according to Stauffer, the total Protestant community in Zhili was just over 22,000, as compared to a Catholic population in the province of more than 578,000.) Latourette, *Christian Missions*, 319, 323, 537–38; MacGillivray, ed., *Protestant Missions*, 675; Stauffer, ed., *Christian Occupation*, 63.

39. Liao Yizhong, Li Dezheng, and Zhang Xuanru, *Yihetuan*, 109. On the establishment of boxing grounds in southeastern Zhili near the Shandong border, see HJZH, 161–68 (Jingzhou and Fucheng), 183–86 (Zaoqiang), 187, 190 (Hengshui), 192 (Ji), 192–94 (Wuyi).

40. Typical was the observation of the missionary Charles A. Killie (American Presbyterian North) from Sanhe county (35 miles east of Beijing) in mid-May: The Boxer movement "is spreading like wildfire all over this district. Where two months ago it was practically unknown, today there are scores of active societies" (letter, May 16, 1900, in *FRUS*, 131). For a detailed account of the types and spatial distribution of altars and boxing grounds in the Tianjin area, based mainly on oral history materials, see Nakamura Tatsuo [Zhongcun Daxiong], "Qingmo Tianjin," 263–83, esp. 272–83.

41. Although not reflected in contemporary written documentation, oral history materials indicate that the other trigrams were also represented in the Tianjin area, the *li* trigram being the most common (after the *kan* and *qian* trigrams); TDYYDB, 35. For a reference to the numerous *li* trigram altars established in Jinghai county, see Shen Desheng (80), Jinghai county, Senior Brother-Disciple, TDYYDB, 118–19. See also Liao Yizhong, Li Dezheng, and Zhang Xuanru, *Yihetuan*, 40–41. There were also *li* trigram units in the southern part of Zhili. Men Wentun (85), Fucheng county, Feb. 1966, HJZH, 168.

42. For a sampling of such notices, see Chen Zhenjiang and Cheng Xiao, *Yihetuan wenxian*, 73–81, 85–91, 94–110, 114–24, 129–33, 171. In a more explicitly religious context, one might, with Susan Naquin (*Millenarian Rebellion*, 216),

308   translate *zhenzhu* "true master." The references to *zhenzhu* in the notices circulated under the Boxer name in 1900 generally have strongly antidynastic connotations, the term *zhenzhu* being used to refer to the authentic sovereign, in contrast
with the current ruler of the Qing, who is by implication a false ruler.

43. Some of the most sophisticated arguments advanced in support of a
Boxer–White Lotus link are in Cheng Xiao, "Minjian zongjiao," 147–63. Cheng
stresses the antidynastic implications of the connection and contends that, given
the danger of being openly identified with the illegal White Lotus sect, the absence
in Boxer posters of reference to such characteristic White Lotus ideas as the Eternal
Venerable Mother was very likely deliberate.

44. See, for example, Sawara Tokusuke and Ouyin, *Quanshi*, 250; TDYYDB, 35;
Doar, "The Boxers," 106–107. *Li* trigram Boxers also wore red (TDYYDB, 35), as did
of course the Boxers' female associates, the Red Lanterns. A Chinese refugee from
Beijing in the summer of 1900 described the shifts in Boxer dress as he made his
way south. In addition to red and yellow, some Boxers wore black turbans, others
black-and-white or blue-and-white spotted ones. *NCH*, Aug. 15, 1900, p. 356.

45. Sometimes, also, a few small villages would join forces to establish a boxing
ground in one of them. See Guo Xiuxing (80) and Guo Kuizhang (75), Fucheng
county, Feb. 1966, HJZH, 163–64.

46. Zhang Jincai (83), a former Boxer from Gaojia village in the western suburbs of Tianjin, states that at the *wen* boxing ground in the village, fighting skills
were also practiced (TDYYDB, 122). But in another instance it was alleged that Boxers
attached to the *wen* altar did not take part in combat (ibid., 153; see also ibid.,
125–26, 144). One of four Boxer altars in Zhuozhou, near the capital, was a *wen* unit
affiliated with the *zhen* trigram; its members, who were said to be well-to-do and literate, handled the preparation of documents for the military units. Xin Hanzhang
(85), Zhuozhou, HDYYDJ, Dec. 24, 1973, 005:No. 7. For examples of the *wen-wu* distinction in southern Zhili, see Sun Lianjia (78), Jing county, Feb. 1966, HJZH, 169;
Wang Laozhi (86), Hengshui county, Feb. 1966, ibid., 187. The Red Spears in the
twentieth century, whom Tai Hsüan-chih sees as coming directly out of the Boxer
tradition, also were organized into military (*wu*) and civil (*wen*) divisions. Tai
Hsüan-chih, *Red Spears*, 33.

47. But also sometimes because he was older or literate or a large landowner or
possessed some other trait traditionally conferring prestige in the villages of North
China. See, for example, Yuan Fushun (80), Fucheng county, Feb. 1966, HJZH, 164;
Jing county Boxer movement historical materials, ibid.; Wang Lianyuan (82) and
Wang Daliang (75), Fucheng county, Feb. 1966, ibid., 166; Han Lianbi (79), Jing
county, Feb. 1966, ibid.; Sun Lianjia (78), Jing county, Feb. 1966, ibid., 167; Niu
Peijun (54), Jing county, ibid., 168; Sun Yusheng (81), Jing county, Feb. 1966, ibid.

48. For the various meanings of "Hongdengzhao," see the last section of ch. 4.
"Hongdengzhao" is rendered "Red Lantern Shining" in Esherick, *Origins*, 136 and
passim; "Red Lantern Illuminating" in "An Eulogy of Red Young Fighters," 12; and
"Red Lanterns" in Chi Pen-yu [Qi Benyu], "Patriotism or National Betrayal?" 10,
and Ono Kazuko, *Chinese Women*, 47–53. "Red Lantern Illuminating" is in some
respects the most meaningful translation, as the Hongdengzhao are often referred
to in White Lotus-influenced notices of the summer of 1900 as "lighting a path" or,
more broadly, "showing the way." I generally use "Red Lanterns" in this book for

the sake of readability. Chinese texts during the Cultural Revolution (when the Red Lanterns were widely mythologized) frequently drop the "zhao" and refer to "daughters of the Red Lantern" (Hongdeng er-nü or nü'er).

49. The most detailed information on Red Lantern organization and operating procedures is found in the Hebei, and especially Tianjin-area, oral history materials. See in particular Zhao Qing (72), Jinghai county, Fourth Sister-Disciple, TDYYDB, 135–36; Li Fengzhi (86), Xiong county, Red Lantern, HDYYDJ, Dec. 27, 1973, 011–14. See also TDYYDB, 40–42, 126, 134, 138, 147, 149, 154, 155; the statements of Liu Qingtang, Sun Yi (91), and Wang Shuchun (70), all of Xiong county, in HDYYDJ, 011–14; and the statement of the former Red Lantern Du Darui (94), of Sun village (county unspecified), in ibid.

50. See ch. 9, n. 11.

51. The Boxer siege and subsequent occupation of Zhuozhou are recounted in Liao Yizhong, Li Dezheng, and Zhang Xuanru, Yihetuan, 129–32.

52. Elvin, "Mandarins," 118.

53. Liu Mengyang, Tianjin quanfei, 8–10.

54. William Hopkyn Rees, letter, June 8, 1899, Chichou [Jizhou], excerpted in Purcell, Boxer Uprising, 287. See also ibid., 285–86.

55. The first mention of the Boxers in the foreign press was in the October 2 issue of the North China Daily News in a news item dated Sept. 21, 1899. Purcell, Boxer Uprising, 242.

56. See, for example, the letters of Luella Miner, sent from Tongzhou on Oct. 31 and Nov. 3, 1899, in LMP, box 2, file 6.

57. Letter of Dec. 16, 1899, excerpted in Purcell, Boxer Uprising, 289.

58. MacDonald to Salisbury, Jan. 5, 1900, in PP:1900, 3.

59. The decree of Jan. 11 (in translation) is in ibid., 9–10; the English text of Britain's communication to the Zongli Yamen, dated Jan. 27, is in ibid., 13–14; see also MacDonald's telegraph to Salisbury, Mar. 10, in ibid., 6. The Chinese texts of the ministers' communications (excepting that of the Italian minister) are in Jiaowu jiaoan dang, 6th ser., vol. 1: 41–44.

60. Purcell, Boxer Uprising, 244; Tan, Boxer Catastrophe, 61–62; Esherick, Origins, 286. The court gave up on the militia idea, which had been proposed by a censor, after strenuous objections from Yulu (not Ronglu, as stated by Purcell) and Yuan Shikai.

61. Purcell, Boxer Uprising, 245; Esherick, Origins, 286.

62. Ai Sheng, Quanfei, 448; Yan Baoqi (68), Gaoluo village, Laishui county, HDYYDJ, Jan. 4, 1974, 005:No. 22.

63. Esherick, Origins, 284; Liao Yizhong, Li Dezheng, and Zhang Xuanru, Yihetuan, 125–29.

64. Liao Yizhong, Li Dezheng, and Zhang Xuanru, ibid., 129–43.

65. Esherick, Origins, 284–85; Tan, Boxer Catastrophe, 55; Liao Yizhong, Li Dezheng, and Zhang Xuanru, Yihetuan, 134.

66. The decision to call up the guards was unanimous. See MacDonald's telegraphic dispatch to Salisbury, May 29, 1900, in PP:1900, 30.

67. Liao Yizhong, Li Dezheng, and Zhang Xuanru, Yihetuan, 135–37. The evidence for popular support of the Boxers is extensive and is taken up in later chapters. This support was explicitly noted in early June by Nie Shicheng and his fellow

310   commander Yang Mushi (ibid., 139–40). Esherick (*Origins*, 288) argues that popular support of the Boxers "was often increased by the inevitable mistreatment of innocent villagers by undisciplined soldiers."

68. Esherick, *Origins*, 287.

69. Purcell, *Boxer Uprising*, 246. "It is at least arguable," Purcell concluded, "that the bringing up of the guards added fuel to the fire of anti-foreignism and thus endangered the very individuals it aimed to protect" (ibid., 248).

70. "Instead of being dispersed," Tan writes (*Boxer Catastrophe*, 69), "the Boxers thus won a victory without shedding blood."

71. MacDonald's wire is quoted in Seymour's telegraphic dispatch to the Admiralty, June 10, 1900, in PP:1900, 45.

72. The battle at Langfang was much celebrated by Chinese mythologizers during the Cultural Revolution. See, for example, Ji Yang, "Dabai Ximo'er."

73. Sixty-two men were killed, 212 wounded. Esherick, *Origins*, 288–89; Purcell, *Boxer Uprising*, 249.

74. As Esherick (*Origins*, 303) points out, the "declaration of war" was a curious document, in that it was issued as an edict, not as a formal communication to the foreign powers, and it did not even explicitly indicate that a state of war existed.

75. Since there was no systematic collection of statistics on either the Catholic or Protestant sides, it is hard to get precise counts even of the numbers of foreigners killed as a direct result of the Boxer rising. (One problem, for example, is that foreigners killed in non-Boxer-related anti-Christian incidents in other parts of China in the summer of 1900 were often included indiscriminately among Boxer-related deaths. The most serious such incident was the killing of eleven missionaries in Zhejiang by a militia-led crowd.) On the Protestant side, two sources are in agreement that, excluding the Zhejiang killings, there were 178 deaths in all. See Arthur H. Smith, *China in Convulsion* 2:648; MacGillivray, ed., *Protestant Missions*, Appendix, vi–viii. Nat Brandt has stated that at least 186 Protestant missionaries (including family members) were killed, the majority of them English and most of them belonging to the China Inland Mission; but he doesn't indicate how he arrived at this total or whether the Zhejiang deaths are included in it (Brandt, *Massacre*, 269).

There is still less consensus on the Catholic side, although most tallies are within a reasonably close range of one another. Brandt (*Massacre*, 269) states that Catholic losses totaled 47; Smith (*China in Convulsion* 2:649) gives a figure of 44 Catholics killed and cautions that this total is probably not complete. A well-known contemporary Catholic source, on the other hand, indicates only 38 foreign Catholics as having died at the Boxers' hands (*Les missions catholiques* 33.1699 [Dec. 27, 1901]: 622–24). Esherick (*Origins*, 304–306) has assembled the most accurate figures overall; I follow him with a few minor exceptions. There is much additional detail in Latourette, *Christian Missions*, 508–19.

76. Tan, *Boxer Catastrophe*, 76–92.

77. A rich trove of Chinese sources on the Boxer movement in Shanxi is Qiao Zhiqiang, comp., *Yihetuan zai Shanxi*.

78. Esherick (*Origins*, 304–305) has the right aggregate figure (179) but is far too precise in his assertion that approximately 130 foreigners were killed in Shanxi and 49 in Inner Mongolia. The trouble derives from the fact that contemporary

Protestant reporting did not clearly distinguish between the two areas (partly, it would appear, because missionaries stationed in northern Shanxi went back and forth across the border at will). Thus both Smith, *China in Convulsion* 2:648, and Broomhall, ed., *Last Letters*, 24, give the figure of 159 Protestant lives lost in Shanxi and "over the Mongolian Border," and E. H. Edwards (*Fire and Sword*, 14–16) presents almost the identical total (158) under the heading "The Martyrs of Shansi" (clearly intended here to include Inner Mongolia).

79. Tan, *Boxer Catastrophe*, 157–61; Latourette, *Christian Missions*, 511, 515–16. On the brutal massacres of Chinese civilians carried out by the Russians in the Amur River area in July, see ch. 9. For a comprehensive documentary record of the Manchurian phase of the Boxer story, see *Dongbei Yihetuan dang'an shiliao*.

80. For a detailed account of the Baoding killings, from the missionary perspective, see Ketler, *Paotingfu*.

81. Sixty-four *zhou* and *xian* in the province experienced harvest shortages in 1900. Li Wenhai et al., eds., *Zaihuang*, 669–70. See also Li Di, *Quan huo ji* 2:440, 447, 450, 452.

82. The containment of the Boxers in Henan appears, at least in part, to have been a result of the influence of Huguang Governor-General Zhang Zhidong, one of the lower Yangzi officials most active in seeking to prevent the southward spread of the uprising. Wu Yingguang, "Dui Henan de yingxiang," 9–10.

83. Tan, *Boxer Catastrophe*, 157–61.

84. See ch. 6.

85. The foreigners estimated that there were over 5,000 Chinese casualties. The number of killed and wounded on the foreign side was 750–775, over 300 of whom were Japanese. Walsh, "Herbert Hoover," 40; Duiker, *Cultures in Collision*, 140; *NCH*, July 25, 1900, p. 168; Robert L. Meade, letter, Tientsin, July 18, 1900.

86. Numerous accounts of the siege of the legations were published by survivors. Many of these are used in Fleming's *The Siege at Peking*.

87. Ibid., 211; Purcell, *Boxer Uprising*, 252. According to the detailed breakdown supplied by U.S. minister Conger, 78 foreigners were killed and 179 wounded. Dispatch to Hay, Sept. 1, 1900, in *FRUS*, 190. Esherick (*Origins*, 306) is in serious error in attributing only 14 foreign casualties to the siege.

88. In a memorial submitted just prior to taking his life, Li was devastating in his critique of the Chinese army's performance. Among other things, he noted that fleeing troops, "as they passed the villages and towns, . . . set fire and plundered, . . . so that there was nothing left for the armies under my command to purchase, with the result that men and horses were exhausted" (translated in Tan, *Boxer Catastrophe*, 110).

89. For a brief but lively account of the march of the relief expedition to the capital and the final lifting of the siege of the legations, see Fleming, *The Siege*, 177–210.

90. Duiker, *Cultures in Collision*, 184–86. A much more detailed account is in Li Dezheng, Su Weizhi, and Liu Tianlu, *Baguo lianjun*, 322–93. On the difficulties von Waldersee had with the forces of the other powers under his command, see Kelly, *Negotiations*, 53–55.

91. Quoted in Fleming, *The Siege*, 253. In more general terms, two weeks after the relief of the siege, U.S. minister Conger reported from Beijing: "There are now

here 30,000 troops. If they remain this winter famine will ensue. Military occupation by so many powers is creating irreparable devastation and bringing terrible punishment upon innocent people." Dispatch to Hay, Aug. 29, 1900, in *FRUS*, 199.

92. Quoted in Kelly, *Negotiations*, 52. The German foreign secretary von Bülow, apprehensive lest the Kaiser's aggressive posturing should send the wrong message to the other powers, tried unsuccessfully to keep the speech from appearing in the press in its entirety (ibid.). On the unusually harsh German response to the Boxer crisis, see also Schrecker, *Imperialism*, 135–37.

93. The most detailed discussions in English of the negotiations leading up to the Boxer Protocol are in Tan, *Boxer Catastrophe*, 129–56, 215–36, and Kelly, *Negotiations*. Tan (*Boxer Catastrophe*, 162–214) also has a comprehensive account of the diplomatic efforts to end the Russian occupation of Manchuria. Although in time the foreign powers remitted their shares of the Boxer indemnity or applied them to purposes beneficial to China, this did little for the immediate fortunes of the Manchus. A full study of the indemnity and subsequent remissions is in Wang Shuhuai, *Gengzi peikuan*.

94. This point is made by Prasenjit Duara in his *Culture, Power, and the State*, 2, 58.

PART 2 / Prologue: The Experienced Past

1. Barnes, *Flaubert's Parrot*, 38; see also 90.

2. Trachtenberg, " 'Bullets Tore Holes in the Water,' " *NYT*, June 6, 1994, A15.

3. The quoted phrase is from Mrs. Chauncey Goodrich, "Besieged," 52. For one of the more thoughtful of the many published accounts of the siege, see Allen, *Siege*. The best manuscript account I have seen is Luella Miner's journal, in LMP, box 1, file 1.

4. This is a paraphrase of the words of Leo Hershkowitz, whose thinking on history is summarized in Douglas Martin, "A 'Bum' Gleans the Discarded to Find History," *NYT*, July 28, 1990, 23.

5. The "life experiences" of the ethnographer, Renato Rosaldo writes, "both enable and inhibit particular kinds of insight." In his own work with the Ilongot people of northern Luzon in the Philippines, Rosaldo was initially unequipped, in terms of his own experience, to imagine the rage accompanying the bereavement of Ilongot men and the particular means (the killing of a fellow human being and the severing and tossing away of the victim's head) by which this rage was vented. Such empathic understanding came only with the accidental death of his wife during field research. Rosaldo, "Introduction," 1–21 (esp. 19).

6. Fussell, *The Great War*, ch. 2.

7. Goodrich, "Besieged," is quite good on this.

8. Bärbel Bohley, in an interview of 1992. *NYT*, Aug. 12, 1992, A4.

9. Davies, *World of Wonders*, 141.

10. Boorstin, "The Historian," 29.

11. Which, unfortunately for Buckner's place in history, Boston lost. At a video taping at Shea Stadium in January 1988, TV crew members, during breaks, "peered down at the snow-filled seats and pointed to where they had been when Mookie Wilson's grounder slithered through Bill Buckner's legs, now a moment in history,

like Pearl Harbor, Bobby Thomson's homer and the death of Elvis." *NYT*, Jan. 17,
1988, S3.

12. Burns, "How Should History Be Taught?" *NYT*, Nov. 22, 1986, 31. The changeability of the past in consequence of unforeseen future occurrences is framed in philosophical language by David Carr (29, 173).

13. Boyer and Nissenbaum, *Salem Possessed*, 25–30. The authors note that, even at the time, the same exact behavior could be defined as satanic possession or spiritual awakening. In the summer of 1692 a Boston servant girl, Mercy Short, soon after running an errand that took her to the jail where many of the Salem witches happened to be incarcerated while awaiting trial, began to exhibit the bizarre symptoms that had by then come to be taken as proof of bewitchment. Mercy's minister, Cotton Mather, however, appraised her as one whose soul had been awakened and treated the episode "not as an occasion for securing witchcraft accusations but as an opportunity for the religious edification of the community" (ibid., 25).

14. Hobsbawm, " Introduction," 13.

15. Personal communication, Shen Tong, Spring 1990. Shen reiterated this point in a talk at Harvard University, Oct. 24, 1990. As a participant, he emphasized, he could not have an "umbrella" picture of the Tiananmen events; he could only know what he himself had experienced.

16. Robin Munro, a leading proponent of the view that most of the killing took place elsewhere in the capital, has contended that, inasmuch as Tiananmen Square extends over 100 acres, "no single eyewitness could hope to encompass the complex and confusing sequence of events that unfolded there on the night of June 3–4." Munro, "Remembering," 401.

17. Journal, June 26, 1900, in LMP, box 1, file 1.

18. Christopher Martin, *The Boxer Rebellion*; Purcell, *The Boxer Uprising*; Tan, *The Boxer Catastrophe*. The Boxer uprising is labeled a "fiasco" in *Turmoil at Tiananmen*, 25.

19. Weber, "History Is What Historians Do," 13.

20. Madsen, *Morality and Power*, 26.

21. I exclude from this statement, of course, those villagers who, after fleeing China, became involved in the research of Madsen and his associates in Hong Kong. Such persons were no longer experiencers. They had, to a greater or lesser extent, become "historians," in the sense that their primary activity had become to assist in a process of inquiry aimed at elucidating the original experience. See, in particular, Madsen's discussion of the contributions of Ao Meihua, an interviewee who became his research assistant (ibid., xi–xv).

22. The distinction between biographical (or in this case autobiographical) consciousness and historical consciousness was made by Shen Tong in reference to his participation in the demonstrations in Beijing in the spring of 1989. Shen observed that, for him, there were "two Tiananmen Squares," the one he personally experienced, which was full of confusion and excitement and remained an ongoing part of his consciousness, and the one created by the Western media, which quickly faded from view after the June 4 crackdown. Likening his experience to a "voyage" or "journey," Shen noted that although Tiananmen as an *event* was "over," his own sense of involvement in the movement that resulted in it began before the spring

314   of 1989 and continued after it. Tiananmen, for Shen Tong, was clearly a "paradigmatic moment." Talk, Harvard University, Oct. 24, 1990.

23. Eva Jane Price, *China Journal*, 237.

24. *NYT*, Jan. 19, 1991, 10; Mar. 2, 1991, 1; Mar. 10, 1991, E14. "It was," asserted an
editorial in the *Times*, "as if two wars, not just one, ended with the American-led
coalition's quick and decisive victory over Iraq" (*NYT*, Mar. 10, 1991, E14).

25. Myerhoff, *Number Our Days*, 222.

2. Drought and the Foreign Presence

1. Liu Zhenguo (80), Qihe county, Dec. 1965, SYDZX, 86; Yu Longxing (80),
Chiping county, Mar. 1960, ibid., 88; Zhang Kexin (81), Gaotang county, Mar.
1960, ibid., 89–90; Zhang Xunxiu (80), Chiping county, Feb. 1960, ibid., 91–92. See
also Yu Xunchen (74), Chiping county, Mar. 1960, ibid., 88; Wang Yumei (78),
Chiping county, Mar. 1960, ibid., 89; Cao Shengrui (83), Chiping county, Jan.
1966, ibid., 90; Zhao Hongzhu (75), Chiping county, Feb. 1960, ibid., 91; Chen
Tingxian (93), Gaotang county, Feb. 1966, ibid., 92.

2. Esherick, *Origins*, 177; the quotation, from *North-China Herald* missionary
correspondents, is in ibid.

3. Report of Pu Liang, GX 25/1/7 (Feb. 16, 1899), as quoted in Lin Dunkui,
"Shehui zaihuang," 215–16. Conditions were especially bad, according to Pu, in the
flooded areas south of the river.

4. Elvin, "Mandarins," 118.

5. Lin Dunkui, "Shehui zaihuang," 214–15.

6. In his account of the drought-induced famine that took place in the central
Shaanxi plain (Guanzhong) in 1928–1931, Eduard Vermeer (*Economic Development*, 30) elaborates on the meaning and critical importance of timeliness. A different illustration of the importance of timely rainfall is afforded by the Ethiopian
experience, which suggests that drought can bring human disaster not only to normally arid or marginal agriculture areas but also to areas where rainfall is relatively
abundant and cultivation normally successful (see Wetherell, Holt, and Richards,
"Drought in the Sahel," 139). In parts of East Africa, where as in China heavy rains
and flooding often follow in the wake of drought, Somali prayers expressly beseech
God to send rain that will bring relief from drought without causing damage and
devastation by flooding. See Baker, "Study of Drought," 76.

7. See Li Wenhai et al., eds., *Zaihuang*, 650–75; *Zhongguo jin wubainian hanlao*, 220–21, 331–32.

8. Bohr, *Famine in China*, xv–xvi, 17, 26. See also He Hanwei, *Huabei de da
hanzai*.

9. The horror of the famine of the 1870s in Shandong and Shanxi is graphically
portrayed in Bohr, *Famine in China*, 13–26. On the historical and psychological
significance of the fact that famines were, in most societies, recurrent events,
David Arnold writes: "It was the terror of their possible, even probable, return that
kept them alive in myth and memory, made cultivators anxiously scan the heavens before planting or harvesting or sleep uneasily when the air was rife with
rumours of impending war or drought" (*Famine*, 16). Presumably playing on popular memory of the 1870s, English Baptist missionary George B. Farthing is
alleged to have dispersed a Taiyuan crowd in the summer of 1900 by reminding

them of the many lives foreigners had saved during earlier "famine times" (Edwards, *Fire and Sword*, 297).

10. Some of the differences are explored suggestively in Esherick, *Origins*, 281–82.

11. This is not to say that, even in the context of a major drought covering a large area, there will not be isolated, localized interruptions of the drought pattern. Heavy rains fell in early April 1900 along the Zhili-Shandong border (Esherick, *Origins*, 281). A missionary in Sanhe county, some 35 miles east of Beijing, reported in mid-May that the rains of a week before in the capital "have not reached this part of the country" (Charles A. Killie, letter, May 16, 1900, in FRUS, 131). The rains Killie referred to, which occurred elsewhere in Zhili as well, did not in general last long enough to break the drought pattern in the province (NCH, May 30, 1900, p. 968). Thus, in the Tianjin region, the *North-China Herald's* correspondent reported "an hour or two of fairly heavy rain" on June 7 (ibid., June 20, 1900, p. 1113), but by the end of the month was forced to conclude: "There has been no rain, and there are no crops. There is every prospect of pestilence and famine" (ibid., July 11, 1900, p. 52).

Later in the summer, on the other hand, although the situation remained unchanged in parts of North and Northwest China (most dramatically, in Shanxi and Shaanxi), in other parts, including the central Zhili area, there were definite signs that the drought was beginning to lift: *TYJ*, 152; Liu Mengyang, *Tianjin quanfei*, 27–28; Zhongfang Shi, *Gengzi jishi*, 30; Gao Nan, *Riji*, 149–50; Hua Xuelan, *Riji*, 108–109; Luella Miner, journal, Beijing, June 19 and July 4, 1900, in LMP, box 1, file 1.

12. *Famine*, 12–13. Arnold observes that sometimes, as in Portugal in 1521, in England in 1594–1596, in Russia in 1601–1603, or in Ireland in 1846–1851, famines were so severe and protracted that they did not need specific names and came to be known simply as "*the* Famine" or "the Great Hunger" (ibid., 13). An especially dramatic instance of this phenomenon was supplied by the sociologist Gilberto Freyre, who wrote (in 1948) that "when a Brazilian hears one speak of 'drought' . . . , he thinks immediately of Ceará [the area of northeastern Brazil where in 1877 an estimated 500,000 people perished from hunger and disease] and '77. One place and one date." Quoted in ibid., 13–14.

13. Dando, *Geography*, 11.

14. NYT, May 5, 1991, sec. 8, p. 5S. When, after many years of disappointment, the Brazilian soccer team reached the semifinals of the 1994 World Cup, its coach was referred to as "a rainmaker on the verge of ending Brazil's 24-year title drought" (ibid., July 12, 1994, B7).

15. A law partner, for example, who brings in a lot of business (NYT, Oct. 22, 1993, B7). In his denial that he would become a rainmaker for the Manhattan law firm he had recently joined, former New York Governor Mario Cuomo elaborated on the meaning of the term: "I'm not good as a rainmaker, if you mean by a rainmaker somebody whose dazzling wit, charm and social niceties would lure people into the law firm." "However," he added in an aside, ". . . my reputation is such that we will gain a little precipitation even without my incantations." NYT, Feb. 8, 1995, B5.

16. Dando, *Geography*, 11. G. B. Silberbauer's research on the G/wi-speaking hunter-gatherers of Botswana led him to conclude that "despite the many attempts

316   to establish objective criteria, drought is essentially a subjectively defined phenomenon perceived by its sufferer in terms of his disappointed expectations of rain, the degree of discomfort or danger he experiences, and, sometimes, his dissonant cognition of his circumstances." Silberbauer, "Social Hibernation," 112.

17. Cooke, "Problem of Drought," 7.

18. And the weather in particular. "Uncertainty" is a frequently encountered term in climatological writing. See, for example, two books by W. J. Maunder: *The Uncertainty Business: Risks and Opportunities in Weather and Climate* and *The Human Impact of Climate Uncertainty: Weather Information, Economic Planning, and Business Management.*

19. Ramage, *Great Indian Drought*, 2–4.

20. The same is true in parts of Nigeria, where prolonged drought is sometimes attributed to faults committed by a chief or more generally by the government (Bernus, "Éleveurs," 146).

21. Ocko, "Righting Wrongs," 57, 154; see also 138–39, 174. In both of these cases, it is worth noting, the injustice was suffered by women. Since women are identified with *yin* (the female principle), which in turn is associated with wetness, it is logical for drought to result when women are treated unfairly. In the past, female stones ("*yin*-stones") were beaten with whips to induce rain in time of drought. Eberhard, *Dictionary*, 323.

One of the stories told about the daughter of the Lin family who became the goddess Mazu (Tianhou) is that, in the course of a drought-related famine in Putian county, Fujian, in the tenth century, the Putian magistrate announced that a virtuous person was needed to perform rain-inducing ceremonies. Lin was called on and, almost immediately after her performance of the ceremonies, a heavy rain fell. Rubinstein, "Revival of the Mazu Cult," 91.

According to the sixteenth-century Arab traveler Ali Akbar, every Chinese city had special quarters for prostitutes who were the wives and daughters of high officials who had been executed for serious crimes. One of the special duties of these women was to pray for rain in time of drought. Since, if their prayers did not meet with success, they were liable to be incarcerated and beheaded, it was customary for them, before going to the local temple to carry out their rain prayers, to bid farewell to their loved ones and make known their last wishes. Aliakebaer [Ali Akbar], *Jixing*, 107–11. I am grateful to Ellen Widmer for calling this source to my attention.

22. Liu Dapeng, *Riji*, GX 27/2/28 (Apr. 16, 1901), 13–14.

23. The text of the poem is in Chen Zhenjiang and Cheng Xiao, *Yihetuan wenxian*, 59–61.

24. Prah, "Aspects of Drought," 87.

25. Hitchcock, "Response to Drought," 91–92, 96.

26. Ramage, *Great Indian Drought*, 3.

27. Aaron Smith, *Some temporal advantages . . .* ; Prince, *Natural and moral government*.

28. Boston radio station WEEI, June 19–20, 1988. The general consensus of the onlookers in Ohio, according to the radio announcer (Charles Osgood), was to believe in rather than doubt the potential efficacy of the rainmaking ceremony.

29. Pomeranz, "Water to Iron," 62–99. For an early Western description of the Handan rain shrine, see Arthur H. Smith, *Village Life*, 170.

30. Bohr, *Famine in China*, 33–34.

31. The killing of animals was, from the standpoint of Buddhism, a highly polluting act and provoked the anger of the gods. It was customary, therefore, in time of drought, for such killing to be prohibited.

32. See, for example, the anonymous work *Yu nan riji*, 161; another anonymous work *Yong rao lu*, 247; Liu Mengyang, *Tianjin quanfei*, 8; report of Guantao county (Shandong) magistrate, GX 26/6/20 (July 16, 1900), in *Shandong Yihetuan anjuan, shang*, 435; Courtenay H. Fenn, "A Remarkable Disaster," *The Evangelist*, in Mrs. S. P. Fenn, comp., "Peking Siege-Book," 15–16. Olivia Ogren (of the China Inland Mission) reported that the local official of Yongning, Shanxi, where she and her husband were stationed, was "so eager . . . to obtain rain that, finding his prayers in the temple had failed, he even secretly asked my husband how to pray to the God of Heaven and Earth" ("Conflict of Sufferings," 65; see also Forsyth, comp. and ed., *China Martyrs*, 148–50). In the middle and lower Yangzi provinces (especially Hubei), where drought was also a problem in the summer of 1900, it was much the same, prayers for rain being offered up by the people and officials, fasts being proclaimed, and bans placed on the slaughter and sale of livestock. See *NCH*, June 13, 1900, p. 1063 (Yichang, Hubei); June 27, 1900, p. 1155 (Suizhou, Hubei); July 18, 1900, p. 120 (Yichang), p. 141 (Liangjiang).

33. *NYT*, Dec. 8, 1990, A1, A10. The same themes ("many have grown anxious about what the next year may bring") were highlighted in *NYT*, Dec. 16, 1990, 26.

34. Pertinent here is David Arnold's observation that "the human consequences of a cyclone in Bangladesh are immeasurably greater than those of a cyclone pounding the Florida coast—not because the nature of the cyclone is inherently different but because some societies are infinitely more vulnerable to the effects of famine and natural disaster than others" (*Famine*, 7). A telling illustration of Arnold's point was the situation in California, Arizona, and Nevada, as these states in December 1990 prepared for their fifth consecutive dry year. In response, citrus farmers were ready to buy water at any cost, while other farmers prepared to switch to crops that used less water and urban residents were faced with severe restrictions on lawn-watering, car-washing, swimming pool use, and home showers. If a comparable drought had occurred in the North China plain at any time in the late imperial era, widespread famine would almost certainly have resulted. See *NYT*, Dec. 25, 1990, 1, 7.

35. The Indian drought ultimately took two million lives, mostly the very young and very old. Ramage, *Great Indian Drought*, 2–4.

36. Letters of Oct. 31 and Nov. 3, 1899, in LMP, box 2, file 6. American minister Edwin H. Conger made essentially the same point (see n. 61 below). See also *NCH*, Feb. 28, 1900, p. 354.

37. Sawara Tokusuke and Ouyin, *Quanshi*, 244; Yuan Chang, memorial of Gengzi 5/22 (June 18, 1900), in *YHT* 4:162; Li Wenhai et al., eds., *Zaihuang*, 668. The connection between the prolonged drought and the spread of contagious disease in the capital was also noted by Mrs. Courtenay Fenn in a letter of May 29, 1900, in Mrs. S. P. Fenn, "Peking Siege-Book," 7 (inset). Tang Yan, a teacher in a private academy in Huaian county (in northwestern Zhili), took the train from Tianjin to Beijing on April 29. The countryside was completely barren, he reported, owing to its not having rained since the previous autumn. When he got

318 to the capital, he added, there were Boxers everywhere. Tang Yan, *Gengzi xixing*, 471. For a graphic description of the impoverished look of the countryside around Beijing, owing to the drought, see Emma Martin, diary, May 26, 1900, 35.

38. Bainbridge, "Besieged," 3–4. Friends of the Beijing official Gao Nan wrote him in early July that sizable numbers of people in Zhili were beginning to experience serious hunger (*egui tai duo*). Gao Nan, *Riji*, GX 26/6/9 (July 5, 1900), 150.

39. Gao Nan, *Riji*, GX 26/5/19 (June 15, 1900), 145.

40. Liu Xizi, *Jin xi biji*, 75.

41. Wang Fengji (79), TDYYDB, 144. "The nine months' drought, with the consequent fears of impending famine," wrote the *North-China Herald's* Tianjin correspondent, ". . . have been of inestimable value to the Boxers in their propaganda. Scarcity of food is so terrible a foe that political sedition is a welcome diversion to many." *NCH*, June 20, 1900, p. 1113; also ibid., p. 1125.

42. Liu Mengyang, *Tianjin quanfei*, 8–10. For a description similar to Liu Mengyang's, see *Tianjin zhengsu*, 961.

43. Corbin, "Shansi Mission," 3.

44. Sawara and Ouyin, *Quanshi*, 244; excerpts from gazetteers in Qiao Zhiqiang, comp., *Yihetuan zai Shanxi*, 135–37, 142–48; Li Wenhai et al., eds., *Zaihuang*, 665–67. Olivia Ogren (CIM) described the situation in Yongning, Shanxi: "The people very quickly turned from fearing to trusting the Boxers. As soon as they came, the crowds of famine sufferers who had before threatened us ceased coming, for they had a new ally to destroy us and allow rain to come again." Cited in Forsyth, comp. and ed., *China Martyrs*, 151.

45. Esherick, *Origins*, 281.

46. TYJ, 152. For other examples of Tianjin-area Boxers returning to farming in the wake of rain, see Liu Mengyang, *Tianjin quanfei*, 28; Yuan Chang, *Riji*, 348.

47. Yu Keyi (78), Juye county, Feb. 1960, SYDZX, 66. See also Yuan Luanyu, Juye county, 1960, ibid., 66–67.

48. Lin Dunkui, "Shehui zaihuang," 220. Chen Zhenjiang also makes a strong case for the critical importance of natural disasters in general, and drought in particular, in the generation and progress of the Boxer movement. See his "Huabei youmin."

49. Bird, Journal entry. In a letter to her brother from Taigu the day before (June 24, 1900), Bird had written: "with the country in this state, what will come if the rains do not come? It seems impossible that it can be peace" (ibid).

50. Letter of July 1, 1900, ibid. See also Bird's letter of July 2, 1900, ibid. On July 11, a fellow Taigu missionary Dwight H. Clapp penned these words in his diary: "The weather still continues very hot and dry; Another good rain would do much to settle matters" (Clapp).

51. Partridge. In a letter of July 14, 1900, Partridge struck similar themes: "it was so dry, and men were starving everywhere." Quoted in Edwards, *Fire and Sword*, 296.

52. Price, *China Journal*, 231; see also 236. Similar observations were made by Price's husband, C. W. Price (diary entry, excerpted in Edwards, *Fire and Sword*, 269).

53. Excerpted in Forsyth, comp. and ed., *China Martyrs*, 148–49; see also her "Conflict of Sufferings," 65–66. See also Broomhall, ed., *Martyred Missionaries*, 18, 77.

54. Quoted in Forsyth, comp. and ed., *China Martyrs*, 367.

55. Letter, Tung Cho [Tongzhou], May 25, 1900.

56. Journal, May 29 and 30, 1900, LMP, box 1, file 1.

57. Journal, June 19, 1900, ibid. After an earlier, but apparently less penetrating, downpour on May 7, Bessie Ewing (ABCFM) in Beijing had made a similar observation: "The 'Boxers' will be busy now [planting their fields], so they wont [sic] have time to bother the Christians" (Ewing, letter of May 11, 1900). See also Ewing's prior letter of Apr. 9, 1900, where she noted that for over a year and a half there had not been enough rain in the Beijing area for farmers to plant their grain (ibid.). For additional commentary by Beijing-area missionaries on the relationship between the drought and the threat to foreigners, see Bessie McCoy, letter, May 28, 1900, in Mrs. S. P. Fenn, "Peking Siege-Book," 1; Courtenay H. Fenn, letter, May 3, 1900, in ibid., 3 (excerpted from *New York Tribune*).

58. Simcox, letter, Apr. 12, 1900, Paotingfu [Baoding], *China Supplement* (Oct. 1900), 279, excerpted toward end of Mrs. S. P. Fenn, "Peking Siege-Book" (n.p.); Pitkin, letter, June 2, 1900, in Sarah Boardman Goodrich, "Journal," June 6, 1900, 6–7; Miner, "Last Rites."

59. From the account of Dr. G. W. Guinness, as excerpted in Forsyth, comp. and ed., *China Martyrs*, 219.

60. Smith, *China in Convulsion* 1:219.

61. Conger to Secretary of State John Hay, May 8, 1900, *FRUS*, 122. Conger had earlier linked the drought to mounting problems (including Boxer-related unrest) in northwestern Shandong. See his dispatch to Hay, Dec. 7, 1899, ibid., 77.

62. MacDonald to Salisbury, May 21, 1900, in PP:1900, p. 105.

63. Bird, journal entry, June 25, 1900; see also Clapp, diary letter, Taigu, Shanxi, July 7 and 15, 1900; Luella Miner, journal, Beijing, June 25, 1900, in LMP, box 1, file 1.

64. Luella Miner, journal, Beijing, June 17, 1900, in LMP, box 1, file 1.

65. Miner, journal, Tongzhou, June 7, 1900, in LMP, box 1, file 1.

66. Miner, journal, Beijing, June 23, 1900, in LMP, box 1, file 1; Clapp, diary letter, Taigu, Shanxi, July 13, 1900; see also Clapp's comment, after voicing his fears for the safety of missionaries elsewhere in Shanxi: "Ah this is serious business for poor China! But in the end [it] will be for the furtherance of the Kingdom of God. Of this I feel sure. I have felt for many years that Satan would stir up a great persecution for China one of these days & it is coming now. It is a time of testing & sifting too" (diary letter, Taigu, Shanxi, July 6, 1900). "Overshadowing every other impression made by the events of the past Summer," wrote Mary Porter Gamewell in the aftermath of the lifting of the siege of the legations, "is the indelible impression that God's hand move[d] through it all. The final result is His will." Gamewell, "History," 64.

67. Sarah Boardman Goodrich, letter, Tung Cho [Tongzhou], May 28, 1900. (I have inserted an apostrophe in the original, which reads "Gods soldiers.") Murray Rubinstein describes the "military cast of mind" as "an inherent element in the mission enterprise." See his "The Wars They Wanted," 271.

68. An exception was Olivia Ogren's assertion, in June 1899, that the people of Yongning, Shanxi, were already suffering from "famine" occasioned by "drought." See text above.

69. *The Boxer Rising*, 9.

70. Esherick, *Origins*, 299. The original may be found in *Yihetuan shiliao, shang*, 18; Chen Zhenjiang and Cheng Xiao, *Yihetuan wenxian*, 34. For two other almost identical notices, see ibid., 30–33; Sawara Tokusuke and Ouyin, *Quanluan*, 112. A shorter version of the text translated by Esherick was circulated orally in the Shandong-Zhili border area. See Zhang Zhizhen (84), Liyuantun, Nangong, Hebei, 1960, SYDZX, 315–16; Chen Zhenjiang and Cheng Xiao, *Yihetuan wenxian*, 31–32.

71. Chen Zhenjiang and Cheng Xiao, ibid., 32. The first jingle circulated initially in Shandong and Zhili and traveled from there to various parts of Henan. Li Di, *Quan huo ji* 2:447; Wu Yingguang, "Dui Henan de yingxiang," 8; "Yihetuan yundong shiqi Henan," 155.

72. Chen Zhenjiang and Cheng Xiao, *Yihetuan wenxian*, 15–16.

73. Chen Zhenjiang and Cheng Xiao, *Yihetuan wenxian*, 18. The text of a very similar notice that was circulated mainly in the Tianjin area is in ibid., 19–20. Sometimes notices taking the form of a direct message from the Jade Emperor were addressed to the Boxers themselves. In one such notice, the original Chinese text of which is no longer extant, the Jade Emperor, after enumerating the multiple sins of the foreign devils (including their nonadherence to China's religious teachings and defamation of the native gods), issues the following instructions: "The will of heaven is that the telegraph wires be first cut, then the railways torn up, and then shall the foreign devils be decapitated. In that day shall the hour of their calamities come. The time for rain to fall is yet afar off, and all on account of the devils." The original of this placard was posted in the western part of Beijing and dated Apr. 29, 1900. The version given here is an English translation that appeared in PP:1900, p. 105; reprinted in Allen, *Siege*, 18–19. A translation back into Chinese, along with explanatory notes, is in Chen Zhenjiang and Cheng Xiao, *Yihetuan wenxian*, 14–17.

74. Chen Zhenjiang and Cheng Xiao, ibid., 49. Another notice directed at Christians was posted in Zhengding prefecture in western Zhili and subsequently made its way to nearby Shanxi. Qiao Zhiqiang, comp., *Yihetuan zai Shanxi*, 3–4.

75. For a sampling, in addition to the ones already cited, see Qiao Zhiqiang, ibid., 1, 4–5; *Shanxi sheng gengzinian jiaonan*, 510; and, especially, Chen Zhenjiang and Cheng Xiao, *Yihetuan wenxian*, 22–23, 26–28, 41–42, 47–48, 49–50, 84. A variation on the logic in the notices discussed here was related by a foreign observer: "The Boxer propagandists proclaimed . . . ['the railways and telegraphs and other hated inventions of the foreign devil'] to be the causes of the long-continued drought. They said that the ponderous locomotives and rumbling trains pressed heavily the head of the Dragon and that his beneficient [*sic*] exhalations were smothered and no clouds could form in the heavens." Bainbridge, "Besieged," 3–4.

76. See, for example, their analysis of a notice circulated in Shanxi (*Yihetuan wenxian*, 47–48). Li Wenhai and Liu Yangdong take a similar position; see their "Shehui xinli fenxi," 4–5.

77. Esherick, *Origins*, 300. He also makes the claim that "popular support for the Boxers was almost universal in the countryside" (289). Roland Allen stated authoritatively that the leaders of the Boxer movement really believed that the northern Chinese drought "was due to the presence of foreigners and to the evil influence of the foreign doctrine" (Allen, *Siege*, 6).

78. Emma Martin, diary, May 15, 1900, 29.

79. This included some of the most careful and astute observers on both sides. Liu Mengyang (*Tianjin quanfei*, 7) felt that only 20 percent of the Chinese population was sufficiently discerning to reject the message of the Boxers; Yuan Chang (*Riji*, 346–47) regarded the support for the Boxers in Zhili, after the shift of the movement's core to that province, as near-universal. For the observations of Robert Hart see ch. 3.

80. Deuteronomy 11:13–21.

81. Both examples are cited in Arnold, *Famine*, 15.

82. Gottlieb, "Menstrual Cosmology," 62–64.

83. Hitchcock, "Response to Drought," 92.

84. Arnold, *Famine*, 15–16. During the disastrous flooding that struck parts of the American Midwest in summer 1993, a Des Moines woman responded to President Clinton's visit to a stricken area as follows: "He can't play with God and nature. He'll do what he can. But this happened because God wanted it." *NYT*, July 15, 1993, B10.

85. Geertz, "Thick Description," 12.

86. Arnold, *Famine*, 77.

87. Cohn, *Pursuit*, 212.

88. This kinship is noted in Elvin, "Mandarins," 121.

89. Dikötter, *Discourse of Race*, esp. ch. 2.

90. On the application of the *Hanjian* label, see Kwong, "T'i-Yung Dichotomy," 264–68.

91. Elvin, "Mandarins," 134*n*71; Entenmann, "Clandestine Catholics," 23.

92. See ch. 9, n. 84. An important exception to this general pattern is Chen Zhenjiang; see n. 48 above.

93. For examples, see ch. 3, n. 65; the Juye incident of November 1, 1897, was reported in some quarters to have been instigated by a former bandit seeking, for reasons of personal revenge, to destroy the career of the Juye magistrate (Esherick, *Origins*, 126, 371*n*9).

94. Boyer and Nissenbaum, *Salem Possessed*, 2.

95. Chalmers Johnson, *Peasant Nationalism*. The controversy is summarized in Paul A. Cohen, *Discovering History*, 169–72.

96. Two very different examples of Cultural Revolution memoir literature are Gao Yuan, *Born Red*, and Yang Jiang, *Six Chapters*. Much of the literary production of British soldiers on the Western Front between 1914 and 1918 is housed in the Imperial War Museum. Fussell made extensive use of it in his marvelous study, *The Great War and Modern Memory*. For Menocchio's testimony before the Inquisition, see Ginzburg, *Cheese*.

97. The main published oral history testimony is in *SYDZX*. See also Lu Yao and Cheng Xiao, *Yihetuan yundong*, 365–85, 393–428; HJZH. There are extensive unpublished oral history transcripts collected by the Shandong University History Department and housed at that institution. On a visit to Nankai University in 1987 I was able to examine and xerox a sizable quantity of unpublished oral history materials gathered by various institutions in that city. These included transcripts of surveys done during the early and mid-1970s in selected counties in Hebei (HDYYDJ) and a lengthy report (accompanied by interview protocols) covering the Tianjin

322   area, based on interviews (done in 1958) with 1,114 individuals (including 123 former Boxers), carried out by the Class of 1956 of Nankai University's History Department, in conjunction with the Tianjin Historical Museum and the Tianjin City Cultural Office. The latter survey report was compiled by the Class of 1956 and distributed in mimeographed form in August 1960 (TDYYDB).

    The limitations of oral history testimony are all, of course, variable. For example, the interviewing conducted in the 1950s in the Tianjin region was not as hampered by the age of the respondents as that done in the early and mid-1970s in a broader area of Hebei; the reliability of the latter interviewing, moreover, was further undermined by the fact that the Cultural Revolution, when a specific and strongly mythologized construction of the Boxer experience was required fare throughout China, was still in progress, inevitably influencing both the questions of the interviewers and the respondents' answers. In a candid conversation of September 5, 1987, with Lu Yao, the prime mover behind the Shandong oral history surveys and chief editor of the published portion of those surveys (SYDZX), Professor Lu readily acknowledged other limitations on the interviewing process: the technology used in the 1960s (when most of the Shandong surveys were done) was quite primitive; students, who did most of the interviewing, did not have tape recorders and therefore had to write very fast, as a consequence of which some of the original transcripts are difficult to decipher. Another obstacle was the language barrier presented by local dialects; sometimes the problems in this regard could be quite serious, as when, for example, interviewers found it impossible to tell whether a peasant respondent was saying Yihe*tuan* or Yihe*quan* and, because the person in question was illiterate, could not ask him (or her) to write the identifying character. For further detail on the procedures followed in the Shandong oral history surveys of the 1960s, see Kwong, "Oral History," 34–37.

    98. Stauffer, ed., *Christian Occupation*, 38. The exact figure given for 1889 is 37,287.

    99. Latourette, *Christian Missions*, 329; Paul A. Cohen, "Christian Missions," 557.

    100. The Protestant missionary body in China more than doubled, going from 1,296 in 1889 to 2,818 in 1900 (Latourette, *Christian Missions*, 606; Wehrle, *Britain*, 12). The increase in Catholic missionaries, less sizable, was from 639 in 1890 to 886 in 1900 (Latourette, *Christian Missions*, 329; Cohen, "Christian Missions," 554).

    101. This was owing in large measure to the dramatic growth of the German Society of the Divine Word, whose numbers increased from four in 1887 to forty-three in 1901. Esherick, *Origins*, 93.

    102. Railway development in Manchuria, partly under Russian auspices, was more extensive and was a prime target of Boxer activity in the summer of 1900. There were no railways in Shanxi. Railway construction in Shandong began in 1899; the first lines were not completed, however, until well after the suppression of the Boxer rising. Schrecker, *Imperialism*, 105–24. Although in the years from 1897 to 1900 China witnessed "the first real surge" of railway construction in its history, as of 1900, in the entire country, there were only 665 miles of track. The United States, by way of comparison, had about 175,000 miles of mainline track as of 1894. Huenemann, *Dragon*, 47, 60, 76.

    103. The latter estimate is Elvin's ("Mandarins," 120). Although Dengzhou (Penglai), on the northern coast of peninsular Shandong and for many years an

important center of American Protestant operations, experienced the "Boxer madness" in the form of rumors and people practicing boxing, no Boxer altar apparently was established in the city and no one was killed. Pruitt, *Daughter of Han*, 151.

104. Elvin, "Mandarins," 120.

105. In Salem, in 1692, a large majority of the total group of accused witches were outsiders, over 80 percent of them living beyond the bounds of Salem Village. Boyer and Nissenbaum, *Salem Possessed*, 190.

106. According to the recollections of Liu Baotong (78), a former Boxer from the area just west of Tianjin: "That year [1900] we all fled from famine [*taohuang*]. When we came back we had to fry up barnyard grass to eat; there were no crops in the fields." TDYYDB, 146. See also Fan (Pan?) Shuchun (74), Jing county, Feb. 1966, HJZH, 176.

107. The drought in Shanxi continued into spring 1901, resulting in widespread starvation. See Hu Sijing, *Lü bei ji*, 524; Liu Dapeng, *Riji*, 11, 13–14, 16. Drought-related famine was even more severe in Shaanxi in the early months of 1901. For a graphic description, see Tang Yan, *Gengzi xixing*, 485; also Hu Sijing, *Lü bei ji*, 527, and Forsyth, comp. and ed., *China Martyrs*, 8.

108. See her *Death Without Weeping*, esp. 128–66.

109. Arnold (*Famine*, 19), commenting on the "horror of famine" in earlier times, points out that "the more protracted and intense the crisis the more the normal order of things collapsed and gave way to all that was abnormal and horrific." Corbin ("Shansi Mission," 3) attributed the radical change in the behavior of the population of Shanxi mainly to the "long drouth": "Though ordinarily so peaceful and inoffensive as to have given a byword to North China, the people of Shansi seemed to have been aroused to demoniacal fury by the Boxer craze of 1900."

3. Mass Spirit Possession

1. Xie Jiagui (86), Chiping county, Dec. 1965, SYDZX, 200 (for additional oral testimony on spirit possession in Shandong, see ibid., 200–203); Sawara Tokusuke and Ouyin, *Quanshi*, 238–39; extract from letter of unnamed county magistrate, Beijing, in ibid., 251 (I have departed slightly from the French translation in Dunstheimer, "Religion et magie," 360–61; for an oral history account of spirit possession by a former Boxer from southern Zhili, see Wang Laozhi [86], Hengshui county, Feb. 1966, HJZH, 185); *Anze xianzhi*, 140; interview with Jia Xianju, Aug. 1959, in Qiao Zhiqiang, comp., *Yihetuan zai Shanxi*, 150.

2. Ch'en described the Boxers as "the most important religious uprising in the world . . . in the present century" ("Nature and Characteristics," 287).

3. See, for example, Li Wenhai and Liu Yangdong, "Shehui xinli fenxi"; Cheng Xiao, "Minjian zongjiao"; Xu Xudian, "Yihetuan yuanliu."

4. According to an elderly informant from Chiping county, Shandong, the reason for facing southeast, sometimes accompanied by performance of the *koutou*, was that this was the general direction (from the vantage point not only of Chiping in northwestern Shandong but also of many of the other locations in North China where the Boxers became active in 1900) of Peach Blossom Mountain (Taohuashan) in Feicheng county, Shandong; Peach Blossom Mountain was said to have seventy-two grottoes, each inhabited by gods and immortals (Wang Yumei [78], Chiping county, Mar. 1960, SYDZX, 199). Seventy-two was an auspicious

324   number in Chinese popular culture. See Elliott, *Spirit Medium Cults*, 170; Eberhard, *Dictionary*, 262.

5. On the near-universal prevalence of religious trance behavior, out of 488 societies for which ethnographic data is available, 437 or 90% are reported to have one or more "institutionalized, culturally patterned forms of altered states of consciousness" (Bourguignon, "Introduction," 9–11). The following description of possession trance in sub-Saharan Africa could as easily apply to the Boxers, in all of its details: "*Possession trance* . . . refers to a condition in which a person is believed to be inhabited by the spirit of another person or a supernatural being. During this 'possession' . . . the person is in an altered state of consciousness, evidenced by one or more of the following: talking and acting like the inhabiting spirit, lapsing into a coma-like state, speaking unintelligibly, exhibiting physical symptoms such as twitching, wild dancing, frothing at the mouth, and so on. Upon regaining his original identity, the person generally retains no conscious memory of the activity of the spirit." Greenbaum, "Societal Correlates," 42.

6. Guan He, *Quanfei*, 477. For another account of variations in possession behavior (not specifically limited to any one place), see Sawara and Ouyin, *Quanshi*, 271.

7. Zhang Jincai (83), Third Brother-Disciple, western suburbs of Tianjin, TDYYDB, 123.

8. Naquin, *Shantung Rebellion*, 100.

9. Their technique was called Shaolin Spirit Fighting (Shaolin shenda); see Chen Zhenjiang and Cheng Xiao, *Yihetuan wenxian*, 63. For an overview of the many other Qing sects, antecedent to the Boxers, that believed in the efficacy of charms, practiced spirit possession, and claimed invulnerability to weapons, see Cheng Xiao, "Minjian zongjiao," 153–56.

10. Kuhn, "Maoist Agriculture."

11. Benton, *Mountain Fires*, 213. (Benton translates Dadao as "Great Knives" instead of "Big Swords.") See also ibid., 240, for reference to a local Daoist belief that eating cinnabar could confer invulnerability to swords and bullets. As we shall see in ch. 4, "dirty" things—cloth, water, and so on—were also believed by the Boxers to be powerful inhibitors of their invulnerability magic.

12. Ibid., 257.

13. Tai Hsüan-chih, *Red Spears*, esp. 41–58. Tai (passim) refers to a number of other groups in the twentieth century that had invulnerability rituals centering on spirit possession. Some scholars, of whom Tai Hsüan-chih is a leading example, believe the Red Spears to have been an offshoot of the Boxers.

14. Ibid., 65. Tai Hsüan-chih believes the Armor of the Iron Gate to have evolved from the Red Lanterns of 1900.

15. Ibid. Note the similarity of this invulnerability ritual to that used by Wang Lun's rebels in 1774 (above).

16. Duara, *Culture*, 123.

17. According to one estimate, there were some 60 million practitioners of qigong in China as of 1990. On the qigong craze (re) that began to sweep the country in the early 1980s, see NYT, Sept. 4, 1990, A4. For a perceptive analysis of some of the ways in which qigong has functioned in the contemporary Chinese world, see Nancy N. Chen, "Urban Spaces."

18. Myron Cohen, "Being Chinese," 125.

19. Eberhard, *Guilt and Sin*, 21.

20. Smith, *Village Life*, 172. Along the same lines, during a drought in Nanling county, Anhui, in the late 1920s, "a god was publicly tried by the magistrate for neglect of duty, condemned, left in the hot sun to see how he liked it himself, and finally, after enduring every kind of insult, was broken in pieces." Shryock, *Temples of Anking*, 97; see also Duara, *Culture*, 283n55.

21. Myron Cohen, "Being Chinese," 129.

22. I have relied for information on, and understanding of, Chinese spirit mediumship mainly on the following works: Elliott, *Spirit Medium Cults*; Potter, "Cantonese Shamanism"; Jordan, *Gods*, 67–86; Kleinman, *Patients and Healers*; Anagnost, "Politics and Magic"; Margery Wolf, *A Thrice-Told Tale*; Seaman, "In the Presence of Authority"; Gould-Martin, "*Ong-ia-kong*,"; Jerome Ch'en, *Highlanders*, 182–83.

23. Potter, "Cantonese Shamanism," 326; see also ibid., 327, 337.

24. For example, in Singapore and to a lesser extent in Taiwan it may be accompanied by mortification of the flesh, but in many other settings such mortification appears to play no role at all (see Elliott, *Spirit Medium Cults*, 51–56, 149–57; Jordan, *Gods*, 78–84). Again, although it appears to be relatively rare, in certain parts of China, such as the Xunzhou region of Guangxi and the Canton area, during trance, the soul of the possessed person sometimes takes a journey to the world of the spirits. Potter, "Cantonese Shamanism," 322; Weller, *Resistance*, 71–72.

25. This point is cast in more generalized form by Raymond Firth in his foreword to Beattie and Middleton, eds., *Spirit Mediumship*, xi.

26. Potter ("Cantonese Shamanism," 345) sees the spirit medium in the Canton area as the "high priestess of [the] black half of the villagers' supernatural world. She rules over the dark world inhabited by the malevolent ghosts of the unsuccessful, the discontented, the abnormal, and the exploited. Her major function in village society is to deter these discontented and dangerous beings from wreaking their vengeance on the living villagers."

27. See, for example, the descriptions of spirit-medium trance recorded in Gould-Martin, "*Ong-ia-kong*," 46–47; Potter, "Cantonese Shamanism," 322–29, 334–36; Elliott, *Spirit Medium Cults*, 63–65; Jordan, *Gods*, 75–76.

28. This was of course one of the two main ideas contained in the most famous of the Boxers' slogans: "Fu [Bao] Qing mieyang" (Support [Protect] the Qing, destroy the foreign [or foreigner]). The first two lines of a jingle circulated in the Tianjin area ("Yihetuan, Ba guo bao, Yao da guizi, Hongdengzhao") conveyed the same thought ("The Boxers protect the country . . ."). See TDYYDB, 157.

29. Bourguignon, "An Assessment," 326–27.

30. Weller, *Resistance*, 76–77. For a broader analysis of Boxer empowerment that includes spirit possession but also looks beyond it to other empowering facets of the Boxer thought world, see Kobayashi Kazumi, "Minshū shisō," 245–50, 261–62.

31. Weller, *Resistance*, 78.

32. Ibid., 76–77.

33. Horton, "Types of Spirit Possession," 19. In a similar vein, Beattie suggests that the great public ceremonies and feasts of the past among the Nyoro of Bunyoro

326   in East Africa, which centered on possession ritual, "may . . . almost be said to constitute a Nyoro traditional theatre" ("Spirit Mediumship," 168). For other examples of the entertainment value of possession dance, see Colson, "Spirit Possession," 88; Southall, "Spirit Possession," 235.

34. Beattie and Middleton, "Introduction," xxviii. For biting criticism of the (in his view) excessive interest of anthropologists in the "expressive or theatrical" aspect of possession, see Lewis, *Ecstatic Religion*, 22–23.

35. Jordan, *Gods*, 78–84. Elliott (*Spirit Medium Cults*, 62) notes that worshipers in Singapore expect to be impressed by the noise and spectacle of a *tâng-ki*'s performance as much as by the efficacy of the cures given.

36. Jordan, *Gods*, 79–80.

37. Margery Wolf, *A Thrice-Told Tale*, 103. Because of her understanding of the purpose of such physical self-abuse, Wolf (ibid.) questions the use of the term "mortification" to characterize it. Like Jordan and Wolf, Per-Arne Berglie interprets the more spectacular behavior sometimes accompanying Tibetan spirit possession (such as the throwing of glowing charcoal) as intended "to show the audience the powers of the gods and impress on it the reality of their presence" (Berglie, "Spirit-Possession," 165).

38. Johnson, "Actions," 30–31. The impact of opera on Boxer possession has been widely noted. Particularly informative, because of the author's knowledge of Chinese theater, is Doar, "The Boxers," passim. Esherick (*Origins*, 63–67, 328–31) makes some useful observations, as does Jerome Ch'en in his pioneering article, "The Nature and Characteristics of the Boxer Movement," 298–99. Mark Elvin was, I believe, the first to apply the concept of "political theater" to the interactions between Boxer religious behavior and Chinese opera and fiction. Elvin, "Mandarins," 124.

39. Bourguignon makes the point that, although the capacity to experience altered states of consciousness has a psychobiological basis and is universal among human beings, the behavior that takes place during possession trance is culturally patterned and must therefore be studied by ethnographic means. "Introduction," 13–15.

40. Useful information on these performances is in Tanaka, "Social and Historical Context."

41. Liu Mengyang, *Tianjin quanfei*, 8. "When the Boxer gods presented themselves," Chen Duxiu wrote, "their speech was modeled on the spoken parts in the operas and their gestures were modeled on the prescribed movements of the opera actors" ("Kelinde bei," 454–55).

42. Chen Duxiu (ibid., 454–55) pointed to traditional opera as one of five principal causes of the Boxer uprising. Jiang Zhiyou (Guanyun), a close associate of Liang Qichao, in 1904 blamed the military defeat of the Boxers on the fighting methods they had learned from actor-warriors (Doar, "The Boxers," 94–95). The fusion of the distinction between actors and warriors, suggested by Jiang, calls to mind a similar fusion of the roles of actor and priest, as discussed in David Johnson, "Actions," 29–31.

43. This would, of course, not apply in all cases. Boxers drawn from the ranks of demobilized soldiers—to cite the most conspicuous exception—would have had some degree of formal military training and even, possibly, live combat experience.

44. Seaman, "In the Presence of Authority," 71.

45. Yang, *Religion in Chinese Society*, 22.

46. Tsai, "Historical Personalities," 35.

47. Elliott, *Spirit Medium Cults*, 76–77.

48. Duara, *Culture*, 139–48; see also Watson, "Standardizing the Gods."

49. Doar, "The Boxers," 111–18. Doar has an interesting discussion of the relationship between the operatic influence on the Boxers and the fact that Guandi, in addition to being the God of War, was also the patron god of actors.

50. Duara, *Culture*, 139.

51. De Groot, *Religious System* 6:1277–78; an illustration of five daggers with general's-head hilts appears facing p. 1278.

52. The full texts of both of these invocations, along with two others, are in Elliott, *Spirit Medium Cults*, 170–71. For a similar invocation, also calling on the assistance of "divine warriors" (spirit soldiers), see de Groot, *Religious System* 6:1273. On the Third Prince, see Elliott, 76–77.

53. Beattie, "Spirit Mediumship," 167.

54. Middleton, "Spirit Possession," 225–26. See also Beattie and Middleton's "Introduction" (xxviii), where they note a possible parallel between the African examples and the inception of classical drama in the possession rituals of ancient Greece.

55. Margery Wolf, *A Thrice-Told Tale*, 8, 94, and passim.

56. For evidence that this generalization may hold even for contemporary Chinese mainland society, see Anagnost, "Politics and Magic." On the prevalence of shamanism throughout China during the late Qing and Republican periods, see Sutton, "Pilot Surveys."

57. Liu Mengyang, *Tianjin quanfei*, 7.

58. Liu Xizi, *Jin xi*, 75. Further evidence of the widespread popular acceptance of Boxer supernatural claims is supplied in Yang Tianhong, "Yihetuan 'shenshu,'" 195. See also Esherick, *Origins*, 67.

59. Hart, *Essays*, 8. A young American missionary reported to Roland Allen in May, after interviews with local officials and gentry in the Boxer-saturated country between Beijing and Baoding, that "the influence which the Boxer superstition exercised over the minds of these men was appalling. Men who could talk quietly and reasonably about every other subject, the moment the Boxers were mentioned raved like lunatics, and professed unswerving faith in the most childish and incredible stories about their supernatural powers." Allen, *Siege*, 25.

60. Letter of July 10, 1900. In a similar vein, Louise Partridge, one of Bird's colleagues, commented that the Boxer movement in Shanxi "has swept over the country like a flood carrying all before it" (letter of July 2, 1900). A CIM missionary, after relating some of the more far-fetched stories about the Boxers that had circulated in Yongning, Shanxi, wrote: "The early fears and suspicions which the people had of the Boxers were soon exchanged for unbounded confidence, and they quickly enrolled themselves as their followers" (Ogren, "Conflict of Sufferings," 65). Nigel Oliphant wrote in his siege diary that the populace of Beijing had "vast respect" for the "miraculous powers" of the Boxer chief in the capital (Oliphant, *Diary*, 26).

61. See SYDZX, 200–203; TDYYDB, 123, 126, 128, 133, 136, 145, 147.

62. Chen Zhenjiang, emphasizing the importance of the latter group, goes so far as to characterize North China in the waning years of the nineteenth century as

328   a "society of the mobile unemployed" (*youmin shehui*). See his "Huabei youmin,"
230–45.

63. Zhongfang Shi, *Gengzi jishi*, 25; Li Yuanshan (79), Boxer, Tianjin, TDYYDB,
133; also ibid., 47; Xin Hanzhang (85), Zhuo county, HDYYDJ, Dec. 24, 1973,
005:No. 7, p. 2. Contributions of grain and money from the rich were not always
voluntary. A jingle circulated in Laishui county went (in free translation): "The
Senior Brother-Disciple is going into trance; from the rich rice is demanded. The
Second Brother-Disciple is ascending the altar; if not rice, then money." Liu Qing
(83) and Liang Chun (86), Shiting commune (Laishui county), ibid., Jan. 1, 1974,
005:No. 7.

Some Boxers, we are told, turned down contributions of food and grain, saying
that they had magic cooking pots, the food contents of which were never depleted
(*TYJ*, 142). Along similar lines, Guan He (*Quanfei*, 470) tells of a Boxer support
organization called the Armor of the Earthenware Pots (Shaguozhao), the members of which, after completing their training course, were able to fill empty pots
with an inexhaustible supply of food. See also Kobayashi Kazumi, "Minshū shisō,"
248–49).

64. Sun Shaotang (75), Boxer, Tianjin, TDYYDB, 146.

65. Zhongfang Shi (*Gengzi jishi*, 22) noted that when the Boxers in Beijing bore
a grudge against someone from former days, they would falsely accuse the person
of being a "secondary hairy one" (*ermaozi*, i. e., either a Christian or someone with
close connections with foreigners) and kill him and sometimes his entire family,
even including the children. Liu Mengyang (*Tianjin quanfei*, 20, 22, 35) reported
similar behavior in Tianjin. A former Boxer, in accounting for the strict procedures
the Boxers allegedly followed before putting a Christian to death, recalled that
"since in those days there were some people who, for reasons of personal
vengeance, accused such-and-such a person of being a straight eye [Christian], if
we relied on such one-sided claims without checking them out, would we not
wrong good people?" Li Zhende (81), Duliu, TDYYDB, 126.

Among foreigners, Rowena Bird wrote: "All that is necessary now to get rid of a
man someone hates is to suggest that he is hired by foreigners to set fire to houses
or poison wells, and he is at once killed without question—in this way many are
killed who have no connection at all with us" (letter, July 9, 1900, Taigu, Shanxi;
see also Bird's letters of July 6 and 10, and her journal entries of July 3, 5, 6, 9, 15).
After the defeat of the Boxers, it was reported that Christians in Shanxi behaved in
the exact same way, filing charges against people they didn't like, even if these persons had had no connection whatever to the Boxers. See Liu Dapeng, *Riji*, GX
27/4/5 (May 22, 1901), 16.

66. See the testimony of Wang Fengji, a former Boxer from the Tianjin area (ch.
2, n. 41).

67. Elite accounts take frequent note of the coercive behavior of the Boxers
toward the resident populations of Beijing and Tianjin. See, for example, Guan He,
Quanfei, 471, 474–79; Liu Mengyang, *Tianjin quanfei*, 8–11, 13, 18, 23, 31–32; *TYJ*,
143, 147–48; Tang Yan, *Gengzi xing*, 472–74. The analogy in this respect between
the Boxers and the Red Guards in the late 1960s was not lost on contemporary
detractors of the Cultural Revolution (see Wang Hsueh-wen, "A Comparison").

68. Liu Mengyang, *Tianjin quanfei*, 19.

69. Johnson, "Actions," 31–32. As an example of the operaticization of "real life," Perry Link has noted that, in watching the student demonstrators in Tiananmen Square in spring 1989, he almost thought he was viewing scenes from a Chinese opera, as one unit after another marched under their respective banners and groups of hunger-strikers echoed one another in the stylized chanting of "*Women bupa si*" ("We do not fear death"). Informal comments at Four Anniversaries conference, Annapolis, Sept. 1989.

70. Dhomhnaill, "Why I Choose to Write in Irish," 28; Gould-Martin, "*Ong-ia-kong*," 62n3.

71. Cheng Xiao, "Minsu xinyang," 296–301. On the Patriarch's Assembly and the resemblance of its practices to those of the Boxers, see also Hu Zhusheng, "Yihetuan de qianshen," 8; Esherick, *Origins*, 56–57. Additional evidence of the relative receptivity of northern Chinese, culturally and/or socially, to the experience of possession is found in the fact that, when Pentecostal Christianity became established in China in the first decades of the twentieth century, the main native churches—the True Jesus Church (Zhen Yesu jiaohui), the Jesus Family (Yesu jiating), and the Spiritual Gifts Church (Ling'enhui)—all either originated in North China or had their main centers of strength there. The possession practices of the Spirit Boxers were, in Daniel Bays's judgment, "similar to one of the key Pentecostal religious experiences, the 'infilling' of the Holy Spirit which comes with Holy Spirit baptism and often brings supernatural powers" (see his "Indigenous Protestant Churches," 141n27). It may also be worth noting, in terms of Cheng Xiao's analysis, that the True Jesus Church (the largest of the Chinese Pentecostal churches) was militantly antiforeign in its orientation (ibid., 135, 138).

72. Wang Lianfa (82), Duliu, HDYYDJ, Mar. 16, 1976, 003–07:No. 2. The modern meaning of *tongzijun*, "boy scouts," clearly is inapplicable here. Another oral history informant, this one from southern Zhili, described a contingent of 200 Shandong Boxers who arrived in Jingzhou one evening as consisting of half grownups and half youngsters. The latter, who ranged in age from 14 to 16 *sui* (13 to 15 by Western counting), were known as the "children's brigade" (*wawadui*). Sun Lianjia (78), Jing county, Feb. 1966, HJZH, 175; the same expression is used in Cao Shi'an (83), Jing county, Feb. 1966, ibid., 178, and Sun Yusheng (81), Jing county, Feb. 1966, ibid., 180. A contemporary patriotic print referred to Boxers engaged in an attack on foreign forces as "Youth United in Righteousness" (*Yihe tongzi*) (Toynbee, ed., *Half the World*, 324). For other references to the youthfulness of the Boxers, see Sawara and Ouyin, *Quanshi*, 238–39, 251, 271; interview with Jia Xianju, Aug. 1959, in Qiao Zhiqiang, comp., *Yihetuan zai Shanxi*, 150; Liu Mengyang, *Tianjin quanfei*, 8; *TYJ*, 145, 148. Among contemporary foreign accounts, Rowena Bird wrote: "One of the dreadful things about this Boxer movement in Shansi is the part that young boys—only children, take in it. Often in a killing affair the children take the lead" (journal, June 28, 1900). Louise Partridge referred to the movement in Shanxi as having "been taken up by boys mostly" (letter of July 2, 1900). Edith Nathan (CIM, Shanxi) wrote: "Truly these 'Child Boxers' are devilish, and a device of the devil. We in England know little of what the power of Satan can do over the mind of a child" (letter of July 12, 1900, in Broomhall, ed., *Last Letters*, 34). "The spread of the Boxer movement," Arthur H. Smith asserted in more general terms, "was largely through young boys who were put under the influence of something

330   like hypnotism, or mesmerism" (*China in Convulsion* 2:661). According to an eyewitness of the Boxer attack on Seymour's forces at Langfang on June 12, "many" of the attackers were "quite boys" (quoted in Fleming, *The Siege*, 77).

Among scholars, Mark Elvin ("Mandarins," 123) describes the Boxer movement as "a children's crusade, in which the young were manipulated by their elders." Other secondary accounts taking special note of the Boxers' youth are Kobayashi Kazumi, "Minshū shisō," 245–46; Jerome Ch'en, "Nature and Characteristics," 296, 298, and "Origin," 81; Dunstheimer, "Religion et magie," 342, 345–46, 358–59.

73. Boyer and Nissenbaum, *Salem Possessed*, 28–29.

74. Rawski, "Problems," 406.

75. This belief is discussed by ter Haar in "Images of Outsiders."

76. Elliott, *Spirit Medium Cults*, 46–47. See also Margery Wolf, A *Thrice-Told Tale*, 107; Jordan (*Gods*, 71) states that a "*tâng-ki* is a man whose natural life is thought to be short (hence the term *tâng*, 'lad'), and who has been granted an extension, as it were, in order that he may serve his god." Still other terms for "medium" which incorporate *tong* are briefly discussed in ibid., 67–68n10, and in de Groot, *Religious System* 6:1269.

77. Sawara and Ouyin, *Quanshi*, 271. The same authors at an earlier point in their account present another interpretation of the Boxers' recruitment of young males. This interpretation, clearly premised on the view of the Boxers as a rebellious movement (evidently White Lotus-inspired), maintained that, over several years, as the power of the Boxers spread, the youth recruited earlier would become highly trained and strengthened in their faith in the Boxer cause and would rise up en masse in response to their leaders' summons. Ibid., 239.

78. Letter of May Nathan, late July 1900, in Broomhall, ed., *Last Letters*, 38.

79. Ogren, "Conflict of Sufferings," 72 (emphasis supplied).

80. Dunstheimer, "Religion et magie," 342; Hou Bin, "Yihetuan de zuzhi," 68–69.

81. Field, "Spirit Possession," 7. Zulu possession, for example, is often accompanied by "avoidance of food and consequent emaciation" (S. G. Lee, "Spirit Possession," 140). The Alur, on the other hand, present a clear exception to Field's rule, neither patients nor acolytes being "predisposed towards dissociation by prolonged lack of food" (Southall, "Spirit Possession," 244).

82. Leonard, "Spirit Mediums," 170. Although it is possible that the betel nut itself may act as a trance-inducing agent in certain circumstances, Leonard's investigations indicate that such is probably not the case in Palau.

83. Pressel, "Umbanda," 310.

84. Siikala, "Siberian Shaman's Technique," 112.

85. Elliott, *Spirit Medium Cults*, 62; see also ibid., 47. Elliott claims that the lowered body temperature of *tâng-ki* prior to trance has been empirically verified (ibid., 62). Some *tâng-ki* in Taiwan, according to Jordan (*Gods*, 76), also empty their stomachs while going into trance.

86. Emily Brontë, *Wuthering Heights*, 395–96. Heathcliff's behavior in the final chapter of the novel displays other characteristic features of trance behavior as well, including abnormal speech and breathing. His mood changes at this climactic juncture also recall some of the psychological "stigmata" of slow starvation, as catalogued by Nancy Scheper-Hughes (*Death Without Weeping*, 138).

87. Field ("Spirit Possession," 7) is quite explicit on this point. The exact way in which it happens, however, is as yet not well understood (Björkqvist, "Ecstasy," 76–77).

88. Nelly Dean, the faithful family servant and chief narrator in *Wuthering Heights*, claims after Heathcliff's death to be persuaded that "he did not abstain [from food] on purpose: it was the consequence of his strange illness, not the cause" (Emily Brontë, *Wuthering Heights*, 405).

89. And also by the impoverished, chronically hungry Nguni Bantu of South Africa. Gussler ("Social Change," 115–23) finds a high correlation among the Nguni between relative susceptibility to *ukuthwasa* ("possession-illness") and undernourishment or malnourishment.

90. See the summary of recent research in this area (including her own) in Felicitas D. Goodman, *Ecstasy*, 39. Goodman does not address the issue of hunger pain specifically. It is interesting to note also, in relation to the "vision quest" of the Maya, the growing literature on the complex interconnections among bloodletting, the release of endorphins, the absence of pain in the course of self-mutilation, and the experience of altered consciousness. See, for example, Furst, "Fertility,"; Schele and Miller, *Blood of Kings*, 177.

91. Shack, "Hunger." Bourguignon would distinguish the two forms of deprivation anxiety operating among the Ojibwa and Gurage as "objective" (social) and "subjective" (personal). Spirit possession, she hypothesizes, acts as a compensatory response, either elevating the status (or otherwise increasing the power) of people who are relatively deprived in societal terms ("objective instrumental compensation") or providing emotional satisfaction (derived from the trance experience itself) to those who experience personal deprivation ("subjective expressive compensation"). Bourguignon, "An Assessment," 327–29.

92. Shack, "Hunger," 39. On this point, see the discussion of *delírio de fome* ("the madness of hunger") in Scheper-Hughes, *Death Without Weeping*, esp. 128–66.

93. I do not wish to be misunderstood here as interpreting religious experience in general as a simple function of anxiety; I concur fully in the following words of I. M. Lewis (*Ecstatic Religion*, 24): "My starting point . . . is precisely that large numbers of people in many different parts of the world do believe in gods and spirits. . . . My objective is not to explain away religion. On the contrary, my purpose is to try to isolate the particular social and other conditions which encourage the development of an ecstatic emphasis in religion."

94. The phrase is Cheng Xiao's; see his "Minsu xinyang," 297.

95. We have seen examples of this in ch. 2, above. The use of such sanctions in the context of deprivation-related possession is, however, by no means universal. See Bourguignon, "An Assessment," 328–29.

4. Magic and Female Pollution

1. Liu Mengyang, *Tianjin quanfei*, 12–13, 16.

2. Ai Sheng, *Quanfei*, 449–50.

3. Memorial of *gengzi* 5/22 (June 18, 1900), in *YHT* 4:162; in a memorial of *gengzi* 6/*zhong* (July 7–16, 1900), Yuan, who on July 28, 1900, was executed for his outspoken opposition to the throne's pro-Boxer policy, wrote that, after more than twenty

332   days of attacks on the legation compound, only a few foreign soldiers had been killed, while the bones of dead Boxers lay scattered all about the entrance to East Jiaomin Lane (ibid., 163). Other examples of elite Chinese mockery of Boxer invulnerability claims are: Yang Diangao, *Gengzi dashi ji*, 79, 88; Liu Mengyang, *Tianjin quanfei*, 39; Liu Xizi, *Jin xi*, 81–82; Ai Sheng, *Quanfei*, 460; *Yu nan riji*, 163, 171; Tang Yan, *Gengzi xixing*, 486; Ye Changchi, *Riji*, 443–44; Guan He, *Quanfei*, 490; Lu Wantian, *Beijing shibian*, 434 (Lu was a Chinese Methodist). For an account that is more sympathetic to the Boxers in general and their invulnerability claims in particular, see Liu Yitong, *Minjiao xiangchou*, 183–96 (esp. 183, 185, 191).

4. Journal, Beijing, June 14, 1900, in LMP, box 1, file 1. Nigel Oliphant, describing an encounter that took place on June 14 between Boxers and British marines in the capital (very possibly the same as that recounted by Miner), reported that, after being fired on by the British, the Boxers "all threw themselves on the ground, praying, according to the Boxer custom, to be saved from the bullets, and the marines, thinking they were praying for mercy, ceased fire. Then one of their leaders rushed forward with a huge poleaxe and was shot dead by the sergeant. Then the whole crowd retreated." Oliphant, *Diary*, 13.

5. Quoted in Forsyth, comp. and ed., *China Martyrs*, 276; see also the account of John Ross (United Presbyterian Church), in ibid., 302–303. The Tianjin correspondent for the *North-China Herald* reported (in a dispatch dated June 8) that a lot of foreigners in the city eagerly awaited the attack of the Boxers, so they could prick the bubble of Boxer invulnerability claims (which "Chinese of all classes believe"). *NCH*, June 20, 1900, p. 1113.

6. Yang Tianhong, "Yihetuan 'shenshu,' " 194.

7. Douglas, *Purity*, 58.

8. Yang Tianhong, "Yihetuan 'shenshu,' " 197.

9. Ai Sheng, *Quanfei*, 444. As an example of a noncombat demonstration of Boxer invulnerability powers, a former Boxer from the Tianjin area recalled the visit to his village of one "Troublemaker Han" ("Han Daodan"). With his musket, "he fired at people's backs and sure enough the shot didn't penetrate. Han said this was because of the help of the gods, and everyone believed him." Li Changqing (77), Nankai district of Tianjin, Second Brother-Disciple, TDYYDB, 120. For another example of demonstration invulnerability, see Wang Enpu, northern suburbs of Tianjin, Second Brother-Disciple, TDYYDB, 143. Unlike some Boxer disparagers, Ai Sheng was prepared to distinguish between what he viewed as plausible and implausible claims: "A Boxer from my county told me: 'A boxing teacher from a certain village tied a red string around a huge stone roller and after chanting a few words proceeded to lift it. Everyone was amazed. The boxing teacher said: "This doesn't nearly exhaust my skills. I can tie a thin piece of cord around the spire of a church and drag [the whole thing] down effortlessly." Is that miraculous or not?' I said: 'That's an opera stunt. He can only lift the stone roller; he can't drag a church down. If he could drag down [a church], what is he waiting for? He just uses the stone roller to trick people.' " Ai Sheng, *Quanfei*, 458. See also Liu Mengyang, *Tianjin quanfei*, 8. The boxing teacher referred to by Ai Sheng's Boxer informant may well have been the Tianjin Boxer leader, Zhang Decheng, who, according to a former Boxer from Zhang's home place, boasted that with a piece of red rope he could hoist a stone roller to the top of a tree. Li Zhende (81), Duliu, TDYYDB, 125.

10. Brody. "Lucking Out: Weird Rituals and Strange Beliefs," *NYT*, Jan. 27, 1991, S11.

11. Ibid.

12. Douglas, *Purity*, 68, 72.

13. Sarah Boardman Goodrich, letter, Tong Cho [Tongzhou], May 25, 1900. See also Goodrich's letters of May 28, May 30, and June 3, 1900.

14. See ch. 2, n. 66.

15. Gustav Jahoda writes of "superstition"—and I would make the same claims for religious and magical ritual generally—that it provides "at least the subjective feeling of predictability and control," thereby reducing the anxiety that is apt to be aroused in threatening situations marked by uncertainty as to probable outcome. Jahoda, *Superstition*, 130, 134.

16. It is worth noting that people in other cultures have also relied on invulnerability magic for protection in combat. In the religious rioting unleashed by the Islamic sect, the 'Yan Tatsine, against Nigerian security forces in 1980, the insurrectionists were said to have used rituals, tattoos, invincibility charms, and "magic sand" to protect themselves against the bullets of their adversaries (Lubeck, "Islamic Protest," 370, 386). I am indebted to Lidwien Kapteijns for this reference. Earlier in the twentieth century, the Lugbara followers of the Kakwa prophet and diviner Rembe, after performing specified rituals, went into battle "berserk and believing in the power of the *Yakan* water to turn bullets into water." Middleton, "Spirit Possession," 227–28.

17. Chen Zhenjiang and Cheng Xiao, *Yihetuan wenxian*, 153–54. The original Chinese reads: "Dizi zai hongchen, bizhu qiangpao men; qiangpao yiqi xiang, shazi liangbian fen."

18. *TYJ*, 148–49, 151. The Chinese cook for the family of the Tianjin customs official, E. B. Drew, often told Mrs. Drew "how wonderful it was" that the Boxers "could not be killed," and that "if a bullet should happen to hit them and enter the body, they could easily take it right out again through the mouth." Mrs. E. B. Drew, diary, 14.

19. Liu Mengyang insisted that the real reason the foreign guns stopped firing was simply that there had been a lull in the fighting. See Liu Mengyang, *Tianjin quanfei*, 31, 34.

20. Tang Yan, *Gengzi xixing*, 471; see also Zhongfang Shi, *Gengzi jishi*, 12. In Shanxi, according to CIM missionary Olivia Ogren, it was reported that as soon as foreign troops attacked, the Boxers would "fly away to heaven, out of the reach of bullets." Ogren, "Conflict of Sufferings," 72; see also ibid., 65.

21. *TYJ*, 148, 151. Someone told Liu Mengyang (*Tianjin quanfei*, 24) in late June that when Cao Futian found himself downstairs in a foreign building with a lot of foreigners upstairs, he threw a metal coin upstairs and the heads of the foreigners instantly fell to the ground. The same person informed Liu that he had personally seen Cao decapitate a bunch of foreigners in a building simply by waving a stick at them. The person who claimed to have witnessed this told Liu: "I saw it with my own eyes. It's not fabricated."

22. Li Yuanshan (79), Boxer, Tianjin, TDYYDB, 134. Since the same character—*qiang*—is used for both "gun" and "spear," it is sometimes impossible to tell which meaning is intended.

23. Shen Desheng (80), Jinghai county, Senior Brother-Disciple, TDYYDB, 119.

24. *Yu nan riji*, 163; Liu Mengyang, *Tianjin quanfei*, 9, 36. Before his unit left the Tianjin area to take part in the fighting in the capital, one former Boxer reported, they all went to the home of the top local Red Lantern, the Holy Mother of the Yellow Lotus (see below in text), to ask for magic charms to make them invulnerable to firearms. Guo Shirong (75), TDYYDB, 138.

25. Zhao Qing (72), Jinghai county, Fourth Sister-Disciple, TDYYDB, 136; also ibid., 41; TYJ, 146; Liu Mengyang, *Tianjin quanfei*, 36. The Holy Mother of the Yellow Lotus, whose original name was Lin Hei'er, became a central figure in Cultural Revolution mythologization of the Boxer movement (see ch. 9). For a brief but well-documented biography, see Liao Yizhong, "Lin Hei'er."

26. Liu Yitong, *Minjiao xiangchou*, 183, 185. See also ibid., 190–91, where the Boxers, by mumbling some phrases and waving their banners, are reported by Liu to have protected a grain shop in the Xidan area of the capital.

27. Tang Yan, *Gengzi xixing*, 472.

28. Ibid. For another report (this time from Renqiu county, Zhili) of Boxer-set fires harming only the homes of Christians, see Sawara Tokusuke and Ouyin, *Quanshi*, 250.

29. Zhongfang Shi, *Gengzi jishi*, 12. See also Yang Diangao, *Gengzi dashi ji*, 79.

30. Liu Yitong, *Minjiao xiangchou*, 183–84. For a slight variation on the same story, see Guan He, *Quanfei*, 468.

31. Liu Mengyang, *Tianjin quanfei*, 8.

32. Sun Shaotang (75), TDYYDB, 147.

33. Yang Diangao, *Gengzi dashi ji*, 82.

34. *TYJ*, 147.

35. Yang Diangao, *Gengzi dashi ji*, 82. I am indebted to Susan Naquin for the characterization of foreign technological "magic" as "world-shrinking." Red Lantern flying claims, as well as the boasts of the Boxers that they were able to set fire to foreign steamships at sea, may well, she suggests, have been seen at the time as a kind of "equalizer" — a response in kind to the magic seemingly inherent in foreign artillery (and, one might add, the telegraph, with its ability to send invisible messages over vast distances apparently instantaneously).

36. Liu Mengyang, *Tianjin quanfei*, 17. The extreme skeptic Guan He gave a quite different account of Red Lantern wind-management skills. Tianjin people, according to Guan, all said that in order for the fires burning in the city to reach the foreign concession area, a northwest wind was needed. Yet, day after day, the wind blew only from the southeast. The Red Lanterns, despite the use of their magic, were unable to cause the wind to shift direction. Guan He, *Quanfei*, 478. As another example of the striking parallelism between Boxers and Christian missionaries noted in chapter 2, the missionaries, too, were convinced that they were the beneficiaries of supernatural wind-management assistance. See n. 69 below.

37. According to Hu Sijing (*Lü bei ji*, 488), Red Lanterns learned to fly by placing a copper dish filled with water before a god and walking around it continuously crying out "fly." After doing this for forty-eight days they were able to fly. For a slightly different version of this training procedure, which took only five days to master, see *TYJ*, 141. During the Cultural Revolution, a former Red Lantern recalled a ritual in which, twice daily, all the Red Lanterns circled a copper basin.

But, as was characteristic of Cultural Revolution references to the Red Lanterns, she omitted any mention of the magical purpose of the procedure. Li Fengzhi (86), Xiong county, HDYYDJ, Dec. 27, 1973, 011–14. In the Tianjin oral history materials from the late 1950s, when ideological constraints were less austere, a retired railway worker (non-Boxer) claimed that, despite his initial skepticism regarding the Red Lanterns' flying skills, at the time he actually had seen red lanterns in the sky at night. Li Fengde (75), TDYYDB, 149.

38. *TYJ*, 141. At one point, according to Liu Mengyang (*Tianjin quanfei*, 37), it was reported (and widely believed) in Tianjin that half of the Japanese capital had been burned down by Red Lanterns using their magical skills.

39. *Yu nan riji*, 163. For another reference to Red Lantern incendiary powers, see Yuan Chang, *Riji*, 346.

40. *TYJ*, 149. Similarly, Tai Hsüan-chih (*Red Spears*, 52) asserts that when Red Spear invulnerability rituals didn't work, "the grand master laid the blame on members, claiming that insincerity or failure to perform the rituals properly had prevented the spirits from descending into their bodies." Although Big Sword Society members in southwestern Shandong in the mid-1890s did not have spirit possession as part of their repertoire, they explained failures in their invulnerability rituals in much the same way. When one of them sustained a sword wound (called *loudao* or "a slip of the sword"), the teacher said it was because he was not sincere in his heart. Liu Changru (72), Heze county, 1960, SYDZX, 16.

41. Shen Desheng (80), Jinghai county, Senior Brother-Disciple, TDYYDB, 119–20. Another former Boxer from Tianjin said that the leaders constantly exhorted the rank and file not to be money-mad or take things that didn't belong to them. "If you were greedy for money, when you were fighting on the front lines you wouldn't be protected against swords and spears [or guns] [*bibuliao daoqiang*]." Guo Shirong (75), TDYYDB, 137; see also ibid., 47.

42. Liu Mengyang, *Tianjin quanfei*, 36.

43. *TYJ*, 148. See also Liu Mengyang, *Tianjin quanfei*, 24, 32. Zhongfang Shi (*Gengzi jishi*, 24) reported that when Boxers in Beijing were asked why, with such superiority in numbers and after such a long time period, they still had not been able to achieve victory over the foreigners, they simply replied that it wasn't the right time yet, that when the right time arrived the foreigners would, as a matter of course, be obliterated.

44. *TYJ*, 152.

45. Liu Yitong, *Minjiao xiangchou*, 186.

46. Zhongfang Shi, *Gengzi jishi*, 13–14. Aside from the ravaging of commercial establishments, according to U.S. minister Conger, "over three thousand houses were destroyed, and many people perished in the flames." Dispatch to Hay, June 18, 1900, in *FRUS*, 151.

47. Oliphant, *Diary*, 25–26.

48. A former Tianjin Boxer explained the Boxer prohibition against contact with women in terms of "the fear that the gods would be offended and our magic wouldn't work" (*fa buling*). Zhang Jincai (83), Third Brother-Disciple, western suburb of Tianjin, TDYYDB, 123.

49. See Eberhard, *Dictionary*, 309.

50. Esherick, *Origins*, 54.

51. Naquin, *Shantung Rebellion*, 100–101.

52. Lu Hsun [Xun], "Ah Chang," 367. For an interesting variation on this theme, see Eberhard, *Dictionary*, 202–203.

53. The Taiping prohibition included husbands and wives, who (in theory at least) were domiciled separately. Prohibitions specifically relating to spousal contact are seldom encountered in Boxer materials, possibly because so many Boxers were still boys. An exception is the assertion by a former Boxer from southern Zhili that people who wanted to become Boxers "could not sleep with their wives." Wang Laozhi (86), Hengshui county, Feb. 1966, HJZH, 186.

54. See, for example, Buckley and Gottlieb, "A Critical Appraisal," 6; Delaney, "Mortal Flow," 89; Beyene, *From Menarche*, 106–107 (on Greek taboos). Buckley and Gottlieb (24, 32) also make it clear that the view of menstruation as a polluting force, although widely held, is a cultural construction and is far from universal. Among the Rungus of Sabah, Malaysia, for example, menstruation is not considered polluting at all and a menstruating priestess is able to communicate effectively with her spirit familiar (see Appell, "The Rungus of Borneo," 110–11). Again, although the prevailing view of *male* Yurok Indians in northwestern California was that there existed a strong antipathy between menstruous women and the world of spirits, recent analysis shows that at least some portion of Yurok *women* viewed menstruation as entirely positive, a time when they could attain spiritual ascendancy (Buckley, "Menstruation," 197). Charlotte Furth has raised the related question of the degree to which "the power of pollution" in the Chinese world reflected not only the beliefs of males but also the experience of women; see her "Blood, Body, and Gender," 44.

55. Tai Hsüan-chih, *Red Spears*, 50.

56. Elliott, *Spirit Medium Cults*, 48–49.

57. Ahern, "Power and Pollution," 280–81. See also Margery Wolf, *Women*, 95. For a fascinating account of popular Chinese conceptions of the physical basis for female pollution, as embodied in the Blood Bowl Sutra rite performed at the funerals of women in Taiwan, see Seaman, "Sexual Politics."

58. Ahern, "Power and Pollution," 281; also ibid., 278.

59. In the Boxer world, it is important to emphasize, the polluting power of women reflected a set of male myths and fantasies. Since our sources for reconstructing these myths and fantasies are all male-authored, we can only speculate on the degree to which contemporary Chinese women shared in them.

60. The first justification is found in *TYJ*, 142, the second in Guan He, *Quanfei*, 470.

61. Liu Yitong, *Minjiao xiangchou*, 187.

62. Douglas, *Purity*, 102. "Pollution can be committed intentionally," Douglas also writes, "but intention is irrelevant to its effect—it is more likely to happen inadvertently" (ibid., 113).

63. Liu Mengyang, *Tianjin quanfei*, 16; *TYJ*, 153. A former Boxer, in his account of an engagement his unit fought with a foreign cavalry unit near the railway in Tianjin, recalled that the two lead horses of the foreigners were indeed ridden by women. The reason he gave for the high casualty figures sustained by the Boxer side, however, was that foreign spies hidden in the rush ponds in the Hedong district of the city had fired on them. Li Changqing (77), Nankai district of Tianjin, Second Brother-Disciple, TDYYDB, 121.

64. *TYJ*, 151.

65. Ibid., 145.

66. Freri, ed., *Heart of Pekin*, 29–30.

67. Liu Yitong, *Minjiao xiangchou*, 184, 191, 193–94; Hua Xuelan, *Riji*, 109; Zhongfang Shi, *Gengzi jishi*, 28. For another example of foreign use of pregnant women to foil Boxer invulnerability magic, see Liu Yitong, *Minjiao xiangchou*, 189. Hua Xuelan, the source of the allegation concerning the ten-thousand woman flag, heard it in conversation with friends after dinner and hesitated to vouch for its accuracy. Although this was among the more bizarre of the stories that circulated at the time, none of which presumably had much basis in fact, I am persuaded that, in the atmosphere of excitement, uncertainty, and anxiety that prevailed in North China in the summer of 1900, the level of acceptance of such accounts not only among the Boxers but among the population at large was very high. The heightened willingness of people, in such situations, to suspend their normal standards of judgment is discussed in chapter 5.

68. Vinchon, "La culte," 132–33. Richard Madsen says that, in interviews elsewhere in the province with Chinese Catholic descendants of families that lived through the Boxer experience, he heard stories of a similar nature. There is evidence (as yet unsubstantiated), he adds, that the story of Mary's deliverance of the Catholics from the Boxers is central to the identity of the Catholic community of Donglü, a town just south of Baoding which is the site of the recently completed "Our Lady of China" shrine, the largest church in the country. Personal communication, August 1, 1995.

69. When a heavy wind was on the point of spreading a blaze from the Hanlin Academy to the British Legation, according to Mary Porter Gamewell, the wind suddenly died down: "The same voice that spoke to the sea 1900 years ago spoke that violent wind into quiet" (Gamewell, "History," 61). Sarah Boardman Goodrich wrote of the besieged in the legation quarters: "We have had many wonderful answers to prayer, twice at least in turning the wind away from us when it seemed as if our houses must certainly catch fire" ("Journal," June 28, 1900, p. 29). And Bishop Favier, sequestered in the Northern Cathedral in Beijing, reported that when retreating Boxers on June 15 set fire to the houses adjoining the cathedral on the south, the cathedral itself and its occupants were "preserved by God, who changed the direction of the wind in our favor" (diary, June 15, 1900, in Freri, ed., *Heart of Pekin*, 26).

Along parallel lines, when a force of several thousand Boxers threatened to overpower the Catholic community of Guo Family village in southeastern Zhili in July 1900, the local missionary prayed for heavy rains that would form a cordon of water around the village and prevent the Boxers from entering. His prayers were answered by a terrific storm, which had exactly the desired effect. It was assumed, without question, that the storm had been sent by the Virgin Mary. Vinchon, "La culte," 133.

70. Vinchon, "La culte," 132–33.

71. Ying-ho Chiang, "Literary Reactions," 100; Liu Yitong, *Minjiao xiangchou*, 194. According to Liu (ibid.), on June 28 Prince Duan, the staunchest supporter of the Boxers at court, had personally mounted the steeple of the cathedral and captured and killed the devil prince, so that the Boxers should henceforth experience

338   little difficulty in vanquishing the other defenders. Zhongfang Shi's account of
Favier (Gengzi jishi, 28), although less bizarre than that of Liu Yitong, also speaks
of an "old devil" inside the cathedral who specialized in harming people with his
black magic. It appears that in one form or another this belief was widely held at
the time.

72. As was clearly recognized by foreigners at the time. "During the whole of
yesterday," Elwood G. Tewksbury, Arthur H. Smith, and W. T. Hobart wrote from
Beijing in a letter of June 15, "the entire horizon was filled with smoke from the
countless fires in every direction, *and this most dangerous weapon the Boxers hope
to use constantly and effectively against us*" (emphasis supplied), cited in Sarah
Boardman Goodrich, June 18 entry of "Journal," 18. W. E. Bainbridge described
fire as the Boxers' "favorite weapon" (Bainbridge, "Besieged," 24). During the
siege of the legations, fire control became an important part of the daily activity
of the besieged. See, for example, Emma Estelle Martin, diary, June 21, 1900, pp.
55–56.

73. Liu Mengyang, *Tianjin quanfei*, 24, 32; *TYJ*, 148.

74. From a notice posted in Tianjin, in Chen Zhenjiang and Cheng Xiao,
Yihetuan wenxian, 41. For other examples, see ibid., 18, 20, 22; Qiao Zhiqiang,
comp., *Yihetuan zai Shanxi*, 5–6. This same essential calamity-aversion logic
appears to be used the world over; it is often encountered in the United States in
chain letters.

75. Recorded in Chen Zhenjiang and Cheng Xiao, *Yihetuan wenxian*, 143. This
incantation was derived from a Shandong Spirit Boxer incantation, the text of
which is also in ibid. In one form or another it was widely circulated in the Beijing-
Tianjin area during the Boxer summer. My translation makes no attempt to capture the rhyming pattern of the original. Another incantation which the Boxers
instructed Tianjin residents to place on their doors is found in ibid., 170–71.

76. See, for example, Yang Diangao, *Gengzi dashi ji*, 84; Zhongfang Shi,
Gengzi jishi, 12; Liu Yitong, *Minjiao xiangchou*, 185, 187; Hua Xuelan, *Riji*, 102;
TYJ, 148; Guan He, *Quanfei*, 475. The reason for the injunction to burn incense
throughout the night may have been the belief that people were better able to protect themselves against evil spirits by staying awake (see Tang Yan, *Gengzi xixing*,
473; Hua Xuelan, *Riji*, 102). In the atmosphere of fear and intimidation that prevailed in both Beijing and Tianjin, local elites often found it convenient to comply with Boxer orders (sometimes for fear that, if they did not, word of it would get
to the Boxers via their household servants). Zhongfang Shi (*Gengzi jishi*, 13) thus
wrote on June 14: "Starting yesterday my household each night has faced southeast,
burned incense, and prayed, respectfully beseeching heaven and earth to safeguard the health of my mother and the security of my family." See also Guan He,
Quanfei, 475.

77. After the burning down of the three churches in Tianjin on June 14, for
example, the Boxers ordered all families to abstain from meat for three days (Liu
Mengyang, *Tianjin quanfei*, 13; see also ibid., 11). For seven days, according to
another account, men and women in Tianjin were to eat vegetarian meals only
(*TYJ*, 147).

78. See, for example, Yang Diangao, *Gengzi dashi ji*, 84; Tang Yan, *Gengzi xixing*, 473; Zhongfang Shi, *Gengzi jishi*, 12; *TYJ*, 148.

79. This was one of the less commonly encountered restrictions. See Liu Mengyang, *Tianjin quanfei*, 11.

80. See, for example, ibid., 13; Zhongfang Shi, *Gengzi jishi*, 12; Liu Yitong, *Minjiao xiangchou*, 187.

81. Sun Shaotang, a former Boxer from Tianjin, for example, recalled that the Boxers at one point instructed all households in the city to paste red paper on their windows or at their kitchen entrances (TDYYDB, 147). "Red in China," Arthur P. Wolf has written, "is more than an expression of joy; it is also a prophylactic color, a means of warding off evil." See his "Chinese Kinship and Mourning Dress," 193–94. See also Watson, "Of Flesh and Bones," 167–68.

82. Yang Diangao, *Gengzi dashi ji*, 87. See also Hua Xuelan, *Riji*, 104.

83. The text of the notice is reproduced in Qiao Zhiqiang, comp., *Yihetuan zai Shanxi*, 3. For examples of the blood-smearing magic attributed to foreigners and native Christians in Tianjin, see Liu Mengyang, *Tianjin quanfei*, 11; for similar examples in Beijing, and the magic used by the Boxers to counteract it, see Yang Diangao, *Gengzi dashi ji*, 86; for Shanxi, see Liu Dapeng, *Suoji*, 35. The Boxers' enemies were accused, among other things, of using dogs' blood to inscribe red circles on the main entrances of people's homes; unless this magic was counteracted, the members of the household would kill each other within seven days. Dogs' blood, especially the blood of black dogs, was commonly used to symbolize human menstrual blood. See Eberhard, *Dictionary*, 186; Naquin, *Shantung Rebellion*, 101; Seaman, "Sexual Politics," 392.

84. Zhongfang Shi, *Gengzi jishi*, 13, 19, 21–22. Writing "Precious Sword of the Red Heaven" on one's door was also a means of affording protection in situations fraught with danger (such as kalpa calamity). Chen Zhenjiang and Cheng Xiao, *Yihetuan wenxian*, 171–72.

85. Guan He, *Quanfei*, 475; Liu Mengyang, *Tianjin quanfei*, 11, 19. For another example of conflicting instructions to the populace of Tianjin, see ibid., 30.

86. Yang Diangao, *Gengzi dashi ji*, 88.

87. Liu Mengyang, *Tianjin quanfei*, 13. See in this connection Guan He's account (*Quanfei*, 476) of his family's flight from Tianjin, in which he states that his wife's rickshaw was covered with a red quilt so that the Boxers would not consider her impure and kill her.

88. Guan He, *Quanfei*, 474.

89. TYJ, 147–48.

90. TYJ, 147. The reason women were not to touch their feet to the ground was presumably that the ground was considered to be, as Ahern puts it, "full of dirty stuff" ("Power and Pollution," 270).

91. Eberhard, *Dictionary*, 261.

92. Chen Zhenjiang and Cheng Xiao, *Yihetuan wenxian*, 46–47, 112–14. A slightly different version of the notice containing these orders was circulated in Shanxi; see Qiao Zhiqiang, comp., *Yihetuan zai Shanxi*, 5–6. In his diary, Hua Xuelan says (*Riji*, 111) that, although he and a friend, finding the Boxers' prohibitions intolerable, consumed cooked food as usual on the seventh day, the womenfolk in his household adhered to the orders scrupulously. Also, according to what he had heard, many other families both within and without Beijing didn't light fires on this day.

340   93. *TYJ*, 147. I have translated the jingle freely in order to convey something of the original rhyming structure: "Fünü bushutou, kanqu yangren tou, fünü buguo-jiao, shajin yangren xiao hehe." A similar jingle was chanted, at the Boxers' urging, by the population of Zhuozhou (Chen Zhenjiang and Cheng Xiao, *Yihetuan wen-xian*, 131). In southern Guangdong a hairdressing (*shutou*) ritual was performed before marriage to signal a girl's transition to adulthood (see Topley, "Marriage Resistance," 67, 82–83; also Stockard, *Daughters*, 72). It is therefore possible (although somewhat speculative) that "not dressing one's hair" (*bushutou*) (trans-lated in the text as "don't dress their locks") is here intended to have the additional meaning of "not marry." By remaining unmarried, women would be freed of a major source of uncleanness and thus, by removing from the environment a crip-pling obstacle to the effective functioning of Boxer magic, advance the cause of the Chinese side in the conflict with the foreigners. During the Cultural Revolution, when the Red Lanterns were presented in heavily mythologized form (see ch. 9), *bushutou* became a clear symbol of youthful rebellion and female emancipation from an oppressive Confucian moral code.

94. I am grateful to Ruby Watson for suggesting this analogy.

95. Although the Red Lanterns were far and away the best known and most active organization of females in 1900, and the only one consisting almost entirely of girls and teenagers, there were reports of Green Lanterns (Qingdengzhao), Blue Lanterns (Landengzhao), and Black Lanterns (Heidengzhao), the former two of which were apparently composed of widows (TDYYDB, 40; Liu Mengyang, *Tianjin quanfei*, 9; Liu Dapeng, *Suoji*, 30). Liu Dapeng states that there was also an organ-ization of Christian women in the Taiyuan area, who were called White Lanterns (Baidengzhao) and had magic so powerful it could overcome that of the Boxers and Red Lanterns. He notes a number of instances in which the Boxers managed to kill these women or punish them in some other way (*Suoji*, 30).

96. *Yu nan riji*, 163. On a more general level, Li Xisheng writes that the Boxers regarded themselves as no match for the Red Lanterns (*zi wei buru*) (Li Xisheng, *Guobian*, 18). Also not in fear of "dirty things," according to rumors heard (with skepticism) by Zhongfang Shi (*Gengzi jishi*, 24), were the "black corps" Boxers. These people were said to have entered Beijing on July 21: "They cover their heads with black kerchiefs and wear dark shirts and trousers and yellow waistbands. Armed with double-edged swords, they don't fear dirty things and gunfire is unable to get near their bodies."

97. Liu Yitong, *Minjiao xiangchou*, 182; Chen Zhenjiang and Cheng Xiao, *Yihetuan wenxian*, 24–25. A photograph of the original of this request is in *YHT*, vol. 1, front.

98. For references to the Red Lanterns in Shandong, see *SYDZX*, 17, 66–67, 80, 85. For Shanxi, the contemporary Taiyuan resident Liu Dapeng supplies detailed information in his *Suoji*, 29–30.

99. Liu Mengyang, *Tianjin quanfei*, 9. Some of the towns with Red Lantern altars are listed in TDYYDB, 40. To train to become a Red Lantern appears to have become something of a fad among teenagers in Tianjin in the spring and summer (see *TYJ*, 141). On the arduous regimen required of trainees, see Zhao Qing (72), Fourth Sister-Disciple, Jinghai county, TDYYDB, 135–36.

100. Liu Mengyang, *Tianjin quanfei*, 9; also ibid., 37. There was not always a clear line between the general Boxer prohibition against looking at females or having contact with them, because they were a source of pollution, and the more specific injunction, in the case of the Red Lanterns, not to look at them, out of a sense of awe and respect. A former Boxer from Duliu claimed that, although Duliu had its contingent of Red Lanterns, "we never saw them. In those days the Boxers had a rule that you weren't permitted to gaze on females casually." Li Zhende (81), Duliu, TDYYDB, 126. See also Zhang Jincai (83), Third Brother-Disciple, western suburb of Tianjin, ibid., 123.

The same confusion between reverence and pollution-aversion is found in the later oral history materials gathered in Hebei in the 1970s. A former Red Lantern reported that the Boxers came to the Red Lantern altar every day to pay their respects before the image of the Venerable Mother Guanyin (Guanyin laomu). When the time came for them to perform this ritual, the senior sister-disciple shut the gate and hung the Guanyin image outside. When the Boxers were done, they called out: "Please take it down." Li Fengzhi (86), Xiong county, HDYYDJ, Dec. 27, 1973, 011–14.

A former Boxer recalled: "When our village defenses fell, the Red Lanterns didn't run over to us. We had rules, and they weren't allowed to come here." Sun Yi (91), Xiong county, ibid., n.d., 011–14. The separate location of Red Lantern and Boxer training areas is confirmed in Wang Shuchun (70), Xiong county, ibid., n.d., 011–14; Xin Hanzhang (85), Zhuozhou, ibid., Dec. 24, 1973, 005:No. 7. The general prohibition against looking at any woman is alluded to in Liu Qing (83) and Liang Chun (86), Laishui county (Shiting commune), ibid., Jan. 1, 1974, 005:No. 7. It is possible that in some places and in certain circumstances the taboo against Boxer contact with women was not observed. One very elderly former Red Lantern recalled that in her village the daughter-in-law of the senior brother-disciple of the Boxers was the senior sister-disciple of the local contingent of Red Lanterns and that the two groups ate their meals together. Du Darui (94), Sun village (county unspecified), ibid., n.d., 011–14.

101. Chen Zhenjiang and Cheng Xiao, *Yihetuan wenxian*, 75. Yuan Chang, in a diary excerpt dated July 18, 1900, refers to the Red Lanterns as Armor of the Red Lantern (Yuan Chang, *Riji*, 346). On the interchangeability of the Red Lantern and other fighting techniques emphasizing invulnerability, as perceived by both Christian observers and oral history informants in Shandong, see Esherick, *Origins*, 227.

102. In Chen Zhenjiang and Cheng Xiao, *Yihetuan wenxian*, 78; for other texts of a similar nature, see ibid., 73–95.

103. Some contemporaries, of course, did link the Boxers to the White Lotus. The most famous was Lao Naixuan, whose influential pamphlet *Yihequan jiaomen yuanliu kao* and other writings are found in YHT 4:431–39, 449–74, 477–90. Esherick (*Origins*, 220) states that "among contemporary observers it was usually those most hostile to the Boxers . . . who were most apt to argue for the White Lotus origins of the group." This may indeed be so with respect to the Boxers specifically, but it did not carry over to commentary on the Red Lanterns.

104. Chinese women typically could expect to undergo excruciating torments in Hell unless ceremonially purified at their funerals by the male members of their

342   families (Grant, "Spiritual Saga," 226). Such ritual purification is an important function of the Mulian story cycle, as pointed out by Grant and other contributors to Johnson, ed., *Ritual Opera*. It is also the main point of the Blood Bowl Sutra ritual, as enacted in Taiwan at women's funerals. In this rite, men perform ritually the most horrible act imaginable. They symbolically drink the blood of their birth and in so doing free their mother "from the bonds of her existence as a woman and allow her to be reincarnated as a higher being." Seaman, "Sexual Politics," 395.

    105. See, for example, Zhao Qing (72), Jinghai county, Fourth Sister-Disciple, TDYYDB, 135; Liu Mengyang, *Tianjin quanfei*, 9; Yuan Chang, *Riji*, 346. Zhao Qing stated that she was only twelve *sui* (eleven) when she joined the Red Lanterns. Another former Red Lantern, Li Fengzhi, was only thirteen *sui* (twelve). Li's mother was so anxious over her daughter's becoming a Red Lantern that she agreed to it only on the proviso that she, the mother, could come along as the group's cook (which she did). Li Fengzhi (86), Xiong county, HDYYDJ, Dec. 27, 1973, 011–14.

    106. In Europe in the early 1990s the average age of menarche was 12.8; in 1840 it was 16.5, in 1880, 16.0 (Rees, "Menarche"; Hughes and Jones, "Intake," 329; see also Frisch, "Demographic Implications"). Although there are a number of factors believed to affect the age of onset of menstruation (genetic influences, socioeconomic conditions, general health and well-being, nutrition, the type of exercise engaged in, and so forth) and there is some uncertainty as to the exact role nutrition plays, there seems to be broad agreement that poor diet (especially a diet low in protein) has a delaying effect. According to one major study done by an international team of scientists, focusing mainly on nutrition and based on survey data collected in 1983 from 65 largely rural counties from all over China, the average age of menarche in the Chinese countryside at the time was seventeen (Chen Junshi et al., *Diet*, 750) (I am indebted to Dr. Walter C. Willett of the Harvard School of Public Health for calling my attention to this study). Other studies of Chinese (specifically Han) females from rural backgrounds, also based on data collected in the 1980s but from much more limited samples, have come up with a significantly lower average menarcheal age, ranging from 13.83 to 14.40 (Xi Huanjiu et al., "Yuejing chuchao nianling"; Shen Yue et al., "Jiating yinsu"; W. S. Lin et al., "The Menarcheal Age of Chinese Girls"). Whichever of these sets of figures is closer to the truth, it seems reasonable to assume that, at the turn of the century, when the diet of most rural Chinese was far worse than in the 1980s, the average age of menarche was substantially higher than it is now, comparable to, if not higher than, the average age of menarche in Europe in the nineteenth century.

    107. One of Ahern's informants told her: "Menstruation is like one-hundredth of a birth" ("Power and Pollution," 270). The traditional period of childbearing pollution in China lasted, according to Topley ("Marriage Resistance," 73), from the fifth month of pregnancy until 100 days after a child's birth (a total of eight to nine months), which would mean that a married woman in her childbearing years would have been in a seriously polluted state a good bit of the time.

    108. Grant, "Spiritual Saga," 227. Liu Xiang nü, another example of this form of heroine noted by Grant, did in fact marry, although, as Daniel Overmyer observes, it was hardly a "normal marriage." What Liu Xiang nü valued, Overmyer contends, was "meditation, not sex and children." There was, therefore, "a strong implicit

resistance to marriage" in the *baojuan* in which her story is told. Overmyer, "Values," 251. The full story of Liu Xiang nü is told in ibid., 245–50. For a Chinese Catholic variation on the theme of marriage resistance as a vehicle for the leading of a life of religious purity and devotion, see Entenmann, "Christian Virgins."

109. Topley, "Marriage Resistance," 67–88, esp. 75, 79. Stockard, in her in-depth treatment of the various strategies of marriage resistance in the silk-reeling areas of southern Guangdong, revises some of Topley's earlier analysis.

110. One of the few exceptions is the oral history testimony of the former Red Lantern, Zhao Qing. Zhao's account is informative. But the discussion of her motives for becoming a member of the Red Lanterns (along with, she claims, all the other girls in Ziya, the market town in Jinghai county in which she lived) is so consistent with the standard Communist rhetoric of the 1950s that it is hard to know how much credence to give it. Zhao states that she joined partly as an act of rebellion against her parents, who, because she was their only offspring, had betrothed her at age six, and partly because it was an opportunity to fight the foreigners. Zhao Qing (72), Jinghai county, Fourth Sister-Disciple, TDYYDB, 135. Zhao Qing (with the grass radical over the character for her given name, making it "Jing") was again hauled out to represent the voice of the Red Lanterns during the campaign against Liu Shaoqi in the early stages of the Cultural Revolution. Her faithful reflection of the prevailing party line, in these circumstances, was beyond dispute. See Zhao Jing, "Yihetuan shi gemingde!"

111. Liu Mengyang, *Tianjin quanfei*, 19–20.

112. Sawara Tokusuke and Ouyin, *Quanshi*, 272; Ying-ho Chiang, "Literary Reactions," 291.

113. Guan He, *Quanfei*, 487–88. The Holy Mother of the Yellow Lotus was also described as a prostitute in *TYJ*, 146. What actually became of the Holy Mother isn't clear. For an account differing in some details from Guan He's, see Liu Mengyang, *Tianjin quanfei*, 56. The author of *TYJ* (158) says she was killed in action, rather than captured by foreign forces. Liao Yizhong, "Lin Hei'er" (100–101n8) reviews the several theories concerning her fate.

114. *Quanfei jilüe*, Jingtu:4a-b; *Jing-Jin quanfei jilüe*, Jingtu:4a-b.

115. As an indication of the mood of intimidation prevailing in the summer of 1900, Guan He (*Quanfei*, 488) tells of an incident that occurred when he was staying at the home of a family named Liu in Qing county (just south of Tianjin). One day Old Liu, who was a man of some education, called to Guan to come outside and see the Armor of the Red Lantern. Pointing to a dark cloud in the sky, he said: "Those countless women dressed in red are the Armor of the Red Lantern." Guan didn't see a thing, but he noted that everyone in the streets was talking about it, gesticulating animatedly, certain that what they saw in the sky was none other than the Armor of the Red Lantern. And Old Liu echoed everything said by the rest. Guan was perplexed. Only later did he realize that Liu, as a self-protective stratagem, had faked the whole thing. See the similar account in Ye Changchi, 5/8 (June 4, [1900]), *Riji*, 441.

116. I am indebted here to Ann S. Anagnost, who applies Lévi-Strauss's idea of "gravitational field" to the practice and social acceptance of "the shaman and his magic" in contemporary China. See Anagnost, "Politics and Magic," 47; also Lévi-Strauss, "The Sorceror," 162.

5. Rumor and Rumor Panic

1. The locus classicus is the ancient text *Zhanguo ce* (Intrigues of the Warring States): "It was perfectly clear that there was no tiger in the marketplace. But after three people said there was, a tiger materialized."

2. Ye Changchi, 5/28 (June 24, [1900]), *Riji*, 453; Liu Mengyang, *Tianjin quan-fei*, 11; C. W. Price, diary, between June 15 and 23, 1900, Fen Chou Fu, Shansi [Fenzhou, Shanxi], as excerpted in Edwards, *Fire and Sword*, 269–70 (note the intriguing parallel to the Red Lanterns' power, with their fans, to change the direction and strength of the winds); Guan He, *Quanfei*, 469; Liu Dapeng, *Suoji*, 41 (on the black wind, see Chen Zhenjiang and Cheng Xiao, *Yihetuan wenxian*, 76–77, and Naquin, *Millenarian Rebellion*, 12).

3. Rosnow, "Inside Rumor," 484–96 (quoted phrases from 488). There appears to be a lack of consensus among rumor researchers over whether individuals are more or less critical in their evaluation of rumors when their personal involvement in the content of the rumor is high (see ibid., 487).

4. Quoted in Goleman, "Anatomy of a Rumor," C5. See also Rosnow and Fine, *Rumor*, 11, 81–93, 131.

5. Rosnow, "Inside Rumor," 488.

6. Li Wenhai and Liu Yangdong, "Shehui xinli fenxi," 10–11.

7. Pruitt, *Daughter of Han*, 151.

8. Guan He, *Quanfei*, 468.

9. Liu Dapeng, *Suoji*, 39–42 (quote from 39).

10. *NCH*, June 13, 1900, p. 1064 (also ibid., June 20, 1900, p. 1113); Newton letters, excerpted in unidentified newspaper clippings, in Mrs. S. P. Fenn, "Peking Siege-Book," 10 (insert).

11. Letter, May 4, 1900, in LMP, box 2, file 6.

12. According to Liu Mengyang, *Tianjin quanfei*, 11, incense shops in Tianjin completely sold out after the Boxers ordered families to burn incense continuously.

13. Ibid., 19.

14. Journal, Beijing, Aug. 1, 1900, in LMP, box 1, file 1.

15. This is a common source of rumors generally. In September 1992, people in Dade County, Florida, simply refused to accept the official tally of only fourteen deaths directly attributable to Hurricane Andrew. "The devastation has been so tremendous," an engineer inspecting the damage stated, "that you can't believe that people survived." One rumor alleged that there were a thousand bodies buried in a mass grave in Florida City. *NYT*, Sept. 5, 1992, 6.

16. Liu Mengyang, *Tianjin quanfei*, 10.

17. Wang Enpu, northern suburbs of Tianjin, Second Brother-Disciple, TDYYDB, 144.

18. Goodrich, "Journal," June 30 and July 8, 1900, pp. 32, 42–43; Martin, diary, July 27, 1900, p. 83.

19. *TYJ*, 153–54.

20. Published examples are: Toynbee, ed., *Half the World*, 324–25; Thomson, *China and the Powers*, facing p. 122; Fitzgerald, *Horizon History*, 354; Zhang Haipeng, ed., *Jindaishi tuji*, 106.

21. See Liao Yizhong, "Zhang Decheng."

22. Although not in the form of a rumor, a similar fantasy was reflected in the testimony of a former Boxer, who recalled: "Whenever the Boxers fought, we won. Whatever we pointed at burst into flames. Because of this, the foreigners at the time really were afraid and would send people to make peace with us." Zhang Jincai (83), Third Brother-Disciple, western suburbs of Tianjin, TDYYDB, 124.

23. *TYJ*, 158. According to Liao Yizhong, "Zhang Decheng" (93–94), Zhang did in fact return to the Duliu area after the fall of Tianjin, in the hope of reviving the movement, and was killed not long after by local gentry-led militia. See also Chen Zhenjiang and Cheng Xiao, *Yihetuan wenxian*, 28–29; and the oral history testimony of a Duliu man (Li Zhende) who served under Zhang Decheng, in TDYYDB, 129–30. Liu Dapeng reported a flurry of Boxer-indestructibility rumors in Taiyuan in early 1901. The Boxers were said to have become active again, doing their drilling at night to avoid discovery. See his *Riji*, GX 27/1/21 (Mar. 11, 1901), 12.

24. Guan He, *Quanfei*, 469. A similar symbolic meaning is implied in a story told after the fall of Tianjin. At the time, word had it that there were still a lot of Red Lanterns in circulation, as attested by the fact that boats in Duliu could be seen with red lanterns suspended from their sterns. The rumor was that when foreigners laid eyes on these red lanterns they became so terrified they exclaimed "What's this? The Red Lanterns have risen again?" and never again returned to Duliu. Li Tinghuai (78), non-Boxer, Duliu, TDYYDB, 154.

25. Li Wenhai and Liu Yangdong, "Shehui xinli fenxi," 13–14. The full text of the "Twenty-Five Article Treaty" is in Chen Zhenjiang and Cheng Xiao, *Yihetuan wenxian*, 53. Chen and Cheng (55) state that there were many fabricated treaties of this sort circulated in the summer of 1900 in different parts of China; they supply information on one that made its appearance in Shaoxing, Zhejiang, in *gengzi 6/chu* (late June, early July).

26. Liu Mengyang, *Tianjin quanfei*, 8.

27. Quoted in Edwards, *Fire and Sword*, 269. Rowena Bird, of the same mission, commented in a similar vein (journal, June 25, 1900; see also Corbin, "Shansi Mission," 3).

28. Ogren, "Conflict of Sufferings," 65.

29. Allen, *Siege*, 67–68.

30. Butler, "Dame Rumor," 24.

31. Jeffrey S. Victor's study of the satanic cult rumor panic in Jamestown, New York, in 1988 suggests that "threat rumors . . . have the paradoxical effect of satisfying the need for information in matters of uncertainty and also of increasing people's collective anxiety." Victor, *Satanic Panic*, 40–41; also ibid., 38.

32. Goleman, "Anatomy of a Rumor," C1.

33. Philip Kuhn has written on a sorcery panic centered on queue-clipping that took place in 1768; see his *Soulstealers*. A queue-clipping panic of 1876 is discussed in ter Haar, *White Lotus Teachings*, 263–66.

34. Sawara Tokusuke and Ouyin, *Quanluan*, 116.

35. Liu Dapeng, *Suoji*, 39–40, 42. On the frequency of false alarms in Taiyuan in the summer of 1900, see also the interview (Aug. 1959) with Jia Xianju, who was eighteen *sui* and living in Taiyuan at the time, in Qiao Zhiqiang, comp., *Yihetuan zai Shanxi*, 150. Rowena Bird, in her journal entry of July 10, reported panic in

346   Tung Fan Ts'un (Dunfang village) at the news that foreign soldiers were coming. "Many," she wrote, "jumped into wells."

36. Tang Yan, *Gengzi xixing*, 474.

37. Hong Shoushan, *Shishi*, 94.

38. Memorial of GX 26/6/28 (July 24, 1900), in *Yihetuan dang'an shiliao* 1:366.

39. Liu Mengyang, *Tianjin quanfei*, 50. "At every gate," wrote photographer James Ricalton, "men, women and children were trampling and jostling in their efforts to escape to the country and to outlying villages" (Ricalton, *China*, 232). In the climactic days of the Battle of Tianjin, when the city was in a state of extreme turmoil, the friend of a Chinese bookkeeper, who had moved his family to the foreign firm that employed him, rushed in and announced that since the foreign troops had gone down to defeat and the Chinese government forces and Boxers were about to come, he should quickly take his family and flee the foreign concession. The bookkeeper's family tried to escape but found their way blocked by foreign troops. They returned to their hiding place, only to find that the friend's report had been a rumor. *Yu nan riji*, 170.

40. Gamewell, "History," 50. "Saturday June 9th," Gamewell added a few pages later, "was the day of the patron saint of the Boxers. Rumor, that seemed true, said that the Empress had given out that the troops might slaughter all foreigners in the city" (ibid., 52).

41. Letter, originally printed in the *New York Tribune*, excerpted in Mrs. S. P. Fenn, "Peking Siege-Book," 3.

42. Fei's account, excerpted from Luella Miner's *Two Heroes of Cathay*, is in Eva Jane Price, *China Journal*, 264.

43. Fei Qihao, after a close call, did indeed escape harm and later studied at Oberlin College. Rowena Bird was killed at Taigu, Shanxi, on July 31.

44. Rosnow, "Inside Rumor," 486.

45. Jahoda, *Superstition*, 133.

46. Fussell, *Wartime*, 36. It is interesting to compare Fussell's observations on the importance of narrative as a means of enabling us to deal with "unmediated actuality" in a wartime setting with the late Anatole Broyard's thoughts about narrative's comparable importance in helping people cope with critical illness—another life situation marked by high levels of mortal danger and uncertainty. "My initial experience of illness," Broyard wrote, "was as a series of disconnected shocks, and my first instinct was to try to bring it under control by turning it into a narrative. Always in emergencies we invent stories. We describe what is happening, as if to confine the catastrophe. The patient's narrative keeps him from falling out of his life into his illness. Like a novelist, he gives his anxiety a shape." Broyard, "Good Books."

47. See unidentified newspaper clippings, in Mrs. S. P. Fenn, "Peking Siege-Book," 3–16, 50. The *New York Times* of July 5 announced "ALL FOREIGNERS IN PEKING DEAD" (3). As an example of the irresponsible journalism denounced by the *New York Tribune*, the front-page article in the *Times* of July 16 carried the following headlines: "DETAILS OF THE PEKING TRAGEDY—FOREIGNERS ALL SLAIN AFTER A LAST HEROIC STAND—SHOT THEIR WOMEN FIRST."

48. Blake, "Collective Excitement."

49. Victor, *Satanic Panic*, 18–19. See also Cohn, "Myth of Satan." Victor (47) makes the added point that satanic cult rumors were most likely to be believed by

Americans suffering from anxiety owing to economic stress and looking for a scapegoat for their troubles. A similar analysis was put forward by the deputy mayor of the depressed port of Calais, France, who felt that "a growing sense of insecurity and an increasing concern about the future" lay behind the eruption of mass hysteria that gripped the city in the fall of 1992. Racism, rather than satanism, appears to have been the driving force in this case. The scapegoat was a dark-skinned young man of partly Tunisian descent, who was accused, among other things, of abducting, raping, beheading, and eviscerating blond children. Not a shred of evidence in support of these charges was discovered. *NYT*, Oct. 30, 1992, A3.

50. See Cohen, *China and Christianity*, 45–58; *Jinzun shengyu bixie quantu*. The most comprehensive collection of anti-Christian lore, as circulated during the period from 1861 to 1899, is in Wang Minglun, ed., *Fan yangjiao*.

51. Cohen, *China and Christianity*, 55, 305n33.

52. The words of American minister Frederick F. Low, as cited in ibid., 231.

53. Ter Haar, "Images of Outsiders."

54. Wang Enpu, northern suburbs of Tianjin, Second Brother-Disciple, TDYYDB, 143.

55. Liu Yitong, *Minjiao xiangchou*, 184.

56. Ibid., 195. During the siege the foreigners did in fact dine on horse meat with some regularity.

57. Guan He, *Quanfei*, 471; see also ibid., 489. The "straight eyes" appellation is used by many of the former Boxers from the Tianjin area whose words are recorded in TDYYDB, 118–47.

58. Ye Changchi, 5/28 (June 24, [1900]) and 5/25 (June 21), *Riji*, 453.

59. Longgu shanren [Guo Zeyun], *Gengzi shijian*, 131.

60. Sarah Boardman Goodrich, "Journal," June 15, 1900, p. 13. The girls, according to Goodrich (ibid.), "bravely refused to lie. . . . Some were killed, and some fled."

61. *TYJ*, 151.

62. *Yong rao lu*, 5/13 (June 9, [1900]), 250.

63. Ibid.

64. I have been unable to examine Yun's diary directly. It is cited in Li Wenhai and Liu Yangdong, "Shehui xinli fenxi," 13. Li and Liu (ibid.) use Yun Yuding to illustrate the distinction they draw between two basically different kinds of rumors prevalent at the turn of the century: one, reflecting the "superstitious mentality" (*mixin sixiang*) of the Boxers and referring to things that could not possibly have occurred (such as Red Lanterns flying or Boxers causing foreign ships at sea to burst into flames spontaneously), the other embodying charges against the Christians that, although not in fact true, were at least scientifically plausible.

65. On these legends, see Brunvand, *Vanishing Hitchhiker*; Ellis, "Introduction."

66. See Campion-Vincent, "Baby-Parts Story"; Victor, *Satanic Panic*, 73–75 and passim; Rosnow and Fine, *Rumor*, 21–22, 42ff.

67. Statement of Dr. E. H. Edwards of the Baptist Missionary Society, as quoted in Forsyth, comp. and ed., *China Martyrs*, 367; Liu Mengyang, *Tianjin quanfei*, 11; Boxer notice, in Qiao Zhiqiang, comp., *Yihetuan zai Shanxi*, 3; report of Jizhou (in Shuntian prefecture) Battalion Captain Xie Dian'en, GX 26/5/30 (June 26, 1900), in *Yihetuan dang'an shiliao* 1:193; Liu Dapeng, *Suoji*, 35, 46; Rowena Bird, letter, July 10, 1900; Pruitt, *Daughter of Han*, 151.

348

68. In Qiao Zhiqiang, comp., *Yihetuan zai Shanxi*, 3.

69. Liu Dapeng, *Suoji*, 35, 46. On the use of human urine to negate the effects of harmful magic (in this case paper objects), see ter Haar, *White Lotus Teachings*, 265. This is, as the author notes, the "logical counterpart of the use of clear water to make magic work" (ibid., 176; also 265).

70. Liu Dapeng, *Suoji*, 35; Edwards, in Forsyth, comp. and ed., *China Martyrs*, 367; Smith, *China in Convulsion* 2:659–60.

71. Liu Dapeng, *Suoji*, 35.

72. Theodora M. Inglis, letter, Beijing, May 30, 1900, in Mrs. S. P. Fenn, "Peking Siege-Book," 1–2.

73. Elvin, "Mandarins," 134n80.

74. Smith, *China in Convulsion* 2:659–60. The charge was reported by the American minister Edwin H. Conger in a dispatch to Secretary of State John Hay, May 8, 1900, in *FRUS*, 122. Evidence of the charge's circulation in Zhili is in: Chen Zhenjiang and Cheng Xiao, *Yihetuan wenxian*, 23, 41, 107–109; Charles A. Killie, letter, Sanhe county, May 16, 1900, *FRUS*, 131; *NCH*, May 30, 1900, pp. 966–67; ibid., June 6, 1900, p. 1022; Luella Miner, letter, Tongzhou, May 4, 1900, in LMP, box 2, file 6; memorial of Zhili Governor-General Yulu, GX 26/4/19 (May 17, 1900), in *Yihetuan dang'an shiliao* 1:91; report of Jizhou Battalion Captain Xie Dian'en, in ibid., 193; Yang Diangao, *Gengzi dashi ji*, 86; Bessie McCoy, letter, Beijing, May 28, 1900, excerpted in Mrs. S. P. Fenn, "Peking Siege-Book," 1; Theodora M. Inglis, letter, Beijing, May 30, 1900, in ibid., 1–2; Allen, *Siege*, 25. In Shanxi: Edwards, in Forsyth, comp. and ed., *China Martyrs*, 367; Ogren, "Conflict of Sufferings," 65; Liu Dapeng, *Suoji*, 34–35, 42, 45–47; Forsyth, comp. and ed., *China Martyrs*, 34; Herbert Dixon (English Baptist Mission), diary, July 11, 1900, in ibid., 51; *Shanxi sheng gengzinian jiaonan*, 510; Rowena Bird, letter, Taigu, July 6, 1900; Bird, journal, Taigu, July 3 and 6, 1900; memorials of Shanxi Governor Yuxian, GX 26/6/12 (July 8, 1900) and GX 26/6/14 (July 10, 1900), in *Yihetuan dang'an shiliao* 1:263, 281. In Shandong: Pruitt, *Daughter of Han*, 151.

75. Chen Zhenjiang and Cheng Xiao, *Yihetuan wenxian*, 107. See also ibid., 23, 41, 108; *Shanxi sheng gengzinian jiaonan*, 510; Qiao Zhiqiang, comp., *Yihetuan zai Shanxi*, 5; Liu Dapeng, *Suoji*, 34–35. Chen and Cheng note (23) that the items typically included in these remedies functioned, in standard herbal medicine, to calm the stomach, nourish the kidney, and act as antidotes to poison or as astringents.

76. Liu Dapeng, *Suoji*, 46.

77. Letter, July 6, 1900. In a letter of July 9 Bird wrote: "All that is necessary now to get rid of a man someone hates is to suggest that he is hired by foreigners to set fire to houses or poison wells, and he is at once killed without question — in this way many are killed who have no connection at all with us." See also Bird's journal, July 3 and 6.

78. Elvin, "Mandarins," 118–19.

79. *NCH*, Jan. 6, 1893, p. 10.

80. *NCH*, June 25, 1897, pp. 1126, 1129, 1136; Sept. 3, 1897, p. 448; Sept. 10, 1897, pp. 486–87.

81. *NCH*, Sept. 24, 1897, pp. 579–80; Oct. 8, 1897, p. 654; Dec. 19, 1898, p. 1147. The abrupt fading of rumor panics is particularly noticeable, of course, when a specific date that has been fixed for a cataclysmic event passes without the cataclysm

occurring. This is what happened in the flood panic of 1872. It also happened in the case of the satanic cult panic of 1988 in Jamestown, New York. When May 13 (Friday the thirteenth), the date set for the kidnapping and ritual murder of a blonde, blue-eyed virgin and other horrible occurrences came and went, people suddenly ceased to believe the stories that had only recently paralyzed them with fear and were even able to laugh at their former concerns. See Victor, *Satanic Panic*, 36, 41–42. Elvin ("Mandarins," 122–23) notes that during the summer of 1900 also "there was a curious combination of simple-minded gullibility followed by a swift reassertion of common sense," as initial enthusiasm for Boxer practices and claims gave way to growing skepticism.

82. Philip Kuhn, *Soulstealers*; ter Haar, "Images of Outsiders" and *White Lotus Teachings*, 173–95, 263–81. A kidnapping scare erupted in Wuhan, Yichang, and other areas of Hubei in the summer of 1900, occasioned partly by drought-related anxiety, partly by rumors that to secure the bridges for the Beijing-Hankou railway, then under construction, children had to be buried beneath the foundations. It was charged that foreigners practiced "mesmerism" and, simply by touching children, were able to gain complete control over them. *NCH*, June 13, 1900, pp. 1063, 1065; June 20, 1900, p. 1111; June 27, 1900, pp. 1157–58; July 4, 1900, p. 14.

83. Ter Haar, "Images of Outsiders."

84. See Victor, *Satanic Panic*, 52–53, 65, 73–75, 76, 123–30; Campion-Vincent, "Baby-Parts Story."

85. These examples are all drawn from Loewenberg, "Rumors."

86. Gordon, *Labor*, 177. I am indebted to Yoshihisa Tak Matsusaka for this reference. As a sign of what can only be called progress, in early news coverage of the Kobe earthquake of January 1995 no tensions were reported between Japanese and ethnic Koreans. Indeed, members of the two groups were said to have come to each other's assistance in coping with the disaster. *NYT*, Jan. 22, 1995, 8.

87. Nkpa, "Rumors." Of course, just because rumors of well-poisoning are commonplace doesn't mean that real well-poisoning cannot occur in wartime. A medic from the notorious Japanese biological experimentation group during World War II, Unit 731, admitted to having helped poison Chinese rivers and wells (*NYT*, Mar. 17, 1995, A12). It is also worth noting that, although well-poisoning rumors may be most common in situations in which the survival of an entire community is at stake, there is nothing to keep them from occurring in less cataclysmic circumstances. During the May Fourth movement, Jeffrey Wasserstrom points out, some of the anti-Japanese violence in Shanghai was precipitated by reports that Japanese nationals were poisoning that city's water and food supplies. See his *Student Protests*, 70.

6. Death

1. Ai Sheng, *Quanfei*, 456.

2. Li Yuanshan (79), Boxer from Tianjin, TDYYDB, 133. The charge of indiscriminate killing having been frequently leveled against the Boxers during the first half of the twentieth century, it is not surprising to find a certain level of defensiveness concerning the subject in the oral history materials. See also Xin Hanzhang (85), Zhuo county, HDYYDJ, Dec. 24, 1973, 005:No. 7, p. 3.

350   3. Allen, *Siege*, 292–93. U. S. commissioner William W. Rockhill, who visited the capital in September, elaborated on Allen's observations: "Between Tientsin and Pekin the country for several miles on either side of the highroad has been abandoned by the Chinese. . . . A few peasants may now and then be seen hiding in the fields of corn or sorghum, trying to cut some of the now ripe grain, but when their presence is detected by the foreign soldiers traveling along the road or on the river, they are exposed to being shot at. I saw several corpses along the road, evidently those of peasants shot in this manner." Dispatch to Hay, Shanghai, Oct. 1, 1900, in *FRUS*, 205. The crops referred to by Allen and Rockhill had been made possible by the summer rains. Four months earlier, when the Jiangnan teacher Tang Yan made the trip by train from Tianjin to Beijing, he described a landscape that, as far as the eye could see, was absolutely barren as a result of the drought. Tang Yan, *Gengzi xixing*, 471.

    4. Liu Mengyang, *Tianjin quanfei*, 23; see also ibid., 20–21. Arthur H. Smith accounted for the Boxer penchant for cutting their victims to pieces—and often burning them—by citing the belief (which he claimed was widely prevalent at the time) that Christians would rise from the dead within three days "unless energetic steps were taken to prevent it." *China in Convulsion* 2:660.

    5. Hong Shoushan, *Shishi*, 100. The numbers Hong supplies for people killed and homes burned down are in the "millions" rather than the "thousands." I have treated them as pseudonumbers and translated them accordingly.

    6. Sarah Boardman Goodrich, "Journal," Aug. 20, 1900, 78.

    7. Isaacs, *Images of Asia*, 139–40.

    8. James Hevia's pioneer study of the symbolism of foreign retributive behavior greatly advances our understanding of the psychological dimension, but we still lack a first-rate conventional account of what happened; see Hevia, "Leaving a Brand." On the Chinese side, see Li Dezheng, Su Weizhi, and Liu Tianlu, *Baguo lianjun*, 322–93.

    9. Ai Sheng, *Quanfei*, 448, 461, 464. For a Catholic account of the Gaoluo massacre, with somewhat different details, see Freri, *Heart of Pekin*, 8–10. In the Hebei region oral history materials, a man claiming to be the grandson of the Boxer chief of Gaoluo village described the May 12 event as an armed encounter between Boxers and Christians, with heavy casualties on both sides. Among Christian children alone, he reported, there were several dozen killed. Since all the Christians were placed together in a mass grave, it was impossible to tell how many there were. Yan Baoqi (68), Gaoluo village, Laishui county, HDYYDJ, Jan. 4, 1974, 005:No. 22. For another example of the Boxer practice of throwing Christian victims into wells, see Qu Jiujiang (79), Zaoqiang county, Feb. 1966, HJZH, 186.

    10. Guan He, *Quanfei*, 483. A former Tianjin-area Boxer recalled that south of his village (Gao Family village) there was an unmarked burial pit. Christians ("straight eyes"), when captured, were put to death in the pit. Zhang Jincai (83), Third Brother-Disciple, western suburbs of Tianjin, TDYYDB, 123.

    11. Liu Mengyang, *Tianjin quanfei*, 28.

    12. Ogren, "Conflict of Sufferings," 83. For many other stories of the torments suffered by Chinese Christians at the hands of the Boxers, see Forsyth, comp. and ed., *China Martyrs*, 346–82.

    13. Fenn, diary, 87.

14. Liu Mengyang, *Tianjin quanfei*, 18, 24.

15. Ricalton, *China*, 197–98. See also *NCH*, July 11, 1900, 52, 82. The agent of a traveling circus, who was in Tianjin during the early fighting and then escaped to Shanghai, described the scene as he was leaving the city on July 2: "The muddy Peiho [Baihe] was lined on both banks with hundreds of dead Chinese in all stages of decomposition, beheaded and mutilated in every way" (ibid., 83–84). "Every day," the *North-China Herald* reported, "some 50 to 100 bodies are jammed against the pontoon bridge and are creating a pestilence" (ibid., July 18, 1900, 141; July 25, 1900, 198).

16. Ricalton, *China*, 195; also 193.

17. Guan He, *Quanfei*, 482. In Beijing, according to Zhongfang Shi, the bodies of countless Christians, slaughtered in late June, were simply left in an open area with neither clothing nor coffins. In the summer heat, the stench of the rotting corpses could be smelled a hundred paces away. Because the relatives of the victims were afraid to bury them, the bodies decomposed completely. An analogous situation was encountered in the aftermath of the execution of the anti-Boxer official Xu Jingcheng on July 28. No one prepared the corpse for burial and it wasn't removed from the execution site until afternoon of the second day. It was very hot at the time, there were flies and maggots everywhere, and the foul odor was suffocating. Zhongfang Shi, *Gengzi jishi*, 17–18, 30. The date Zhongfang Shi gives for Xu's execution, August 11, is incorrect.

18. Diary, 107.

19. Oliphant, *Diary*, July 12, 1900, 115.

20. "Inside the Circle" (corrected typed draft).

21. Zhongfang Shi, *Gengzi jishi*, 30–31.

22. Tang Yan, *Gengzi xixing*, 478.

23. Journal, Beijing, Aug. 16, 1900, in LMP, box 1, file 1.

24. *TYJ*, 156–57. Ricalton (*China*, 232–34) offered a not dissimilar account of the flight of refugees after the foreign advance into the Chinese city.

25. Liu Mengyang, *Tianjin quanfei*, 43. See also ibid., 40–42.

26. Liu Mengyang, *Tianjin quanfei*, 48.

27. Ibid., 55.

28. Sawara Tokusuke and Ouyin, *Quanshi*, 288–89.

29. Journal, Aug. 16, 1900, in LMP, box 1, file 1. Curiously, only a week earlier, Miner, in a mood of obvious frustration, had confided to her journal her growing impression "that the only way to ensure lasting peace to poor, distracted China, is for this foreign army to come to Peking and reek [sic] a vengence [sic] which will be understood in the most remote, mountain-locked hamlet in her domains" (ibid., Aug. 8, 1900).

30. Steel, *Through Peking's Sewer Gate*, 54.

31. The most articulate among missionary defenders of looting was Gilbert Reid; see his "Ethics of Loot." On the American missionaries' justification of force during the Boxer crisis, which provoked satirical responses from Mark Twain and Finley Peter Dunne ("Mr. Dooley"), see Miller, "Ends and Means," 273–80.

32. Michael Hunt describes the performance of the American troops in Beijing as "exemplary" (*A Special Relationship*, 196). The Japanese record was also highly praised by contemporaries, who tended to reserve their strongest criticism for the Russians and Germans (ibid.; see also Hunt's "Forgotten Occupation," 525–526).

33. "The violence of the German troops," Chester Tan writes, "made the Chinese people detest and fear them more than any other foreign force." Tan, *Boxer Catastrophe*, 145.

34. Gao Shaochen, *Yongqing*, 421–39, esp. 429–31.

35. Liu Xizi, *Jin xi*, 95–102 (quotation from 95).

36. Wang Enpu, northern suburbs of Tianjin, Second Brother-Disciple, TDYYDB, 143.

37. In addition to the judgments, already cited, of James Ricalton and Luella Miner, Emma Martin wrote: "It is just outrageous the way the allied powers especially the soldiers have behaved in China." Letter, Jan. 12, 1901, quoted in Hunter, *Gospel*, 171.

38. A twelve-year-old Tutsi orphaned as a result of a massacre by government soldiers in Rwanda in 1994 told a reporter: "They [the soldiers] told us we were inyenzi" ("insects"). "And then they began to kill us" (*NYT*, Sept. 16, 1994, A3). "The crucial fact that the killers must forget," Natalie Zemon Davis has written of the religious violence between Catholics and Protestants in sixteenth-century France, "is that their victims are human beings" (Davis, *Society*, 181). For an illuminating discussion of the psychological mechanisms underlying dehumanization (including the interesting observation that, for self-protective purposes, dehumanization of the other is regularly accompanied by a corresponding dehumanization of the self), see Bernard, Ottenberg, and Redl, "Dehumanization."

39. Laurie Lee, *A Moment of War*, 161.

40. Yang Mushi, *Dianwen*, 347; Ai Sheng, *Quanfei*, 447.

41. "History, June," 3. After the first week of the Chinese siege of the foreign settlement, Hoover, more explicitly, described the Boxers as "hordes of fanatics, who, now also armed with foreign weapons, were even more to be feared, for they had what the soldiers possessed little of—courage to assault" ("Inside the Circle"). "At Tientsin," Michael Hunt has written, confirming Hoover's observation, "the Americans suffered heavy losses when the Chinese failed to live up to their reputation for military cowardice" ("Forgotten Occupation," 502). For more on the combat value of the Boxers' "fanaticism," see NCH, Aug. 1, 1900, 224.

42. Interview with Lieutenant von Krohn, NCH, July 25, 1900, 201. See also Fleming, *The Siege*, 77.

43. Allen, *Siege*, 288.

44. *Yu nan riji*, 171. A variation on this account, possibly describing the same battle, was offered by a former Boxer: "During the fighting in the city [Tianjin], the Boxers had the worst of it. The Boxers were up front, the government soldiers in the rear. When the fighting started and there was firing from both sides, the Boxers were attacked from front and rear and suffered heavy casualties." Li Jiusi (78), western suburbs of Tianjin, TDYYDB, 132.

45. Liu Mengyang, *Tianjin quanfei*, 39.

46. Liu Xizi, *Jin xi*, 87–88. Liu Xizi refers here to the Battle of North Hollow (Beiwa dazhan), recounted in the biographical sketch of Liu Shijiu in TDYYDB, 112, and also, in greater detail, in ibid., 98–100. In his oral testimony, Liu Baotong (78), who was in Liu Shijiu's unit, says that when the local peasants returned to their fields the following year there were bones strewn about everywhere (ibid., 146). In another war also marked by the youth of its participants, World War II, Paul Fussell

tells us "the most common cry" among the severely wounded was "Mother!" (*Wartime*, 52). The Herman Melville line, from his poem "The March into Virginia," is quoted in ibid.

47. Miner's account was published, under the title "Ti-to and the Boxers: A True Story of a Young Christian's Almost Miraculous Escape from Death at the Hands of Bold Cut-throats," in *The Ram's Horn*. The version used here is in LMP, box 4, file 1.

48. Butler, "Dame Rumor," 24.

49. Ricalton, *China*, 221.

50. Letter, Beijing, Aug. 18, 1900, in Steel, *Through Peking's Sewer Gate*, 21.

51. Upham, log, July 17, 1900.

52. Ibid., Aug. 14, 1900.

53. Steel, *Through Peking's Sewer Gate*, 21, 23.

54. Kinman, letter, Yokohama, Dec. 4, 1900. Lest it be thought that Kinman had a tendency to exaggerate the vulnerability of the enemy and the invulnerability of the U.S. Marines, in an earlier letter of June 27, 1899, written from Cavite in the Philippines, he commented: "It is all a dam lie about only 15 or 20 of our boys being killed in these fights and 3000 or 4000 insurgents. There are hundreds of our boys killed in nearly every fight and the next day the papers say 20 or 30 killed." Ibid.

55. Fussell, *Wartime*, 61.

56. Goodrich, "Journal," 27; see also Emma Martin, diary, 71.

57. Upham, June 29, 1900. In his log entry for the following day (June 30), Upham, after recounting another loophole death, commented: "those Chinks have got it down pat, they can put 5 shots out of six through a loop hole three inches square and dont need a field glass to do it either."

58. Steel, *Through Peking's Sewer Gate*, 54, 55–56, 64.

59. Hoover, "Inside the Circle."

60. Martin, diary, 44.

61. "With the arrival of the Relief and the removal of the black fear of massacre," Hoover wrote, "the people of the centre became themselves again" (the "centre" referring to the central area of the foreign settlement, where the civilian population had congregated during the initial part of the siege) ("Inside the Circle"). Elsewhere Hoover observed that the arrival of the relief column on June 26 marked the end of the first phase of the siege. "It was destined to continue another 18 days, but the assured safety of the Garrison from massacre now removed the more dramatic element of the situation, which became a game of military tactics and diplomacy" ("History, June" 10–11).

62. Diary, June 24, 1900, 57–58.

63. Tang Yan, *Gengzi xixing*, 473. The substance of the woman's remarks is interesting. As of the time she made them, it is indeed true that very few foreigners had lost their lives, even fewer in the capital and its environs, which very likely was her frame of reference. On the other hand, although it is certainly possible, as the woman suggested, that the figures for women and children killed greatly outnumbered those for men, there is no hard evidence to support such a claim.

64. Hoover, "The Period from May 28th."

65. "Inside the Circle." Apparently, one didn't have to go out of doors to be endangered. A number of foreigners were actually struck by bullets while lying in their beds. Drew, diary, 40.

66. Hoover, "Inside the Circle."

67. See the entries in Bishop Alphonse Favier's diary for June 23, 25, July 7, 23, in Freri, *Heart of Pekin*, 32–33, 39, 45.

68. Diary, July 10 and 11, 1900, ibid., 40.

69. Diary, Aug. 12, 1900, ibid., 52.

70. Diary, July 1, Aug. 2, 5, and 15, 1900, ibid., 36, 49, 54; see also ibid., 38, 44, 46, 50, 51.

71. The 43 French and Italian marines who defended the Northern Cathedral were drawn from the 450 or so troops originally stationed in the legation quarter. See Duiker, *Cultures in Collision*, 101.

72. While accurate figures for the number of foreigners among the besieged are available, estimates of the number of Chinese vary wildly from one source to another. There were approximately 880 foreigners in the legation quarter at the beginning of the siege. Allen asserts that, when the Protestant missionaries evacuated the Methodist Episcopal mission on June 20, they brought with them 1,700 Chinese Christians (mostly, one presumes, Protestants). He also says that, although the total Catholic population was estimated by the *Times* correspondent (Morrison) at 1,200, one of the men responsible for the organization of Chinese labor during the siege assured him it was closer to 2,000, a figure also supported by most missionaries in the British legation. If the higher figure for Catholics is accepted, we get a total population of 4,580 in the legation compound at the start of the siege. Arthur Smith gives a lower figure of 1,662 for the Catholic component among the besieged, which, if the other components are kept constant, would produce a total population of 4,242. Luella Miner suggests a still lower aggregate count, referring at one point in her diary to "this multitude of nearly 4,000." From these figures, I estimate the total Chinese population in the legations during the siege at somewhere between 2,900 and 3,700. Allen, *Siege*, 85–86, 104; Smith, *China in Convulsion* 1:359; Miner, diary, July 19, 1900, in LMP, box 1, file 1.

73. Diary, July 18, 1900, in LMP, box 1, file 1.

74. Favier, letter, Tianjin, Sept. 1900, in Freri, *Heart of Pekin*, 12.

75. Miner, diary, July 19, 1900, in LMP, box 1, file 1.

76. Oliphant, *Diary*, 66; Allen, *Siege*, 256. As an example of the mental erasure of Chinese from foreign accounts, Mary Porter Gamewell lists as one of the ten providences of God during the siege: "notwithstanding presence of contagious diseases, there was no epidemic, the general health was good, though little children suffered and six died." This was, of course, the mortality rate of foreign children alone; if that of Chinese children had been included, the figure would have been far in excess of six. Gamewell, "History," 61.

77. Luella Miner wrote: "Seventy children have died among the Catholics, who are far less careful than our people about sanitary conditions, and whose priests give them little care." Diary, Aug. 2, 1900, in LMP, box 1, file 1. See also Smith, *China in Convulsion* 1:320.

78. This information is supplied in Lu Wantian, *Beijing shibian*, 418.

79. Oliphant, *Diary*, July 1, 1900, 66.

80. Diary, Aug. 5, 1900, in LMP, box 1, file 1.

81. Lu Wantian, *Beijing shibian*, 407, 409.

82. Ricalton, *China*, 241.

83. Zhongfang Shi, *Gengzi jishi*, 14. The American minister, Conger, reported a much heavier toll in lives. Dispatch to Hay, June 18, 1900, *FRUS*, 151.

84. Zhongfang Shi, *Gengzi jishi*, 15.

85. Ibid., 22. See also ibid., 25.

86. Guan He, *Quanfei*, 475.

87. Ibid., 477, 490.

88. *Yu nan riji*, 169–70. On the pervasive fear of spies within the foreign community in Tianjin in the summer of 1900, Mrs. E. B. Drew wrote: "There was always a fear that spies would get into the settlement, or were there already in the person of our servants. There was a great feeling of distrust of all the Chinese" (diary, 22).

89. *TYJ*, 143.

90. Guan He, *Quanfei*, 476–77.

91. Ye Changchi, GX 26/5/27 (June 23, 1900), *Riji*, 446.

92. Guan He, *Quanfei*, 476.

93. Ibid., 489.

94. Liu Mengyang, *Tianjin quanfei*, 15.

95. See ch. 3, n. 65.

96. Zhongfang Shi, *Gengzi jishi*, 25; see also Yang Diangao, *Gengzi dashi ji*, 83.

97. Yang Diangao, ibid., 86; Zhongfang Shi, *Gengzi jishi*, 12–13; Alitto, *Last Confucian*, 29. According to one account, consumers of foreign books actually were killed on occasion. Gao Nan, GX 26/6/5 (July 1, 1900), *Riji*, 149.

98. Liu Mengyang, *Tianjin quanfei*, 10; Guan He, *Quanfei*, 471. A Chinese refugee who had fled from the north to Shanghai stated that the order to change the name of rickshaws emanated from the Boxers in Beijing and was followed all over North China (*NCH*, Aug. 15, 1900, p. 356). Other examples of name changes in Tianjin are listed in Sun Shaotang (75), Boxer, TDYYDB, 146.

99. Liu Mengyang, *Tianjin quanfei*, 32–33. Liu (ibid.) also detailed Boxer attacks on a number of other Tianjin firms specializing in foreign commodities.

100. Pruitt, *Daughter of Han*, 152.

101. Guan He, *Quanfei*, 474.

102. Liu Mengyang, *Tianjin quanfei*, 40–41.

103. Guan He, *Quanfei*, 475–76.

104. Ibid., 475. Some days later, as we have seen, Guan and his family did flee.

105. Zhongfang Shi, *Gengzi jishi*, 30.

106. Diary, June 11–13, 1900, 45.

107. "Journal," June 19, 1900, 20–21. The pain experienced by missionaries who, in seeking safety for themselves, were forced to "desert" their Christian followers is articulated in Miner, journal, Tungchow [Tongzhou], June 7, 1900, in LMP, box 1, file 1.

108. See, for example, Clapp, diary letter, Taigu, July 13–14, 1900; Bird, journal, Taigu, July 13, 1900.

109. Eva Jane Price, *China Journal*, 231–32. See also her letter of Aug. 1, ibid., 235–36.

110. Partridge.

111. Letter, June 2, 1900, Baoding, in Goodrich, "Journal," 6–7.

112. Letter, Tianjin, Aug. 3, 1900 (original spelling and punctuation retained).

356

113. Allen, *Siege*, 23–24.

114. Journal and letter, Taigu, July 13, 1900.

115. For details, see Forsyth, comp. and ed., *China Martyrs*, 68–69.

116. Entitled "The Twentieth Century," in Hoffman, *Hang-Gliding from Helicon*, 121.

PART 3 / Prologue: The Mythologized Past

1. Keegan, *Face of Battle*; Fussell, *The Great War*, especially the brilliant evocation of life in the trenches in ch. 2 ("The Troglodyte World"). Similar studies are Linderman's *Embattled Courage* and Fussell's more recent *Wartime*.

2. Schwarcz, "Remapping May Fourth," 23.

3. Ibid., 24.

4. García Márquez, *The General in His Labyrinth*. The quoted reference to Bolívar's womanizing is from an interview with García Márquez cited in the *NYT*, June 26, 1989, C13.

5. Greenhouse, "Protecting Its Mystique," *NYT*, May 27, 1993, A1, A24.

6. Januszczak, *Sayonara, Michelangelo*.

7. G. R. Elton speaks of "the fear of the demolished myth" (Elton, *Return to Essentials*, 6). While García Márquez claimed to be "absolutely certain" that *The General in His Labyrinth* captured "the way Bolívar really was," Belisario Betancour, the former president of Columbia, "said the book left him feeling 'an immense desolation' as well as 'an impression of anguish and infinite sadness' that would force readers to 'rethink the world, amidst sobs' " (*NYT*, June 26, 1989, C17). A flyer announcing a lecture to be given on Dec. 6, 1990, at the Isabella Stewart Gardner Museum in Boston stated: "For many people, the restoration of the Sistine Ceiling has robbed it of its most sublime qualities." In a letter dated May 25, 1993, Supreme Court Chief Justice William H. Rehnquist, speaking for "a majority of the active Justices of the Court," expressed surprise and disappointment at the Library of Congress's decision to release Justice Marshall's papers so precipitately. *NYT*, May 26, 1993, D21.

8. Marilynne Robinson, in "Writers," 34.

9. Slotkin, *Gunfighter Nation*.

10. Bickers, "History, Legend," 81–84.

11. For insightful commentary on modern Chinese historical consciousness and the retrospective importance of the Opium War as "the beginning of a prolonged process of enforced 'modernization,' " see Jiwei Ci, *Dialectic*, 25–27, 248–49n.

12. I refer here specifically to *historical* mythologization. Autobiographical mythologization, briefly mentioned below but otherwise barely addressed in this book, is in important respects different from other forms, the greatest difference being the merging of subject and object in the mythologization process.

13. For a discussion of the contradictory ways in which the French Revolution ("*la mère de nous tous*") has remained alive in the present, see Barker, "Teaching," 17–18. Indicative of its aliveness is Barker's assertion that "if you lecture on the French Revolution, you must immediately show your colors in a way not required by many other historical subjects" (17).

14. The new sensitivity toward the shaping role of gender, ethnicity, and the environment that emerged in the United States in the 1960s has done much, for

example, to shift the angle of vision of a new generation of historians of the American West. See Bernstein, "Unsettling the Old West"; Brinkley, "The Western Historians."

15. Hobsbawm, "Introduction," 13.

16. This is not too different from the claim philosophers of science have made regarding the creation of scientific theory. The best-known example is Thomas S. Kuhn (in *The Structure of Scientific Revolutions*). Mary Hesse summarizes the position she has taken in a number of her writings as follows: "Scientific theory is a particular kind of myth that answers to our practical purposes with regard to nature." Hesse, "Aristotle's Shadow," *NYT*, Oct. 22, 1989, 24E.

17. Alpern, "New Myths," 35. Alpern refers here specifically to the *unintended* mythmaking of *historians*, as distinct from the deliberate mythologization of non-historians. The issue of intentionality has been squarely joined in the Afrocentrism controversy in the United States, some scholars viewing the infusion of more Afrocentric material into high school and college curricula as a blatant attempt "to improve black students' self-esteem rather than to correct the historical record," others seeing improved black self-esteem as very possibly a by-product, but not the primary purpose, of Afrocentric scholarship. Marriott, "Afrocentrism," *NYT*, Aug. 11, 1991, 18.

18. Wilford, *Columbus*, 249–62 (quotes from 249, 252). The emotions aroused by competing mythologizations of Columbus were very much in evidence in the summer of 1991 in Philadelphia when, to mark the 500th anniversary of Columbus's landing in America, the City Council voted to change the name of Delaware Avenue (almost four miles long) to Christopher Columbus Boulevard. Italian-American groups had pushed for the change. But an Apache Indian active in the Stop the Name Change coalition said his group did not wish to honor a man who stood for "the enslavement of people of color" (*NYT*, Aug. 25, 1991, 27L). A year later, a group of Native American protesters in Boston elicited the following response from the grand marshal of the planned Columbus Day parade: "We're Italian-Americans, and they've taken all our heroes away from us. . . . Columbus is the last hero we have. . . . He discovered America. Why don't they leave the guy alone?" *NYT*, Oct. 11, 1992, 18.

19. Wilford (*Columbus*, ix–x) speaks of "the poorly charted waters of ambiguity and conflicting documentation everywhere Columbus went and in everything he did." The historian Richard L. Kagan takes issue with Wilford on this point, contending that "in fact, our knowledge of the history he [Wilford] calls 'mysterious' is remarkably complete." Richard L. Kagan, "Discovery of Columbus," 27.

20. The key work sparking the controversy is the multivolume study (in progress) by Bernal entitled *Black Athena*.

21. Barmé, "Beijing Days," 43; see also his "Confession, Redemption, and Death," 78.

22. Schell, "Introduction," 12.

23. I am grateful to Andrew Walder for providing me with this example, which he obtained in an interview with a former worker activist in Cambridge on June 9–10, 1990. Although at the end of the nineteenth century the phrase "*daoqiang bu ru*" (as opposed to other formulaic allusions to invulnerability) appears to have been more commonly encountered among the Big Swords than among the Boxers

358 (Esherick, *Origins*, 228), in the course of the twentieth century it came to be associated in people's minds mainly with the Boxers.

24. Greene, *Hsiang-Ya Journal*, xiii.

25. Liu Xinwu, "What Is 'New' in Post-Mao Literature?"

26. Myerhoff, *Number Our Days*, 37. On a more general level, Shelley E. Taylor argues that, to a significant degree, the operations of the healthy mind are marked less by a concern for accuracy than by the ability to engage in "creative self-deception" (Taylor, *Positive Illusions*). David Carr, while acknowledging that individuals in the course of "composing and constantly revising" their autobiographies are much concerned with coherence, is less willing than either Myerhoff or Taylor to yield on the governing importance of truth and truthfulness to people so engaged. Carr, *Time*, 75–78, 98–99, 171–72.

27. Boyer and Nissenbaum, *Salem Possessed*, 22.

28. Ying-ho Chiang, "Literary Reactions," Part 1, esp. 18, 96–100, 147n12.

29. See ch. 5, n. 20.

30. "Bianzhe de hua," prefacing Zhang Shijie, comp., *Hongying dadao*, 2. The value of popular Boxer stories for fostering patriotism and proper socialist values is discussed at length in Wei Gang, "Yihetuan gushi."

31. In Lao She, *Lao She wenji, juan* 12, 109–81; the circumstances surrounding the writing of the play are recounted in Lao's postscript, in ibid., 182–86. Alternately titled *Yihetuan* (The Boxers), the play first appeared in print in a combined issue of *Juben* (Drama), February-March 1961.

32. For a somewhat less standard account of the Boxers, see Feng Jicai's *Yihequan* (The Boxers), a long historical novel coauthored with Li Dingxing and published in 1977; the novel focuses on the part taken by Zhang Decheng and others in the defense of Tianjin in July 1900. Some of the ambiguities in its treatment of the Boxers are pointed out in David Der-wei Wang, *Fictional Realism*, 296–98.

33. "Zooming in on May 19" (originally published as "5.19 changjingtou" in 1986), in Barmé and Jaivin, eds., *New Ghosts, Old Dreams*, 265–78, esp. 275–76.

34. I rely here on Barmé's summary and analysis in his "Wang Shuo," 51–60. The literal translation of the title of Wang's work is "Whatever you do, don't treat me as a human." The reason for the choice of "No man's land" is given in ibid., 52–53.

35. A brief account of the visit is in Buck, "The 1990 International Symposium," 116–17. More on the Zhao Sanduo memorial is found in a booklet published by the Wei county government and party committee marking the memorial's establishment: *Zhao Sanduo he ta lingdao de Yihetuan*.

36. A prime example is the superbly successful educational project "Facing History and Ourselves," which, according to one of its flyers, seeks "to reach young people with instruction in the Nazi Holocaust and the Armenian Genocide as examples of what happens when morality breaks down."

37. Allen, *Siege*, 261–63. A medal actually was made to commemorate the experience, but a different design was used.

38. Miner, journal, Aug. 16, 1900, in LMP, box 1, file 1.

39. Seligson, "Bewitched."

40. Or, alternatively, it may be to draw energy from the past to warn against the recurrence of a purportedly analogous but not identical phenomenon in the present. In early November 1992 the 54th anniversary of Kristallnacht—the night of

November 9, 1938, when the Nazis destroyed thousands of Jewish homes, shops, and synagogues all over Germany—was commemorated in Berlin and other German cities by large-scale demonstrations protesting the wave of antiforeign violence that, in the months since German unification, had been unleashed mainly against recent immigrants from the Middle East and Southeast Asia. *NYT*, Nov. 9, 1992, A1, A8.

41. Seligson, "Bewitched," 10. "Lest We Forget" is of course a key theme of Holocaust commemoration as well.

42. *NYT*, June 19, 1988, 1S, 6S.

43. In Schama, *Citizens*, to take a celebrated example, central place is given to what the author calls "the painful problem of revolutionary violence" (xv).

44. Qiao Wen, "Baguo lianjun," *Renmin ribao (haiwai ban)*, Aug. 20, 1990, 2. See also ibid., Aug. 15, 1990, 1; Aug. 16, 1990, 4.

7. The New Culture Movement and the Boxers

1. Levenson, *Confucian China* 1:123. Compare to Hu Shi's formulation in a speech given at Yanjing University in 1925 and set down in writing the following year: "Twenty-five years ago the enemy of the missionary enterprise [referring to the Boxers] was ignorant superstition. Twenty-five years later the difficulty facing the missionary enterprise is enlightened rationalism [*lixingzhuyi*]." Hu Shi, "Jiaohui jiaoyu," 730. See also the English version of this speech: Hu Shih [Hu Shi], "The Present Crisis in Christian Education," 435.

2. Cohen, *China and Christianity*, 267–68.

3. See, for example, Li Xisheng, *Guobian*, passim; Yun Yuding, *Chongling chuanxin lu*, 52; Hong Shoushan, *Shishi*, passim; Chai E, *Gengxin*, passim. See also the following press accounts: *Shenbao*, July 1 and Aug. 19, 1900, in *YHT* 4:171–74; *Guowenbao*, n.d., in *YHT* 4:174–76; *Zhongwai ribao*, June 17 and 18, 1900, in *YHT* 4:183–85.

4. Hong Shoushan, *Shishi*, 90. Note also the titles of the following two works: Yuan Chang, *Luanzhong riji can'gao* (Draft fragments of a diary kept during the disorders), and Liu Mengyang, *Tianjin quanfei bianluan jishi* (An account of the Boxer bandit disorders in Tianjin).

5. Liu Mengyang, *Tianjin quanfei*, 7; Hong Shoushan, *Shishi*, 90.

6. Yun Yuding, *Chongling chuanxin lu*, 47.

7. See, for example, Liu Mengyang, *Tianjin quanfei*, 13.

8. Yuan Chang, *Riji*, 346.

9. Liu Mengyang, *Tianjin quanfei*, 7.

10. For a survey, mainly drawing on journalistic writing, see Horikawa Tetsuo, "Giwadan undō." The negative posture of reform-minded Chinese toward the Boxers was also frequently expressed in poetry and fiction. See Ying-ho Chiang, "Literary Reactions," 96–100, 147n12, 271–327.

11. Alitto, *Last Confucian*, 22. Liang was so convinced that the Boxers were a disaster that he took the sizable risk of publicly urging action against them, even after they had gained the Empress Dowager's support (ibid., 27).

12. "Quanfei zhi luan wei fu shengzhu er cun Zhongguo shuo" (The Boxer turmoil as a means of restoring the emperor and preserving China), cited in Kung-chuan Hsiao, *A Modern China*, 237.

13. Liang Qichao, "Xiaoshuo yu qunzhi," 9; Lyell, *Lu Hsün's Vision*, 61. Liang's main purpose in this essay was not to fault fiction but to call attention to its enormous power in shaping popular attitudes and beliefs.

14. See Don C. Price, "Popular and Elite Heterodoxy."

15. There were some early revolutionaries, among them Sun Yat-sen, who came to the Boxers' defense. Sun's views are summarized in Kuang-chung Chen, "A Semiotic Phenomenology," 73–74. See also Don C. Price, "Popular and Elite Heterodoxy" and ch. 8 below.

16. Zou Rong, *Gemingjun*, 331–64, esp. 332, 349. For a translation of Zou's pamphlet, see Tsou Jung, *The Revolutionary Army*.

17. Lu Hsun [Lu Xun], *The True Story of Ah Q*, 120.

18. Lu Hsun [Lu Xun], *A Madman's Diary*, passim.

19. See Duara, "Knowledge and Power."

20. This jotting, "Yihequan zhengfule yangren" in Chinese, is signed pseudonymously by Zhiyan (One with exceptional insight) and is found in the "Suiganlu" (Random thoughts) section of *Meizhou pinglun*, no. 1, Dec. 22, 1918. The author appears to have been Chen Duxiu. See his *Wencun*, *juan* 2:1–2.

21. Chiang Monlin, *Tides*, 43–44; on Wang Xinggong, see Lutz, *Chinese Politics*, 34–35; Hu Shi, "Jiaohui jiaoyu," 730 (see also Hu Shih, "The Present Crisis," 435). In a diary entry of July 26, 1914, Hu wrote: "Whenever in my reading of history I come to the Opium War, the Anglo-French War, and the like, I always regard China as having been in the right; but when I come to the war of 1900 I never regard the Boxer bandits as having been in the right." Hu Shi, *Liuxue riji* 2:315.

22. As we have seen, Guan Yu, Zhang Fei, and Zhao Yun were from the *Romance of the Three Kingdoms* and Sun Wukong was the "Monkey King" from *Journey to the West*. Huang Santai came from *Peng Gong an* (Cases conducted by Magistrate Peng) and Huang Tianba from *Shi Gong an* (Cases conducted by Magistrate Shi). The last two titles were popular novels from the nineteenth century which portrayed the ideal official, who always took the side of the common people and brought the bad guys to justice.

23. Chen Duxiu, "Kelinde bei," 449–58, esp. 453–55, 458.

24. Lu Xun, "Suiganlu," no. 37, 514–15.

25. Chen Tiesheng, "Quanshu," 218–19.

26. Lu's response appears immediately after Chen Tiesheng's piece, on 219–21.

27. Schneider, *Ku Chieh-kang*, 124.

28. Cited in Hayford, *To the People*, 12.

29. It was still widely encountered among educated Chinese in the Deng Xiaoping era. One scholarly analysis of "the students' aversion to cross-class coalition" during the protest demonstrations in Beijing in 1989 contends that it stemmed in part from "an elitist view of themselves as morally and politically superior to the uneducated masses." Perry and Fuller, "China's Long March," 669. See also Myron L. Cohen, "Being Chinese," 113–14; Link, *Evening Chats*, 106–107.

30. Myron L. Cohen ("Being Chinese," 129–30) writes: "Attacks on superstitions represent efforts by those who are cultural outsiders (by birth, self-definition, or both) to gain control over and to remake society. These efforts on the part of Communists and non-Communists alike have been in the context of a hostility pronounced to such a degree as to warrant consideration of the entire historical

process as cultural warfare." On the periodic campaigns of the Chinese state against "superstition" and other popular beliefs and practices deemed potentially inimical to state interests, see Duara, "Knowledge and Power." Chang-tai Hung has written about the elimination of the gods and temples of popular religion under the auspices of the "Superstition Destruction movement" (*Pochu mixin yundong*) in *Going to the People*, 160.

31. During the Cultural Revolution years, to note one of the exceptions, the Boxers and Red Lanterns came in for warm praise from radical Chinese-Americans in New York and San Francisco. A Red Guard party was formed in the latter city. In New York, an organization calling itself I Wor Kuen (Cantonese for Yihequan or "Boxers") started publishing a bimonthly (sometimes monthly) bilingual magazine called *Getting Together* (*Tuanjiebao* in Mandarin) in February 1970. An editorial entitled "I Wor Kuen" in the second number clearly indicated the group's stance: "I Wor Kuen fighters were not frightened away by the foreigners' weapons because they believed that spiritual understanding and unity among people were more important than weapons in deciding the outcome of a war. . . . I Wor Kuen . . . believed in the equality and potential power of liberated women. Tens of thousands of liberated women fought against foreigners alongside of the men in units such as the Red Lantern Brigade. . . . The patriotic rebels of the Taipings and I Wor Kuen lit the spark which started the gigantic fire for the liberation of Chinese [*sic*] and world's peoples." *Getting Together* 1.2 (Apr. 1970): 2 (English-language section).

32. Shoup, "In Peking."

33. For commentary on this cartoon, see Utley, "American Views," 122.

34. Leyda, *Dianying*, 4–6.

35. Paine's novel was published in ten installments. It subsequently appeared in book form under the modified title *The Dragon and the Cross*. The common tendency among contemporary foreigners to conflate the "Boxers" and "Big Knives" (the Big Sword Society) is clearly evidenced in a news item in *The Youth's Companion* 74.25 (June 21, 1900): 322.

36. Isaacs, *Images of Asia*, 106.

37. Foster, "China and the Chinese," 382.

38. Ibid., 436–38.

39. The "murderous Boxer Uprising" loomed large in Part 1 of *Life*'s three-part pictorial survey of the historical background to the emergence of "the young fanatics of the Communist Red Guard" in the fall of 1966 ("Behind Mao's Red Rule: The 100 Violent Years," *Life*, Sept. 23, Sept. 30, and Oct. 7, 1966). Witke (*Comrade Chiang Ch'ing*, 349) described the "xenophobic behavior" of the Red Guards during their assault on the office of the British chargé d'affaires in 1967 as seeming "to recapitulate the Boxers' more express and virulent program to purge China of all foreign influence."

8. Anti-Imperialism and the Recasting of the Boxer Myth

1. The cultural iconoclasm of the New Culture movement and the angry nationalism of the political demonstrations that erupted on May 4, 1919, in the Chinese capital are often conflated into the "May Fourth movement" or "May Fourth era." For an insightful analysis of the problems this causes, see Furth, "May Fourth in History."

2. Ku Hung-ming [Gu Hongming], *Papers*, 80, 94–95. Gu Hongming's view of the Boxers as a patriotic force, who "ought to convince the world that the Chinese are not unwilling to fight," was by his own admission not very far from that of Sir Robert Hart, whose countrymen thought he had (in Gu's words) "lost his wits when he prophesied about the future of 'Boxerism' in China" (ibid., 78). For more on Gu, see Arkush, "Ku Hung-ming." Hart referred to the Boxers quite explicitly as patriots in his *Essays*, 4, 53–54. Arthur von Rosthorn, the Austrian chargé d'affaires at the time of the siege, also saw the Boxers as "patriots," whose anger toward the foreigners was entirely justified. Mackerras, *Western Images*, 69–70.

3. Originally published Dec. 22, 1900, and reprinted in Ku Hung-ming, *Papers*, 96.

4. "Zhuke pingyi" (A dialogue between a host and his guest), as translated in Schwartz, *In Search of Wealth and Power*, 142.

5. Schiffrin, *Sun Yat-sen*, 275; Chen Kuangshi, "*Kaizhilu*," 875.

6. "Yihetuan you gong yu Zhongguo." The *Kaizhilu* article is the main focus of Nohara Shirō, "Giwadan undō." Chen Kuangshi's researches establish the article's author as Guan Gong, a pen name for Zheng Guanyi (Chen Kuangshi, "*Kaizhilu*," 876). Other reformers and revolutionaries who valued the Boxers for their patriotic spirit are discussed in Don C. Price, "Popular and Elite Heterodoxy"; also (in regard to revolutionaries in particular) in Kubota Bunji, "Giwadan hyōka."

7. Yixian [Sun Yat-sen], "Zhina baoquan fenge helun," 601, as translated in Schiffrin, *Sun Yat-sen*, 312.

8. Rankin, *Elite Activism*, 285.

9. *Anhui suhuabao*, 1905, nos. 13–15. See also Feigon, *Chen Duxiu*, esp. 60–68.

10. Chen, as we have just seen, had been alert to issues of patriotism and anti-imperialism during the immediate post-Boxer period. His sensitivities at that time, however, appear to have been directed more to the humiliations inflicted on China by imperialism than to the courageous resistance to imperialism of the Boxers. On the shift in Chen's views on the Boxers after May Fourth, see Richard C. Kagan, "From Revolutionary Iconoclasm," 71–72; Carrère d'Encausse and Schram, *Marxism and Asia*, 223–24.

11. Lutz, *Chinese Politics*, 131. On the telegram to the nation of the directors of the Anti-Imperialist Federation (Beijing, Aug. 10, 1924), see Wieger, ed., *Chine moderne* 5:228.

12. Chen Duxiu, "Cuowu de guannian."

13. Chen Duxiu, "Jiaoxun," 17.

14. [Peng] Shuzhi, "Diguozhuyi," 646.

15. Cai Hesen, "Guomin geming."

16. The fullest treatment of the May Thirtieth movement in English is Rigby, *The May 30 Movement*; in Chinese, see Li Jianmin, *Wusa can'an*.

17. Tang Xingqi, "Wusa yundong"; see also Rigby, *The May 30 Movement*, 121.

18. On this point in particular see Wasserstrom, "The Boxers as Symbol."

19. [Qu] Qiubai, "Yihetuan yundong"; see also Rigby, *The May 30 Movement*, 121–23.

20. Li Dazhao, "Sun Zhongshan." Li's article, dated Mar. 12, 1926, was included in a special commemoratory issue of *Guomin xinbao*. It was reprinted in Li Dazhao, *Li Dazhao xuanji*, 537. See also Meisner, *Li Ta-chao*, 174.

21. Long Chi, "Feiyue yundong," 1727.

22. Lutz, *Chinese Politics*, 131. I have not seen *Fei Jidujiao tekan*.

23. Lutz, *Chinese Politics*, 133.

24. Spence, *To Change China*, 179.

25. Wieger, ed., *Chine moderne* 6:265.

26. A foreign precedent for this was supplied at the time of the siege of the legations in a cartoon in the *San Francisco Chronicle* entitled "The Real 'Boxers' "; the cartoon depicted the foreign powers nailing China into a coffin in preparation for dividing it up. *The Literary Digest* 21.2 (July 14, 1900): 34; see also Utley, "American Views," 117.

27. I. Hu, "Did the Boxer Uprising Recur in 1925?" (esp. 33, 38).

28. As an example of the local media's capacity to shape local attitudes, William F. Prohme, in the aftermath of the antiforeign actions of Guomindang (Nationalist) troops in Nanjing in late March 1927, reported from Shanghai on April 4: "Shanghai . . . is thick with the atmosphere of anti-Nationalist propaganda generated by the local British press. The correspondents are working in and affected by this atmosphere." Prohme, "Outrages at Nanking."

29. Quoted in Wasserstrom, "The Boxers as Symbol," 20.

30. Rigby, *The May 30 Movement*, 146–47. Along similar lines, a China-based British naval officer recorded in his journal for January 17, 1925: "The trouble at Shanghai gets worse every day. . . . There are other serious things as well; such as anti-foreign risings in Hankow. It looks as if there might be another Boxer rising." Quoted in Bickers, "History, Legend," 84.

31. Wasserstrom, "The Boxers as Symbol," 20. Wasserstrom (ibid.) cites a contemporary German correspondent who observed that, whenever "an occidental resident of Shanghai, particularly of the older generation, mentions hatred of foreigners, the memory of the Boxer outbreak always lurks somewhere in the background of his mind, like a mediaeval incomprehensible spook." Quoted from *The Living Age* 326 (Sept. 1, 1925): 241.

32. Letter from Frederick Hough, Shanghai, July 28, 1927, in *The Nation* 125.3252 (Nov. 2, 1927): 478–79. "It is true that the camera doesn't lie," Hough observed, "but it's wonderful what a lying camera man can do with a picture."

33. See Wasserstrom, "The Boxers as Symbol," 26.

34. *China in Chaos*, 1.

35. Ibid., 15, 42–43 (news item dated Tayeh [Daye], Hupeh [Hubei], Jan. 6, 1927), 43–44, 46, 51 (dated Shanghai, Mar. 21, 1927).

36. Although my focus here has been on Westerners and on the decade of the 1920s, Paul S. Reinsch reports that at the time of the May Fourth demonstrations in the summer of 1919 "the Japanese, who were feeling the full force of the popular thrust, tried to brand it anti-foreign and to reawaken memories of the Boxer period." Reinsch, *An American Diplomat*, 371.

37. Cited in Rigby, *The May 30 Movement*, 112.

38. Tiansheng, "Yang Yihetuan."

39. Lutz, *Chinese Politics*, 65–66, 145.

40. Wieger, ed., *Chine moderne* 6:242.

41. Cited in Rigby, *The May 30 Movement*, 72.

42. Wieger, ed., *Chine moderne* 6:205.

43. Hu Shih [Hu Shi], "The Present Crisis," 434–35, 437. The contrast between nationalism and Boxerism was again drawn by Hu in an interview with a *Baltimore Sun* reporter in Beijing on July 29: "This nationalist movement in China is quite different from the blind reaction against foreign aggression in the closing years of the last century. Instead of that blind reaction we have conscious advocacy of nationalism." Cited in Rigby, *The May 30 Movement*, 107.

44. Cai Yuanpei, "Xuanyan"; a similar text, in French, in the form of a letter from Paris, received in Beijing July 27, 1925, is in Wieger, ed., *Chine moderne* 6:232–35.

45. Letter to Xu Guangping, June 13, 1925, as cited in Rigby, *The May 30 Movement*, 109.

46. For example, Luella Miner, whom the reader will recall as one of the besieged in the legations in 1900, in early 1927 specifically distinguished what was then taking place—"China is in the throes of a real revolution"—from "the 1900 trouble" (letter, Tsinan [Jinan], Jan. 1, 1927, LMP, box 2, file 1). Even when discussing the "intense suffering" caused by the anti-Christian activity, Miner insisted that it was "not the least like the Boxer outbreak" (letter, Tsinan, Feb. 5, 1927, ibid.). A partial exception to this "liberal" pattern was a novel by Louise Jordan Miln entitled *It Happened in Peking* (1926). Miln, instead of distancing the Boxers from Chinese nationalism (which she strongly supported), saw them as patriotic harbingers of this force. She even went a step further and transferred many of the negative traits customarily reserved for the Boxers (and often, by extension, the Chinese in general) to the Westerners themselves: "We gave China the brutal injustice of the Arrow War; we have given her a thousand examples of barbarian greed, cruelty, dishonesty, ruthless chicanery that have beat the drum calling her millions to a new patriotism, a patriotism no longer free to build in peace, but goaded and stung to resent, resist and defend." Miln, ibid., 224, as cited in Foster, "China and the Chinese," 425 (Foster mistakenly has "Arrow Law" instead of "Arrow War").

47. Wasserstrom, "The Boxers as Symbol," passim, supplies other examples of this perspective (which he labels the "sympathetic" view).

48. Hu Shih [Hu Shi], "The Present Crisis," passim.

49. High, "China's Anti-Christian Drive."

50. "China's War of Independence," *The Nation* 124 (Jan. 19, 1927): 54.

51. "China—Vaccinated," *The Nation* 124 (Feb. 23, 1927): 198.

52. For a full account of the Nanjing incident, see Lutz, *Chinese Politics*, 232–45. According to Lutz (234), in the incident's aftermath, "the shadow of the Boxer Rebellion influenced the perceptions of many" on both sides. A good example on the foreign side was the publication *China in Chaos* (discussed earlier).

53. "Yellow Peril or White?" *The Nation* 124 (Apr. 13, 1927): 387.

54. " 'Bolshevist' China," *The Nation* 124 (Apr. 20, 1927): 420.

55. Aron, "How the West Was Lost," 3–6. A variation on the bivocal mythologization of Daniel Boone is found in the contradictory myths of American national origins that, according to Leo Marx, continue to exert a strong hold on our collective imagination. "Thus," Marx writes, "the trans-Atlantic migration of white settlers has been represented both as a triumph of 'civilization' over wild, undeveloped nature (or 'barbarism'), and as a recovery of 'the natural'—a liberating retreat—

from the oppressive, overdeveloped, hierarchical societies of the Old World." Marx, *The Pilot*, xii.

56. Chang-tai Hung, "Female Symbols of Resistance," 173.

9. *The Cultural Revolution and the Boxers*

1. For an illuminating discussion of "ideological hegemony," a concept derived from Gramsci, see Shue, "Powers of State," 214–18.

2. The use of the Boxers in attacks against the Soviet Union extended into the early 1980s, well beyond the end of the Cultural Revolution, and therefore cannot be considered exclusively a Cultural Revolution phenomenon.

3. Qi Benyu, "Aiguozhuyi haishi maiguozhuyi?" References to Qi's piece here are to the English translation found (under the name Chi Pen-yu) in *Peking Review* 15 (Apr. 7, 1967): 5–16. As with all writings of major political importance, Qi's article was promptly disseminated throughout the country. It took up the entire first two pages and part of a third of the *People's Daily* (*Renmin ribao*) of Apr. 1, 1967, and was for the next several weeks an almost daily focal point of discussion in that paper's columns. On the circumstances relating to the article's writing, see Schram, ed., *Chairman Mao*, 337n4; Goldman, *China's Intellectuals*, 146. Mao, in a talk with an Albanian military delegation on Aug. 31, 1967, described the publication of Qi's article as marking a "crucial stage" in the development of the Cultural Revolution; in Selden, ed., *People's Republic of China*, 558.

4. Terrill, *White-Boned Demon*, 272–73.

5. For details see Chi Pen-yu [Qi Benyu], "Patriotism or National Betrayal?" 5–6; Witke, *Comrade Chiang Ch'ing*, 234–36. Other possible motives are suggested in Leyda, *Dianying*, 273.

6. Yao Hsin-nung [Yao Xinnong], the author of the play, also did the original scenario for the film adaptation. Over his protestations, the film's director and producer added several scenes of their own, including a substantially new ending that, as it turned out, was the basis for much of the eventual Maoist animus against the film. See Ingalls, "Introduction," 14, 17–19.

7. Ingalls, "Introduction," 19.

8. Goldman, *China's Intellectuals*, 75, 147; Witke, *Comrade Chiang Ch'ing*, 234. Goldman relies on Qi Benyu and Witke on Jiang Qing herself for the characterization of Liu's assessment of the film. Whether he really described it as "patriotic" remains unclear. After *Qinggong mishi's* formal repudiation in Qi Benyu's article, Mao, ever unpredictable, ordered (in May 1967) that the film be screened once again all over China, this time accompanied by propaganda carefully pointing out its profoundly poisonous character. Witke, *Comrade Chiang Ch'ing*, 235–36; Ingalls, "Introduction," 17, 22.

9. Chi Pen-yu [Qi Benyu], "Patriotism or National Betrayal?" 7, 9–12.

10. Two collections of these political cartoons are *Dadao Liu Shaoqi manhua ji*, published in May 1967 in Shanghai; and *Dadao Liu Shaoqi yilianhuan manhua ce*, published in April 1967 in Shanghai.

11. This was (as elaborated in chapter 4) much less true of the place occupied by the Red Lanterns in the thought world of the Boxers (see also Kobayashi Kazumi, "Minshū shisō," 247–48, 257). For reference to the Red Lanterns in Western writings, see Esherick, *Origins*, 297–98; Purcell, *Boxer Uprising*, 165, 233,

366 235, 238; Ch'en, "Nature and Characteristics," 296, 298, 303; Dunstheimer, "Religion et magie," 346. A leading Japanese historian of Chinese women, Ono Kazuko, devotes a chapter to the Red Lanterns in her *Chinese Women in a Century of Revolution, 1850–1950*, but it is only a few pages in length (47–53). The Red Lanterns do not fare much better in Chinese scholarship. A 47-page bibliography of articles on the Boxers covering all periods except for the Cultural Revolution has only two items on the Red Lanterns (see Wu Shiying, "Baokan wenzhang suoyin"). The two articles are: Song Jiaheng and Pan Yu, "Funü qunzhong," and Wang Zhizhong, " 'Hongdengzhao' kaolüe." There are also scattered references to the Red Lanterns in Chen Zhenjiang and Cheng Xiao, *Yihetuan wenxian*; TDYYDB; HDYYDJ, and *SYDZX*.

12. In the 86-page *Yihetuan yundong*, 11, 28; in the 128-page English-language edition of the same work, *The Yi Ho Tuan Movement of 1900*, 20, 43.

13. *Yihetuan zai Tianjin*, 58–61.

14. See, for example, Wu Wenying, "Hongdengzhao"; Geming lishi yanjiusuo, " 'Hongdengzhao.' "

15. See Hongdengzhao zhandoudui, "Cong *Xiuyang* dao *Qinggong mishi*."

16. Mackerras, *The Chinese Theatre*, 207; Bell Yung, "Model Opera," 147; Mackerras, *The Performing Arts*, 22; Mowry, *Yang-pan hsi*, 60–63 and passim. Mackerras describes *The Red Lantern* as "probably the most famous" of the model operas (*The Chinese Theatre*, 207).

17. *The Red Lantern*, 362.

18. *The Story of the Modern Peking Opera "The Red Lantern"*, 35, 42–43. Witke (*Comrade Chiang Ch'ing*, 153) conjectures that Jiang Qing named the opera after the Red Lanterns, who had enjoyed a limited presence in her native Shandong at the turn of the century.

19. Beijing Shifan Daxue Jinggangshan Gongshe Zhongwenxi lianhe dadui Tingjin bao bianjibu, "Wuchanjieji wenyi," 8; *Current Background* (American Consulate General, Hong Kong) 831 (July 24, 1967): 19.

20. In 1936, for example, Jiang Qing (then named Lan Ping) had badly wanted to play the lead role of Sai Jinhua in Xia Yan's new play of that title. *Sai Jinhua*, like *The Inside Story of the Qing Court*, took place against the backdrop of the Boxer rising. Moreover, since its heroine used her contacts with high-level foreigners to save the lives of numerous Chinese, it was generally perceived in the 1930s—when it was first produced and when China was embattled against the Japanese—as a patriotic play. When Xia Yan, who was not a special admirer of Jiang Qing's, chose someone else for the part of Sai, Jiang was enraged. Sai Jinhua was now transformed in her mind into a "treacherous whore," who unaccountably had been permitted to "speak for China" and eclipse the role played by the "heroic mass movement" of the Boxers (Terrill, *White-Boned Demon*, 102–103). Twenty years later, in what turned out to be a dress rehearsal for the "reversal of verdicts" on *The Inside Story of the Qing Court*, Sai Jinhua, in the context of the campaign against Tian Han, Xia Yan, and other playwrights of the older generation, was redefined (one can only assume with Jiang Qing's enthusiastic backing) as a work of national betrayal. Mu Hsin [Xin], "Reactionary Thought." See also Gray and Cavendish, *Chinese Communism*, 103.

21. "Zan 'Hongdengzhao.' "

22. Fudan Daxue Lishixi er hongweibing, "Jicheng he fayang." Other articles in this issue also draw parallels between the Red Lanterns and the Red Guards. See especially Shanghai tiyu zhanxian geming zaofan silingbu and Lu Xun bingtuan Dongfanghong zhandoudui, "Jiehuo 'Hongdeng' nao geming"; Huadong Shida Lishixi and Hong haichao, " 'Hongdengzhao' ming yang tianxia." For a particularly elaborate comparison between the Red Lanterns and Red Guards, see " 'Hongdengzhao' de geming zaofan jingshen hao de hen."

23. See, for example, " 'Hongdengzhao' de geming zaofan jingshen wansui"; Zhao Jing, "Yihetuan shi gemingde!" 4; Wu Wenying, "Hongdengzhao."

24. Rodzinski, *A History of China* 1:376n.

25. In this regard, it is worth emphasizing, there was a fundamental difference between the parallels Cultural Revolution mythologizers drew between the Boxer and Cultural Revolution periods and the parallels drawn by serious historians. For a suggestive listing of the latter, see Blunden and Elvin, *Cultural Atlas*, 154–55.

26. Ke Fu, "Cong 'Qieyang jie' dao 'Fandi lu.' " For a contemporary reference to Boxer street-name changes, see *NCH*, Aug. 15, 1900, p. 356.

27. Sun Daren, " 'Hongdengzhao.' "

28. An early Red Guard manifesto, alluding to the famous novel *Journey to the West*, proclaimed that revolutionaries were "Monkey Kings," whose "supernatural powers" and "magic," derived from "Mao Tse-tung's great invincible thought," were to be used "to turn the old world upside down, smash it to pieces, pulverize it, create chaos and make a tremendous mess, the bigger the better!" *Peking Review* 9.37 (Sept. 9, 1966): 21.

29. For numerous examples see Chen Zhenjiang and Cheng Xiao, *Yihetuan wenxian*, passim. Whether these millenarian writings, very likely of White Lotus inspiration, are to be viewed as Boxer writings, thereby supplying strong evidence of White Lotus influence on the intellectual content of the Boxer movement, or as the writings of White Lotus and other religious sectarians who were taking advantage of the upsurge of Boxer activity in North China in the spring and summer of 1900 to openly proclaim their own—non-Boxer—message is a matter of some dispute among historians. Chen and Cheng clearly view them as Boxer writings. Esherick (*Origins*, 300–301, 405–406n89) takes the opposite view.

30. Apart from brief mention in passing, the last piece I have seen that addresses the Red Lanterns—and much more extensively their male Boxer counterparts—in the context of the attack on "China's Khrushchev" for his praise of *The Inside Story of the Qing Court* is Xiao Renwu, "Weida de Yihetuan yundong."

31. "Down with Ch'i Pen-yü"; "Information about Ch'i Pen-yü."

32. Goldman, *China's Intellectuals*, 166.

33. See, for example, "Hong xiao jiang zan," 3 (trans. in *Survey of the China Mainland Press* 3934 [May 8, 1967]: 12); Xiao Renwu, "Weida de Yihetuan yundong"; Wu Wenying, "Hongdengzhao"; Sun Daren, " 'Hongdengzhao.' "

34. Hunan sheng Dongli Jichang gongren lilun xiaozu, "Fandi fanfeng pi Kong-Meng"; see also Tianjin tielu diyi zhongxue lilun yanjiu xiaozu, "Yihetuan fandi sao Qingchao." Other articles written in conjunction with the anti-Confucian campaign focused on the Boxer movement in general, with only passing reference to the Red Lanterns. See, for example, Lishixi qi'erji gongnongbing xueyuan, "Fandi fanfeng"; Wu Yannan, "Fan-Kong douzheng."

35. For the use of female symbols in the battle against "imperialism" and "feudalism" in Chinese spoken drama in World War II, see Chang-tai Hung, "Female Symbols of Resistance," 170.

36. My summary of the Lin Hei'er legend is drawn mainly from Liu Rong and Xu Fen, "Hongdeng nü'er song." For other fairly detailed accounts of the legend, see Hunan sheng Dongli Jichang, "Fandi fanfeng pi Kong-Meng"; Tianjin tielu, "Yihetuan fandi sao Qingchao." Some sources identify Lin Hei'er as a boatman's daughter rather than daughter-in-law.

37. The Chinese were not the only ones to mythologize the Red Lantern leader. In 1919 Metro Pictures Corporation produced a film, *The Red Lantern*, which told the story of the tragic love of a Chinese half-caste girl and the son of an American Protestant missionary against the background of the Boxer Rebellion. The film, based on a novel by Edith Wherry, was an extravaganza: 800 Chinese "extras" were imported from all parts of California and garbed at the Nazimova studios. One episode in the film (as recounted in *Moving Picture World*, Mar. 22, 1919, p. 1643) depicted "the sudden, seemingly miraculous appearance of the Goddess of the Red Lantern [presumably Lin Hei'er], borne on a gilded palanquin carried by sixteen men. . . . To the Chinese this meant that she was to be a deliverer. The Boxers seized upon the circumstance to put her, like a Joan of Arc, at the head of their forces which sought to drive Europeans from China." Quoted in Leyda, *Dianying*, 30–31; see also Jones, *Portrayal*, 15.

38. The most recent example was the 1989 crackdown in Beijing. Wasserstrom discusses the same pattern in connection with student martyrdom in the May Thirtieth Incident (*Student Protests*, 110–11).

39. See Solomon and Masataka Kosaka, eds., *Soviet Far East*, especially the chapters by Solomon and Kosaka, Harry Gelman, and Yao Wenbin.

40. Both quotations are cited in Pollack, *Sino-Soviet Rivalry*, 19–20.

41. By the Soviet Science Publishing House. Although Tikhvinsky's book may have been excerpted in *Cankao xiaoxi* (Reference news) and/or translated in its entirety for internal (*neibu*) circulation, there was no openly published Chinese-language edition. An English translation entitled *Modern History of China* came out too late (1983) to be used in the campaign. The Chinese critiques that I have seen appear to be based on the original Russian version. I have not seen this version, but I have consulted the English edition and, if it is a reasonably faithful translation, Chinese characterizations of the treatment of the Boxers in the original Russian edition do not seem at all exaggerated.

42. For examples of Chinese critiques of the book that focus on themes other than the Boxers, see: Song Bin, "Da Eluosi shawenzhuyi," 86–94, trans. in *Selections from People's Republic of China Magazines* (Hong Kong: American Consulate General), 850 (Dec. 16, 1975): 23–35; Nei Menggu Daxue Menggu shi yanjiushi, "Huangyan," 98–109, trans. in *Selections from People's Republic of China Magazines* 885 (Aug. 23, 1976): 19–39; Wu Yinnian, "Baquanzhuyi de 'jiezuo,'" 121–31, trans. in *Selections from People's Republic of China Magazines* 878 (July 6, 1976): 16–32.

43. See, for example, Beijing Shida Lishixi ernianji kaimenbanxue xiao fendui, "Weida de fandi geming douzheng"; Ge Tian and Gong Zhu, "Wenming shizhe haishi qinlüe qiangdao?"; Wu Wenxian, "Sha E wuzhuang," 29–30; Jin Yan, "Sha

E qinzhan Dongbei," 90; Sun Kefu and Guan Jie, "Yihetuan yundong de guanghui," 68–70; Lishixi qisanji pixiu xiaozu, "Yihetuan fandi jingshen."

44. See, for example, Ge Tian and Gong Zhu, "Wenming shizhe haishi qinlüe qiangdao?" 23; Wu Wenxian, "Sha E wuzhuang," 31; Shi Lan, "Wuchi de beipan," 95–96; Jin Yan, "Sha E qinzhan Dongbei," 90; Sun Kefu and Guan Jie, "Yihetuan yundong de guanghui," 69; Dong Wanlun, " 'Jiangdong liushisi tun' he lao shahuang de qin Hua baoxing," 92; Bi Sisheng, "Chi Suxiu," 69.

45. Beijing Shida Lishixi, "Weida de fandi geming douzheng."

46. Ibid., 62; see also Sun Kefu and Guan Jie, "Yihetuan yundong de guanghui," 68–69; Wu Wenxian, "Sha E wuzhuang," 30.

47. Wu Wenxian, "Sha E wuzhuang," 25. The book in question, which contained colored photographs, was titled *Al'bom' sooruzheniia Kitaiskoi vostochnoi zheleznoi dorogi, 1897–1903* (A photographic record of the construction of the Chinese Eastern Railway, 1897–1903).

48. Shi Lan, "Wuchi de beipan," 97; Zhong E, "Huangyan yan'gaibuliao lishi," 67.

49. See, for example, Bi Sisheng, "Chi Suxiu," 69; Lishixi qisanji, "Yihetuan fandi jingshen," 51–52; Wu Wenxian, "Sha E wuzhuang," 29.

50. This was not dissimilar to the Chinese government's efforts, post-Tiananmen, to recover its standing as a member of the community of civilized nations by reminding the world in August 1990 of the atrocities committed by foreigners in Beijing in the Boxer summer (see prologue to this part).

51. Beijing Shida Lishixi, "Weida de fandi geming douzheng," 61. The supplier of this information, a branch secretary of the Communist Party from the Tianjin area, included (ibid.) in his account a jingle alleged to have been widely circulated in the area in 1900: "In the Tianjin garrison and the city of Beijing, The harm visited by the foreigners has indeed been great. The robbing and looting have been beyond reckoning, The killing and arson completely routine."

52. Ge Tian and Gong Zhu, "Wenming shizhe haishi qinlüe qiangdao?" 21–22; also Sun Kefu and Guan Jie, "Yihetuan yundong de guanghui," 71; Lishixi qisanji, "Yihetuan fandi jingshen," 53.

53. These massacres really did take place, and Chinese accounts of them are no more grisly than Western scholarly accounts, although some of the details vary. See, especially, Lensen, *The Russo-Chinese War*, 89–103. Lensen's narrative is based on an extensive reading of Russian sources.

54. The ensuing description of the Russian massacres at Hailanpao and Jiangdong Liushisitun is drawn mainly from Dong Wanlun, " 'Jiangdong liushisi-tun' he lao shahuang de qin Hua baoxing," 90–91, and Zhong E, "Huangyan yan'-gaibuliao lishi," 68–69. Of the many other Cultural Revolution accounts of the massacres, see especially Wu Wenxian, "Sha E wuzhuang," 31; Lishixi qisanji, "Yihetuan fandi jingshen," 53; and Jin Yan, "Sha E qinzhan Dongbei," 87.

55. *Dongsansheng zhenglüe*, cited by Dong Wanlun, " 'Jiangdong Liushisitun' he lao shahuang de qin Hua baoxing," 91.

56. Ibid.

57. Zhong E, "Huangyan yan'gaibuliao lishi," 68. See also Wu Wenxian, "Sha E wuzhuang," 31.

370   58. Ge Tian and Gong Zhu, "Wenming shizhe haishi qinlüe qiangdao?" 20, 23–24.

59. Shi Lan, "Wuchi de beipan," 98; Sun Kefu and Guan Jie, "Yihetuan yundong de guanghui," 73–74; Lishixi qisanji, "Yihetuan fandi jingshen," 53; Jin Yan, "Sha E qinzhan Dongbei," 86. A slight variation on this theme charged Tikhvinsky and other Soviet revisionist historians with attacking the Boxers in order to attack contemporary national liberation movements in Asia, Africa, and Latin America, as well as China and other socialist countries that, upholding the Marxist-Leninist line, supported such movements. See Wei Hongyun, "Yingxiong qu hubao," 75–76.

60. Sun Kefu and Guan Jie, "Yihetuan yundong de guanghui," 68.

61. Dong Wanlun, " 'Jiangdong liushisi tun' de lishi," 100. See also Gao Yuanchao, "Dongbei renmin," 75.

62. The use of military language in connection with the commune movement is discussed in T. A. Hsia, *Metaphor*, 1–15; on its use during the Cultural Revolution, see Dittmer and Chen, *Ethics*, 29–33.

63. Zhong E, "Huangyan yan'gaibuliao lishi," 72.

64. As it did also, it may be noted, in the aftermath of the suppression of the popular demonstrations in Beijing in the spring of 1989. See, for example, the photo essay *Beijing fengbo jishi*. "This album," the editors write in the introduction, "with its abundant pictures, will help our readers understand the whole story of and truth about the turmoil and the present situation in Beijing." On the intense "concern with facticity" characterizing Chinese government narratives of Tiananmen, see Wasserstrom, "Afterword," 269.

65. See, in particular, Zhao Jing, "Yihetuan shi gemingde!"

66. See, for example, Wu Wenying, "Hongdengzhao," 4; " 'Hongdengzhao' zan"; Sun Daren, " 'Hongdengzhao.' "

67. Geming lishi yanjiusuo et al., " 'Hongdengzhao,' " 4.

68. Wang Zhizhong, " 'Hongdengzhao' kaolüe," 65–67. There is some evidence of such involvement in the Tianjin oral history materials. But it tends to be heavily mythologized. Thus, in an account of the heroism displayed by the Boxers in the famous clash with Russian soldiers at Tianjin's Laolongtou Railway Station, one respondent asserted: "In the assault on Laolongtou Station, the Red Lanterns also took part. We called them 'the executioners' [*guizishou*] because, during the fighting, they took the lead in killing the foreigners." Li Yuanshan (79), Boxer, Tianjin, TDYYDB, 134.

69. The quoted phrase is from Ai Sheng, *Quanfei*, 447.

70. For an interesting analysis of Red Lantern magic and the role it played in the Boxer movement, see Wang Zhizhong, " 'Hongdengzhao' kaolüe," 64–66.

71. Also violating this picture—and therefore suppressed—were the magical healing powers ascribed to Lin Hei'er in contemporary writings and the evidence that she may have been a prostitute in her pre-Red Lantern existence (ibid., 67–68; see also ch. 4).

Pre- and post-Cultural Revolution Communist writings, although often extolling the heroic part the Red Lanterns took in the struggle against imperialism, make no effort to conceal the religious and magical capacities attributed to them. See, for example, Huang Ning, *Yihetuan*; Mingqing, *Yihetuan*, 32–38; Zhao Qing (72), Jinghai county, Fourth Sister-Disciple, TDYYDB, 135–36; Mu Wenzhen (77), Tianjin, non-Boxer, ibid., 154–55; Song Jiaheng and Pan Yu, "Funü qunzhong"; Li Junhe, " 'Huanglian shengmu"; Jin Jiarui, *Yihetuan shihua*, 100; and Liao Yizhong, "Lin Hei'er." A similar contrast between Cultural Revolution and pre- and post-Cultural Revolution treatment of religious aspects of the Taipings is noted in Weller, "Historians and Consciousness," 741–44.

72. Li Tu, "Lishi de tie'an." A book that came out in 1978 dealt with the massacres in politicized language but made no reference at all to the Tikhvinsky volume. See Li Guang and Zhang Xuanru, *Dongbei*, 89–92.

73. Xue Xiantian, "Hailanpao can'an sinan renshu."

74. Xue Xiantian, "Jiangdong liushisi tun can'an."

75. Wang Zhizhong, " 'Hongdengzhao' kaolüe," 63–69, 85.

76. For a variety of reasons, some of them no doubt self-evident, much more writing was done in the immediate post-Cultural Revolution years on the Amur massacres than on the Red Lanterns. Accounts of the massacres that were still quite politicized included: Heilongjiang sheng bowuguan lishibu et al., comps., *Heilongjiang Yihetuan*, 23–26; *Sha E qin Hua shi*, 291–94. On the more scholarly side, see the following compilations of source materials: Yao Xiuzhi and Wei Xiangpeng, comps., "Can'an ziliao"; "Hailanpao yu Jiangdong liushisi tun can'an waiwen ziliao"; Ishimitsu Makiyo, "Liuxue beiju."

77. Two early examples of this were the following articles by Wang Zhizhong: "Fengjian mengmeizhuyi" and "Ruhe pingjia Yihetuan." See Buck, ed., *Recent Chinese Studies*, 7–8.

78. Esherick, *Origins*, xvi.

79. For summaries and assessments of the positions taken by Boxers scholars on a range of issues during the 1980s, see "Disanci Yihetuan yundong shi xueshu taolunhui jianjie"; Sun Zhanyuan, "Yihetuan yundong yanjiu."

80. It was clear, for example, from a highly politicized exchange that took place in 1985–86 that the old question of "patriotism" vs. "national betrayal," as framed by Qi Benyu in 1967, was still alive almost two decades later. See Liao Zonglin, "Tan gengzi," 3 (trans. in *Foreign Broadcast Information Service Daily Report: China*, No. 238:K9–K12 [Dec. 11, 1985]); and Jiang Weifan and Han Xibai, "Aiguo yu maiguo wenti," 3 (trans. in *Foreign Broadcast Information Service Daily Report: China*, No. 054:K7–K9 [Mar. 20, 1986]). See also Sun Zuomin's vigorous defense of the peasantry as the great motive force in Chinese history in his response to the iconoclastic views of Wang Zhizhong: "Yihetuan yundong pingjia" (trans. in Buck, ed., *Recent Chinese Studies*, 196–219). (Buck's comments on Sun are in his "Editor's Introduction," in ibid., 7–8.)

81. See, for example, *Shandong Yihetuan anjuan; SYDZX; Yihetuan shiliao; Choubi oucun.*

82. On the social psychology not only of the Boxers but of the population of North China generally at the time of the Boxer episode, see Li Wenhai and Liu Yangdong, "Shehui xinli fenxi." On the influence of popular religion on the Boxers, see in particular Chen Zhenjiang and Cheng Xiao, *Yihetuan wenxian*; also Cheng Xiao, "Minjian zongjiao."

83. See, for example, the articles in *Yihetuan yundong yu jindai Zhongguo shehui.*

84. Li Wenhai and Liu Yangdong, in their otherwise excellent article on the social psychological setting of the Boxer movement, continue to use the term *mixin*

372   more or less uncritically to refer to the ideas of the Boxers. Qi Qizhang asserted in 1980 that, while there were differences among historians concerning the antifeudal nature of the Boxers, the "anti-imperialist and patriotic" nature of the Boxer movement was something "acknowledged by all" (Qi Qizhang, "Yihetuan yundong pingjia," 97). In his 1990 survey of Chinese Boxer scholarship of the preceding decade, Sun Zhanyuan wrote ("Yihetuan yundong yanjiu," 72): "The virtually unanimous view in academic circles is that the Boxer movement was an anti-imperialist and patriotic movement; the focus of debate has been on whether or not the Boxers are to be categorized as an old-style peasant war (or peasant revolution), whether or not they were a national war against foreign [aggression], and such questions." Even the iconoclastic Wang Zhizhong, while calling for a more careful definition of the exact nature of the anti-imperialist role played by the Boxers, fully accepted the overall anti-imperialist discourse I have referred to: "That [the Boxers] played a memorable part in the unending anti-imperialist struggle of the Chinese people is something that is universally acknowledged" ("Fandi zuoyong," 56). For a well-regarded text treatment of the Boxer movement that operates more or less uncritically within the anti-imperialist discourse, see Liao Yizhong, Li Dezheng, and Zhang Xuanru, *Yihetuan.*

85. The historian and Marxist theorist Li Shu came about as close as anyone to suggesting that "anti-imperialism" was a label superimposed on the Boxers by later historians: "The slogan of the Boxers," Li asserted in a 1980 speech, "was 'destroy the foreigner.' We sympathize with those peasants who over eighty years ago suffered oppression and humiliation at the hands of foreign aggressors, and it stands to reason that we interpret 'destroy the foreigner' as anti-imperialism. But it is beyond a doubt that their understanding of 'destroy the foreigner' at the time was mistaken. The foreigner cannot be destroyed." Li Shu, "Zhong-Xi wenhua wenti."

86. It is significant, in this light, that Li Shu, in his speech at the 1980 conference marking the eightieth anniversary of the Boxer uprising, hardly referred to the Boxers at all. He took the occasion instead to address the more general problem of how Chinese should view Western culture—as *ti* (essence) or as *yong* (practical use)—and how Chinese and Western cultures should be combined in a new cultural synthesis in the future. Li Shu, ibid.

87. Chiang Monlin [Jiang Menglin], *Tides,* 43.

88. Wasserstrom, " 'Civilization' and Its Discontents."

89. One of the major events of the "culture fever" (*wenhua re*) that began around 1983–84 was the showing (in summer 1988) of the six-part television series, *Heshang* (River elegy), which addressed the issue of Chinese cultural identity in the most frontal way. The series and the controversies it excited are discussed in Wakeman, "All the Rage"; for a fuller treatment, see Su Xiaokang and Wang Luxiang, *Deathsong.* For a stimulating discussion of the problems involved in "being Chinese" in contemporary China, see Myron Cohen, "Being Chinese," 125–33.

Conclusion

1. Ricoeur argues forcefully that even the work of Braudel and other members of the Annales school, although proclaiming itself to be nonnarrative in character, has embedded in it a concealed narrative structure. See, especially, *Time and*

Narrative, vol. 1, ch. 6, on "Historical Intentionality." See also Carr, *Time*, 8–9, 175–77.

2. The oral history materials, which give us the fullest Boxer evocations of their own experience, clearly are inadequate for this purpose, both because they are not contemporary and because they are structured to a substantial extent by the consciousness not of the respondents but of their interrogators. The judicial confessions of Boxers scattered among the documents housed at the First Historical Archives at the Palace Museum in Beijing are, if the ones I examined are any indication, brief, stylized, and not terribly informative. See, for example, the confession of Guo Dunyuan, GX 26/intercalary 8/11 (Oct. 4, 1900), in Junjichu lufu zouzhe: Nongmin yundong, file 1763.

At the most superficial level, we know that some Boxers previously fought in the Sino-Japanese War and others may have gone on to involvement with the Red Spears (Perry, *Rebels*, 153, 200). We also know, from the Shandong oral history accounts, the occupations of many of the respondents as of the 1960s. None of these materials, however, comes close to supplying us with the kind of intimate biographical tracking (including pre-Boxer or post-Boxer life experience or both) that is readily available in such foreign accounts of the period as Steel's *Through Peking's Sewer Gate* (including the introduction by George W. Carrington), Eva Jane Price's *China Journal*, and Miner's papers (the journal in particular).

3. Don C. Price, "Popular and Elite Heterodoxy."

4. Mary C. Wright discusses the growing shift away from this identification with the Taipings as the Guomindang under Chiang Kai-shek (Jiang Jieshi) became more and more wedded to stability and order and less and less to revolutionary change ("From Revolution to Restoration").

5. Uhalley, "Li Hsiu-ch'eng"; Harrison, *Peasant Rebellions*, 128.

6. Sullivan, "The Controversy," 2–3, 14.

7. Schiffrin, *Sun Yat-sen*, 23.

8. Harrison, *Peasant Rebellions*, 260.

9. Constable, "Christianity."

10. Davies, *World of Wonders*, 58.

11. Myerhoff, *Number Our Days*, 37, 222.

12. "My paramount object in this struggle," Lincoln wrote Horace Greeley on Aug. 22, 1862, "is to save the Union and is *not* either to save or destroy slavery. If I could save the Union without freeing *any* slave, I would do it." *The People Shall Judge* 1:768–69.

13. Almost 75 percent of those interned were American citizens. German-Americans, Italian-Americans, and German or Italian nationals living in the United States encountered difficulties only when there were specific grounds for believing them to be enemy agents.

GLOSSARY

A Q *zhengzhuan*	阿Q正傳
Ai Sheng	艾聲
Anhui suhuabao	安徽俗話報
Baidengzhao	白燈照
baifa	敗法
baojia	保甲
bao-Qing	保清
baotu	暴徒
Benming	本明
bi (hamper)	閉
bi (scamper)	避
bianluan	變亂
bibuliao daoqiang	避不了刀槍
bihuo men zhou	閉火門咒
bipao zhi fa	避砲之法
bu wei qiangpao	不畏槍炮
bushutou	不梳頭
Cai Hesen	蔡和森
Cai Yuanpei	蔡元培
Cao Futian	曹福田
chang	場
Chen Duxiu	陳獨秀
Chen Tiesheng	陳鐵生
Cixi (Empress Dowager)	慈禧太后
da shijie	大師姐
da shixiong	大師兄
Dadaohui	大刀會
Damengquan	大夢拳
Daoguang	道光
daoqiang buru	刀槍不入

daozei	盜賊
daquan	打拳
diangun buchu	電棍不觸
Dong Fuxiang	董福祥
Dong Wanlun	董萬侖
Dongyangche	東洋車
Duan (Prince)	端親王
egui tai duo	餓鬼太多
er shijie	二師姐
er shixiong	二師兄
ermaozi	二毛子
fa buling	法不靈
fandi aiguo	反帝愛國
Fei Jidujiao tekan	非基督教特刊
feidi	飛地
fengjian mixin	封建迷信
Fengshen yanyi	封神演義
Fu-Qing mieyang	扶清滅洋
furen pi	婦人皮
fushen	附身
fushui	符水
Gailiang nü'er jing	改良女兒經
Gangyi	剛毅
Gao Shaochen	高紹陳
Gaoluo	高洛
geminghua	革命化
Gemingjun	革命軍
Gu Hongming	辜鴻銘
Gu Jiegang	顧頡剛
Guan He	管鶴
Guan Yu	關羽
Guandi	關帝
Guangong	關公
Guangxu	光緒
Guansheng	關聖
Guanyin laomu	觀音老母
gui (deceitful)	詭
gui (spirit)	鬼
guidao	鬼道
guidaozhuyi	鬼道主義
guiwang	鬼王
guizishou	劊子手
guochi	國恥

Hailanpao	海蘭泡
Han Daodan	韓倒蛋
Han Guniang	韓姑娘
Handan	邯鄲
Hanjian	漢奸
hanzai	旱災
He Xiangu	何仙姑
Heidengzhao	黑燈照
heifengkou	黑風口
hong	紅
Hong Xiuquan	洪秀全
Hongdeng ji	紅燈記
Hongdengzhao	紅燈照
Hongdengzhao (Armor of the Red Lantern)	紅燈罩
Hongdengzhao zhandoudui	紅燈照戰鬥隊
Hongquan	紅拳
hongtian baojian	紅天寶劍
Hongweibing	紅衞兵
Houquan	猴拳
Hu Jijiao	胡犄角
Hu Shi	胡適
Hualanhui	花籃會
Huang Santai	黃三太
Huang Tianba	黃天霸
Huanglian shengmu	黃蓮聖母
Huanhou	桓侯
huiwu	穢物
huo	惑
Jiang Menglin	蔣夢麟
Jiang Qing	江青
Jiangdong Liushisitun	江東六十四屯
jiangshen futi	降神附體
jiangshen re	降神熱
jiangtong	降童
jiao	剿
jiaoan	教案
jie	劫
Jindao shengmu	金刀聖母
jingbu	經布
Jinzhongzhao	金鐘罩
Jiu tian xuannü	九天玄女
junjiang tou	軍將頭
kan	坎
Kang Youwei	康有為

ketou	磕頭
kong po qi shu	恐破其術
kongdi, chongdi, qindi	恐帝, 崇帝, 親帝
Kongming	孔明
koutou	叩頭
kuangre shaonian	狂熱少年
Kuangren riji	狂人日記
Landengzhao	藍燈照
Lanzihui	籃子會
Lao She	老舍
li	離
Li Bingheng	李秉衡
Li Dazhao	李大釗
Li Hongzhang	李鴻章
Li Shiyu	李世瑜
Li Tiemei	李鐵梅
Li Xiucheng	李秀成
Li Yuhe	李玉和
Li Zhongpeng (Jingshu)	李仲彭 (經述)
Liang Ji	梁濟
Liang Qichao	梁啟超
Liang Shuming	梁漱溟
Lin Hei'er	林黑兒
Lishan laomu	梨山老母
Liu Bei	劉備
Liu Dapeng	劉大鵬
Liu Mengyang	劉孟揚
Liu Shaoqi	劉少奇
Liu Shiduan	劉士端
Liu Shijiu	劉十九
Liu Xiang nü	劉香女
Liu Xinwu	劉心武
Liu Xizi	柳溪子
Liu Yitong	劉以桐
lixingzhuyi	理性主義
Liyuantun	梨園屯
Long Chi	龍池
loudao	漏刀
Lü Dongbin	呂洞賓
Lu Wantian	鹿完天
Lu Xun	魯迅
luan	亂
luanmin	亂民
Lüzu (Hall)	呂祖堂
Mai Menghua	麥孟華

maocao	毛草
Mazu	媽祖
Meihuaquan	梅花拳
Miaoshan	妙善
Minbao	民報
mixin	迷信
mixin sixiang	迷信思想
Nantang	南堂
Nayancheng	那彦成
neigong	內功
Nie guizi	聶鬼子
Nie Shicheng	聶士成
Nü'er jing	女兒經
Peng Gong an	彭公案
Peng Shuzhi	彭述之
po qi fa	破其法
Pochu mixin yundong	破除迷信運動
Qi Benyu	戚本禹
qian	乾
Qianwan bie ba wo dang ren	千萬別把我當人
qigong	氣功
qing	請
Qing (Prince)	慶親王
Qingdengzhao	青燈照
Qinggong mishi	清宮秘史
Qinggong yuan	清宮冤
Qinglianjiao	青蓮教
qiu	求
qiushen futi	求神附體
Qu Qiubai	瞿秋白
quan	拳
quanchang	拳場
quanfei	拳匪
quanfei zhi luan	拳匪之亂
quanshu	拳術
renao	熱鬧
Ronglu	榮祿
rouqiu fen	肉丘墳
San taizi	三太子
sancong side	三從四德
Sanguo yanyi	三國演義
sao-Qing	掃清

Senluo (Temple)	森羅殿
Shaguozhao	沙鍋罩
Shaliuzhai	沙柳寨
shangfa	上法
shanhuo	煽惑
shao	燒
Shaolin shenda	少林神打
Shaseng	沙僧
shehui xianxiang	社會現象
shen	神
shen bu fushen	神不附身
shenbing	神兵
Shengxian (sect)	聖賢教
Shenquan	神拳
Shi Gong an	施公案
shiba kui	十八魁
shixiong	師兄
Shuihu zhuan	水滸傳
shuizai	水災
shun-Qing	順清
Song Qing	宋慶
Sui-Tang yanyi	隋唐演義
Sun Bin	孫臏
Sun Wukong	孫悟空
taipingche	太平車
tan	壇
Tang Xingqi	唐興奇
Tang Yan	唐晏
Tangseng	唐僧
taohuang	逃荒
Tianhou	天后
Tiebu shan	鐵布衫
Tieguanzhao	鐵關罩
tongji (tâng-ki)	童乩
tongzijun	童子軍
tongzituan	童子團
tuan	團
tuanfei	團匪
wan nü mao	萬女旄
Wang Lun	王倫
Wang Luoyao	王洛要
Wang Shuo	王朔
Wang Xinggong	王星拱
Wang Zhizhong	王致中
wawadui	娃娃隊

wen	文
wenhua re	文化熱
wenming zhi geming	文明之革命
wu	武
Wu Song	武松
Wu Wenxian	吳文銜
wuhe zhi zhong	烏合之眾
wuhui	污穢
Wusheng laomu	無生老母
xiajiang	下降
xiandaihua	現代化
Xiangdao zhoubao	嚮導週報
Xiantiandao	先天道
Xincheng	心誠
Xing-Qing mieyang	興清滅洋
xinsheng shiwu	新生事物
Xiuge jinzhen	綉閣金箴
Xiyouji	西遊記
Xu Yingkui	許應騤
Xuanzang	玄奘
Xue Xiantian	薛銜天
Yan Fu	嚴復
Yan Shuqin	閻書勤
yang (foreign)	洋
yang (male principle)	陽
Yang Diangao	楊典誥
Yang Futong	楊福同
Yang Mushi	楊慕時
yang Yihetuan	洋義和團
Ye Changchi	葉昌熾
Ye Mingchen	葉名琛
yeman de paiwai	野蠻的排外
yeman zhi geming	野蠻之革命
Yihe	義和
Yihe shen tuan	義和神團
Yihe tongzi	義和童子
Yihequan	義和拳
Yihetuan	義和團
yimin	義民
yin	陰
ying	硬
yinhun zhen	陰魂陣
Yinyangquan	陰陽拳
youmin	游民
youmin shehui	游民社會

382	Yu Qingshui	于清水
	Yu Xian	豫咸
	Yuan Chang	袁昶
	Yuan Shikai	袁世凱
	Yulu	裕祿
	yumin	愚民
	Yun Yuding	惲毓鼎
	Yuxian	毓賢
	zai	宰
	Zeng Guofan	曾國藩
	Zhang Decheng	張德成
	Zhang Fei	張飛
	Zhang Rumei	張汝梅
	Zhang Zhidong	張之洞
	Zhao Qing	趙青
	Zhao Sanduo	趙三多
	Zhao Yun	趙雲
	Zhao Zilong	趙子龍
	zhen	震
	zhenzhu	真主
	zhiyan	直眼
	Zhongfang Shi	仲芳氏
	Zhu Bajie	豬八戒
	Zhu Hongdeng	朱紅燈
	Zhu-Qing mieyang	助清滅洋
	Zhuang (Prince)	莊親王
	Zhuge Liang	諸葛亮
	zi wei buru	自謂不如
	Zizhulin	紫竹林
	Zou Rong	鄒容
	zun wang rang yi	尊王攘夷
	Zushihui	祖師會

BIBLIOGRAPHY

Ahern, Emily M. "The Power and Pollution of Chinese Women." In Wolf, ed., *Studies in Chinese Society*, 269–90.

Ai Sheng. *Quanfei jilüe* (A brief account of the Boxer bandits). In *Yihetuan* 1:441–64.

Aliakebaer [Ali Akbar]. *Zhongguo jixing* (Notes on a trip to China). Beijing: Sanlian Shudian, 1988.

Alitto, Guy. *The Last Confucian: Liang Shu-ming and the Chinese Dilemma of Modernity*. Berkeley: University of California Press, 1979.

Allen, Roland. *The Siege of the Peking Legations*. London: Smith, Elder, 1901.

Alpern, Stanley B. "The New Myths of African History." *Bostonia* 2 (Summer 1992): 34–40, 68–69.

American Board of Commissioners for Foreign Missions (hereafter, ABCFM) (Congregationalist). Papers. Houghton Library, Harvard University.

Anagnost, Ann S. "Politics and Magic in Contemporary China." *Modern China* 13.1 (Jan. 1987): 41–62.

Anhui suhuabao (Anhui common speech journal). 1905.

Anze xianzhi (Anze [Yueyang] county gazetteer). 1932 ed. Excerpted in Qiao Zhiqiang, comp., *Yihetuan zai Shanxi diqu shiliao*, 140–41.

Appell, Laura W. R. "Menstruation Among the Rungus of Borneo: An Unmarked Category." In Buckley and Gottlieb, eds., *Blood Magic*, 94–112.

Arkush, R. David. "Ku Hung-ming (1857–1928)." *Papers on China* 19 (Dec. 1965): 194–238.

Arnold, David. *Famine: Social Crisis and Historical Change*. Oxford: Basil Blackwell, 1988.

Aron, Stephen. "How the West Was Lost: The Transformation of Kentucky from Daniel Boone to Henry Clay." Ph.D. diss., University of California, Berkeley, 1990.

Bainbridge, W. E. "Besieged in Peking." In Lou Hoover Papers, Boxer Rebellion: Diaries, Herbert Hoover Presidential Library.

Baker, S. J. K. "A Background to the Study of Drought in East Africa." In Dalby, Church, and Bezzaz, eds., *Drought in Africa 2 / Sécheresse en Afrique 2*, 74–82.

Barker, Nancy Nicholas. "Teaching the French Revolution." *Perspectives* 28.4 (Apr. 1990): 17–18.

384 Barmé, Geremie. "Beijing Days, Beijing Nights." In Jonathan Unger, ed., *The Pro-Democracy Protests in China: Reports from the Provinces*, 35–58. Armonk, N.Y.: M. E. Sharpe, 1991.

——. "Confession, Redemption, and Death: Liu Xiaobo and the Protest Movement of 1989." In George Hicks, ed., *The Broken Mirror: China After Tiananmen*, 52–99. Chicago: St. James Press, 1990.

——. "Wang Shuo and *Liumang* ('Hooligan') Culture." *Australian Journal of Chinese Affairs* 28 (July 1992): 23–64.

Barnes, Julian. *Flaubert's Parrot*. New York: Vintage, 1990.

Bastid-Bruguière, Marianne. "Currents of Social Change." In Fairbank and Liu, eds., *The Cambridge History of China* 11:535–602.

Bays, Daniel H., ed. *Christianity in China: The Eighteenth Century to the Present*. Stanford: Stanford University Press, 1996.

——. "Indigenous Protestant Churches in China, 1900–1937: A Pentecostal Case Study." In Steven Kaplan, ed., *Indigenous Responses to Western Christianity*, 124–43. New York: New York University Press, 1995.

Beattie, John. "Spirit Mediumship in Bunyoro." In Beattie and Middleton, eds., *Spirit Mediumship and Society in Africa*, 159–70.

Beattie, John and John Middleton, eds. *Spirit Mediumship and Society in Africa*. New York: Africana Publishing, 1969.

"Behind Mao's Red Rule: The 100 Violent Years." *Life*, Sept. 23, Sept. 30, and Oct. 7, 1966.

Beijing fengbo jishi (The truth about the Beijing turmoil). Beijing: Beijing Chubanshe, 1989.

Beijing Shida Lishixi ernianji kaimenbanxue xiao fendui. "Weida de fandi geming douzheng burong wumie: Hebei sheng Langfang diqu gongnongbing he Yihetuan yundong canjiazhe nuchi Suxiu gongji Yihetuan de miulun" (It is not permitted to slander the great anti-imperialist revolutionary struggle: Workers, peasants, and soldiers and Boxer movement participants of the Langfang region of Hebei province angrily denounce the falsehoods in the Soviet revisionists' attack on the Boxers). *Beijing Shifan Daxue xuebao* 2 (1975): 60–66.

Beijing Shifan Daxue Jinggangshan Gongshe Zhongwenxi lianhe dadui *Tingjin bao* bianjibu. "Wuchanjieji wenyi de yizhan hongdeng—Zan geming xiandai jingju yangbanxi *Hongdeng ji*" (A red lantern of proletarian literature and art—In praise of *The Red Lantern*, a model revolutionary Beijing opera on a contemporary theme). *Renmin ribao* (People's daily), May 29, 1967, 8.

Benton, Gregor. *Mountain Fires: The Red Army's Three-Year War in South China, 1934–1938*. Berkeley: University of California Press, 1992.

Berglie, Per-Arne. "Spirit-Possession in Theory and Practice: Séances with Tibetan Spirit-Mediums in Nepal." In Holm, ed., *Religious Ecstasy*, 151–66.

Bernal, Martin. *Black Athena: The Afroasiatic Roots of Classical Civilization*. Multivolume work (in progress). New Brunswick, N.J.: Rutgers University Press, 1987–.

Bernard, Viola W., Perry Ottenberg, and Fritz Redl. "Dehumanization." In Nevitt Sanford, Craig Comstock et al., eds., *Sanctions for Evil: Sources of Social Destructiveness*, 102–24. San Francisco: Jossey-Bass, 1973.

Bernstein, Richard. "Unsettling the Old West: Now Historians Are Bad-Mouthing the American Frontier." *New York Times Magazine*, Mar. 18, 1990, 34–35, 56–59.

Bernus, Edmond. "Les Éleveurs face à la Sécheresse en Afrique Sahélienne: Exemples Nigériens." In Dalby, Church, and Bezzaz, eds., *Drought in Africa 2 / Sécheresse en Afrique 2*, 140–47.

Beyene, Yewoubdar. *From Menarche to Menopause: Reproductive Lives of Peasant Women in Two Cultures*. Albany: State University of New York Press, 1989.

Bi Sisheng. "Weida de fandi aiguo douzheng buke wu: Chi Suxiu dui Yihetuan yundong de edu gongji" (The great anti-imperialist patriotic struggle is not to be treated disrespectfully: A denunciation of the Soviet revisionists' venomous attack on the Boxer movement). *Shandong Shiyuan xuebao* 6 (1975): 68–72.

Bickers, Robert A. "History, Legend, and Treaty Port Ideology, 1925–1931." In Bickers, ed., *Ritual and Diplomacy: The Macartney Mission to China, 1792–1794*, 81–92. London: British Association for Chinese Studies in association with Wellsweep Press, 1993.

Bird, Rowena. Letters, journal. In Alice M. Williams Miscellaneous Papers (Shansi Mission), file 12, ABCFM, Papers.

Björkqvist, Kaj. "Ecstasy from a Physiological Point of View." In Holm, ed., *Religious Ecstasy*, 74–86.

Blake, Reed H. "The Relationship Between Collective Excit ment and Rumor Construction." *Rocky Mountain Social Science Journal* 6 (1969): 119–26.

Blunden, Caroline and Mark Elvin. *Cultural Atlas of China*. New York: Facts on File, 1983.

Bohr, Paul Richard. *Famine in China and the Missionary: Timothy Richard as Relief Administrator and Advocate of National Reform, 1876–1884*. Cambridge: East Asian Research Center, Harvard University, 1972.

" 'Bolshevist' China." *The Nation* 124 (Apr. 20, 1927): 420.

Boorstin, Daniel J. "The Historian: 'A Wrestler with the Angel.' " *New York Times Book Review* (hereafter, *NYTBR*), Sept. 20, 1987, 1, 28–29.

Bourguignon, Erika. "An Assessment of Some Comparisons and Implications." In Bourguignon, ed., *Religion, Altered States of Consciousness, and Social Change*, 321–39.

——. "Introduction: A Framework for the Comparative Study of Altered States of Consciousness." In Bourguignon, ed., *Religion, Altered States of Consciousness, and Social Change*, 3–35.

——, ed. *Religion, Altered States of Consciousness, and Social Change*. Columbus: Ohio State University Press, 1973.

Boxer Rising, The: A History of the Boxer Trouble in China (reprinted from *Shanghai Mercury*). 2d ed. Shanghai: Shanghai Mercury, 1901.

Boyer, Paul and Stephen Nissenbaum. *Salem Possessed: The Social Origins of Witchcraft*. Cambridge: Harvard University Press, 1974.

Brandt, Nat. *Massacre in Shansi*. Syracuse: Syracuse University Press, 1994.

Brinkley, Alan. "The Western Historians: Don't Fence Them In." *NYTBR*, Sept. 20, 1992, 1, 22–27.

Brody, Jane E. "Lucking Out: Weird Rituals and Strange Beliefs." *New York Times*, Jan. 27, 1991, S11.

Brontë, Emily. *Wuthering Heights* (1847). New York: Pocket Books, n.d.

386   Broomhall, Marshall, ed. *Last Letters and Further Records of Martyred Missionaries of the China Inland Mission*. London: Morgan and Scott, 1901.

——, ed. *Martyred Missionaries of the China Inland Mission with a Record of the Perils and Sufferings of Some Who Escaped*. London: Morgan and Scott, 1901.

Broyard, Anatole. "Good Books About Being Sick." *NYTBR*, Apr. 1, 1990, 28.

Brunvand, Jan Harold. *The Vanishing Hitchhiker: American Urban Legends and Their Meanings*. New York: Norton, 1981.

Buck, David D. "The 1990 International Symposium on the Boxer Movement and Modern Chinese Society." *Republican China* 16.2 (Apr. 1991): 113–20.

——, ed. *Recent Chinese Studies of the Boxer Movement*. Armonk, N.Y.: M. E. Sharpe, 1987.

Buckley, Thomas. "Menstruation and the Power of Yurok Women." In Buckley and Gottlieb, eds., *Blood Magic*, 187–209.

Buckley, Thomas and Alma Gottlieb. "A Critical Appraisal of Theories of Menstrual Symbolism." In Buckley and Gottlieb, eds., *Blood Magic*, 3–50.

Buckley, Thomas and Alma Gottlieb, eds. *Blood Magic: The Anthropology of Menstruation*. Berkeley: University of California Press, 1988.

Burns, Michael. "How Should History Be Taught?" *New York Times*, Nov. 22, 1986, 31.

Butler, Smedley D. "Dame Rumor: The Biggest Liar in the World." *American Magazine* 111 (June 1931): 24–26, 155–56.

Cai Hesen. "Yihetuan yu guomin geming" (The Boxers and the national revolution). *Xiangdao zhoubao* 81 (Sept. 3, 1924): 652–54.

Cai Yuanpei. "Cai Yuanpei xiang geguo xuanyan" (Cai Yuanpei's manifesto to all countries). July 30, 1925. In Luo Jialun, ed., *Geming wenxian* (Revolutionary documents), Series 18:36–41. Taibei: Zhengzhong Shuju, 1957.

Campion-Vincent, Véronique. "The Baby-Parts Story: A New Latin American Legend." *Western Folklore* 49.1 (Jan. 1990): 9–25.

Carr, David. *Time, Narrative, and History*. Bloomington: Indiana University Press, 1986.

Carrère d'Encausse, Hélène and Stuart R. Schram. *Marxism and Asia: An Introduction with Readings*. London: Allen Lane, 1969.

Chai E. *Gengxin jishi* (A record of the events of 1900–1901). In *Yihetuan* 1:301–33.

Chen Duxiu. *Duxiu wencun* (Collected writings of Chen Duxiu). Hong Kong: Yuandong Tushu Gongsi, 1965.

——. "Ershiqi nian yilai guomin yundongzhong suo de jiaoxun" (Lessons to be derived from the national movements of the past twenty-seven years). *Xin qingnian* 4 (Dec. 20, 1924): 15–22.

——. "Kelinde bei" (The von Ketteler Monument). *Xin qingnian* 5.5 (Nov. 1918): 449–58.

——. "Women duiyu Yihetuan liangge cuowu de guannian" (Our two mistaken conceptions concerning the Boxers). *Xiangdao zhoubao* 81 (Sept. 3, 1924): 645–46.

Ch'en, Jerome. *The Highlanders of Central China: A History, 1895–1937*. Armonk, N.Y.: M. E. Sharpe, 1992.

——. "The Nature and Characteristics of the Boxer Movement: A Morphological Study." *Bulletin of the School of Oriental and African Studies* 23.2 (1960): 287–308.

———. "The Origin of the Boxers." In Ch'en and Nicholas Tarling, eds., *Studies in the Social History of China and South-East Asia: Essays in Memory of Victor Purcell*, 57–84. Cambridge: Cambridge University Press, 1970.

Chen Junshi, T. Colin Campbell, Li Junyao, and Richard Peto. *Diet, Life-style, and Mortality in China: A Study of the Characteristics of 65 Chinese Counties*. Oxford: Oxford University Press, 1990 (jointly published in the United States by Cornell University Press and in China by the People's Medical Publishing House).

Chen, Kuang-chung. "A Semiotic Phenomenology of the Boxers' Movements: A Contribution to a Hermeneutics of Historical Interpretation." Ph.D. diss., University of Illinois, Urbana-Champaign, 1985.

Chen Kuangshi. "*Kaizhilu* yu Yihetuan" (*Kaizhilu* and the Boxers). In *Yihetuan yundong yu jindai Zhongguo shehui guoji xueshu taolunhui lunwen ji*, 875–83.

Chen, Nancy N. "Urban Spaces and Experiences of *Qigong*." Paper presented at Association for Asian Studies annual meeting, Los Angeles, Mar. 1993.

Chen Tiesheng. "Quanshu yu quanfei" (The art of boxing and the Boxer bandits). *Xin qingnian* 6.2 (Feb. 1919): 218–19.

Chen Zhenjiang. "Huabei youmin shehui yu Yihetuan yundong" (The mobile unemployed society of North China and the Boxer movement). In *Yihetuan yundong yu jindai Zhongguo shehui guoji xueshu taolunhui lunwen ji*, 230–45.

Chen Zhenjiang and Cheng Xiao. *Yihetuan wenxian jizhu yu yanjiu* (Explications and studies of Boxer writings). Tianjin: Tianjin Renmin, 1985.

Cheng Xiao. "Minjian zongjiao yu Yihetuan jietie" (Popular religion and the Boxers' posters). *Lishi yanjiu* 2 (1983): 147–63.

———. "Minsu xinyang yu Quanmin yishi" (Folk beliefs and Boxer consciousness). In *Yihetuan yundong yu jindai Zhongguo shehui guoji xueshu taolunhui lunwen ji*, 284–311.

Chi Pen-yu [Qi Benyu]. "Patriotism or National Betrayal?—On the Reactionary Film *Inside Story of the Ching Court*." *Peking Review* 15 (Apr. 7, 1967): 5–16. Translation of article originally published in *Hongqi* (Red flag) 5 (Mar. 1967): 9–23.

Chiang Monlin [Jiang Menglin]. *Tides from the West: A Chinese Autobiography*. New Haven: Yale University Press, 1947.

Chiang, Ying-ho. "Literary Reactions to the Keng-tzu Incident (1900)." Ph.D. diss., University of California, Los Angeles, 1982.

China in Chaos. Shanghai: North-China Daily News and North-China Herald, 1927.

China Records Project. Divinity School Library, Yale University.

"China's War of Independence." *The Nation* 124.3211 (Jan. 19, 1927): 54.

"China—Vaccinated." *The Nation* 124.3216 (Feb. 23, 1927): 198.

Choubi oucun (Retained working notes). Edited by Zhongguo shehui kexueyuan jindaishi yanjiusuo he Zhongguo diyi lishi dang'anguan (Modern History Institute of Chinese Academy of Social Sciences and the First Historical Archive of China). Beijing: Zhongguo Shehui Kexue, 1983.

Ci, Jiwei. *Dialectic of the Chinese Revolution: From Utopianism to Hedonism*. Stanford: Stanford University Press, 1994.

Clapp, Dwight H. Diary letter. In Alice M. Williams Miscellaneous Papers (Shansi Mission), file 12, ABCFM, Papers.

388   Cohen, Myron L. "Being Chinese: The Peripheralization of Traditional Identity." *Daedalus* 120.2 (Spring 1991): 113–34.

Cohen, Paul A. *China and Christianity: The Missionary Movement and the Growth of Chinese Antiforeignism, 1860–1870*. Cambridge: Harvard University Press, 1963.

———. "Christian Missions and Their Impact to 1900." In Fairbank, ed., *The Cambridge History of China* 10:543–90.

———. *Discovering History in China: American Historical Writing on the Recent Chinese Past*. New York: Columbia University Press, 1984.

Cohn, Norman. "The Myth of Satan and His Human Servants." In Mary Douglas, ed., *Witchcraft Confessions and Accusations*, 3–16. London: Tavistock, 1970.

———. *The Pursuit of the Millennium: Revolutionary Millenarians and Mystical Anarchists of the Middle Ages*. Rev. and expanded ed. New York: Oxford University Press, 1970.

Colson, Elizabeth. "Spirit Possession Among the Tonga of Zambia." In Beattie and Middleton, eds., *Spirit Mediumship and Society in Africa*, 69–103.

Constable, Nicole. "Christianity and Hakka Identity." In Bays, ed., *Christianity in China*.

Cooke, H. J. "The Problem of Drought in Botswana." In Hinchey, ed., *Symposium on Drought in Botswana*, 7–20.

Corbin, Paul Leaton. "The Shansi Mission (June 1907)." In Miscellaneous Personal Papers, Manuscript Group No. 8, box no. 5 (Irrenius J. Atwood folder), China Records Project.

Dadao Liu Shaoqi manhua ji (A collection of cartoons attacking Liu Shaoqi). Compiled by Hongweibing Shanghai shi dongfeng zaofan bingtuan (The Red Guard east wind rebel corps of Shanghai). Shanghai, May 1967.

Dadao Liu Shaoqi yilianhuan manhua ce (A volume of cartoon strips attacking Liu Shaoqi). Compiled by Hongweibing Shanghai shi disan silingbu Hongkou tixiao Mao Zedong sixiang hongweibing zongbu. Shanghai, Apr. 1967.

Dai Xuanzhi. *Yihetuan yanjiu* (A study of the Boxers). Taibei: Zhongguo Xueshu Zhuzuo Jiangzhu Weiyuanhui, 1963.

Dalby, David, R. J. Harrison Church, and Fatima Bezzaz, eds., *Drought in Africa 2 / Sécheresse en Afrique 2*. London: International Africa Institute, 1977.

Dando, William A. *The Geography of Famine*. London: Edward Arnold, 1980.

Darnton, Robert. *The Great Cat Massacre and Other Episodes in French Cultural History*. New York: Vintage, 1985.

Davies, Robertson. *World of Wonders*. New York: Penguin, 1981.

Davis, Natalie Zemon. *Society and Culture in Early Modern France*. Stanford: Stanford University Press, 1975.

De Groot, J. J. M. *The Religious System of China: Its Ancient Forms, Evolution, History and Present Aspect, Manners, Customs and Social Institutions Connected Therewith* (1892–1910). 6 vols. Rpt., Taipei: Literature House, 1964.

Delaney, Carol. "Mortal Flow: Menstruation in Turkish Village Society." In Buckley and Gottlieb, eds., *Blood Magic*, 75–93.

Dhomhnaill, Nuala Ní. "Why I Choose to Write in Irish: The Corpse That Sits Up and Talks Back." *NYTBR*, Jan. 8, 1995, 3, 27–28.

Dikötter, Frank. *The Discourse of Race in Modern China*. Stanford: Stanford   389
   University Press, 1992.

Ding Mingnan. "Guanyu Zhongguo jindaishishang jiaoan de kaocha" (An examination of the church cases in modern Chinese history). *Jindaishi yanjiu* 1
   (1990): 27–46.

"Disanci Yihetuan yundong shi xueshu taolunhui jianjie" (A summary account of
   the third academic conference on the history of the Boxer movement). *Renmin
   ribao*, June 2, 1986.

Dittmer, Lowell and Chen Ruoxi. *Ethics and Rhetoric of the Chinese Cultural
   Revolution*. Berkeley: Center for Chinese Studies, Institute of East Asian Studies,
   University of California, 1981.

Doar, Bruce. "The Boxers and Chinese Drama: Questions of Interaction." *Papers
   on Far Eastern History* 29 (Mar. 1984): 91–118.

Dong Wanlun. " 'Jiangdong liushisi tun' de lishi he lao shahuang de baoxing lu:
   Tongchi Suxiu wei lao shahuang qin Hua bianhu" (The history of "the sixty-
   four villages of Jiangdong" and the record of atrocities committed by the old
   czars: A scathing denunciation of Soviet revisionism's defense of the old czars'
   aggression against China). *Yanbian Daxue xuebao* 1 (1976): 93–101.

———. " 'Jiangdong liushisi tun' he lao shahuang de qin Hua baoxing: Bo Suxiu wei
   lao shahuang qin Hua zuixing de wuchi bianhu" ("The sixty-four villages of
   Jiangdong" and the atrocities committed by the old czars in their aggression
   against China: A refutation of the Soviet revisionists' shameless defense of the
   crimes committed by the old czars in their aggression against China). *Wen-
   shizhe* 1 (1976): 85–92.

Dongbei Yihetuan dang'an shiliao (Archival materials on the history of the Boxers
   in the Northeast). Compiled by the Liaoning sheng dang'an guan (Archival
   office of Liaoning province) and Liaoning shehui kexueyuan lishi yanjiusuo
   (Historical research institute of the Liaoning academy of social sciences).
   Shenyang: Liaoning Renmin, 1981.

Douglas, Mary. *Purity and Danger: An Analysis of the Concepts of Pollution and
   Taboo*. New York: Routledge, 1991.

"Down with Ch'i Pen-yü." *Survey of the China Mainland Press* 4158 (Apr. 16, 1968):
   14–15. Translated from *Wen'ge fengyun* 3 (Mar. 1968).

Drew, Mrs. E. B. Diary. In Lou Hoover Papers, Boxer Rebellion: Diaries, Herbert
   Hoover Presidential Library.

Duara, Prasenjit. *Culture, Power, and the State: Rural North China, 1900–1942*.
   Stanford: Stanford University Press, 1988.

———. "Knowledge and Power in the Discourse of Modernity: The Campaigns
   Against Popular Religion in Early Twentieth-Century China." *Journal of Asian
   Studies* 50.1 (Feb. 1991): 67–83.

Duiker, William J. *Cultures in Collision: The Boxer Rebellion*. San Rafael, Calif.:
   Presidio, 1978.

Dunstheimer, G. G. H. "Le mouvement des Boxeurs: Documents et études pub-
   liés depuis la deuxième Guerre mondiale." *Revue historique* 231.2 (April-June
   1964): 387–416.

———. "Religion et magie dans le mouvement des Boxeurs d'après les textes chi-
   nois." *T'oung Pao* 47.3–5 (1959): 323–67.

390 Eberhard, Wolfram. *A Dictionary of Chinese Symbols: Hidden Symbols in Chinese Life and Thought*. Translated by G. L. Campbell. London: Routledge, 1986.

———. *Guilt and Sin in Traditional China*. Berkeley: University of California Press, 1967.

Edwards, E. H. *Fire and Sword in Shansi: The Story of the Martyrdom of Foreigners and Chinese Christians*. Edinburgh and London: Oliphant Anderson and Ferrier, 1903.

Elliott, Alan J. A. *Chinese Spirit Medium Cults in Singapore* (1955). Rpt., London: Athlone, 1990.

Ellis, Bill. "Introduction." *Western Folklore* 49.1 (Jan. 1990): 1–7.

Elton, G. R. *Return to Essentials: Some Reflections on the Present State of Historical Study*. Cambridge: Cambridge University Press, 1991.

Elvin, Mark. "Mandarins and Millenarians: Reflections on the Boxer Uprising of 1899–1900." *Journal of the Anthropological Society of Oxford* 10.3 (1979): 115–38.

Entenmann, Robert E. "Christian Virgins in Eighteenth-Century Sichuan." In Bays, ed., *Christianity in China*.

———. "Clandestine Catholics and the State in Eighteenth-Century Szechwan." *American Asian Review* 5.3 (Fall 1987): 1–45.

Esherick, Joseph W. *The Origins of the Boxer Uprising*. Berkeley: University of California Press, 1987.

"Eulogy of Red Young Fighters, An." American Consulate General, *Survey of China Mainland Press* (Hong Kong) No. 3934 (May 8, 1967): 12 (translation of *Guangming ribao* editorial of Apr. 27, 1967).

Ewing, Bessie. Letters. In Charles E. and Bessie Ewing Papers (North China Mission), box 3, file 23, ABCFM, Papers.

Fairbank, John K., ed. *The Cambridge History of China*, vol. 10: *Late Ch'ing, 1800–1911*, Part 1. Cambridge: Cambridge University Press, 1978.

Fairbank, John K. and Kwang-Ching Liu, eds. *The Cambridge History of China*, vol. 11: *Late Ch'ing, 1800–1911*, Part 2. Cambridge: Cambridge University Press, 1980.

Feigon, Lee. *Chen Duxiu: Founder of the Chinese Communist Party*. Princeton: Princeton University Press, 1983.

Feng Jicai with Li Dingxing. *Yihequan* (The Boxers). 2 vols. Beijing: Renmin Wenxue, 1977.

Fenn, Courtenay Hughes. Diary. In Miscellaneous Personal Papers. Manuscript Group No. 8, box no. 69, China Records Project.

Fenn, Mrs. S. P., comp. "Peking Siege-Book." In Miscellaneous Personal Papers, Manuscript Group No. 8, box no. 68, China Records Project.

Field, M. J. "Spirit Possession in Ghana." In Beattie and Middleton, eds., *Spirit Mediumship and Society in Africa*, 3–13.

Fitzgerald, C. P. *The Horizon History of China*. New York: American Heritage, 1969.

Fleming, Peter. *The Siege at Peking* (1959). Rpt., Hong Kong: Oxford University Press, 1986.

Forsyth, Robert Coventry, comp. and ed. *The China Martyrs of 1900: A Complete Roll of the Christian Heroes Martyred in China in 1900 with Narratives of Survivors*. London: Religious Tract Society, 1904.

Foster, John Burt. "China and the Chinese in American Literature, 1850–1950."   391
Ph.D. diss., University of Illinois, 1952.

Freri, J., ed. *The Heart of Pekin: Bishop A. Favier's Diary of the Siege, May-August 1900*. Boston: Marlier, 1901.

Frisch, Rose E. "Demographic Implications of the Biological Determinants of Female Fecundity." *Social Biology* 22.1 (1975): 17–22.

Fudan Daxue Lishixi er hongweibing. "Jicheng he fayang 'Hongdengzhao' de geming zaofan jingshen" (Carry on and develop the spirit of revolutionary rebellion of the "Red Lanterns"). *Wenhuibao*, Apr. 14, 1967, 4.

Furst, Peter T. "Fertility, Vision Quest, and Auto-Sacrifice: Some Thoughts on Ritual Blood-Letting Among the Maya." In Merle Greene Robertson, ed., *The Art, Iconography, and Dynastic History of Palenque, Part III: The Proceedings of the Segunda Mesa Redonda de Palenque*, 181–93. Pebble Beach, Calif.: Robert Louis Stevenson School, 1976.

Furth, Charlotte. "Blood, Body, and Gender: Medical Images of the Female Condition in China, 1600–1850." *Chinese Science* 7 (1986): 43–66.

——. "May Fourth in History." In Benjamin I. Schwartz, ed., *Reflections on the May Fourth Movement: A Symposium*, 59–68. Cambridge: East Asian Research Center, Harvard University, 1972.

Fussell, Paul. *The Great War and Modern Memory*. New York: Oxford University Press, 1975.

——. *Wartime: Understanding and Behavior in the Second World War*. New York: Oxford University Press, 1989.

Gamewell, Mary Porter. "History of the Peking Station of the North China Mission of the Woman's Foreign Missionary Society of the Methodist Episcopal Church." In Miscellaneous Personal Papers, Manuscript Group No. 8, box no. 73, China Records Project.

Gao Nan. *Gao Nan riji* (The diary of Gao Nan). In *Gengzi jishi*, 143–246.

Gao Shaochen. *Yongqing gengxin jilüe* (A summary account of Yongqing county in 1900–1901). In *Yihetuan* 1:417–39.

Gao Yuan. *Born Red: A Chronicle of the Cultural Revolution*. Stanford: Stanford University Press, 1987.

Gao Yuanchao. "Yihetuan shiqi Dongbei renmin de kang E douzheng: Jian ping Qihewensiji zhi liu de wuchi lanyan" (The Northeast people's struggle against Russia during the Boxer era: Along with a critique of the shameless slanders of Tikhvinsky and Company). *Jilin Shida xuebao* 2 (1976): 70–73, 75.

García Márquez, Gabriel. *The General in His Labyrinth*. Translated by Edith Grossman. New York: Knopf, 1990.

Ge Tian and Gong Zhu. "Shi wenming shizhe haishi qinlüe qiangdao? — Cong Yihetuan fankang Sha E qinlüe de bingqi he yizhang Sha E de fangeming 'gaoshi' tan qi" (Emissary of civilization or aggressor bandit? — An account based on the weapons used by the Boxers to resist Czarist Russia's aggression and a Czarist Russian counterrevolutionary "proclamation"). *Wenwu* 3 (1975): 19–24.

Geertz, Clifford. "Thick Description: Toward an Interpretive Theory of Culture." In Geertz, *The Interpretation of Cultures*, 3–30. New York: Basic Books, 1973.

392   Geming lishi yanjiusuo (The revolutionary history research institute) et al. " 'Hongdengzhao' de geming zaofan jingshen wansui" (Long live the revolutionary rebel spirit of the "Red Lanterns"). *Guangming ribao*, Apr. 27, 1967, 4.

Gengzi jishi (A record of the events of 1900). Compiled by Zhongguo shehui kexueyuan jindaishi yanjiusuo jindaishi ziliao bianjishi (Section for editing of materials on modern history of the Modern History Institute, Chinese Academy of Social Sciences). Beijing: Zhonghua, 1978.

Getting Together (Tuanjiebao). New York, N.Y. Feb. 1970 et seq.

Ginzburg, Carlo. *The Cheese and the Worms: The Cosmos of a Sixteenth-Century Miller*. Translated by John and Anne Tedeschi. Baltimore: Johns Hopkins University Press, 1980.

Goldman, Merle. *China's Intellectuals: Advise and Dissent*. Cambridge: Harvard University Press, 1981.

Goldstein, Jonathan, Jerry Israel, and Hilary Conroy, eds. *American Views of China: American Images of China Then and Now*. Bethlehem, Pa.: Lehigh University Press, 1991.

Goleman, Daniel. "Anatomy of a Rumor: It Flies on Fear." *New York Times*, June 4, 1991, C1, C5.

Goodman, Felicitas D. *Ecstasy, Ritual, and Alternate Reality: Religion in a Pluralistic World*. Bloomington: Indiana University Press, 1988.

Goodrich, Mrs. Chauncey. "Besieged in Pekin." *The Youth's Companion* 75.5 (Jan. 31, 1901): 52–53.

Goodrich, Sarah Boardman. "Journal of 1900" and letters. In Miscellaneous Personal Papers, Manuscript Group No. 8, box no. 88, China Records Project.

Gordon, Andrew. *Labor and Imperial Democracy in Prewar Japan*. Berkeley: University of California Press, 1991.

Gottlieb, Alma. "Menstrual Cosmology Among the Beng of Ivory Coast." In Buckley and Gottlieb, eds., *Blood Magic*, 55–74.

Gould-Martin, Katherine. "*Ong-ia-kong*: The Plague God as Modern Physician." In Arthur Kleinman, Peter Kunstadter, E. Russell Alexander, and James L. Gate, eds., *Culture and Healing in Asian Societies: Anthropological, Psychiatric, and Public Health Studies*, 41–67. Boston: G. K. Hall, 1978.

Grant, Beata. "The Spiritual Saga of Woman Huang: From Pollution to Purification." In Johnson, ed., *Ritual Opera, Operatic Ritual*, 224–311.

Gray, Jack and Patrick Cavendish. *Chinese Communism in Crisis: Maoism and the Cultural Revolution*. New York: Praeger, 1968.

Great Britain, Parliamentary Papers. *China No. 3 (1900): Correspondence Respecting the Insurrectionary Movement in China*. London: Her Majesty's Stationery Office, 1900. Cited as PP:1900.

Greenbaum, Lenora. "Societal Correlates of Possession Trance in Sub-Saharan Africa." In Bourguignon, ed., *Religion, Altered States of Consciousness, and Social Change*, 39–57.

Greene, Ruth Altman. *Hsiang-Ya Journal*. Hamden, Conn.: Archon, 1977.

Greenhouse, Linda. "Protecting Its Mystique." *New York Times*, May 27, 1993, A1, A24.

Guan He. *Quanfei wenjian lu* (A record of things seen and heard concerning the Boxer bandits). In *Yihetuan* 1:465–92.

Gussler, Judith D. "Social Change, Ecology, and Spirit Possession Among the 393 South African Nguni." In Bourguignon, ed., *Religion, Altered States of Consciousness, and Social Change*, 88–126.

"Hailanpao yu Jiangdong liushisi tun can'an waiwen ziliao" (Foreign-language materials on the massacres of Hailanpao and the sixty-four villages of Jiangdong). Translated by Xue Xiantian et al. *Jindaishi ziliao* 1 (1981): 122–45.

Harrison, James P. *The Communists and Chinese Peasant Rebellions: A Study in the Rewriting of Chinese History*. New York: Atheneum, 1971.

Hart, Robert. *"These from the Land of Sinim": Essays on the Chinese Question*. London: Chapman and Hall, 1901.

Hayford, Charles W. *To the People: James Yen and Village China*. New York: Columbia University Press, 1990.

He Hanwei. *Guangxu chunian (1876–79) Huabei de da hanzai* (The great drought in North China in the early Guangxu period [1876–79]). Hong Kong: Zhongwen Daxue Chubanshe, 1980.

"Hebei diqu Yihetuan yundong diaocha jilu" (Transcripts of surveys of the Boxer movement in the Hebei region). Unpublished. Cited as HDYYDJ.

"Hebei Jingzhou, Zaoqiang, Hengshui diqu Yihetuan diaocha ziliao xuanbian" (Selected survey materials on the Boxers from the Jingzhou, Zaoqiang, Hengshui region of Hebei), comp. Shandong daxue lishixi Zhongguo jindaishi jiaoyanshi (Shandong University history department, modern Chinese history teaching and research section). *Shandong daxue wenke lunwen jikan* 1 (1980): 157–94. Cited as HJZH.

Heilongjiang sheng bowuguan lishibu et al., comps. *Heilongjiang Yihetuan de kang E douzheng* (The Heilongjiang Boxers' struggle against Russia). Ha'erbin: Heilongjiang Renmin, 1978.

Hershatter, Gail. "The Subaltern Talks Back: Reflections on Subaltern Theory and Chinese History." *Positions: East Asia Cultures Critique* 1.1 (Spring 1993): 103–30.

Hesse, Mary. "Aristotle's Shadow." *New York Times*, Oct. 22, 1989, 24E.

Hevia, James. "Leaving a Brand on China: Missionary Discourse in the Wake of the Boxer Movement." *Modern China* 18.3 (July 1992): 304–32.

High, Stanley. "China's Anti-Christian Drive." *The Nation* 120.3128 (June 17, 1925): 681–83.

Hinchey, Madalon T., ed. *Symposium on Drought in Botswana*. Gabarone, Botswana: Botswana Society in collaboration with Clark University Press, 1979.

Hitchcock, R. K. "The Traditional Response to Drought in Botswana." In Hinchey, ed., *Symposium on Drought in Botswana*, 91–97.

Hobsbawm, Eric. "Introduction: Inventing Traditions." In Hobsbawm and Terence Ranger, eds., *The Invention of Tradition*, 1–14. Cambridge: Cambridge University Press, 1983.

Hoffman, Daniel. "The Twentieth Century." In Hoffman, *Hang-Gliding from Helicon: New and Selected Poems, 1948–1988*. Baton Rouge: Louisiana State University Press, 1988.

Holm, Nils G., ed. *Religious Ecstasy: Based on Papers Read at the Symposium on Religious Ecstasy Held at Åbo, Finland, on the 26th–28th of August 1981*. Stockholm: Almqvist and Wiksell International, 1982.

394   Hong Shoushan. *Shishi zhilüe* (A summary record of contemporary events). In *Yihetuan* 1:85–103.

"Hong xiao jiang zan" (In praise of the young red generals). *Guangming ribao*, Apr. 27, 1967, 3.

" 'Hongdengzhao' de geming zaofan jingshen hao de hen" (The revolutionary rebel spirit of the "Red Lanterns" is very fine). *Beijing ribao*, Apr. 27, 1967, 4.

" 'Hongdengzhao' de geming zaofan jingshen wansui" (Long live the revolutionary rebel spirit of the "Red Lanterns"). *Guangming ribao*, Apr. 27, 1967, 4.

" 'Hongdengzhao' zan" (In praise of the "Red Lanterns"). *Jiefang ribao*, Apr. 23, 1967.

Hongdengzhao zhandoudui (The Red Lantern fighting force). "Cong *Xiuyang* dao *Qinggong mishi* de maiguozhuyi bixu chedi pipan" (The theme of national betrayal extending from *How to be a Good Communist* to *The Inside Story of the Qing Court* must be thoroughly criticized). *Hongdengbao* (Red Lantern), May 9, 1967. Reprinted in *Hongweibing ziliao* (Red guard materials), 8:2149. Washington, D.C.: Center for Chinese Research Materials, Association of Research Libraries, 1975.

Hoover, Herbert. "History of Inside the Circle" (corrected typed draft). In Lou Hoover Papers, Boxer Rebellion: Drafts, box no. 14, Herbert Hoover Presidential Library.

——. "History, June, 17th. to 23rd., 1900." In Lou Hoover Papers, Boxer Rebellion: Drafts, Herbert Hoover Presidential Library.

——. "The Period from May 28th. to June 17th." In Lou Hoover Papers, Boxer Rebellion: Drafts, Herbert Hoover Presidential Library.

Hoover, Lou. Papers concerning Boxer Rebellion. Herbert Hoover Presidential Library, West Branch, Iowa.

Horikawa Tetsuo. "Giwadan undō to Chūgoku no chishikijin" (The Boxer movement and China's intellectuals). *Gifu daigaku kenkyū hōkoku (Jimbun kagaku)* 15 (Feb. 1967): 35–42.

Horton, Robin. "Types of Spirit Possession in Kalabari Religion." In Beattie and Middleton, eds., *Spirit Mediumship and Society in Africa*, 14–49.

Hou Bin. "Shi lun Yihetuan de zuzhi ji qi yuanliu" (An exploratory discussion of Boxer organization and origins). *Shandong daxue wenke lunwen jikan* 1 (1980): 62–73.

Hsia, T. A. *Metaphor, Myth, Ritual and the People's Commune*. Berkeley: Center for Chinese Studies, Institute of International Studies, University of California, 1961.

Hsiao, Kung-chuan. *A Modern China and a New World: K'ang Yu-wei, Reformer and Utopian, 1858–1927*. Seattle: University of Washington Press, 1975.

Hu, I. "Did the Boxer Uprising Recur in 1925?" *Chinese Students' Monthly* 21.3 (Jan. 1926): 33–38.

Hu Shi. *Hu Shi liuxue riji* (Hu Shi's diary while studying abroad). 4 vols. Taibei: Taiwan Shangwu, 1959.

——. "Jinri jiaohui jiaoyu de nanguan" (The present crisis in Christian education). In *Hu Shi wencun* (Collected writings of Hu Shi), 3:728–36. 4 vols. Taibei: Yuandong Tushu Gongsi, 1953.

Hu Shih [Hu Shi]. "The Present Crisis in Christian Education." *Religious Education* 20.6 (Dec. 1925): 434–38.

Hu Sijing. *Lü bei ji* (Writings from the back of a donkey). In *Yihetuan* 2:481–533.

Hu Zhusheng. "Yihetuan de qianshen shi zushihui" (The Boxers' predecessor was the Patriarch's Assembly). *Lishi yanjiu* 3 (1958): 8.

Hua Xuelan. *Gengzi riji* (A diary of 1900). In *Gengzi jishi*, 99–141.

Huadong Shida Lishixi and Hong haichao. "'Hongdengzhao' ming yang tianxia/Hongweibing wei zhen quanqiu" (The fame of the "Red Lanterns" spreads throughout the world/The might of the Red Guards shakes the entire globe). *Wenhuibao*, Apr. 14, 1967, 4.

Huang Ning. *Yihetuan* (The Boxers). Beijing: Kaiming Shudian, 1950.

Huenemann, Ralph Wm. *The Dragon and the Iron Horse: The Economics of Railroads in China, 1876–1937*. Cambridge: Council on East Asian Studies, Harvard University, 1984.

Hughes, R. E. and Eleri Jones. "Intake of Dietary Fibre and the Age of Menarche." *Annals of Human Biology* 12.4 (1985): 325–32.

Hunan sheng Dongli Jichang gongren lilun xiaozu. "Yihetuan fandi fanfeng pi Kong-Meng" (The Boxers opposed imperialism and feudalism and criticized Confucius and Mencius). *Changsha ribao*, Dec. 28, 1974, 3.

Hung, Chang-tai. "Female Symbols of Resistance in Chinese Wartime Spoken Drama." *Modern China* 15.2 (1989): 149–77.

——. *Going to the People: Chinese Intellectuals and Folk Literature, 1918–1937*. Cambridge: Council on East Asian Studies, Harvard University, 1985.

Hunt, Michael. "The Forgotten Occupation: Peking, 1900–1901." *Pacific Historical Review* 48.4 (Nov. 1979): 501–29.

——. *The Making of a Special Relationship: The United States and China to 1914*. New York: Columbia University Press, 1983.

Hunter, Jane. *The Gospel of Gentility: American Women Missionaries in Turn-of-the-Century China*. New Haven: Yale University Press, 1984.

Ingalls, Jeremy. "Introduction." In Yao Hsin-nung, *The Malice of Empire*, 11–29. Translated by Jeremy Ingalls. Berkeley: University of California Press, 1970.

"Information about Ch'i Pen-yü." *Survey of the China Mainland Press* 4159 (Apr. 17, 1968): 4–5. Translated from *Hong dianxun*, Mar. 27, 1968.

Isaacs, Harold. *Images of Asia: American Views of China and India*. New York: Capricorn, 1962.

Ishimitsu Makiyo. "Heilongjiangshang de liuxue beiju" (Sanguinary tragedy on the Amur). Translated by Jin Yuzhong. *Jindaishi ziliao* 1 (1981): 146–76.

Jahoda, Gustav. *Psychology of Superstition*. Harmondsworth, Middlesex, Eng.: Penguin, 1969.

Januszczak, Waldemar. *Sayonara, Michelangelo: The Sistine Chapel Restored and Repackaged*. Reading, Mass.: Addison-Wesley, 1990.

Ji Yang. "Yihetuan dabai Ximo'er" (The Boxers' crushing defeat of Seymour). In *Zhongguo renmin fandi douzheng de gushi* (Stories of the anti-imperialist struggles of the Chinese people), 91–100. Shanghai: Shanghai Renmin, 1974.

Jiang Weifan and Han Xibai. "Ye tan gengzi shibianzhong de aiguo yu maiguo wenti" (A further discussion of the question of patriotism and betrayal in reference to the 1900 incident). *Guangming ribao*, Mar. 5, 1986, 3.

Jiaowu jiaoan dang (Archives of church affairs and disputes involving missionaries and converts). Compiled by Zhongyang yanjiuyuan jindaishi yanjiusuo

396   (Modern History Institute, Academic Sinica). 21 vols. in 7 series, cover-
        ing period 1860–1912. Taibei: Zhongyang Yanjiuyuan Jindaishi Yanjiusuo,
        1974–1981.

Jin Jiarui. *Yihetuan shihua* (A historical narrative of the Boxers). Beijing: Beijing
        Chubanshe, 1980.

Jin Yan. "Yihetuan yundong shiqi Sha E qinzhan Dongbei de zuixing he Zhong-
        guo renmin de fankang" (Czarist Russia's criminal invasion and occupation of
        the Northeast in the Boxer period and the resistance of the Chinese people).
        Tianjin Shiyuan xuebao 5 (1975): 86–90.

Jing-Jin quanfei jilüe (A brief chronicle of the Boxer bandits in Beijing and Tianjin).
        Hong Kong: Xianggang Shuju, 1901.

Jinzun shengyu bixie quantu (Heresy exposed in respectful obedience to the Sacred
        Edict: A complete picture gallery). In *The Cause of the Riots in the Yangtse
        Valley: A "Complete Picture Gallery."* Hankow, 1891.

Johnson, Chalmers. *Peasant Nationalism and Communist Power: The Emergence of
        Revolutionary China, 1937–1945.* Stanford: Stanford University Press, 1962.

Johnson, David. "Actions Speak Louder Than Words: The Cultural Significance
        of Chinese Ritual Opera." In Johnson, ed., *Ritual Opera, Operatic Ritual,*
        1–45.

——, ed. *Ritual Opera, Operatic Ritual: "Mu-lien Rescues His Mother" in Chinese
        Popular Culture.* Berkeley: Chinese Popular Culture Project, University of
        California, 1989.

Johnson, David, Andrew J. Nathan, and Evelyn S. Rawski, eds., *Popular Culture in
        Late Imperial China.* Berkeley: University of California Press, 1985.

Jones, Dorothy B. *The Portrayal of China and India on the American Screen,
        1896–1955: The Evolution of Chinese and Indian Themes, Locales, and Char-
        acters as Portrayed on the American Screen.* Cambridge, Mass.: Center for
        International Studies, MIT, 1955.

Jordan, David K. *Gods, Ghosts, and Ancestors: The Folk Religion of a Taiwanese
        Village.* Berkeley: University of California Press, 1972.

Junjichu lufu zouzhe (Reference copies of Grand Council memorials). First
        Historical Archives, Palace Museum, Beijing.

Kagan, Richard C. "From Revolutionary Iconoclasm to National Revolution:
        Ch'en Tu-hsiu and the Chinese Communist Movement." In F. Gilbert Chan
        and Thomas H. Etzold, eds., *China in the 1920s: Nationalism and Revolution,*
        55–72. New York: New Viewpoints, 1976.

Kagan, Richard L. "The Discovery of Columbus." NYTBR, Oct. 6, 1991, 3, 27–29.

Ke Fu. "Cong 'Qieyang jie' dao 'Fandi lu' " (From "Cut off the foreigners street" to
        "Anti-imperialism road"). *Renmin ribao,* Apr. 24, 1967, 4.

Keegan, John. *The Face of Battle: A Study of Agincourt, Waterloo, and the Somme.*
        New York: Viking, 1976.

Kelly, John S. *A Forgotten Conference: The Negotiations at Peking, 1900–1901.*
        Geneva: Librairie E. Droz, 1963.

Ketler, Isaac C. *The Tragedy of Paotingfu: An Authentic Story of the Lives, Services,
        and Sacrifices of the Presbyterian, Congregational, and China Inland Mission-
        aries who Suffered Martyrdom at Paotingfu, China, June 30th and July 1, 1900.*
        New York: Fleming H. Revell, 1902.

Kinman, Harold. Letters. In Personal Collection 331 (Kinman), History and Museum Division, Marine Corps (Navy Department), Personal Papers.

Kleinman, Arthur. *Patients and Healers in the Context of Culture: An Exploration of the Borderland Between Anthropology, Medicine, and Psychiatry.* Berkeley: University of California Press, 1980.

Kobayashi Kazumi. "Giwadan no minshū shisō" (The popular thought of the Boxers). In *Kōza Chūgoku kingendaishi 2: Giwadan undō* (Lectures on the modern and contemporary history of China, 2: The Boxer movement), 237–66. Tokyo: Tokyo Daigaku Shuppankai, 1978.

Ku Hung-ming [Gu Hongming]. *Papers from a Viceroy's Yamen: A Chinese Plea for the Cause of Good Government and True Civilization in China.* Shanghai: Shanghai Mercury, 1901.

Kubota Bunji. "Giwadan hyōka to kakumei undō" (The revolutionary movement and the evaluation of the Boxers). *Shisō* 17 (Nov. 1976): 1–33.

Kuhn, Philip A. "Maoist Agriculture and the Old Regime." In Marie-Claire Bergère and William Kirby, eds., *China's Mid-Century Transitions: Continuity and Change on the Mainland and on Taiwan, 1945–1955.* Cambridge: Harvard University Press, forthcoming.

———. *Soulstealers: The Chinese Sorcery Scare of 1768.* Cambridge: Harvard University Press, 1990.

Kuhn, Thomas S. *The Structure of Scientific Revolutions.* 2d ed. Chicago: University of Chicago Press, 1970.

Kwong, Luke S. K. "Oral History in China: A Preliminary Review." *Oral History Review* 20.1–2 (Spring-Fall 1992): 23–50.

———. "The T'i-Yung Dichotomy and the Search for Talent in Late-Ch'ing China." *Modern Asian Studies* 27.2 (1993): 253–79.

Lao Naixuan. *Yihequan jiaomen yuarliu kao* (An examination of the origins and evolution of the Boxer sect). In *Yihetuan* 4:431–39.

Lao She. *Shenquan* (The Spirit Boxers). In Lao She, *Lao She wenji* (The collected writings of Lao She), *juan* 12: 109–86. Beijing: Renmin Wenxue, 1987.

Latourette, Kenneth Scott. *A History of Christian Missions in China.* London: Society for Promoting Christian Knowledge, 1929.

Lee, Laurie. *A Moment of War: A Memoir of the Spanish Civil War.* New York: New Press, 1991.

Lee, S. G. "Spirit Possession Among the Zulu." In Beattie and Middleton, eds., *Spirit Mediumship and Society in Africa,* 128–56.

Lensen, George Alexander. *The Russo-Chinese War.* Tallahassee: Diplomatic Press, 1967.

Leonard, Anne P. "Spirit Mediums in Palau: Transformations in a Traditional System." In Bourguignon, ed., *Religion, Altered States of Consciousness, and Social Change,* 129–77.

Levenson, Joseph. *Confucian China and Its Modern Fate,* vol. 1, *The Problem of Intellectual Continuity.* Berkeley: University of California Press, 1958.

———. "The Day Confucius Died." *Journal of Asian Studies* 20.2 (Feb. 1961): 221–26.

Levi, Primo. *The Drowned and the Saved.* Translated by Raymond Rosenthal. New York: Summit, 1988.

398   Lévi-Strauss, Claude. "The Sorceror and His Magic." In Lévi-Strauss, *Structural Anthropology*, 161–80. Translated by Claire Jacobson and Brooke Grundfest Schoepf. Garden City, N.Y.: Anchor, 1967.

Lewis, I. M. *Ecstatic Religion: A Study of Shamanism and Spirit Possession.* 2d ed. London: Routledge, 1989.

Leyda, Jay. *Dianying: An Account of Films and the Film Audience in China.* Cambridge, Mass.: MIT Press, 1972.

Li Dazhao. "Sun Zhongshan Xiansheng zai Zhongguo minzu gemingshishang zhi weizhi" (The place of Mr. Sun Yat-sen in the history of the Chinese national revolution). *Guomin xinbao* (Mar. 1926). Reprinted in Li Dazhao, *Li Dazhao xuanji* (Selected works of Li Dazhao), 537–44. Beijing: Renmin, 1962.

Li Dezheng, Su Weizhi, and Liu Tianlu. *Baguo lianjun qin Hua shi* (A history of the Eight-Power Allied Force's aggression against China). Jinan: Shandong Daxue Chubanshe, 1990.

Li Di. *Quan huo ji* (A record of the Boxer calamity). 2 vols. Preface dated 1905.

Li Guang and Zhang Xuanru. *Yihetuan yundong zai Dongbei* (The Boxer movement in the Northeast). Jilin: Jilin Renmin, 1981.

Li Jianmin. *Wusa can'an hou de fan-Ying yundong* (The anti-British movement after the May Thirtieth massacre). Taibei: Zhongyang Yanjiuyuan Jindaishi Yanjiusuo, 1986.

Li Junhe. " 'Hongdengzhao' de lingxiu—Huanglian shengmu" (The leader of the "Red Lanterns"—Holy Mother of the Yellow Lotus). *Tianjin ribao*, Aug. 5, 1961.

Li Shiyu. "Yihetuan yuanliu shitan" (An exploration into the origins and development of the Boxers). *Lishi jiaoxue* 2 (1979): 18–23.

Li Shu. "Zhong-Xi wenhua wenti" (The question of Chinese and Western cultures). *Lishi yanjiu* 3 (1989): 50–55.

Li Tu. "Lishi de tie'an: Sha E qinzhan Jiangdong liushisi tun de zuixing" (The ironclad evidence of history: Czarist Russia's criminal seizure of the sixty-four villages of Jiangdong). *Nanjing Daxue xuebao* 2 (1977): 75–81.

Li Wenhai et al., eds. *Jindai Zhongguo zaihuang jinian* (A chronological record of modern Chinese famines). Changsha: Hunan Jiaoyu Chubanshe, 1990.

Li Wenhai and Liu Yangdong. "Yihetuan yundong shiqi shehui xinli fenxi" (A social-psychological analysis of the Boxer movement era). In *Yihetuan yundong yu jindai Zhongguo shehui* (The Boxer movement and modern Chinese society), 1–25. Compiled by Zhongguo Yihetuan yundong shi yanjiuhui (Association for study of the history of the Boxer movement of China). Chengdu: Sichuan Sheng Shehui Kexueyuan Chubanshe, 1987.

Li Xisheng. *Gengzi guobian ji* (A chronicle of the national troubles of 1900). In *Yihetuan* 1:9–44.

Liang Qichao. "Lun xiaoshuo yu qunzhi zhi guanxi" (On the relationship between fiction and social order). In Liang Qichao, *Yinbingshi wenji* (Collected essays from the Ice-drinkers' Studio), vol. 4, *juan* 10:6–10. 16 vols. Taibei: Taiwan Zhonghua, 1960.

Liao Yizhong. "Lin Hei'er" (Lin Hei'er). In Lin Zengping and Li Wenhai, comps., *Qingdai renwu zhuan'gao* (Draft biographies of Qing figures). Second Part (*xiabian*), 3:98–101. Shenyang: Liaoning Renmin, 1987.

———. "Zhang Decheng" (Zhang Decheng). In Lin Zengping and Li Wenhai, eds.,   399
Qingdai renwu zhuan'gao (Draft biographies of Qing figures). Second Part
(xiabian), 3:92–94. Shenyang: Liaoning Renmin, 1987.

Liao Yizhong, Li Dezheng, and Zhang Xuanru. Yihetuan yundong shi (A history of
the Boxer movement). Beijing: Renmin, 1981.

Liao Zonglin. "Tan gengzi shibianzhong de aiguo yu maiguo wenti" (A discussion
of the question of patriotism and betrayal in reference to the 1900 incident).
Guangming ribao, Nov. 27, 1985, 3.

Lin Dunkui. "Shehui zaihuang yu Yihetuan yundong" (Social famines and the
Boxer movement). In Yihetuan yundong yu jindai Zhongguo shehui guoji
xueshu taolunhui lunwen ji, 213–29.

Lin, W. S., A. C. N. Chen, J. Z. X. Su, F. C. Zhu, W. H. Xing, J. Y. Li, and G. S.
Ye. "The Menarcheal Age of Chinese Girls." Annals of Human Biology 19.5
(1992): 503–12.

Linderman, Gerald F. Embattled Courage: The Experience of Combat in the
American Civil War. New York: Free Press, 1987.

Link, Perry. Evening Chats in Beijing: Probing China's Predicament. New York:
Norton, 1992.

Lishixi qi'erji gongnongbing xueyuan. "Fandi fanfeng po gangchang: Yihetuan de
fan-Kong douzheng" (Oppose imperialism, oppose feudalism, destroy the feudal ethical code: The Boxers' struggle against Confucius). Zhongshan Daxue
xuebao 1 (1975): 93–96.

Lishixi qisanji pixiu xiaozu. "Yihetuan fandi jingshen wandai chuan: Chi Suxiu
Lin Biao yihuo wumie gongji Yihetuan de miulun" (Carry on for ten thousand
generations the anti-imperialist spirit of the Boxers: A denunciation of the slanderous attack of the Soviet revisionists and the Lin Biao bunch against the
Boxers). Guiyang Shiyuan 4 (1976): 51–53.

Liu Dapeng. Qianyuan suoji (Sundry information from the Qian Garden). In Qiao
Zhiqiang, comp., Yihetuan zai Shanxi diqu shiliao, 26–76.

———. Tuixiangzhai riji (A diary from the Tuixiang Study). In Qiao Zhiqiang,
comp., Yihetuan zai Shanxi diqu shiliao, 11–25.

Liu Mengyang, Tianjin quanfei bianluan jishi. (An account of the Boxer bandit disorders in Tianjin). In Yihetuan 2:1–71.

Liu Rong and Xu Fen. "Hongdeng nü'er song" (In praise of the daughters of the
Red Lantern). Tianjin Shiyuan xuebao 2 (1975): 78–82, 77.

Liu Xinwu. "What Is 'New' in Post-Mao Literature?" Talk, Harvard University, Oct.
6, 1987.

———. "Zooming in on May 19." Translated by Geremie Barmé. In Barmé and
Linda Jaivin, eds., New Ghosts, Old Dreams: Chinese Rebel Voices, 265–78. New
York: Times Books, 1992.

Liu Xizi. Jin xi biji (A cautionary account of the area west of Tianjin). In Yihetuan
2:73–138.

Liu Yitong. Minjiao xiangchou dumen wenjian lu (A record of things seen and
heard concerning the mutual hatred of the people and the Christians in the capital). In Yihetuan 2:181–96.

Lively, Penelope. Moon Tiger. New York: Harper and Row Perennial Library, 1989.

400   Loewenberg, Richard D. "Rumors of Mass Poisoning in Times of Crisis." *Journal of Criminal Psychopathology* 5 (July 1943): 131–42.

Long Chi. "Feiyue yundong yu jiuqi jinian" (The movement for treaty abolition and the commemoration of September 7). *Xiangdao zhoubao* 170 (Sept. 10, 1926): 1726–27.

Longgu shanren [Guo Zeyun]. *Gengzi shijian* (A poetic examination of the events of 1900). In *Yihetuan shiliao* (Historical materials on the Boxers), 1:28–154. Edited by Zhongguo shehui kexueyuan jindaishi yanjiusuo "Jindaishi ziliao" bianjizu (The "Modern historical materials" editorial group of the Modern History Institute of the Chinese Academy of Social Sciences). 2 vols. Beijing: Zhongguo Shehui Kexue, 1982.

Lu Hsun [Lu Xun]. "Ah Chang and the 'Book of Hills and Seas.' " In Lu Hsun, *Selected Works of Lu Hsun* 1:363–70.

——. *A Madman's Diary.* In Lu Hsun, *Selected Works of Lu Hsun* 1:8–21.

——. *Selected Works of Lu Hsun.* 4 vols. Peking: Foreign Languages Press, 1956.

——. *The True Story of Ah Q.* In Lu Hsun, *Selected Works of Lu Hsun* 1:76–135.

Lu Jingqi. "Zhao Sanduo Yan Shuqin" (Zhao Sanduo and Yan Shuqin). In Dai Yi and Lin Yanjiao, eds. *Qingdai renwu zhuan'gao* (Draft biographies of Qing figures), Second Part (*xiabian*), 1:210–17. Shenyang: Liaoning Renmin, 1984.

Lu Wantian. *Gengzi Beijing shibian jilüe* (A brief account of events in Beijing in 1900). In *Yihetuan* 2:395–438.

Lu Xun. "Suiganlu" (Random thoughts), no. 37. *Xin qingnian* 5.5 (Nov. 1918): 514–15.

Lu Yao. "Guanxian Liyuantun jiaoan yu Yihequan yundong" (The church case in Liyuantun, Guan county, and the Boxer movement). *Lishi yanjiu* 5 (1986): 77–90.

——. "Lun Yihetuan de zuzhi yuanliu" (On the organizational origins of the Boxers). In *Yihetuan yundong shi taolun wenji* (Collected essays on the history of the Boxer movement), 65–97. Compiled by Qi-Lu Shushe bianjibu (Qi-Lu Book Company editorial department). Jinan: Qi-Lu, 1982.

——. "The Origins of the Boxers." Translated by K. C. Chen and David D. Buck. In Buck, ed., *Recent Chinese Studies of the Boxer Movement,* 42–86.

——, ed. *Yihequan yundong qiyuan tansuo* (Probings into the origins of the Boxer movement). Jinan: Shandong Daxue Chubanshe, 1990.

Lu Yao et al., comps. *Shandong Yihetuan diaocha ziliao xuanbian* (Selections from survey materials on the Shandong Boxers). Jinan: Qi-Lu, 1980. Cited as SYDZX.

Lu Yao and Cheng Xiao. *Yihetuan yundong shi yanjiu* (Studies on the history of the Boxer movement). Jinan: Qi-Lu, 1988.

Lubeck, Paul M. "Islamic Protest Under Semi-Industrial Capitalism: 'Yan Tatsine Explained." *Africa* 55.4 (1985): 369–89.

Lutz, Jessie Gregory. *Chinese Politics and Christian Missions: The Anti-Christian Movements of 1920–28.* Notre Dame, Ind.: Cross Cultural Publications, 1988.

Lyell, William A., Jr. *Lu Hsün's Vision of Reality.* Berkeley: University of California Press, 1976.

MacGillivray, D., ed. *A Century of Protestant Missions in China (1807–1907), Being the Centenary Conference Historical Volume.* Shanghai: American Presbyterian Mission Press, 1907.

Mackerras, Colin. *The Chinese Theatre in Modern Times: From 1840 to the Present*   401
Day. Amherst: University of Massachusetts Press, 1975.

——. *The Performing Arts in Contemporary China*. London: Routledge and Kegan
Paul, 1981.

——. *Western Images of China*. Oxford: Oxford University Press, 1989.

Madsen, Richard. *Morality and Power in a Chinese Village*. Berkeley: University of
California Press, 1984.

Marriott, Michael. "Afrocentrism: Balancing or Skewing History?" *New York
Times*, Aug. 11, 1991, 1, 18.

Martin, Christopher. *The Boxer Rebellion*. London: Abelard-Schuman, 1968.

Martin, Douglas. "A 'Bum' Gleans the Discarded to Find History." *New York Times*,
July 28, 1990, 23.

Martin, Emma Estelle. Diary. In Miscellaneous Personal Papers, Manuscript
Group No. 8, box no. 137, China Records Project.

Marx, Leo. *The Pilot and the Passenger: Essays on Literature, Technology, and
Culture in the United States*. New York: Oxford University Press, 1988.

Maunder, W. J. *The Human Impact of Climate Uncertainty: Weather Information,
Economic Planning, and Business Management*. London: Routledge, 1989.

——. *The Uncertainty Business: Risks and Opportunities in Weather and Climate*.
London: Methuen, 1986.

Meade, Robert L. Letters. In Personal Collection 147 (Leonard), History and
Museum Division, Marine Corps (Navy Department), Personal Papers.

Meisner, Maurice. *Li Ta-chao and the Origins of Chinese Marxism*. Cambridge:
Harvard University Press, 1967.

Middleton, John. "Spirit Possession Among the Lugbara." In Beattie and
Middleton, eds., *Spirit Mediumship and Society in Africa*, 220–31.

Millard, Thomas F. *The New Far East*. New York: Scribner's, 1906.

Miller, Stuart Creighton. "Ends and Means: Missionary Justification of Force in
Nineteenth-Century China." In John K. Fairbank, ed., *The Missionary
Enterprise in China and America*, 249–82. Cambridge: Harvard University
Press, 1974.

Miln, Louise Jordan. *It Happened in Peking*. New York: Frederick A. Stokes, 1926.

Miner, Luella. Journal, letters. In Luella Miner Papers (North China Mission), box
1, file 1; box 2, files 1, 6; box 4, file 1. ABCFM, Papers. Cited as LMP.

——. "Last Rites for the Pao-ting-fu Martyrs." *The Advance*, Aug. 1, 1901.

——. "Ti-to and the Boxers: A True Story of a Young Christian's Almost Miraculous
Escape from Death at the Hands of Bold Cut-throats." In Luella Miner Papers
(North China Mission), box 4, file 1, ABCFM, Papers.

Mingqing. *Yihetuan* (The Boxers). Shanghai: Shidai Shuju, 1950.

*Missions catholiques, Les: Bulletin hebdomadaire illustré de l'Oeuvre de la
Propagation de la Foi*. Lyons, 1868 et seq.

Mowry, Hua-yuan Li. *Yang-pan hsi: New Theater in China*. Berkeley: Center for
Chinese Studies, University of California, 1973.

Mu Hsin [Xin]. "On the Reactionary Thought of the Play, *Sai Chin Hua*:
Dissecting and Analyzing a So-Called 'Famous Play' of the Thirties." *Current
Background* 786 (May 16, 1966): 15–36. Translated from *Guangming ribao*, Mar.
12, 1966.

402   Munro, Robin. "Remembering Tiananmen Square: Who Died in Beijing, and Why." In Suzanne Ogden, Kathleen Hartford, Lawrence Sullivan, and David Zweig, eds., *China's Search for Democracy: The Student and the Mass Movement of 1989*, 393–409. Armonk, N.Y.: M. E. Sharpe, 1992.

Myerhoff, Barbara. *Number Our Days*. New York: Simon and Schuster, 1978.

Nakamura Tatsuo [Zhongcun Daxiong]. "Qingmo Tianjin xian de xiangzhen jiegou yu Yihetuan zuzhi" (The structure of villages and towns in Tianjin county in the late Qing and Boxer organization). In *Yihetuan yundong yu jindai Zhongguo shehui guoji xueshu taolunhui lunwen ji*, 263–83.

Naquin, Susan. *Millenarian Rebellion in China: The Eight Trigrams Uprising of 1813*. New Haven: Yale University Press, 1976.

———. *Shantung Rebellion: The Wang Lun Uprising of 1774*. New Haven: Yale University Press, 1981.

Nei Menggu Daxue Menggu shi yanjiushi. "Huangyan gaibianbuliao lishi: Bo Suxiu cuangai woguo Zhonga'erbu lishi de wuchi lanyan" (Lies cannot change history: In refutation of the shameless slanders perpetrated by the Soviet revisionists in their falsification of the history of our Zunghar tribe). *Lishi yanjiu* 2 (1976): 98–109.

Nkpa, Nwokocha K. U. "Rumors of Mass Poisoning in Biafra." *Public Opinion Quarterly* 41.3 (Fall 1977): 332–46.

Nohara Shirō. "Giwadan undō no hyōka ni kanshite" (On the evaluation of the Boxer movement). *Senshū shigaku* 1 (1968): 1–24.

North-China Herald and Supreme Court and Consular Gazette. Cited as NCH.

Ocko, Jonathan. "Righting Wrongs: Concepts of Justice in Late Imperial China." Unpublished manuscript.

Ogren, Olivia. "A Great Conflict of Sufferings." In Broomhall, ed., *Last Letters and Further Records of Martyred Missionaries of the China Inland Mission*, 65–83.

Oliphant, Nigel. *A Diary of the Siege of the Legations in Peking During the Summer of 1900*. London: Longmans, Green, 1901.

Ono Kazuko. *Chinese Women in a Century of Revolution, 1850–1950*. Edited by Joshua A. Fogel. Stanford: Stanford University Press, 1989 (original Japanese edition 1978).

Overmyer, Daniel L. "Values in Chinese Sectarian Literature: Ming and Ch'ing Pao-chüan." In Johnson, Nathan, and Rawski, eds., *Popular Culture in Late Imperial China*, 219–54.

Paine, Ralph D. *The Cross and the Dragon*. Serialized in ten installments in *The Youth's Companion*, beginning 85.49 (Dec. 7, 1911): 661–63, concluding 86.6 (Feb. 8, 1912): 72–73.

———. *The Dragon and the Cross*. New York: Scribner's, 1912.

Partridge, (Mary) Louise. Letters. In Alice M. Williams Miscellaneous Papers (Shansi Mission), file 12, ABCFM, Papers.

[Peng] Shuzhi. "Diguozhuyi yu Yihetuan yundong" (Imperialism and the Boxer movement). *Xiangdao zhoubao* 81 (Sept. 3, 1924): 646–52.

People Shall Judge, The: Readings in the Formation of American Policy. 2 vols. Chicago: University of Chicago Press, 1949.

Perry, Elizabeth J. *Rebels and Revolutionaries in North China, 1845–1945*. Stanford: Stanford University Press, 1980.

Perry, Elizabeth J. and Ellen V. Fuller. "China's Long March to Democracy." 403
World Policy Journal (Fall 1991): 663–85.

Pollack, Jonathan D. *The Sino-Soviet Rivalry and Chinese Security Debate*. Santa
Monica, Calif.: Rand Corporation, 1982.

Pomeranz, Kenneth. "Water to Iron, Widows to Warlords: The Handan Rain
Shrine in Modern Chinese History." *Late Imperial China* 12.1 (June 1991):
62–99.

Potter, Jack M. "Cantonese Shamanism." In Wolf, ed., *Studies in Chinese Society*,
321–45.

Prah, K. K. "Some Sociological Aspects of Drought." In Hinchey, ed., *Symposium
on Drought in Botswana*, 87–90.

Pressel, Esther. "Umbanda in São Paulo: Religious Innovation in a Developing
Society." In Bourguignon, ed., *Religion, Altered States of Consciousness, and
Social Change*, 264–318.

Price, Don C. "Popular and Elite Heterodoxy toward the End of the Ch'ing." In
Kwang-Ching Liu and Richard Shek, eds., *Heterodoxy in Late Imperial China*.
Berkeley: University of California Press, forthcoming.

Price, Eva Jane. *China Journal, 1889–1900: An American Missionary Family During
the Boxer Rebellion*. New York: Scribner's, 1989.

Prince, Thomas. *The natural and moral government and agency of God in causing
droughts and rains: A sermon at the South Church in Boston, Thursday Aug. 24,
1749. Being the day of the general thanksgiving, in the province of the
Massachusetts, for the extraordinary reviving rains, after the most distressing
drought which have been known among us in the memory of any living*. Boston:
Kneeland and Green's, 1749.

Prohme, William F. "The Outrages at Nanking." *The Nation* 124.3223 (Apr. 13,
1927): 388.

Pruitt, Ida. *A Daughter of Han: The Autobiography of a Chinese Working Woman*.
Stanford: Stanford University Press, 1967 (pbk. rpt.).

Purcell, Victor. *The Boxer Uprising: A Background Study*. Cambridge: Cambridge
University Press, 1963.

Qi Benyu. "Aiguozhuyi haishi maiguozhuyi?—Ping fandong yingpian *Qinggong
mishi*" (Patriotism or national betrayal?—On the reactionary film *Inside Story of
the Qing Court*). *Hongqi* 5 (Mar. 1967): 9–23. Reprinted in *Renmin ribao*, Apr.
1, 1967, 1–3.

Qi Qizhang. "Guanyu Yihetuan yundong pingjia de ruogan wenti" (Certain problems concerning appraisal of the Boxer movement). *Dongyue luncong* 4 (1980):
97–104.

Qiao Wen. "Baguo lianjun zai Beijing de baoxing" (The atrocities committed by
the eight-nation force in Beijing). *Renmin ribao (haiwai ban)*, Aug. 20, 1990, 2.

Qiao Zhiqiang, comp. *Yihetuan zai Shanxi diqu shiliao* (Historical materials on the
Boxers in the Shanxi area). Taiyuan: Shanxi Renmin, 1980.

[Qu] Qiubai. "Yihetuan yundong zhi yiyi yu Wusa yundong zhi qiantu" (The significance of the Boxer movement and the future of the May Thirtieth movement). *Xiangdao zhoubao* 128 (Sept. 7, 1925): 1167–72.

Quanfei jilüe (A brief chronicle of the Boxer bandits). Shanghai: Shangyang Shuju,
1903.

404 Ramage, C. S. *The Great Indian Drought of 1899*. Boulder, Colo.: Aspen Institute for Humanistic Studies, 1977.

Rankin, Mary Backus. *Elite Activism and Political Transformation in China: Zhejiang Province, 1865–1911*. Stanford: Stanford University Press, 1986.

Rawski, Evelyn S. "Problems and Prospects." In Johnson, Nathan, and Rawski, eds., *Popular Culture in Late Imperial China*, 399–417.

Red Lantern, The. Translated by Yang Hsien-yi and Gladys Yang. In Walter J. Meserve and Ruth I. Meserve, eds., *Modern Drama from Communist China*, 328–68. New York: New York University Press, 1970.

Rees, Margaret. "Menarche When and Why?" *The Lancet* 342.8884 (Dec. 4, 1993): 1375.

Reid, Gilbert. "The Ethics of Loot." *The Forum* 31.5 (July 1901): 581–86.

Reinsch, Paul S. *An American Diplomat in China*. Garden City, N.Y.: Doubleday, Page, 1922.

Renmin ribao (People's daily).

Ricalton, James. *China Through the Stereoscope: A Journey Through the Dragon Empire at the Time of the Boxer Uprising*. New York: Underwood and Underwood, 1901.

Ricoeur, Paul. *Time and Narrative*, vol. 1. Translated by Kathleen McLaughlin and David Pellauer. Chicago: University of Chicago Press, 1984.

Rigby, Richard W. *The May 30 Movement: Events and Themes*. Folkstone, Kent: Dawson, 1980.

Robinson, Marilynne. "Writers and the Nostalgic Fallacy." *NYTBR*, Oct. 13, 1985, 1, 34–35.

Rodzinski, Witold. *A History of China*, vol. 1. Oxford: Pergamon, 1979.

Rosaldo, Renato. "Introduction: Grief and a Headhunter's Rage." In Rosaldo, *Culture and Truth: The Remaking of Social Analysis*, 1–21. Boston: Beacon Press, 1989.

Rosnow, Ralph L. "Inside Rumor: A Personal Journey." *American Psychologist* 46.5 (May 1991): 484–96.

Rosnow, Ralph L. and Gary Alan Fine. *Rumor and Gossip: The Social Psychology of Hearsay*. New York: Elsevier, 1976.

Rubinstein, Murray. "The Revival of the Mazu Cult and of Taiwanese Pilgrimage to Fujian." In *Harvard Studies on Taiwan: Papers of the Taiwan Studies Workshop*, vol. 1 (Cambridge: Fairbank Center for East Asian Research, Harvard University, 1995), 89–125.

——. "The Wars They Wanted: American Missionaries' Use of *The Chinese Repository* Before the Opium War." *The American Neptune* 48.4 (Fall 1988): 271–82.

Satō Kimihiko [Zuoteng Gongyan]. "Yihetuan minzhong de quanliguan" (The Boxer masses' conception of state authority). In *Yihetuan yundong yu jindai Zhongguo shehui guoji xueshu taolunhui lunwen ji*, 884–903.

Sawara Tokusuke [Zuoyuan Dujie] and Ouyin. *Quanluan jiwen* (A record of things heard concerning the Boxer disorders). In *Yihetuan* 1:105–234.

——. *Quanshi zaji* (Miscellaneous notes on Boxer affairs). In *Yihetuan* 1:235–99.

Schama, Simon. *Citizens: A Chronicle of the French Revolution*. New York: Knopf, 1989.

Schele, Linda and Mary Ellen Miller. *The Blood of Kings: Dynasty and Ritual in* 405
Maya Art. New York: George Braziller, in association with Kimbell Art Museum,
Fort Worth, 1986.

Schell, Orville. "Introduction." In *Children of the Dragon: The Story of Tiananmen
Square*. Compiled by Human Rights in China. New York: Collier, 1990.

Scheper-Hughes, Nancy. *Death Without Weeping: The Violence of Everyday Life in
Brazil*. Berkeley: University of California Press, 1992.

Schiffrin, Harold Z. *Sun Yat-sen and the Origins of the Chinese Revolution*.
Berkeley: University of California Press, 1970.

Schneider, Laurence A. *Ku Chieh-kang and China's New History: Nationalism
and the Quest for Alternative Traditions*. Berkeley: University of California
Press, 1971.

Schram, Stuart, ed. *Chairman Mao Talks to the People: Talks and Letters, 1956–1971*.
New York: Pantheon, 1974.

Schrecker, John E. *Imperialism and Chinese Nationalism: Germany in Shantung*.
Cambridge: Harvard University Press, 1971.

Schwarcz, Vera. "Remapping May Fourth: Between Nationalism and Enlighten-
ment." *Republican China* 12.1 (Nov. 1986): 20–35.

Schwartz, Benjamin I. *In Search of Wealth and Power: Yen Fu and the West*.
Cambridge: Harvard University Press, 1964.

Seaman, Gary. "In the Presence of Authority: Hierarchical Roles in Chinese
Spirit Medium Cults." In Arthur Kleinman and Tsung-yi Lin, eds., *Normal
and Abnormal Behavior in Chinese Culture*, 61–74. Dordrecht, Holland: D.
Reidel, 1981.

———. "The Sexual Politics of Karmic Retribution." In Emily Martin Ahern and
Hill Gates, eds., *The Anthropology of Taiwanese Society*, 381–96. Stanford:
Stanford University Press, 1981.

Selden, Mark, ed. *The People's Republic of China: A Documentary History of
Revolutionary Change*. New York: Monthly Review Press, 1979.

Seligson, Susan. "Bewitched, Bothered . . . and Bewitched: Three Hundred Years
of Salem's Dark History." *New England Monthly*, Sept. 1990, 10–12.

Sha E qin Hua shi (A history of Czarist Russia's aggression against China) (1975).
Compiled by Fudan Daxue Lishixi *Sha E qin Hua shi* bianxiezu (*Sha E qin
Hua shi* compilation group of the Fudan University History Department). Rev.
ed. Shanghai: Shanghai Renmin, 1986.

Shack, William A. "Hunger, Anxiety, and Ritual: Deprivation and Spirit Possession
Among the Gurage of Ethiopia." *Man: The Journal of the Royal Anthropological
Institute*, n.s., 6.1 (Mar. 1971): 30–43.

Shandong Yihetuan anjuan (Archival records concerning the Shandong Boxers).
Compiled by Zhongguo shehui kexueyuan jindaishi yanjiusuo jindaishi zi-
liao bianjishi (Section for editing of materials on modern history of the
Modern History Institute, Chinese Academy of Social Sciences). 2 vols. Jinan:
Qi-Lu, 1981.

Shanghai tiyu zhanxian geming zaofan silingbu and Lu Xun bingtuan Dongfanghong zhandoudui. "Jieguo 'Hongdeng' nao geming/Wusi wuwei yong xiang-
qian" (Carry on the revolutionary tradition of the "Red Lanterns"/Selflessly and
fearlessly forever forge ahead). *Wenhuibao*, Apr. 14, 1967, 4.

406 *Shanxi sheng gengzinian jiaonan qianhou jishi* (A complete account of the church difficulties in Shanxi province in 1900). In *Yihetuan* 1:493–523.

Shen Tong. Talk, Harvard University, Oct. 24, 1990.

Shen Yue, Shen Bo, Xu Weiheng, and Li Yu. "Jiating yinsu dui nü'er chuchao nianling de yingxiang" (Effects of family factors on daughter's menarcheal age). *Renleixue xuebao* 7.2 (May 1988): 128–32.

Shi Lan. "Wuchi de beipan: Chi Qihewensiji zhi liu dui Yihetuan yundong de feibang" (Shameless betrayal: A denunciation of the slanderous treatment of the Boxer movement by Tikhvinsky and his ilk). *Lishi yanjiu* 5 (1975): 95–98.

Shoup, Samantha Whipple. "In Peking." *The Independent* 52.2697 (Aug. 9, 1900): 1901.

Shryock, John. *The Temples of Anking and Their Cults: A Study of Modern Chinese Religion.* Paris: Librairie Orientaliste Paul Geuthner, 1931.

Shue, Vivienne. "Powers of State, Paradoxes of Dominion: China 1949–1979." In Kenneth Lieberthal, Joyce Kallgren, Roderick MacFarquhar, and Frederic Wakeman, Jr., eds., *Perspectives on Modern China: Four Anniversaries*, 205–25. Armonk, N.Y.: M. E. Sharpe, 1991.

Siikala, Anna-Leena. "The Siberian Shaman's Technique of Ecstasy." In Holm, ed., *Religious Ecstasy*, 103–21.

Silberbauer, G. B. "Social Hibernation: The Response of the G/wi Band to Seasonal Drought." In Hinchey, ed., *Symposium on Drought in Botswana*, 112–20.

Slotkin, Richard. *Gunfighter Nation: The Myth of the Frontier in 20th-Century America.* New York: Atheneum, 1992.

Smith, Aaron. *Some temporal advantages in keeping covenant with God: considered and applied in two discourses from Lev. 26, 3, 4. Delivered June 15th 1749. Being a day of publick fasting, on occasion of extream drought.* Boston: S. Kneeland, 1749.

Smith, Arthur H. *China in Convulsion.* 2 vols. New York: Fleming H. Revell, 1901.

———. *Village Life in China: A Study in Sociology.* New York: Fleming H. Revell, 1899.

Solomon, Richard H. and Masataka Kosaka, eds. *The Soviet Far East Military Buildup: Nuclear Dilemmas and Asian Security.* Dover, Mass.: Auburn House, 1986.

Song Bin. "Da Eluosi shawenzhuyi de huobiaoben: Ping Qihewensiji zhubian de Zhongguo jindaishi" (A living specimen of great Russian chauvinism: A critique of *The History of Modern China* edited by Tikhvinsky). *Lishi yanjiu* 5 (1975): 86–94.

Song Jiaheng and Pan Yu. "Yihetuan yundongzhong de funü qunzhong" (Female masses in the Boxer movement). *Shandong Daxue xue bao (lishi ban)* 2 (1960): 54–60.

Southall, Aidan. "Spirit Possession and Mediumship Among the Alur." In Beattie and Middleton, eds., *Spirit Mediumship and Society in Africa*, 232–72.

Spence, Jonathan. *To Change China: Western Advisers in China, 1620–1960.* Boston: Little, Brown, 1969.

Stauffer, Milton T., ed. *The Christian Occupation of China: A General Survey of the Numerical Strength and Geographical Distribution of the Christian Forces in China Made by the Special Committee on Survey and Occupation, China Continuation Committee, 1918–1921*. Shanghai: China Continuation Committee, 1922.

Steel, Richard A. *Through Peking's Sewer Gate: Relief of the Boxer Siege, 1900–1901*. Edited by George W. Carrington. New York: Vantage, 1985.

Steiger, George Nye. *China and the Occident: The Origin and Development of the Boxer Movement*. New Haven: Yale University Press, 1927.

Stockard, Janice E. *Daughters of the Canton Delta: Marriage Patterns and Economic Strategies in South China, 1860–1930*. Stanford: Stanford University Press, 1989.

Story of the Modern Peking Opera "The Red Lantern," The. Peking: Foreign Languages Press, 1972.

Su Xiaokang and Wang Luxiang. *Deathsong of the River: A Reader's Guide to the Chinese TV Series Heshang*. Translated by Richard W. Bodman and Pin P. Wan. Ithaca, N.Y.: Cornell East Asian Series, 1991.

Sullivan, Lawrence R. "The Controversy over 'Feudal Despotism': Politics and Historiography in China, 1978–82." *Australian Journal of Chinese Affairs* 23 (Jan. 1990): 1–31.

Sun Daren. "'Hongdengzhao' geming zaofan jingshen song" (In praise of the revolutionary rebel spirit of the "Red Lanterns"). *Guangming ribao*, Apr. 27, 1967.

Sun Kefu and Guan Jie. "Yihetuan yundong de guanghui yong cun: San ping Qihewensiji zhubian de Zhongguo jindaishi" (The glory of the Boxer movement will last forever: Three criticisms of *The History of Modern China* edited by Tikhvinsky). *Liaoning Daxue xuebao* 6 (1975): 68–74.

Sun Zhanyuan. "Shinianlai Yihetuan yundong yanjiu shuping" (A review of research on the Boxer movement during the past decade). *Xin Hua wenzhai* 9 (1990): 69–72. Excerpted from *Shandong shehui kexue* 3 (1990).

Sun Zuomin. "Guanyu Yihetuan yundong pingjia de jige wenti" (A few questions concerning appraisal of the Boxer movement). In *Yihetuan yundong shi taolun wenji* (Collected articles on the history of the Boxer movement), 185–206. Jinan: Qi-Lu, 1982. Translated in Buck, ed., *Recent Chinese Studies of the Boxer Movement*, 196–218.

Sutton, Donald. "Pilot Surveys of Chinese Shamans, 1875–1945: A Spatial Approach to Social History." *Journal of Social History* 15.1 (Fall 1981): 39–50.

Tai Hsüan-chih. *The Red Spears, 1916–1949*. Translated by Ronald Suleski. Ann Arbor: Center for Chinese Studies, University of Michigan, 1985.

Tan, Chester C. *The Boxer Catastrophe*. New York: Columbia University Press, 1955.

Tanaka, Issei. "The Social and Historical Context of Ming-Ch'ing Local Drama." In Johnson, Nathan, and Rawski, eds., *Popular Culture in Late Imperial China*, 143–60.

Tang Xingqi. "Wusa yundong zhi yiyi" (The significance of the May Thirtieth movement). *Xiangdao zhoubao* 121 (July 16, 1925): 1115–16.

Tang Yan. *Gengzi xixing jishi* (A record of the imperial progress westward in 1900). In *Yihetuan* 3:467–87.

Taylor, Dr. and Mrs. Howard. *Hudson Taylor in Early Years: The Growth of a Soul*. 2d ed. London: Morgan and Scott, 1912.

408   Taylor, Shelley E. *Positive Illusions: Creative Self-Deception and the Healthy Mind.* New York: Basic Books, 1989.

Ter Haar, Barend J. "Images of Outsiders: The Fear of Death by Mutilation." Unpublished paper.

———. *The White Lotus Teachings in Chinese Religious History.* Leiden: E. J. Brill, 1992.

Terrill, Ross. *The White-Boned Demon: A Biography of Madame Mao Zedong.* New York: William Morrow, 1984.

Thomson, H. C. *China and the Powers: A Narrative of the Outbreak of 1900.* London: Longmans, Green, 1902.

"Tianjin diqu Yihetuan yundong diaocha baogao" (Report on the survey of the Boxer movement in the Tianjin area). Compiled by Nankai daxue lishixi 1956 ji (Class of 1956 of the History Department of Nankai University), unpublished. Undated reissue of original 1960 mimeographed version. Cited as TDYYDB.

Tianjin tielu diyi zhongxue lilun yanjiu xiaozu. "Yihetuan fandi sao Qingchao— Hongdengzhao pi Ru po lijiao" (The Boxers opposed imperialism and swept away the Qing—The Red Lanterns assailed the Confucians and broke out of the conventional moral code). *Tianjin ribao,* Sept. 24, 1974, 2.

Tianjin yiyue ji (An account of one month in Tianjin). In *Yihetuan* 2:141–58. Cited as TYJ.

Tianjin zhengsu yange ji (An account of the evolution of political customs in Tianjin). In *Yihetuan shiliao* (Historical materials on the Boxers), 961–63. Edited by Zhongguo shehui kexueyuan jindaishi yanjiusuo "Jindaishi ziliao" bianjizu ("Modern historical materials" editorial group of the Institute of Modern History, Chinese Academy of Social Sciences). 2 vols. Beijing: Zhongguo Shehui Kexue, 1982.

Tiansheng. "Duiyu yang Yihetuan zhi suo gan" (My reactions to the foreign Boxers). *Guowen zhoubao* 2.22 (June 14, 1925): 2.

Tikhvinsky, S. L., ed. *Modern History of China.* Moscow: Progress Publishers, 1983. Translation of *Novaia istoriia Kitaia.* Moscow: Soviet Science Publishing House, 1972.

Topley, Marjorie. "Marriage Resistance in Rural Kwangtung." In Margery Wolf and Roxane Witke, eds., *Women in Chinese Society,* 67–88. Stanford: Stanford University Press, 1975.

Toynbee, Arnold, ed. *Half the World: The History and Culture of China and Japan.* New York: Holt, Rinehart and Winston, 1973.

Trachtenberg, Alan. " 'Bullets Tore Holes in the Water.' " *New York Times,* June 6, 1994, A15.

Tsai, Wen-hui. "Historical Personalities in Chinese Folk Religion: A Functional Interpretation." In Sarah Allan and Alvin P. Cohen, eds., *Legend, Lore, and Religion in China: Essays in Honor of Wolfram Eberhard on His Seventieth Birthday,* 23–42. San Francisco: Chinese Materials Center, 1979.

Tsou Jung [Zou Rong]. *The Revolutionary Army: A Chinese Nationalist Tract of 1903.* Translated by John Lust. The Hague: Mouton, 1968.

Turmoil at Tiananmen: A Study of U.S. Press Coverage of the Beijing Spring of 1989. Cambridge: Joan Shorenstein Barone Center on the Press, Politics, and Public Policy, John F. Kennedy School of Government, Harvard University, 1992.

Uhalley, Stephen, Jr. "The Controversy over Li Hsiu-ch'eng: An Ill-Timed Centenary." *Journal of Asian Studies* 25.2 (Feb. 1966): 305–17.

United States. *Papers relating to the Foreign Relations of the United States, 1900.* Washington, D.C.: GPO, 1902. Cited as *FRUS.*

Upham, Oscar J. "Log of seige [*sic*] of Pekin." In Personal Collection 504 (Upham), History and Museum Division, Marine Corps (Navy Department), Personal Papers.

Utley, Jonathan G. "American Views of China, 1900–1915: The Unwelcome but Inevitable Awakening." In Goldstein, Israel, and Conroy, eds., *American Views of China,* 114–31.

Vermeer, Eduard B. *Economic Development in Provincial China: The Central Shaanxi Since 1930.* Cambridge: Cambridge University Press, 1988.

Vernon, John. "Exhuming a Dirty Joke." *NYTBR,* July 12, 1992, 1, 34–35.

Veyne, Paul. *Writing History: Essay on Epistemology.* Translated by Mina Moore-Rinvolucri. Middletown, Conn.: Wesleyan University Press, 1984. Original French ed. published 1971.

Victor, Jeffrey S. *Satanic Panic: The Creation of a Contemporary Legend.* Chicago: Open Court, 1993.

Vinchon, Albert, S.J. "La culte de la Sainte Vierge du Tche-li sud-est: Rapport présent au Congrès marial de 1904." *Chine, Ceylan, Madagascar: Lettres missionnaires français de la Compagnie de Jésus (Province de Champagne)* 18 (Mar. 1905): 125–33.

Wakeman, Frederic, Jr. "All the Rage in China." *New York Review of Books,* Mar. 2, 1989, 19–21.

Walsh, Tom. "Herbert Hoover and the Boxer Rebellion." *Our Heritage in Documents* (Spring 1987): 34–40.

Wang, David Der-wei. *Fictional Realism in Twentieth-Century China: Mao Dun, Lao She, Shen Congwen.* New York: Columbia University Press, 1992.

Wang Hsueh-wen. "A Comparison of the Boxers and the Red Guards." *Issues and Studies: A Monthly Journal of World Affairs and Communist Problems* 4.1 (Oct. 1967): 1–14.

Wang Minglun, ed. *Fan yangjiao shuwen jietie xuan* (Selected writings and notices opposing the Western religion). Jinan: Qi-Lu, 1984.

Wang Shuhuai. *Gengzi peikuan* (The Boxer indemnity). Taibei: Zhongyang yanjiuyuan jindaishi yanjiusuo, 1974.

Wang Zhizhong. "Fengjian mengmeizhuyi yu Yihetuan yundong" (Feudal obscurantism and the Boxer movement). *Lishi yanjiu* 1 (1980): 41–54.

——. " 'Hongdengzhao' kaolüe" (A brief examination of the "Red Lanterns"). *Shehui kexue* (Gansu) 2 (1980): 63–69, 85.

——. "Lun Yihetuan yundong de fandi zuoyong" (The anti-imperialist role of the Boxer movement). *Shehui kexue* (Gansu) 3 (1983): 56–66.

——. "Ye tan ruhe pingjia Yihetuan yundong" (A further word on how to appraise the Boxer movement). *Guangming ribao,* Aug. 19, 1980.

Wasserstrom, Jeffrey. "Afterword: History, Myth, and the Tales of Tiananmen." In Wasserstrom and Elizabeth J. Perry, eds., *Popular Protest and Political Culture in Modern China: Learning from 1989,* 244–80. Boulder: Westview, 1992.

410 ———. "The Boxers as Symbol: The Use and Abuse of the Yi He Tuan." Unpublished paper, 1984.

———. " 'Civilization' and Its Discontents: The Boxers and Luddites as Heroes and Villains." *Theory and Society* 16 (1987): 675–707.

———. *Student Protests in Twentieth-Century China: The View from Shanghai.* Stanford: Stanford University Press, 1991.

Watson, James L. "Of Flesh and Bones: The Management of Death Pollution in Cantonese Society." In Maurice Bloch and Jonathan Parry, eds., *Death and the Regeneration of Life*, 155–86. Cambridge: Cambridge University Press, 1982.

———. "Standardizing the Gods: The Promotion of T'ien Hou ('Empress of Heaven') Along the South China Coast, 960–1960." In Johnson, Nathan, and Rawski, eds., *Popular Culture in Late Imperial China*, 292–324.

Weber, Eugen. "History Is What Historians Do." *NYTBR*, July 22, 1984, 13–14.

Wehrle, Edmund S. *Britain, China, and the Antimissionary Riots, 1891–1900.* Minneapolis: University of Minnesota Press, 1966.

Wei Gang. "Yihetuan gushi de shidai jingshen he yishu tedian" (The contemporary spirit and distinguishing artistic features of the Boxer stories). In *Zhongguo jindai wenxue lunwen ji (1949–1979): Xiju, minjian wenxue juan* (Essays on modern Chinese literature [1949–1979]: Drama and popular literature volume), 557–65. Beijing: Zhongguo Shehui Kexue, 1982.

Wei Hongyun. "Du you yingxiong qu hubao: Bo Qihewensiji dui Yihetuan geming jingshen de feibang" (Only heroes drive out tigers and leopards: A refutation of Tikhvinsky's slanderous treatment of the revolutionary spirit of the Boxers). *Nankai Daxue xuebao* 3 (1976): 74–76.

Weller, Robert P. "Historians and Consciousness: The Modern Politics of the Taiping Heavenly Kingdom." *Social Research* 54.4 (Winter 1987): 731–55.

———. "Popular Tradition, State Control, and Taiping Christianity: Religion and Political Power in the Early Taiping Rebellion." In Li Qifang, ed., *Zhongguo jindai zhengjiao guanxi guoji xueshu yantaohui lunwen ji* (Proceedings of the First International Symposium on Church and State in China: Past and Present), 183–206. Taibei: Danjiang Daxue Lishixi, 1987.

———. *Resistance, Chaos, and Control in China: Taiping Rebels, Taiwanese Ghosts, and Tiananmen.* Seattle: University of Washington Press, 1994.

Wetherell, H. I., J. Holt, and P. Richards. "Drought in the Sahel: A Broader Interpretation, with regard to West Africa and Ethiopia." In Hinchey, ed., *Symposium on Drought in Botswana*, 131–41.

White, Hayden. "The Question of Narrative in Contemporary Historical Theory." *History and Theory* 23.1 (Feb. 1984): 1–33.

Wieger, Léon, ed. *Chine moderne*, vols. 5–6. Hien-hien [Xianxian]: Imprimerie de Hien-hien, 1924–25.

Wilford, John Noble. *The Mysterious History of Columbus: An Exploration of the Man, the Myth, the Legacy.* New York: Knopf, 1991.

Witke, Roxane. *Comrade Chiang Ch'ing.* Boston: Little, Brown, 1977.

Wolf, Arthur P. "Chinese Kinship and Mourning Dress." In Maurice Freedman, ed., *Family and Kinship in Chinese Society*, 189–207. Stanford: Stanford University Press, 1970.

———, ed. *Studies in Chinese Society.* Stanford: Stanford University Press, 1978.

Wolf, Margery. *A Thrice-Told Tale: Feminism, Postmodernism, and Ethnographic Responsibility*. Stanford: Stanford University Press, 1992.

——. *Women and the Family in Rural Taiwan*. Stanford: Stanford University Press, 1972.

Wright, Mary C. "Introduction: The Rising Tide of Change." In Wright, ed., *China in Revolution: The First Phase, 1900–1913*, 1–63. New Haven: Yale University Press, 1968.

——. "From Revolution to Restoration: The Transformation of Kuomintang Ideology." *Far Eastern Quarterly* 14.4 (Aug. 1955): 515–32.

Wu Shiying. "Yihetuan yundong shi baokan wenzhang suoyin" (A listing of newspaper and periodical articles on the history of the Boxer movement). In *Yihetuan yundong shi lunwen xuan* (Selected essays on the history of the Boxer movement), 545–92. Beijing: Zhonghua, 1984.

Wu Wenxian. "Sha E wuzhuang zhenya Heilongjiang Yihetuan de zuizheng: *Xiuzhu Dongqing tielu tupian ce (1897–1903)*" (Proof of Czarist Russia's criminal use of armed force to suppress the Heilongjiang Boxers: *Al'bom' sooruzheniia Kitaiskoi vostochnoi zheleznoi dorogi, 1897–1903* [A photographic record of the construction of the Chinese Eastern Railway, 1897–1903]). *Wenwu* 3 (1975): 25–33.

Wu Wenying. "Hongdengzhao" (The Red Lanterns). *Beijing ribao*, Apr. 27, 1967, 4.

Wu Yannan. "Yihetuan yundong he fan-Kong douzheng" (The Boxer movement and the anti-Confucian struggle). *Jilin Shida xuebao* 3 (1976): 60–62, 81.

Wu Yingguang. "Yihetuan qiyi ji qi houguo—dui Henan de yingxiang" (The Boxer uprising and its consequences: The impact on Henan). Translated by Tao Feiya. *Yihetuan yanjiuhui tongxun* (The Boxer Study Association newsletter), 3 (Apr. 1987): 5–15.

Wu Yinnian. "Baquanzhuyi de 'jiezuo': Ping Mosike chuban de *Zhongguo jindaishi*" ("Masterpiece" of hegemonism: A critique of *The History of Modern China*, published in Moscow). *Lishi yanjiu* 2 (1976): 121–31.

Xiao Renwu. "Weida de Yihetuan yundong" (The great Boxer movement). *Guangming ribao*, Aug. 30, 1967.

Xi Huanjiu, Gu Xuejing, Li Zeshan, Wang Huiya, Sun Chao, and Lin Qi. "Yuejing chuchao nianling de yanjiu" (A study of menarcheal age). *Renleixue xuebao* 6.3 (Aug. 1987): 213–21.

Xu Xudian. "Yihetuan yuanliu chuyi" (My humble view on the origins and development of the Boxers). In *Shandong daxue wenke lunwen jikan* (Collected essays in the humanities from Shandong University) 1 (1980): 23–35.

Xue Xiantian. "Hailanpao can'an sinan renshu jiujing you duoshao?" (How many people actually died in the Hailanpao massacre?). *Lishi yanjiu* 1 (1980): 173–76.

——. "Jiangdong liushisi tun can'an yanjiu" (A study of the massacre in the sixty-four villages of Jiangdong). *Jindaishi yanjiu* 1 (1981): 235–54.

Yang, C. K. *Religion in Chinese Society: A Study of Contemporary Social Functions of Religion and Some of Their Historical Factors*. Berkeley: University of California Press, 1961.

Yang Diangao. *Gengzi dashi ji* (A record of the main events of 1900). In *Gengzi jishi*, 79–98.

412   Yang Jiang. *Six Chapters from My Life "Downunder."* Translated by Howard Goldblatt. Seattle: University of Washington Press, 1984.

Yang Mushi. *Gengzi jiaoban quanfei dianwen lu* (Selected telegrams concerning the suppression of the Boxer bandits in 1900). In *Yihetuan* 4:329–62.

Yang Tianhong. "Yihetuan 'shenshu' lunlüe" (A summary discussion of the "magical powers" of the Boxers). *Jindaishi yanjiu* 5 (1993): 189–204.

Yao Xiuzhi and Wei Xiangpeng, comps. "Hailanpao yu Jiangdong liushisi tun can'an ziliao" (Materials on the massacres of Hailanpao and the sixty-four villages of Jiangdong). *Jindaishi ziliao* 1 (1981): 101–21.

Ye Changchi. *Yuandulu riji chao* (Selections from the diary of the Yuandu Studio). Compiled by Wang Jilie. In *Yihetuan* 2:439–80.

"Yellow Peril or White?" *The Nation* 124 (Apr. 13, 1927): 387.

Yi Ho Tuan Movement of 1900, The. Peking: Foreign Languages Press, 1976.

Yihetuan (The Boxers). Edited by Jian Bozan et al. 4 vols. Shanghai: Shenzhou Guoguang She, 1951. Cited as *YHT*.

Yihetuan dang'an shiliao (Archival materials on the Boxers). Edited by Guojia dang'an ju Ming-Qing dang'an guan (The Ming-Qing archives division of the national archives bureau). 2 vols. Beijing: Zhonghua, 1959.

Yihetuan shiliao (Historical materials on the Boxers). 2 vols. Edited by Zhongguo shehui kexueyuan jindaishi yanjiusuo "Jindaishi ziliao" bianjizu ("Modern history materials" editorial group of the Modern History Institute of the Chinese Academy of Social Sciences). Beijing: Zhongguo Shehui Kexue, 1982.

"Yihetuan you gong yu Zhongguo shuo" (On the Boxers' contributions to China). *Kaizhilu* (1901). Reprinted in Zhang Nan and Wang Renzhi, eds., *Xinhai geming qian shinian jian shilun xuanji*, vol. 1, *ce* 1:59–60.

Yihetuan yundong (The Boxer movement). Compiled by Zhongguo jindaishi congshu bianxiezu (Compilation group for *History of Modern China* series). Shanghai: Shanghai Renmin, 1972.

"Yihetuan yundong shiqi Henan renmin de fandi douzheng" (The anti-imperialist struggle of the people of Henan during the Boxer movement era). Jointly written by Kaifeng Shifan Xueyuan lishixi (The history department of Kaifeng Normal College) and Zhongguo kexueyuan Henan fenyuan lishi yanjiusuo (The historical research institute of the Henan branch of the Chinese Academy of Sciences). In Zhongguo kexueyuan Shandong fenyuan lishi yanjiusuo (Historical research institute of Shandong branch of Chinese Academy of Sciences), comp., *Yihetuan yundong liushi zhounian jinian lunwen ji* (Collected essays in commemoration of the sixtieth anniversary of the Boxer movement), 147–66. Beijing: Zhonghua, 1961.

Yihetuan yundong yu jindai Zhongguo shehui (The Boxer movement and modern Chinese society). Chengdu: Sichuan Sheng Shehui Kexueyuan, 1987.

Yihetuan yundong yu jindai Zhongguo shehui guoji xueshu taolunhui lunwen ji (Collected papers presented at the international conference on the Boxer movement and modern Chinese society). Compiled by Zhongguo Yihetuan yanjiuhui (Chinese association for Boxer research). Jinan: Qi-Lu, 1992.

Yihetuan zai Tianjin de fandi douzheng (The anti-imperialist struggle of the Boxers in Tianjin). Compiled by Tianjin shi lishi yanjiusuo, Tianjin shihua bianxiezu

(The history research institute of Tianjin and the Tianjin historical narrative compilation group). Tianjin: Tianjin Renmin, 1973.

Yixian [Sun Yat-sen]. "Zhina baoquan fenge helun" (The arguments for preserving or dismembering China). *Jiangsu* 6 (Nov. 1903). Reprinted in Zhang Nan and Wang Renzhi, eds., *Xinhai geming qian shinian jian shilun xuanji*, vol. 1, ce 2:601.

Yong rao lu (A record of troubles needlessly brought on). In *Gengzi jishi*, 247–65.

Youth's Companion, The. 1900, 1911–1912.

Yu nan riji (A daily record of my encounters with misfortune). In *Yihetuan* 2:159–73.

Yuan Chang. *Luanzhong riji can'gao* (Draft fragments of a diary kept during the disorders). In *Yihetuan* 1:335–49.

Yun Yuding. *Chongling chuanxin lu* (A true account of the Guangxu emperor). In *Yihetuan* 1:45–55.

Yung, Bell. "Model Opera as Model: From *Shajiabang* to *Sagabong*." In Bonnie S. McDougall, ed., *Popular Chinese Literature and Performing Arts in the People's Republic of China, 1949-1979*, 144–64. Berkeley: University of California Press, 1984.

"Zan 'Hongdengzhao' " (In praise of the "Red Lanterns"). *Wenhuibao*, Apr. 14, 1967. Reprinted in *Renmin ribao*, Apr. 17, 1967, 3.

Zhang Haipeng, ed. *Jianming Zhongguo jindaishi tuji* (A concise pictorial history of modern China). Beijing: Changcheng Chubanshe, 1984.

Zhang Nan and Wang Renzhi, eds. *Xinhai geming qian shinian jian shilun xuanji* (Selected essays on current topics written during the ten-year period preceding the 1911 revolution). Hong Kong: Sanlian Shudian, 1962.

Zhang Shijie, comp. *Hongying dadao* (The red-tasseled sword). Shanghai: Shaonian Ertong Chubanshe, 1961.

Zhao Jing. "Yihetuan shi gemingde!" (The Boxers were revolutionary!). *Guangming ribao*, Apr. 24, 1967, 4.

Zhao Sanduo he ta lingdao de Yihetuan (Zhao Sanduo and the Boxers he led). Wei county, 1986.

Zhiyan [pseudonym]. "Yihequan zhengfule yangren" (The Boxers' conquest of the Westerners). *Meizhou pinglun* (The weekly critic), no. 1, Dec. 22, 1918.

Zhong E. "Huangyan yan'gaibuliao lishi: Bo Suxiu wumie Yihetuan he meihua lao shahuang de miulun" (Lies cannot cover up history: A refutation of Soviet revisionism's fallacies of slandering the Boxers and prettifying the old czars). *Lilun xuexi* 5 (1975): 66–72, 62.

Zhongfang Shi. *Gengzi jishi* (A record of the events of 1900). In *Gengzi jishi*, 9–77.

Zhongguo jin wubainian hanlao fenbu tu ji (Annual maps showing the distribution of drought and flood in China during the last five hundred years). Compiled by Zhongyang qixiangju, Qixiang kexue yanjiuyuan (Meteorological Science Research Institute, Central Meteorology Bureau). Beijing: Ditu Chubanshe, 1981.

Zou Rong. *Gemingjun* (The revolutionary army). In Chai Degeng et al., eds., *Xinhai geming* (The 1911 revolution), 1:331–64. 8 vols. Shanghai: Renmin, 1957.